Beginning ASP.NET

using VB.NET

Rob Birdwell

Ollie Cornes

Chris Goode

Ajoy Krishnamoorthy

Juan T. Llibre

Christopher L. Miller

Neil Raybould

David Sussman

Chris Ullman

Wrox Press Ltd. ®

Beginning ASP.NET

Published by Wrox Press Ltd,
Arden House, 1102 Warwick Road, Acocks Green,
Birmingham, B27 6BH, UK
Printed in the United States
ISBN 1861005040

Trademark Acknowledgements

Wrox has endeavored to provide trademark information about all the companies and products mentioned in this book by the appropriate use of capitals. However, Wrox cannot guarantee the accuracy of this information.

Credits

Authors
Rob Birdwell
Ollie Cornes
Chris Goode
Ajoy Krishnamoorthy
Juan T. Llibre
Christopher L. Miller
Neil Raybould
David Sussman
Chris Ullman

Additional Material
Jon Duckett
James Hart
John Kauffman
Matt Reynolds
Dan Squier

Technical Architect
Dan Squier

Technical Editors
Alessandro Ansa
Ewan Buckingham
Jake Manning

Category Manager
Kirsty Reade

Production Manager
Simon Hardware

Production Team
Mark Burdett
Abbie Forletta
Emma Eato
Natalie O'Donnell

Index
Bill Johncocks

Cover
Dawn Chellingworth

Author Agents
Avril Corbin
Laura Jones

Project Administrator
Louise Carr

Technical Reviewers
Kenneth Avellino
Russ Basiura
Paul Bradzonis
Kyle Burns
Steve Celius
Paul Churchill
Ollie Cornes
Edgardo D'Andrea
Slavomir Furman
John Godfrey
Michael Green
Mark Harrison
Erik Hougaard
Rob Howard
Daniel Kent
Ajoy Krishnamoorthy
Vidar Langberget
Don Lee
Dianna Leech
Juan T. Llibre
Gleydson de Macedo
Ron Miller
Fredrik Normen
Ken Schaefer
Steve Schofield
David Schultz
Keyur Shah
Marc Simkin
Imar Spaanjaars
Andrew Stopford
Tom Washington
Sanjeev Yadav

Proof Reader
Diana Skeldon
Miriam Robinson

About the Authors

Rob Birdwell

Rob Birdwell makes his home in Corvallis, Oregon along with his wife and three beautiful children. He works at Hewlett-Packard and moonlights as a musician, composer, and songwriter. He first became interested in programming when he discovered he could make a machine play one of his musical melodies. His current interests include all facets of .NET technology and especially the C# language. His hobbies include swimming, tennis and playing his trumpet in various ensembles. Rob would like to thank his wife, Christel, and children for their patience and support while he endeavored to make a small contribution to this wonderful book.

Ollie Cornes

Ollie Cornes has been working with the Internet and the Microsoft platform since the early '90s. In 1999 he co-founded a business-to-business Internet company and until recently was their Chief Technical Officer.

Prior to that his various roles involved programming, technical authoring, network management, writing, leading development projects and consulting. He has worked with Demon Internet, Microsoft, Saab, Travelstore and Vodafone. Ollie holds a degree in computer science and is Microsoft certified.

When he's not working he spends his time devouring books on human potential and practicing Chinese internal martial arts, meditation and healing. He also juggles fire and knives.

Chris Goode

Chris is a Technical Architect in the .NET team at Wrox, currently specializing in ASP.NET. She lives in Birmingham (that's UK, not Alabama), and has a house full of old computers. Chris started programming at the age of 10 on her Atari 65XE, and has always enjoyed spending time with as much technology as possible. She has a degree in Mechanical Engineering, but decided that the engineering world wasn't for her. She's now back firmly in the world of computers, finding that life at Wrox combines the fun stuff with the work stuff pretty well.

I'd like to thank my family for putting up with me over the years, and for buying me my first computer. Good luck to my brother, Rob, who should be getting his A-Level results at about the same time this book comes out. Thanks to Dan for giving me the chance to be involved in this book. Special thanks go to James for all his time, patience and support.

Ajoy Krishnamoorthy

Ajoy Krishnamoorthy is a consultant with over 5 years of experience, working in Microsoft technologies such as ASP, VB, IIS, MTS and most recently .NET. He writes regularly for leading online publications. He received Bachelors degree in Electronics and Communication and Masters degree in Systems and Information. He is currently working for his Masters in Business Administration at Fisher College of Business, Ohio State University. His interests include writing, hanging out with friends and travel. He is originally from Chennai, India and currently lives in Columbus, Ohio with his wife Vidhya. He and his wife are excited to have their first child in October. He can be reached at ajoyk@ajoys.net.

This would not have been possible without an understanding and supportive wife. Thank you Vidhya, you are the best. I also want to thank my family for their support and encouragement. Finally, thanks to Wrox Press and its wonderful people for this opportunity.

Juan T. Llibre

Juan T. Llibre is the Director of the Computer Sciences and Distance Education departments at Universidad Nacional Pedro Henríquez Ureña in Santo Domingo, Dominican Republic.

He has been a consultant to the Caribbean Export Development Agency and the Dominican Republic's Central Bank and is currently the Technical Architect for the Caribbean Virtual University, a Distance Education consortium composed of 30 Caribbean Universities, which will go online in 2002. He's also planning what he calls a "killer app" for Caribbean Tourism.

Juan has been an Active Server Pages Microsoft MVP for 4 years and can regularly be found in the newsgroups and mailing lists, offering advice on ASP and ASP.NET in English and Spanish.

He co-authored Wrox's "Beginning ASP 2.0" and "Beginning ASP 3.0", and has been a Technical Reviewer for over a dozen books on ASP and its related technologies.

When he isn't writing, reviewing, seeing students and running the school, producing Distance Education courses, or hanging out with developers, he takes off to a beach hut with a high-speed connection, because "…a man must have some fun, too!".

He has three daughters, Jonquil, Anthea and Isabelle, and two grandsons, David and Keenan.

Christopher Miller

Christopher Miller began his development in the early 1980's with Atari Basic, migrating to GW Basic, QuickBasic, and finally to Visual Basic, where he's lived and breathed, since 1992. He is currently a business consultant with Crossoft Inc of Pittsburgh, PA, specializing in Intranet architecture and design. He's also president of the Pittsburgh ASP / .NET User Group (http://www.pghasp.org).

When he's not entrenched in a project, he spends his time working on his personal site, www.chrisandstacy.com, or pretending to exercise by playing hockey.

His current projects include an adaptive Intranet framework tool and other .NET-based Web Service applications. He holds a business degree from Pensacola Christian College of Florida, and all major Microsoft certifications (MCSE+I, MCSD, MCT, MCDBA).

Neil Raybould

Neil is working as a software developer and technical writer with Crossoft Incorporated, north of Pittsburgh, Pennsylvania. He has given several presentations on ASP and ASP.NET related topics in the Pittsburgh area. Growing up in Emporia, Virginia, Neil used lawn-mowing profits in 1981 to buy a Commodore VIC-20. His current interests have progressed to include .NET and wireless applications. But, sometimes, Neil still longs for the days of CBM Basic, tape cassette drives, PEEKs and POKEs, and 3.5 K RAM.

Neil holds a BS (Virginia Tech), an MBA (Duquesne University), and MCSD and MCDBA certifications.

To my wife Vicky. You are such a blessing to me. Thank you so much for your encouragement and patience.

To the newest Raybould, due August 27, 2001. We can't wait to meet you!

David Sussman

David Sussman spent most of his professional life as a developer before realizing that writing was far more fun. He specializes in Internet and data access technologies, and spends much of his time delving into beta technologies. He's just moved house, so now has no money left to add more components to his ludicrously expensive hi-fi. You can reach him at davids@ipona.co.uk.

Chris Ullman

Chris Ullman is a Computer Science graduate who came to Wrox six and half years ago, when 14.4 modems were the hottest Internet technology and Netscape Navigator 2.0 was a groundbreaking innovation. Since then he's applied his knowledge of HTML, server-side web technologies, Java and Visual Basic to developing, editing and authoring books.

When not trying to reconstruct the guts of his own PC or trying to write extra chapters in a hurry, he can be found either playing keyboards in a psychedelic band, The Beemen (http://www.beemen.com), tutoring his cats in the way of eating peacefully from their own food bowl and not the one next to theirs, or hoping against hope that this is the year his favourite soccer team, Birmingham City, can manage to end their exile from the Premier League. A selection of Chris's non-computer related writings on music, art and literature can be found at http://www.atomicwise.com.

Chris would like to thank everybody who has worked with him at Wrox and assisted him in the last six and half years here and helped make it such a great stay. While he would like to mention everybody individually, there just isn't space, and he would undoubtedly miss names out, but particular thanks goes out to my author agents over the last two years, Sarah Bowers and Avril Corbin. Also thanks on this book is due to the editorial team Dan Squier, Ewan Buckingham, Jake Manning and Alessandro Ansa, whose tireless work ensured that the book turned out as good as it is.

Lastly but most importantly Chris would like to thank his wife Kate for her eternal love and support throughout all of his authoring ventures.

Table of Contents

Table of Contents

Table of Contents

Table of Contents

Introduction

ASP.NET is the latest incarnation of Microsoft's Active Server Pages (ASP) – a powerful server-based technology from Microsoft, designed to create dynamic and interactive HTML pages for your World Wide Web site, or corporate intranet. ASP.NET also constitutes a core element in Microsoft's .NET vision, providing web-based access to an immensely powerful new development environment, .NET; in this respect alone, it's a great leap ahead of all previous versions of ASP.

This purpose of this book is to teach you how to use ASP.NET to write web pages, whose content can be programmatically-generated from scratch every time the page is viewed. This not only saves you a lot of effort in presenting and updating your web pages, but also offers tremendous scope for adding sophisticated functionality to your site. This book will answer the fundamental questions:

- ❑ What is ASP.NET?
- ❑ How do I get install ASP.NET and get it up and running?
- ❑ How does it work?
- ❑ How can I use it to produce dynamic, interactive web applications?

We'll answer these questions in a thorough and comprehensive way, with plenty of fully working examples. Even if you're totally new to this technology, you will gain a deep understanding of what ASP.NET is all about, and learn how you can harness it to build powerful web applications.

Who Is This Book For?

This book is aimed at relatively inexperienced web builders who are looking to enrich their sites with dynamically-generated content, and want to learn how to start building web applications using ASP.NET. Developers who have a little experience with previous versions of ASP (and are looking to move over to ASP.NET), may also find this book helpful in getting a simple grasp on what ASP.NET is, what it does, and how we can use it.

> **This is a Wrox *Beginning...* series book, so we will aim to teach you everything you need to know from scratch. If you already have some experience of programming ASP.NET or VB.NET, you may be more comfortable starting at a somewhat quicker pace with the natural follow-up title *Professional ASP.NET* (Wrox Press, ISBN 186004-88-5).**

We appreciate that most (if not all) of the web authors and developers who take up ASP.NET, are reasonably familiar with simple HTML, so we won't spend lots of time on it teaching you to suck eggs. If you don't already know HTML, we suggest you take some time to get familiar with it before trying to learn about ASP.NET. There are plenty of good HTML tutorials available, both in books and on the Web.

There are two kinds of beginners for whom this is the ideal book:

❑ You're a **beginner to programming** and you've chosen ASP.NET as the technology with which to get started. Great choice! ASP.NET is not only easy and fun, but it's also very useful, and very, very powerful. This book will hold your hand throughout.

❑ You can program in another language, but you're a **beginner to web programming**. Again, this is a great choice! You may still have a few lessons to learn about programming in .NET, but this book will introduce you to how it does things in terms you'll understand.

Most importantly, you don't need to know anything more than the basic ins and outs of how to put your own web page together. If you've never written a single line of any programming language, then you have to nothing to fear – this is the book for you. The bottom line is as follows:

> **This book will teach you how to write ASP.NET applications.**

What Does This Book Cover?

This book was written as Microsoft released the Beta 2 version of ASP.NET. This release is almost feature complete, and stable enough for developers to begin learning about and using the new technology as well as deploying live sites. Microsoft already has several live sites running on the beta release, which have proved faster than their older counterparts. While we can't guarantee that the final release version will be identical, you can be sure that almost all of the concepts, examples, and explanations we provide are accurate within the timeframe of the first full version of .NET.

In this book, we attempt to explain just what ASP.NET is all about, how you can use it, and what you can use it for. The book can be broken down into four main sections:

An Introduction to ASP.NET

In Chapters 1 to 3, we shall introduce some of the core concepts behind the Web and look at how ASP.NET adds to the range of web programming technologies already available. We'll take you through the process of installing the Microsoft .NET Framework (on which ASP.NET relies), and demonstrate some simple applications. We'll start to consider how ASP.NET works behind the scenes, and introduce some simple techniques for generating web pages with ASP.NET.

Programming ASP.NET

Chapters 4 through 7 go on to look at various ways in which we can store and manipulate data in our programs, look at controlling the order in which commands are executed, and consider some simple issues of code structure.

Objects in ASP.NET

Objects and the principles of object-oriented programming (OOP) play a fundamental role in .NET, so Chapters 8 through 11 will familiarize you with the notion of OOP, the philosophy behind it, and the ways in which we can use objects to write more effective code.

Practical ASP.NET

The final section of the book will discuss and demonstrate various techniques for making your web applications useful in the real world. Chapters 12 through 19 will consider topics such as error handling, data access, configuration, and building code components and web services.

What Do I Need to Run ASP.NET?

In order to answer this, we need to consider the role that we'll be playing in this book – namely that of the web developer or Webmaster. In this role, we'll be writing web pages, publishing them on a web server, and testing them to see what they look like and whether they work. This is just a list of items that you will need. Don't worry if you can't locate all the bits and pieces just yet, as we'll be looking at where to get them from in the opening chapter:

- ❑ A text editor (such as Windows Notepad).

- ❑ A web browser (any one should do, since the hard work is all done on the server).

- ❑ An ASP.NET-compliant web server (ASP.NET requires IIS 5.0 or later – this means that you'll need to be running Windows 2000 or Windows XP).

- ❑ The .NET Framework (currently available in several different varieties – unless you have access to the full ".NET Framework SDK", which features documentation, tutorials, and a download size of over 100Mb, we suggest you download the slightly more modest but no less functional 18Mb "ASP.NET Premium Edition" from www.aspnet.com).

> **The code in this book will not work with the -1 release of ASP.NET.**

In order to make full use of .NET's data access functionality (which we look at in later chapters), you must make sure that you have version 2.7 or later of the Microsoft Data Access Components (MDAC2.7) installed on the same machine as your web server. We'll also assume you have a copy of Microsoft Access from which to access the sample data. Other databases such as MSDE and SQL Server are also fine, but most of the examples we show will require a little tweaking in order to work with these alternative databases.

> *Specifically for the purposes of this book, we discourage you from using a web page editor such as FrontPage, or a full development tool like Visual Studio. While these are powerful tools that can be very helpful in a development environment, they will often add their own code to your web pages automatically. This can often make it harder to see what's going on, and can, at this level, really get in the way of what we're supposed to be demonstrating in a particular example...*

When we browse pages on the Web, or even on a local intranet, the browser and the web server software are generally hosted on two *different* physical machines. Note however, that it's quite possible to run your text editor, browser, and web server simultaneously on the *same* machine. Indeed, web developers often use this technique as they write, test, rewrite and tweak their ASP.NET pages.

Conventions

We've used a number of different styles of text and layout in this book to help differentiate between the different kinds of information. Here are examples of the styles we used and an explanation of what they mean.

Code has several fonts. If it's a word that we're talking about in the text – for example, when discussing a `For ... Next` loop, it's in this font. If it's a block of code that can be typed as a program and run, then it's also in a gray box:

```
<?xml version 1.0?>
```

Sometimes we'll see code in a mixture of styles, like this:

```
<?xml version 1.0?>
<Invoice>
    <part>
        <name>Widget</name>
        <price>$10.00</price>
    </part>
</invoice>
```

In cases like this, the code with a white background is code we are already familiar with; the line highlighted in gray is a new addition to the code since we last looked at it.

Advice, hints, and background information comes in this type of font.

> **Important pieces of information come in boxes like this.**

Bullets appear indented, with each new bullet marked as follows:

- ❑ **Important Words** are in a bold type font.
- ❑ Words that appear on the screen, or in menus like the File or Window, are in a similar font to the one you would see on a Windows desktop.
- ❑ Keys that you press on the keyboard like *Ctrl* and *Enter*, are in italics.

Customer Support

We've tried to make this book as accurate and enjoyable as possible, but what really matters is what the book actually does for you. Please let us know your views, either by returning the reply card in the back of the book, or by contacting us via email at feedback@wrox.com.

Source Code and Updates

As we work through the examples in this book, you may decide that you prefer to type in all the code by hand. Many readers prefer this, because it's a good way to get familiar with the coding techniques that are being used.

Whether you want to type the code in or not, we have made all the source code for this book available at our web site at the following address:

http://www.wrox.com/

If you like to type in the code, you can use our files to check the results you should be getting - they should be your first stop if you think you might have typed in an error. If you don't like typing, then downloading the source code from our web site is a must!

Either way, it'll help you with updates and debugging.

Errata

We've made every effort to make sure that there are no errors in the text or the code. However, to err is human, and as such, we recognize the need to keep you informed of any mistakes as they're spotted and corrected. Errata sheets are available for all our books at http://www.wrox.com. If you find an error that hasn't already been reported, please let us know. For more information on this, see Appendix G at the end of the book.

Our web site acts as a focus for other information and support, including the code from all Wrox books, sample chapters, previews of forthcoming titles, and articles and opinions on related topics.

1

Getting Started With ASP.NET

ASP.NET is a new and powerful technology for writing dynamic web pages. It's a convergence of two major Microsoft technologie's, Active Server Pages (ASP) and .NET. ASP is a relative old-timer on the web computing circuit and has provided a sturdy, fast, and effective way of creative dynamic web pages for more than five years now. .NET is the new kid on the block and is a whole suite of technologies designed by Microsoft with the aim of revolutionizing the way in which all programming development is conducted in the future and the way companies carry out business. Therefore, as a conjunction of the two, ASP.NET is a way of creating dynamic web pages while making use of the innovations present in .NET.

The first great thing to note about ASP.NET is that you don't need to know anything about ASP to get started. All you need is a little bit of HTML knowledge for building your own web pages, and you're away! ASP.NET is a more powerful technology than its older namesake, not only can it produce dynamic web pages, but it can tailor them to the browser you are using. Better still, it comes complete with a wide range of predefined controls ready for you to use in your own projects, saving you time, and making you more productive.

So, what can you do with ASP.NET? It'd probably be quicker to list what you can't! One of the most eye-catching new innovations is the way you can create your applications, so you ca write them in VB.NET, Jscript, C# (a new Java-like language from Microsoft), or even a combination of them all – you'll choose the best language for the job, or whichever language compliments your skills best.

Within your applications ASP.NET allows you to customise pages for a particular user, keep track of user's details as they move through a website and store information about them in a database of self-describing XML file. You can alter the layout of pages at the click of a button, add and remove files from your machines (if you have the appropriate permissions) and even draw on the logic of other applications without having to download them first.

In this first chapter we'll be mainly concerned with ASP.NET's installation process. We'll start with a quick introduction to the world of web servers, dynamic web pages, and a little bit about what ASP.NET is, but what we really aim to achieve is to get you running a fully functional web server, with a fully functional ASP.NET installation. By the end of the chapter you'll have created a short ASP.NET test page, to check that both the web server and ASP.NET are working as intended. Don't worry we'll have a look at some of the most common pitfalls encountered, just in case things don't go as planned!

The topics to be discussed are:

- ❑ Static Web Pages
- ❑ Dynamic Web Pages
- ❑ An overview of the different technologies for creating dynamic web pages, including ASP.NET
- ❑ Installing Internet Information Services (IIS)
- ❑ Installing the .NET Framework
- ❑ Testing and Troubleshooting your installation

What Is A Static Web Page?

If you surf around the Internet today, you'll see that there are lots of static web pages out there. What do we mean by a **static** web page? Essentially, it's a page whose content consists of some HTML code that was typed directly into a text editor and saved as an .htm or .html file. Thus, the author of the page has already completely determined the *exact* content of the page, in HTML, at some time before any user visits the page.

Static web pages are often quite easy to spot; sometimes you can pick them out by just looking at the content of the page. The content (text, images, hyperlinks, etc.) and appearance of a static web page is *always* the same – regardless of *who* visits the page, or *when* they visit, or *how* they arrive at the page, or any other factors.

For example, suppose we create a page called Welcome.htm for our website, by writing some simple HTML like this:

```
<hmtl>
<head><title>A Welcome Message</title></head>
<body>
  <h1>Welcome</h1>
  Welcome to our humble web site. Please feel free to view our
  <a HREF="contents.htm">list of contents</a>.
  <br><br>
  If you have any difficulties, you can
  <a href="mailto:webmaster@wrox.com">send e mail to the webmaster</a>.
</body>
</html>
```

Whenever any client comes to our site to view this page, it will look like this. The content of the page was determined *before* the request was made – at the time the webmaster saved the .htm file to disk:

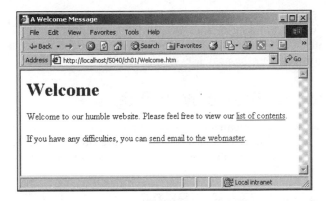

How Are Static Web Pages Served?

Ok, so let's think for a moment about how a static, pure-HTML page finds its way onto a client browser:

1. A web author writes a page composed of pure HTML, and saves it within an .htm file on the server

2. Sometime later, a user types a page request into their browser, and the request is passed from the browser to the **web server**

3. The web server locates the .htm page and converts it to an HTML stream

4. The web server sends the HTML stream back across the network to the browser

5. The browser processes the HTML and displays the page

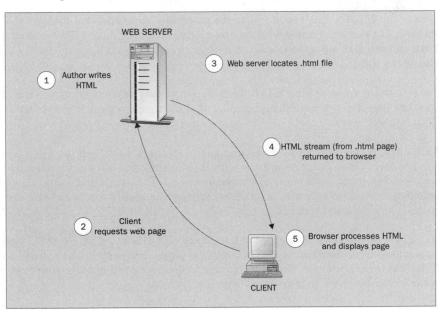

Static, pure-HTML files like `Welcome.htm` make perfectly serviceable web pages. We can even spruce up the presentation and usability of such pages by adding more HTML to create frames and tables. However, there's only so much we can achieve by writing pure HTML, precisely because their content is completely determined *before* the page is ever requested.

The Limitations of Static Web Pages

For example, suppose we want to enhance our Welcome page – so that it displays the current time or a special message that is personalized for each user. These are simple ambitions, but they are impossible to achieve using HTML alone. If you're not convinced, try writing a piece of HTML for a web page that displays the current time, like this:

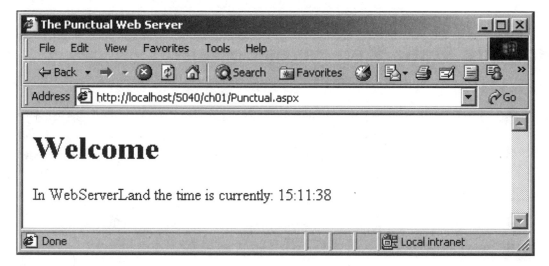

As you type in the HTML, you'll soon realize the problem – you know that the user will request the page sometime, but you don't know *what the time will be* when they do so! Hard-coding the time into your HTML will result in a page that will lways claim that the time is the same (and will almost always display the wrong time).

In other words, trying to write pure HTML for a web page that displays the time – but you can't be sure of the *exact* time that the web page should display until the time the page is requested. It can't be done using HTML alone.

Also HTML offers no features for personalizing your web pages, each web page that is served is the same for every user. There's also no security with HTML, the code is there for everybody to view, and there's nothing to stop you from copying somebody else's HTML code and using it in your own web page. Static pages might be very fast, as quick as copying a small file over a network, but they are quite limited without any dynamic features.

Since we can't create our page by saving our hard-coded HTML into a file *before* the page is requested, what we need is a way to generate the HTML *after* the page is requested. There are two ways of doing this; we'll look at them both now. Before we go any further, we need to make sure everybody is up to speed on the terminology we've introduced here.

What is a Web Server?

A **web server** is a piece of software that manages web pages and makes them available to 'client' browsers – via a local network or over the Internet. In the case of the Internet, the web server and browser are usually on two different machines, possibly many miles apart. However, in a more local situation, we might set up a machine that runs the web server software, and then use a browser on the *same* machine to look at its web pages. It makes no difference whether we access a remote web server (that is, a web server on a different machine to our browser application) or a local one (web server and browser on the same machine), since the web server's function – to make web pages available to all – remains unchanged. It might well be that you are the only person with access to our web server on your own machine, as would be case if you were running a web server from our home machine. Nevertheless, the principles remain the same.

While there are many web servers available (the commonest ones being Apache, IIS and Iplanet's Enterprise server) we're only going to talk about one in this book Microsoft's IIS 5. This is because it is the only web server that will run ASP.NET. The web server comes as part of the installation for both Windows 2000 and Windows XP. IIS version 5.0 comes with Windows 2000, and IIS version 5.1 with Windows XP; however, there is very little to distinguish the two, and we shall treat them in this chapter as the same product. We'll look at how we go about installing IIS shortly; however first let's take a look at its role in helping to create dynamic web pages.

How are Dynamic Web Pages Served?

To fully understand the nature of dynamic web pages, we first need to look at the limitations of what we can and can't do with a static web page.

Two Ways of providing Dynamic Web Page Content

Even though we're only going to be creating dynamic web pages in this book using one of these methods, you need to be aware of the two different ways of doing it, as the underlying principles for both feature heavily throughout the book.

Client-Side Dynamic Web Pages

In the client-side model, modules (or plug-ins) attached to the browser do all the work of creating dynamic pages. The HTML code is typically sent to the browser along with a separate file containing a set of **instructions**, which is referenced from within the HTML page. However, it is also quite common to find these instructions intermingled with the HTML codes. The browser then uses them to generate pure HTML for the page when the user requests the page – in other words, the page is generated **dynamically** on request. This produces a HTML page, which is sent back to the browser.

So, in this model, our set of five steps now becomes six:

1. A web author writes a set of instructions for creating HTML, and saves it within an .htm file. The author also writes a set of instructions in a different language. This might be contained within the .htm file, or within a separate file.

2. Sometime later, a user types a page request into their browser, and the request is passed from the browser to the web server.

3. The web server locates the .htm page, and may also have to locate a second file that contains the instructions.

4. The web server sends both the newly created HTML stream and instructions back across the network to the browser.

5. A module within the browser processes the instructions and returns it as HTML within the .htm page – only one page is returned, even if two were requested.

6. The HTML is then processed by the browser which displays the page

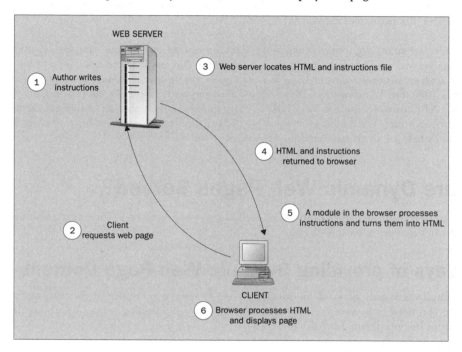

Client-side technologies have fallen out of favor in recent times, as they take a long time to download, especially if we have to download a second file with a separate set of instructions. In some cases, we might have to download several files of separate instructions. A second drawback is that each browser interprets these instructions in different ways, so we have no way of guaranteeing that if Internet Explorer understands them, whether Netscape Navigator or Opera will. An other major drawbacks are that it is a problem to write client-side code that uses server-side resources such as databases, because it is interpreted at client-side. Also all code for client-side scripting is available to everybody, which can be undesirable.

Server-Side Dynamic Web Pages

With the server-side model, the HTML source is sent to the web server with an intermingled set of **instructions**. Again this set of instructions will be used to generate HTML for the page at the time the user requests the page. Once again, the page is generated dynamically upon request. Our set of five steps once more becomes six, however, with the subtle twist regarding where the processing of instructions is done:

1. A web author writes a set of instructions for creating HTML, and saves these instructions within a file

2. Sometime later, a user types a page request into their browser, and the request is passed from the browser to the web server

3. The web server locates the file of instructions

4. The web server follows the instructions in order to create a stream of HTML

5. The web server sends the newly created HTML stream back across the network to the browser

6. The browser processes the HTML and displays the page

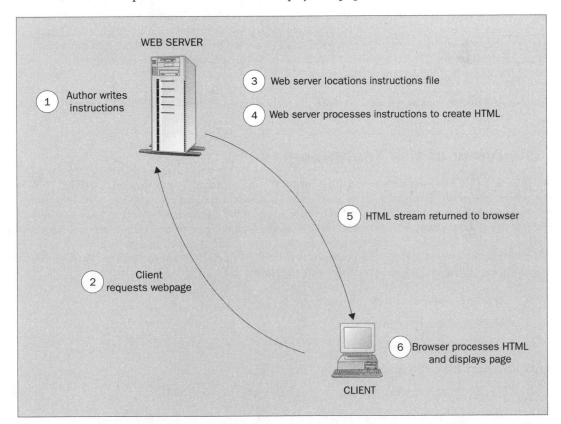

The twist is that all the processing is done on the server, before the page is sent back to the browser. One of the key advantages this has over the client-side model is that only the HTML code describing the finished page is actually sent to the browser. This means that our page's logic is hidden away on the server, and that we can safely assume that most browsers should be able to at least have a go at displaying it. ASP.NET as you might have gathered, follows the server-side model.

In fact either process of serving a dynamic web page is only slightly different from the process of serving a static web page – there's just one extra step involved (Step 5 on the client or Step 4 on the server). But in both cases this difference is crucial – the HTML that defines the web page is not generated until *after* the web page has been requested. For example, we can use either technique to write a set of instructions for creating a page that displays the current time:

```
<html>
<head><title>The Punctual Web Server</title></head>
<body>
   <h1>Welcome</h1>
   In Webserverland, the time is exactly
    <INSTRUCTION: write HTML to display the current time>
</body>
</html>
```

In this case, we can compose most of the page using pure HTML. It's just that we can't hard-code the current time. Instead, we can write a special code (which would replace the highlighted line here) that instructs the web server to generate that bit of HTML during Step 5 on the client, or Step 4 on the server, at the time the page is requested. We'll return to this example later in the chapter, and we'll see how to write the highlighted instruction using ASP.NET.

Now we're going to look at the various different technologies, including ASP.NET and see how the logic is supported in each.

An Overview of the Technologies

We just seen that there are also two distinct models for providing dynamic content. ASP.NET falls into the server-side model. However, we're going to look at what we consider to be the most important technologies in both models, as we will reference some of the client-side models in later chapters, particularly if we mention old style ASP. Not all of the technologies work in the same way as ASP.NET, but they all allow the user to achieve the same end-result – that of dynamic web applications. If ASP.NET is not an ideal solution to your problems, then you might want to consider these following technologies, taking into account the following questions:

❑   Are they supported on the platform you use?

❑   Are they difficult to learn?

❑   Are they easy to maintain?

❑   Do they have a long-term future?

❑   Do they have extra capabilities, such as being able to parse XML?

❑   Are a lot of people already using them – are there a lot of tools available?

❑   Are the support, skills, and knowledge required to use them readily available?

We're now going to give a quick overview of what each one does, and in doing so, try to give you an idea of where ASP.NET (and the ASP technology that preceded it) fits in to the big picture.

Client-Side Technologies For Providing Dynamic Content

Each of these technologies relies on a module (or plug-in) built into the browser to process the instructions we talked about earlier. The client-side technologies are a mishmash of scripting languages, controls, and fully fledged programming languages.

JavaScript

JavaScript is the original browser scripting language, and is not to be confused with Java. Java is a complete application programming language in its own right. Netscape had originally developed a scripting language, known as LiveScript, to add interactivity to their web server and browser range. It was introduced in the release of the Netscape 2 browser, when Netscape joined forces with Sun and in the process, they changed its name to **JavaScript**. JavaScript borrows some of its syntax and basic structures from Java (which in turn borrowed ideas from C), but has a different purpose – and evolved from different origins (LiveScript was developed separately to Java).

For example, while JavaScript can control browser behavior and content, it isn't capable of controlling features such as file handling. In fact, JavaScript is actively prevented from doing this for security reasons. Think about it: you wouldn't want a web page capable of deleting files on your hard drive, now would you? Meanwhile, Java can't control the browser as a whole, but it can do graphics and perform network and threading functions.

Javascript is much easier to learn than Java. It is designed to create small, efficient, applications that can do many things, from performing repetitive tasks, to handling events generated by the user (such as mouse clicks, keyboard responses, and so on).

Microsoft introduced their own version of JavaScript, known as **JScript**, in Internet Explorer 3.0 and have supported it ever since right up to, and including IE6. It has only minor differences from the Netscape version of the language, although in older versions of both browsers, the differences were originally quite a lot wider.

VBScript

In Internet Explorer 3.0, Microsoft also introduced their own scripting language, **VBScript**, which was based on their Visual Basic programming language. VBScript was intended to be a direct competitor to JavaScript. In terms of functionality, there isn't much difference between the two; it's more a matter of personal preference – VBScript has a similarly reduced functionality. Visual Basic developers sometimes prefer VBScript because VBScript is, for the most part, a subset of Microsoft's Visual Basic language. However, it enjoys one advantage that makes it more attractive to novice programmers, in that, unlike JavaScript, it isn't case-sensitive and is therefore less fussy about the particulars of the code. Although this "advantage", makes it a lot slower and less efficient.

The biggest drawback is that there isn't a single non-Microsoft browser that supports VBScript for client-side scripting. For a short while there were some proprietary plug-ins for Netscape that provided VBScript support, but these never took off. You'll find that JavaScript is much more widely used and supported. If you want to do client-side scripting of web pages on the Internet then JavaScript is the only language of choice. Indeed Microsoft themselves have replaced VBScript in their .NET framework, with VB.NET. VBScript should only be considered when working on Intranet pages where it is known that all clients are IE on Windows.

With both JavaScript and VBScript there is a module, known as a script engine, built into the browser that dynamically processes the instructions, or script, as it is known in this case.

ActiveX Controls

An **ActiveX control** is a self-contained program (or component), written in a language such as C++ or Visual Basic. When added to a web page, it provides a specific piece of client-side functionality, such as a bar chart, timer, client authentication, or database access. ActiveX controls are added to HTML pages via the `<object>` tag, which is now part of the HTML standard. ActiveX controls can be executed by the browser when they are embedded in a web page.

There is a catch. ActiveX controls were developed by Microsoft, and despite being compatible with the HTML standard, they are not supported on any Netscape browser prior to version 6 (which, at time of writing, was still in beta) without an ActiveX plug-in. Without this, they will only function on Internet Explorer. Also, unlike VBScript, ActiveX is able to manipulate items on the user's machine such as the files or Windows registry. For this reason it is very often considered a security risk and is not even allowed through firewalls. Consequently, ActiveX controls still can't really be considered either a common or a cross-platform way of making your pages dynamic and are falling out of use.

Java applets

Java is a cross-platform language for developing applications. When Java first hit the Web in the mid-1990s, it created a tremendous stir. The idea is to use Java code in the form of **applets**, which are essentially Java components that can be easily inserted into web pages with the aid of the `<applet>` tag.

Java enjoys better functionality than scripting languages, offering better capabilities in areas such as graphic functions and file handling. Java is able to provide these powerful features without compromising security because the applets run in what is known as a sandbox – which prevents a malicious program downloaded from the web from doing damage to your system. Java also boasts strong database support through JDBC.

Microsoft and Netscape browsers both have built-in Java support via something known as the Java Virtual Machine (JVM), and there are several standard `<object>` and non-standard `<applet>` tags that are used to add Java applets to a web page. These tags tell the browser to download a Java file from a server and execute it with the Java Virtual Machine built into the browser. Of course, this extra step in the web page building phase means that Java applets can take a little while to download, and can take even longer to process once on the browser. So, while smaller Java applets (that provide features such as drop-down menus and animations) are very popular on the Web, larger ones are still not as widespread as scripted pages.

Although the popularity of Java today isn't quite what some people expected, it makes an ideal teaching tool for people wishing to break out into more complex languages; and its versatility makes it well suited for programming web applications.

Curl

A very recent innovation comes from a company partly set up by Tim Berners-Lee (the innovator behind the Web and the HTML language). Curl is another programming language like Java, but unlike Java, where a second file (or more) has to be downloaded with the HTML file, it completely replaces the HTML source and the Java files. It relies on a Curl plug-in having been installed on your browser first, and currently only works on very recent browsers. The advantage are that the download time is faster than Java, and also you don't have to worry about integrating different languages into the page, as Curl is capable of providing the same features as both Java and JavaScript.

Curl is still in the very early stages of development, although the first version has been released, and more details can be obtained at http://www.curl.com.

Server-Side Technologies For Providing Dynamic Content

Each of these technologies relies on a modular attachment added onto the web server rather than the browser. Consequently, only HTML, and any client-side script, is sent back to the browser by the web server. In other words, none of the server-side code is sent back. Server-side technologies have a more consistent look and feel than client-side ones, and it doesn't take that much extra learning to move between some of the server-side technologies (excepting CGI).

CGI

The **Common Gateway Interface** (**CGI**) is a mechanism for creating scripts on the server, which can then be used to create dynamic web applications. CGI is a module that is added to the web server. It has been around for quite a bit longer than even ASP, and right now, a large proportion of dynamically created web pages are created using CGI and a scripting language. However, it's incorrect to assume that CGI does the same job as ASP.NET or ASP. Rather, CGI allows the user to invoke another program (such as a Perl script) on the web server to create the dynamic web page, and the role of CGI is to pass the user supplied data to the this program for processing. However, it does provide the same end result – a dynamic web application.

You should be aware that CGI has some severe shortcomings:.

❑ It is not easy for a beginner to learn how to program such modules.

❑ CGI requires a lot of server resources, especially in a multiuser situation.

❑ It adds an extra step to our server–side model of creating dynamic content: namely, it's necessary to run a CGI program to create the dynamic page, before the page is processed on the server.

What's more, the format in which CGI receives and transmits data means that the data is not easily manipulated by many programming languages, so you need one with good facilities for manipulating text and communicating with other software. The most able programming languages that can work on any operating system for doing this are C, C++ and Perl. While they can adequately do the job for us, they are some of the more complex languages to learn. Visual Basic doesn't offer adequate text handling facilities, and is therefore rarely used with CGI.

Despite this, CGI is still very popular with many big web sites, particularly those running on UNIX operating systems. It also runs on many different platforms, which will ensure its continued popularity.

ASP

Active Server Pages (ASP) is now dubbed "Classic ASP" and if you see this term in the book, we will be using it to describe any ASP that isn't ASP.NET. ASP commonly relied on either of the JavaScript or VBScript scripting languages (although it was also possible to use any scripting language installed on Windows, such as PerlScript) to create dynamic web pages. ASP is a module (the asp.dll file) that you attach to your web server, and it then processes the JavaScript/VBScript on the web server, and turns it into HTML, before sending it into the server, rather than doing it on the browser.

ASP lets us use practically any of the functionality provided by Windows, such as database access, e-mailing, graphics, networking, and system functions, and all from within a typical ASP page. However, ASP's shortcomings are that it is very, very slow performance wise. It is also restricted to using only scripting languages. It can't do all the things that a fully-fledged programming language can. Secondly, the scripting languages, being like "junior" versions of full programming languages, took a lot of shortcuts to make the language smaller. Some of these shortcuts make their programs longer and more complicated than is otherwise necessary. As we're going to see, ASP.NET rectifies a lot of this by making code more structured, easier to understand, and shorter.

JSP

JavaServer Pages (**JSP**) is a technology that allows you to combine markup (HTML or XML) with Java code to dynamically generate web pages. The JSP specification is implemented by several web servers, as opposed to ASP which is only supported under IIS, and plug-ins are available that allow you to use JSP with IIS 4.0/5.x. One of the main advantages of JSP is the portability of code between different servers. JSP is also very powerful, faster than ASP, and instantly familiar to Java programmers. It allows the Java program to leverage the aspects of the Java2 platform such as JavaBeans and the Java 2 libraries. JavaServer Pages isn't directly related ASP, but it does boast the ability to embed Java code into your web pages using server-side tags. More details can be found at the official site at http://www.javasoft.com/products/jsp/index.html and at the JSP FAQ at http://www.esperanto.org.nz/jsp/jspfaq.html.

ColdFusion

ColdFusion (http://www.macromedia.com/software/coldfusion/) also enables servers to access data as the server builds an HTML page. ColdFusion is a module installed onto your web server. Like ASP, ColdFusion pages are readable by any browser. ColdFusion also utilizes a proprietary set of tags, which are processed by the ColdFusion Server software. This server software can run on multiple platforms, including IIS, Netscape Enterprise Server and Unix/Apache. The major difference is that while ASP.NET solutions are built primarily with programming languages and objects, ColdFusion utilizes HTML-like tags, which encapsulate functionality. A drawback is that the ColdFusion software doesn't come for free and indeed you could find yourself paying well in excess of a thousand dollars for the privilege of running Cold Fusion on your web server.

PHP

PHP (originally **Personal Home Pages**, but more recently **PHP HyperText Preprocessor**) is another scripting language for creating dynamic web pages. When a visitor opens the page, the server processes the PHP commands and then sends the results to the visitor's browser, just as with ASP.NET or ColdFusion. Unlike ASP.NET or ColdFusion, however, PHP is open-source and cross-platform. PHP runs on Windows NT and many Unix versions, and it can be built as an Apache module and as a binary that can run as a CGI. When built as an Apache module, PHP is especially speedy. A downside is that you have to download PHP separately and go through a series of quite complex steps to install it and get it working on your machine. Also PHP's session management was non-existent until PHP 4, and still is even now,inferior to ASP's even now.

PHP's language syntax is similar to C and Perl. This might prove a barrier to people with no prior programming experience, but if you have a background in either language then you might want to take a look. PHP also has some rudimentary object-oriented features, providing a helpful way to organize and encapsulate your code. You can find more information about PHP at http://www.php.net.

ASP.NET

So why are you telling me about all these other technologies if we're only going to be learning about ASP.NET you might be wondering? Hopefully you'll see a similarity between the technologies, and this will aid your understanding of ASP.NET.

ASP.NET also relies on a module attached to the web server. However, the ASP.NET module (which is a physical file called `aspnet_isapi.dll`) doesn't do all of the work itself; it passes some on to the .NET Framework to do the processing for it. Rather than going into ASP.NET in this subsection here, it's time to start talking about it as a separate entity in its own right, as this is the focus of the book.

What is ASP.NET?

We're going to be asking this question a lot throughout the book, and each time we ask it, we're going to give you a slightly more in-depth answer. If we were we to give you a full answer now, you'd be overwhelmed by as-yet meaningless jargon. So, you'll probably be aware of some unanswered questions each time we describe it.

Our original definition, right at the very start of the chapter, was "ASP.NET is a new and powerful technology for creating dynamic web pages", and this still holds true. However, as you now know, it isn't the only way to deliver dynamic web pages, so let's refine our definition a little to read:

> **A new and powerful** server-side **technology for creating dynamic web pages.**

Secondly, ASP.NET isn't the only thing that we're interested in. In fact, it's one of a set of technologies that comprise the **Microsoft .NET Framework**. For now, you can think of this as a giant toolkit for creating all sorts of applications, and in particular, for creating applications on the Web. When we come to install ASP.NET, we will also be installing the .NET Framework at the same time, and we'll be using bits and pieces of the .NET Framework throughout the book.

How does ASP.NET differ from ASP?

Steady on! We're just getting to this part. ASP, as we've said is restricted to using scripting languages, mainly JavaScript or VBScript (although it can be any scripting language supported by the Windows system). We add ASP code to our pages in the same way as we do client-side script, and this leads to problems such as messy coding and restricted functionality. ASP.NET has no such problems.

First off ASP.NET allows you to use a far greater selection of full programming languages and also allows you to utilize to the full the rich potential of the .NET Framework. It helps you create faster, more reliable dynamic web pages with any of the programming languages supported by the .NET Framework. Typical languages supported natively are VB.NET, C# and a new version of JavaScript called JScript.NET. On top of this it is expected that third party developers will create versions of Perl, Python, and many others to work in ASP.NET. And no, before you ask, we don't expect you to be know any of these programming languages. We're going to choose one language, VB.NET, and teach you ASP.NET with it. We've chosen VB.NET as it's arguably the simplest for beginners, and it can do pretty much anything that the other languages we mentioned can as well. Lastly, and most importantly we've chosen VB.NET as it comes free with ASP.NET – so when you install ASP.NET you get VB.NET as well.

At this stage, you might be thinking, "Hang on, I've got to figure out VB.NET, then I've got to get a handle on ASP.NET – that sounds like an awful lot to learn." Don't worry; you won't be learning two languages. ASP.NET, as we said right from the beginning, is not a language – it is a technology. This technology is accessible, via a programming language. What we're going to be doing is teaching you ASP.NET features as we teach you VB.NET. So in other words, you will be creating your web pages using VB.NET and using ASP.NET to drive it. However, before you rush out and get a VB.NET book instead, we will be approaching the language from the angle of creating dynamic web pages only.

In summation, ASP.NET is a server-side technology that lets us use fully-fledged programming languages to create your web pages.

I'm still confused about ASP, ASP.NET, and VB.NET

It's really important to get these terms separate and distinct in your mind, so before we move on to actually installing and running ASP.NET, we're going to go back and redefine them just to make sure:

❑ ASP – a server-side technology for creating dynamic web pages that only lets you use scripting languages

❑ ASP.NET – a server-side technology for creating dynamic web pages that lets you use any fully-fledged programming language supported by .NET

❑ VB.NET – our chosen programming language for writing code in ASP.NET

Now it's time to get it all installed.

The Installation Process

Installation is going to be done in three steps. We're going to install the web server first, next, we're going to install the prerequisites required for ASP.NET to work, and then, lastly, we're going to install ASP.NET Premium Edition or .NET Framework SDK (which also contains ASP.NET).

> SDK stands for Software Development Kit, and the only real difference with SDK's is the huge amounts of extra documentation and examples they supply.

Anybody who is familiar with ASP might be used to it being installed automatically with the web server, and thereby doing it all in one step. This is true – classic ASP is still installed with the web server, however ASP.NET currently is only available as a separate download. This means you will have to download ASP.NET from Microsoft's web site or from CD (if you have one). However, before you can install ASP.NET, it is necessary to have a working web server.

If you have installed IIS 5.x already, or have installed either the Windows 2000 Server or Advanced Server operating system, then the good news is that you can skip this section, and go straight onto the section about installing the .NET Framework. However for the rest of us, you will have to pay careful attention to the next section.

Installing the IIS 5.x Web Server

We'll look at the installation process for IIS on Windows 2000 Professional and Windows XP Professional together, as they don't differ significantly. The main difference is that Windows 2000 installs IIS 5.0, while Windows XP installs IIS 5.1. The options for installing are exactly the same, the only thing that might differ is the look of the dialog boxes. However, the options you need to select are still the same.

Before you install it though, it's worth noting that we might not have to do much in this initial stage, as it's possible you're already running IIS 5.x. We'll describe a process for checking whether this is the case as part of the installation process. You should also note that to install anything (not just ASP.NET, but literally anything) on Windows 2000/XP you need to be logged in as a user with administrative rights. If you're uncertain of how to do this, we suggest you consult your Windows documentation. Right let's get started!

Try It Out – Locating and/or installing IIS 5.x on my Web Server machine

1. Go to the control panel (Start | Settings | Control Panel) and select the Add/Remove Programs icon. The following dialog will appear, displaying a list of your currently installed programs:

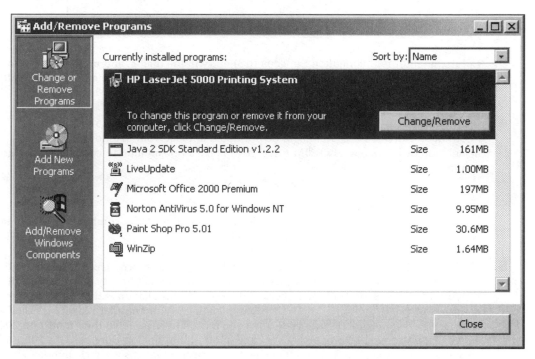

2. Select the Add/Remove Windows Components icon on the left side of the dialog, to get to the screen that allows you to install new windows components:

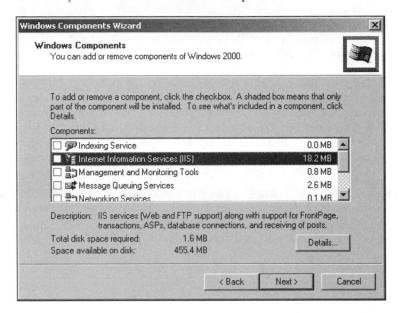

3. Locate the Internet Information Services (IIS) entry in the dialog, and note the checkbox that appears to its left. Unless you installed Windows 2000 via a custom install and specifically requested IIS, it's most likely that the checkbox will be unchecked (as shown above).

4. If the checkbox is *cleared*, then check the checkbox and click on Next to load Internet Information Services 5.x. You might be prompted to place your Windows 2000/XP installation disk into our CD-ROM drive. It will take a few minutes to complete. Then go to Step 5.

OR

If the checkbox is *checked* then you won't need to install the IIS 5.x component – it's already present on your machine. Go to Step 6 instead.

5. Click on the Details button – this will take you to the dialog shown below. There are a few options here, for the installation of various optional bits of functionality. For example, if the World Wide Web Server option is checked then our IIS installation will be able to serve and manage web pages and applications. If you're planning to use FrontPage 2000 or Visual InterDev to write your web page code, then you'll need to ensure that the FrontPage 2000 Server Extensions checkbox is checked. The Internet Information Services Snap-In is also very desirable, as you'll see later in the chapter, so ensure that this is checked too:

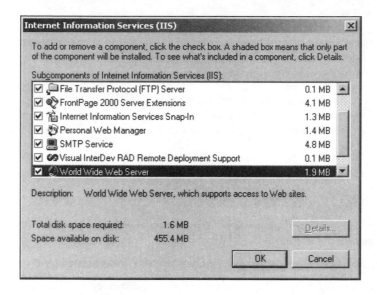

> **For the purpose of this installation, make sure all the checkboxes in this dialog are checked; then click on OK to return to the previous dialog.**

6. There's one other component that we'll need to install, for use later in this book – it's the Script Debugger. If you scroll to the foot of the Windows Components Wizard dialog that we showed above, you'll find a checkbox for Script Debugger. If it isn't already checked, check it now and click on Next to complete the installation. Otherwise, if both IIS 5.x and the script debugger are already present, you can click on Cancel to abort the process:

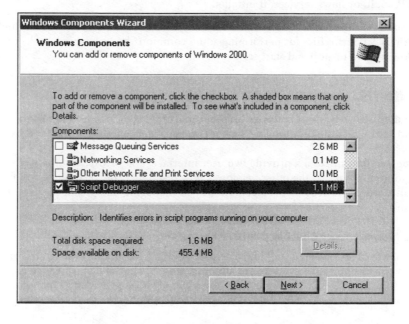

How It Works

Web Services starts up automatically as soon as your installation is complete, and thereafter, whenever you boot up Windows – so you don't need to run any further startup programs, or click on any short-cuts as you would to start up Word or Excel.

IIS installs most of its bits and pieces on your hard drive, under the \WinNT\system32\inetsrv directory; however, more interesting to us at the moment is the \InetPub directory that is also created at this time. This directory contains subdirectories that will provide the home for the web page files that we create.

If you expand the InetPub directory, you'll find that it contains several subdirectories:

❑   \iissamples\homepage contains some example classic ASP pages

❑   \iissamples\sdk contains a set of subdirectories that hold classic ASP pages which demonstrate the various classic ASP objects and components.

❑   \scripts is an empty directory, where ASP.NET programs can be stored.

❑   \webpub is also empty. This is a 'special' virtual directory, used for publishing files via the Publish wizard. Note that this directory only exists if you are using Windows 2000 Professional Edition.

❑   \wwwroot is the top of the tree for your web site (or web sites). This should be your default web directory. It also contains a number of subdirectories, which contain various bits and pieces of IIS. This directory is generally used to contain subdirectories which hold the pages that make up our web site – although, in fact, there's no reason why you can't store your pages elsewhere. We'll be discussing the relationship between physical and virtual directories later in this chapter.

❑   \ftproot, \mailroot and \nntproot should form the top of the tree for any sites that use FTP, mail, or news services, if installed.

❑   In some versions of Windows , you will find an \AdminScripts folder which contains various VBScript files for performing some common "housekeeping" tasks on the web server, allowing you to stop and start services.

Working with IIS

Having installed IIS web server software onto our machine, we'll need some means of administering its contents and settings. In this section, we'll meet the user interface that is provided by IIS 5.x.

In fact, some versions of IIS 5.x provide two user interfaces the MMC, and the PWS interface. We're only going to look at one, as the other version is now obsolete. The version we will use is the **Microsoft Management Console (MMC)** that is a generic way of managing all sorts of services. Let's take a quick look at it now.

The Microsoft Management Console (MMC)

The beauty of the MMC is that it provides a central interface for administrating all sorts of services that are installed on your machine. We can use it to administrate IIS – but in fact, when we use it to administrate other services the interface looks roughly the same. The MMC is provided as part of the Windows 2000 operating system – in fact, the MMC also comes with older Windows server operating systems.

The MMC itself is just a shell – on its own, it doesn't do much at all. If we want to use it to administer a service, we have to add a **snap-in** for that service. The good news is that IIS 5.x has its own snap-in. Whenever you need to administer IIS, you can simply call up the Internet Services Manager MMC console by selecting Start | Control Panel |Administrative Tools |Internet Services Manager.

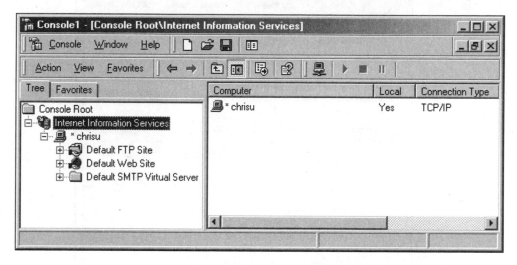

Having opened the IIS snap-in within the MMC, you can perform all of your web management tasks from this window. The properties of the web site are accessible via the Default Web Site node. We'll be using the MMC more a little later in the chapter.

Testing the Installation

The next thing to do is test the web server to see if it is working correctly, and serving pages as it should be. We've already noted that the web services should start as soon as IIS has been installed, and will restart every time you start your machine. In this section, we'll try that out.

In order to test the web server, we'll start up a browser and try to view some web pages that we know are already placed on the web server. In order to do that, we'll need to type a **URL** (Uniform Resource Locator) into the browser's Address box, as we often do when browsing on the Internet. The URL is an http://... web page address which indicates which web server to connect to, and the page we want to view.

What URL do we use in order to browse to our web server? If your web server and web browser are connected by a local area network, or if you're using a single machine for both web server and browser, then it should be enough to specify the name of the web server machine in the URL.

Identifying your Web Server's Name

By default, IIS will take the name of your web server from the name of the computer. You can change this in the machine's network settings. If you haven't set one, then Windows will generate one automatically – note that this automatic name won't be terribly friendly; probably something along the lines of "P77RTQ7881". To find the name of your own web server machine, select Start | Settings | Network and Dial-up Connections, and from the Advanced menu select Network Identification. The Network Identification tab will display your machine name under the description Full computer name:

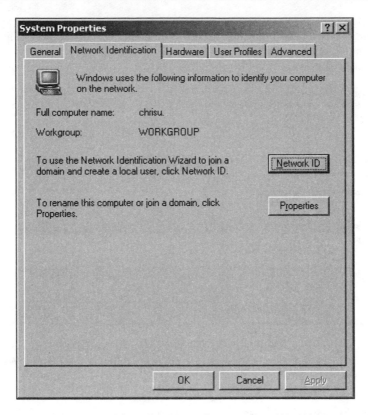

My machine has the name chrisu, and (as you can see here, and in the earlier screenshot of the MMC dialog) my web server has adopted the same name. Browsing to pages on this machine across a local area network (or, indeed, from the same machine), I can use a URL that begins http://chrisu/...

There are a couple of alternatives if you're using the same machine as both web server and browser. Try http://127.0.0.1/... – here, 127.0.0.1 is the loopback address that causes requests to be sent to a web server on the local machine. Alternatively, try http://localhost/... – 'localhost' is an alias for the 127.0.0.1 address – you may need to check the LAN settings (in your browser's options) to ensure that local browsing is not through a proxy server.

> **Throughout the book, in any examples that require you to specify a web server name, the server name will be shown as localhost, implicitly assuming that your web server and browser are being run on the same machine. If they reside on different machines, then you simply need to substitute the computer name of the appropriate web server machine.**

Browsing to a Page on your Web Server

Now you know the name of your web server, and that web services are running; you can view some classic ASP pages hosted on your web server by browsing to them with your web browser. Let's test out this theory by viewing our default home page:

Try It Out – Testing the Web Service

1. To verify that web services are working, start up your browser and type http://*my_server_name*/localstart.asp into the address box. (My server is named chrisu, so I typed in http://chrisu/localstart.asp.) Now press *Enter*; and (if all is well) you should get to see a page like this one:

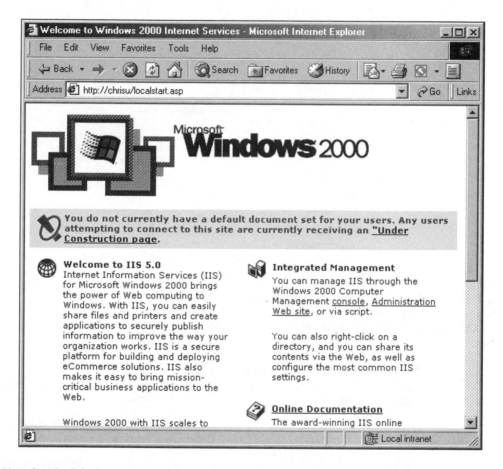

Note that the default page we see here uses the .asp extension, denoting a Classic ASP page. Support for ASP3 is provided as part of the standard IIS5.x web server program.

What do you do if this doesn't work?

If you don't get this page, then take a look at the following steps as we try to resolve the problem. If it's not working correctly, then most likely you'll be greeted with this screen:

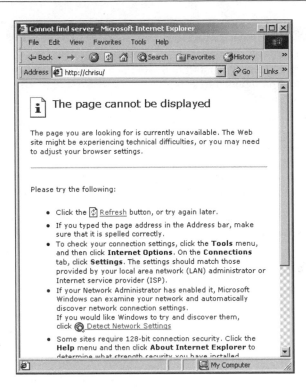

If you get this page then it can mean a lot of things, however one of the most likely problems is that your Web services are not switched on. To switch on Web services, you'll first need to start the IIS admin snap-in that we described earlier in the chapter (select Start | Run, type MMC and hit OK; then select Open from the MMC's Console menu and locate the iis.msc file from the dialog. Alternatively, just use the shortcut that you created there).

Now, click on the + of the root node in the left pane of the snap-in, to reveal the Default sites. Then right-click on Default Web Site, and select Start:

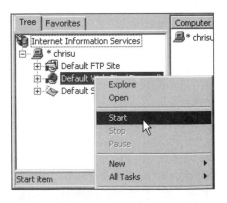

If it's still not working then here are a few more suggestions, which are based on particular aspects of your PC's setup. If you're running on a network and using a proxy server (a piece of software that manages connections from inside a firewall to the outside world – don't worry if you don't have one, they're mainly used by big businesses), there's a possibility that this can prevent your browser from accessing your web server. Most browsers will give you an opportunity to bypass the proxy server:

❑   If you're using Internet Explorer, you need to go to View | Internet Options (IE4) or Tools | Internet Options (IE5/IE6) and select the Connections tab. In IE5/IE6 press the LAN Settings button and select Bypass the proxy server for local addresses. In IE4, this section forms part of the Connections dialog.

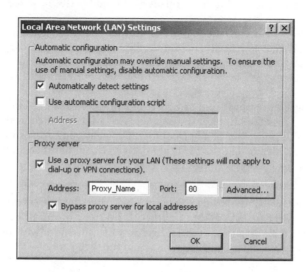

❑   If you're using Netscape Navigator (either version 4.x or 6.x) and you are having problems then you need to turn off all proxies and make sure you are accessing the Internet directly. To do this, select Edit | Preferences; in the resulting dialog select Advanced | Proxies from the Category box on the left. Then on the right, select the Direct Connection to Internet option, and hit OK. Although you won't be browsing online to the Internet, it'll allow Netscape Navigator to recognize all variations of accessing local ASP.NET pages – such as http://127.0.0.1, http://localhost, etc.

You may hit a problem if your machine name is similar to that of some web site out there on the Internet – for example, if your machine name is jimmyd but there also happens to be a public web site out there called http://www.jimmyd.com. When you type http://jimmyd into your browser's address box, expecting to view a page on your local web server, you unexpectedly get transported to http://www.jimmyd.com instead. If this is happening to you, then you need to make sure that you're not using a proxy server in your browser settings – again, this can be disabled using the Internet Options | Connection dialog or the Edit | Preferences dialog.

Lastly, if your web server is running on your home machine with a modem, and you get an error message informing you that your web page is offline, this could in fact be a misperception on the part of the web server. This can be corrected by changing the way that your browser looks for pages. To do this, select View | Internet Options (IE4) or Tools | Internet Options (IE5/IE6), choose the Connections tab and select Never dial a connection.

Of course, you might encounter problems that aren't answered above. In this case, the chances are that it's related to your own particular system setup. We can't possibly cover all the different possible configurations here; but if you can't track down the problem, you may find some help at one of the web sites and newsgroups listed later in this chapter.

Managing Directories on your Web Server

Before we install ASP.NET, we need to make one last pit stop in IIS. This is because when you come to run your ASP.NET pages, you need to understand where to place your pages, and how to make sure you have the permission to access them. As this is governed by IIS, now seems as good a time as any.

These days, many browsers are sufficiently advanced that you can use them to locate and examine files and pages that exist on your computer's hard disk. So, for example, you can start up your browser, type in the physical location of a web page (or other file) such as `C:\My Documents\mywebpage.html`, and the browser will display it. However, this isn't real web publishing at all:

❑ First, web pages are transported using a protocol called HTTP – the HyperText Transfer Protocol. Note that the http:// at the beginning of a URL indicates that the request is being sent by HTTP. Requesting C:\My Documents\mywebpage.html in your browser doesn't use HTTP, and this means that the file is not delivered and handled in the way a web page should be. No server processing is done in this case. We'll discuss this in greater detail when we tackle HTTP in Chapter 2.

❑ Second, consider the addressing situation. The string C:\My Documents\mywebpage.html tells us that the page exists in the \My Documents directory of the C: drive of the hard disk *of the machine on which the browser is running*. In a network situation, with two or more computers, this simply doesn't give enough information about the web server.

However, when a user browses (via HTTP) to a web page on some web server, the web server will need to work out where the file for that page is located on the server's hard disk. In fact, there's an important relationship between the information given in the URL, and the physical location (within the web server's file system) of the file that contains the source for the page.

Virtual Directories

So how does the relationship between the information given in the URL, and physical location work? In fact, it can work by creating a second directory structure on the web server machine, which reflects the structure of your web site. It sounds like it could be complicated, but it doesn't have to be. In fact, in this book it's going to be very simple.

The first directory structure is what we see when we open Windows Explorer on the web server – these directories are known as **physical directories**. For example, the folder `C:\My Documents` is a physical directory.

The second directory structure is the one that reflects the structure of the web site. This consists of a hierarchy of **virtual directories**. We use the web server to create virtual directories, and to set the relationship between the virtual directories and the real (physical) directories.

When you try to visualize a virtual directory, it's probably best not to think of it as a directory at all. Instead, just think of it as a nickname or alias for a physical directory that exists on the web server machine. The idea is that, when a user browses to a web page that is contained in a physical directory on the server, they don't use the name of the *physical* directory to get there, instead, they use the physical directory's nickname.

To see how this might be useful, consider a web site that publishes news about many different sporting events. In order to organize his web files carefully, the Webmaster has built a physical directory structure on his hard disk, which looks like this:

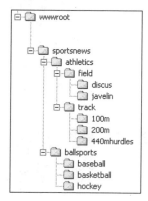

Now, suppose you visit this web site to get the latest news on the Javelin event in the Olympics. If the URL for this web page were based on the physical directory structure, then the URL for this page would be something like this:

http://www.oursportsite.com/sportsnews/athletics/field/javelin/default.asp

That's Okay for the Webmaster, who understands his directory structure; but it's a fairly unmemorable web address! So, to make it easier for the *user*, the Webmaster can assign a *virtual* directory name or *alias* to this directory – it acts just like a nickname for the directory. Here, let's suppose we've assigned the virtual name javelinnews to the c:\inetpub\...\javelin\ directory. Now, the URL for the latest Javelin news is:

http://www.oursportsite.com/javelinnews/default.asp

By creating virtual directory names for all the directories (such as baseballnews, 100mnews, 200mnews, etc.) it's easy for the user to type in the URL and go directly to the page they want:

http://www.oursportsite.com/baseballnews/default.asp
http://www.oursportsite.com/100mnews/default.asp
http://www.oursportsite.com/200mnews/default.asp

Not only does this save the user from long, unwieldy, URLs – it also serves as a good security measure, because it hides the physical directory structure from all the web site visitors. This is good practice, otherwise hackers might be able to work out and access our files if they know what the directory structure looked like. Moreover, it allows the Webmaster's web site structure to remain independent of the directory structure on his hard drive – so he can move files on his disk between different physical folders, drives, or even servers, without having to change the structure of his web pages. There is a performance overhead to think about as well, as IIS has to expend effort translating out the physical path. It can be a pretty costly performance wise to have too many virtual directories.

Let's have a crack at setting up our own virtual directories and permissions (please note that these permissions are set automatically if you use the FrontPage editor to create a new site – so don't use FrontPage to set up this site for you unless you know what you're doing).

Try It Out – Creating a Virtual Directory and Setting Up Permissions

Now let's take a quick look at how you can create your own virtual directory. We'll use this directory to store the examples that we'll be creating in this book. We don't want to over complicate this example by creating lots of directories, so we'll demonstrate by creating a single physical directory on the web server's hard disk, and using the IIS admin tool to create a virtual directory and make the relationship between the two:

1. Start Windows Explorer and create a new physical directory named `BegASPNET`, in the root directory of your hard drive. For example, `C:\BegASPNET\`:

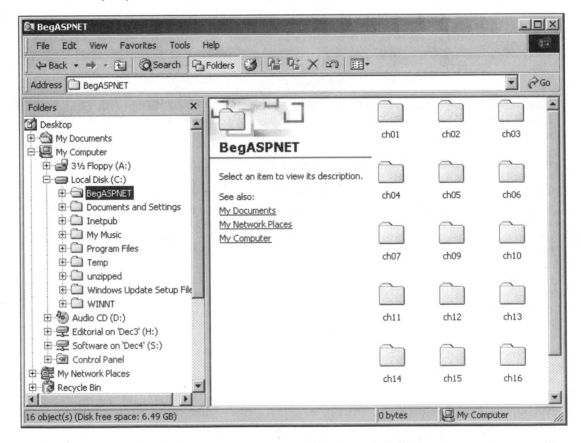

2. Next, start up the IIS admin tool (using the MMC, as we described earlier). Right-click on **Default Web Site,** and from the menu that appears select New | Virtual Directory. This starts the **Virtual Directory Creation Wizard,** which handles the creation of virtual directories for you and the setting up of permissions as well. You'll see the splash screen first, which looks like this. Click on Next:

3. Type 5040 (an abbreviation of the book's ISBN, found on the back cover) in the Alias text box; then click Next:

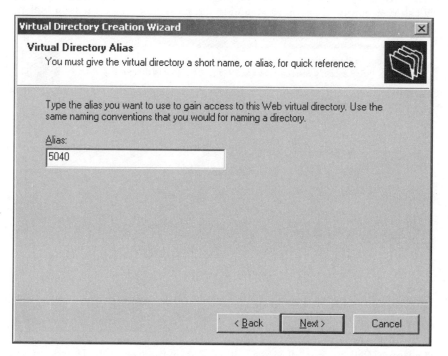

4. Click on the Browse... button and select the directory \BegASPNET that you created in Step 1. Then click Next:

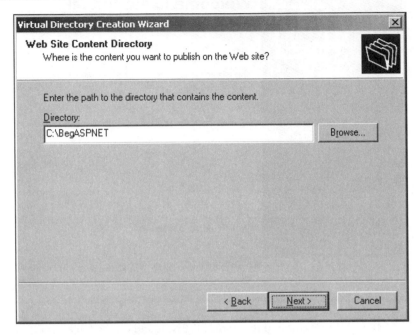

5. Make sure that the Read and Run scripts checkboxes are checked, and that the Execute checkbox is empty. Click on Next, and in the subsequent page, click on Finish:

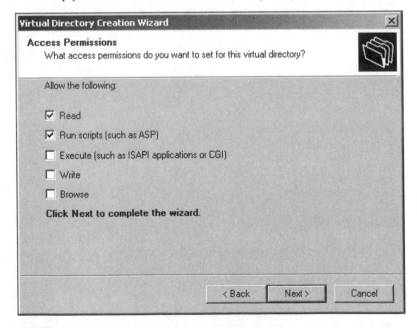

6. The BegASPNET virtual directory will appear on the tree in the IIS admin window:

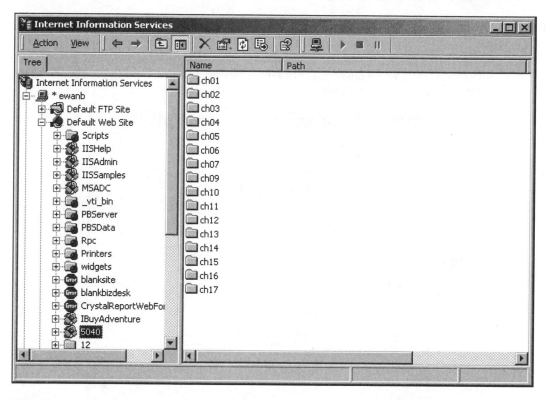

How It Works

We just created a physical directory called BegASPNET, this directory will be used throughout the book to store our code examples. The download files from wrox.com are also designed to follow this structure. Within this directory we recommend that you create a sub-directory for each of the chapters in order to keep things tidy (this needn't be a virtual directory – just a physical one.)

You've also created a virtual directory called 5040, which you created as an alias for the physical BegASPNET directory. If when we create Chapter 1 examples you place the ASP.NET files in the physical C:\BegASPNET\ch01 directory; you can use the browser to access pages stored in this folder. You'll need to use the URL http://my_server_name/5040/ch01/...

You should also note that the URL uses the alias /5040 – IIS knows that this stands for the directory path C:\BegASPNET. When executing ASP.NET pages, you can reduce the amount of typing you need to do in the URL, by using virtual directory names in your URL in place of the physical directory names.

We also set the permissions read and run – these must be set or the IIS security features will prevent you from running any ASP.NET pages. The Execute checkbox is left empty as allowing others to run applications on your own machine is a sure way of getting viruses or getting hacked. We'll take a closer look at permissions now, as they are so important. If you don't assign them correctly you may find that you're unable to run any ASP.NET pages at all – or worse still, that anybody at all can access your machine, and alter (even delete) your files via the Web.

Permissions

As we've just seen, we can assign permissions to a new directory as we create it, by using the options offered in the Virtual Directory Wizard. Alternatively, we can set permissions at any time, from the IIS admin tool in the MMC. To do this, right-click on the 5040 virtual directory in the IIS admin tool, and select Properties. You'll get the following dialog:

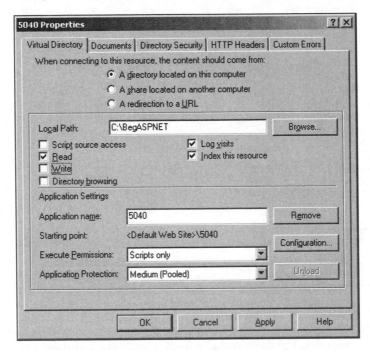

It's quite a complicated dialog, and it contains a lot of options – not all of which we wish to go into now.

Access Permissions

The four check boxes on the left are of interest to us, as they govern the types of access for the given directory and dictate the permissions allowed on the files contained within that directory. Let's have a look at what each of these options means:

❑ **Script source access** – This permission enables users to access the source code of an ASP.NET page. It's only possible to allow this permission if the Read or Write permission has already been assigned. But we generally don't want our users to be able to view our ASP.NET source code, so we would usually leave this checkbox unchecked for any directory that contains ASP.NET pages. By default, all directories created during setup have Script Source Access permission disabled. You should leave this as is.

❑ **Read** – This permission enables browsers to read or download files stored in a home directory or a virtual directory. If the browser requests a file from a directory that *doesn't* have the Read permission enabled, then the web server will simply return an error message. Note that when the folder has Read permission turned off, HTML files within the folder cannot be read; but ASP.NET code within the folder can still be run. Generally, directories containing information that you want to publish (such as HTML files, for example) should have the Read permission enabled, as we did in our Try It Out.

❑ **Write** – If the write permission on a virtual directory is enabled, then users will be able to create or modify files within the directory, and change the properties of these files. This is not normally turned on, for reasons of security and we don't recommend you alter it.

❑ **Directory Browsing** If you want to allow people to view the contents of the directory (that is, to see a list of all the files that are contained in that directory), then you can allow this by checking the Directory Browsing option.

If someone tries to browse the contents of a directory that has Directory Browsing enabled but Read disabled, then they may receive the following message:

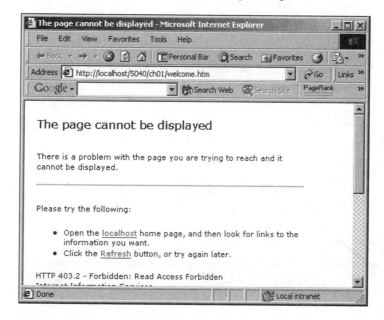

> For security reasons, we'd recommend disabling this option unless your users specifically need it – such as when transferring files using FTP (file transfer protocol), from your web site . If you don't know what FTP is, then we recommend this strongly, as you obviously don't need it!

Execute Permissions

There's a dropdown list box near the foot of the Properties dialog, labeled Execute permissions – this specifies what level of program execution is permitted on pages contained in this directory. There are three possible values here – None, Scripts only, or Scripts and Executables:

❑ Setting Execute permissions to None means that users can only access static files, such as image files and HTML files. Any script-based files of other executables contained in this directory are inaccessible to users. If you tried to run an ASP.NET page, from a folder with the permission set to None, we would get the following – note the Execute Access Permission forbidden message in the page:

37

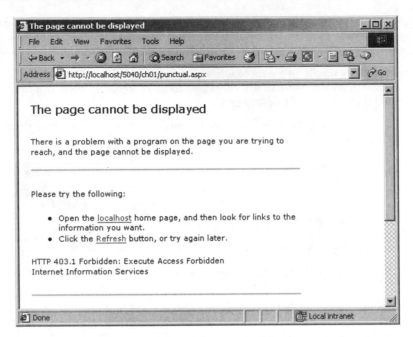

❑ Setting **Execute** permissions to **Scripts Only** means that users can also access any script-based pages, such as ASP.NET pages. So if the user requests an ASP.NET page that's contained in this directory, the web server will allow the ASP.NET code to be executed, and the resulting HTML to be sent to the browser.

❑ Setting **Execute** permissions to **Scripts and Executables** means that users can execute any type of file type that's contained in the directory. It's generally a good idea to avoid using this setting, in order to prohibit users from executing potentially damaging applications on your web server.

For any directory containing ASP.NET files that you're publishing, the appropriate setting for the **Execute** permissions is **Scripts Only**. Now you've started to familiarize yourself with IIS, you're ready to prepare your machine for the installation of ASP.NET itself.

Prerequisites for installing ASP.NET

Before you can install ASP.NET or the .NET Framework you will need to install the Microsoft Data Access Components (MDAC) version 2.7 or later. This is a set of components that will enable you to use ASP.NET to communicate with databases and display the contents of your database on a web page. Without these components installed you won't be able to run any of the database examples in this book. This will affect examples as early as Chapter 2, so please don't skip this stage! Although you might already have an earlier version of MDAC installed (such as 2.5 if you're using Windows 2000), unless you have specifically upgraded, in all likelihood you won't have the most up to date version and will still need to upgrade.

The Microsoft Data Access Components is a small download (roughly 5 or 6 MB) available for free from Microsoft's site at http://www.microsoft.com/data.

As of writing, Microsoft hadn't yet placed 2.7 at the above URL, as it was still in beta. If you can only find version 2.6 at this location, we suggest trying http://www.microsoft.com/downloads/release.asp?ReleaseID=30134 Alternatively you can look at http://msdn.microsoft.net for a list of the latest .NET resources.

The installation for MDAC 2.7 is pretty straightforward, but we'll run through it quickly just to make sure that everything is clear.

Try It Out – Installing MDAC 2.7

1. MDAC 2.7 comes as file `MDAC_typ_dnld.exe` that you will need to run. Once you have run it, it will ask you for a location where you wish to download the files. Type in an appropriate location:

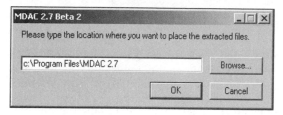

2. In fact rather confusingly, it seems only to download one file, `MDAC_TYPE.EXE` to the pre-specified location. If you run this EXE file, then it will begin the installation process.

3. After agreeing to the terms of the license, there's a good chance that you will be asked to reboot our system, it will tell you this in advance.

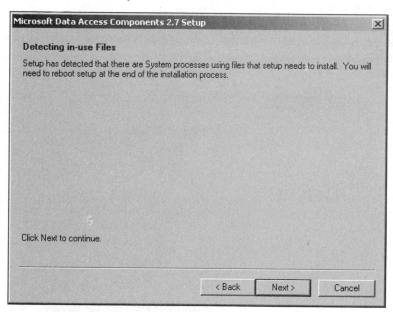

4. Then the installation process will continue without requiring further intervention, although you might have to wait for a system reboot, if one was specified earlier.

You're now ready to install ASP.NET.

Installing ASP.NET and the .NET Framework SDK

We're almost ready to install ASP.NET, but there are two important points to be made beforehand.

First, there are two different types of installation available from Microsoft's site, the .NET Framework SDK and ASP.NET. The .NET Framework SDK already contains ASP.NET, so you do not need to download both separately. You only need to download one. Both downloads contain ASP.NET, VB.NET, and the .NET Framework.

The **ASP.NET Premium Edition** download is a smaller, streamlined download that only contains the bare bones needed for you to run ASP.NET and the .NET framework. None of the extra documentation or samples will be included. The size differential between the two is pretty big (ASP.NET is 18MB while the .NET Framework SDK is a staggering 123MB), so unless you have the .NET Framework SDK on CD (which you can order from the Microsoft site) or broadband high-speed Internet access, you'll probably want to download the ASP.NET version.

Don't worry, this won't affect your ability to run the examples in this book – everything's been written so that it will run on the ASP.NET Premium Edition. While you won't have direct access to the help files, all support materials are available online at Microsoft's http://www.asp.net site.

Don't worry about replacing an existing Classic ASP installation, since ASP.NET will be installed alongside ASP and they will both continue to work with no action from us.

We'll now walk you through a typical installation of both ASP.NET Premium Edition and the .NET Framework SDK. The installation process is the same for Windows 2000 and Windows XP, so once again we're only going to detail the installation process on the former. Although the wizard looks a bit different on XP, it asks for exactly the same things.

Try It Out – Installing ASP.NET

1. Click on setup.exe and after confirming that you do want to install ASP.NET Premium, and after a short interval, you are propelled into the setup wizard:

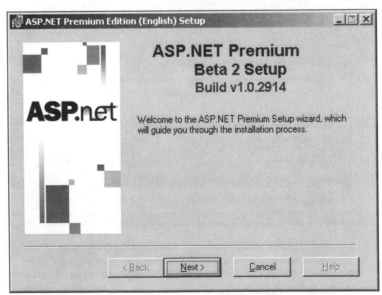

2. Click on Next and accept the License agreement to continue. The next dialog after the license agreement will ask you where you wish to install ASP.NET:

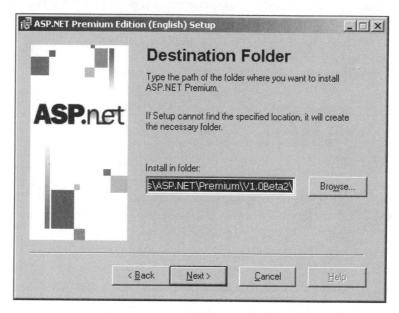

3. Unless you have good reason to, we suggest leaving the location as the one specified by the setup wizard, and then click on Next. ASP.NET will now install without further intervention:

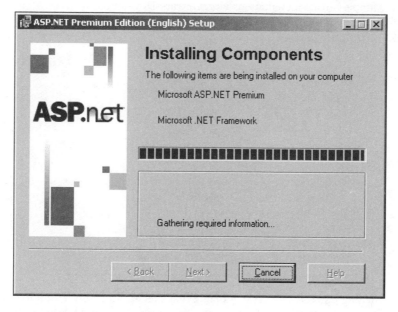

4. You will be notified when installation has finished, and unlike with the MDAC 2.7, you probably won't have to reboot. We can now go to the testing section and check everything is working.

Installing the .NET Framework SDK

1. Click on `setup.exe` and after confirming that you do want to install the NET Framework SDK package, and after an interval of a few minutes, you are propelled into the setup wizard:

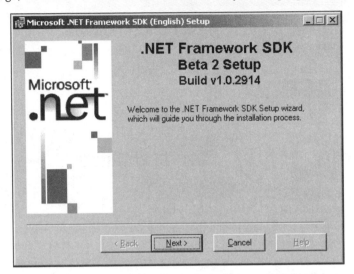

2. Click on **Next** and accept the License agreement to continue. The next dialog after the license agreement will ask you which different pieces of the SDK you need to install. You should check all of them, although if you're short of hard drive space, you could choose to omit the SDK_Samples or documentation. The Software Development Kit is essential:

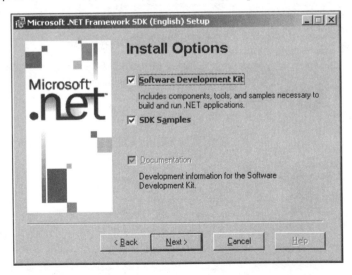

3. After clicking on **Next** you get to a dialog that specifies the destination folder for the different .NET Framework SDK samples and bits and pieces. You can choose to install these wherever you want. More importantly there is a checkbox at the foot of the dialog, which asks you to register environment variables. This checkbox should be checked, as we will use the environment variables in later chapters:

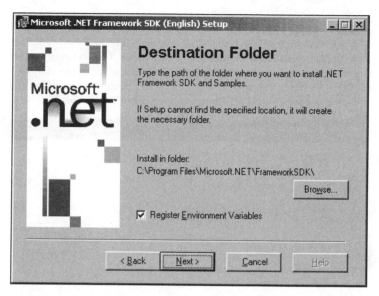

Click on Next and the .NET Framework SDK will install without further ado. It shouldn't require a reboot.

Troubleshooting Hints and Tips

The installation process is very straightforward, and will work on the majority of machines. However, sometimes the particular configuration of your machine will prevent it from installing. Unfortunately we can't cover all of the possible eventualities, but if it doesn't work on yours, you should check that you have enough hard disk space, as this is the most common cause of problems. Also try to ensure that the installation process isn't curtailed half way, as no installer is completely foolproof at removing all the different bits and pieces of the aborted install and it can cause problems when you try to reinstall, and leave you needing to reformat your hard drive to get it to work correctly. Other than that, check the list of newsgroups and resources later in this chapter.

ASP.NET Test Example

Ok, we've now reached the crux of the chapter, checking to see if everything is working correctly. Do you remember the punctual web server code that we talked about earlier in the chapter – in which we wanted to write a web page that displays the current time? We'll return to that example now. As you'll see it's quite a simple bit of code, but it should be more than enough to check that ASP.NET is working Okay.

Try It Out – Your first ASP.NET web page

1. Open up a text editor and type in the following code:

```
<script language="vb" runat="server">
Sub Page_Load()
time.text=Hour(Now) & ":" & Minute(Now) & ":" & Second(Now)
End Sub
</script>

<html>
<head><title>The Punctual Web Server</title></head>
<body>
  <h1>Welcome</h1>
  In WebServerLand the time is currently:
<asp:label id="time" runat="server" />
</body>
</html>
```

We strongly suggest (and will assume throughout) that you use Notepad to code all the examples in this book, since it will always do precisely what you ask it to and no more. It's therefore a lot easier to track down any problems you're having, and is a great deal easier than troubleshooting problems caused by FrontPage or similar web page editors.

2. Save this page as `punctual.aspx`. Make sure that you save it in the physical folder you created earlier `C:\BegASPNET\Ch01\`.

When you save the file, you should double-check that your new file has the correct suffix. It should be `.aspx`, since this is how you tell the web server that the page contains ASP.NET code. Be aware that Notepad (and many other text editors) consider `.txt` to be the default. So in the **Save** or **Save As** dialog, make sure that you change the **Save As** type to read **All Files**, or **All Files(*.*)**,or enclose the path and filename in quotes.

3. Now start up your browser and type in the following: http://localhost/5040/punctual.aspx

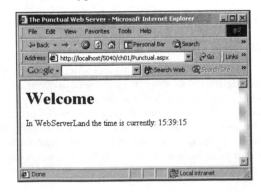

4. Now click on the refresh button of the browser and the displayed time will change. In effect the browser is showing a new and different instance of the same page.

5. Now on your browser select View Source or similar, (depending on which browser you're using) from the browser menu to see the HTML source that was sent from the web server to the browser. The result is shown below. You can see that there is no ASP.NET code to be seen, and nothing before the first <html> tag – the ASP.NET code has been processed by the web server and used to generate pure HTML, which is hard-coded into the HTML source that's sent to the browser:

```
Punctual[1] - Notepad
File  Edit  Format  Help

<html>
<head><title>The Punctual web server</title></head>
<body>
  <h1>welcome</h1>
  In webServerLand the time is currently:
<span id="time">15:39:15</span>
</body>
</html>
```

Here, you can see the HTML that was sent to the browser when I Refreshed the page at 15.39:15.

6. As we mentioned before, you can expect this to work in any browser – because the ASP.NET is processed on the web server. If you have another browser available, try it out.

How It Works

Easy wasn't it? (If you didn't get it to work first time, then don't rush off to email technical support just yet – have a little look at the next section, *ASP.NET Troubleshooting*, first.) Now let's take a look at the ASP.NET code that makes this application tick.

Of course, there is only one block of ASP.NET code (ignoring the server control) in the whole program. It's enclosed by the <script> and </script> tags:

```
<script language="vb" runat="server">
Sub Page_Load()
time.text=Hour(Now) & ":" & Minute(Now) & ":" & Second(Now)
End Sub
</script>
```

The script delimiters specify which code needs ASP.NET to run, and we'll look at them in detail in the next chapter. If we ignore the <script> tags for the time being, and just think of them as ASP.NET code delimiters, then we're left with just three lines. If we further ignore the Sub Page_Load and End Sub lines, which are standard to many ASP.NET programs, and which we'll be discussing in Chapter 3, we're left with one line. This line:

```
time.text=Hour(Now) & ":" & Minute(Now) & ":" & Second(Now)
```

tells the web server to go off and run the VB.NET `Now()` function **on the web server**. The VB.NET `Now()` function returns the current time **at the web server**. It returns the values of the `Now()` function divided up into hour, minute, and second values. The result of this function is returned as part of the `<ASP: label>` control, further down the page. We'll be looking at this control in Chapter 3.

If the web server and browser are on different machines, then the time returned by the web server might not be the same as the time kept by the machine you're using to browse. For example, if this page is hosted on a machine in Los Angeles, then you can expect the page to show the local time in Los Angeles – even if you're browsing to the page from a machine in Cairo.

This example isn't wildly interactive or dynamic, but it illustrates that we can ask the web server to go off and do something for us, and return the answer **within the context** of an HTML page. Of course, by using this technique with things like HTML forms and other tools, we'll be able to build a more informative, interactive, interface with the user.

ASP.NET Troubleshooting

If you had difficulty with the example above, then perhaps you fell into one of the simple traps that commonly snare new ASP.NET programmers, and that can be easily rectified. In this section we'll look at a few common errors and reasons why your script might not run. If you did have problems, maybe this section will help you to identify them.

Program Not Found, or the Result of the ASP.NET isn't being Displayed, or the Browser tries to Download the File

You'll have this problem if you try to view the page as a local file on your hard drive, like this:

C:\BegASPNET\ch01\punctual.aspx

You'll also get this problem if you click on the file in Windows Explorer. If you have Microsoft FrontPage or Visual Studio.NET installed, then it will start up and attempt to help you to edit the code. Otherwise, your browser may display a warning message, or most likely it will ask you which application you wish to use to open up the ASPX file:

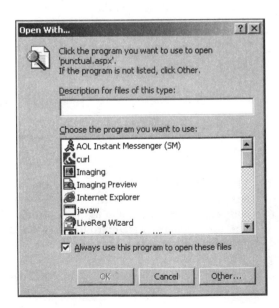

Older browsers may try to download the file:

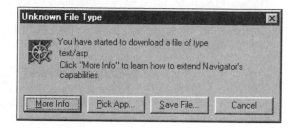

The Problem

This is because you're trying to access the page in a way that doesn't cause the ASP.NET page to be requested **from the web server**. Because you're not requesting the page through the web server, the ASP.NET code doesn't get processed – and that's why you don't get the expected results.

To call the web page through the web server and have the ASP.NET code processed, you need to reference the web server in the URL. Depending on whether you're browsing to the server across a local network, or across the Internet, the URL should look something like one of these:

http://localhost/5040/ch01/punctual.aspx
http://www.distantserver.com/5040/ch01/punctual.aspx

Page Cannot be Displayed: HTTP Error 403

If you get a 403 error message, then it's probably because you don't have permission to execute the ASP.NET code contained within the page – notice the **Execute Access Forbidden Error** in the middle of the page:

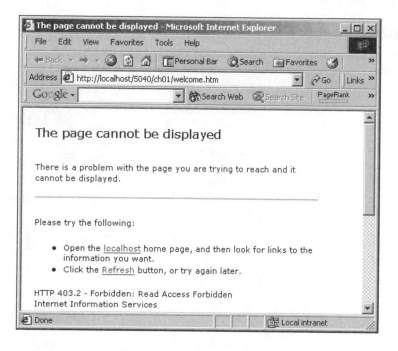

As you'll recall, permissions are controlled by the properties of the virtual directory that contains the ASP.NET page. To change these properties, you'll need to start up the IIS admin snap-in in the MMC, as we described earlier in the chapter. Find the BegASP.NET virtual directory in the left pane, right-click on it and select Properties. This will bring up the BegASP Properties dialog that we met earlier in the chapter:

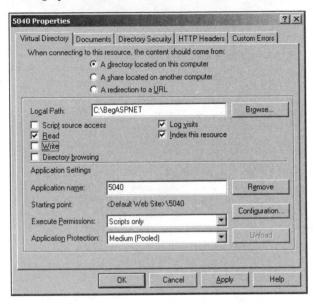

Here, you'll need to check that the value shown in the Execute Permissions box is "Scripts only" or "Scripts and Executables" –but definitely **NOT** "None".

Page Cannot Be Found: HTTP Error 404

If you get this error message then it means that the browser has managed to connect to the web server successfully, but that the web server can't locate the page you've asked for. This could be because you've mistyped the URL at the browser prompt. In this case, we'll see a message like this:

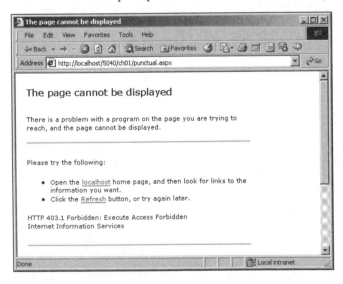

If you get this page, then you might suspect one of the following errors:

❑ A simple typing error in the URL, for example. http://localhost/5040/ch01/punctually.aspx

❑ A wrong directory name, for example. http://localhost/5040/punctual.aspx instead of http://localhost/5040/ch01/punctual.aspx

❑ Including a directory separator (/) after the file name, for example. http://localhost/5040/ch01/punctual.aspx/

❑ Using the directory path in the URL, rather than using the alias, for example. http://chrisu//BegASPNET/ch01/punctual.aspx

❑ Saving the page as .html or .htm, rather than as an .aspx, for example. http://localhost/5040/ch01/punctual.htm

❑ Or as above, you've used the name of the physical directory rather than the virtual one for example.

http://localhost/BegASPNET/ch01/punctual.aspx

Of course, it may be that you've typed in the URL correctly, and you're **still** experiencing this error. In this case, the most likely cause is that you have used Notepad to save your file and that (when you saved the file) it used its default Save As Type setting, which is Text Documents (*.txt). This automatically appends a .txt suffix to the end of your file name. In this case, you will unwittingly have finished up with a file called punctual.aspx.txt.

To check if that is what happened, go to Windows Explorer, and view the (physical) folder that contains the file. Go to the Tools menu and select Folder Options.... Now, in the View tab, ensure that the Hide file extensions for known file types is unchecked, as shown here:

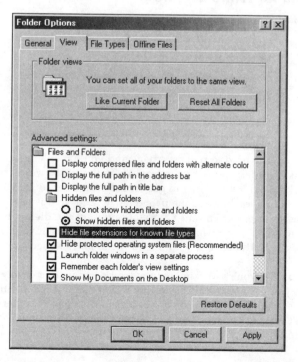

Now click **OK** and return to view your file in Windows Explorer. You may well see something like the following:

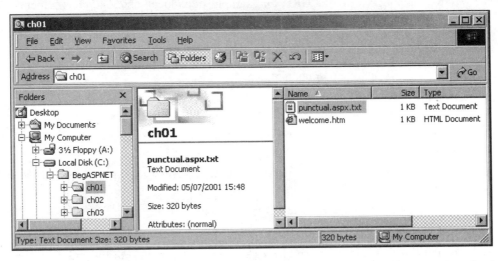

As you can see, Notepad has been less than honest in its dealings with you: when you thought that you had saved your file as `punctual.aspx`, it had inconveniently saved it as `punctual.aspx.txt`. Not surprisingly, your web server won't be able to find your file if it's been renamed accidentally. To correct the filename, right click on the it in the right pane above, select **Rename** from the dropdown menu that appears and remove the .txt at the end.

Web Page Unavailable While Off-line

Very occasionally, you'll come across the following message box:

This happens because you've tried to request a page and you haven't currently got an active connection to the Internet. This is a misperception by the browser (unless your web server isn't the same machine as the one you're working on) – it is trying to get onto the Internet to get your page when there is no connection, and it's failing to realize that the page you've requested is present on your local machine. One way of retrieving the page is to hit the **Connect** button in the dialog; but that's not the most satisfactory of solutions (since you might incur call charges). Alternatively, you need to adjust the settings on your browser. In IE5/IE6, select the **File** menu and uncheck the **Work Offline** option.

This could also be caused if you're working on a network and using a proxy server to access the Internet. In this case, you need to bypass the proxy server or disable it for this page, as we described in the section *Browsing to a Page on your Web Server*, earlier in the chapter. Alternatively, if you're using a modem and you don't need to connect, you can correct this misperception by changing the way that IE looks for pages. To do this, select the **Tools | Connections** option and select **Never dial a connection**.

I Just Get a Blank Page

If you see an empty page in your browser, then it probably means that you managed to save your `punctual.aspx` without entering any code into it, or that you didn't remember to refresh the browser.

The Page Displays the Message but not the Time

If the web page displays the message "In Webserverland, the time is exactly " – but doesn't display the time – then you might have mistyped the code. For example, you may have mistyped the name of the control:

```
time.text=Hour(Now) & ":" & Minute(Now) & ":" & Second(Now)
```

and:

```
<asp:label id="hour" runat="server" />
```

The name of the control "hour", must match the first word in the line of ASP.NET code, otherwise the control won't be able to identify it.

I Get an Error Statement Citing Server Error

If you get a message stating that the page cannot be displayed, and citing a server error such as:

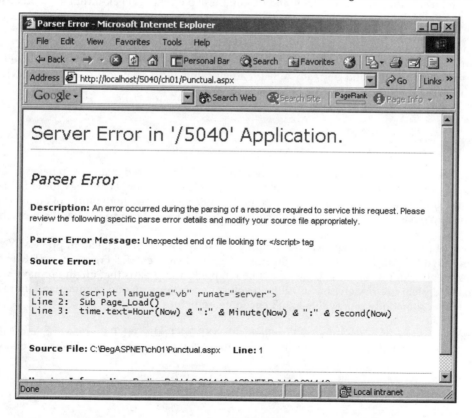

then it means that there's an error in the ASP.NET code itself. Usually, there's additional information provided with the message. For example, you'd get this error message if you omitted the closing `</script>` tag on your code. To double-check that this isn't the case, use the sample `punctual.aspx` from the Wrox site at http://www.wrox.com.

I Have a Different Problem

If your problem isn't covered by this description, it's worth testing some of the sample ASP.NET pages that are supplied with the QuickStart tutorials at http://www.asp.net. These should help you to check that IIS has actually installed properly. You can always uninstall and reinstall if necessary, although before you try this, rebooting the server first might help.

You can get support from http://p2p.wrox.com, which is our web site dedicated to support issues in this book. Alternatively, there are plenty of other web sites that are dedicated to ASP and ASP.NET. In fact you will find very few sites focus on just one of the two technologies. Here are just a few:

http://www.asp.net
http://www.asptoday.com
http://www.asp101.com
http://asptracker.com
http://www.15seconds.com
http://www.4guysfromrolla.com

There are lots of solutions, discussions, and tips on these pages, plus click-throughs to other related pages. Moreover, you can try the newsgroups available on www.asp.net such as aspngfreeforall.

You should now have successfully downloaded, set up and installed both IIS and ASP.NET, and got your first ASP.NET application up and running. If you've done all that, you can pat yourself on the back, make a cup of tea, and get ready to learn about some of the principles behind ASP.NET in the next chapter.

Summary

We started the chapter with a brief introduction to ASP.NET and to dynamic web pages in general and we looked at some of the reasons why you'd want to use a server-side technology for creating web pages. We looked at some of the history behind dynamic web pages, in the form of an overview of the other technologies. This very brief introduction to ASP.NET will be expanded in the next chapter.

The bulk of the chapter though, was taken up by a description of the installation process. You must have installed IIS 5.0/5.1, MDAC 2.7 and either ASP.NET or the .NET Framework SDK to be able to progress at all with this book, so please don't be tempted to skip parts that might not have worked. We've listed plenty of resources that will help you get everything up and running, and there's rarely a problem that somebody somewhere hasn't encountered before.

The next chapter covers the software installed with ASP.NET, the .NET Framework, and will build up in much greater detail what ASP.NET does, what the .NET Framework is, and how the two work together.

Anatomy of an ASP.NET Page

Before we get stuck into using all the fantastic features that ASP.NET has to offer, we're going to take a little time to step through the mechanics behind it. After all, we've not really got a fix on how ASP.NET works its magic yet, and although we don't need to know everything about it, it's going to be very helpful later on if we have an idea of what's going on behind the scenes.

We will be covering the following points:

- ❑ What the .NET Framework is, and what it does.
- ❑ What ASP.NET is, what it does, and how it relies on the .NET Framework.
- ❑ The role of the Common Language Runtime.
- ❑ Core concepts of ASP.NET.
- ❑ Some examples of ASP.NET and the .NET Framework in action.

Since this chapter's mostly quite theoretical, I'm also including a few examples towards the end, demonstrating just how flexible and powerful ASP.NET really is.

So, first of all, let's consider the big beef behind it all – namely, the .NET Framework.

What is .NET?

I recently attended one of Microsoft's .NET roadshows, and between talks, one of the speakers was giving out free software to anyone in the audience who could answer one of several simple questions. He challenged the audience by asking them to define what they thought .NET was. Tellingly, in a room full of experienced developers, not a single hand was raised. He moved on quickly, and instead chose to ask what a 'delegate' in the C# language was, and was greeted with a much larger response, to this potentially much more baffling question.

You may have come across lengthy discourses from journalists and Microsoft's rival companies, claiming that even Microsoft doesn't have a clear idea of what it is, and it's certainly true to say that it could have been made somewhat clearer than it has been. Accusations of it being "vaporware" (that is all hype, and no substance) ring hollow, however, if you scratch below the surface and start taking a look at the different bits and pieces that go to make it up.

In fact, **.NET** is a catchall term that embraces Microsoft's core strategy, plans, and vision for the forseeable future. At the heart of this strategy is the **.NET Framework**, which provides the core technology that underpins it all. The Framework itself consists of several components, of which ASP.NET is just one.

.NET is designed to help solve many fundamental problems faced by programmers. Many of these issues concern rather involved programming concepts that are beyond the scope of this book – suffice it to say, it takes care of a great deal of the hard work involved in building large, reliable applications. It also blurs the line between writing applications to run locally on your own machine and writing applications that can be accessed over the Web. What's more, it doesn't bring with it all the overheads traditionally associated with 'simple' programming frameworks – that is, we don't need to write complex code in a high-powered language to get some fairly impressive speed out of our .NET programs.

In the course of this section, we'll break down this mysterious entity piece by piece, take a brief look at its main features, and consider the function of each one.

> *The aim of this book is to get you writing ASP.NET web applications, therefore we're not going to try and detail every single aspect of the Framework. In many cases, all we really need to know is what its elements can do for us, and what they need from us in order to do it. Other elements provide us with important functionality, and these will merit further discussion. In this way, we hope you'll get more than a simple knowledge of ASP.NET, but also a sense for how it fits in with the .NET Framework as a whole.*

We can break down our discussion of the .NET Framework into a few specific topics:

❑ MS Intermediate Language – all the code we write is compiled into a more abstract, trimmed-down form before it's executed. Whichever .NET language is used to write the code, the trimmed code that's created from it is defined using MSIL: the Common Language of .NET.

❑ The Common Language Runtime (CLR) – this is a complex system responsible for executing the MSIL code on the computer. It takes care of all the nitty-gritty tasks involved in talking to Windows and IIS.

❑ The .NET Framework Class Libraries – these are code libraries containing a mass of tremendously useful functionality, which we can very easily bolt into our own applications to make complex tasks much more straightforward.

❑ The .NET Languages – these are simply programming languages that conform to certain specific structural requirements (as defined by the Common Language Specification), and can therefore be compiled to MSIL.

❑ ASP.NET – this is how the .NET Framework exposes itself to the Web, using IIS to manage simple pages of code, so that they can be compiled into full .NET programs. These are then used to generate HTML that can be sent out to browsers.

Before we go into any detail though, we need to take a careful look at some fundamental code concepts and terminology.

From Your Code to Machine Code

As you probably know, computers understand everything in terms of binary bits – sequences of ones and zeros that represent instructions and data – hence the enthusiastic use of the word 'digital', to describe anything even vaguely related to computers. We refer to these binary instructions as **machine code**. Obviously, for most humans it's totally impractical to remember the particular sequence of ones and zeros that prints "Hello World" (let alone one that defines a sophisticated web application), so we use programming languages as a **layer of abstraction**. We gloss over much of the possible functionality offered by the bitstream, and abstract it away as human-readable commands; many of these may even correspond to real words.

Once we've written some code in a human-friendly language, we need to convert it into machine code, and this process is called **compilation** – we literally compile the human-readable instructions into machine-readable instructions. Part of this compilation process involves hardwiring information regarding the local environment into the compiled code, so that it can make the most efficient use of all the machine resources available to it.

> *The particular sequences of bits that make up a specific hardware instruction varies from one type of processor to another. This is why you'll not get Windows to run on one of those nice colorful iMacs – we can say that these systems aren't* **binary compatible**.

For many years, there's been a simple choice between two types of compilation:

❑ **pre-compiled code** – This is code that we compile before we need to use it, so that it's ready and waiting to be executed on the hardware. This makes for very fast execution, as the compiler has the opportunity to spend time considering the full set of code, and **optimize** it to get the most out of the specific set of instructions available on the local system. We've compiled it on a specific machine, however, therefore we're now either tied to using it on that machine, or we need to set up another machine with the same system and all the same resources as our own.

❑ **interpreted code** – This code gets compiled as and when we decide to execute it. We're therefore, not tied down to a specific machine in the same way, since the compiler can wire up resources as required. We don't get the performance advantage, however, since we have to wait for the compiler to interpret the code, and it doesn't get the chance to fully optimize the code we've written.

Introducing a Common, Intermediate Language

When we write a program to run on the .NET Framework – perhaps using VB.NET or C# – we must always compile this human-readable code before using it. The way that .NET's compilers are designed however, means that this only takes us half way to the usual binary code that presents such problems of portability. In fact, they compile our code into a special format, called the MS Intermediate Language (MSIL). Some optimization can be done as part of this process, since the MSIL's structure doesn't have to be as easily human-readable as our original code. Consequently, it doesn't have to be nearly so verbose, clearly structured, or neatly arranged.

When we execute this MSIL, we effectively pass it on to the CLR, which is really the cornerstone of the .NET Framework. Just as the .NET Framework lies at the heart of Microsoft's .NET vision, the Common Language Runtime (CLR) lies right at the heart of the Framework. Its main purpose is to take care of executing any code that's been fed into it, and to deal with all the nightmarishly complicated jobs that Windows and IIS require doing in order to work properly. The CLR uses another compiler – the **JIT (Just-In-Time) compiler** – to compile to true machine code, and make any last minute, machine-specific optimizations to the program, so that it can run as quickly as possible on the specific machine it inhabits.

> **MSIL is .NET's famous** Common Language**, and is designed to give us the best of both worlds: the structural optimization of pre-compiled code along with the portability of interpreted code.**

Most importantly, MSIL itself is not at all machine-specific, so we can execute it on any machine that has the CLR installed. In essence, once we've written some .NET code and compiled it, we can copy it to any machine with the CLR installed, and execute it there.

While the CLR currently only exists in a form that's compatible with Windows (9x, NT, 2000, and XP versions), moves are already afoot to build a version for the Unix-based operating system FreeBSD.

MSIL can also be generated from any human-readable language with a compatible structure. VB.NET, C# and JScript.NET are all ".NET-compliant" languages; that is, they conform to a **Common Language Specification** that guarantees they can be faithfully compiled to MSIL. We can therefore, use these and any other compliant languages *interchangably* within our applications – once a set of files have been compiled to MSIL, they're all effectively written in the same language!

Objects, Objects Everywhere

In order to properly grasp how .NET works, you need to have at least a notional idea of what we mean when we talk about **objects**. Just about everything you come across within the .NET Framework is implemented as a software object – we can in fact describe .NET as an **object-oriented environment**. What does that mean, then?

An object is a self-contained unit of functionality – almost like a miniature program. It holds data, and lets us (or code that we write), access and manipulate that data in simple, well-defined ways. By defining particular classes of objects (in a **class definition**) to do very specific tasks, we can define methods of access that are very well suited to the particular things we're going to do with that object. We can therefore wrap up all sorts of complex processes into a few very specific instructions.

For example, let's consider a publishing company – there are many different jobs defined within the company, such as Manager, Editor, Author Agent, and Web PR. Once we've established the basic jobs that an Editor needs to do (edit chapters, review chapters, send chapters to authors for rewrites and so on) we probably don't need to know all the gory details of how they do those jobs. You could simply say "Dan, please edit chapter 2", and leave him to get on with it. You might also say, "Dan, is the chapter edited yet?", and assume the editor could tell you whether or not it was.

This is essentially how objects make our lives as programmers easier – in this instance, there's an Editor class, from which template we've built an Editor type object called Dan. We can instruct the object to Edit, Review, or Return To Author, and we can ask it about its state, that is, whether its EditComplete information is set to True or False. Just to reiterate: we don't need to know *how* our Editor object Dan does this – we just need to know a few specific ways in which to instruct it, and how to ask it for information.

The advantages of this type of programming are fairly obvious – we don't need to worry about how each object does its job, so it's a whole lot easier to build large, complex (but at the same time reliable) applications. We simply hook together lots of job-specific objects in simple, well-defined ways to make something large yet relatively stable – somewhat analogous to building a skyscraper out of Lego bricks!

The .NET Base Classes

One very important feature of the .NET Framework, and one that saves us from potentially hideous amounts of tedious coding is its **base class library**. This contains an enormous amount of ready-written code that you can include in any of your programs to simplify all sorts of useful tasks.

The base framework classes cover a multitude of different functions. For instance, you'd expect to be able to display text, but what happens if you want to perform more specialized graphical operations,

such as draw a circle or a rectangle? Or add an animated image to an ASP.NET page? These functions are all provided in a number of base classes that are grouped together under a **namespace** called `System.Drawing`.

> **Namespaces are used by .NET to group together classes in functionally similar groups. In terms of our earlier business analogy, this is equivalent to a departmental grouping. For example, all the jobs directly involved with producing book content (Editor, Author Agent, Project Administrator) are classified as being within Editorial. Likewise, jobs involving the layout and printing of the physical book (Cover Designer, Illustrator) can be classified as being within the Production department.**

We can import these classes into our ASP.NET pages, by simply adding a **directive** to the top of the file. For example, if we want to make use of all the classes defined in the System.Drawing namespace, we just say:

```
<%@ Import Namespace=System.Drawing %>
```

This literally *directs* the Framework to apply a specific setting to the page as a whole: in this case, importing the classes in `System.Drawing` for use in our page.

There are a whole variety of .NET classes, from classes that look after generating graphics to classes that help to simplify data access. We'll see some examples that rely on our importing namespaces towards the end of the chapter. After you've run them, you might try removing them and seeing what error messages are produced!

So why does .NET do this? Why can't you have access to all the classes you need, all of the time? One reason is performance. The more you include in an application, the slower it will run. It makes sense, therefore, to only include the bits you need to use, or the most commonly used classes. In fact, a selection of the most commonly used classes is included by default anyway. This concept of including classes has been a standard feature in many programming languages, such as Java, for a long time now.

The Class Browser

How can I get a list of these pre-defined .NET classes, you might be wondering? One great tool that makes all of this more transparent is the .NET Framework class browser. This is an ASP.NET application that lists the main Framework classes defined on whatever machine it's being run from. The class browser application is available as part of the Quickstart Tutorials that are provided along with the .NET Framework SDK. If you have these installed, you'll be able to run it locally from:

http://localhost/quickstart/aspplus/samples/classbrowser/vb/classbrowser.aspx

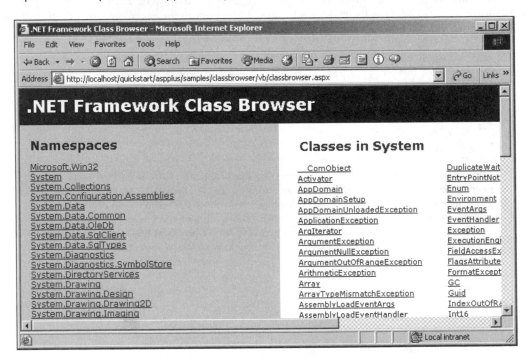

If you've only installed the ASP.NET Premium edition, then you won't have the class browser installed. It is possible, however, to access the class browser online at:

http://www.gotdotnet.com/quickstart/aspplus/samples/classbrowser/vb/classbrowser.aspx

Of course, this will list the System classes available on *that* site's web server (the standard set of base classes under the System namespace). You won't be able to browse any additional namespaces – such as custom namespaces or add-ins that you've installed – or configure the browser application. Nevertheless, you should find that it covers most of your needs. It really is a very handy tool for students and developers alike. You'll almost certainly find the class browser useful in later chapters, as much of the book will be concerned with exploring .NET's various classes.

How ASP.NET works

For most purposes, we can simply think of ASP.NET pages as just like normal HTML pages that have certain sections marked up for special consideration. When .NET is installed, the local IIS web server is automatically configured to look out for files with the extension `.aspx` and to use the ASP.NET module (a file called `aspnet_isapi.dll`) to handle them.

Technically speaking, this module **parses** the contents of the ASPX file – it breaks them down into separate commands in order to establish the overall structure of our code. Having done this, it arranges the commands within a pre-defined class definition – not necessarily together, and not necessarily in the order in which we wrote them. That class is then used to define a special ASP.NET `Page` object, and one of the tasks this object then performs is to generate a stream of HTML that can be sent back to IIS, and from here, back to the client:

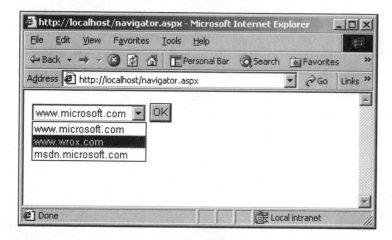

We'll take a more detailed look at various aspects of this process as we progress through the book – in particular, Chapters 10 and 14 will explore the Page object, and discuss some of the specific things it can do for us.

For now though, we're more concerned with the immediate business of getting a page up and running. The first stage is to let the web server identify your web page as an ASP.NET page.

Saving your ASP.NET files with a .aspx suffix

In the last chapter, we defined an ASPX .NET page simply by saving some appropriate code in a file with the extension `.aspx`. This is important because, all ASP.NET pages are identified by the `.aspx` suffix that is attached to the end of the filename. Only pages with `.aspx` will be sent to ASP.NET for processing. Even pure HTML files with a `.aspx` suffix will be sent for processing, so don't give a standard HTML page the `.aspx` suffix, because this will adversely affect performance.

Although it's possible to use the `<script>` tags in a `.htm` file, anything you put between them won't be interpreted as ASP.NET code. Instead, it will be sent to the browser for client-side execution, which is unlikely to work, because only HTML can be executed on the browser. If you try to include any ASP.NET code within these tags, then the script will not be executed, and your web page won't look the way you intended.

Now that we know how to identify an ASP.NET page using the extension .aspx, we now need to consider how to identify specific sections of code within those pages.

Inserting ASP.NET code into our web pages

If we place any kind of server-side code (not just ASP.NET code) within our web page source files, then we need to label it so that the server can identify it as server-side code, separate from the HTML code, and therefore arrange for it to be dealt with correctly. The best way to delimit ASP.NET code from the HTML code in your pages is by using <script> tags, with the runat attribute set to server. This indicates the target host for processing the code: the web server.

The default when using the <script> tag is for the script to be executed on the browser (client-side), so if you're writing a server-side script, then you must remember to specify this.

As we know, ASP.NET itself is not a language, but a technology for creating dynamic pages. It allows us to use fully-fledged programming languages to define sections of code within our pages. The default language for coding in ASP.NET is VB.NET – to define a page that uses VB.NET, you can simply include a Page directive at the top of the page as follows:

```
<%@ Page language="VB" %>
```

To define some code, we can then do the following:

```
<script language="VB" runat="server">
... Visual Basic.NET declarations go here ...
</script>
```

We've already specified VB.NET as our language of choice, therefore the language attribute in the above example isn't essential, and can be omitted. It serves to clarify which language we're using, however, so let's leave it in.

To define a page in a different language – C# for example – you can do the following:

```
<%@ Page language="C#" %>

<script language="C#" runat="server">
... C# declarations go here ...
</script>
```

In both of these snippets, all code enclosed with the <script> element must be in the language specified.

Although we can place server-side <script> blocks at just about any point within an ASPX, any code we put *inside* them must be **declarations**, that is, we're declaring sections of code that we'll be using later on, but they won't actually be executed until some other code triggers them.

A class definition is one type of declarative code – it's not code we actually want the CLR to execute as soon as it's been spotted. Rather we want to say: "here's some code that we want to use later on". We'll look at this topic in more detail when we get to Chapter 5.

The logical question is, therefore: how do we trigger our page code in the first place? The solution is to use the following structure:

```
<script language="VB" runat="server">
  sub Page_Load(source As Object, e As EventArgs)
... Visual Basic.NET code goes here ...
  end sub
</script>
```

We won't go into detail explaining this format – suffice to say, when the page is loaded, the declarative block that we've labeled `sub Page_Load()` is triggered automatically. Any code we want to run when the page starts up, we can put straight into here.

Try It Out – Inserting server-side (ASP.NET) code

In this example, we're only concerned with how we insert code, not with how the ASP.NET code works, so the code is quite trivial. We're just going to demonstrate how web pages are affected by the placement of ASP.NET code:

1. Using your preferred text editor, create a new document and type in the following code:

```
<html>
  <head>
    <title>Inserting ASP.NET code Example</title>
  </head>
  <body>
    Line1: First HTML Line<br />
    Line2: Second HTML Line<br />
    Line3: Third HTML Line<br />
  </body>
</html>
```

2. Save this as `message.aspx` in your test directory; if you've followed the steps from Chapter 1, this will be `C:\BegASPNET\ch02\`.

3. Open your browser, and call up http://localhost/5040/ch02/message.aspx :

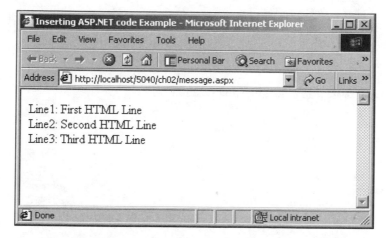

4. Now go back to the code page of `message.aspx`, and place the following code into it:

```
<script language="VB" runat="server">
Sub Page_Load()
 Response.Write ("First ASP.NET Line<br />")
 Response.Write ("Second ASP.NET Line<br />")
 Response.Write ("Third ASP.NET Line<br />")
End Sub
</script>
```

```
<html>
  <head>
    <title>Inserting ASP.NET code Example</TITLE>
  </head>
  <body>
    Line1: First HTML Line<br />
    Line2: Second HTML Line<br />
    Line3: Third HTML Line<br />
  </body>
</html>
```

5. Save this as `message2.aspx`, and view this example in your browser, by typing in the URL: http://localhost/5040/ch02/message2.aspx. You should get a similar result, however this time, we can see the results from the ASP.NET code we just added above the HTML:

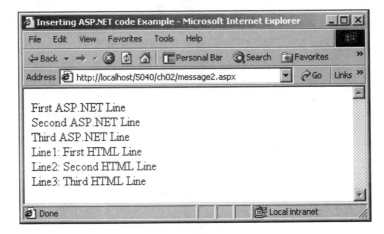

6. Now cut the code between the `<script>` tags (including the `<script>` and `</script>` tags), and paste it into the following position:

```
<html>
<head>
<title>Inserting ASP.NET code Example</title>
</head>
<body>
Line1: First HTML Line<br />
Line2: Second HTML Line<br />
Line3: Third HTML Line<br />
```

```
<script language="VB" runat="server">
Sub Page_Load()
Response.Write ("First ASP.NET Line<br />")
Response.Write ("Second ASP.NET Line<br />")
Response.Write ("Third ASP.NET Line<br />")
End Sub
</script>
</body>
</html>
```

7. Save this as `message3.aspx`.

8. Call up `message3.aspx` in your browser:

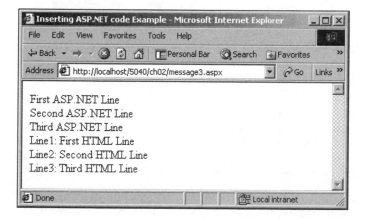

How It Works

The first thing to note is that although this is ASP.NET code, we're not actually creating a dynamic web page. All we're doing is demonstrating the order in which ASP.NET code and HTML are executed. The next point is that all three of these examples use the `.aspx` suffix – despite the fact the first page, `message.aspx` only contained HTML code. As far as the web server is concerned therefore, all three pages are ASP.NET pages. This demonstrates that HTML is treated in the same way in both pure HTML pages and ASP.NET pages.

The code in the first page just displays a number of HTML lines and some plain text:

```
<html>
<head>
<title>Inserting ASP.NET code Example</TITLE>
</head>
<body>
Line1: First HTML Line<br />
Line2: Second HTML Line<br />
Line3: Third HTML Line<br />
</body>
</html>
```

When the code is parsed in your browser, the lines are displayed in order, as you might expect.

In the second web page, `message2.aspx`, we have a combination of some pure HTML, some plain text, and a little server-side script. By using `runat="server"`, we specified that the following script (the highlighted lines) should be processed on the server, before the page is sent to the browser:

```
<script language="VB" runat="server">
Sub Page_Load()
 Response.Write ("First ASP.NET Line<br/>")
 Response.Write ("Second ASP.NET Line<br/>")
 Response.Write ("Third ASP.NET Line<br/>")
End Sub
</script>
<html>
<head>
<title>Inserting ASP.NET code Example</TITLE>
</head>
<body>
Line1: First HTML Line<br/>
Line2: Second HTML Line<br/>
Line3: Third HTML Line<br/>
</body>
</html>
```

The ASP.NET code is placed within a subroutine called `Page_Load()`. Whenever ASP.NET loads up a page it executes any code contained within the `Page_Load()` subroutine first. If you place code in this subroutine that spits out text to the browser for example, this text will always precede any text from the HTML part of the file. Note also that any code placed within the `<script>` blocks must always be placed in a subroutine otherwise it won't work.

The ASP.NET code uses a statement `Response.Write` to display three ASP.NET lines, and as you might expect, these three lines are displayed before the HTML lines. We'll talk a little more about `Response.Write` in Chapter 3.

In the last example, we move the ASP.NET code to come after the HTML lines:

```
<body>
Line1: First HTML Line<br />
Line2: Second HTML Line<br />
Line3: Third HTML Line<br />
<script language="VB" runat="server">
Sub Page_Load()
Response.Write ("First ASP.NET Line<br />")
Response.Write ("Second ASP.NET Line<br />")
Response.Write ("Third ASP.NET Line<br />")
End Sub
</script>
```

Yet the browser still displays the ASP.NET code first.

This is the reason; the web server first scans the file to see if there is a `<script runat="server">` tag. If there is one then it arranges for the `script` to be processed first. The ASP.NET code is in the `Page_Load()` subroutine, which always runs as soon as the page is loaded, therefore the ASP.NET output always appears first, even if the `<script>` tag is not at the top of the code page. In other words, the server takes no notice of the position of the `<script>` tag relative to other elements of the page.

There's an important lesson to be learned here; namely, that if you place ASP.NET code in the `Page_Load()` subroutine within the `<script>` tag, it will always be processed before the HTML code.

Other ways to use code in an ASP.NET page

We now know how to output text to a browser using ASP.NET. Unfortunately, anything we output from ASP.NET will always precede the rest of the HTML, which is pretty awkward if we want to insert ASP.NET output anywhere else on the page. We will now therefore look at a couple of ways we can interweave ASP.NET output with HTML.

It's actually possible to incorporate code into our pages much more directly. If we specify a **render code block** (also known as an **inline code block**), any code it contains is executed as part of the page rendering process (this is the process by which we get our Page object to send back HTML for the browser to display). We can write render code blocks like this:

```
<%
Response.Write ("hello world!")
%>

<html>
  <body>
    Line1: First HTML Line<br />
    <% Response.Write ("First ASP.NET Line<br />") %>
    Line2: Second HTML Line<br />
    <% Response.Write ("Second ASP.NET Line<br />") %>
    Line3: Third HTML Line<br />
    <% Response.Write ("Third ASP.NET Line<br />") %>
  </body>
</html>

<%
Response.Write ("Goodbye!")
%>
```

We can write code that executes wherever you put it, whether that's inside the HTML `<head>` tags, inside the `<body>`, or even right at the end of the page. While this saves on keystrokes, however, it ultimately makes for quite intractable code. We therefore, encourage you to try and find alternatives wherever possible, and we'll spend quite a lot of the next chapter looking at one particular, very powerful way of doing this, using **server controls**. Separating the ASP.NET code from the HTML not only makes the code easier to read, but means that its a great deal easier to strip out either and reuse them in another page.

> *As we'll see later on in the book, we can even separate code and HTML blocks into separate files. For now though, we'll keep them together for clarity's sake.*

We recommend (and will actively practice throughout the book) placing the ASP.NET code in a declarative code block near the top of the file, and just before the line of first `<html>`:

```
<script language="VB" runat="server">
... ASP.NET code here ...
</script>

<html>
... HTML code here ...
</html>
```

Try-It-Out – Interweaving ASP.NET Output with HTML

Now, you may still be wondering: "how do we intersperse static content with dynamic content if the code and the HTML are separated like this?" Let's take a quick look at how to get round this very problem; you'll soon realise that this doesn't restrict us nearly as much as you might think.

1. Enter the following code and save it is `interweave1.aspx`:

```
<html>
<head>
<title>Interweaving ASP.NET code and HTML Example</title>
</head>
<body>
Line1: First HTML Line<br />
<% Response.Write ("First ASP.NET Line<br />") %>
Line2: Second HTML Line<br />
<% Response.Write ("Second ASP.NET Line<br />") %>
Line3: Third HTML Line<br />
<% Response.Write ("Third ASP.NET Line<br />") %>
</body>
</html>
```

2. Point your browser to `interweave1.aspx`:

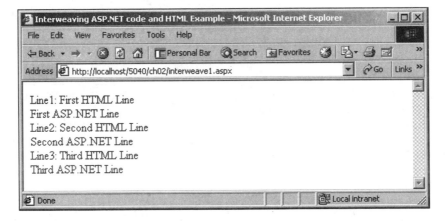

3. Although this method works, there are some major drawbacks, as we mentioned earlier. Luckily for us, there's another way to interweave ASP.NET output with HTML. Enter the following code and save it as `interweave2.aspx`:

```
<script language="VB" runat="server">
Sub Page_Load()
  Message.Text="The ASP.NET line"
End Sub
</script>

<html>
<head>
```

```
<title>Inserting ASP.NET code Example</TITLE>
</head>
<body>
First HTML Line<br/>
<asp:label id=Message runat="server"/> <br />
Second HTML Line<br/>
</body>
</html>
```

4. Browse to `interweave2.aspx`:

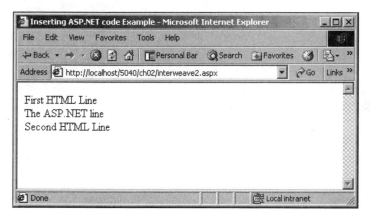

How It Works

You might have noticed that in the first web page, `interweave1.aspx`, we didn't use the declarative `<script>` block at all. Instead, we inserted lines of ASP.NET code between the HTML using `<%...%>` delimiters, these lines of code are called **inline code blocks**:

```
<html>
<head>
<title>Inserting ASP.NET code Example</title>
</head>
<body>
Line1: First HTML Line<br />
<% Response.Write ("First ASP.NET Line<br />") %>
Line2: Second HTML Line<br />
<% Response.Write ("Second ASP.NET Line<br />") %>
Line3: Third HTML Line<br />
<% Response.Write ("Third ASP.NET Line<br />") %>
</body>
</html>
```

As the server reads the page, it neatly inserts the output of the ASP.NET code exactly where we specified it with the inline code blocks. Unfortunately, even though this technique can be handy sometimes, there are some drawbacks to using inline code blocks like this. Not only does our ASP.NET code get jumbled up with HTML (and therefore becomes very difficult to reuse in another program), but it also becomes very difficult to maintain. Making modifications to code that uses inline code blocks interspersed with HTML markup, means having to comb through all the HTML to find the relevant lines; if the ASP.NET code were kept separate in a declarative code block, this would be much simpler.

In `interweave2.aspx`, we solve all these problems by returning to the declarative `<script>` block at the head of the document that contains all the ASP.NET code:

```
<script language="VB" runat="server">
Sub Page_Load()
   Message.Text="The ASP.NET line"
End Sub
</script>
```

This time, instead of having the `Response.Write` statements that send text to the browser as we did in the `previous Try-it-Out`, we have just one line of code in which we define the text that we want to insert – "`The ASP.NET line`".

The following section contains the HTML markup, but notice that we have now added a special marker (highlighted) that tells ASP.NET where to insert the text that we specified earlier in the declarative code block:

```
<html>
<head>
<title>Inserting ASP.NET code Example</TITLE>
</head>
<body>
First HTML Line<br/>
<asp:label id=message runat="server"/> <br />
Second HTML Line<br/>
</body>
</html>
```

This marker is known as a **sever control** which we will be exploring in more detail in subsequent chapters. The `id` attribute of the server control corresponds with the line of code in the `<script>` block in which we specify the text to display. Now we can insert ASP.NET output anywhere we want on the page, while maintaining a clear separation between ASP.NET code and HTML, or between content (ASP.NET code) and presentation (HTML).

The .NET Framework/ASP.NET in Action

This has been a very theory-heavy chapter, and you're probably dying for some examples now, so let's get stuck into a couple. We've still not looked at much ASP.NET code therefore, we're going to throw in quite a lot of commands that won't necessarily make a lot of sense to you at this stage. We will break down the basic tasks that our code is performing, however, and you may like to refer back to this example as you progress through the book, so that you can build up a more detailed picture of what it's doing as your understanding grows.

One thing that ASP.NET makes very straightforward (particularly compared to the Classic ASP approach), is the process of binding your web page to a database.

Binding to a database

With previous versions of ASP, binding to a database has been, quite frankly, a bit of nightmare. For most people, the key reason for using ASP, and now a key reason for using ASP.NET, is the ability to connect a web page to a database, and to be able to browse and even update it. Prior to ASP.NET, this would have taken quite a bit of coding. A major step forward is the way that it is now possible to bind your web pages to a database using minimal amounts ASP.NET code. ASP.NET provides a set of server controls that cut down, and almost completely eliminate, the need for separate coding.

We'll use one of the example databases provided with the .NET Framework, the grocertogo database – which is in Access format, and build a quick web page that allows us to browse the contents of the Products table, one of four tables contained with the database. If you only have ASP.NET Premium Edition then modify the lines beginning with "strConnect += "Data Source=", to point to any database you have on your system.

Try It Out – Binding to a Database

1. Open your web page editor of choice, and type in the following:

```
<%@ Import Namespace="System.Data" %>
<%@ Import Namespace="System.Data.OleDb" %>
<script language="vb" runat="server">
Sub Page_Load(Sender As Object, E as EventArgs)
  Dim objConnection As OleDbConnection
  Dim objCommand As OleDbDataAdapter
  Dim strConnect As String
  Dim strCommand As String
  Dim DataSet1 As New DataSet

  strConnect =  "Provider=Microsoft.Jet.OLEDB.4.0;"
  strConnect += "Data Source=C:\Program Files\Microsoft.NET\FrameworkSDK\"
  strConnect += "Samples\quickstart\aspplus\samples\grocertogo\data"
  strConnect += "\grocertogo.mdb;"
  strConnect += "Persist Security Info=False"

  strCommand = "SELECT ProductName, UnitPrice FROM products"
  objConnection = New OleDbConnection(strConnect)
  objCommand = New OleDbDataAdapter(strCommand, objConnection)
  objCommand.Fill(DataSet1, "products")
  DataGrid1.DataSource=DataSet1.Tables("Products").DefaultView
  DataGrid1.DataBind()
End Sub
</script>
<html>
<head>
<title>Data Grid Control example</title>
</head>
<body>
<asp:DataGrid id="DataGrid1" runat="server"  />
</body>
</html>
```

2. Save this as datacontrol.aspx.

3. Open this page in your browser:

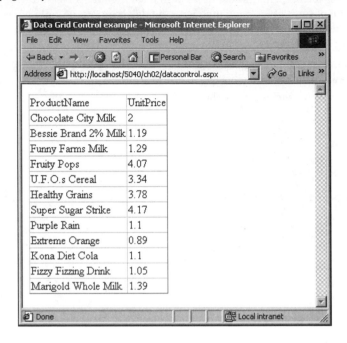

How It Works

All the ASP.NET looks quite daunting, but it's just there to supply the necessary connection information to the database control. We're not going to enter into a big discussion about how this control works, but we will have a quick overview of the ASP.NET that connects us to our database:

```
Sub Page_Load(Sender As Object, E as EventArgs)
   Dim objConnection As OleDbConnection
   Dim objCommand As OleDbDataAdapter
   Dim strConnect As String
   Dim strCommand As String
   Dim DataSet1 As New DataSet

   strConnect =  "Provider=Microsoft.Jet.OLEDB.4.0;"
   strConnect += "Data Source=C:\Program Files\Microsoft.NET\FrameworkSDK\"
   strConnect += "Samples\quickstart\aspplus\samples\grocertogo\data"
   strConnect += "\grocertogo.mdb;"
   strConnect += "Persist Security Info=False"

   strCommand = "SELECT ProductName, UnitPrice FROM products"
   objConnection = New OleDbConnection(strConnect)
   objCommand = New OleDbDataAdapter(strCommand, objConnection)
   objCommand.Fill(DataSet1, "products")
   DataGrid1.DataSource=DataSet1.Tables("Products").DefaultView
   DataGrid1.DataBind()
End Sub
```

Without breaking down the code line by line, there are three things going on, that we need to discuss. These are the three things critical to our getting data back from the database. Two of them are provided by the following lines:

```
strConnect =   "Provider=Microsoft.Jet.OLEDB.4.0;"
strConnect += "Data Source=C:\Program Files\Microsoft.NET\FrameworkSDK\"
strConnect += "Samples\quickstart\aspplus\samples\grocertogo\data"
strConnect += "\grocertogo.mdb;"
strConnect += "Persist Security Info=False"
```

The first is the `Provider=` section. We don't want to qualify what a provider is yet, but it is this section that tells ASP.NET what type of database we are using. In this case, we are using an Access database.

The second part is also contained within this line. This tells us where the database we wish to query with ASP.NET is physically located on the web server. In this case it is the sample database, which is installed with the .NET Framework, and should be located at:

C:\Program Files\Microsoft.NET\FrameworkSDK\Samples\quickstart\aspplus
\samples\grocertogo\data\

This is a long string and doesn't fit on one line it is therefore good practice to break it up into smaller strings and concatenate them together using the + symbol as we did in the code.

The last piece of information that ASP.NET requires is to know exactly what we want from the database. The following line provides that:

```
strCommand = "SELECT ProductName, UnitPrice FROM products"
```

It tells us that we only want information from the `ProductName` and `UnitPrice` parts of the database. The rest of the ASP.NET code is concerned with putting this information in a way that ASP.NET can understand. It is then displayed using the `DataGrid` control.

All that the `DataGrid` control receives, is raw information in the following format "Chocolate City Milk", "2", "Bessie Brand 2% Milk", "1.19" and so on. The Data Grid control provides the display information, and creates the HTML table in which the information is presented.

Binding to a simple XML doc

It doesn't stop there either, the capabilities that ASP.NET has for connecting to databases extend to many other different data sources as well. We'll now look at how we can use the data controls to connect to a quick XML document.

Let's alter our example now so that we can demonstrate the flexibility of the `DataGrid` control, and bind it to the contents of the XML document. In fact, we'll go one step further, and create the XML document as well, and then use the control to bind to it, displaying the contents within a table, just as it would with a database.

Try It Out – Binding to a simple XML document

1. Open up your web page editor, and type in the following:

```xml
<?xml version="1.0"?>
<artist>
  <item>
    <name>Vincent Van Gogh</name>
    <nationality>Dutch</nationality>
    <movement>Post Impressionism </movement>
    <birthdate>30th March 1853</birthdate>
  </item>
  <item>
    <name>Paul Klee </name>
    <nationality>Swiss </nationality>
    <movement>Abstract Expressionism </movement>
    <birthdate>18th December 1879</birthdate>
  </item>
  <item>
    <name>Max Ernst </name>
    <nationality>German </nationality>
    <movement>Surrealism </movement>
    <birthdate>2nd April 1891</birthdate>
  </item>
</artist>
```

2. Save this as `artists.xml`, and make sure you save it in the **C:\BegASPNET\ch02** folder.

3. Keeping your web page editor open, and add the following:

```vb
<%@ Page language="VB" runat="server" %>
<%@ Import namespace="System.Data" %>
<%@ Import namespace="System.XML" %>

<script language="vb" runat="server">
  Sub Page_Load()
    Dim xmlFilename As String
    xmlFilename= "C:\BegASPNET\ch02\artists.xml"
    Dim newDataSet As New DataSet
    newDataSet.ReadXML(xmlFilename)
    DataGrid1.DataSource = newDataSet
    DataGrid1.DataBind()
  End Sub
</script>

<html>
  <head>
    <title>Data Grid Control example</title>
  </head>
  <body>
    <asp:DataGrid id="DataGrid1" runat="server"  />
  </body>
</html>
```

4. Save this as `datacontrol2.aspx`.

5. View this on your browser, it should look like this:

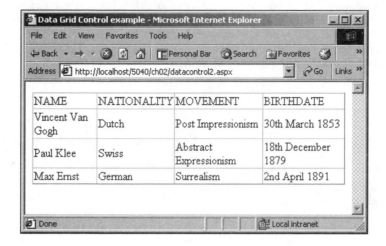

How It Works

The code in this example is much more straightforward. Our XML file is pretty much like a database table. We've kept it simple, so that you can see what is happening. `Artists.XML` has three entries, for three artists. Each artist's entry is structured like this. The artist's individual entry is held with a single set of item tags:

```
<item>
   <name>Artist's Name</name>
   <nationality>Artist's Nationality</nationality>
   <movement>Artist's Movement</movement>
   <birthdate>Artist's Birthday</birthdate>
</item>
```

There are four elements: one for name, one for nationality, one for movement, and one for birthday. The data on the artists is stored between the tags. Once again, we use the `DataGrid` control to format the information as an HTML table, as once again all it receives is raw text.

The ASP.NET that connects with the XML document is much simpler than the code we used to connect with the database. It only has two purposes. The first is to provide the physical location of the XML file:

```
Dim xmlFilename As String = "C:\BegASPNET\ch02\artists.xml"
```

The second is to read the contents of the XML document and make it available in ASP.NET code:

```
newDataSet.ReadXML(xmlFilename)
```

The rest of the code attaches the XML document data to the Data Grid control.

Summary

This chapter has been quite theory-heavy, so I've deliberately kept it quite short to prevent it becoming too overwhelming. Hopefully, your understanding of exactly what ASP.NET is has been broadened considerably. We have now seen that when we request an ASPX page from the web server:

❑ Its contents are passed to the ASP.NET module, which parses them into a .NET-compliant class definition, and compiles this to MSIL.

❑ This Page class is used to instantiate an object within the Common Language Runtime, and this generates HTML that's returned to IIS, and from there sent back to the client browser.

This is quite a bit more complex than the idea of a web page being interpreted and then displayed!

Most of the hard work involved takes place within the "black box" of the .NET Framework. This can call upon a wide range of functionality, which is therefore, also available to our web pages. We've learned how to insert ASP.NET code into our web pages, and seen a quick example of one of the data controls in action.

In the next chapter, we're going to look at creating HTML forms, and using client-submitted data to generate content for our web pages dynamically.

3

Forms and HTML Server Controls

One of the most common tasks any web developer will perform is collecting and storing information from the user. It could simply be the name and email of a user, it might range across a whole gamut of details including address, phone number, fax details, credit card number, and delivery address. Whatever the information you want to gather, the processing cannot be performed within the confines of HTML on the browser alone. Therefore, you need to send the information to the web server for processing. Once the web server has extracted the requisite information, an updated version of the page, or a separate second page, is returned to the user.

The method by which information is transmitted via web pages, is termed a **form**, and in HTML, there are specialized tags for dealing with this. HTML forms contain a set of HTML controls, such as text boxes, check boxes, and drop down lists, all of which aid the passage of information from the user to the server. On top of this, ASP.NET adds its own extra controls for dealing with forms. With these, ASP.NET introduces some new concepts to the control of forms. Previously, for example, when you selected a particular form control, the web browser dealt with the entire handling of the form data until it was passed to the web server. A new feature of the .NET framework, offers extra features, such as remembering what text you've typed into a text box, or what selection you made in a list box between page refreshes.

While we're going to be using some ASP.NET code to handle the interchange of form data, we will be using ASP.NET as a means to an end. To keep things clear, we're not going to start explaining exactly how it all works until later chapters, but by the end of the chapter, you will understand how to send information between browser and server via ASP.NET code. You'll also be introduced to some of the terminology associated with this process.

In this chapter we will cover:

- ❑   The client-server model of the web
- ❑   HTTP request and HTTP response
- ❑   HTML forms and web forms
- ❑   HTML form controls
- ❑   Server Controls
- ❑   The business example that forms the framework of the next few chapters

Forms in the Real World

The main focus of the chapter is forms, and implicitly, the transfer of data from the browser to the server. Before we start delving into the inner workings of the form, we'll describe a few situations in which forms would be required in the business world, to see what kind of things they are used for. If you take a look at a few commercial web sites, you'll find that forms are usually provided in the same kinds of situations, such as:

❑ To take information from a user. This could be for the purpose of registration, the purchase of a product, or joining an email list/form/newsgroup

❑ To take note of a user's particular set of preferences so that we can customize other pages in the site to include relevant information, and exclude things that don't interest the user

❑ To provide a questionnaire or survey on how a business may go about improving the service that they offer

❑ To act as front end for a forum or newsgroup, where a user can enter and edit their text online

These are just a few examples of some common everyday situations. To take this one step further, and to try and tie things in with the real world, later on in the chapter, we're going to describe a simple business situation that we will return to over the next few chapters. While we won't be building one single stand-alone application with this recurring example, we will be building different bits and pieces, which might logically form part of one standalone application.

Our hypothetical situation is this: A fictional business, Feiertag Holidays, require a web site, which will allow users to view different destinations within Europe, and then browse through details of different hotels at each destination. If the user wishes to make a booking, they are referred to a travel agent who can arrange the reservation particulars. The main advantage of using this example is that rather than having to create a unique page for each separate destination and each separate hotel, as might have to be done in the real world, we should be able to create a generic page, dynamically generated by ASP.NET, which fills in details about each destination, and therefore, requires a lot less coding.

In this chapter, we're just going to approach one facet of the task, namely how to select a destination, and how ASP.NET forms can be used to expedite the process. Before we get into that, However it's best to take a quick overview of forms, and see the ways in which ASP.NET affects them.

Web Pages, HTML Forms and Web Forms

With the introduction of any new technology comes new terminology and jargon. ASP.NET is no different in this respect. With ASP.NET, even the terms you use to describe a simple web page have been amended to more accurately describe the processes that are going on within them. To start getting into the concept of forms, let's start with an agreed common base line, the **web page**.

Everybody reading this should know what a web page is; it's just a bundle of HTML code that is placed on a machine, known as a web server, which makes that page available to all and sundry. Whether that page contains text, graphics, movies, sound, or bits and pieces of other languages/technologies, or whether it was dynamically generated, is of no concern to us.

A **HTML form** is a web page that contains one or more **form controls** (grouped together inside an HTML <form> element) that allow the user to enter information on the web page and send that information back to the web server. Commonly used form controls include buttons, textboxes, checkboxes, and dropdown lists.

Although you don't need anything more than HTML to send form data to the server, the server needs some sort of extra technology (in this case, ASP.NET) to actually *do* anything with the information it receives. HTML forms are typically saved with the suffix .html (or sometimes .htm).

The term **web form** refers to the grouping of two distinct blocks of code:

❑ The HTML template containing page layout information and ASP.NET server controls (see below). This is responsible for the presentation of the web form on the browser.

❑ The ASP.NET code that provides the web form's processing logic. This is responsible for generating dynamic content to be displayed within the web form. This content is typically exposed via server controls defined in the HTML presentation block.

> **Although a web form may also be an HTML form (that is, there's nothing to stop us using <form> elements inside an ASPX), remember that these two entities are defined in quite distinct terms.**

When we start using ASP.NET within our web pages, we can use a new breed of ASP.NET **server controls** within our HTML. Not only do they duplicate the functionality of many HTML elements (including the form controls), but they also do a lot more besides. A server control takes the form of an *HTML-like* element marking a point in the page at which the server needs to generate corresponding true-HTML elements. The advantage this offers over an HTML control lies in the fact that it will also produce a server-side object; since this object is used to provide content for the true-HTML element on the finished page, we can assign this content from just about anywhere in our code.

As we've already seen, the ASP.NET code can be specified in a <script> block that may occur at any point within the ASPX file. We're keeping it at the top of the code page, to help clarify the separation of presentation and content. As we'll see in Chapter 15 though, we can ultimately place the ASP.NET code into a completely separate file (a technique known as code behind). What's important, is that you recognize that when we talk about a web form, we're referring to both these sections, regardless of where they are, or how they're organized.

So we know that it is possible for web forms to use normal HTML form controls, but ASP.NET also comes with its own set of web form controls that are run on the server, and we will be using these in preference most of the time, because they are able to remember the state of the different controls, such as what text has been typed into a text box. These ASP.NET controls are run within specially modified HTML <form runat="server"> tags, and these are **ASP.NET forms**.

There are four different terms here that we need to be clear about before we go any further and look at them in any more detail:

❑ A web page is any page that contains just HTML (they can also contain script/other languages not covered by this book, but in this book a web page will refer to pages containing only HTML)

❑ A HTML form is an HTML element that contains HTML form controls

❑ A web form is any page that combines ASP.NET code with an HTML template

❑ An ASP.NET form is a form inside a web form, that contains ASP.NET server controls

Our discussion of forms is essentially a discussion of how to transmit data from a browser back to the web server, therefore we need to start out by considering the whole process of data transmission on the Web, so that we can put the role of forms into context. Let's now look at how web browsers and web servers work together to make web pages available to the world.

Simple Web Theory

When we installed ASP.NET in Chapter 1, the installation was broken down into stages, because we installed several different pieces of software. One of these pieces of software was the web server, whose main job is to make your web pages available to all and sundry. Another job of the web server is to provide an area (typically in a directory or folder structure) in which to organize and store your web pages, or whole web site.

When you use the Web to view a web page, you will automatically be making contact with a web server. The process of submitting your URL is called 'making a **request**' to the server. The server interprets the URL, locates the corresponding page, and sends back the code to create the page as part of what is called the **response** to the browser. The browser then takes the code it has received from the web server and compiles a viewable page from it. The browser is referred to as a **client** in this interaction, and the whole interaction as a **client-server relationship**.

Client-Server

This term describes the workings of the Web, by outlining the distribution of tasks. The server (the web server) stores, interprets data, and distributes data (that is compiled into web-pages), and the client (browser) accesses the server to get at the data. From now on, whenever we use the term client, we are just referring to the browser.

To understand what is going on in greater detail, we need to briefly discuss how the client and server communicate over the internet using the HTTP protocol.

The HTTP Protocol

The Internet is a network of interconnected nodes. It is designed to carry *information* from one place to another. When the user tells the browser to fetch a web page, a message is sent from the browser to the web server.

This message is sent using Hypertext Transfer Protocol (or HTTP). HTTP is the protocol used by the World Wide Web in the transfer of information from one machine to another – when you see a URL prefixed with http://, you know that the internet protocol being used is HTTP.

The message passed from the browser to the web server asking for a particular web page is known as an **HTTP request**. When the web server receives this request, it checks its stores to find the appropriate page. If the web server finds the page, it bundles up the HTML in an **HTTP response**, and sends this back across the network to the browser. If the web server cannot find the requested page, it issues a response that features an appopriate error message, and dispatches *that* page to the browser.

Here's an illustration of the process, as we understand it so far:

HTTP is known as a **stateless** protocol. This is because HTTP doesn't know whether the HTTP request that has been made, is part of an ongoing correspondence, or just a single message, just as the same way your postman won't know whether your letter is the first asking your local hi-fi company for a refund on the piece of junk they sold you, or the fifteenth one penned in giant green capital letters demanding that they give you the refund and a brand new stereo system on top.

The reason HTTP is stateless, is that it was only intended to retrieve a single web page for display. The Internet would be very slow and might even collapse if permanent connections needed to be maintained between browsers and servers, as people moved from one page to another. Think about the extra work HTTP would have to do if it had to worry about whether you had been connected for one minute or whether you had been idle for an hour, and needed disconnecting. Then multiply that by a million for all the other users. Instead, HTTP makes the connection and delivers the request, and then returns the response and disconnects. The downside of this is that HTTP can't distinguish between different requests however, and can't assign different priorities, so it won't be able to tell whether a particular HTTP request is the request of a user, or the request of a virus infected machine, that has been set up to hit a government web server 1000 times an minute. It will treat all requests equally with the same status, as there are no ways for HTTP to determine where the request originated.

There is still quite a lot of technical detail missing here, so let's dig further down and take a closer look at HTTP.

How HTTP Works

When a request for a web page is sent to the server, this request contains more than just the desired URL. There is a lot of extra information that is sent as part of the request. This is also true of the response – the server sends extra information back to the browser. It's these different types of information that ASP.NET can make use of, and that we'll look at in this next section.

A lot of the information that is passed within the HTTP message is generated automatically, and the user doesn't have to deal with it directly, so you don't need to worry about transmitting such information yourself. While you don't have to worry about creating this information yourself, you should be aware that it is being passed between machines as part of the HTTP request and HTTP response – because the ASP.NET code that we write can allow us to have a direct effect on the exact content of this information.

Every HTTP message assumes the same format (whether it's a client request or a server response). We can break this format down into three sections: the request/response line, the HTTP header, and the HTTP body. The content of these three sections is dependent upon whether the message is an HTTP request or HTTP response – so we'll take these two cases separately.

Let's just pause and illustrate our understanding of the process now:

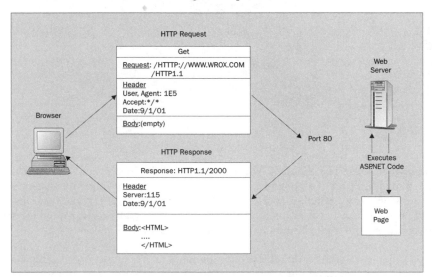

We can see that the HTTP request and HTTP response have broadly similar structures, and that there is information common to both that is sent as part of the HTTP header.

There are other pieces of information that can only be known to either the browser or the server, and are only sent as part of either the request or response, so it makes sense to examine their constituent parts in greater detail. These pieces of information, such as the server name, the date, the acceptance code returned by the server if it finds a web page, are all termed **environment** or **server variables**. They are easily readable when using ASP.NET code, and indeed, we will be interrogating them in later chapters, and using the results they return to customize our web forms for a particular user.

The HTTP Request

The browser sends the HTTP request to the web server, and it contains the following three listed elements:

- ❑ The Request line
- ❑ The HTTP header
- ❑ The HTTP body

The Request Line

The first line of every HTTP request is the request line, which contains three pieces of information:

❏ An HTTP command, known as a method

❏ The file name, and the path in the server directory structure of the resource that the client is requesting from the server.

❏ The version number of HTTP

So, an example request line might look like this:

```
GET/Testpage.htm HTTP/1.1
```

The method is used to tell the server how to handle the request, and usually consists of a GET or POST command. These basically tell the server to find some particular data. We'll look at these methods shortly. There are a number of other methods supported by HTTP – including PUT, DELETE, TRACE, CONNECT, and OPTIONS. As a rule, you'll find that these are less common, and for this reason, they are beyond the scope of this discussion. If you want to know more about these, take a look at document RFC 2068, which you can find at http://www.rfc.net.

The HTTP Header

The next bit of information sent is the HTTP header. This contains details of what document types the client will accept back from the server, like the type of browser that has requested the page, the date, and general configuration information. The HTTP request's header contains information that falls into three different categories:

❏ **General**: contains information about either the client or server, but not specific to one or the other

❏ **Entity**: contains information about the data being sent between the client and server

❏ **Request**: contains information about the client configuration and different types of acceptable documents

An example HTTP header might look like this:

```
Accept: */*
Accept-Language: en-us
Connection: Keep-Alive
Host: www.wrox.com
Referer: http://webdev.wrox.co.uk/books/SampleList.aspx?bookcode=5040
User-Agent: Mozilla (X11; I; Linux 2.0.32 i586)
```

As you can see, the HTTP header is composed of a number of lines; each line contains the description of a piece of HTTP header information, and its value. For example, the user agent line refers to the type of browser that made the request. The accept-language indicates the human-readable language used within the web page; in this case, US English. There are many different lines that can be contained in a HTTP header, and most of them are optional, so HTTP has to indicate when it has finished transmitting the header information. To do this, a blank line is used.

You can see among the lines of information sent is the `User-Agent`, or browser. This is interesting, because we have already talked about one of the advantages of ASP.NET – it can customize web forms to a particular browser. We didn't give any indication of how it did that though, and we indicated that as HTTP is stateless, it, on its own, has no idea who a particular user is. We can now see that this information is packaged up within the HTTP request, and in later chapters we will show you how ASP.NET can unpack, and indeed act on the information contained.

The HTTP Body

The HTTP request body will contain any data that is being sent to the server – for example, data that the user typed into an HTML form (we'll see examples of this later in the book). Otherwise, the HTTP request body will be empty. Data can actually be sent in the URL line (thus, still leaving the request body empty), if the `GET` method is used in the HTTP request line, but we'll discuss this in a moment.

The HTTP Response

The HTTP response is sent by the server back to the client browser, and contains the following three elements:

❑ The Response line
❑ The HTTP header
❑ The HTTP body

The Response Line

The response line contains only two bits of information:

❑ The HTTP version number
❑ An HTTP status code that reports the success or failure of the request

An example response line might look like this:

```
HTTP/1.1 200 OK
```

First of all, we can see the HTTP version number – this isn't significant, there are only two versions 1.0 and 1.1 and it just tells the server which format was used to package up the request. The version number is followed by the status code. This example returns the HTTP status code 200, which represents the message 'OK'. This denotes the success of the request, and that the response contains the required page or data from the server. Error code values are three-digit numbers, where the first digit indicates the class of the response. There are five classes of response:

Code class	Description
100-199	These codes are informational – they indicate that the request is currently being processed.
200-299	These codes denote success – that the web server received and carried out the request successfully.
300-399	These codes indicate that the request hasn't been performed, because the information required has been moved.

Code class	Description
400-499	These codes denote a client error – that the request was incomplete, incorrect, or impossible.
500-599	These codes denote a server error – that the request appeared to be valid, but that the server failed to carry it out.

The HTTP Header

The HTTP response header is similar to the request header, which we discussed above. In the HTTP response, the header information again falls into three types:

- ❑ General: contains information about either the client or server, but is not specific to one or the other
- ❑ Entity: contains information about the data being sent between the client and the server
- ❑ Response: Information about the server sending the response, and how it can deal with the response

Once again, the header consists of a number of lines, and uses a blank line to indicate that the header information is complete. Here's a sample of what a header might look like, with the name of each line down the side:

```
HTTP/1.1 200 OK                                     – the response line
Date: Mon, 1st Nov 1999, 16:12:23 GMT               – the general header
Server: Microsoft-IIS/5.0                           – the response header
Last-modified: Fri, 29th Oct 1999, 12:08:03 GMT     – the entity header
```

We've already discussed the first line, the second is self-explanatory. On the third line, `Server`, indicates the type of software the web server is running, and as we are requesting a file somewhere on the web server, the last bit of information refers to the last time the page we are requesting was modified.

The header can contain much more information than this, or different information, depending on what is requested. If you want to know more about the different types of information contained in the three parts of the header, you'll find them listed in RFC 2068 (Sections 4.5, 7.1 and 7.2), that you can find at http://www.rfc.net.

The HTTP Body

If the request was successful, then the HTTP response body contains the HTML code (together with any script that is to be executed by the browser), ready for the browser to use. Additional HTTP requests are used to retrieve any other resource, such as images, dictated by the HTML code returned after the first request.

Where ASP.NET Fits in with the .NET Framework

In the last chapter, we saw some of the major concepts involved in .NET framework. In this chapter, we've already gained a better understanding of how a browser sends a web page request, and how the web server sends the page back to the browser. What we're going to do now is to tie the two together, as this will help us understand what is happening when we use forms and server-side controls.

Let's sum up the 5-step process for delivering a web page:

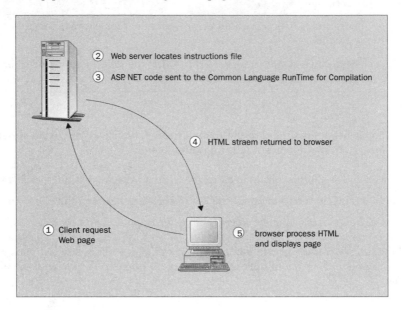

1. The client requests a web page.

2. The web server needs to locate the page that was requested; and if it's an ASP.NET page then this code will need to be processed in order to generate the HTML that is returned to the browser.

3. If the name of the web page is suffixed with `.aspx`, the server sends it to the `aspnet_isapi.dll` (which is attached to the web server) for processing. The `aspnet_isapi.dll` doesn't actually do much itself, it just forwards the ASP.NET code to the Common Language Runtime. We looked at what role this performs in the last chapter, and here we'll just treat it as a black box. If the ASP.NET code hasn't been compiled before, it is compiled and then it is executed, and pure HTML comes out the other end. In this way the HTML is created **dynamically**.

4. The HTML stream is returned to the browser.

5. The browser displays the web page.

There are a lot of advantages to generating a page dynamically: you can return information to the user based on their responses in a form, you can customize web pages for a particular browser, you can personalize information (and utilize a particular profile for each individual), and much more beyond the static text and graphics that pure HTML returns. This is down to the fact that the code we write is interpreted at the time it is requested.

Now we have a basic understanding of how the web works, it's time to get stuck into forms. We'll begin by looking at HTML forms, as they are much misunderstood. Also, once you know about HTML forms, the ASP.NET server controls begin to look familiar, as the HTML form controls perform many of the same functions as their server-side counterparts.

HTML Forms

In HTML, forms are important, as they provide the only means by which a user can input data and send it back to the web server. The method via which this is accomplished is the <form> tag. You can use the <form> tag to specify the page you wish the data to be sent to, along with the method by which you wish to transmit the form data – this is mentioned in the request line of the form transmission as we saw earlier.

The <form> tag

The <form> tag is a container tag. It is used purely to denote the set of form controls that the developer intends to use to convey information back to the server. It adds no extra presentational features itself, in other words the form itself is invisible. In Netscape browsers, prior to version 6, form controls cannot be displayed without the <form> tag. In other words, all form controls, such as text boxes and radio buttons, must be placed within <form> tags, otherwise they won't be displayed at all in Netscape. On the other hand, IE and Opera can still display the form controls without the <form> tag, but if you want to send the form data back to the server, then the form controls have to be contained with a set of <form> tags; there needs to be a <form> tag for the page to send its data to the server. We'll take a look at the <form> tag in more detail now.

While the <form> tag supports eleven attributes (as defined by the HTML 4.01 standard), there are only two that we really need to worry about:

❑ action – specifying the web page we want to receive our form data

❑ method – specifying the HTTP method by which our form data is transmitted

The other attributes, which include name *(with which we can reference the form from client-side code) and* target *(to specify a different window or frame in which to load the returned page), are all useful in themselves. They're not immediately relevant to the current discussion however, so we will not be looking at them here. For more information, you may want to take a look at "HTML 4.01 Programmer's Reference" from Wrox Press (ISBN 1861005334)*

The action Attribute

The first of the <form> tag's attributes, action, defines the name of the web page that will receive the form data. A typical action attribute in a HTML form might look like this:

```
<form action="nextpage.aspx"  ... >
...
```

We've referenced an .aspx page here as HTML forms have to work in conjunction with another technology. This is still a HTML form though. ASP.NET forms have a specialized set of attributes that are not part of the HTML 4.01 standard.

When you submit a form (send it to the web server), you need to specify the name of the web page that the information will be returned to. It could possibly be the same page as the one that received the information, but for our early examples, we will be using a separate second page.

One last thing we need to say about this attribute: make sure it points to a valid page; otherwise you will generate a page error.

The method Attribute

The second attribute defines the method of transmission of the form data. As we mentioned earlier, there are plenty of different possible methods, but in practice, you'll only ever use two of them: you guessed it, GET or POST.

The GET Method

The GET method is the default method, and is normally used to retrieve files from a web server, as we shall see shortly. When it is used in conjunction with a <form> tag though, it *sends* the form data to the web server. Form data sent to the server is appended to the end of the URLs in the form of name/value pairs, attached with a question mark for example:

```
?firstname=Vervain
```

The first part of this name/value pair is the name, which acts as an identifier. The second part is the value that you wish to store. The name and value are taken from a form element like a text box or a checkbox. The name of the form element (textbox and so on.) is the name used in the GET method, and the content the user has written in the form element is the value. Here 'firstname' is the name, while 'Vervain' is the value. This can be appended to the URL as follows:

```
http://www.nonexistentserver.com/asppages/form.aspx?firstname=Vervain
```

The browser automatically appends the information to the URL when it sends the page request to the web server. You can add more than one name/value pair to a URL if you separate each pair with an ampersand (&). With two name/value pairs, the end of the URL might look like this:

```
?firstname=Vervain&surname=Delaware
```

As part of the URL it would look like this:

```
http://www.nonexistentserver.com/asppages/form.aspx?firstname=Vervain&surname=Dela
ware
```

The part appended to the URL is known as a **query string**.
This is how you can still pass information between the browser and server, while leaving the HTTP body empty – it is transferred in the URL.

Occasionally, you might want to pass spaces in the values that make up the query string. For instance, if you had a form that had a <textarea> tag, and someone had typed in the following reply:

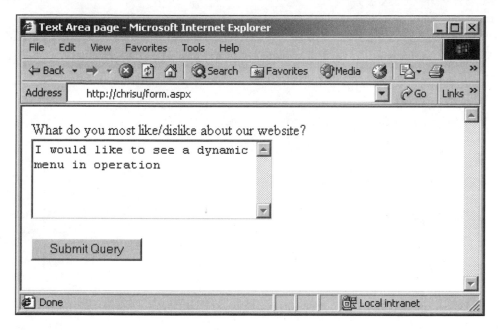

The line "I would like to see a dynamic menu in operation", contains several spaces that need to be represented. In such cases, the plus sign replaces the spaces:

```
http://chrisu/form.html?TextArea=I+would+like+to+see+a+dynamic+menu+in+operation
```

Some of you will be thinking, "But what happens if you want to put an plus sign in the `<textarea>`? How is that represented within a query string?" In this case, the character or operator in question has to be replaced by a code, which signifies this particular character. This is known as **URL encoding**.

URL Encoding

There is a set of characters that can't appear in a URL, and therefore by association, can't appear in a query string either, so they have to be URL encoded.

The encoding process requires you, the user or developer, to do precisely nothing. It's all done for you. The web browser takes the offending character, whether a bracket or an addition sign, and replaces it with a **code value**. The code is always the same, and we have listed the most common characters and their code values for you in the table beneath:

Some of the above characters have to be encoded, or they would adopt another meaning in the query string – as we saw above, the plus sign is used to denote a space in the query string, and the question mark denotes the start of a query string.

The previous query string with the URL code value for a space in place of the plus sign would look like this:

Character	URL encoding	Character	URL encoding
Tab	%09	,	%2C
Space	%20	.	%2E
!	%21	/	%2F
"	%22	:	%3A
#	%23	;	%3B
%	%25	<	%3B
&	%26	>	%3C
(	%28	=	%3D
)	%29	?	%3F
+	%2B	@	%40
\	%5C	,	%2C

http://chrisu/form.aspx?TextArea=I%20would%20like%20to%20see%20a%20dynamic%20me
nu%20in%20operation

Having talked about the different ways in which query strings can be created by the browser, let's see an example of GET sending form data to the server.

Try It Out – The GET Method

1. Type in the following code:

```
<html>
  <head>
    <title>Test Form page</title>
  </head>
  <body>
    <form action="nextpage.aspx" method="get">
      Enter your name into the text box:
      <input name="TextBox" name="text">
      <br />
      <br />
      <input type="Submit" value="Submit Query">
    </form>
  </body>
</html>
```

Remember that all this code can be downloaded from the Wrox web site at www.wrox.com.

2. Save this as `formsubmit.html`.

3. If you run the above code then you will see the following (I have filled in the box):

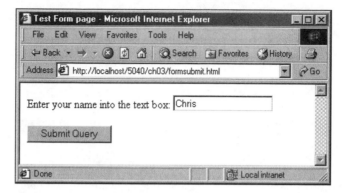

4. This now a fully active HTML form. If you click on the button however, you will generate an error message, saying something similar to the one below:

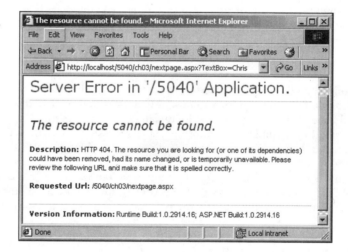

You will notice that after Description, *we are informed that the status code here is 404. You may recall from the table a few pages ago that error codes 400-499 denote a client error – that the request was incomplete, incorrect, or impossible. If the response line contains a 404, then the web server failed to find the requested resource. In this case, we are trying to submit the form to a web page that does not exist.*

How It Works

This form is active in the sense that, despite the error message, the information is still passed to the server as you can see the information in the browser. It is visible in the address line in the screenshot above that the form data has been appended to the URL, although without an active web page to receive the details, the information is currently useless, and doesn't provide any function. Many newcomers to HTML make the mistake of assuming that the browser can somehow deal with the contents of the form, and results can be returned within the context of a HTML page. Forms however don't actually work like this. They rely on the presence of another technology to process the details.

In this example, we use the text box control and the submit button control to capture and submit the name:

```
<input name="TextBox" type="text">
<br />
<br />
<input type="Submit">
```

The `<form>` tag tells the browser where to send the form data, and by what method to transmit the name:

```
<form action="nextpage.aspx" method="get">
```

All we've done is transmit the information, in the following format, to the server, appended to the URL:

```
?TextBox=Chris
```

This is a typical name/value pair, `TextBox` being the name and `Chris` being the value. If we want to make use of it in ASP.NET, then we need another page to process the information, as we shall see shortly.

GET isn't the only method that can be used to transmit data. As the default, it's perhaps the most popular, but the POST method provides an equally suitable alternative. In fact there are many situations in which you might choose to use POST in preference.

The POST Method

One disadvantage you might have discerned from using query strings is the rather public nature of their transmission. If you don't want the information sent to appear in the URL, then you will have to rely on the POST method instead. This works almost identically to the GET method, the only difference being that the form information is sent in the *body* of the HTTP request rather than as part of the URL. We'll see why this makes a difference when we come to discuss the workings of HTTP shortly.

POST can also allow a greater amount of information to be transmitted. Some web servers have a limit on the amount of text you can transmit as part of a URL. Using the POST method avoids this problem. Apart from this, for all intents and purposes, the two methods provide the same functionality and level of performance.

Let's take a look at an example of POST in action.

Try It Out – The POST method

1. Go back and open up the page `formsubmit.html` and change the line highlighted in gray as follows:

```
...
<body>
<form action="nextpage.aspx" method="post">
Enter your name into the text box:
<input name="TextBox" type="text">
...
```

2. Save this file `formsubmit2.html`.

3. Open it up in the browser, fill in some information, and submit it:

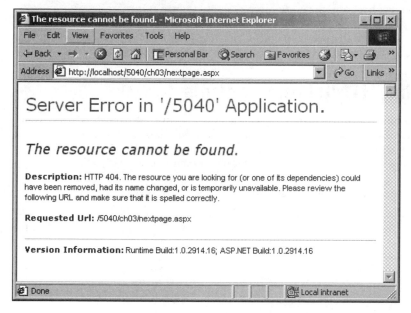

How It Works

Once again, we get an error message., as we are trying to submit the form to a page that does not exist. This time, there is no evidence that the form data has reached the server; you'll just have to take our word for it that it has. There are no name/value pairs listed in the address bar, but the data is actually accessible to the ASP.NET code in the same way. It's just been tucked away, that's all. Apart from that, there is no difference between the two examples.

We'll see shortly how we can use ASP.NET to return data from the form and where the form data is placed when you use the POST method, however before we do that, we need to eliminate any confusion by taking a quick look at when it is better to use GET or POST.

Do I Use GET or POST?

There's a mixture of opinion on this one, some people say you should almost never use the GET method, due to its insecurity and limit on size imposed by some web servers.

Others maintain that you can use GET to retrieve information, while POST should be used whenever you modify data on the web server. There are no hard and fast rules though; these are just guidelines.

One feature of POST is that pages loaded with POST cannot be properly book-marked, whereas pages loaded with GET contain all the information needed to reproduce the request right in the URL. In many cases, you can bookmark the result of a form submission (a search on Alta Vista, for example) by using the GET method, and this is why most search engines use GET. Additionally, the POST method itself isn't secure – while the information is placed in the HTTP body and isn't immediately visible, the information isn't encrypted, and could still be obtained by a hacker without too much difficulty. To make sure it is secure, you would need to use a secure connection to a secure server, which the HTTP protocol on its own cannot provide.

Which method you use depends on what you want to the form to do. If you do use GET, be aware of its shortcomings and its indiscreet nature. If you use POST, beware that it can't be book-marked by search engines, and just because it is more discreet doesn't mean it is more secure.

We've now discussed the pros and cons of sending and receiving information in forms, so lets move on to the practical methods we have at our disposal for transmitting form data.

Embedding HTML Form controls

Before we look at how to return information from a form control with ASP.NET, let's do a quick tour and refresher through the many form controls that HTML offers. For the majority of HTML form controls, you will use the <input> tag we saw earlier to place them on the web page, and for those that have their own specialist tags, the attributes they require are broadly similar.

The HTML form controls you might use on a typical web page are:

HTML Form Control	Appearance	Description	Implementation
Text boxes	text here...	Text boxes are single line fields for typing text into.	Uses the <input> tag, with the type attribute set to text
Text areas	Several lines of text...	Text areas are multiple line boxes for typing text into.	Uses the <textarea> tag
Radio Buttons	⊙ ○	Radio buttons are multiple choice buttons that allow only one, mutually exclusive answer.	Uses the <input> tag, with type set to radio
Check boxes	☑ ☐	Check boxes are single and multiple choice buttons that allow several, independent answers.	Uses the <input> tag, with type set to checkbox
List boxes	A ▾ A B C	List boxes are buttons which reveal a drop-down menu, from which you're allowed to select one or more options.	Uses the <select> tag
Submit uttons	Submit Query	Submit buttons submit HTML forms to the web server.	Uses the <input> tag, with type set to submit

HTML Form Control	Appearance	Description	Implementation
Reset buttons	Reset	Reset buttons reset the contents of an HTML form that hasn't already been submitted.	Uses the `<input>` tag, with `type` set to `reset`
Normal Buttons	Click here	Normal buttons trigger whatever event they are connected to.	Uses the `<input>` tag, with `type` set to `button`
Password fields	********	Password fields are like text boxes, but with one important difference, anything you type into them is disguised by an asterisk.	Uses the `<input>` tag, with `type` set to `password`
Hidden fields	No visual appearance	Hidden fields are set in the HTML, and are sent along with other form data.	Uses the `<input>` tag, with `type` set to `hidden`

As you can see, the `<input>` tag deals with the broad majority of HTML form controls, so we'll take a closer look at it.

The `<input>` tag has only four attributes that we will make use of:

- ❑ `name` – Is used to identify the control in ASP.NET code.
- ❑ `type` – Specifies which type of form control you are using. Valid options are Submit, Reset, Radio, Check, Hidden, Text and Password.
- ❑ `value` – Not strictly necessary for all controls, but can be used to specify a default value for some button or text controls.
- ❑ `checked` – If you wish to pre-select a radio control, so that a particular choice is selected when the user first sees the page, you can add the CHECKED attribute to a particular `<input>` tag.

These attributes of the `<form>` tag are all you need to be able to access and manipulate form controls with ASP.NET code.

Textbox and Submit Button

We've already used the two basic controls you will find on many forms. The first was the textbox, or text field, which accepts text from the user.

The textbox is the default form control – that is to say, if you don't specify a particular type (using the TYPE attribute), the browser will assume that you wish to insert a text box in your page. You can specify a text box in a page as follows:

```
<form action="nextpage.aspx" method="GET">
   Enter your name into the text box:
   <input name="TextBox" type="text">
</form>
```

Of course, the text box doesn't do anything on its own – it needs to be submitted to the web server. To do this, you need to add a 'submit' button control to your page.

We create a submit button control by setting the `<input>` tag's `type` attribute set to `submit`. By default, the button will display the words **Submit Query**, unless you specify a different value attribute. The submit button is essential to every form, so to get the above form to work, you would need to add the following:

```
<form action="nextpage.aspx" method="GET">
  Enter your name into the text box:
  <input name="TextBox" type="text">
  <input type="Submit" value="Submit Query">
</form>
```

It isn't necessary to assign a name to the submit button, as you won't need to access/manipulate it with ASP.NET code.

Previously in this chapter, we created an HTML form, and submitted data to the server. We didn't however return anything. So now we'll add to our previous example, by creating a second page – a web form that can receive the information, and return it to the user as part of a simple message. Remember that we're not going into great detail with the code in this chapter. The main thing is to grasp the key concepts of forms, and become familiar with some of the terminology involved.

Try It Out – Getting a Response back from the Form

1. Type in the following code:

```
<html>
<head>
  <title>Test Response page</title>
</head>
<body>
 <script runat="server" language="VB">
 Sub Page_Load()
   Response.Write("Well how are you doing, " +Request.QueryString("TextBox") +"?")
 End Sub
 </script>
</body>
</html>
```

This code, as with all code in the book, can be downloaded from http://www.wrox.com

2. Save this as `nextpage.aspx`

3. Go back, run the first form you created (`formsubmit.html` – not `formsubmit2.html`, which won't work) in your browser, and you will see something like the following:

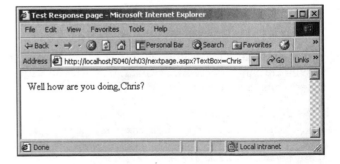

How It Works

The ASP.NET code, encompassed by `<script>` tags, is able to make use of the information supplied on the form:

```
<script runat="server" language="VB">
  Sub Page_Load()
   Response.Write("Well how are you doing, "+ Request.QueryString("TextBox") +"?")
  End Sub
</script>
```

The code that performs this only really requires the following line of code:

```
Response.Write("Well how are you doing,"+ Request.QueryString("TextBox") +"?")
```

Don't worry, the code itself will become clear when we come to look at it in more detail. You will notice that this line of code is surrounded by `Sub Page_Load()` and `End Sub` statements that we introduced in the previous chapter; you must place any code that you want ASP.NET to execute as soon as the web form loads in these statements. They just delimit a block of code.

The line `Response.Write` is used to display text to the screen, and everything contained between quotation marks is displayed exactly as you see it. The part of the line that reads:

```
Response.Write ("Well how are you doing,")
```

will just display the words **Well how are you doing,** on the web page. It's the section of code in the middle of this statement that returns the information from the form on the previous web page. The line:

```
Request.QueryString("TextBox")
```

actually refers to the contents of the text box. There are three separate parts we can split this into:

❑ The first, `Request`, just refers to the fact you are sending HTTP request to the web server.

❑ The second part refers to a particular part of the HTTP request; that is the `QueryString`. In the page `formsubmit.html`, we specified that we wanted to store the form data as a `QueryString` by setting the `method` attribute to `GET` (that's why we tell you not to use `formsubmit2.html`, as this uses `POST`). Now, because we want to reference that information, we need to explicitly tell ASP.NET that we want to retrieve information from a `QueryString`. It won't return anything if you use `POST`, as `Querystring` can only retrieve information from forms sent with `GET`.

❑ The third part is the most important, it references the form control name `TextBox`. We created this name ourselves in the `name` attribute of the `<input>` tag in `formsubmit.html`.

In `formsubmit.html`, when we created the text box with the `<input>` tag, we used the `name` attribute to create a name for the control:

```
<input name="TextBox" type="text">
```

Now in ASP.NET, we can access the contents of the control by referring to this name in parentheses and quotation marks. So ASP.NET takes the line `Request.QueryString("TextBox")`, and substitutes it with the user-supplied contents of the textbox. As I typed the name `Chris`, this text is substituted by ASP.NET, and if we could pause the workings of the server at this point, the result ASP.NET is generating would look like this:

```
Response.Write ("Well how are you doing, " + "Chris" + "?")
```

In this case, we use plus signs '+' to glue the different sections of our text together. Anything that appears within quotation marks is treated as pure text by ASP.NET, anything outside quotation marks, within the parentheses is treated as something that ASP.NET needs to process. Now there is nothing else that needs processing, the text is glued together to produce the message:

Well how are you doing, Chris?

How It Doesn't Work

Before we race through the other HTML form controls and explain how we can return information from the radio buttons, check boxes, drop down lists, and the like, we need to explain that in many ways this is the old way of doing things. The mechanism of submitting forms used by HTML to return data from just about any server-side technology, such as Cold Fusion or PHP, and as we have just demonstrated, by using ASP.NET, isn't efficient as it could be. It provides no continuity of information such as text held in controls between pages. ASP.NET though provides much better facilities for dealing with form data. It replaces all of the HTML form controls we've just mentioned with its own server-side equivalents, and while it is using the HTML form controls underneath to achieve its ends, the user doesn't get to see this, and therefore, doesn't have to know about any of it. All you need to be concerned with is the ASP.NET server controls.

Now we've looked at HTML forms, and seen how they are transmitted back and forth between the client and server. We haven't however seen how ASP.NET itself handles the contents of forms. To do this, we're going to look at a form control and see how we can use ASP.NET to return information from it. Again, we're not going to go into any great depth here into explaining how the ASP.NET code works, we will return to this in later chapters.

Introduction to Server Controls

In this chapter, we're going to concentrate on one particular group of server-side controls known as the HTML server controls. These are all form controls that can be used just like their HTML form control equivalents, the main difference being that they are actually constructed dynamically on the server and then sent out complete. There's another difference we'll need to look at first though.

As we explained earlier when using HTML form controls, we use a modified version of the `<form>` tag in ASP.NET. The ASP.NET version of the `<form>` tag looks like this:

```
<form runat="server">
... ASP.NET form...
</form>
```

It takes only one attribute (runat="server"), which tells the web server that it should process the form itself, rather than just sending it out to the browser (which won't be able to interpret this ASP.NET-specific attribute). Even though we haven't specified the contents of the method and get attributes, ASP.NET is able to handle this itself and provide its own values. In fact, all ASP.NET forms are sent by the POST method. If they are not sent by the POST method (in other words if you try and override it, you will not be able to use the information in the form.) We have a new version of the <form> tag, but how does that compare with the HTML version?

The <form> tag allows us to process form controls on the server. ASP.NET introduces its own customized versions of these controls. The ASP.NET server controls were introduced to solve many of the problems associated with the HTML form controls. For instance, if you go forward from a form on almost any web site, and then jump back again to make a correction, you will find that all of the information has disappeared. This is because HTTP is stateless, as we mentioned earlier; it has no concept of who is connecting to it, or when, it just answers requests for a connection. However, ASP.NET now takes over some of these responsibilities of looking after and persisting this data.

ASP.NET Server Controls

In this next section, we're going to be demonstrating how each of the ASP.NET server controls work, and compare the way they are used to the way their equivalent HTML form control passed information. We'll also demonstrate how we can start achieving our ambition of separating the presentational code (HTML) from the code that provides the content (ASP.NET).

The <asp:label> control

We'll start with a small, but very useful little control, the <asp:label> control. This control provides an alternative way of displaying text on your web page. It is actually vital to us if we want to separate our HTML from our ASP.NET code.

You might have noticed earlier, that there were one or two glitches when using our Response.Write method of displaying code, if you played around with it or altered it in anyway. For instance, let's go back to our previous example, with formsubmit.html and nextpage.aspx:

```
<html>
<head>
  <title>Test Response page</title>
</head>
<body>
  <script RUNAT="SERVER" LANGUAGE="VB">
    Sub Page_Load()
    Response.Write("Well how are you doing,"+ Request.QueryString("TextBox") +"?")
    End Sub
  </script>
</body>
</html>
```

and instead, lay the text out slightly differently:

```
<html>
<head>
  <title>Test Response page</title>
</head>
<body>
```

101

```
Well how are you doing,
  <script RUNAT="SERVER" LANGUAGE="VB">
    Sub Page_Load()
      Response.Write(Request.QueryString("TextBox"))
    End Sub
  </script>
?
</body>
</html>
```

We are still supplying the same text, but we are now placing it within the body of the HTML code, rather than within the ASP.NET code. Despite the fact that we haven't altered the logic of the program in any way, we have actually changed the output, so that it no longer makes the same sense:

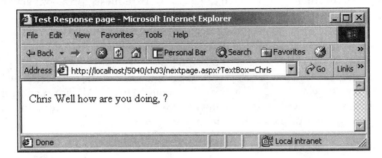

OK, it still makes some sense at least, but our ASP.NET code is no longer in the correct position. The ASP.NET code is compiled and returned to the browser first, the HTML is created second. Imagine you had a page where you were relying on the ASP.NET code to supply values within the text for a customized web page, such as the date, or the name of the user. It would make life very difficult if you could only return them at the top of the page, before any text in the HTML. This is where the <asp:label> control comes in useful, because instead of using the Response.Write statement to display text, or even HTML code, you can use the <asp:label> control.

The <asp:label> control attributes

The <asp:label> control is just like any other HTML form control in that it has a collection of attributes you can set. We won't list them all, but ones you might wish to use are:

- ❑ BackColor – sets the background color of the label

- ❑ ForeColor – sets the foreground color of the label

- ❑ Height – sets the height in pixels of the label

- ❑ ID – sets a unique identifier for that particular instance of the label

- ❑ Text – sets the text that you want the label to display

- ❑ Visible – sets whether the label control is currently visible on the page, must be either true or false

- ❑ Width – sets the width of the label control

If you want a full detailed list of the attributes that the `<asp:label>` control supports (or indeed any HTML server control), and if you have already installed the Quickstart tutorials when you installed the .NET framework SDK, then you can use a handy tool known as the class browser, which you can run from the following URL:

http://localhost/quickstart/aspplus/samples/classbrowser/vb/classbrowser.aspx?namespace=System.Web.UI.WebControls

On the right hand side of the page, you can find a list of all the controls, from label and dropdownlist, to checkbox and the likes. Clicking on the link for a particular control will a reveal a list of allowable attributes under the name Properties. We won't be supplying a list of attributes for the other controls, as, generally, they each support the same attributes, and this information is easily obtainable from the above URL.

One other attribute not mentioned on the lists for any of the controls, but supported by all of them is the attribute `runat`, which is always set to `server`. This is to explicitly indicate that this particular control should be run on the server, not the browser.

<asp:label>control examples

To create the control with the minimum of information needed, you can just supply the `runat` and `id` attributes:

```
<asp:label id="Message1" runat="server">Hello</asp:label>
```

The `id` attribute is used to uniquely identify the `<asp:label>` control so you can refer to it in your ASP.NET code. The `runat="server"` attribute tells the server to process the control and generate HTML code to be sent to the client.

Let's look at another example. If you wanted to set the color of a text message to red, you could set it like this:

```
<asp:label id="Message1" forecolor="red" runat="server">Hello</asp:label>
```

Alternatively, you can use the `text` attribute. This way, everything can be contained within the opening tag, in which case you need to close the tag in the following way:

```
<asp:label id="Message1" forecolor="red"  text="Hello" runat="server" />
```

Here, we omit the closing tag, and just supply a closing / to indicate that the tag is closed. Throughout the book, if the tag hasn't been closed, then we will use this latter notation in preference to having a closing tag.

The `<asp:>` prefix indicates that this control is part of the set of built in ASP.net controls. It is possible to create custom controls, which have prefixes of the developer's choice. We will look at this later in the book.

Let's now take a look at an example of how we can use the `<asp:label>` control to display some text at requisite places within our web page. In this example, we'll assume that values of the user's name and the destination they selected on our holiday web, site have already been passed across, and that all we need to do is output a message displaying confirmation that we have received the user's details.

Try It Out – Using the <asp: label> control

1. Rouse your web page editor from its slumber and type in the following text:

```
<html>
<head>
  <title>Label Control page</title>
</head>
<body>
  <h1>Feiertag Holidays</h1>
  <br /><br />
  Thank you
  <asp:label id="Message1" runat="server" text="Chris"/>
    you have selected to receive information about
  <asp:label id="Message2" runat="server" text="Oslo"/>
.   The information pack will be sent out within the next 24 hours.
</body>
</html>
```

2. Save this as `labelcontrol.aspx`.

3. View this page in your browser:

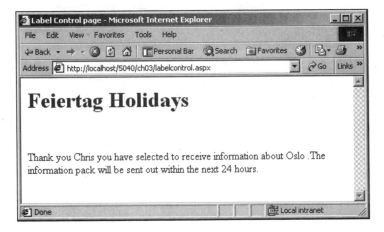

How It Works

There isn't much to explain here. Our <asp:label> controls fit neatly within the HTML code:

```
<h1>Feiertag Holidays</h1>
<br /><br />
Thank you
<asp:label id="Message1" runat="server" text="Chris"/>
  you have selected to receive information about
<asp:label id="Message2" runat="server" text="Oslo"/>
  .The information pack will be sent out within the next 24 hours.
</body>
```

For all intents and purposes, the <asp:label> control could be an HTML control. The only thing that differentiates it is the fact that it, is executed on the server. The only way you can note this is by checking the underlying HTML source code that is sent back to the browser:

```
<h1>Feiertag Holidays</h1>
<br /><br />
Thank you
<span id="Message1">Chris</span>
  you have selected to receive information about
<span id="Message2">Oslo</span>
  .The information pack will be sent out within the next 24 hours.
</body>
```

The <asp:label> controls are translated into HTML <span> tags, to which they are functionally equivalent.

This still leaves one question unanswered though. How do we get hold of the <asp:label> control within our ASP.NET code? Well, we can do this by adding some ASP.NET code at the head of the HTML, as in the following example. First delete the text attribute from both <asp:label> controls:

```
...
<asp:label id="Message1" runat="server" />
you have selected to receive information about
<asp:label id="Message2" runat="server" />
...
```

Now add the following ASP.NET code:

```
<script language="vb" runat="server">
  Sub Page_Load()
    Message1.text = "Vervain"
    Message2.text = "Madrid"
  End Sub
</script>
<html>
<head>
  <title>Label Control page</title>
...
```

If you run the example above, you'll see that the output has changed:

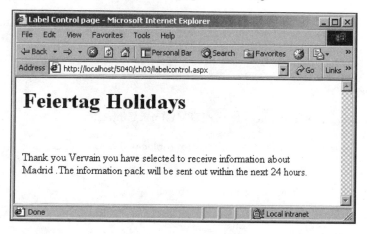

Once again, it's the code within the Sub Page_Load() and End Sub sections that's important. The code that makes the transformation is really quite simple. The first line:

```
Message1.text = "Vervain"
```

Message1 refers to the identity of our first <asp:label> control, while text refers to its text attribute. Basically we're saying change the <asp:label> Message1 control's text attribute to "Vervain". The second line:

```
Message2.text = "Madrid"
```

Just does the same for the Message2 <asp:label> control, setting the type attribute to Madrid. This is reflected in the final display of our web form. This ASP.NET code has allowed us to directly influence the contents of the <asp:label> control, and set it separately independently from our HTML code.

Let's now move on to a more complex control.

The <asp:dropdownlist> control

The <asp:dropdownlist> control is one of the best controls for demonstrating the usefulness of having a form control processed on the server-side.

Before we move onto the <asp:dropdownlist> control, let's pause to look at the HTML form control equivalent. Dropdown List boxes are implemented in HTML using the <select> and <option> tags. For each option, you would have a separate opening and closing <option> tag inside the <select> tag. A list box can be defined in HTML as follows:

```
<select name="list1">
  <option>Madrid</option>
  <option>Oslo</option>
  <option>Lisbon</option>
</select>
```

To create an ASP.NET dropdown list control that did exactly the same, you'd need to define it in the following way:

```
<asp:dropdownlist id="list1" runat="server">
  <asp:listitem>Madrid</asp:listitem >
  <asp:listitem >Oslo</asp:listitem >
  <asp:listitem >Lisbon</asp:listitem >
</asp:dropdownlist >
```

There are three important differences to the HTML form control:

❑ The <asp:dropdownlist> tag directly replaces the <select> tag

❑ The <asp:listitem> tag replaces the <option> tag

❑ The id attribute replaces the name attribute

Up until now, in all HTML form controls, the `name` attribute has been used to pass the identity of the form control to the ASP.NET code. The `id` attribute, for all but form controls, provides exactly this function for any other HTML tags. The server-side control is therefore, being brought up to date, by using the `id` attribute to perform this function, rather than the `name` attribute.

The `<asp:label>` control has many attributes to help customize its appearance. We're not going to describe them here – once again you can find out more details using the class browser tool. There is one attribute of interest however, which we will look at now.

The `selectionmode` attribute is used to determine whether you can select multiple or only select single items from the list box. By default it is set to single, but you do have the option of using multiple.

Visually, the `<asp:dropdownlist>` control is identical to the HTML dropdown list control, it's what's going on behind the scenes that is different. The best way to explain this is to look at an example. We'll create a form that asks the user to select the particular holiday destination they wish to know more about.

Try It Out – Using the <asp:dropdownlist> control

1. Start your web page editor and type in the following:

```
<script runat="server" language="vb">
  Sub Page_Load()
    if Request.Form("list1") <> "" then
      Message.text = "You have selected " + Request.Form("list1")
    end if
  End Sub
</script>
<html>
  <head>
    <title>Drop Down List Example</title>
  </head>
  <body>
    <asp:label id="message" runat="server"/>
    <br />
    <form runat="server">
    Which city do you wish to look at hotels for?<br /><br />
    <asp:dropdownlist id="list1" runat="server">
      <asp:listitem>Madrid</asp:listitem>
      <asp:listitem>Oslo</asp:listitem>
      <asp:listitem>Lisbon</asp:listitem>
    </asp:dropdownlist>
    <br /><br /><br /><br />
    <input type="Submit">
    </form>
  </body>
</html>
```

2. Save this as `listpage.aspx` this time.

3. Run `listpage.aspx` in your browser:

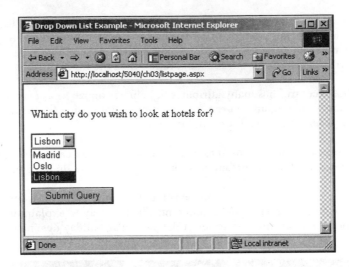

4. Select an option and click on **Submit Query**:

5. Now, click on the **View** menu and select **Source**. You should see something like the following, don't worry if there are items like an extra couple of `<br />` tags, the code has been tailored to your personal browser:

```
<html>
  <head>
    <title>Drop Down List Example</title>
  </head>
  <body>
    <span id="message">You have selected Lisbon</span>
    <form name="ctrl0" method="post" action="listsubmit.aspx" id="ctrl0">
    <input type="hidden" name="__VIEWSTATE"
value="dDwtMTg2MjQ4MjEzO3Q8O2w8aTwxPjs+O2w8dDxwPHA8bDxUZXh0O00z47bDxZb3UgaGF2ZSBzZWx
lY3RlZCBMaXNib247Pj47Pjs7Pjs+Pjs+" />
```

```
         Which city do you wish to look at hotels for?<br /><br />
         <select name="list1" id="list1" size="4">
           <option value="Madrid">Madrid</option>
           <option value="Oslo">Oslo</option>
           <option selected="selected" value="Lisbon">Lisbon</option>

         </select>
         <br /><br />

         <input type="Submit">
         </form>
      </body>
   </html>
```

How It Works

This is our first real look at what the ASP.NET code has been doing. As you can see, everything that has been returned to the browser, has been returned as HTML code. Secondly, this is the only page we are using, in direct contrast to our two-page approach with HTML forms. To explain how it works, we're going to reference the source code that we can view in our browser, and compare it to our original ASPX code.

Let's start by jumping into the <form> section of the script. The very first thing we do with the form is set a new attribute:

```
<form runat="server">
```

This tells ASP.NET that we intend this form to be run on the server. If we compare this line to what has been returned to the browser, we can see a large difference:

```
<form name="ctrl0" method="post" action="listsubmit.aspx" id="ctrl0">
```

ASP.NET has generated four new attributes. The name and id attributes serve the same purpose, uniquely identifying the form, but it's the other two that are of interest. As we described earlier, HTML forms require a page to receive the form data, and a method of transmission. We didn't specify either of these in our .aspx code, so ASP.NET code specified them for us. The action attribute actually points to the same page that we have run, so the answers are returned to our first page. It also specifies the post method by default.

The main item on the form is the <asp:dropdownlist> control:

```
   Which city do you wish to look at hotels for?<br /><br />
   <asp:dropdownlist id="list1" runat="server">
     <asp:listitem>Madrid</asp:listitem>
     <asp:listitem >Oslo</asp:listitem>
     <asp:listitem >Lisbon</asp:listitem>
   </asp:dropdownlist>
```

It's crucial to note how this is rendered. If you view the source code that's been sent back to the browser, you should see something like this:

```
<input type="hidden" name="__VIEWSTATE" value="dDwtMTg2MjQ4MjEzO3Q8O2w8aTwxPjs+O2
   w8dDxwPHA8bDxUZXh0Oz47bDxZb3UgaGF2ZSBzZWxlY3RlZCBMaXNib247Pj47Pjs7Pjs+Pjs+" />

Which city do you wish to look at hotels for?<br /><br />
<select name="list1" id="list1" size="4">
  <option value="Madrid">Madrid</option>
  <option value="Oslo">Oslo</option>
  <option selected="selected" value="Lisbon">Lisbon</option>
</select>
```

The lower of the two is just a <select> HTML form control; this is the HTML output of a
dropdownlist. Note that it's had one of the <option> tags altered to reflect the selection we made
before we submitting the form.

It's however, the first line that is of particular note. This is a hidden control called __VIEWSTATE,
whose value is an encoded representation of the overall state of the form (as it was when last submitted).
This is used by ASP.NET to keep track of *all* the server control settings from one page refresh to
another – otherwise, our dropdown listbox would revert to a static default setting every time we
submitted a value.

It may not be immediately obvious how useful this can be – consider a registration form in which you
have to enter a full set of personal details; if you forget to fill in a required field, and then submit the
form, you may well be prompted with the same form again. Perhaps the field you missed will be
highlighted, but unless the page has been very carefully coded (or is running off a sophisticated
technology like ASP.NET), all the data you just entered will have to be put in again. Thanks to
__VIEWSTATE, all that data is automatically persisted through to the refreshed page, and we (as
developers) haven't even to raise a finger!

We don't need to try and interpret the value contained in the value attribute is – it's only really
designed to means much to ASP.NET itself). However, it's important to note that this attribute is what
allows the form to keep track of the state of server control between page moves and page refreshes.
Indeed when we ran through the example you might have noticed that even refreshing the page, doesn't
alter the selection you have made.

So we can see that the ASP.NET server control passes the form data to the ASP.NET code, it's just up to
the ASP.NET code to access it. It's the little section of script at the head of the ASPX code that returns
the data from the form:

```
<script runat="server" language="vb">
  Sub Page_Load()
    if Request.Form("list1") <> "" then
      Message.text = "You have selected " + Request.Form("list1")
    end if
  End Sub
</script>
```

There are three lines of code here. We won't dissect this code fully here (we'll come to that later in the
book), but in plain terms, the code is saying if a selection has been made in the list box, then we will
display a message confirming the choice the user made. If they haven't made a choice, then we won't
display anything in the <asp:label> control.

We use the `Request.Form("list1")` line to actually return the data from our dropdown list box. `Request` merely refers to the HTTP request. As we have already noted, ASP.NET has automatically adjusted the form's method attribute to `POST`. To get at information transferred by `POST`, as part of the form's body, we use the `Form` statement. Lastly, `("list1")` refers to the identifier of our dropdown list control.

So our message is constructed as follows:

"You have selected " + "Lisbon"

Where does `Message.text` come into all of this? `Message`, as you might have already noticed, is the unique identifier of our `<asp:label>` control. We use `Message.text` to display the message, as this refers to the text that this particular `<asp:label>` control will display. You can find the `<asp:label>` control just underneath the `<body>` tag on our ASPX page:

```
<body>
  <asp:label id="message" runat="server"/>
  <br />
```

In this way, we can ensure that the first time a user logs on, there is no message displayed in the `<asp:label>` control, but every time the user returns subsequently to the page, there is a message displayed. We will be looking at how the particular `if` and `end if` statements work in a later chapter.

As hidden fields play a crucial role in this example, let's take a quick digression to look at how they work in more detail, as the way in which they work is slightly different to the other HTML form controls.

Hidden controls

Hidden controls are simply controls that are not visible on the rendered form. We can set their contents separately and then they are packaged up along with any other form information. Hidden fields are very commonly used throughout ASP.NET code, and are often generated automatically to transmit data.

Hidden form controls cannot be set directly by the user's actions, since the user is necessarily unaware of them. It is possible however to set hidden controls as the indirect result of a user's actions. To create a hidden control, you set the `<input>` tag's type attribute to `hidden`, and pass the information you wish to send to the server in the value attribute:

```
<input name="hidden1" type="hidden" value="green">
```

In the next example, we'll look at how we can use a hidden control to pass a value from one web page to a web form.

Try It Out – Using hidden fields

1. Poke your web page editor in the ribs to wake it up and type up the following:

```
<script runat="server" language="vb">
  Sub Page_Load()
    if Request.Form("hidden1") <> "" then
```

```
            Message.text = "The hidden control contained the value: " + _
                           Request.Form("hidden1")
        end if
    End Sub
</script>
<html>
  <head>
    <title>Hidden Control Example</title>
  </head>
  <body>
    <asp:label id="message" runat="server"/>
    <form runat="server">
      <input name="hidden1" type="hidden" value="green">
      <input type="Submit" VALUE="Click here to submit hidden control">
    </form>
  </body>
</html>
```

2. Save this as `hiddenpage.aspx`.

3. Open up `hiddenpage.aspx` in your browser:

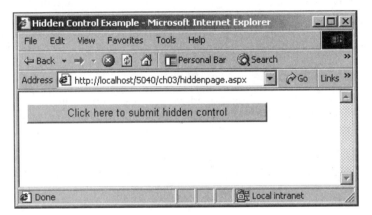

4. Click on the submit button to see the result of the value that was passed:

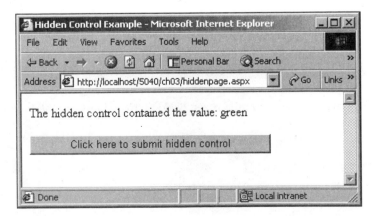

How It Works

The use of the hidden field isn't entirely obvious from this example. You can see that it is used to pass hidden values, but given that the value in this example is set by the HTML, it doesn't offer any advantage over other form controls.

We've set the `runat` attribute of the `<form>` tag to server in this page, just as we did in the previous example:

```
<form runat="server">
```

We've create a hidden control on our first page `hiddensubmit.html`:

```
<input name="hidden1" type="hidden" value="green">
```

As before, ASP.NET will change the underlying code, and set the method attribute to `POST`:

```
<form name="ctrl0" method="post" action="hiddenpage.aspx" id="ctrl0">
```

Choosing `POST` will ensure that the user doesn't actually see that any information has passed across to the server. Once the information has been received on the server, our `<asp:label>` control can display text in the normal way via our ASP.NET code.

```
<asp:label id="message" runat="server"/>
```

We've set the identifier of the `<asp:label>` control to `message` again. This identifier is referenced by our ASP.NET code at the top of the page:

```
<script runat="server" language="vb">
  Sub Page_Load()
    if Request.Form("hidden1") <> "" then
      Message.text = "The hidden control contained the value: " +
Request.Form("hidden1")
    end if
  End Sub
</script>
```

Here the code is almost identical to the ASP.NET code that we used in the dropdown list control example. In fact, the only difference is that instead of passing the list control, `list1`, we substitute it with the name of our hidden control, `Hidden1`. Once again, the information is passed in the HTTP request body, along with the form. We use the `Form` command and the `("hidden1")` identifier to access the contents of our hidden control.

The hidden control is being used as "memory" between two web pages. Normally, information is lost between one page and another, unless actively submitted by the user. Now we have a method of remembering our own data that we set, passing it between pages, and making it available to ASP.NET code.

The <asp:listbox> control

The third HTML server control, <asp:listbox>, is very much related to the first. In fact, we mentioned the HTML form control <select> that creates dropdown list boxes; well, the <asp:listbox> is a server-side equivalent of using the <select> tag with the size attribute set to the maximum number of options possible. In fact, the only differences with this control are the facts that it doesn't drop down and that it is capable of multiple selections.

The <asp:listbox> has the following format:

```
<asp:listbox id="list1" runat="server">
  <asp:listitem>Madrid</asp:listitem >
  <asp:listitem >Oslo</asp:listitem >
  <asp:listitem >Lisbon</asp:listitem >
</asp:listbox>
```

In the ASP.NET code the <asp:listbox> tag now replaces the <asp:dropdownlist> tag, the <asp:listitem> tag, which delimits each of the list-box options, is the same for both controls.

Let's take a look at a quick example, where we alter our previous example to use a listbox instead of a dropdown list control. We'll also alter it to allow multiple selections as well.

Try It Out – Using the <asp:listbox> control

1. Open up the listpage.aspx and make the following amendments:

```
<script runat="server" language="vb">
  Sub Page_Load()
    if Request.Form("list1") <> "" then
      Message.text = "You have selected " + Request.Form("list1")
    end if
  End Sub
</script>
<html>
  <head>
    <title>Drop Down List Example</title>
  </head>
  <body>
    <asp:label id="message" runat="server"/>
    <br />
    <form runat="server">
    Which city do you wish to look at hotels for?<br /><br />
    <asp:listbox id="list1" runat="server" selectionmode="multiple">
      <asp:listitem>Madrid</asp:listitem>
      <asp:listitem>Oslo</asp:listitem>
      <asp:listitem>Lisbon</asp:listitem>
    </asp:listbox>
    <br /><br /><br /><br />
    <input type="Submit">
    </form>
  </body>
</html>
```

2. Save this as `listpage2.aspx`.

3. Run this page in your browser, and use the ctrl, or shift keys to select multiple choices:

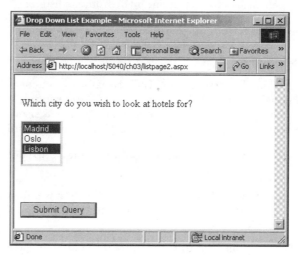

4. Click on Submit Query to see the following:

How It Works

As you can see, minimal changes have been made to alter this example and get it working with a listbox control, as opposed to a dropdown listbox. All we have changed is the type of control:

```
<asp:listbox id="list1" runat="server" selectionmode="multiple">
  <asp:listitem>Madrid</asp:listitem>
  <asp:listitem>Oslo</asp:listitem>
  <asp:listitem>Lisbon</asp:listitem>
</asp:listbox>
```

Most notably, we have kept the `id` attribute the same, as this allows us to refer to the control in the same way in the ASP.NET code. We have added a `selectionmode` attribute that allows us to make multiple selections. As you can see from the output from the browser, the browser automatically appends a comma between each of the selections made from the listbox.

Let's move on to some different types of control.

The <asp:textbox> control

This server control is ASP.NET's version of the HTML textbox form control. In fact, it doubles up and also provides the functionality of the HTML `<textarea>` form control. In fact, text areas are simply text boxes that feature multiple lines, thus allowing you to put in larger quantities of text. The textbox control is also able to supply the functionality of the HTML form password control.

To be able to cover the remit of three HTML form controls, the `<asp:textbox>` control needs some extra attributes:

❑ `textmode` – specifies whether you want the control to have one line (don't set it), or many lines (set it to multiline), or have a single line of masked content (set it to password if you want to conceal the text that's been entered)

❑ `rows` – specifies the number of rows you want the textbox to have, and will only work if `textmode` is set to `multiple`

❑ `columns` – specifies the number of columns you want the textbox to have, and will also only work if `textmode` is set to `multiple`

If you wish to provide any default text that appears in the control, you can either set place it between the opening and closing tags:

```
<asp:textbox id="text1" runat="server">Default text here...</asp:textbox>
```

Or set it in the text attribute:

```
<asp:textbox id="text1" runat="server" text="Default text here..."/>
```

Now we'll create a short example that uses the textbox control to ask for the name and address of the user, and a password as well. Previously in HTML, this would require three different types of control, here we shall only use the one `<asp:textbox>` control.

Try It Out – Using the <asp:textbox> control

1. Time to start your web page editor again and type in the following:

```
<script runat="server" language="vb">
  Sub Page_Load()
    if Request.Form("text1") <> "" then
      Message1.text = "You have entered the following name: " +
Request.Form("text1")
    end if
    if Request.Form("text2") <> "" then
      Message2.text = "You have entered the following address: " +
Request.Form("text2")
```

```
      end if
      if Request.Form("text3") <> "" then
        Message3.text = "You have entered the following password: " +
Request.Form("text3")
      end if
    End Sub
</script>
<html>
  <head>
    <title>Text Box Example</title>
  </head>
  <body>
    <asp:label id="message1" runat="server" />
    <br />
    <asp:label id="message2" runat="server" />
    <br />
    <asp:label id="message3" runat="server" />
    <br />
    <form runat="server">
      Please enter your name:
      <asp:textbox id="text1" runat="server" />
      <br /><br />
      Please enter your address:
      <asp:textbox id="text2" runat="server" rows=5 textmode="multiline" />
      <br /><br />
      Please enter your chosen password:
      <asp:textbox id="text3" runat="server" textmode="password" />
      <br /><br />
      <input type="Submit">
    </form>
  </body>
</html>
```

2. Save this as `textboxpage.aspx`.

3. Open `textboxpage.aspx` in your browser, and type in some details:

4. Click on Submit Query to see the results:

How It Works

Within the form, we have created three types of textbox control:

```
<asp:textbox id="text1" runat="server" />
<br /><br />
Please enter your address:
<asp:textbox id="text2" runat="server" rows=5 textmode="multiline" />
<br /><br />
Please enter your chosen password:
<asp:textbox id="text3" runat="server" textmode="password" />
```

The first is identified as text1, and requires no other attributes other than of id and runat. This is displayed as a single text field. The second control, text2, is a multiline textbox (which will render as a text area), and requires that we set the textmode attribute to multiline, so that we can set the number of rows we wish this text box to have. Here, we have set it to five for the address. Lastly, we create a third control, text3, which we set to password with the textmode attribute. This, again, will display a single line text field, but any text typed into it is obscured by a set of asterisks.

To display the results from three sets of controls, we have used three separate <asp:label> controls:

```
<asp:label id="message1" runat="server" />
<br />
<asp:label id="message2" runat="server" />
<br />
<asp:label id="message3" runat="server" />
```

Each one is identified with a different `id` attribute. In this way, we can pass information from our three text boxes to a separate label control. The job of assigning text values to these three label controls falls to the ASP.NET code contained within `<script>` tags at the top of the page.

The code that assigns the values is very repetitive:

```
<script runat="server" language="vb">
  Sub Page_Load()
    if Request.Form("text1") <> "" then
      Message1.text = "You have entered the following name: " +
Request.Form("text1")
    end if
    if Request.Form("text2") <> "" then
      Message2.text = "You have entered the following address: " +
Request.Form("text2")
    end if
    if Request.Form("text3") <> "" then
      Message3.text = "You have entered the following password: " +
Request.Form("text3")
    end if
  End Sub
</script>
```

For the first control, we take the text information, and assign it to the first label control. This will display the name information. For the second control, we take the text information from the second textbox control, and assign it to the second asp label control, and we do likewise for the third. The line breaks from the multi-line control (second textbox control) won't display in the label on the result page. Next, we surround each statement with the `if` and `end if` tags, because we want to check each control individually before displaying its contents, in this way only, the controls that have contents will be displayed. So if you only entered information into the name field, only one message would be displayed. Go ahead, try it and see.

The *<asp:radiobutton>* and *<asp:radiobuttonlist>* controls

In HTML, radio buttons are used when there a multiple set of choices, but you want the user to select only one of the choices. If they click on a second selection, after making a first, the first selection is removed and replaced by the second. Radio buttons are implemented in HTML using the `<input>` tag, and setting the type attribute to `radio`. Every radio button on the page needs to have its own `<input type="radio">` tag. Each radio button within a particular group must have the same `name` attribute.

The `<asp:radiobutton>` and `<asp:radiobuttonlist>` controls work in a different way to their HTML forms equivalent. No longer do they necessarily exclude each other. In HTML radio buttons were assigned the same identifier using the `name` attribute, as below:

```
A<input name="radio1" type="radio">
B<input name="radio1" type="radio">
C<input name="radio1" type="radio">
```

This would ensure only one radio button could be selected. The `<asp:radiobutton>` however control actively forbids you from doing this. If you try and set each radio button to have the same identifier with the `<asp:radiobutton>` control (remembering that HTML form controls use the `name` attribute, while HTML server controls use the `id` attribute), then you'd generate an error:

```
A<asp:radiobutton id="radio1" runat="server" />
B<asp:radiobutton id="radio1" runat="server" />
C<asp:radiobutton id="radio1" runat="server" />
```

Instead, you have to use the `<asp:radiobuttonlist>` control to get the functionality that you'd typically associate with radio buttons. The `<asp:radiobuttonlist>` works in the same way as listboxes, in that the `<asp:radiobuttonlist>` control contains a set of options that are set using the `<asp:listitem>` tag with one for each option:

```
<asp:radiobuttonlist id="radio1" runat="server">
  <asp:listitem id="option1" runat="server" value="A" />
  <asp:listitem id="option2" runat="server" value="B" />
  <asp:listitem id="option3" runat="server" value="C" />
</asp:radiobuttonlist>
```

This would look as follows:

     ⦿ A

     ◯ B

     ◯ C

The identifier for the whole control is set only in the `id` attribute of the `<asp:radiobuttonlist>` control, and it is this that is used to return the selected item to ASP.NET.

We'll now create a quick example that uses a group of radio buttons to decide which destination a user has selected on a HTML form, and relays that information back to the user. We will only allow the user to select one destination.

Try It Out – Using the `<asp:radiobutton>` control

1. Crank up your web page editor of choice and type in the following:

```
<script runat="server" language="vb">
  Sub Page_Load()
    if Request.Form("radio1") <> "" then
      Message.text = "You have selected the following: " + Request.Form("radio1")
    end if
  End Sub
</script>
<html>
  <head>
    <title>Radio Button List Example</title>
  </head>
  <body>
    <asp:label id="message" runat="server" />
    <br /><br />
    Which city do you wish to look at hotels for?
    <br /><br />
    <form runat="server">
      <asp:radiobuttonlist id="radio1" runat="server">
        <asp:listitem id="option1" runat="server" value="Madrid" />
```

```
            <asp:listitem id="option2" runat="server" value="Oslo" />
            <asp:listitem id="option3" runat="server" value="Lisbon" />
          </asp:radiobuttonlist>
          <br /><br />
          <input type="Submit">
        </form>
      </body>
    </html>
```

2. Save this as `radiopage.aspx`.

3. View `radiopage.aspx` in your browser:

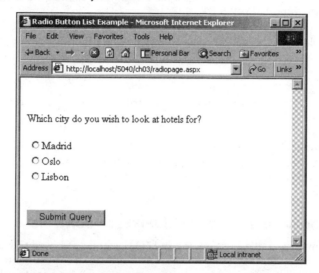

4. Select a button, and click on **Submit Query**:

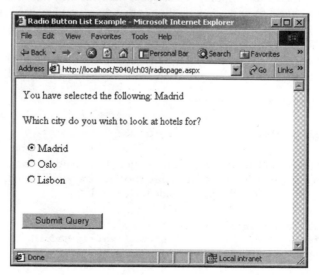

121

How It Works

The `radiopage.aspx` page has three radio buttons, for Madrid, Oslo, and Lisbon:

```
<asp:radiobuttonlist id="radio1" runat="server">
  <asp:listitem id="option1" runat="server" value="Madrid" />
  <asp:listitem id="option2" runat="server" value="Oslo" />
  <asp:listitem id="option3" runat="server" value="Lisbon" />
</asp:radiobuttonlist>
```

We have assigned each of the radio buttons their respective values, and used the `<asp:radiobuttonlist>` control, to place them within the same group. We use the `radio1` identifier to return them to the ASP.NET code.

In the ASP.NET code at the top of the page delimited within the `Sub Page Load` and `End Sub` statements, we have used the familiar three lines to return the information from the form:

```
if Request.Form("radio1") <> "" then
  Message.text = "You have selected the following: " + Request.Form("radio1")
end if
```

This is again used to display some plain text in `<asp:label>` control, if there has been a selection made on the radio buttons. If a radio button is selected, then the message `"You have selected the following: "` is followed by the contents of `Request.Form("radio1")`. This is then displayed on the web form.

The <asp:checkbox> and <asp:checkboxlist> controls

Check boxes are similar to radio buttons, and in HTML, they were used to allow multiple choices from a group of buttons. With the `<asp:checkboxlist>` control, it is possible to create them in groups, but unlike radio buttons, it isn't possible to restrict the ability of the user to select just one possible answer from a group of checkboxes; they can select as many as they like. The other fundamental difference between a checkbox and a radio button is that once you have selected a checkbox you are able to deselect it.

We're not going to spend too long examining them, as most of the same principles that we followed in the `<asp:radiobutton>` and `<asp:radiobuttonlist>` examples apply.

A typical `<asp:checkbox>` looks like this:

```
<asp:checkbox id="check1" runat="server" />
```

If we want to use an array of checkboxes we can contain them inside a `<asp:checkboxlist>` control. We need to set an id attribute for the `<asp:checkboxlist>` control itself, and create a `<asp:listitem>` control for each option inside the control:

```
<asp:checkboxlist id="check1" runat="server">
  <asp:listitem id="option1" runat="server" value="Madrid" />
  <asp:listitem id="option2" runat="server" value="Oslo" />
  <asp:listitem id="option3" runat="server" value="Lisbon" />
</asp:checkboxlist>
```

Checkboxes are most typically used when you have single yes/no answers, or you wish the user to be able to make a multiple set of selections, and be able to deselect them as well.

In our next exercise, we're going tweak our previous example, so that it uses our established holiday code to allow the user to select more than one option for a particular destination.

Try It Out – Using the <asp:checkbox> control

1. Open up the `radiopage.aspx` and amend the code highlighted in gray, as follows:

```
<script runat="server" language="vb">
  Sub Page_Load()

    Dim s As String = "You have selected the following items:<br />"

    If check1.Items(0).Selected Then s = s & check1.Items(0).Text & "<br />"
    If check1.Items(1).Selected Then s = s & check1.Items(1).Text & "<br />"
    If check1.Items(2).Selected Then s = s & check1.Items(2).Text & "<br />"

    Message.Text = s
  End Sub
</script>
<html>
<head>
  <title>Check Box List Example</title>
</head>
<body>
  <asp:label id="message" runat="server" />
  <br /><br />
  Which city do you wish to look at hotels for?
  <br /><br />
  <form runat="server">
    <asp:checkboxlist id="check1" runat="server">
      <asp:listitem id="option1" runat="server" value="Madrid" />
      <asp:listitem id="option2" runat="server" value="Oslo" />
      <asp:listitem id="option3" runat="server" value="Lisbon" />
    </asp:checkboxlist>
    <br /><br />
    <input type="Submit">
  </form>
</body>
</html>
```

2. Save this as `checkpage.aspx`.

3. Open `checkpage.aspx` in your browser, and select more than one option:

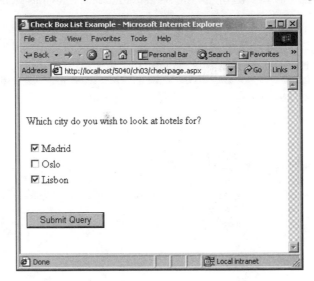

4. Then click on Submit Query:

How It Works

Very little has visibly changed within the body of our `checkpage.aspx` page – all we've done is change the HTML control to an `<asp:checkboxlist>`, and then change the actual name of control to reflect this:

```
<asp:checkboxlist id="check1" runat="server">
  <asp:listitem id="option1" runat="server" value="Madrid" />
..<asp:listitem id="option2" runat="server" value="Oslo" />
..<asp:listitem id="option3" runat="server" value="Lisbon" />
</asp:checkboxlist>
```

We've however, had to completely overhaul our ASP.NET code:

```
Dim msg As String = "You have selected the following items:<br />"

If check1.Items(1).Selected Then msg = msg & check1.Items(1).Text & "<br />"
If check1.Items(2).Selected Then msg = msg & check1.Items(2).Text & "<br />"
If check1.Items(3).Selected Then msg = msg & check1.Items(3).Text & "<br />"

Message.Text = s
```

In fact, we've introduced a whole new way of determining which checkboxes are checked. The `If...Then` construct that we've applied to each of the items in the list, is something we'll be introducing properly in a couple of chapters' time. It's not complex though: we specify a condition (in this case, the value of each item's `Selected` attribute), and if it's logically `True` (that is, the item *is* currently selected), an operation is carried out.

Here's another new construct: a variable assignment. The first line in this block creates a `String` variable (again, we'll be looking at variables in depth very shortly). This essentially just declares a label 'msg' which refers to a space in the computer's memory that we can use to hold a sequence of characters, or **string**. We set it up with a simple heading, and then add country names on the end, according to which checkboxes have been selected. Finally, we assign its final value (a long string of HTML) to the `Text` attribute of the Message label, so that it can be seen on the page.

As you can see, checkboxes work in a slightly different way from radio buttons. Each time you add a value, rather than replacing it, the value is added to the contents of (`"check1"`) with a comma automatically added to split the two up. However, for all other intents and purposes, you use them in the same way.

One last point to note about checkboxes, though, is that you might want to treat each checkbox within a group as a separate entity, rather than have them all grouped together. In which case you could set each of them as separate `<asp:checkbox>` controls to reflect this:

```
<asp:checkbox id="check1" runat="server" Text="Madrid"/>
<asp:checkbox id="check2" runat="server" text="Oslo"/>
<asp:checkbox id="check3" runat="server" text = "Lisbon"/>
```

The `text` attribute here specifies the text that will appear next to the checkbox. The checkbox itself will not return a value, to find out if it is checked or not we need to add some ASP.NET code to test if the `Checked` attribute is `True` or `False`; it will be True if the checkbox is checked.

Combination of controls on one page

OK, so we've looked at all of the major form controls, bar one. This final one works in a different way, as we shall see shortly. While it should now be a breeze to return information from any of them, how about returning information from the whole load of them on one page?

We'll now put together a quick example where we will return data from each of the different types of form control on the page we have considered so far. We will use this to demonstrate how a simple front-end might look for the Feiertag Holidays site, and return all of the information that a user has submitted. We also aim to show which form controls are most suitable for a particular kind of task.

Try It Out – The Business Example

1. Open your web page editor and type in the following code:

```
<html>
<head>
  <title>Holiday page</title>
</head>
<body>
  <form action="holidayresponse.aspx" method="post">
    <h1>Feiertag Holidays</h1>
    Please enter your details here.
    <br /><br />
    Name:<asp:textbox id="FullName" runat="server" />
    <br /><br />
    Address:<asp:textbox id="Address" rows="5" textmode="multiline" runat="server"
/>
    <br /><br />
    Sex -
    <asp:radiobuttonlist id="sex" runat="server">
      <asp:listitem value="Male" />
      <asp:listitem value="Female" />
    </asp:radiobuttonlist>
    Please select the destination you would like details on:
    <asp:dropdownlist id="Destination" runat="server">
      <asp:listitem value="Madrid" />
      <asp:listitem value="Barcelona"/>
      <asp:listitem value="Lisbon"/>
      <asp:listitem value="Oslo"/>
      <asp:listitem value="Prague"/>
    </asp:dropdownlist>
    <br /><br />
      <input type="Submit">
      <input type="Reset">
  </form>
</body>
</html>
```

2. Save this as `holidaypage.aspx`.

3. Keeping your web page editor open, type in the following:

```
<script runat="server" language="vb">
  Sub Page_Load()
    Response.Write ("<b>Name:</b> " + Request.Form("FullName") + "<br />")
    Response.Write ("<b>Address:</b> " + Request.Form("Address") + "<br />")
    Response.Write ("<b>Sex:</b> " + Request.Form("Sex") + "<br />")
    Response.Write ("<b>Destination:</b> " + Request.Form("Destination") + "<br />")
  End Sub
```

```
</script>
<html>
<head>
  <title>Holiday page</title>
</head>
<body>
  <br /><br />
  These details have been entered into our database, you should receive a
confirmation email from us shortly.
<br /><br />
</body>
</html>
```

4. Save this as `holidayresponse.aspx`.

5. Open `holidaypage.aspx` and type in some details:

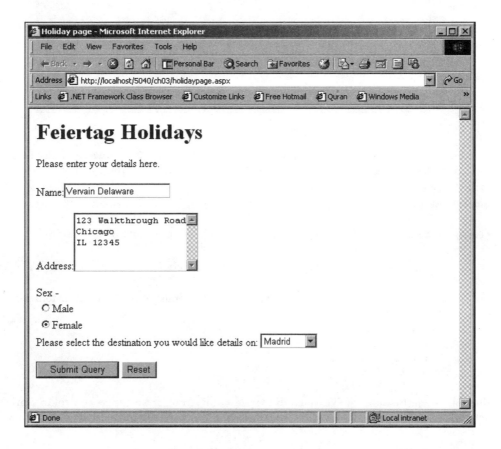

6. Click on Submit Query:

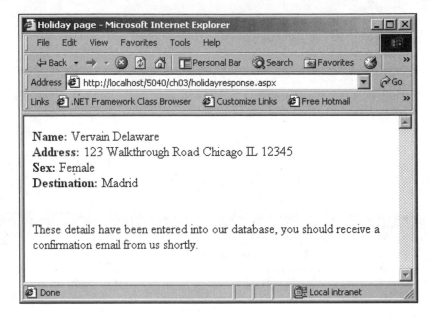

How It Works

We've seen all of the form controls (with the exception of the new one that we shall discuss shortly) on the holidaypage.aspx page before. We use a textbox to collect the user's name:

```
Name:<asp:textbox id="FullName" runat="server" />
```

We also use a textbox to capture the user's address, which will presumably have multiple lines of text:

```
Address:<asp:textbox id="Address" rows="5" textmode="multiline" runat="server" />
```

We use radio button list control to select the sex, as a person must either be male or female:

```
<asp:radiobuttonlist id="sex" runat="server">
  <asp:listitem value="Male" />
  <asp:listitem value="Female" />
</asp:radiobuttonlist>
```

For the holiday destinations, we've opted to use the <asp:dropdownlist> control to conserve space on the page. We could have used radio buttons, but this might have ended up looking clumsy:

```
<asp:dropdownlist id="Destination" runat="server">
  <asp:listitem value="Madrid" />
  <asp:listitem value="Barcelona"/>
  <asp:listitem value="Lisbon"/>
  <asp:listitem value="Oslo"/>
  <asp:listitem value="Prague"/>
</asp:dropdownlist>
```

In addition to our submit button for submitting the form, we've also added a reset button:

```
<input type="Submit">
<input type="Reset">
```

All that the reset button does is reset all of the form controls on the page to their original state, before the user entered any information. Of course, it can't be used once the form has been submitted.

Before we move on to the next page, there is one small detail that might have escaped your attention:

```
<form action="holidayresponse.aspx" method="post">
```

We've set the form, but not used the `runat="server"` attribute. "Why?" you might wonder. Well the `runat="server"` setting prohibits us from moving to another page because it automatically creates an `action` attribute within our first page specified. If we try to override it by setting the `action` attribute to another page, it won't have any effect, and we will be returned to the original page. Since we want to progress to a second page, we've chosen not to set the `runat="server"` attribute, and instead specify ourselves how the form is sent and where it is sent to.

When we submit our first page, we transmit the form data stored within each control as part of the HTTP request. Consequently, that's where we need to tell our second page to look for the data, so as to display it using `Response.Write`:

```
Response.Write ("Name: " + Request.Form("FullName") + "<br />")
Response.Write ("Address: " + Request.Form("Address") + "<br />")
Response.Write ("Sex: " + Request.Form("Sex") + "<br />")
Response.Write ("Destination: " + Request.Form("Destination") + "<br />")
```

Since we gave each control a separate name, we just reference each name in turn to get back the data from the form.

Summary

This chapter has seen us dabble with ASP.NET code for the first time. While some of the examples might have seemed quite repetitive, it is necessary to be comfortable with how you go about handling all the different HTML server controls, as they will crop up frequently and we won't spend any time going back over how they work.

We introduced the ASP.NET server controls in preference to using the HTML form controls, and demonstrated that the server-side counterparts of many of the HTML form controls offer extra functionality over their client-side counterparts. In particular we saw how we could use the `<asp:label>` control to display text and how we could use the other controls such as `<asp:dropdownlist>`, `<asp:textbox>` and `<asp:radiobutton>` in situations in place of the HTML form controls.

Our next chapter, we will look at how we can store information within our ASP.NET pages.

Storing Information in VB.NET

One of the most important concepts in any programming language is the ability to persist data from one command to another. Suppose we write some code that asks a user to input their name – how can we store this information long enough to use it? How do we store other types of data, such as numbers and dates? In addition, what if several users have all provided similar pieces of data – how does the computer know how to match up the information provided to the user who provided it? This can all be done using **variables**.

Variables are fundamental to programming – they let you assign a label to an area of memory in which you can store just about any type of information. A programming language lets you create variables, assign values to them, access their contents, and reuse those values in your code. It will enable you to perform mathematical functions, calculate new dates, manipulate text, count the length of sentences, and perform many other functions.

VB.NET is a **strongly typed** language, which means that any variable at all will have a well-defined data type associated with it, such as String, Integer, or Date. Consequently, it can always identify how the variable's value should be interpreted: numbers will be treated as numbers, character strings as text (even if they consist of numbers), and dates can be seen as proper dates (and not just complicated long division sums such as: 5/10/2001).

In the course of this chapter, we'll be looking at each of the main data types available in VB.NET, and the consequences of not assigning them. We'll look at some basic arithmetic operators and see how we can use them with variables. We'll consider the most suitable data types for the kind of operation you wish to perform.

Next, we'll move on to the topic of structured data, by which means you can store your items of data in specific structures. In this chapter, we'll look at arrays, which are indexed collections of variables, and in the next, we'll introduce XML, a separate language that doesn't use variables, but provides us with another way to store structured information.

As you may have noticed, we've now started talking about VB.NET instead of ASP.NET, and this is intentional. Although we're still in the process of learning ASP.NET, the implementation of variables is one particular feature that's implemented as part of the underlying .NET language we use to write it. Although this is a very important topic, it would undoubtedly be confusing to cover exactly how variables are implemented in every single language that ASP.NET supports. This chapter will, therefore, discuss how VB.NET variables are created and stored – we'll continue to create ASP.NET pages throughout the chapter, but most of the specific issues and syntax we introduce will relate specifically to VB.NET. Other languages will follow the same general format, but with some differences. For example in C# the method of structuring your code and ending code statements differs from VB.NET, but the basic ideas and techniques remain the same.

In this chapter we'll look at:

❑ What a Variable is

❑ Data Types

❑ Performing simple calculations with data types

❑ Arrays

What is a Variable?

A **variable** is a label or reference to a container in memory that is allocated a name by the programmer. By label, we mean like the little labels you used to have on your clothing when you went to school. These containers in memory can be used to store pieces of information that will be used in the program. Think of variables as you might think of boxes. They're simply repositories for information that you wish to store. The variable doesn't actually contain the information, but shows you where the information can be found. It will however essentially look as though the variable does store the information.

For example, here are three variables – they contain a string of text, a numerical value, and a date respectively:

```
Dim CapitalCityOfUK As String
Dim NumberOfStates As Integer
Dim IndependenceDay As Date

CapitalCityOfUK = "London"
NumberOfStates = 50
IndependenceDay = #7/4/1863#
```

Any variable is empty until you put information into it (although the memory space is reserved while the code runs). You can then look at the information inside the variable, get the information out, or replace the information with new data. In fact, variables are essential for storing data in any computer language, VB.NET certainly not least!

Declaration

You'll notice that before we assign value to each of our variables, there is an equivalent line at the top that has preceded it. This line declares what type the variable is. As we hinted in our introduction, VB.NET needs data types explicitly defining so that it knows how to deal with the contents of the variable. You can define the different data types, using the process of declaration.

Declaration is an important fact of life in programming, and in ASP.NET, you should be taking care to declare your variables whether using VB.NET, C# or JScript.NET. All variables should be declared **before** they are used within a program or web page.

In VB.NET, a variable declaration is made with the keyword `Dim`, which is short for 'dimension'. This rather odd-looking incantation tells VB.NET that you're setting up a new variable. What this does is set aside the name and space for the variable in memory. Until the variable is assigned a value, it contains nothing (bear in mind zero is a value, so it won't contain zero or even a blank space).

For example, the first line here declares a variable as a string type with the name `strCarType`; the second line assigns a string value to that variable:

```
Dim strCarType As String
strCarType = "Buick"
```

It's also possible to declare a variable, and assign a value to it, in one line:

```
Dim strCarType As String = "Buick"
```

For the time being, in this chapter, we're going to stick to declaring, and assigning a value as two different operations and perform them on two lines. In later chapters, once you're happy with this, you'll see us moving to one line.

Finally, it's also possible to declare several variables all of the same type on the same line:

```
    Dim strCarType1, strCarType2, strCarType3 As String
    strCarType1 = "Buick"
    strCarType2 = "Cadillac"
    strCarType3 = "Pontiac"
```

You can then assign each of the variables values, as we have done.

Let's look at an example here. We'll take the three variables we introduced at the beginning of the chapter and assign them values, then display those values within three separate `<asp:label>` controls.

Try It Out – Using Variables

1. Open your web page editor and type in the following:

```
<script language="vb" runat="server">
Sub Page_Load()
  Dim CapitalCityOfUK As String
  Dim NumberOfStates As Integer
  Dim IndependenceDay As Date
```

```
   CapitalCityOfUK = "London"
   NumberOfStates = 50
   IndependenceDay = #7/4/1863#

   Display1.Text = CapitalCityOfUK
   Display2.Text = NumberOfStates
   Display3.Text = IndependenceDay
   End Sub
</script>

<html>
<head>
<title>Creating Variables Example</title>
</head>
<body>
   The contents of CapitalCityOfUk is:
   <asp:label id="Display1" runat="server" />
   <br>The contents of NumberOfStates is:
   <asp:label id="Display2" runat="server" />
   <br>The contents of IndependenceDay is:
   <asp:label id="Display3" runat="server" />
</body>
</html>
```

2. Save this as `C:\BegASPNET\Ch04\variable.aspx`

3. Open `variable.aspx` in your browser and view it, it will look something like this:

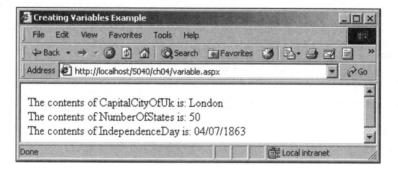

4. Now go back to the example and add the following line:

```
...
Dim IndependenceDay As Date

CapitalCityOfUK = "London"
NumberOfStates = 50
IndependenceDay = #7/4/1863#
NumberOfDaysInJuly = 31

Display1.text = CapitalCityOfUK
...
```

5. Save this as `variable.aspx` and run the same example again:

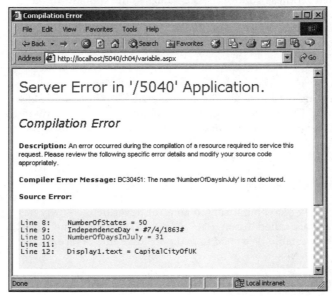

This time an error is generated, because the variable `NumberOfDaysInJuly` hasn't been declared.

How It Works

We've separated the code into different stages. The first section declares each of the variables we wish to use in the example:

```
Dim CapitalCityOfUK As String
Dim NumberOfStates As Integer
Dim IndependenceDay As Date
```

We want to use text in the `CapitalCityOfUk` variable, so we declare it as a `String`, we wish to convey numerical information in the `NumberOfStates` variable, so we declare it as an `Integer` and we wish to store the date of Independence Day as a `Date`.

In the next section, having declared the variables, we are now free to assign values to each:

```
CapitalCityOfUK = "London"
NumberOfStates = 50
IndependenceDay = #7/4/1863#
```

We assign the value of "`London`" to the `CapitalCityOfUK` variable. We've surrounded the value with quotes; this is to let VB.NET know that we are supplying a piece of text to the variable. If we wished to supply a value to a purely numerical variable, we would remove the quotation marks. This is, in fact, what we've done in the second variable. As we're assigning the variable `NumberOfStates` an integer value, we can omit the quotation marks. Finally, we assign a date to our variable `IndependenceDay`. To delimit a date, we use the hash mark identifiers. Once again, this indicates to VB.NET that the information supplied to the variable is in date format.

In the last section, we've created three `<asp:label>` controls called `Display1`, `Display2`, and `Display3`. We then set these control's `Text` values to the contents of our three variables:

```
Display1.Text = CapitalCityOfUK
Display2.Text = NumberOfStates
Display3.Text = IndependenceDay
```

Our web form duly displays the contents of our variables. You might be wondering what stops the three controls from supplying the literal text "CapitalCityOfUK", "NumberOfStates", and "IndependenceDay"? The answer is the absence of quotation marks. Anything inside quotation marks is interpreted as text. Anything not contained in them is treated as a variable, numeric value or object.

We then went on to amend our example to add another line:

```
NumberOfDaysInJuly = 31
```

This line looks perfectly okay, but it caused an error nevertheless – why has it done this? If we look at the line, it sets a variable called `NumberOfDaysInJuly` to the value `31`. The problem is, that we haven't declared this variable. We need to add a separate line before we used the variable in this way:

```
Dim NumberOfDaysInJuly As Integer
```

If we had done this then we would have been free to use it, and the error would not have occurred.

Now we've seen just how important data types are in our ASP.NET web forms. We haven't however, discussed what the possible data types are and when you should use them. Let's look at this now.

Simple data types

There are 12 different built-in data types in VB.NET. We can divide them up into three areas, numerical types, textual types and lastly a set of miscellaneous types. Although there are 12, we will only be talking about 11 here, as the final one, the `Object` data type, is not one we will use at this level of programming.

Numeric

You can assign almost any number to a variable. We can create variables and assign whole numbers, fractions, and even negative floating-point numbers, depending on their data type:

```
Dim IntegerNumber1 As Integer
Dim DecimalNumber2 As Decimal
Dim FloatingPointNumber3 As Float

IntegerNumber1 = 76
DecimalNumber2 = 2.5356
FloatingPointNumber3 = -1.4E06
```

We use floating-point numbers to represent very small or very large decimals such as 0.00000123 or 1.14E-6 or 1.87E17.

You'll notice two of the numbers shown above are written in Exponential Form. If you don't know what this is, it allows a large number to be squeezed into a smaller amount of digits, at the expense of some of its accuracy. To remove the exponent, simply multiply the number to the left of the 'E' by the number to the right as a power of ten. Taking the numbers above as an example this means moving the decimal point six places to the left in the first case (as the exponent is negative) and moving it 17 places to the right in the second case (as the exponent is positive).

Numeric data types make up the vast majority of VB.NET's built-in data types, representing 7 of the 12 possible types.

Integer

`Integers` are simply whole numbers. Examples of integers are 3, 12, and –5,127. The `integer` data type can handle whole numbers within the range –2,147,483,648 to 2,147,483,647. For numbers that are outside this range the `long` type is used, which we'll see shortly.

Byte

`Bytes` are integers within the range 0 to 255. They're used for very basic arithmetic. It's a useful type, because the method in which data is made available, means that a variable can be easily stored by the computer within a single `byte`, which is the computer's basic storage unit, and any processing or arithmetic done with them is, therefore, faster.

Short

The `short` data type is a form of `integer`, but as the name implies, can only accept a relatively small range of values. The range of values is –32,768 to 32,767.

Long

The `long` type is very similar to the integer type, but supports a much larger range. A `long` variable can contain a value in the range -9,223,372,036,854,775,808 to 9,223,372,036,854,775,807.

Single

The `single` type can hold single precision floating-point numbers, within the range -3.402823E38 to -1.401298E-45 (for negative values), and 1.401298E-45 to 3.402823E38 (for positive values).

Double

The `double` type holds double precision floating point numbers. This means that it will support a much larger range than the `single` type. In reality, this range is -1.79769313486232E308 to -4.94065645841247E-324 (for negative values), and 4.94065645841247E-324 to 1.79769313486232E308 (for positive values).

Decimal

The `decimal` subtype accepts numbers with up to twenty-eight decimal places. With zero decimal places, it can support numbers with a largest possible value of +/- 79,228,162,514,264,337,593,543,950,335. With twenty-eight decimals places, the largest value it can support becomes much smaller, at +/- 7.9228162514264337593543950335. This is the type used for storing currency values.

Textual Data Types

There are just two data types for storing text. As you might have surmised, text can be anything, so a data type that stores text, stores pretty much everything. The `String` data type is the most commonly used one to hold any length of text from a character to many lines. There is another separate data type `char`, which stores one character of text coded as a number, which we'll see in a moment.

String

The `string` type will identify everything you store in it as text, even if you supply it with a mixture of text and numerical data, numerical data alone, or even date information. For example, the following code creates a `string` variable called `CarType`, with the value `"Buick"`, a `string` variable called `CarEngineSize`, with the value `"2.0"`, and a `string` variable called `DatePurchased`, with the value `"July 4, 1999"`:

```
Dim CarType As String
Dim CarEngineSize As String
Dim DatePurchased As String

CarType = "Buick"
CarEngineSize = "2.0"
DatePurchased = " July 4, 1999"
```

As mentioned earlier, `string` values are usually encapsulated in double quotation marks, so they can be differentiated visually from numerical values, without having to reference their actual declarations.

Note that you can't perform mathematical functions on `strings`, even if their contents are purely numerical. Hence, if you try to add the two `strings` `"12"` and `"14"` together, as shown in the following example, you won't get the result `"26"` that you might have anticipated, but `"1412"` instead (we get 1412 here because we add `Number2` to `Number1` – if we added `Number1` to `Number2`, we'd get 1214):

```
Dim Number1 As String
Dim Number2 As String
Dim Number3 As String

Number1 = "12"
Number2 = "14"
Number3 = Number2 + Number1      'Will produce "1412"
```

This is because, while the `string` variable itself seemingly accepts different types of data, as it is a `string`, it is only holding a textual representation of those types, such as `Integer` or `Date`. Therefore, while it might appear to you that `Number1` contains a number, the original declaration, and the presence of quotation marks, indicate that it is to be treated as text.

We'll cover the process of joining, or concatenating, `strings` later in this chapter. VB.NET also provides a number of special functions with which you can manipulate strings. These functions allow you to measure the length of a `string`, truncate a string at the beginning or end, return certain characters from a given string, or even convert a string into its numerical equivalent. We'll look at string manipulation and conversion later, in a future chapter, as it requires the use of specialist .NET objects.

A basic rule of thumb, is that strings are normally used for storing words or alphanumeric information – numeric information is normally stored in the appropriate numeric subtype. The exceptions to this rule would be any number that you absolutely will not perform math with, such as telephone numbers and social security numbers, which are usually better stored as strings.

Char

The char data type is a bit of a strange one, because it stores text as a number. By this, we mean you place a single character in a variable, defined as a char, and it is stored as a number between 0 and 65535.

> *Unicode is an international standard code for representing characters numerically that overcomes the problems of different encoding systems. It is language, platform and program independent. More information about Unicode can be obtained from www.unicode.org*

If you were to display the contents of a char variable, you'd still see a text character, despite the manner in which it is stored. A variable using the char data type could be declared as follows – note the 'C' is used after the quotes to indicate that this is a char and not a string:

```
Dim Letter As Char
Letter = "Q"C    'This would be stored as 81
```

The Char data type is mainly used by people designing their own customized character sets.

Other Data Types

It's a bit of a cop out to group the next couple of data types together, as they have nothing in common, but it's a good reminder that there are more types of data that VB.NET can store than just numbers and text.

Date

We're treating the date data type separately from the numerical types. Dates must be defined in the mm/dd/yyyy format, for example, 12/15/1984. Date values are delimited using the # symbol. The date type can store any value between January 1, year 1 and December 31,9999. You can define a variable to store a date as follows:

```
Dim Date1 As Date

Date1 = #12/07/1984#
```

The Date data type is also used to store time information as well. You can configure it to store time, as follows:

```
Dim Time1 As Date

Time1 = #16:25:05#
```

The time ranges store can be anything between `00:00:00` and `23:59:59`.

Boolean

`Boolean` variables can be set to one of two values, namely `True` or `False`. In VB.NET, if you convert these values to an integer type then they convert to the values -1 and 0 respectively. When other numeric types are converted to Boolean values, 0 becomes `False` and all other values become `True`. When Boolean values are converted to other data types, `False` becomes 0 and True becomes 1. The discrepancy between True being -1 when converted to a VB.NET integer, and +1 when converted to other data types, is due to VB.NET's legacy support for older Visual Basic code.

Boolean variables can be used to record the state of a variable; inasmuch as if a variable isn't `True`, then it must be `False`. They can be set when a user performs a certain action, (like opening a form) and can be used to determine a certain course of action:

```
Dim blnVariable

blnVariable = False
If blnVariable = False Then 'do this
...
Else 'do that
...
```

Note that `True` or `False` should not be in quotes.

Naming Variables

As we go, we'll look at the different types of variables, how to assign values to them, and how to use them in expressions. We'll also talk about the kinds of names you should give your variables. For example, while the variable names we've used above reflect their contents in a reasonably self-explanatory way, the meanings of the variables in the following expressions are less obvious:

```
Dim a as Integer
Dim varBoolean as Boolean

a = 1*10+73
varBoolean = true
```

They're not particularly helpful, are they? It's really up to the programmer to find a suitable name for his variable when his?her creates it. Ideally, you should find a name that is meaningful to someone else who subsequently reads your code. At the same time, excessively long variable names are unwieldy and easy to mistype, so you should avoid these too. If the variable names are chosen well, then the thinking behind the apparent gobbledygook in expressions like those above will become clearer. It's a good idea to make variable names descriptive even if this means making them longer. Here are some quick tips:

❑ `DateStart` and `DateEnd` are better then `StartDate` and `EndDate`, as these two related functions will then come next to each other in an alphabetically sorted search

❑ Variables like `Price`, `Name`, and `Number` are confusing, because there are usually more than one of these, like `NameFirst`, `NameLast`, `NameSpouse`, `PriceBuy`, or `PriceSell`

❑ Variable names that coincide with data types aren't allowed, so `Dim Integer as Integer` would cause an error

- ❏ Avoid confusing abbreviations, such as `datFDOM` for first day of month – the acronym FDOM could stand for other things

- ❏ Never use the same variable name for two different variables, no matter how sure you are that they will not conflict

- ❏ Variable names with multiple words, should have the first letter of words capitalized, such as `InputType`

In most languages, the name of a variable can be almost anything you choose, but there are usually a few restrictions:

- ❏ There are usually restrictions on which characters you can use in your variable names. In VB.NET, there are the restrictions that all variable names must begin with a letter and must not contain an embedded period/full-stop or a space. In fact, you're better off avoiding symbols altogether, other than underscores, to keep your code readable and to guarantee it will work as intended.

- ❏ Case-sensitivity is another important issue. VB.NET is case-insensitive, which means that you can use upper- and lower-case characters to refer to exactly the same variable. For example, VB.NET will interpret `counter` and `COUNTER` as the same variable. On the other hand, other languages such as C# or JScript.NET, are both case sensitive and will interpret `counter` and `COUNTER` as two entirely different variables.

Naming Conventions

If we have many variables in a program, we need a way to keep track of which of them contain which types of information, as it may not be evident from the name alone. Okay, you could go back and look up the declarations, but if you've declared a thousand different variables in your application, do you really want to trawl through the whole lot of them looking for just one?

The fact that we can convert variables from one type to another – as we will see in Chapter 8 – makes this 'tracking' even more important. The sensible answer is to use a good naming convention. By doing so, you can tell at a glance whether you're using an integer, a string, or a date, and can manipulate it in a consistent way.

Naming conventions aren't compulsory, can't be enforced, and generally it's up to the programmer as to which convention they apply, but the most common one, known as **Hungarian notation**, is to use the first three letters of a variables name to distinguish the sub type. The fourth letter of the variable is then typed in upper case, to indicate that this is where the actual variable name starts.

Here's the suggested naming convention: we'll be using it in our applications throughout the rest of the book:

Data Type	Prefix	Example
Boolean	`bln`	`blnMember`
Byte	`byt`	`bytByte`
Char	`chr`	`chrChar`

Table continued on following page

141

Data Type	Prefix	Example
Date	dat	datToday
Double	dbl	dblDouble
Decimal	dec	decDecimal
Integer	int	intSalary
Long	lng	lngLong
Single	sng	sngSingle
Short	sho	shoShort
String	str	strTextBox

In keeping with just about everything in life, there's also a different version of this form, called short Hungarian notation, which is common with Microsoft and recommended in their MSDN .NET documentation. You can find a copy of this alternative version of the convention at http://msdn.microsoft.com/library/default.asp?url=/library/en-us/dnw98bk/html/variablenameshungariannotation.asp. As the longer version is more descriptive, we'll stick to using that instead. Ultimately the choice of naming convention is a decision for the programmer however and every option is fine as long as it is used consistently

Operators

Of course, variables aren't much use unless you can manipulate them in some way. To manipulate them typically you'd use **operators**. An operator is a symbol that carries out a predefined operation on the operands and generates a result. If $X=1+2$, then X is a variable, $=$ is an operator, and, 1 and 2, are operands. We have already seen one or two examples of basic data manipulation using operators in this chapter, but in this section, we'll introduce the concepts more formally.

Assignment Operator

The familiar 'equal' sign ($=$) is probably the most common operator in computing. You've already seen it used several times to **assign** values to our variables. The variable **name** goes on the left; the variable **value** goes on the right:

```
Number1 = 2
```

VB.NET doesn't enforce spaces either side of the 'equal' sign, but you may prefer to include some to make your code easier to read.

Mathematical Peculiarities

You can also use the assignment operator to increase (or decrease) the value of variables using the following, mathematically unsound, formula:

```
Dim intNumber1As Integer

intNumber1 = 2
intNumber1 = intNumber1 + 1
```

Mathematicians will be scratching their heads, wondering how `intNumber1` can be equal to `intNumber1` plus 1: it's similar to saying $2 = 2 + 1$, which is impossible. The answer is, of course, that it can't. In VB.NET, expressions are evaluated from right to left. Thus, in this example `intNumber1 + 1` is evaluated first, and assigned to `intNumber1` at the end. The equals sign takes on the role of an **assignment operator**, as it is assigning a new value to `intNumber1`. It's a way of saying whatever the old value of `intNumber1` is, take that and add 1 to it. Now this value constitutes the new value of `intNumber1`.

Arithmetic Operations

The arithmetic operations available in VB.NET are:

Addition	+	Exponentiation	^
Subtraction	−	Negation	−
Multiplication	*	Modulus	MOD
Division	\		

Here is a very simple example: we'll assign values to the variables `intNumber1` and `intNumber2` before adding them together, and assigning the result to a third variable, `intNumber3`:

```
Dim intNumber1 As Integer
Dim intNumber2 As Integer
Dim intNumber3 As Integer

intNumber1 = 14
intNumber2 = 12
intNumber3 = intNumber1 + intNumber2
```

Due to this, `intNumber3` will contain the value 26.

You can also use brackets (parentheses) to influence the order in which a calculation is performed. For example, in the following code we divide the variable `intNumber2` by 6 and add the result to the variable `intNumber1`:

> *A quick reminder, normal mathematical procedure is to start inside the innermost parentheses and work from left to right performing exponentiation. Next, go left to right performing multiplication and division, and then finally go left to right performing addition and subtraction. Then repeat the above steps again for the next innermost set of parentheses, until you've calculated the expression. ALL programming languages will use these rules for performing arithmetic.*

```
Dim intNumber1 As Integer
Dim intNumber2 As Integer
Dim intNumber3 As Integer

intNumber1 = 14
intNumber2 = 18
intNumber3 = intNumber1 + (intNumber2/6)
```

First, the computer evaluates the contents of the brackets, following normal mathematical procedure: intNumber2 is divided by 6 and yields the result 3. This is added to the value of intNumber1, and the result of this – 17 – is assigned to the variable intNumber3.

Adding parentheses is a good idea to make your code more readable, even when parentheses may not be technically required for the evaluation to occur correctly.

Let's have a go at a quick example that performs a simple calculation of tax. To do this we need to create three variables, one for earnings, one for the tax percentage, and one for the total. We're going to deduct the earnings by whatever percentage the tax rate is set to, and display the output in our old friend the <asp:label> control.

Try It Out – Performing a Calculation on an ASP.NET page

1. Type in the following code into your web page editor:

```
<script language="vb" runat="server">
Sub Page_Load()
  Dim intEarn As Integer
  Dim intTax As Integer
  Dim decTotal As Decimal
  intEarn = 150
  intTax = 23
  decTotal = intEarn - ((intEarn/100)*intTax)
  Display1.Text = decTotal
End Sub
</script>

<html>
<head>
  <title>Declaring Variables</title>
</head>
<body>
  Your total earnings after tax are $
  <asp:label id="Display1" runat="server" />
</body>
</html>
```

2. Save this as C:\BegASPNET\ch04\tax.aspx

3. View this in your browser:

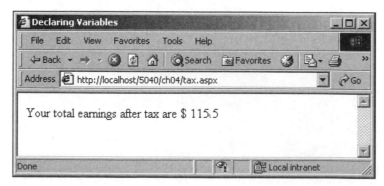

How It Works

There are only seven lines of ASP.NET code (excluding the event handling) in this program. The first three declare three variables, `intEarn` for the earnings, `intTax` for the tax rate, and `decTotal` for our final amount:

```
Dim intEarn As Integer
Dim intTax As Integer
Dim decTotal As Decimal
```

In the next line, we set the value of the earnings to 150, and the tax rate to 23:

```
intEarn = 150
intTax = 23
```

The `decTotal` variable is where the calculation is performed. To gain our percentage, we first have to calculate what 23% of the earnings are: this is done by dividing the earnings by 100 and multiplying the result by the tax rate. Brackets are used to indicate the order of calculation within the expression:

```
decTotal = intEarn - ((intEarn/100)*intTax)
```

Finally, we return the value of `decTotal`, as text in the `<asp:label>` control called `Display1`:

```
Display1.Text = decTotal
```

You could calculate tax deductions for any percentage rate, and any earnings, by altering the values of `intEarn` and `intTax`.

Concatenating Strings

It makes sense to add integers together, using expressions such as 2 + 3, or `intNumber1 + intNumber2` (as we showed above), but what happens if you wish to 'add' strings together? It doesn't make much sense to add them in the arithmetic sense – `"Beans"` plus `"Rice"` doesn't have a tangible meaning. VB.NET allows us to 'add' strings together in a different sense however – using a process known as **concatenation**.

The Shorthand Way

In .NET there are two ways of doing this, we'll look at the shorthand way here, as it is much simpler, but strictly speaking it isn't the correct way in .NET. It does work, however performs exactly the same task, and gives you a more intuitive feel for how the process of concatenation works.

With the "shorthand" way when two strings are concatenated, the second string is attached at the end of the first string, creating a new string. In order to concatenate two strings we use the ampersand operator (&). Let's run through a few examples.

Microsoft has insisted on leaving the + operator for concatenating strings as well, and this can be used in place of ampersand. Using ampersand however, is preferable as your code will be more readable – that is, it will be evident you are concatenating strings, not adding numbers.

We can concatenate the strings `"Helter"` and `"Skelter"`, as follows:

```
Dim strConcatenate As String

strConcatenate = "Helter" & "Skelter"
```

Here, the result of the concatenation is the string `"HelterSkelter"`, which will be assigned to the variable `strConcatenate`, of type `String`. You should note that VB.NET doesn't automatically put in spaces. You can also concatenate a number of `strings` within the same expression. Here, we'll concatenate three strings, one of which is a space (which is also a string, since a space is a character):

```
Dim strConcatenate As String

strConcatenate = "Helter" & " " & "Skelter"
```

Now, `strConcatenate` will contain the string `"Helter Skelter"`. You can concatenate as many `string` variables, as you like.

```
Dim strFirst As String
Dim strExclamationLine As String

strFirst = "Never "
strExclamationLine = strFirst & strFirst & strFirst & strFirst & strFirst
```

Then `strExclamationLine` will contain the line `"Never Never Never Never Never "`.

Another way of doing the same thing is to use the `+=` operator:
```
Dim strFirst As String
Dim strExclamationLine As String

strFirst = "Never "

strExclamationLine = strFirst
strExclamationLine += strFirst
strExclamationLine += strFirst
strExclamationLine += strFirst
strExclamationLine += "No Way"
```

`strExclamationLine` will then contain the line `"Never Never Never Never No Way"`.

Comparing String Variables

Although you can't add or subtract strings numerically, comparison operators are a kind of exception to this. These can be used to help compare and sort text into alphabetical order. If you wished to find out which came first in the alphabet Anteater or Ape, the following code could be used:

```
Dim strAnimal1 As String
Dim strAnimal2 As String

strAnimal1 = "Anteater"
strAnimal2 = "Ape"
If strAnimal1 < strAnimal2 Then Display1.Text = "Anteater"
If strAnimal2 < strAnimal1 Then Display1.Text = "Ape"
```

Note that a lower case 'a' is considered greater than an upper case 'A'.

It doesn't take a genius to figure out that the program will return **Anteater**. If you were comparing the contents of variables, which depend on input from users however, then this can alphabetically sort data for you without the need to refer to a database.

Constants

There will be occasions when you want a value assigned to a variable to remain constant throughout the execution of the code. A good example is statewide sales tax. This value will rarely change, yet when calculating the total of a shopping basket, you'll probably need to refer to it several times. Even if the tax is changed, you'd still only need to refer to one value, and you'd only want to update one value. To represent the sales tax you can you use something other than a variable, called a constant.

Constants are like variables except that, once they have been assigned a value, they don't change. Many programming languages provide an explicit facility for constants, by allowing the programmer to assign an initial value to the them, and subsequently forbidding any alteration of that value. The main reason you'd assign a value to a constant, is to prevent its accidental alteration.

VB.NET supports constants with the `Const` keyword being used to define them. By convention, constants are named in upper case:

```
Const ABSOLUTEZERO As Integer = -273
```

If you then tried to assign another value to `ABSOLUTEZERO`, such as:

```
ABSOLUTEZERO = 0
```

The change would be rejected and an error message produced. Constants remain in force for the duration of the script, just as variables do. It isn't possible to amend their value once they have been set. Constants make your code easier to read and maintain, as they require less updating and if you choose a self-explanatory name, they make your code easily understandable. They also give a performance increase over variables, as well.

Structured data types

We've now finished discussing data types for single pieces of information. Next, we're going to move on to look at how we can store related information together. VB.NET has several structures for storing data in this manner – ranging from dictionary objects and hash-tables (see Chapter 11), to Arrays and XML.

We'll begin our discussion of structured data types by looking at arrays, which are their simplest form.

Arrays

Arrays are used to store a series of related data items that are connected by an index number appended to the end of the variable. You could use them to store the names of the Marx brothers, for instance:

```
Dim strMarx(5) As String

strMarx(0) = "Groucho"
strMarx(1) = "Harpo"
strMarx(2) = "Chico"
strMarx(3) = "Zeppo"
strMarx(4) = "Gummo"
strMarx(5) = "Karl"
```

You don't have to store something in each item of the array, however and you don't even have to store it sequentially:

```
Dim strHouse(4) As String

strHouse(1) = "Mr Jones"
strHouse(4) = "Mr Goldstein"
strHouse(3) = "Mrs Soprano"
```

Arrays are particularly useful if you want to manipulate a whole set of data items as though they were one. For example, if you want to adjust the pay rates for a set of five employees, then the difficult way of doing it is the following:

```
Dim intEmployeePay(4) As Integer

intExtraPay = 10
intEmployeePay(0) = intEmployeePay(0) + intExtraPay
intEmployeePay(1) = intEmployeePay(1) + intExtraPay
intEmployeePay(2) = intEmployeePay(2) + intExtraPay
intEmployeePay(3) = intEmployeePay(3) + intExtraPay
intEmployeePay(4) = intEmployeePay(4) + intExtraPay
```

This, much simpler, code utilizes your array structure and has exactly the same effect:

```
Dim intEmployeePay(4) As Integer
Dim intExtraPay, intLoop As Integer

intExtraPay = 10
For intLoop = 0 to 4
  intEmployeePay ( intLoop) = intEmployeePay(intLoop) + intExtraPay
Next
```

We'll look at the control structure (For...Next) used to create this in Chapter 6, all you need to realize here is that it does the same thing as the previous snippet of code, but in half the number of lines.

Arrays are also much more versatile than regular variables when dealing with sets of data.

Declaring Arrays

Arrays, like variables, have to be declared using the Dim keyword before you can use them. An array declaration needs an extra parameter at the end however, which is used to specify the size of the array. Apart from that, not much changes. Arrays aren't true data types, as you still have to declare what kind of information they need to store.

For example, we could set up an array to have 50 entries, one for each of the states in the US, with the following statement:

```
Dim StatesInUS(49) As String
```

We'd need to define it as a `String`, to show that all of the variables in the array are strings. Hopefully, you can now see why explicit conversions could be needed. If you were storing 50 bits of information, and 49 of them were strings, and one was an integer, you could run into a lot of problems.

Also, in case you're wondering, the index number 49 isn't a mistake. It is because arrays count from zero upwards in VB.NET, rather than from one. In this case the 50 states are indexed by the 50 different parameter values 0, 1, ... 49.

Now we're ready to look at a small example utilizing some of these concepts. Let's go back and adapt our Feiertag Holidays example from the last chapter, so that we can store information gathered from the user in an array.

Try It Out – Using Arrays

1. Assuming you've typed in `holidaypage.aspx` and `holidayresponse.aspx` from the last chapter, go back and open `holidayresponse.aspx` and amend the following lines:

```
<script runat="Server" language="VB">
Sub Page_Load()
Dim strArrayDetails(3) As String
Dim intLoop As Integer

strArrayDetails(0) = Request.Form("FullName")
strArrayDetails(1) = Request.Form("Address")
strArrayDetails(2) = Request.Form("Sex")
strArrayDetails(3) = Request.Form("Destination")

Response.Write ("<BR>" + strArrayDetails(0))
Response.Write ("<BR>" + strArrayDetails(1))
Response.Write ("<BR>" + strArrayDetails(2))
Response.Write ("<BR>" + strArrayDetails(3))

End Sub
</script>
<html>
<head>
<title>Holiday page</title>
...
```

2. Save this as `holidayresponse.aspx` once again

3. View `holidaypage.aspx` in your browser

4. Enter some details and submit them

5. You will see something similar to the following:

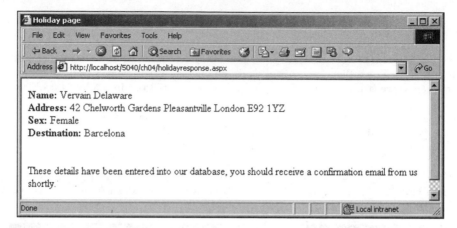

How It Works

Okay, let's see what has changed. The working of the web form `holidaypage.aspx` is no different from the one we used in the last chapter. It simply collects the name, address, sex, intended destination, and whether they want to receive extra information from us. What does change is the `holidayresponse.aspx` page. Instead of displaying the information we receive straight to the screen, we now store it in an array, called `strArrayDetails()`, first.

We start our ASP.NET code by declaring this as an array of string variables:

```
Dim strArrayDetails(3) As String
```

Then we populate our array with the four items of information that the user has provided on the previous form:

```
strArrayDetails(0) = Request.Form("FullName")
strArrayDetails(1) = Request.Form("Address")
strArrayDetails(2) = Request.Form("Sex")
strArrayDetails(3) = Request.Form("Destination")
```

Next we display each of our items again, in turn:

```
Response.Write ("<BR>" + strArrayDetails(0))
Response.Write ("<BR>" + strArrayDetails(1))
Response.Write ("<BR>" + strArrayDetails(2))
Response.Write ("<BR>" + strArrayDetails(3))
```

The first item in the array `strArrayDetails(0)` contains the string value "**Vervain Delaware**" in this example, and is displayed on the screen using `Response.Write`.

> *Yes I'm well aware we advised you to use the `<asp:label>` control to display text on the screen, but in this example, it would make it longer and more difficult to explain!*

Then `strArrayDetails(1)` is displayed, which contains the string value "24 Chelworth Gardens Pleasantville London E92 1YZ" that we assigned earlier. The remaining elements are then displayed in turn. Before, finally the HTML is displayed, and the web form is complete.

Multi-Dimensional Arrays

If you need to keep information of a two-dimensional nature, you can do it by declaring a two-dimensional array. For instance, if you wanted to store a set of related information separately, such as a first and last name, a normal (one-dimensional) array would probably be unsuitable. You can achieve far better results by adding another parameter to your array declaration:

```
Dim str2Darray(3,3) As String
```

This will set up a two-dimensional array of size 4 by 4, which can hold a total of 16 values. You can assign values to a multi-dimensional array by referencing each element of the array through its two-value index. For example, you could use such an array to store first and last names and phone numbers:

```
str2Darray(0,0) = "John"
str2Darray(0,1) = "Doe"
str2Darray(0,2) = "111-111-1111"
str2Darray(1,0) = "Jane"
str2Darray(1,1) = "Doe"
str2Darray(1,2) = "222-222-2222"
```

The first dimension stores the information that is related to one person, while the second dimension holds data of the same type for a different person. Let's have a look at a tabular representation of what is happening:

	0	1
0	**John**	Jane
1	Doe	Doe
2	111-111-1111	222-222-2222

You can see that the contents of `str2DArray(0,0)` is John.

In fact, VB.NET is not limited to arrays of one or two dimensions; you can declare an array with up to 60 dimensions, should you so require. Using anything more than three dimensions is impractical however, and you'd be better off pursuing other solutions (such as databases) if you need more than this. This takes us as far as we need to go with arrays and variables. We'll be using them throughout the rest of this book, so take care to understand them.

This leaves one last form of information storage for us to cover. Arrays, for all their virtues, don't hold any information about the data that they contain. To take our last example, there's nothing about `str2DArray(0,0)` that tells you it contains name information at this location. It could just as easily hold an address, or a telephone number. The array structure doesn't inherently tell us anything of its data's meaning. To gather, store, and transmit data in a more "intelligent" fashion we can use XML.

Summary

This chapter has looked at the use of variables for storing information in VB.NET.

It really can't be stressed enough how important variables are. It is very hard to create a functional program without them. We've looked at how VB.NET implements variables and how you go about placing them in your ASP.NET pages. We have plowed a furrow through the built-in numeric and textual data types and looked at a couple of specialist types like `Boolean`, and `Date`, as well. We then moved on to examine how you can manipulate numbers and perform simple calculations in VB.NET.

In the next chapter, we will be looking at XML (Extensible Markup Language), which is a powerful means of storing structured data in a "variable-free" way.

Exercise Questions

1. What is a variable and how is it related to data types in VB.NET?

2. Use string, integer and date variables to create an ASPX file to display your name, age and date of birth.

3. Arrange the following into groups of Numeric, Textual and Miscellaneous data types, and give an example of a value and a use for each:

   ❑ Integer
   ❑ Char
   ❑ Byte
   ❑ Short
   ❑ Boolean
   ❑ String
   ❑ Long
   ❑ Single
   ❑ Double
   ❑ Date
   ❑ Decimal

4. Write an ASPX file that will multiply the values of two integer variables together. Then modify the example to add, divide and subtract the two numbers. After this experiment with exponential, negation and modulus controls.

5. Create an array containing your 5 favorite singers. Then concatenate the elements of your array into one string, and after the opening sentence "My 5 favorite singers are:", display them in a clear way using the `<asp:label>` control.

Introducing XML

We first came across the topic of **XML** (the **eXtensible Markup Language**) back in Chapter 2, when we mentioned it as a primary method of transporting data in and around .NET applications. One of XML's great strengths is that, unlike with a database, you don't need a separate piece of software to create an XML document, due to its plain text based, self-describing, style. All you need is a text editor, like Notepad.

Like the variables that we discussed in the previous chapter, XML is simply a method of storing data. Unlike variables however, XML aims to store your information in a structured manner that is easy to understand just by looking at the information itself:

```
<artist>
  <name>Vincent Van Gogh</name>
  <nationality>Dutch</nationality>
  <birthdate>30th March 1853</birthdate>
  <movement>Post Impressionism</movement>
</artist>
<artist>
  <name>Max Ernst</name>
  ...
```

You might be wondering why we don't write this as HTML:

```
<p>
  <b>Vincent Van Gogh</b>
  <br/>Dutch
  <br/><i>30th March 1853</i>
  <br/>Post Impressionism
</p>

<p>
  <b>Max Ernst</b>
  ...
```

The simple answer is 'meaning'. With the HTML version, we have lost the meaning of the information. HTML tags don't offer any extra information about our data, like our XML tags did. In fact, we're committing the cardinal sin of mixing up data (our artist information) with presentation (the HTML tags) – something ASP.NET tries hard to avoid.

None of our XML tags contain any implicit styling information the way HTML tags do (that is, the HTML tag <b> makes the text bold, while the XML tag <name> doesn't have any styling information attached to it). We'll explain why that is, and how it works in this next section.

> **We will be using XML on and off throughout the remainder of this book, so it's important that you have a fairly good understanding of its syntax and meaning.**

Tags and Elements

Even those of us who are familiar with HTML, often get the meaning of tags and elements mixed up. Just to clarify, **tags** are the angled brackets (known as delimiters), and the text between them. Here are some examples of tags used in HTML:

❑   <p> is a tag that marks the beginning of a new paragraph

❑   <i> is a tag indicating that the following text should be rendered in italic type

❑   </i> is a tag that indicates the end of a section of text to be rendered in italic type

Elements refer to the tags **plus** their content. The following is an example of an element:

```
<b>Here is some bold text</b>
```

In general terms, a tag is simply a label that tells a user agent (such as a browser), how it should interpret whatever text is enclosed within the tags.

A user-agent is anything that acts on your behalf. You are a user agent working for your boss, your computer is a user agent working for you, your browser is a user agent working for you and your computer, and so it goes on.

Empty elements (such as the <br> element in HTML) have no content, and therefore don't have separate closing tags. Many browsers will simply allow you to specify a single opening tag, and treat that as a complete element. XML however requires us to explicitly close all elements, so we either have to add a closing tag:

```
<br></br>
```

Or use the proper condensed notation for an empty element, which is a tag like this:

```
<br />
```

The following diagram illustrates the parts of an element:

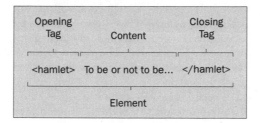

Attributes

Any tag can have an attribute. They take the form of name/value pairs (also referred to as attribute/value pairs). These name/value pairs are very similar to the ones we encountered in Chapter 3 when sending forms. In XML though, they take the following format:

```
<tagname attribute="value">
```

This is where XML is very similar to HTML. For example, in HTML 4.01 the <body> tag can take the following attributes:

class id	dir	lang	style	title
background	bgcolor	alink	link	vlink
text				

It could be defined as follows:

```
<body bgcolor="#000000" alink="#999999" link="#990099"
                        vlink="#888888" text="#999999">
```

Examples of Markup Languages

Let's take a quick look at three markup languages, so we can see where XML fits into the big picture. We'll look at SGML, HTML, and of course XML.

SGML

Standard Generalized Markup Language (SGML) is a markup language that is used to create other markup languages. The most famous language written in SGML is HTML, which we all know and love for its use on the Web. HTML is known as an application of SGML. The problem with SGML is that it is very complicated – hence our interest in XML. XML is a simplified version of SGML, retaining much of SGML's functionality, yet initially designed for use on the web.

Back in 1986, SGML became an international standard (ISO 8879) for defining markup languages, before the Web was even conceived (in fact, SGML has been in existence since the late 1960s). Its purpose was to describe markup languages by allowing the author to provide formal definitions for each of the elements and attributes in the language. This allowed authors to create their own tags relating to their content. In effect, they could write their own markup language using SGML, which is exactly what happens when a new version of HTML is created. The World Wide Web Consortium (W3C) makes up the new tags, and it is up to browser manufacturers to implement them.

As a language SGML is very powerful, but with its power comes complexity, and many of its features are rarely used. It is very difficult to interpret an SGML document without the definition of the markup language, kept in a Document Type Definition (DTD). The DTD is where all the rules for the language are; after all, you cannot create your own markup language without specifying how it should be used. The DTD has to be sent with, or included in, the SGML document so that your custom created tags can be understood.

DTDs are written in a language called Extended Backus-Naur Form (EBNF). The DTD needs to declare the rules of the markup language:

❑ Declare what exactly constitutes markup

❑ Declare exactly what our mark up means

Practically speaking, this means that we have to give details of each of the elements, their order, and say what attributes (and other types of markup) they can take.

HTML

As we just saw, HTML is one particular application of SGML. It describes how information is to be prepared for the World Wide Web. HTML is just a set of SGML rules and, as such, it has a DTD. In fact, there are several DTDs, for the different versions of HTML.

Being far simpler than SGML, and a fraction of its size, HTML is very easy to learn – a factor that quickly made it popular and widely adopted by all sorts of people. It was created by Tim Berners-Lee in 1991 as a way of marking up technical papers so that they could easily be organized and transferred across different platforms for the scientific community. This is not meant to be a history lesson, but it is important to understand the concepts behind HTML if we are to appreciate the power of XML. The idea was to create a set of tags that could be transferred between computers so that others could render the document in a useful format. For example:

```
<h1> This is a primary heading</h1>
<h2>This is a secondary heading</h2>
<pre>This is text whose formatting should be preserved</pre>
<p>The text between these two tags is a paragraph</p>
```

Back then, the scientific community had little concern over the aesthetic appearance of their documents. What mattered to them was that they could transfer them while preserving their meaning. They weren't worried about the color of the fonts or the exact size of their primary heading!

As HTML usage exploded and web browsers started to become readily available, non-scientific users soon started to create their own pages *en masse*. These non-scientific users became increasingly concerned with the aesthetic presentation of their material. Manufacturers of browsers, used to view web sites, were all too ready to offer different tags that would allow web page authors to display their documents with more creativity than was possible using plain ASCII text. Netscape were the first, adding the familiar `<font>` tag, which allowed users to change the actual text font as well as its size and weighting. This triggered a rapid expansion in the number of tags that browsers would support.

With the new tags, however, came new problems. Different browsers implemented the new tags inconsistently. Today we have sites that display signs saying that they are "Best Viewed Through Netscape Navigator" or are "Designed For Internet Explorer." On top of all this, we now expect to be able to produce web pages that resemble documents created on the most sophisticated Desktop Publishing systems.

Meanwhile, the browser's potential as a new application platform was quickly recognized, and web developers started creating distributed applications for businesses, using the Internet as a medium for information and financial transactions.

Drawbacks of HTML

While the widespread adoption of HTML propelled the rise in the number of people on the Web, these users wanted to do an ever-increasing variety of new and more complex things, and weaknesses with HTML became apparent:

❑   HTML has a fixed tag set. You cannot create your own tags that can be interpreted by others.

❑   HTML is a presentation technology. It doesn't carry information about the structure of the content held within its tags.

❑   HTML is "flat". You cannot specify the **relationship one tag has to another tag**, so a hierarchy of data cannot be represented.

❑   Browsers are being used as an application platform. HTML does not provide the power needed to create advanced web applications, at least not to the level at which developers are currently aiming. For example, it does not readily offer the ability for advanced retrieval of information from documents marked up in HTML and it is not easy to process the data within the document, because the text is only marked up for display.

While HTML has proven a very useful way of marking up documents for display in a web browser, a document marked up in HTML tells us very little about its actual content. For most documents to be useful in a business environment, there is a need to know about the document's content. When a document contains content details, then it is possible to perform generalized processing and retrieval on that document. This means that it is no longer suitable for just one purpose – rather than just being used for display on the web, it can also be used as part of an application. Marking up data in a way that tells us about its content makes it self-describing. This means that the data can be re-used in different situations. SGML made this possible, but it is now also possible with XML – which is far simpler and rapidly gaining in popularity.

How XML Came About

The major players in the browser market made it clear that they did not intend to fully support SGML. Furthermore, its complexity prevented many people from learning it. Moves were made to create a simplified version for use on the web, signaling a return to documents being marked up according to their content. In the same way that HTML was designed for technical papers, with tags such as the "heading" and "paragraph", there was a move to allow people greater flexibility. They wanted to create their own tags and markup languages so they could mark up whatever they wanted, however they wanted, with the intention of making it self-describing.

The W3C saw the worth of creating a simplified version of SGML for use on the Web, and agreed to sponsor the project. SGML was put under the knife and several of the non-essential parts were cut, molding it into a new language called XML. This lean alternative is far more accessible, its specification running to around a fifth of the size of the specification that defined SGML.

What is XML?

XML got the name eXtensible Markup Language, because it is not a fixed format like HTML. While HTML has a fixed set of tags that the author can use, XML users can create their own tags (or use those created by others, if applicable) so that they describe the content of the element.

At its simplest level, XML is just a way of marking up data so that it is self-describing. What do we mean by this? Well, as one example, Wrox Press makes details of its books available in HTML over the Web – we might display book details in HTML as follows:

```
<hmtl>
<head>
    <title>Beginning ASP.NET</title>
</head>

<body>
<h1>Beginning ASP.NET</h1>
    <h3>ISBN 1-861005-04-0</h3>

<h4>Authors</h4><br>
<h4>Chris Ullman, Ollie Coombes, John Kauffman, Rob Birdwell, Chris Goode, Daniel
Kent, Srinavasar Sivakumar, Juan Llibre</h4>

<p>US $49.99</p>

<p>ASP.NET is a powerful technology for dynamically creating web site content.
Learn how to create exciting pages that are tailored to your audience. Enhance
your web/intranet presence with powerful web applications.</p>
</body>
</html>
```

That's all you need to do if you want put information about a book on a Web page. It will look something like this:

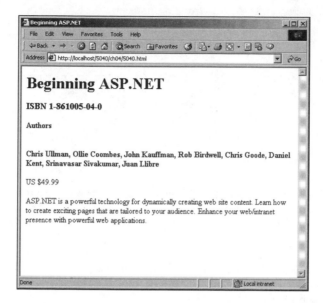

When we are building our web pages, we have lots of data in HTML, but the tags (or markup) don't give you any information about what you are displaying. There is no way that you can tell, from the tags, that you are displaying information about a book. With XML, however, you can create your own tags and make things much more clear.

So, how can we mark up the information in a more logical way, using XML? In the following Try It Out, we will create our first XML document that mimics the data held in the above HTML example.

You will have to be using an up-to-date browser, either IE5/IE6 or Netscape 6 to get this example to work.

Try It Out – My First XML Document

All you need to create an XML document, is a simple text editor; something like Notepad will do just fine for our first example.

1. Fire up your text editor and type in the following, which we will call books.xml. Make sure you type it in exactly as shown, since XML is case sensitive and spaces must be in the correct positions:

```
<?xml version="1.0"?>
<books>
<book>
    <title>Beginning ASP.NET</title>
    <ISBN>1-861005-04-0</ISBN>
    <authors>
        <author_name>Chris Ullman</author_name>
        <author_name>Ollie Coombes</author_name>
```

```
<author_name>John Kauffman</author_name>
      <author_name>Rob Birdwell</author_name>
      <author_name>Chris Goode</author_name>
      <author_name>Daniel Kent</author_name>
      <author_name>Srinavasa Sivakumar</author_name>
      <author_name>Juan Llibre</author_name>
   </authors>
   <description> ASP.NET is a powerful technology for dynamically creating web
site content. Learn how to create exciting pages that are tailored to your
audience. Enhance your web/intranet presence with powerful web
applications.</description>
   <price US="$49.99"/>
</book>
</books>
```

2. Save our file as books.xml to any folder you want on your hard drive. It could be with the other directories on your web server, or it could be completely separate. I've placed all my XML files in a folder called XMLfiles, as a subfolder to this chapter's BegASP.NET directory.

3. To open your XML file in Internet Explorer, just use select **Open** from the file menu and browse to it. Alternatively, you can type in the URL Here is how our XML version of the book details is displayed when we open it in IE5.5:

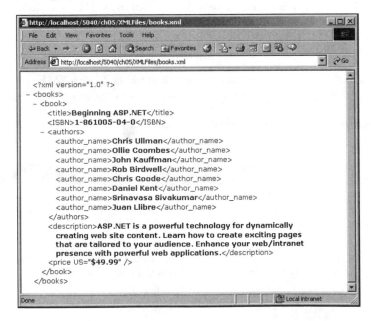

How It Works

Let's go through our code step-by-step and look at exactly what is happening:

```
<?xml version="1.0"?>
```

This is the XML prolog. It tells the receiving application that it is getting an XML document compatible with version one of the XML specification. Note that the XML is in lowercase and that there are no white spaces between the question mark and the opening XML. The question mark at the front denotes that this is a declaration, and not actually an XML element.

All XML documents must have a unique opening and closing tag. <books> is ours, as we have a file containing data about books:

```
<books>
  ...
</books>
```

This is known as the root element. XML tags need to have a corresponding closing tag. Unlike HTML, you cannot miss out end tags and expect your application to accept it. The only exception to this is called an empty element, in which there is no element content. An example of this in HTML, would be an <img> tag. In XML, if you have an empty element you must add a slash before the closing delimiter, such as <tag attribute="value" />.

> Note that XML, unlike HTML, is case sensitive, so <BOOK>, <Book> and <book> would be treated as three different tags.

Within our root element, we are describing data about a specific book, so we use an opening tag that explains what will be contained by the tag. Here we are using <book>:

```
<books>
<book>
  ...
</book>
</books>
```

In the same way that we made sensible opening and closing tags for the document using the <books> element, we use similarly descriptive tags to mark up more details, this time the title of the book and its ISBN (International Standard Book Number – as shown just above the bar code on the back of the book). These go inside the opening and closing <book> tags:

```
<title>Beginning ASP.NET</title>
<ISBN>1-861005-04-0</ISBN>
```

As there are several authors on this book, we'll put the list of authors in nested elements. We start with an opening <authors> tag, and then nest inside this an <author_name> tag for each author. Again, these go between the opening and closing <book> tags. In this example we put them under the ISBN:

```
<authors>
    <author_name>Chris Ullman</author_name>
    <author_name>Ollie Coombes</author_name>
    <author_name>John Kauffman</author_name>
    <author_name>Rob Birdwell</author_name>
    <author_name>Chris Goode</author_name>
    <author_name>Daniel Kent</author_name>
    <author_name>Srinavasa Sivakumar</author_name>
    <author_name>Juan Llibre</author_name>
</authors>
```

The fact that XML format elements are presented in a **hierarchical** structure is very important, because it allows us to work with our data in a more sophisticated way.

Next, we added the description of the book. Here we are using an element called <description>, although it could equally be something like <precis>, <details> or <synopsis>:

```
<description>ASP.NET is a powerful technology for dynamically creating web site
content. Learn how to create exciting pages that are tailored to your audience.
Enhance your web/intranet presence with powerful web applications.</description>
```

Finally, we added the price of the book to the document. Here you can see that we are using an empty element tag, with the closing slash inside it. The currency and amount are actually held within the US attribute:

```
    <price US="$49.99"/>
</book>
```

> **In XML, all attribute values must be contained in double quotes.**

That's all there is to it! You have just created your first XML document. It is plain text, easily human readable, and the tags describe its content and create a hierarchy of related data elements from it.

From this alone, you can tell that we are now talking about a book. Those tags that meant little in our HTML version, such as <h3> and <p>, are gone replaced with tags describing the file's content. This makes things much more logical and it is simple to see what we are talking about.

However does this work in a browser? We can't expect it to look at tags we've just made up and then display the information with headings and paragraphs laid out. Indeed, we saw in our last Try It Out that it doesn't do this; instead, it places the tag names and the data that they contain in the browser window:

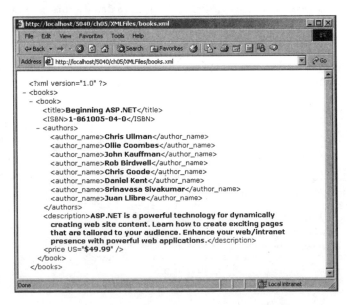

We must remember of course, that HTML is a format specifically designed for displaying information in browsers, while XML is a format concerned with marking up data to make it meaningful for any purpose. Although, as we'll see later in the chapter, we can considerably improve its on-screen display with the use of **Style Sheets**.

The Data Revolution

As computers have found their way into more areas of our work and home life, we are storing ever-increasing amounts of information electronically. The tendency is to think of our business data mainly residing in relational databases, such as SQL Server, Oracle or DB2. The reality, however, is that we probably have more data in other formats:

❑   Quotes and reports in word processor formats, such as Word or Word Perfect

❑   Web pages in HTML

❑   Presentations in PowerPoint

❑   Mail and memos in mail servers such as Exchange and Notes

Some of this data is duplicated and some of it is as good as lost, because not everyone knows how to access it. In addition, the ubiquity of the Internet has meant that we are now trying to share more and more data with people in other physical places.

What has all this got to do with XML? Going back to our book example, Wrox uses the type of information we have just seen for many purposes: for web pages, trade catalogs, public catalogs, information for retail purchasers (bookshops), and so on. Many of these require the information in different formats so we need to be able to use the information in different ways.

The great news is, that if we can mark up our book details just once in XML, we can re-use it for different purposes. As we will see later in this chapter, we can specify formatting rules that can be used to display the XML source to suit each required purpose. Furthermore, we can write programs that can read this source and present it, manipulate it, serve it, or store it, in every imaginable way.

If people want to find out about specific books, they can just collect information about those that they are interested in, rather than wasting bandwidth having to download a large file with a lot of irrelevant data in it. This is because we can easily offer a search facility that goes through <title> elements looking for the title we want. Having said that however, it should be noted that it is not as easy, or efficient, to find data in an XML document as it is in a database.

Breaking Beyond Data Display

Up to now, it may seem as though we have been concentrating on how XML can be an alternative to HTML. Let's quickly expand this view and see the other effects of marking up our data as XML. We will then take a look at some of the associated specifications and techniques that you'll need to learn.

XML is stored and transferred as plain text therefore, it has strong advantages over most other data formats. Its pure text form is non-proprietary so it can span platforms and operating systems – any application that can read pure text can use XML. Also, the data is easy to validate. You may recall that we said SGML uses a DTD to define the rules of any markup language written with it. Well, so does XML. This means that applications can verify the structure and content of an XML file.

Not only can XML be used as a way of presenting data that is marked up as HTML, it is equally useful for many other purposes, including:

- ❑ Data transfer – from the book details we could send details of orders and financial transactions, in XML, that can be understood by any platform

- ❑ Reusable data storage – data can be stored in plain text files rather than pre-purposed formats, such as HTML and proprietary word processor files, making it available to a far wider range of applications

This isn't to say XML is a perfect solution for all data storage. It has problems in allowing concurrent editing of the XML file; in fact it doesn't actually allow concurrent editing. Therefore if one person starts editing a file, after a small amount of time, it will automatically be locked by the operating system. This means no one else can update it during this period. XML won't replace databases for solutions where people are constantly updating and amending the same data. Like most technologies it has it has its specific strengths and weaknesses.

So far we've looked at why XML was created, discussed its structure and its similarities with HTML. Now we're going to move on examine it in more detail. Firstly, we're going to look at the kinds of documents that XML will, and won't, accept and why it is much stricter with regards to formatting than HTML.

Well-formed vs. Valid documents

The XML 1.0 specification lays out two types of XML document, either **well-formed** or **valid**. The distinction between the two is simple:

- ❑ Well-formed documents comply with the rules of XML syntax
- ❑ Valid documents are not only well-formed, they also comply with a DTD

Well-Formed Documents

XML syntax is governed by the XML 1.0 specification. If you understand the specification properly you will have no difficulty in constructing a set of rules to look at a document and decide whether it is in XML or not. If it is, then it can go on to do further processing, if it is not then it can be rejected. Due to the self-descriptive qualities of XML these rules can be applied equally well by either a computer or a human.

The official XML specification states well-formedness as the minimum requirement a document must satisfy in order to be considered as true XML. This specification also features a mixture of other requirements that ensure correct language terms are employed and that the document is logically coherent in the manner defined by the specification (in other words that the terms of the language are used in the right way). You can see the XML specification at http://www.w3.org/tr/xml/. There is also a helpful annotated version available at http://www.xml.com/axml/testaxml.htm.

What are these rules? You'll be pleased to hear that nearly everything we need to know about well-formed documents can be summed up in three rules:

❑ The document must contain one or more elements

❑ It must contain a uniquely named element, no part of which appears in the content of any other element. This is known as the root element

❑ All other elements must be kept within the root element and must be nested correctly

Let's look at how we construct a well-formed document.

The XML Declaration

This is actually optional, although you are strongly advised to use it so that the receiving application knows that it is an XML document and also the version used (at the time of writing this was the only version):

```
<?xml version="1.0"?>
```

Note that "xml" should be in lowercase. Note also that the XML declaration, when present, must not be preceded by any other characters (not even white space). As we saw previously, this declaration is also referred to as the XML prolog.

Elements

As we have already seen, the XML document essentially consists of data marked up using tags. Each start-tag/end-tag pair, with the data that lies between them, is an element:

```
<mytag>Here we have some data</mytag>
```

The start and end tags must be exactly the same, except for the closing slash in the end-tag. Remember that they must be in the same case: <mytag> and <MyTag> would be considered as different tags.

The section between the tags that says, "Here we have some data", is called character data, while the tags either side are the markup. The character data can consist of any sequence of legal characters (conforming to the Unicode standard), except the start element character "<". This is not allowed in case a processing application treats it as the start of a new tag. If you do need to include this character, you can represent it using the entity < as follows:

```
<answer>
  <true>20 > 10</true>
  <false>20 &lt; 10</false>
</answer>
```

Note that we can only ever have one top-level element per XML document. We therefore need to place elements true and false within the element answer for this snippet to be valid as the complete body of an XML document.

Tags can start with a letter, an underscore '_', or a colon ':', followed by any combination of letter, digits, hyphens, underscores, colons, or periods. The only exception is that you cannot start a tag with the letters XML in any combination of upper or lowercase letters.

While it's permissible to use colons in tag names, we don't advise you do so when working with ASP.NET, since your tags may be mistaken for server controls, which use colons to separate a control name from its namespace, for example `<asp:label />`

Here is another example, marking up some details for a hardware store:

```
<inventory>
   <buckets>
      <bucket>
         <make>Addis</make>
         <capacity>3 litres</capacity>
      </bucket>
      <bucket>
         <make>Metro</make>
         <capacity>2.5 litres</capacity>
      </bucket>
   </buckets>
</inventory>
```

If you think back to the three rules at the beginning of this section, you will be able to work out that this is a well-formed XML document. We have more than our one required element. We have a unique opening and closing tag: `<inventory>`, which is the root element and the elements are nested properly inside the root element.

Let's have a look at some more examples to help us get the idea how a well-formed XML document should be constructed.

At the simplest level we could have either:

```
<my_document></my_document>
```

or even:

```
<my_document/>
```

To make sure that tags nest properly, there must be no overlap. So this is correct:

```
<parent>
   <child>Some character data</child>
</parent>
```

While this would be incorrect:

```
<bad_parent>
      <naughty_child>
            Some character data
</bad_parent>
      </naughty child>
```

This is because the closing `</naughty_child>` element is after the closing `</bad_parent>` element.

Attributes

Elements can have attributes. These are values that are passed to the application, but do not constitute part of the content of the element. Attributes are included as part of the element's opening tag, as in HTML. XML attribute values must always be enclosed in quote marks (either single or double quote marks are acceptable). For example:

```
<food healthy="yes">spinach</food>
```

Elements can have as many attributes as you want. You could have:

```
<food healthy="no" tasty="yes" high_in_colesterol="yes">fries</food>
```

To be well-formed, however, you cannot repeat the attribute within an instance of the element. So you could not have:

```
<food tasty="yes" tasty="no">spinach</food>
```

Also, the string values between the quote marks can't contain the characters <, &, ' or ", as they can be interpreted as part of the XML tags. If you need to use these specific characters then they can be represented using CDATA sections, which we look at very shortly.

Other Features

There are also a number of other features of the XML specification that you need to learn if you want to progress to using XML frequently. Unfortunately, there isn't space to cover them all here. We will, however, briefly describe a few of them.

Entities

There are two categories of entity: general entities and parameter entities. Entities are generally used within a document as a way of avoiding having to type out long pieces of text several times. They provide a way of associating a name with your text, so that whenever you need to mention it you can just mention the name instead. As a result, if you have to modify the text, you only have to do it once (rather like the benefits offered by String variables). A typical general entity might look like this:

```
<!ENTITY copyright "@ Feiertag Holidays, Inc., 2001">
```

You can then put the entity into the document as follows:

```
&copyright;
```

Parameter entities are only used within the DTD and for that reason we won't discuss them here.

CDATA Sections

CDATA sections can be used inside elements whenever you need to use character data. They are used to delimit blocks of text that would otherwise be considered as markup. If we wanted to include the whole of the following line, including the tags:

```
<to_be_seen>Always wear light clothing when walking in the dark</to_be_seen>
```

We could use a CDATA section like so:

```
<element>
<! [CDATA[ <to_be_seen>Always wear light clothing when walking in the
dark</to_be_seen> ]]>
</element>
```

The whole line, including the opening and closing <to_be_seen> tags, would not be processed or treated as tags by the receiving application. They are often used when you have HTML tags inside your XML document, and prevents them from being treated as XML tags.

Comments

It is always good programming practice to comment your code – it's so much easier to read if it is commented in a manner that helps explain, reminds you about, or simply points out salient sections of code. It is surprising how code that seemed perfectly clear when you wrote it can soon become a jumble when you come back to it. While the descriptive XML tags often help you understand your own markup, there are times when the tags alone are not enough.

The good news is that comments in XML use exactly the same syntax as those in HTML:

```
<!--I really should add a comment here to remind me about xxxxx -->
```

Of course, to avoid confusing the receiving application, you should not include either the – or –– characters in your comment text.

Processing Instructions

These allow documents to contain instructions for applications using XML data. They take the form:

```
<?NameOfTargetApplication    Instructions for Application?>
```

The target name cannot contain the letters xml in any combination of upper or lower case. Otherwise, you can create your own to work with the processing application (unless there are any predefined by the application at which you are targeting your XML).

In our next Try It Out, we will be looking at badly formed XML. We can tell a lot about whether our XML is well-formed by simply loading it into our browser. It has the ability to tell us about all sorts of errors (although it does let some slip). When you are first writing XML, it is very helpful to do this quick check so that you know your XML is well-formed.

Try It Out – Badly formed XML

1. Open up your books.xml file

2. Remove the opening <book> tag

3. Save the file as bad_book.xml

4. Load it into an up-to-date browser, such as IE5.x/6 or Netscape 6:

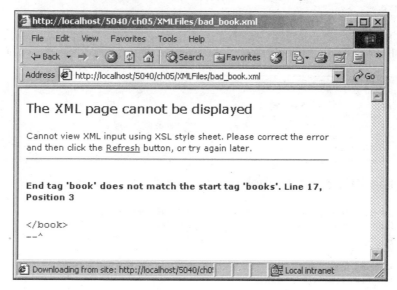

As you can see, the error message is pretty accurate. It more or less explicitly tells you that it was expecting an opening <book> tag. It certainly wouldn't take you long to find out what was wrong.

5. Put the opening book tag in again and change the line:

```
<title>Beginning ASP.NET</title>
```
To:
```
<title>Beginning ASP.NET<title>
```

By simply removing the slash on the closing tag.

6. Save the file again, and open it up in your browser (or simply click the Refresh button, if you have it open already). You should get a result like this:

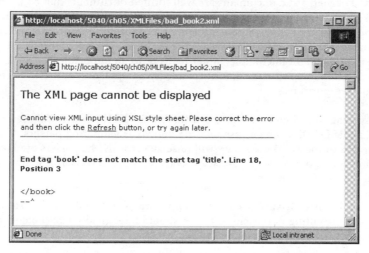

Again, we are not given the exact error, but the browser was expecting a closing <title> tag, which it did not receive.

7. Finally, correct the closing `<title>` tag, and remove the opening quote from the US price attribute. Save the file and refresh your browser. This time you get the exact error:

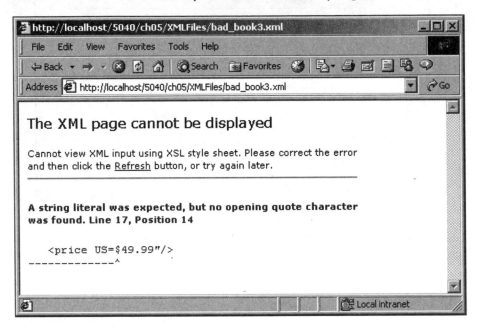

While it is not the most elegant way to test code, it certainly does help find errors quickly. If you have made more than one error, just correct your mistakes one at a time and watch the error messages change.

Valid Documents

As we mentioned earlier, valid documents are well-formed documents that conform to a DTD. When we read a book, manual, or magazine article we rarely notice its structure; if it is well written then the structure will be transparent. Yet, without structure there would be no communication. We may notice headings and paragraphs, but many other aspects pass us by. For one thing this structuring makes the information in the document intelligible, either by us or to an application using it. Furthermore, it means that when a document is parsed, for example by an application, it can be checked for the presence of required portions.

There are many programs, known as parsers, available for XML. Some of these are able to validate a document against its DTD, in which case they are known as validating parsers. If the document does not follow the structure of the DTD the parser will raise an error. XML parsers are included as part of Internet Explorer 5 and onwards, and Netscape Navigator 6 and onwards, hence our need in a previous example to only use these browsers.

Assuming that, in the first instance, we have an appropriate and well-planned structure for a type of document, then the resulting document instances should be logically complete with respect to its predefined structure. In our book example earlier we had:

- ❑ The unique opening and closing tags of `<books>`

- ❑ A `<book>` element, which encapsulates all information on a specific book

- ❑ Followed by a title, in a `<title>` element

- ❑ Then the ISBN in the `<ISBN>` tags

- ❑ Followed by the author, description, and price elements

If we had to exchange a lot of book information in this format, with various different people, there would be many advantages to writing a DTD (or document type definition). Such a book DTD would lay out the structure of how we expect books to be marked up, and while they're not compulsory to create XML files, they do mean that anyone following it will be able to write an XML file about books that would be valid according to our type definitions. In this manner, we could guarantee that any application using the book information, marked up according to our DTD, could understand the document. It could even do a preliminary check to ensure that the document followed our DTD in order to prevent the application showing errors if we passed in the wrong data. You could think of this as being similar to form validation for incoming and outgoing data.

If we wrote an application to processes XML files that conformed to our book DTD, it would be able to process **any** files that conformed to our DTD. In which case, if Wrox had different members of staff all writing XML documents about the books, they could all follow the DTD to make sure that they were valid. Then, should other publishers adopt the same DTD, the bookstores who might make use of our XML files would be able to use the same applications to process the files sent from several different publishers.

It is worth noting however, that there are other techniques on the horizon. The W3C is working on a version of schemas written in XML to be called XML Schemas.

XML Schemas

XML Schemas have several advantages over their DTD counterparts. The group working on the specification has looked at several proposals. The main ones are XML-Data and Document Content Description. Links to both can be found, with all of the submissions and specifications in progress, on the W3C site at http://www.w3.org/tr/.

There are a number of reasons why these XML Schemas will be an advantage over DTDs. Firstly, they use XML syntax rather than Extended Backus-Naur Form, which many people find difficult to learn. Secondly, if you needed to parse the schema, it will be possible to do so using an existing XML parser, rather than having to use a special parser. Another strong advantage is the ability to specify data types in XML Schemas, for the content of elements and attributes. This means that applications using the content will not have to convert it into the appropriate data type from a string. As an example, think about an application that has to add two numbers together, or perform a calculation on a date – using XML Schemas it wouldn't have to convert this data to the appropriate type, from a string, before it could perform the calculation. There will be other advantages too, such as support for namespaces, which we meet shortly. Also, XML Schemas can be easily extended, whereas DTDs cannot be simply extended once written.

Even HTML has DTDs

Being an SGML application, HTML has several SGML DTDs (at the very least, a strict and loose one for each version), and the coming XHTML specification has an XML DTD (as opposed to an SGML DTD). XHTML is a new version of HTML that is designed as an XML application, as opposed to an SGML application. This means that you will be able to parse XHTML documents using an XML parser. You can view an HTML DTD at http://www.w3.org/TR/REC-html40/loose.dtd. According to the HTML standard you should include the following line:

```
<!DOCTYPE HTML PUBLIC "-//W3C//DTD HTML 4.01 //EN">
```

It tells the user agent the location of HTML's DTD. It is often left out because however, practically speaking, it is not necessary and if you are using browser specific tags, which deviate from the specification, it may cause unpredictable results.

Styling XML

So far we've a document (books.xml) using XML to create a self-describing data structure about books. This is a great way to define data, as our tags clearly explain their content and are written in plain text, which is easy to transfer. If we are putting things up on the Web however, we want our pages to look good. As our earlier example showed, even in an XML-aware browser, such as IE5, a plain XML file doesn't look that impressive:

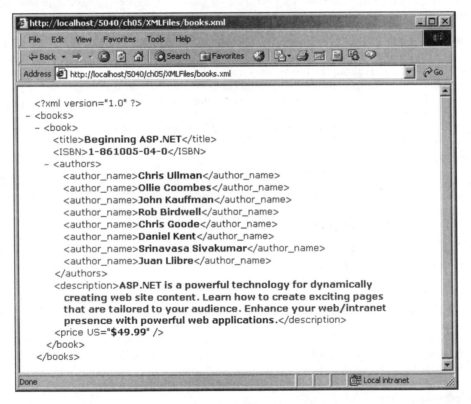

This is because the tags that we have proposed for our book example don't say anything about how the tags should appear on the page, whereas HTML tells the browser how the data should look.

To make it look more attractive we must therfore supply another file, a **style sheet**.

Why Use Style Sheets?

Unfortunately, using style sheets means that we have to use a completely separate language, in a separate file, to declare how we want our document to be presented. They do, however confer the following advantages:

- ❑ They improve document clarity
- ❑ They help reduce download time, network traffic and server load
- ❑ They allow you to modify the presentation of several pages, by altering just one file
- ❑ They allow you to present the same data in different ways for different purposes

Separating rules governing how the content of a document is displayed, like < font > tags, from the content itself is greatly beneficial to our contents clarity.

With a style sheet, all of the style rules are kept in one file and the source document simply links to this file. This means that if several pages use the same type of display (which is often the case as we display an ever-increasing amount of data on web pages) we do not need to repeat the style rules in each page. The browser can download the style sheet and cache it on the client. All other pages can then use the same styling rules. This also means that should you need to change the style of your site – perhaps your company changes its corporate colors – then you do not need to laboriously change every file individually by hand, you just change one style sheet and the changes are propagated across all the pages. Indeed, conversely, it means that you can use the same data, and display it in different ways for different purposes by applying different style sheets.

Cascading Style Sheets

The Cascading Style Sheets Level 1 specification was released by the W3C in late 1996. It has been supported to a large degree in all browsers. Since 1996, a Level 2 specification has been released (May 1998), some of which has been incorporated into Internet Explorer 5 onwards and Netscape version 6 and Opera 5. In addition, at the time of writing, a third level is in progress, but nothing much in the way of this draft standard has made it even into the latest browsers.

Cascading Style sheets are already popular with HTML developers for the same reasons that we have just expanded upon here.

CSS is a rule-based language consisting of two sections:

- ❑ A pattern matching section, which expresses the association between an element and some action
- ❑ An action section, which specifies the action to be taken upon the specified section

For CSS, this means that we have to specify an element and then define how it has to be displayed. If we were to develop a cascading style sheet for our books.xml file, we would have to specify a style for each of the elements that contained markup that we wanted to display.

CSS splits up the browser screen into areas that take a tree-like form, as shown in the following diagram. You can think of this much like the tree that Windows Explorer exposes:

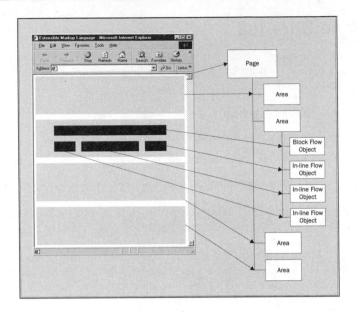

Here we have a page, with several areas. Inside the second area, are a block flow object and a number of in-line flow objects. Using CSS we can specify a style for each of these. Note that the block flow object is taking up the whole line, while the others are on the same line. A block need not contain text or images that take up the whole line – it could simply contain a short title that needs to be displayed in a line of its own.

It is important to decide whether the values are to be displayed in-line or as a block. The difference being that, if they are in-line the next element will be displayed as if it were on the same line as the previous one, whereas if it is displayed as a block, each will be treated separately. We need to make this decision for each object in CSS.

While we cannot cover a full reference to CSS here you should find it fairly easy to catch on and, if you need to investigate a particular implementation, you can always check the specification at http://www.w3.org/style/css/

Let's try it out and write a style sheet for our books.xml file.

Try it Out – Displaying XML with CSS

1. Start by opening up your text editor, and entering the following code:

```
title {
     display:block;
     font-family: Arial, Helvetica;
     font-weight: bold;
     font-size: 20pt;
     color: #9370db;
     text-align: center;
     }
ISBN {
     display:block;
```

```
        font-family: Arial, Helvetica;
        font-weight: bold;
        font-size: 12pt;
        color: #c71585;
        text-align: left;
        }

authors {
        display:inline;
        font-family: Arial, Helvetica;
        font-style: italic;
        font-size: 10pt;
        color: #9370db;
        text-align: left;
        }

description {
        display:block;
        font-family: Arial, Helvetica;
        font-size: 12pt;
        color: #ff1010;
        text-align: left;
        }
```

2. Save the file as `books.css`. We have now finished creating our first style sheet for XML. The only problem is that our `books.xml` file has no way of telling how it should be associated with this style sheet. We will therefore have to add a link to it in our original XML file.

3. To add the link to the style sheet, open up your `books.xml` file again, and add the following line between the XML prolog and the opening `<books>` element.

```
<?xml version="1.0"?>
<?xml:stylesheet href="books.css" type="text/css" ?>
<books>
```

4. Open `books.xml` in your browser and you should see something like this:

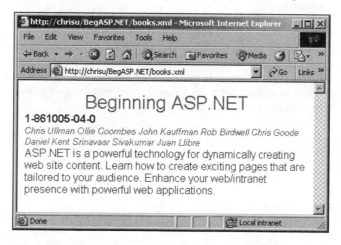

How It Works

CSS files do not need a special header, so we go straight on and declared which elements we needed to display. In this case, we are just adding styling for the `<title>`, `<ISBN>`, `<authors>`, and `<description>` elements. So we add them to the file like this:

```
title {

      }
ISBN  {

      }

authors {

      }

description {

      }
```

This specifies the pattern matching section.

Having declared the elements we want to display, we must associate some action with them. Let's see how to display the content of the <title> element. We want it to be displayed as a block, so within the curly brackets {} we add the directive to display the element as a block:

```
title {
      display:block;
      }
```

This simply specifies that we want to make the title a block level element. We still need to specify the style the title should be displayed in.

> **All properties are specified with a colon delimiting the attribute and values and have a semi-colon after them.**

We added a font to display the content of the `<title>` element. In the screen shot you have just seen the browser is using the Arial font. In case the machine using the file does not have Arial, however we have allowed it to use Helvetica instead. In addition, we want it to appear in the center of the screen, in a size 20pt, bold font, and in a lilac color. So, we add some more action rules, or style elements. As you can see, these are very similar to those used for HTML:

```
title {
      display:block;
      font-family: Arial, Helvetica;
      font-weight: bold;
      font-size: 20pt;
      color: #9370db;
      text-align: center;
      }
```

We can then add some similar rules for the other element content we want to display, for example:

```
authors {
        display:inline;
        font-family: Arial, Helvetica;
        font-style: italic;
        font-size: 10pt;
        color: #9370db;
        text-align: left;
        }
```

You can see from the screen shot that the authors, despite being in separate elements in the books.xml file are displayed on the same line.

Finally, we included an extra line in our books.xml file to tell it to use the correct CSS file:

```
<?xml version="1.0"?>
<?xml:stylesheet href="books.css" type="text/css" ?>
<books>
```

The href attribute acts just like it would in HTML, while the type attribute specifies the type of style sheet that is being attached. This is an example of a **processing instruction**. You may remember us talking about them earlier in the chapter, when we were discussing XML syntax.

> **Remember that because the style sheet link is still in the XML file, the values of the attributes still need to be kept in quotation marks for the XML to be well-formed.**

That's basically all there is to it. If you want to know more about style sheets and how to use them, then we suggest you check out Wrox's *"HTML 4.01 Programmers' Reference" (ISBN 1861005334)*.

While we now have a good idea of how XML works, and how to display it, we still don't know anything about how it works with ASP.NET. We'll look at this now.

Using XML With ASP.NET

We won't actually look at the mechanics of using XML in our ASP.NET pages for another couple of chapters, since we first need to properly introduce objects.

It's worth pointing out however that XML is used in many different ways within ASP.NET, and its usefulness should become increasingly evident as we progress through the book. As we demonstrated briefly back in Chapter 2, it can be used as a data source from which you can extract data – we'll consider this in much more detail when we get on to Chapter 13, in which we'll discuss data sources in general.

XML can also be used as a format to which you can dump database information or object state. It's used in Web Services (which we'll look at in Chapter 18) to transmit data between applications. It's also used in the various configuration files for IIS and ASP.NET (which we're going to focus on in Chapter 20). As you can see it is used for many varying purposes.

This completes our introduction to XML – even if you don't yet fully grasp its significance within ASP.NET, you should at least have some idea of what a useful, flexible, and lightweight information storage structure it can be.

Summary

In this chapter, we've examined the potential of XML as a structured information storage medium. We looked at how it came into being, the job it was designed to do, and its advantages and disadvantages when compared to HTML. We moved on to look at the differences between valid and well-formed XML documents, and how you can use your web browser to provide an indication of whether a document is well-formed. We discussed elements, attributes, entities, and the various other features that make up an XML document, together with the processing instructions that you can include. We examined the creation of Style Sheets to make your XML documents more aesthetically appealing, and the advantages that this approach has over HTML, where presentation and content are combined.

In the next chapter, we will look at the basic structures that VB.NET offers for handling variables and running programs.

Exercise Questions

1. Explain why XML is so useful for storing data.

2. Create an XML file to hold the following employee information:

Company: Wrox Press

employee: Hubert Welsch
employee number: 9862
contact numbers: ext – 346
                home – 8764 35733
length of service: 2 years
department: .NET Team

employee: Paul Crick
employee number: 7461
contact numbers: ext – 399
                home – 2138 90346
length of service: 8 months
department: .NET Team

employee: Alison Freyer
employee number: 7849
contact numbers: ext – 982
                home – 7893 42769
length of service: 4 years
department: Java Team

employee: Sandra Jackson
employee number: 9862
contact numbers: ext – 222
                home – 8974 389743
length of service: 1 year
department: Finance

3. Create a cascading style sheet to display the XML file you have just created. Use font style and alignment, and color to display the employee information in an attractive way.

4. Are the following XML documents well-formed? If not, make the necessary corrections, and explain why your corrections are important in the creation of a well-formed document.

    a.

```
<?xml version="1.0"?>
<shoppingList>
  <title>Shopping List</title>
  <items>
    <fruit items>
      <item>Rasberries</item>
      <item>Apples</item>
      <item>Oranges</item>
    </fruit_items>
    <vegetable_items>
      <item>Carrots</item>
      <item>Onions</item>
      </vegetable_items>
      <other_items>
        <item>Floor cleaner</item>
        <item>Bread</item>
        <item>Toothpaste</item>
        <item>Pasta</item)
      </other_items>
  <items>
</shoppingList>
  <Notes> Don't get cooking apples like last time and post letter to
Harold</Notes>
```

    b.

```
<?xml version="1.0">
<order>
  <salesperson>Sam Clarke</salesperson>
  <customer>Droutledge Waters</customer>
  <item>
    <description>snorkle</description>
    <quantity>37</quantity>
  </item>
  <date>
    <month>7</month>
    <day>6</day>
    <year>2001</year>
  </date>
</order>
```

5. Once you have finished looking at part b, try rearranging this information so that you can view orders that have been placed via Sam Clarke the sales person. Add another order, placed the following week, for 12 goggles, as ordered by Aqua Lake Enterprises.

Control Structures and Procedural Programming

In the first few chapters of this book, you've been writing ASP.NET web forms using VB.NET code. Up until now, you've not been able to use your code for anything but the most trivial of tasks. In fact occasionally, to demonstrate points about how to use Boolean variables or how to populate arrays efficiently, we've had to use structures that we haven't talked about yet. You can breathe a sigh of relief now, as we're going to talk about the fundamental structures – branches, loops, and modules – that go to make up VB.NET.

You might be wondering why we need these structures? The reason is that our ASP.NET programs, given certain conditions, need to be able to skip or repeat lines – or groups of lines. This chapter will teach you ways to change the order that the lines of your code are executed in, and how to repeat the execution of sections of code as necessary.

This chapter covers the three ways that you can use VB.NET with your ASP.NET code to sequence the execution of your lines of code. Respectively, these are:

❑   Deciding which of two or more sections of code to run

❑   Repeating a section of code as many times as needed

❑   Jumping out of the code sequence and executing sections of code in another part of your script

Note that, once again, this chapter refers to using VB.NET in our ASP.NET web forms, and hence the syntax shown in the following examples is specific to VB.NET. If you were to try and work, for example, in C# or JScript.NET, the syntax of the examples would have to be changed appropriately. You'll find that the features introduced in this chapter enable you to write much more complex ASP.NET code and the web forms you will be able to create will now begin to resemble applications, rather than static HTML pages with a few extras bolted on.

We're going to look in this chapter at:

❑   `If ... Then` structures

❑   `Select Case` structures

❑   `For ... Next` loops

- ❑ Do While loops
- ❑ Functions
- ❑ Subroutines
- ❑ Variable scope

A Quick Look at Control Structures

When programming VB.NET, or just about any other computer language, in ASP.NET, we have three types of structures (groups of control statements) to control the order in which the lines of code are executed. These are: branching structures, looping structures, and jumping structures. We'll now look at each of these in more detail.

Overview of Branching Structures

Branching structures work by first performing some type of test. Based on the test results, one set of code will be executed and other sets of code will be skipped. Consider our holiday example from the last two chapters. We might want to test to see if the customer has requested more information before posting them the latest brochure. If they have, then we perform the necessary steps, such as picking up a brochure, putting it in an envelope, and mailing it to them. If they haven't then we skip these steps and just send them information on specific hotels. This is pretty much how VB.NET handles such decisions. In fact there are two types of structure employed to help do this.

The two types of branching structures are:

- ❑ If ... Then ... Else – generally used to select one out of two (or occasionally more) sets of lines to execute based on a condition to be met. A simple example: in a web page featuring news stories, we could choose whether to display the international, or the regional news headlines, depending on a user's preferences. If ... Then is also the tool of choice for complicated comparisons, such as expressions using the terms AND, OR, and NOT.

- ❑ Select Case – generally used to select one set of lines to execute from **many** possibilities. For example, in a page featuring news stories, we could choose which of several icons to include in the page next to the story, depending on whether the story was about politics, business, sport, entertainment, or technology.

Overview of Looping Structures

Looping structures allow the same block of code to be run a number of times. Instead of skipping code – which is what the branching technique does – we **repeat** code. In our holiday example, for each customer that has entered their details and wants more information, you need to get out a brochure, put it in an envelope, address the envelope, then go back and repeat those same steps for the rest of the customers who have done this. This is a real world example of looping. In this chapter, we'll go one further in our holiday example – we may want to generate a page for each person who is going to be staying at a hotel. The construction of those lines (print the description, print the quantity, print the price, put in a line break) would be looped to produce one line for each item ordered:

❑   For ... Next is used to repeat line(s) when, at the beginning of the repetitions, we know exactly how many repetitions we want, or we can use a test (such as the sizeof() function) to determine the amount of repetitions we want. For example, if we know there are five trucks needing a wash, we could repeat five times the set of steps involved in successfully washing a truck.

❑   Do While is used to repeat line(s) when we **don't** know at design time how many repetitions we want. We build into the loop some type of test of condition, which is checked after each loop. The loop will repeat as long as the condition is true.

❑   For ... Each is used when we have a collection of items, but we don't know how many, and we want to repeat the loop for every item in the collection.

Overview of Jumping Structures

Jumping structures allow the programmer to pause the execution of the current code and jump to **another** named code block. For example, we may have written a block of code called ShowOrder that produces lines to show the customer the goods that they ordered. Whenever we want VB.NET to show those lines, we don't have to re-write or copy all of that code. Instead, we just have VB.NET jump out of our current code, execute ShowOrder, and then come back and continue executing our original code. There are two types of jumping controls, which are collectively known as **procedures**:

❑   **Subroutines** can be called using the name of the subroutine, which will run the statements in the subroutine, and then return control to the line following the call

❑   **Functions** can be used to execute some statements which will return an answer to the main body of code

Examples of Control Structures

With these three classes of controls – branching, jumping, and looping – we can solve virtually any programming objective in ASP.NET. In the table below, we've listed several situations we might want to program for, and suggested which class of structure will help us achieve the desired results:

Situation	Solution	Why?
I want ASP.NET to show page A or page B.	Branching	We want to perform only one of two possible events.
I need to show the user which of several meetings they should attend. The meeting displayed is based on which department they belong to.	Branching	We want to write to the page only **one** out of several possible meeting locations.
I want ASP.NET to list each member of the club. The data about each member is held in essentially the same manner, with a name, photo, address and other contact information.	Looping	We will be performing the same set of code (that retrieves a member's name) many times (once for each member, until we list all members).

Table continued on following page

Situation	Solution	Why?
I want to present data in a table.	Looping	We will perform the same code (make a row for a table) again and again until we have built all of the rows needed.
After placing an item that I describe in a catalog page, I want to put in a few lines of information about 'How to Order'. There will be several items across several pages that we need to do this for.	Use a subroutine	We want to pause the main code and perform several lines of **another** set of code that describes 'How to Order'. Then we want to resume the main code. Since the 'How to Order' set of code will be performed at various times across the page, it is best to write it once and call that one piece of code as needed.
I need to calculate prices in several places on each page. The prices will be set according to input from a user form.	Use a function	We will pause building the page, jump out to execute code to calculate the price of an item, and then return to building the page and return the calculated amount. Since we will calculate many prices it is best to write the formula once and have it called when needed.

Let's recap on what we've discussed so far. There are three kinds of statements that control the flow of our code's execution:

❑ Branching statements that perform a test and then execute some lines of code, but not others

❑ Looping statements that execute a set of code again and again

❑ Jumping statements that pause the execution of the current code, jump over to another set of code, and then return to where they started, sometimes bringing values back with them

Now we'll look at branching statements, and see what we can do with them.

Branching Structures in Detail

As we've already mentioned, branching controls perform some type of test. Based on the test results, a set of code will be executed and other sets of code will be skipped.

ASP.NET offers two techniques for branching. `If ... Then` is used when there are only a few choices of outcome. Bear in mind that the more lines you use in `If ... Then`, the more difficult your code will become to follow. It is better to use `Select Case` when there are a lot of outcomes.

For example, if you are making a decision on how to proceed having asked the user "Do you want a confirmation by telephone?" the outcome is either "Yes" (True) or "No" (False), so you would perform the branch using `If ... Then`. But if you ask the user "Do you want confirmation by telephone, fax, FedEx, e-mail, voicemail, or telepathy?" given the number of outcomes, then it is probably better to use `Select Case`.

Before we launch into a detailed examination of how these particular branching structures are used, we need to look at some of the operators that are used within these statements.

Comparison Operators

The comparison operators available in VB.NET are:

Equality	=	Inequality	<>
Less than	<	Greater than	>
Less than or equal to	<=	Greater than or equal to	>=

We've already seen the 'equal' sign (=) in its guise as the assignment operator. You can use it to assign any value to a variable:

```
Dim variable As String
variable = "Here is some text"
```

This statement is saying that the value "Here is some text", should be assigned to the variable variable.

However, it has another guise in VB.NET, to test for equality, as well. In this case, it is used as follows:

```
If number1 = number2 Then
...
```

This statement says, "If the value in number1 is already equal to the value in number2 then we should perform a certain operation". It depends upon the context in which the equals sign is used. If it's used on its own, then it assigns one value to a variable, if it's used as part of an If ... Then statement, then it's being used as a comparison operator. You can also use these operators to compare the values of two operands – such as variables or expressions. The result of the comparison is a Boolean value – that is, either True or False.

The other comparison operators work in the same way. If, for example, you want to compare two numbers to see if one is greater than the other, then you could do the following:

```
If number1 > number2 Then
```

This would test to see whether the first number was greater than the second and would evaluate to either of the Boolean values True or False as a result, depending on the contents of the variables.

Logical Operators

There's also a set of logical operators you can use in your code:

- ❑ AND
- ❑ OR
- ❑ NOT

Actually, there are more than three logical operators, but the others are only required in specialist situations, so we won't be discussing them in this book. Logical operators are used in the same way as comparison operators and the whole expression will evaluate to a `Boolean` value:

```
If number1 = 1 AND number2 = 2 Then
```

They are used to determine a particular course of action. When using AND, both of these conditions have to be True for the condition to be fulfilled. This differs from OR where only one out of the two conditions has to be True for the condition to be fulfilled. If both conditions are true, the condition will also be true:

```
If number1 = 1 OR number2 = 2 Then
```

The third logical operator NOT, simply implies the reverse of the condition. If `number1` isn't equal to 1 then the condition is fulfilled:

```
If NOT number1 = 1 Then
```

When you have a statement containing more than one logical operator, VB.NET decides which ones to execute first according to a simple rule: They're simply executed in the following order, which is known as the order of operator **precedence**.

- ❑ NOT
- ❑ AND
- ❑ OR

Take the following example:

```
If number1 = 1 OR NOT number2 = 1 AND NOT number3 = 1 Then
```

What does this expression actually test for? Well, first it checks that `number2` is not equal to 1, and that `number3` is not equal to 1. Only then does it check that either the result of that AND operation is true, or that `number1` is equal to 1, to calculate the final result of the test. This isn't what you might have expected, reading the expression from left to right.

This expression can be made to read more clearly by adding parentheses, like so:

```
If number1 = 1 OR (NOT number2 = 1 AND NOT number3 = 1) Then
```

You have to beware of these kinds of logical "traps", in the same way as you would using mathematical operators. To prevent your code not working in the way you intend, you should always use parentheses wherever possible.

There's also an important operator which we need to be aware of, which we can also make writing more complex logic like this a lot easier – the inequality operator, <>. This operator looks a little odd, but you can think of it as meaning 'less than or greater than', which, in the case of numbers, is the same as saying 'not equal to'. In fact, you can use the inequality operator to compare strings and other types of value as well.

We can rewrite the above example using this operator as:

```
If number1 = 1 OR (number2 <> 1 AND number3 <> 1) Then
```

Now, that's quite a lot easier to read.

Having looked at the types of operators you can use with branching structures, its time to look at the structures themselves in more detail.

The If ... Then Structure

The basic If ... Then statement has four parts:

❑ An **expression**: that is, a test that evaluates to either true or false

❑ An "**if true**" section of code

❑ An (optional) "**if false**" section of code

❑ An **ending** statement

The first part is the expression, which can be a combination of keywords, operators, variables, and constants. We came across them first in the last chapter. The expression must be Boolean: it must evaluate to either true or false. If the test evaluates True, then only the lines of code in the "If True" section are executed. If the test evaluates False, then only the lines of code in the "If False" section are executed. After either the 'True' or 'False' section is executed, the execution jumps down to the ending statement and continues with the next line of code. There is never a situation where both the true **and** false sections would be executed in a given case.

There are four ways of building If ... Then statements. To select the proper syntax you must answer two questions:

❑ Do I want to do anything if the test is False?

❑ Do I want to execute more than one statement if the test is True?

If ... Then

The first, and simplest syntax is useful if you only want to take action to run one statement in the case of a True condition. Using this method you will not be able to execute any statements if your expression evaluates to False. For example, if a user checks a box to inform you that they have a fax, you want them to enter the number. If they don't check the box then you want to take no action. In this case, you can use a simple one-line syntax:

```
If faxConfirm = "Yes" then Message.Text = "Please enter your fax number."
```

The next most complex syntax is where you want to perform more than one statement in the case of True, but still nothing if the test is False. For example, if the user wants a fax confirmation, then ask for the fax number and jump over to the fax entry page.

In this case, we must write the If ... Then with two changes from the syntax outlined above: the statements must go on their own lines, not the same one as in the simple example above. And, since there is now more than one line for the If ... Then code, we must use a closing line of End If:

```
If faxConfirm = "Yes" Then
  Message.Text = ("Please click below and provide your fax number.")
  Message.Text = Message.Text & _
    "<a href='http://www.On-LineClothier.com/FaxForm'>Click here</a>"
End If
```

If ... Then ... Else

The third level is where you want to perform one or more statements in the case of True, and also one or more lines of code if the test is False. For example, if the user has requested a fax confirmation then ask for the fax number and jump over to the fax entry page. If they haven't requested a fax, then show a line that says that a fax will not be sent. In this situation, we must write the `If ... Then` with a line containing the word `Else` to separate the code that is run in the True case from the code that will run in the False case:

```
If strFaxConfirm = "Yes" then
   Message.Text = "Please enter your fax number."
Else
   Message.Text = "No fax confirmation will be sent."
End If
```

Note that we still write `End If`, not `End Else`.

If ... Then ... ElseIf

There is a fourth level, which is complex, and not used often – although there are some situations where it cannot be avoided. It allows you to choose between several different pieces of code to execute according to complex criteria. To do this, you need to separate each new case with the keyword `ElseIf` (one word), closing the condition as normal with `End If`. You can also include a generic `Else` clause, which will be executed if none of the other cases were chosen. For example, it can be structured like this:

```
If confirm = "Fax" then
   Message.Text = "Please enter your fax number."
ElseIf confirm = "Email" then
   Message.Text = "Please enter your email address"
ElseIf confirm = "Voicemail" then
   Message.Text = "Please enter your voice mail number"
Else
   Message.Text = "No confirmation will be sent."
End If
```

Here we test the data to see if it meets condition 1. If it doesn't, we test it to see if it meets condition 2. If it doesn't meet that either, we test it to see if it meets condition 3, and so on. When our data meets one of the criteria, or the criteria isn't met, the appropriate branch is decided and we arrive at a suitable outcome.

```
There is an alternative structure (Select Case) that provides a simpler solution
to this problem, and we'll be looking at this shortly. Generally, if you are only
testing to see if a variable contains one of several specific values, you will use
Select Case rather than If ... Then ... ElseIf.
```

Summary of Four kinds of If ... Then Control Structures

Situation	Syntax	Example
If test is True do one statement Otherwise do nothing	If test Then statement	If age < 18 Then Message.Text = "You must be 18 or older to order by credit card."

Situation	Syntax	Example

If the test is True
 	
do two or more statements
 	
If the test is False do nothing
	```If test Then```
	
	``` True code line 1```
	``` True code line 2```
	``` ...```
	
	```End If```
		```If age < 18 Then```
		
		``` discount = true```
		
		``` Message.Text = "You are eligible for the student rate of $49."```
		
		```End If```

If the test is True
 	
do one or more statements
 	
If the test is False
 	
do a different set of one or more statements
	```If test Then```
	
	``` True code line 1```
	``` True code line 2```
	
	```Else```
	
	``` False code line 1```
	``` False code line 2```
	
	```End If```
		```If age < 18 Then```
		
		``` discount = true```
		
		``` Message.Text = "You are eligible for the student rate of $49."```
		
		```Else```
		
		``` Message.Text = "The fee for this service is $59."```
		
		```End If```

If the first test is True do one or more statements
 	
Else if the second test is true
 	
do a different set of one or more statements
 	
Else if the nth test is True
 	
do a different set of one or more statements
 	
If all tests are false do nothing
	```If test Then```
	
	``` True code line 1```
	``` True code line 2```
	
	```ElseIf test Then```
	
	``` True code line 1```
	``` True code line 2```
	
	```ElseIf test Then```
	``` True code line 1```
	``` True code line 2```
	
	```End If```
		```If age < 18 Then```
		
		``` discount = true```
		
		``` Message.Text = "You are eligible for the student rate of $49."```
		
		```ElseIf age > 65 Then```
		
		``` discount = true```
		
		``` Message.Text = "You are eligible for the senior rate of $49."```
		
		```ElseIf age > 18 And age < 65 Then```
		
		``` Message.Text = "The fee for this service is $59."```
		
		```End If```

When using the one-line form of If ... Then you do NOT use End If.
When using any multi-line form of If ... Then you MUST use End If.

We're now going to give a quick example that involves a number guessing game. The computer "thinks" of a number between 1 and 10, and you have to guess what it is.

Try It Out – Using the If ... Then Structure

1. *Open up your web page editor and type in the following:*

```
<script language="vb" runat="server">
Sub Page_Load()
  Dim theNumber As Integer
  Dim theGuess As Integer

  theNumber = int(10 * rnd) + 1

  If Request.Form("Guess") <> "" Then
    theGuess = Request.Form("Guess")

    If theGuess > theNumber then
      Message.Text = "<BR><BR>Guess is too high<BR>Try again - it was " _
      & theNumber
    End If

    If theGuess < theNumber then
      Message.Text = "<BR><BR>Guess is too low<BR>Try again - it was " _
      & theNumber
    End If

    If theGuess=theNumber then
      Message.Text = "<BR><BR>Guess is correct!"
    End If
  End If
End Sub
</script>

<html>
<head></head>
<body>
<form runat="server">
  What number am I thinking of?
  <asp:dropdownlist id="Guess" runat="server">
    <asp:listitem>1</asp:listitem>
    <asp:listitem>2</asp:listitem>
    <asp:listitem>3</asp:listitem>
    <asp:listitem>4</asp:listitem>
    <asp:listitem>5</asp:listitem>
    <asp:listitem>6</asp:listitem>
    <asp:listitem>7</asp:listitem>
    <asp:listitem>8</asp:listitem>
    <asp:listitem>9</asp:listitem>
    <asp:listitem>10</asp:listitem>
  </asp:dropdownlist>
  <br>
  <br>
  <input type="submit" value="Submit guess">
  <asp:label id="message" runat="server"/>
</form>
</body>
</html>
```

2. *Save this as* `ifthen.aspx` *in a virtual directory.*

3. *View* `ifthen.aspx` *in your browser:*

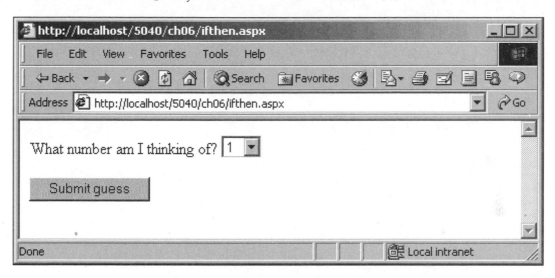

4. *Choose a number and click on Submit guess:*

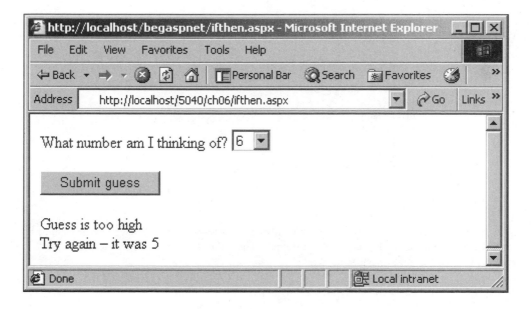

5. *Carry on guessing, until you get the correct answer:*

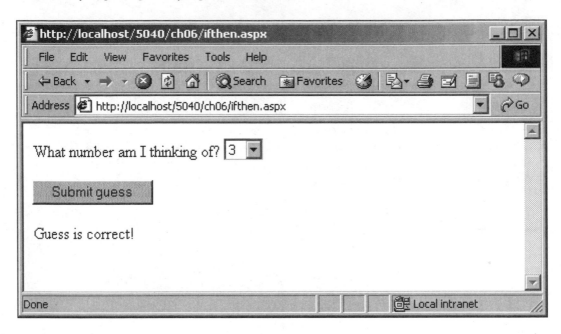

How It Works

As it's such a simple example, it doesn't require too much code. We get the user to enter a guess into the web form with the `<asp:dropdownlist>` control:

```
<asp:dropdownlist id="Guess" runat="server">
  <asp:listitem>1</asp:listitem>
  <asp:listitem>2</asp:listitem>
  <asp:listitem>3</asp:listitem>
  <asp:listitem>4</asp:listitem>
  <asp:listitem>5</asp:listitem>
  <asp:listitem>6</asp:listitem>
  <asp:listitem>7</asp:listitem>
  <asp:listitem>8</asp:listitem>
  <asp:listitem>9</asp:listitem>
  <asp:listitem>10</asp:listitem>
</asp:dropdownlist>
```

Using a dropdown list ensures that we get a valid response back from the user, as they can only choose those that we have approved and placed in the list. The value from the user is passed in the `Request.Form("Guess")` variable.

It's the actual VB.NET code that is most interesting. In our section, we start by defining two variables:

```
Sub Page_Load()
    Dim theNumber As Integer
    Dim theGuess As Integer
```

These two variables respectively contain the number that we randomly generate, and the user's guess:

```
      theNumber = int(10 * rnd) + 1
```

Next, we randomly generate a number. VB.NET has a function called `rnd()`, which will generate a decimal number less than 1 and greater than or equal to zero. To get a random number between 1 and 10, we have to multiply this value by 10, which will generate a number between 0 and 10 (not including 10 itself). We use the `int()` function to round the number down to a whole number between 0 and 9, and then we add 1 to it, giving us what we need: a number from 1 to 10. Any range of random integers in VB.NET can be generated with the following equation:

```
RandomNumber = int((1 + upperbound - lowerbound) * rnd) + lowerbound
```

So we've generated our random number, we've got the guess from the user stored in `Request.Form("Guess")`, all we need to do is compare them, right?

Well, not quite; as this is a web form with just one single page, we need to check to see if the user has ever been there before. As on their first arrival they won't have entered a number, and we don't want to test the random number against an empty variable.

To perform this check, we see if there is any value in the `Request.Form("Guess")` variable. The first time we run the page, there can't be, as the user hasn't guessed yet. Every time the user submits a guess, there will be a value:

```
      If Request.Form("Guess") <> "" Then
```

This line says that if the contents of `Request.Form("Guess")` are not equal to nothing, then run the next bit of code. Remember the inequality operator is <>, and will only evaluate to True, if the two values aren't equal. The two pairs of quotation marks, `""`, are a way of writing an empty string – a string that contains no characters at all. What we're asking is whether the value in `Request.Form("Guess")` is different to an empty string. If there's no value, then it will be considered equal to the empty string. If there is a value there, then it will be considered not-equal. So the first time the user accesses the page, there won't be anything in `Request.Form("Guess")`, and the page execution will jump to the end of the `If ... Then` structure, marked by `End If`. After the related `End If`, is an `End Sub`, so the program ends until the page loads again:

```
      End If
   End Sub
```

You might be wondering, how ASP.NET knows that this is the correct `End If`, as there are several in the code. The answer is that they have been **nested** inside each other. Where there is an `If` statement inside the block of code belonging to another `If` statement, the inner `If` statement has to have a matching `End If` statement, before the outer block can be ended. This means that `If ... Then` blocks can be treated as completely separate self-contained entities:

```
      If Request.Form("Guess")<>"" Then

         Request.Form("Guess") = "", so ignore all this code

      End If
   End Sub
```

There are three separate `If ... Then` structures inside this code:

```
if Request.Form("Guess") <> "" Then
   theGuess = Request.Form("Guess")

   if theGuess > theNumber then
      STRUCTURE 1
   End If

   if theGuess < theNumber then
      STRUCTURE 2
   End If

   if theGuess = theNumber then
      STRUCTURE 3
   End If
End If
```

At this point, it's worth noting that it's useful to indent your code in these structures to keep track of which `End If` statement applies to which `If Then` structure. In this way, it's not only easier to read, but also helps stop you from forgetting to close all of the branching statements.

These are all ignored, unless there is something in the `Request.Form("Guess")` variable. The first time around there isn't.

Second time around, the user has submitted a guess. So, now the `Request.Form("Guess")` test will evaluate to True, and the code inside will be run. Each structure is considered as a separate test in its own right. Before we do the test though, we set our `theGuess` variable to be equal to the contents of `Request.Form("Guess")`, to save us a bit of typing each time we refer to the user's guess:

```
theGuess = Request.Form("Guess")
```

Our first test checks to see whether the guess is bigger than the number:

```
if theGuess > theNumber then
   Message.Text = "<BR><BR>Guess is too high<BR>Try again - it was " _
                                                   & theNumber
End If
```

If it is, then it sets the `<asp:label>` control to display a message informing the user that their guess was too high, along with the number that the user failed to guess.

Our second test checks to see whether the guess is smaller than the number:

```
if theGuess < theNumber then
   Message.Text = "<BR><BR>Guess is too low<BR>Try again - it was " _
                                                   & theNumber
End If
```

In this case we then display a message saying that the guess was too low, and display the number.

Our last test checks to see whether the number is correct, and displays an appropriate message in our `<asp:label>` control:

```
if theGuess = theNumber then
  Message.Text = "<BR><BR>Guess is correct!"
End If
```

That's all there is to this example. However, each time we play this game, a new number is generated, whether we are right or wrong. This is where the concept of state comes in. We can't get ASP.NET to remember the number, without some sort of store between page requests. We'll talk about how to do this when we come to session variables, in Chapter 10.

Select Case Structure

One problem of If ... Then is that it can start getting unwieldy after more than three or four possible outcomes. What happens if you want to show a different page to visitors from each of five departments? What happens if you want to do a calculation based on the user providing one of twelve salary grades? Or if you have different procedures for confirming an order by telephone, fax and e-mail? Your code is going to start looking pretty messy with all of those ElseIfs! You'll also find that your code is going to get slower, the more alternatives you add.

Select Case is the alternative control structure we mentioned earlier for handling branching and it caters much more neatly for these type of situations, by providing a better structure, much better performance and extra readability: anytime you need to make a choice among several answers (more than just True or False) use Select Case.

The syntax for Select Case has five parts:

❑ State which variable to test

❑ State a possible value and what to do if the variable has that value

❑ Repeat for as many possible values as you want to handle

❑ Add an optional catch-all Case Else, in case the variable matches a value you haven't anticipated

❑ End the Select Case control structure

Our first example, below, carries out one of three actions depending on what is contained in the variable confirmation:

```
Select Case confirmation
  Case "Fax"
    Message.Text = "<a href='FaxConfirmation.htm'>Fax</a>"
  Case "Telephone"
    Message.Text = "<a href='telephone.htm'>Telephone</a>"
  Case "Email"
    Message.Text   "<a href='Email.htm'>Email</a>"
End Select
```

VB.NET knows from the first line that you want to compare answers to the contents of the variable confirmation. Next, it will begin testing the contents of the variable against the values shown in the Case lines. When VB.NET finds a match it executes the following code up to the next Case line, and then jumps down to the first line after the End Select statement.

We mentioned in our previous If.... Then example that we used a dropdown list to ensure that the user could only enter a valid answer. When checking user input using Select Case we often need to do the same thing, as string comparisons in VB.NET are case sensitive. If we allow the user to enter text in response to a "Yes/No" question, we must be prepared to handle the fact that "Yes", "yes", and "YES" will all be handled differently. Additionally, we should prepare to handle unexpected inputs (like the user entering "Yeah") as well. This can be done using the Case Else statement as shown here:

```
Select Case question
  Case "yes"
    Message.Text= "Details will be sent."
  Case "YES"
    Message.Text= "Details will be sent."
  Case "Yes"
    Message.Text= "Details will be sent."
  Case "no"
    Message.Text= "We will make further contact by email."
  Case "NO"
    Message.Text= "We will make further contact by email."
  Case "No"
    Message.Text= "We will make further contact by email."
  Case Else
    Message.Text "Your answer " & strQuestion & " is not recognized."
End Select
```

In this example, the user who decided to type Yeah will receive our own custom error message, telling them to try again.

We can further refine this code by having VB.NET test for more than one result on each Case line. As an example, for both "yes" and "YES", we would do the same thing, so we can handle them together:

```
Select Case question
    Case "yes","YES","Yes","Y"
      Message.Text= "Details will be sent."
    Case "no","NO","No","N"
      Message.Text= "We will make further contact by email."
    Case Else
      Message.Text= "Your answer " & strQuestion & " is not recognized."
    End Select
```

This will work fine, but do we really want to spend all that time dreaming up possible cases? VB.NET offers a completely different way to solve the case problem. If you change all input text to uppercase before testing, you can reduce the number of tests needed. The ToUpper() method of the string object will convert a string to uppercase, as follows, before we test it:

```
Dim upperCaseQuestion as String
upperCaseQuestion = question.toUpper
Select Case upperCaseQuestion
  Case "YES","Y"
    Message.Text= "Details will be sent."
  Case "NO","N"
    Message.Text= "We will make further contact by email."
  Case Else
    Message.Text= "Your answer " & strQuestion & " is not recognized."
  End Select
```

We've managed to cut down on the number of test statements that we need to worry about. However, in some situations, such as our previous random number guessing example, it proved more beneficial to use a dropdown list control to limit the range of possible answers.

Let's look at an example that uses `Select Case` to make a more detailed set of selections. In our holidays example we showed how the user could select from a set of destinations. Now we're going to go one better and provide a brief sales pitch depending on which destination the user selects. We will use `Select Case` to decide which pitch to use.

Try It Out – Using Select Case

1. *Open up your web page editor and type in the following:*

```
<script language="vb" runat="server">
Sub Page_Load()
  if Request.Form("Destination") <> "" then
    Select Case(Request.Form("Destination"))
      case "Barcelona"
        Message.Text = "You selected Spain's lively Catalan city"
      case "Oslo":
        Message.Text = "Experience the majesty of Norway's capital city"
      case "Lisbon":
        Message.Text = "Portugal's famous seaport and cultural hub"
      case else
        Message.Text = "you did not select a destination we travel to"
    End Select
  End if
End Sub
</script>

<html>
<head></head>
<body>
  <form runat="server">
  Select your choice of destination:
  <br><br>
  <asp:radiobuttonlist id="destination" runat="server">
    <asp:listitem>Barcelona</asp:listitem>
    <asp:listitem>Oslo</asp:listitem>
    <asp:listitem>Lisbon</asp:listitem>
  </asp:radiobuttonlist>
  <br><br>
  <input type="submit" value="Submit Choice">
  <br><br>
  <asp:label id="message" runat="server"/>
</form>
</body>
</html>
```

2. *Save this as `selectcase.aspx`*

3. View this in your browser:

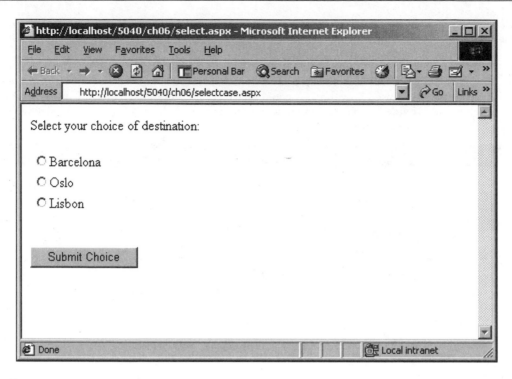

4. *Select two choices and click on* Submit Choice:

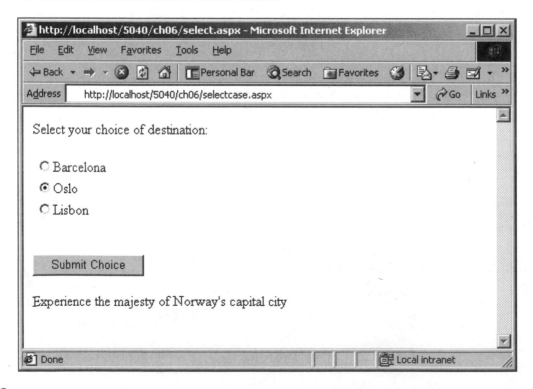

How It Works

There's a lot of code here, but it's probably simpler than the last example we looked at. We have a radio button list control, called `destination`, which allows the user to select a holiday destination:

```
<asp:radiobuttonlist id="destination" runat="server">
  <asp:listitem>Barcelona</asp:listitem>
  <asp:listitem>Oslo</asp:listitem>
  <asp:listitem>Lisbon</asp:listitem>
</asp:radiobuttonlist>
```

This is sent back by the form to the ASP.NET code.

We then test `Request.Form("Destination")` as we did in the last example with `Request.Form("Guess")`. This is to check whether our page has been run before. If it hasn't, then there will be nothing in either of these values, and we can skip to the end of the program and wait until the page is run again:

```
Sub Page_Load()
if Request.Form("Destination") <> "" then
  Select Case Structure
end if
end sub
```

If there is something in the variable, we take the contents and test them against various possibilities:

```
Select Case(Request.Form("Destination"))
  case "Barcelona"
    Message.Text = "You selected Spain's lively Catalan city"
  case "Oslo":
    Message.Text = "Experience the majesty of Norway's capital city"
  case "Lisbon":
    Message.Text = "Portugal's famous seaport and cultural hub"
```

As our page contains one question with three options, we deal with all of these possibilities within our `Select Case` structure. So if we have selected Oslo, then only the code in the `Case "Oslo"` section will be run.

There is a `Case Else` at the end. This should never be generated unless we have made a mistake in matching up the cases we can handle with the options we have presented the user:

```
case else
  Message.Text = "you did not select a destination we travel to"
End Select
```

If they don't select anything, then no message at all is displayed, as this is caught by our `If ... Then` structure. It's a simple example, but hopefully it demonstrates the potential power of case structures. Most importantly, it should be obvious how easy it is to add additional cases to a structure of this type, particularly compared to adding additional code to an `If ... Then ... ElseIf ... Else` structure.

There is one drawback of `Select Case` though, as it doesn't support comparison operators. You can only check for different cases of equality within the terms of the case. This means it might not always be appropriate in some situations (such as our age-range selector above).

These are the main kinds of decision-making structure, now it's time to move on to some looping structures.

Looping Structures In Detail

ASP.NET has several types of looping structures: Do While, Do ... Until, For ... Next and For ... Each. most of the time,However you will only use two of them. Do While and Do ... Until provide the same function with one minor difference in operation, while For ... Each is only used in conjunction with collections, something we will come across in a couple of chapters time.

When you require one of these structures, it's advisable that you decide which to use, depending on whether you know in advance how many loops you want to do. If you **can** determine the number of loops at the point when your program is about to begin the loop (for example, the loop will always be performed exactly ten times, or you have the number of loops stored in a variable), then use For ... Next. If you **do not** know ahead of time how many loops you want to do, and will have to decide after each loop whether to continue, then I suggest using Do While.

The For ... Next Structure

The For ... Next structure has three parts. The first is a line that describes how many times to repeat the loop. Second, comes a set of lines with action statements that carry out the task you want repeated. Finally, there is a line that indicates the end of the action statements and tells VB.NET to go back and repeat the action statements again:

```
For LoopCounter = StartValue To EndValue
    ...Loop Code here...
Next LoopCounter
```

Here is a simple example to get started. Imagine in our holiday example that we need an age declaration from each person going, as some of the adventure holidays require participants to be over a certain age. The company requires each user's signature to be handwritten. To do this, the user has to log in to the company's web site, get the sign-in sheet, and print it. Now, imagine we needed a sheet for five people; this code could be used to do it:

```
For intCounter = 1 to 5
   Message1.Text = Message1.Text & "Attendee Name _____" & _
    "<br /><br />Attendee Age _____<br /><br /><hr /><br />"
Next intCounter
```

From the first line, VB.NET begins the process of running the loop five times. In order to keep count we provide a variable called counter. The lines that will be repeated five times are contained between (but not including) the For ... line and the Next line. In this case, there is one statement needed, to create a line for an attendee to write their name and their age:

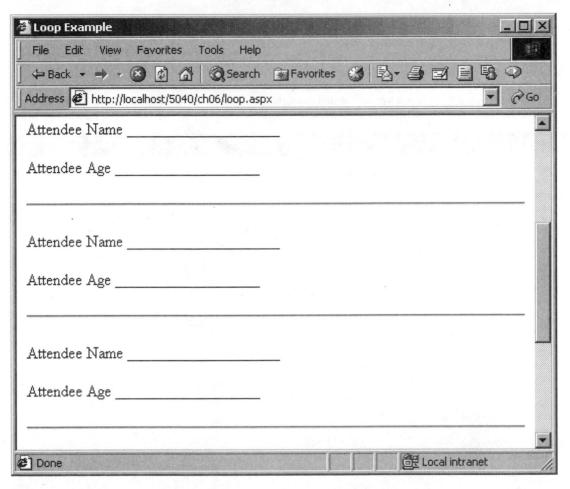

One quick point to note is that, to get the `<asp:label>` control to display five sections for signatures, instead of assigning a value to `Message1.Text`, we have added it to the contents of `Message1.Text`:

```
Message1.Text = Message1.Text & "Attendee Name...
```

This is because if we simply assigned the string to `Message1.Text` each time we went around the loop, we would not achieve the desired effect at all, as each time the assignment was performed, we'd replace the previous contents.

This simple first example assumes that we would always have five attendees. What if that number varied? In that event, we could have a first web page that asked for the number of attendees, and then use that number to determine how many lines to print. We can use `For ... Next` (instead of `Do While`), because **when we start the loop**, we know how many attendees there are.

If we assume that the text field, called `numberAttendees`, contains the number of attendees input by the user, then the responding page can grab the user's data from the field named `numberAttendees` and place it into the variable named `number`. Then we can begin the `For ... Next` loop. This time we don't go up through exactly five cycles. Rather, we go through the number of cycles specified by `number`. Our sign-in sheet is now usable for any number of attendees:

```
number = Request.Form("numberAttendees")
For counter = 1 to number
  Message1.Text = Message1.Text & "Attendee Name _____" & _
   "<br /><br />Attendee Age _____<br /><br /><hr /><br />"
Next counter
```

Okay – let's go and create a version of this example that takes a number from the user and supplies the requisite amount of signature/age sections to declare:

Try It Out – Using For ... Next

5. *Open your web page editor and type in the following:*

```
<script language="vb" runat="server">
Sub Page_load()
  Dim number As Integer
  Dim counter As Integer
  If Request.Form("numberAttendees")<>"" then
    number = Request.Form("numberAttendees")
    Message1.Text = ""
    For counter = 1 to number
      Message1.Text = Message1.Text & _
              "Attendee Name _____<br /><br />" & _
              "Attendee Age _____<br /><br /><hr /><br />"
    Next counter
  End If
End Sub
</script>

<html>
<head>
<title>Loop Example</title>
</head>
<body>
<form runat="server">
Enter the number of attendees(max 6):
<br>
<br>
<asp:dropdownlist id="numberAttendees" runat="server">
  <asp:listitem>1</asp:listitem>
  <asp:listitem>2</asp:listitem>
  <asp:listitem>3</asp:listitem>
  <asp:listitem>4</asp:listitem>
  <asp:listitem>5</asp:listitem>
  <asp:listitem>6</asp:listitem>
</asp:dropdownlist>
<br>
<br>
<input type="submit">
<br>
<br>
<asp:label id="message1" runat="server"/>
</form>
</body>
</html>
```

6. *Save this as* `loop.aspx`.

7. *Open* `loop.aspx` *in your browser:*

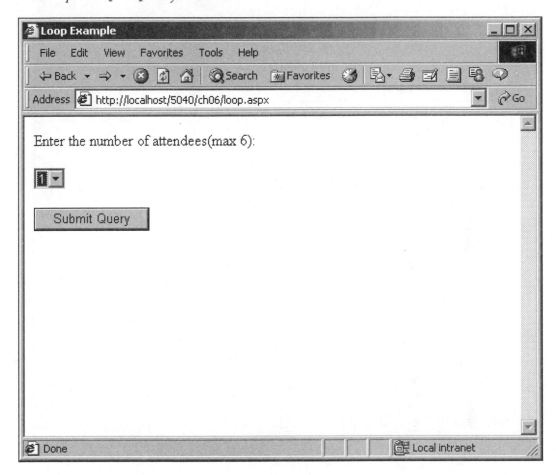

8. *Select a number and check the sheet that appears looks like the next screenshot:*

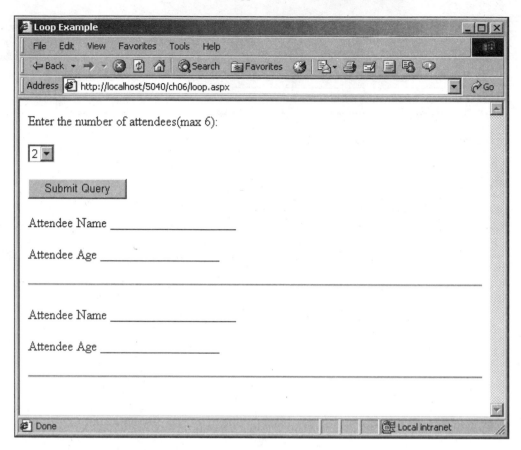

How It Works

In this example we selected "2" from the dropdown box, and two sections for signatures were displayed. The program required just one piece of information from the user in order to create the page:

```
<asp:dropdownlist id="numberAttendees" runat="server">
  <asp:listitem>1</asp:listitem>
  <asp:listitem>2</asp:listitem>
  <asp:listitem>3</asp:listitem>
  <asp:listitem>4</asp:listitem>
  <asp:listitem>5</asp:listitem>
  <asp:listitem>6</asp:listitem>
</asp:dropdownlist>
```

To limit it to a sensible number, we decided to impose a maximum of 6. This control passed the information across under the name numberAttendees.

The VB.NET code only required two variables. The first to hold the number supplied by the user, the second to hold the counter for the loop:

```
Sub Page_Load()
  Dim number As Integer
  Dim counter As Integer
```

Before we could use the loop to display the sections for signatures, we had to check to see whether this was the first time the user had accessed the page, by checking the contents of the Request.Form("numberAttendees") variable. If it was equal to nothing, we would skip the contents, jump to the end of the program, and wait for the user to submit a value:

```
If Request.Form("numberAttendees") <> "" then
  Loop Structure
End If
End Sub
```

Inside this branching structure, if there is a number in the numberAttendees variable, we can deduce this must be the number the user has supplied and assign it to our number variable.

```
number=Request.Form("numberAttendees")
```

Next we blank the contents of our <asp:label> control:

```
Message1.Text =""
```

If someone has used this example once it would work, but then each time the user made a second or third selection, they'd get a whole new set of signature spaces added on top of the ones they had earlier.

Then we can create a loop starting at one, and stopping when it has reached number.

```
For counter = 1 to number
  Message1.Text = Message1.Text & _
         "Attendee Name _____<br /><br />" & _
         "Attendee Age _____<br /><br /><hr /><br />"
Next
```

Each time the loop is executed, and the loop number isn't equal to number, then the <asp:label> control would have an extra section added. When the number of the loop in counter, equals the number held in number, the contents of the loop structure are still executed, however rather than returning to the beginning, the code then carries on past the Next statement and moves on to the statement after.

The Do While Structure

We briefly mentioned the Do While loop earlier in the chapter. You may remember that it's used to repeat a loop when we are not sure how many iterations to perform. So, on each loop it performs a test and continues looping as long as a **specified condition is true** (you can also use the construct Do While NOT, that is, loop while a specified condition **is false**). The Do While loops and For ... Next loops have two significant differences in syntax. First is the difference in key words: For ... Next has only one word (For) in the opening statement and ends with the word Next. Do While has **two** words in the opening statement (Do While) and ends with the word Loop. The code between Do While and Loop continues to run for as long as your specified condition exists.

Differences in Syntax Between For ... Next and Do While Loops

For ... Next Key Words	Do While Key Words
For *LoopCounter* = StartValue To EndValue	Do While loopCounter meets a specified condition
...	...
Lines of code to repeat	Lines of code to repeat, including at least one which may change loopCounter
...	...
Next	Loop

The second difference is the nature of the test to end the looping. For ... Next has a variable for counting, a start point, and an end point. Do While has an expression test: at the beginning of each loop VB.NET checks the expression and if it is True it runs the loop. If the expression is False, then the loop is not run and VB.NET jumps down in the code to the line after Loop.

There is a serious trap that every beginning programmer (and plenty of more experienced ones, too!) fall into: if you start a loop and do not provide a means for it to stop then it will continue forever as an infinite loop.

Most current servers will eventually cut off a given ASP.NET page, since the server needs to attend to other visitors and tries to optimize its resources. If a page seems to be hung up and not loading properly it could be hung because of an unresolved loop, and it can cause your web server not to respond.

The Do While form of looping is perfect for some tasks where it is impossible to know before you start executing the loop, how many times you are going to have to execute it. For example, we could write a page which simulates rolling a dice (by coming up with a random number between one and six) – and keeps rolling it until it gets a six. However, we don't know – at the time of writing our ASP.NET code, or even before we roll the first dice – how many times we'll have to roll the dice to get a six. So, for example, we could write:

```
Dim diceRoll As Integer

Do While diceRoll <> 6
   diceRoll = int(rnd * 6) + 1
   Message1.Text = Message1.Text & "Rolled a: " & diceRoll & "<br />"
Loop
```

VB.NET begins by establishing a variable: diceRoll will track the value of our last dice roll. Next, we begin the Do While loop. The trick is to use the right expression to stop the loop. In this case we will test at the beginning of each loop whether the last dice roll was a six. We then roll the dice, using the random number formula we met earlier, and store the value in diceRoll. Then we print some text from within the loop.

After the loop has executed once, the test is executed again, this time using the value rolled inside the loop. If it wasn't a six, then the loop is run again. If it was a six, then the loop is not executed again – the condition is false.

Let's put this code into an example.

Try It Out – Using Do While

1. *Open your web page editor and type in the following:*

```
<script language="vb" runat="server">
Sub Page_load()
  Dim diceRoll As Integer

  Do While diceRoll <> 6
    diceRoll = int(rnd * 6) + 1
    Message1.Text = Message1.Text & "Rolled a: " & diceRoll & "<br />"
  Loop
End Sub
</script>

<html>
<head>
<title>Do Loop Example</title>
</head>
<body>
  <asp:label id="message1" runat="server"/>
</body>
</html>
```

2. *Save this as* `doloop.aspx.`

3. *View this in your browser:*

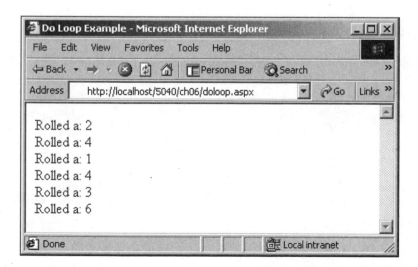

How It Works

We started by declaring a variable:

```
Sub Page_load()
  Dim diceRoll As Integer
```

Then we run the loop. If the last dice roll was anything other than a six, we want to roll again, so we use the inequality operator to tell VB.NET to keep running the loop, so long as the dice roll is not equal to six. We do this because we want the loop to stop once we have a six:

```
Do While diceRoll <> 6
   diceRoll = int(rnd * 6) + 1
   Message1.Text = Message1.Text & "Rolled a: " & diceRoll & "<br />"
Loop
```

When `diceRoll` equals 6, it will stop, and not execute the contents of the loop, instead jumping on to the next statement, beyond the loop. In this case it is:

```
End Sub
```

and this will end the VB.NET code.

Note that it is possible for this code to enter an infinite loop – it is, however, very, very, unlikely that the computer will keep on selecting random numbers forever without selecting a six at some point...

The Do ... Until Structure

You're not restricted by having to place the condition at the beginning of your loop. If you want your condition at the end, this is also possible. The `Do ... Until` structure works as follows:

```
Do
   ...code here...
Loop Until a condition is True
```

So, if you went back to the previous example, it could be amended as follows:

```
Dim diceRoll As Integer

Do
   diceRoll = int(rnd * 6) + 1
   Message1.Text = Message1.Text & "Rolled a: " & diceRoll & "<br />"
Loop Until diceRoll = 6
```

If you go back and amend your program `doloop.aspx`, so that it reads as above, and saved it as `doloop2.aspx`, you will see exactly the same sort of output (but with different numbers, normally):

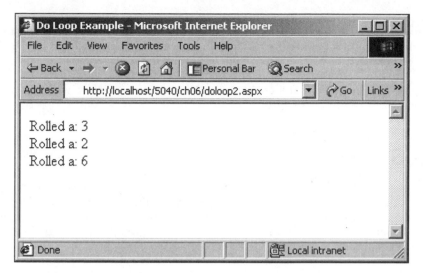

However, there is a very important difference. The difference is that your first block of code would be executed automatically, because we don't check our condition until the end of the loop. So in this way, you can deduce that the contents of this loop will **always** execute at least once, before exiting, while the first occurrence of the loop with Do While might never be executed at all, if the condition was never met. This actually suits our application better, since our original example actually tests the value of the last dice roll before we roll the dice for the first time. This test works, because the variable is initialized with the value of zero, so automatically passes the test and the loop is executed, but this is a slight cheat. The Loop Until version is programmatically a better simulation of the problem we are trying to code.

The rules of when to use Do While...Loop and when to use Do...Loop Until depend on whether actions are taken within the loop that absolutely have to occur at least once no matter what the value of the control variable, or whether there are actions within the loop that absolutely cannot be allowed to execute if the control variable is not acceptable. In the first case, the choice would be the Do ... Loop Until structure while the second case would require the Do While ... Loop.

The For ... Each Structure

Last, but not least is a cousin of the For ... Next statement, the For Each ... Next statement. It works in a similar way to For .. Next, except that it's used for each element inside an array or a collection. We'll meet collections, later, in Chapter 11. For now, you can think of them as being an ordered set of objects. We're not going to cover them in any detail now. However, they're worth a brief mention.

If you remember, in Chapter 4 we looked at arrays, and mentioned that they could be populated using a For ... Next statement. Well, For Each ... Next makes that task even simpler. Here's an example:

```
Dim Item As String
Dim strCities(2)  As String          'Declare an array of string variables
strCities(0) = "London"              'Populate it
strCities(1) = "Paris"
strCities(2) = "Munich"

For Each Item In strCities
   Message.Text = Message.Text & Item & "<BR>"    'List the contents of each
                                                  'item
Next
```

It looks almost identical to For ... Next – the only difference is that you don't have to specify the number of items you want to loop through, VB.NET will simply start with the first item in the array and then repeat the loop until it reaches the last item. In this case, each item is listed on the screen, so, if there were one hundred cities in our array, each one would be displayed by this loop.

We've spent a lot of time looking at these important looping controls. Now, we'll turn our attention to the equally important jumping structures.

Jumping Structures In Detail

As you write more ASP.NET code you'll find that you want to use the same code in more than one place. ASP.NET allows you to write code once, then run it as many times as needed to support the main body of your code. These mini-programs are called procedures. We want ASP.NET to jump away from execution of the main body of code (which is also a procedure itself), run through the commands of a procedure and then return to executing the main body of code.

For example, you may have some code to insert lines of text about how to contact the Sales department. If you would like to have these show up in various places on the page, but want to avoid having to rewrite the code separately each time, you can put them into a procedure, then whenever you want the code to run you can invoke the procedure, rather than rewrite the code.

There are two types of **procedure**:

❏   Subroutines carry out an action. For example, a Sub would be used to carry out the actions of putting text onto a page.

❏   Functions carry out action statements and **return an answer** to your code. A function could be used to calculate a delivery date and return that answer to your main program.

So what are the benefits of using these structures?

Modularization

When you come to write a program, normally you stop and think about what tasks need to be performed, and split the program up into several smaller tasks. Think of these tasks as modules. Programmers write code in modern programming languages using modules and compile these modules into one large application. Modules work as black boxes, with just values going in, or coming out. This makes it easier to test your code: If you know a particular module works without error and, when it's plugged into another new and untested module, it produces wrong results, you can narrow your search down to the untested module straight away.

Also if a module performs a specific task, you can re-use it each time you need to perform that task. So if you put 100 lines of code in one module and call it 10 times in your code, that's 900 lines of code you've saved already! Modularization also makes it easier for you to trace the "flow" of a program from section to section. Imagine one big program that jumped to different places within itself throughout the code. This is bound to become confusing, but with clearly labeled modules connecting to one another, the task of following the flow of a program is made much easier.

Subroutines

Subroutines are easy to write – in fact, we've been writing subroutines already. When we've put code in our pages, we've written it in the following form:

```
<script language="vb" runat="server">
Sub Page_load()
   ...
End Sub
</script>
```

Page_load() is in fact a subroutine, or sub. The code that we write inside this subroutine is executed by ASP.NET whenever our page is loaded – ASP.NET **calls** our subroutine.

We can write subroutines with any name (provided it begins with a letter, and only contains letters, numbers and underscore characters), and call them from within our own code. We write them in exactly the same way as the Page_load() subroutine: The first line consists of the Sub keyword, then the name of our subroutine, followed by a pair of brackets. Then we write the code we want to execute whenever our subroutine is called. Finally, we end the subroutine with the line End Sub.

```
Sub Subroutine_name()
   ...Subroutine code...
End Sub
```

For example, we might write a subroutine to insert a linebreak at the end of a label control:

```
Sub Insert_linebreak()
   Message.text = Message.text & "<BR>"
End Sub
```

We write subroutine definitions like this inside our script tags, at the same level as our Page_load() code – never in between the Sub Page_load() and End Sub lines. We must never nest subroutine (or function) definitions inside one another.

Calling Subroutines

Our example subroutine can be called whenever needed, by using the keyword Call followed by the name of the subroutine, as in the following example:

```
<script language="vb" runat="server">

Sub Insert_linebreak()
   Message.text = Message.text & "<BR>"
End Sub

Sub Page_load()
  Message.text = "First line"
  Call Insert_linebreak()
  Message.text = Message.text & "Second line"
  Call Insert_linebreak()
  Message.text = Message.text & "Third line"
  Call Insert_linebreak()
End Sub

</script>
```

Note that we call our own subroutine from within the code in the `Page_load()` subroutine. When our page is loaded, ASP.NET calls `Page_load()`, and the first line of our code is executed. Then, when the second line is executed, control moves to our subroutine. The line of code in the subroutine is executed, and then control returns to the next line in the `Page_load()` sub. This continues until the end of `Page_load()` is reached, and control is handed back to ASP.NET.

Although you can use the `Call` keyword to call the subroutine, you could just as easily call it without this keyword:

```
Message.text = "First line"
Insert_linebreak()
Message.text = Message.text & "Second line"
Insert_linebreak()
Message.text = Message.text & "Third line"
Insert_linebreak()
```

*As you **cannot** call functions with the `call` keyword, you might choose to use the full version as it makes it more evident in your code that the procedure being called is a subroutine and not a function.*

Passing Parameters

We can make subroutines more versatile by including parameters. This allows the behavior of the subroutine to be varied from one execution to the next. The result of calling the subroutine will depend on data sent from the place in your code where you make the call, into the subroutine. A parameter (sometimes called an argument) is a piece of data that is passed to the subroutine. If we write a subroutine which expects to have a parameter passed to it, we can supply it by placing the piece of data we want to pass inside the brackets after the subroutine name:

```
Call Insert_line("Hello")
```

This passes whatever is in the variable Message into the subroutine. We can build subroutines so that they can expect to receive any number of parameters. In such cases, we provide the parameters by separating them with commas:

```
Call Insert_line_into_label(Message, "Hello")
```

As you can see, we can use variables or strings as parameters for subroutines – in fact, we can use anything which can be evaluated to a value, including mathematical or logical expressions, numbers, or objects.

So, how do we build subroutines which take parameters, and how do we make the code within or subroutines react to the values we pass in?

When we define a subroutine which takes parameters, we need to include declarations in between the brackets after the subroutine's name for variables which will be used to contain the parameters passed in. We declare these parameter variables by specifying a name, and a type, just like we do when using the `Dim` keyword. For example, we can write the following:

```
Sub Insert_line(Line as String)
   Message.text = Message.text & Line & "<BR>"
End Sub
```

This says that the subroutine takes a single argument, a string, and that within this subroutine, the value passed in will be stored in a variable called `Line`. We then use the variable `Line` just like any other variable, and add it to the text of the label `Message`, followed by an HTML linebreak.

There is some more to defining and using parameters, which we'll come to once we've looked at VB.NET's other form of procedure, the function.

Functions

Functions are written in a similar way to subroutines, but with several special characteristics that handle the returning of information.

Defining Functions

First, when you write a function you use `Function` (instead of `Sub`) on the first line and `End Function` (instead of `End Sub`) on the last line. The naming rules of functions are the same as for subroutines – start with a letter, no spaces, and avoid symbols (except underscores). For example, the following function declaration is valid:

```
Function MyFunction(Param As String)
   ... code here ...
End Function
```

As with subroutines, we can declare functions which take any number of parameters, or none at all.

Returning Values

Once the function has done its calculations, it has to report the results back to the calling code. VB.NET provides two methods for performing this operation. You can simply explicitly tell VB.NET which value you want to return, using the `Return` keyword:

```
Function MyFunction(Param As String)
  Return 3
End Function
```

Alternatively, you can use a variable (usable only within this function) that is automatically created when your function is called, with the same name as the function. Whatever value is placed into that variable will be is sent back to VB.NET when the function is finished. For example:

```
Function MyFunction(Param As String)
  MyFunction = 3
End Function
```

In addition, VB.NET makes it possible for our code to specify exactly what type the value returned by the function will be. As usual, we use the `As` keyword, followed by the type. We place the type specification after the function's parameter list:

```
Function MyFunction(Param As String) As Integer
   Return 3
End Function
```

This makes it clear that the function takes a single string as an argument, and returns a value of type `int`.

Calling Functions

You can call a function by just typing its name followed by double parentheses:

```
ReturnedValue = MyFunction("Hello")
```

This line will lead to the function being called, and the return value being placed in the variable `ReturnedValue`. We can use functions which we write ourselves in exactly the same way as the built in functions we used earlier, like `rnd()` and `int()`. We can use the returned value as we have here, to assign it to a variable, or we can use it in a more complex statement:

```
Message.Text = Message.Text & MyFunction("Hello")
```

Passing Parameters By Value

When we call functions and subroutines, we need to understand a little more about what's actually happening when we pass parameters into them. By default, simple data values are passed to functions and subroutines **by value** in VB.NET. This means that when the parameter variables are created inside the function or subroutine, they are all set up to have the value that was passed in. This may seem like it goes without saying, but this has some subtle consequences. Effectively, it means that inside a procedure, we are working with a copy of the original data. Look at the following code:

```
<script language="vb" runat="server">

  Sub Increment(Number as Integer)
    Number = Number + 1
  End Sub

  Sub Page_Load()
    Dim A As Integer
    A = 1
    Increment(A)
    Message.Text = A
  End Sub

</script>

<html>
<head>
<title>Sample Function Page</title>
</head>
<body>
  <asp:label id="Message" runat="server"/>
</body>
</html>
```

We've written a subroutine which takes an integer as a parameter, and increments it. However, when we use this subroutine from our `Page_load()` subroutine, we pass in a variable containing the number 1, but when we display the contents of this variable, we find it hasn't been incremented. Why is this? It is because the data is passed by value.

When `Increment(A)` is called in the above code, the value stored in the variable A (which is 1) is copied into a new variable inside the `Increment()` routine, called `Number`. The `Increment()` routine then adds one to the value stored in this variable – but the value stored in A is left untouched.

Passing by value means that a copy is made for the subroutine or function to play with, and the data in the calling procedure is left untouched.

We can make this default behavior explicit by using the keyword `ByVal` in our function or subroutine definition:

```
Function FindDueDate(ByVal CheckOutDate As Date)
    return datCheckOutDate + 14
End Function
```

While this has no effect at all on the function and what it does, it does help to remind us of how the parameter is being handled.

Passing Parameters By Reference

What happens if you did want the calculation within your function to affect the variable's contents? Well then you could pass the parameter **by reference**. It is possible to pass simple data types by reference by making a small change at the beginning of the function or subroutine definition. Objects are a little different; they are known as reference types, and the default behavior is for them to be passed by reference, not by value. We'll look at what this means in a moment. First, let's amend our Increment sample to use pass-by-reference:

```
<script language="vb" runat="server">

    Sub Increment(ByRef Number as Integer)
      Number = Number + 1
    End Sub

    Sub Page_Load()
      Dim A As Integer
      A = 1
      Increment(A)
      Message.Text = A
    End Sub

</script>

<html>
<head>
<title>Sample Function Page</title>
</head>
<body>
  <asp:label id="Message" runat="server"/>
</body>
</html>
```

All we need to add is the keyword `ByRef` at the front of the parameter passed to the function. Now we find that the increment procedure actually works the way we expect. What happens now is that when the `Increment(A)` call is made, instead of a copy being taken of the value stored in `A`, a second variable is made which points to the same piece of data that `A` points to – a reference to the value in `A` is copied into the `Number` variable inside the procedure. This way, whenever the code inside the subroutine makes a change to the `Number` variable, it is also changing the data in the `A` variable as well.

As mentioned above, this behavior is the default for objects, which are also known as reference types. Look at the following subroutine:

```
Sub AddLineToLabel(Target As Label, Line As String)
    Target.Text = Target.Text & Line & "<BR>"
End Sub
```

This subroutine takes two arguments: a target label control (a label is just an object, so is a reference type), and a string. The idea is that it will add the supplied string to the supplied label control, followed by an HTML linebreak.

Now, we can call this subroutine using code like this:

```
<script language="vb" runat="server">

...

Sub Page_Load()
    AddLineToLabel(Message, "Hello World")
End Sub
</script>

<html>
<head>
<title>Sample Function Page</title>
</head>
<body>
  <asp:label id="Message" runat="server"/>
</body>
</html>
```

The important lines are highlighted. We've declared a label control called `Message`. Within the `Page_Load()` subroutine, then, we can call our subroutine, passing in the label, `Message`, and a string we want adding to it. However, we said before that data passed in as parameters is passed by value, and that this means that a copy is made. Surely this means that within our subroutine, it will be attempting to add text to a copy of the actual label on the page, not the real label? Well, running this page shows this is not the case. The label object is passed by reference – and the subroutine is able to access the original object. This is why objects are called reference types.

For this reason, you might want to consider labeling the parameters of your subroutines and functions with the keywords `ByRef` and `ByVal` even where they don't change the default behavior of the type being passed, to make it clear what is actually going on when you pass in data. For example:

```
Sub AddLineToLabel(ByRef Target As Label, ByVal Line As String)
    Target.Text = Target.Text & Line & "<BR>"
End Sub
```

A Function Example

This example will take the date that the user checked out a book, use a function to calculate the date the book should be returned on, and then display this to the user. We don't want to alter the checkout date in any way in our function so we will pass our parameter by value.

Try It Out – Using Functions

1. *Open up your web page editor again and type in the following:*

```
<script language="vb" runat="server">
  Sub Page_Load()
  Dim DueDate As Date
  Dim CheckOutDate As Date

  CheckoutDate = Now()
  DueDate = FindDueDate(CheckoutDate)
  Message1.text = "<br>Your books were checked OUT on " & Checkoutdate
  Message2.text = "<br>Your books are due on " & DueDate
  End Sub

  Function FindDueDate(CheckOutDate As Date) As Date
      return DateValue(DateAdd("d", 14, CheckOutDate))
  End Function
</script>

<html>
<head>
<title>Sample Function Page</title>
</head>
<body>
  <h2>Thank you for using the On-Line Library.</h2>
  <asp:label id="message1" runat="server"/>
  <asp:label id="message2" runat="server"/>
</body>
</html>
```

2. *Save this as* `function.aspx`

3. *View this in your browser:*

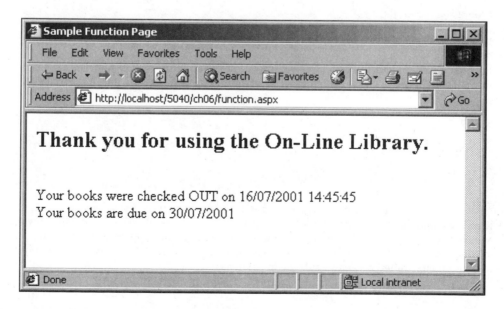

How It Works

Within our VB.NET code there are two procedures. One is the subroutine, `Sub Page_Load()` that is called automatically by ASP.NET, the other is a function, called from within the `Page_Load()` subroutine. We'll start by looking at our function:

```
Function FindDueDate(CheckOutDate As Date) As Date
    Return DateValue(DateAdd("d", 14, CheckOutDate))
End Function
```

It has the relatively mundane task of adding '14' to the date supplied by the user. The only problem is the little matter of date arithmetic. Date arithmetic doesn't involve adding '14' to our date and hoping VB.NET can sort the rest. Indeed it can't, and would generate an error if you tried to do it that way. Instead you need the custom VB.NET `DateAdd` function, which takes three arguments:

```
DateAdd(interval, number, date)
```

The first is the interval you want to add, such as days, weeks, months or years. By specifying `d`, we are saying we want to add `days`. The number we wish to add is '14', hence our second argument. The third is the date we supplied as an argument to the function, `CheckOutDate`. Lastly we use a second function `DateValue`. This simply chops off the time part of any function, leaving only the date. We supply the results of the `DateAdd` function to this function.

So it's a little more complex, but here's a summary of what our function does. It takes the `CheckOutDate` variable as an argument and then uses two VB.NET built-in functions `DateAdd` and `DateValue` to calculate a date 14 days from the date contained in `CheckOutDate`.

To see how `CheckOutDate` is created, let's look at our main procedure. We start by declaring two variables, both of type `Date`. The first is the date returned by the function, the date we have to return the book by, the second is the date we checked the book out on:

```
Sub Page_Load()
Dim DueDate As Date
Dim CheckOutDate As Date
```

The checkout date is calculated using the VB.NET `Now()` function to give today's date. Of course, this function returns the time as well, which we later chop off in our function using `DateValue`:

```
CheckoutDate = Now()
```

Next we run our function, and assign the value returned by it to the variable `varDueDate`:

```
DueDate = FindDueDate(CheckoutDate)
```

You might notice that we're passing in as a parameter a variable which has the same name as the parameter has within the function. there is, in fact, no significance to this whatsoever. We can call the two variables whatever we like – we have simply chosen in both places within the program to store values representing the date on which someone has checked out a book in a variable called `CheckoutDate`. There's nothing to stop us using a completely different name inside the function as follows:

```
Function FindDueDate(HeeBeeGeeBee As Date) As Date
    return DateValue(DateAdd("d", 14, HeeBeeGeeBee))
End Function
```

We've just chosen to call it the same name to make the variable easier to track. If you changed the Try It Out in the above way, it would still work identically.

Lastly we use two `<asp:label>` controls to display our checkout date, and the date we must return the books by:

```
Message1.Text = "<br>Your books are checked OUT on " & datCheckoutdate
Message2.Text = "<br>Your books are due on " & datDueDate
```

Hopefully you can see how VB.NET's own functions and our custom functions blend in with each other. Our own function combines two VB.NET built-in functions together and adds '14' to return its own result. All 3 functions rely on arguments being passed to work correctly. We pass the current date to our function. The function takes the current date and adds 14 to it, using the VB.NET function `DateAdd`, which then passes the new value to the `DateValue` function. When the `DateValue` function chops the time off and returns the value to our function, we're able to display the results.

Variable Scope

Before we looked at our function example, we briefly discussed the concept of passing variables as parameters to and from functions. However we saw that it was possible when passing by value for the variable to have one value inside a function and another outside of it. In fact it was almost as if they were two entirely different variables.

With our ASP.NET programs that didn't contain subroutines and functions, up to now we assumed that when you created a variable it had one unique name to identify it. However now we've admitted our applications could have many subroutines and functions. So what happens to the idea that when you name a variable, it should have a **unique** name? We've just seen that with functions, it doesn't need to. If you use a variable in one subroutine and use a variable with the same name inside another subroutine, far from being able to reuse the contents of the first variable, you have in effect two different variables.

The variable is said to have `scope`. Scope refers to the area in which a variable is used. A variable can exist within a function, and not outside, and this is said to have local scope. A variable that exists across many different subroutines and functions, storing the same value is said to have **global scope**. The idea that a variable need not have influence over the whole contents of a page, but rather only directly over the part of a page you want to use it for, is a powerful one, and confers performance enhancements. VB.NET only has to track it for a short amount of time, rather than the whole lifetime of a page; it uses less memory and when the subroutine that uses the variable is over, the memory is freed up.

Local Variables

So let's have a look at variables that only exist within the confines of a subroutine or function. On the surface this can look very complex, but it is really quite straightforward if you look at it closely. Consider two variables, both with the name `Different`. We'll try to assign different values to these two variables:

```
Dim Different As String

Different = "Hello, I'm variable one"
Different = "Hello, I'm variable two"
```

If you output the value of `Different`, you'd find that it contained the string "Hello, I'm variable two". We've created one variable, and assigning different values to it leads to the previous value being overwritten.

This isn't the case when you declare the variable in two different subroutines. If you defined `Different` twice in two different declarations, then you'd see a different result:

```
Sub Procedure_Number_1()
  Dim Different As String
  Different = "Hello, I'm variable one"
End Sub

Sub Procedure_Number_2()
  Dim Different As String
  Different = "Hello, I'm variable two"
End Sub
```

If you output the value of `Different` in `Procedure_Number_1()`, then you'd get "Hello, I'm variable one". If you return the value of `Different` in `Procedure_Number_2()`, you'd get "Hello, I'm variable two". However, if you **then** go back and run `Procedure_Number_1()` again, you'd get "Hello, I'm variable one" again. Hence, they are effectively two different variables, although they share the same name.

These variables are known as local **variables** (in the Microsoft documentation, they're called procedure-level variables), because they are local to the subroutine that created them. Outside that subroutine, the local variable has no value: this is because the lifetime of the variable ends when the subroutine ends. As these local variables are only in effect for the lifetime of a subroutine, ASP.NET doesn't have to worry about keeping track of them over the whole page. When a local variable is created, it only exists while the subroutine that invoked it is running. Once the program exits the subroutine, the variable's lifetime is over, thus freeing memory and resources, and increasing performance. You cannot create a variable twice within its scope (you're not allowed to use the `Dim` statement twice in the same subroutine with the same variable name). You can't have two variables within the same scope (i.e. same function or subroutine) with the same name.

Block Level Variables

There is also another type of scope, known as block level scope. Block level scope is where you use a set of statements terminated by an `End If`, `Else`, `Loop`, or `Next` statement. So block level variables are local variables that can only be used within a `For ... Next` or `If ... Then ... Else ... End If` type structures.

A variable declared within a block can be used only within that block. In the following example, the scope of the variable `strBlockLevelVariable` is the block between `If` and `End If`, and `strBlockLevelVariable` can no longer be referenced when execution passes out of the block:

```
If intCheck = true Then
  Dim strBlockLevelVariable As String
  strBlockLevelVariable = "Very Short Lived!"
End If
Message1.Text = strBlockLevelVariable
```

`Message1.Text` would contain nothing. The advantage of using this is that you use even less memory than procedure-level variables and could potentially boost performance even further. The disadvantage is that if you aren't careful, you can accidentally declare a variable inside a block, and then try to access it outside the block scope. For this reason, it is a good idea to `Dim` all the procedure-level variables you use within each function or subroutine at the very top of the procedure – before any blocks have begun.

Now, let's take a look at how to use two procedure-level local variables. To demonstrate that they are local we'll make them share the same name during our ASP.NET program.

Try It Out – Creating Procedure-level Local Variables

1. *Start your favorite editor and create the following program:*

```
<script language="vb" runat="server">
Sub Page_Load()
    Response.Write ("<BR />Calling Subroutine 1...")
    Call Subroutine_1()
    Response.Write ("<BR />Calling Subroutine 2...")
    Call Subroutine_2()
    Response.Write ("<BR />Calling Subroutine 1...")
    Call Subroutine_1()
End Sub

  Sub Subroutine_1()
    Dim Different As String
    Different = "<i>Hello I'm the variable Different in Subroutine 1</i>"
    Response.Write (Different)
  End Sub

  Sub Subroutine_2()
    Dim Different As String
    Different = "<b>Hello I'm the variable Different in Subroutine 2</b>"
    Response.Write (Different)
  End Sub
</script>
<html>
<head>
<title>Scope</title>
</head>
<body>
</body>
</html>
```

2. *Save the program as* `local.aspx`

3. *Execute it in your browser of choice:*

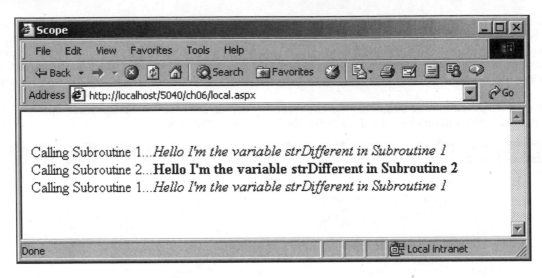

How It Works

This program contains two almost identical subroutines:

```
Sub Subroutine_1
    Dim Different As String
    Different = "<i>Hello I'm the variable Different in Subroutine 1</i>"
    Response.Write (Different)
End Sub

    Sub Subroutine_2
    Dim Different As String
    Different = "<b>Hello I'm the variable Different in Subroutine 2</b>"
    Response.Write (Different)
End Sub
```

However, each of the variables named `Different` is declared and assigned a value within the confines of its respective procedure, and so doesn't exist outside the context of that subroutine. We surround the contents of the variable in subroutine 1 with `<i>` tags, and the contents of the variable in subroutine 2 with `<b>` tags to make them stand out from each other. Neither variable interferes with the running of the other, despite the fact that they both have the same name.

If you asked the ASP.NET program to print the value of `Different` from **outside** either of these subroutines, it would return an error saying that variable hadn't been declared or was out of scope.

In our main program we call these subroutines alternately:

```
Sub Page_Load()
    Response.Write ("<BR>Calling Subroutine 1...")
    Call Procedure_1()
    Response.Write ("<BR>Calling Subroutine 2...")
    Call Procedure_2()
    Response.Write ("<BR>Calling Subroutine 1...")
    Call Procedure_1()
End Sub
```

Hence we can see that the value of Different in Subroutine 1, is not affected by the value of Different in Subroutine 2. Once again we stress here that unless you deliberately intend for some reason to name both variables the same, for readability's sake alone, you should give all your variables unique names.

Global Variables

So, if variables created in subroutines are local to the subroutine that created them, how do you go about ensuring that the value of one variable persists from one subroutine to the next, when you need it to? In other words, how do you extend the lifetime of your variables? The answer comes in the form of global variables. These are variables that are declared **outside** procedures.

The lifetime of a global variable begins at the start of the ASP.NET page and ends at the end of the page, and spans any procedures created within the script. In comparison, local variables contained within a procedure are destroyed when the procedure is exited, and hence the memory space is saved. It's a good idea to use local variables wherever possible, because it makes things easier to read, helps to avoid bugs in code and improves performance. However, there are times when you want to use the same variable throughout many different subroutines.

Try It Out – Using Global Variables

Let's see how we can amend our previous program to include a global level variable. We're going to simply add a new global variable to the program and then display it from inside and outside the subroutines:

1. *Load up the previous program, local.aspx, in your preferred web page editor and add the following lines:*

```
<script language="vb" runat="server">

Dim Global As String ="<br><u>Hello I'm a persistent global variable</u>"

Sub Page_Load()
    Response.Write (Global)
    Response.Write ("<BR>Calling Subroutine 1...")
    Subroutine_1()
    Response.Write ("<BR>Calling Subroutine 2...")
    Subroutine_2()
    Response.Write ("<BR>Calling Subroutine 1...")
    Subroutine_1()
End Sub

  Sub Subroutine_1()
    Dim Different As String
    Different = "<i>Hello I'm the variable Different in " & _
                                        "Subroutine 1</i>"
    Response.Write (Different)
    Response.Write (Global)
  End Sub

  Sub Subroutine_2()
    Dim Different As String
    Different = "<b>Hello I'm the variable Different in " & _
                                        "Subroutine _ 2</b>"
    Response.Write (Different)
    Response.Write (Global)
```

```
   End Sub
</script>
<html>
<head>
<title>Scope</title>
</head>
<body>
</body>
</html>
```

2. *Save it this time as* `global.aspx`

3. *Run this program in your browser.*

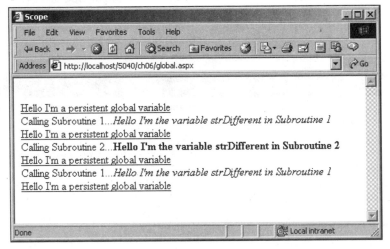

How It Works

We've not changed our original program much; other than adding new text the sole addition is the global variable, `Global`. This variable is declared outside all of the subroutines as follows:

```
Dim Global As String ="<br><u>Hello I'm a persistent global variable</u>"
```

It is also assigned the text `"Hello I'm a persistent global variable"` at the same time. This is because if you declare it first and assign it a value on separate lines, VB.NET will generate an error – remember, we're only allowed to have declarations in our top level script elements, not code, and adding a second line to assign a value to the variable would require us to add a line of code. A `Dim` statement qualifies as a declaration, since it declares a global variable. Similarly, functions and subroutines are allowed because they are declarations. `Global` is then called at various points in the program.

We first display this string from the `Page_load()` subroutine; the second time, from within subroutine 1; the third time from within subroutine 2; and the final time from within subroutine 1, again. Each time, the variable is displayed using the following code, so there's no trickery of any sort:

```
Response.Write (Global)
```

The output shows how global variables and local variables can be used side by side in any ASP.NET program. In fact you can use both procedure-level local variables and block level local variables together, but just be sure to remember what kind of scope each has!

Summary

This chapter has been a whirlwind tour through the key building blocks of VB.NET. The three main structures we looked at were branching structures (`If ... Then` and `Select Case`), looping structures (`For ... Next`, `Do While`, `Do Until`, `For ... Each`) and jumping structures (functions and subroutines). These enable us to control the execution of ASP.NET programs by making decisions about which particular branch to take, by repeating a piece of code several times, or by being able to jump out of a subroutine and in to another, whenever required.

Together with the last few chapters, this gives us a solid grounding in most of the VB.NET coding basics. In the next chapter we will be looking at events and how they are used in ASP.NET programming. They will fundamentally alter the way in which you view your programs in ASP.NET and even how you write them.

Exercises

1. *For each of the following Boolean expressions, say for what values of A each of them will evaluate to True and when they will evaluate to False*

   a. NOT A > 0 OR A > 5

   b. A > 1 AND A < 5 OR A > 7 AND A < 10

   c. A < 10 OR A > 12 AND NOT A > 20

2. Suggest a loop structure which would be appropriate for each of the following scenarios, and justify your choice:

   a. Displaying a set of items from a shopping list, stored in an array

   b. Displaying a calendar for the current month

   c. Looking through an array to find the location of a specific entry

   d. Drawing a chessboard using an HTML table

   Bonus: write an ASP.NET page to perform one of these tasks

3. Write a function that generates a random integer between two integers passed as parameters. Build an ASP.NET page which allows you to enter the lower and upper limits, and generates a set of random numbers in that range.

4. Write an ASP.NET page that displays the number of days until Christmas. You'll need to use the following function:

```
DateDiff(Interval as String, Date1 As Date, Date2 As Date)
```

You need to pass in `"d"` as the interval specifier to get a difference in days.

Modify your page so that it provides the number of days until one of five different public holidays, according to a user's selection.

5. Suggest a situation when you might want to pass variables into a function or subroutine by reference. Write an ASP.NET page to illustrate your example.

Event-driven Programming and Postback

One of the most important features of ASP.NET is the way it allows you to use an event-driven programming model. This isn't a new thing, Windows itself is an event-driven environment. What this means is that nothing happens under Windows unless it is in response to something (an event) that Windows has detected. Example of such events, could be a user clicking on a desktop icon, pressing a key, or opening the Start menu. ASP.NET works in a similar manner.

In ASP.NET, web forms rely on events to trigger the running of code housed in subroutines. As we've just mentioned, this is nothing new, it's been possible to run small sections of client-side code on the user's browser with HTML for a long time. What ASP.NET is doing differently is using **postback**, where additional information is sent back to the server for processing, rather than doing it on the client-side browser. This postback means that information can be sent back to the server when an event is triggered by the user. This is a very powerful concept, as it means we can do things like remembering which option in a list was selected, or what information a user typed into a textbox, between page submissions. We've already seen these features in action in Chapter 3, but so far we've only hinted at what has been going on – now we're going to look at it in more detail.

The event-driven nature of ASP.NET however, doesn't just stop there. It allows us to completely modularize our code into separate functions and subroutines, and only use those sections when a specific situation requiring them has arisen. We're going to see how ASP.NET can pass back information to the user, in response to particular events being generated, in a whole new way; and how this will enable us to create web forms that not only look different from the ones we have seen in previous chapters, but are faster, more efficient and work in a more logical way.

In this chapter we'll look at:

- ❑   What an event is
- ❑   What event-driven programming is
- ❑   ASP.NET "generic" events
- ❑   HTML events
- ❑   ASP.NET server control events
- ❑   The ASP button control
- ❑   Server-side processing of events
- ❑   How the event-driven programming model changes the way in which we program

What is an event?

Let's start by defining exactly what an event is in the real world. For example, a fictional employee, Joe Public, sits in Marketing doing his Sales job, talking to contacts. He can receive information in two ways, one is via the phone, to say things like "We need to re-stock ten cans of jumping beans". When the phone rings, this is an event that he can respond to. He'll answer the phone and take appropriate action, such as sending out an extra ten cans of beans. So an event is just something that happens that can be detected and reacted to.

Extending our example further, Joe Public can also receive news via emails, such as a new policy from the boss, meaning he has to put $1 on all canned goods. This is a different event. Joe Public can also react to the event in any way he chooses. He can phone the stores and say "I'm afraid, I've got to charge you $1 extra for the cans of jumping beans", or he could say, "Stuff it boss! We charge too much for our beans anyway, I'm quitting". So the way that events are responded to is variable, and determined by the individual person, or object.

You can break down our event-driven environment into three chronological sections:

- ❏ An events occurs – for example the phone rings

- ❏ The event is detected by the system – Joe Public hears the phone

- ❏ The system reacts to the event – Joe Public answers the phone

In an operating system such as Windows events occur in a very similar manner. A user clicks the mouse. The mouse sends a message to the Operating System. The Operating System receives the message from the mouse, and generates an `onclick` event. This event is detected by the Operating System and appropriate action taken, such as displaying a menu or highlighting a piece of text.

What is Event-driven Programming?

Event-driven programming fundamentally changes the nature of the programming model. We leave behind the idea of sequential pages being processed on a server, and look instead at proper event-driven programming, where the server responds to events triggered by the user. This may all sound like gobbledygook at the moment, but bear with us. All we mean by this, is that before event-driven programming your programs would execute from top to bottom, like this:

```
Line 1
Line 2
Line 3
Line 4
```

Broadly speaking, "traditional" programming languages (those over ten years old) will start with the first line of your code, process it, move on to the second line, process that, and then move on to the third. Even when functions and subroutines are used it doesn't change the order of execution a great deal – as one procedure calls another, which calls another, and so on. So there is still an ordered sequence of execution.

The concept of event-driven programming changes all of this – with events, this sequential way of doing things is no longer appropriate. Consider the Windows operating system, again. Windows doesn't execute in a sequential fashion. If you click on a menu, you expect the menu to appear instantly, if you double click on an icon, then you expect the corresponding program will run immediately, you don't want to have to wait for Windows to finish whatever it is doing first. Indeed, you don't have to, because Windows is event-driven and able to react to most things instantly. Under the covers, Windows is waiting for an event to occur. As soon as one does it will take the appropriate action to deal with that event.

Without events most Windows programs couldn't run. Windows doesn't run Word, Notepad, or the Calculator by itself, as part of a sequential series of executions, it only loads them when the user requests them. This same principle of programming is being used in ASP.NET. Typically, the code in your web page (not HTML code, but client-side scripting) will be run by the browser, and it will react to your mouse-click by itself. With ASP.NET however, the processing of events is shifted to the server.

ASP.NET Events

Everything in ASP.NET comes down to objects, and in particular the page **object** we mentioned in Chapter 2. Each web form you create is a page object in its own right. You can think of the entire web form as being like an executable program whose output is HTML. Every time a page is called the object goes through a series of stages – initializing, processing, and disposing of information. The page object performs these stages each time the page is called therefore they happen every time a round trip to the server occurs. Each one of these stages can generate events, in the same way that clicking a mouse button can in Windows.

What happens in ASP.NET, is that as you view your ASP.NET web form, a series of events are generated on your web server. The main events that are generated are as follows:

- ❑ Page_Init – Occurs when the page has been initialized. You can use the subroutine Sub Page_Init() associated with it to run code before .NET does certain automatic actions, such as displaying controls on the page. It works in the same manner as Page_Load, but occurs before it.

- ❑ Page_Load – Occurs when the whole page is visible for the first time, but after some details about some of the server controls may have been initialized and displayed, by Page_Init.

- ❑ Control Events are dealt with – Once the ASP.NET server controls have loaded they can respond to click events, the changing of a selection in a list or checkbox, or when a control is bound to a data source. *They are only dealt with when the form is posted back to the server.*

- ❑ Page_Unload – Occurs once the control events in a page have been dealt with, and is an ideal place to shut down database connections, and the like. It isn't compulsory to do this, as .NET will perform these operations for you, but it is good practice to tidy up your code, and the subroutine attached to this event is the ideal place to do it.

> In addition, there is a set of events that the **Page** object supports which are not always fired, such as **PreRender**, which is generated just before the information is written to the browser and allows updates to be made to the page, **Error** which occurs whenever an error is generated on the page and the **CommitTransaction** and **AbortTransaction** events which are fired whenever a transaction is about to be started or cancelled.

We've already said that when a page object is first instantiated it is completely blank. Every time you submit a page, you instantiate a new version of the page object, even if you continually submit the same page. This is because of the **statelessness** of the HTTP protocol. In Chapter 3, we talked about this fact, and how it means that the browser makes a connection to the server with a request for the page, the web server searches for the page and either returns a page or appropriate status message and then shuts down the connection. Everything you wish to do with the page must be performed within this series of stages, before the connection is closed.

What we're getting at here, is each Page object is entirely separate, each time you refresh details or submit information to the same web page, as far as the web server is concerned it is a brand new page and is treated as such. There is **no persistence** of information between pages, and this has to be handled using other means that we will see in later chapters. ASP.NET is however, able to use certain aspects of the ASP.NET server controls to remember the state of information contained within the controls.

To keep things simple, we're going to leave looking at Control events until a little later in the chapter, and first concentrate on getting a solid understanding of the three events that ASP.NET will always call in the lifetime of a page. As we mentioned before, they are Page_Init, Page_Load and Page_Unload.

As we've already mentioned, if you want code to execute on your page before anything else occurs, then you need to associate it with the Page_Init event:

```
<script language="vb" runat="server">
Sub Page_Init()
... code here ...
End Sub
</script>
```

Alternatively, if you want to perform actions, *after* the page has been loaded, *but* before the user has had a chance to submit any information, then the Page_Load() event should be used:

```
<script language="vb" runat="server">
Sub Page_Load()
... code here ...
End Sub
</script>
```

We've used the Page_Load() subroutine for all of our examples so far in this book to make sure that the code that we are writing gets run. Although we could just as easily have placed it in the Page_Init() subroutine.

To clarify this concept, once again, Page_Load is an event that is triggered every time your web form is loaded, and it calls the Sub Page_Load() subroutine. So what's really happening is when the page is loaded, the event is triggered, ASP.NET then detects the event and runs the contents of the subroutine associated with it.

If we look at our code from the last example in Chapter 3, we can see:

```
<script runat="server" language="vb">
Sub Page_Load()
  Response.Write ("<b>Name:</b> " & Request.Form("FullName") & "<br />")
  Response.Write ("<b>Address:</b> " & Request.Form("Address") & "<br />")
  Response.Write ("<b>Sex:</b> " & Request.Form("Sex") & "<br />")
  Response.Write ("<b>Destination:</b> " & Request.Form("Destination") & _
                                                      "<br />")
  Response.Write ("<b>Don't Receive Information from Affiliates:</b> " &
                                      Request.Form("Email") & "<br />")
  Response.Write ("<b>Last option left blank, if no selected</b>")
End Sub
</script>
```

This ASP.NET code is only triggered in response to the `Page_Load()` event occurring. What happens if we take our code and put it into a different subroutine? The answer is that the code will now only run when another event is triggered and calls the new subroutine, or if the subroutine is called from elsewhere in our ASP.NET code.

For example, if you were to move it into a separate subroutine, called `Subroutine_1()` instead, and not associate that subroutine with any event or call it from anywhere else, then the code would never be run:

```
<script runat="server" language="vb">
Sub SubRoutine_1()
  Response.Write ("<b>Name:</b> " & Request.Form("FullName") & "<br />")
  Response.Write ("<b>Address:</b> " & Request.Form("Address") & "<br />")
  Response.Write ("<b>Sex:</b> " & Request.Form("Sex") & "<br />")
  Response.Write ("<b>Destination:</b> " & Request.Form("Destination") & _
                                                      "<br />")
End Sub
</script>
```

Now, if you went back to the example, and changed the code in this way it wouldn't work properly anymore, as this code would no longer be run.

We've looked at `Page_Init` and `Page_Load`, but that leaves us still with the `Page_Unload` event. Like the other two, this will occur every time a page is sent, but the main difference is this event occurs after all of the ASP.NET code in the page has been executed and has completed its tasks. If there are specific actions you wish to take place before the user moves to another page, but after the page has been loaded, then this is the place to do it. The `Page_Unload` event might occur after all other tasks have been performed, but remember as these events are performed as a **single discrete action** on the server, the `Page_Unload` will already have been performed by the time the user gets to see the page.

The only function of this final event, is to give you the chance to perform housekeeping actions, such as closing down objects, before the page is sent back to the user. As `Page_Unload` is performed after the rest of the ASP.NET has been completed, it is not possible to use controls or ASP.NET statements to display code in the associated `Page_Unload()` subroutine either. Typically, not much else is done other than housekeeping and tidying tasks in Page_Unload() and we won't be discussing it in further detail in this chapter.

To summarize, – we've already said that it's not just `Page_Load` that ASP.NET can respond to, there are There are three main events that always occur, regardless of the Custom controls triggered:

❑   `Page_Init()`

❑   `Page_Load()`

❑   `Page_Unload()`

Bearing this in mind, let's have a quick look at an example to see exactly when the code is executed in these first two events and exactly when these events are called:

Try It Out – Putting Code in Event Subroutines

1.   Open up your browser and type in the following:

```
<script language="vb" runat="server">
Dim intGlobal As Integer = 0
Sub Page_Init()
   intGlobal=intGlobal+1
   Message1.Text += "<br>Page_Init has called this line at " & Now() & _
                    " with the value of intGlobal being :" & intGlobal

End Sub
Sub Page_Load()
   intGlobal=intGlobal+1
   Message2.Text += "<br>Page_Load has called this line at " & Now() & _
                    " with the value of intGlobal being :" & intGlobal

End Sub

</script>
<html>
<head>
   <title>Automatic Events Example</title>
</head>
<body>
<form runat="server">
  <input type="submit" value="Click to continue">
  <br />
  <asp:label id="message1" runat="server"/>
  <asp:label id="message2" runat="server"/>
</form>
</body>
</html>
```

2.   Save this as `aspnetevent.aspx`

3.   View this in your browser:

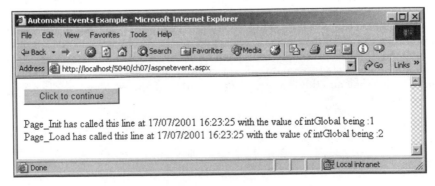

4. Click on the Click to continue button a couple of times:

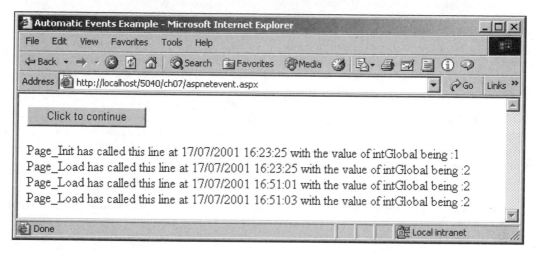

So what's happening here?

How It Works

Our code is simple enough, we start by declaring an integer as a global variable and setting its value to '1':

```
Dim intGlobal As Integer =1
```

Then we declare our two subroutines, starting with `Page_Init()`:

```
Sub Page_Init()
  intGlobal=intGlobal+1
  Message1.text += "<br>Page_Init has called this line at " & Now() & _
                   " with the value of intGlobal being :" & intGlobal
End Sub
```

Here we are incrementing the contents of `intGlobal`, and then adding some text to the contents of our first label control (`Message1`) saying the page has been initialized a with the time it was called and with the contents of our global variable. In our second subroutine, for the `Page_Load()` event, again we increment the contents of intGlobal and then we add some text to a second label control saying that our page has been loaded and display the contents of our global variable:

```
Sub Page_Load()
intGlobal=intGlobal+1
Message2.text += "<br>Page_Load has called this line at " & Now() & _
                 " with the value of intGlobal being :" & intGlobal
End Sub
```

When we run the program our page is initialized, and the global variable has the content '1'. The page is also loaded and this shows the contents of our global variable being '2'. So code that is altered in `Sub Page_Init()` can be also be altered in `Sub Page_Load()`.

Next, we got the user to click on the **Click to Continue** button to submit the form. When we clicked on the button we saw that the only the second message was displayed, however, so by doing this our web form was loaded again. The contents of `intGlobal` stays at '2' however. This harks back to our idea of state. We cannot persist a variable each time we submit a page using variables. So each time you call the page again, you have to use and declare a new set of variables. This is why it remains at '2'. In fact it is possible to persist variables using the `Session` and `Application` objects as we'll see later in Chapter 8, however using normally declared variables as above, you will find they will be re-initialized and re-declared each time.

There is an important anomaly in the page output to be aware of. You should be able to see from this result, that the `Page_Init` event is being called the first time the page is run along with `Page_Load` event, but when the page is submitted only the `Page_Load` message is being displayed the second time around. However the contents of our variable is still '2'. Given that we increment it once in `Page_Init()` and once in `Page_Load()`, `Page_Init()` must still be working.

We can prove this as follows, if we go back to our `Sub Page_Init()` subroutine and remove the line:

```
intGlobal=intGlobal+1
```

Now, when we run out code, `intGlobal` will only return '1'. Thus, we can deduce that `Page_Init` is still being triggered, however it doesn't change the text in our server control after its first use. This is why we've always chosen the `Page_Load` event to associate our code examples with.

This gives you a good idea of the sequence of steps that ASP.NET runs through when you request a page. Between a page being loaded and it being unloaded hoever, there is the potential for the user to generate an event by clicking a button, changing a listbox, and so on. These events are associated with particular ASP.NET server controls. You can set and trigger them in the same way that we've already seen.

Events in HTML

Before we launch into more detail of how these events work in ASP.NET, it helps to look at the way HTML deals with these events.

For those used to writing HTML pages, to understand the advantages of using ASP.NET event handlers, you first need to see how HTML does it. In a form, HTML will usually use the `<input>` tag with the type attribute being set to `Submit` to create a submit button, to send the forms data with. If you wanted to create a button, but didn't wish to send the contents of the form to the server for processing however, you'd need to use the HTML `<input>` tag again, but this time setting the type attribute to `Button`. This button wouldn't do anything at all at the moment; to get it to react to an event you'd need to add some more code to the `<input>` tag. Typically HTML will use a combination of a form and a small piece of client-side script to achieve this. The client-side script is placed in a special event attribute of a HTML tag and the tag is placed inside the form as usual.

This is best demonstrated with an example. We're going create a page with a button that displays a message when the user presses it. Don't worry, you don't have to know any client-side script for this example. You must however be using a modern browser, IE4 and upward, Netscape 6 and upward, or Opera 5 and upward.

Try It Out – Handling an Event in HTML

1. Open up your web page editor and type in the following:

```
<html>
<head>
<title>HTML Event Example</title>
</head>
<body>
<form>
<input type="button" value="Click Me" onclick=
                                    "alert('You have raised an event!')">
</form>
</body>
</html>
```

2. Save it as `htmlevent.htm` (note the HTM suffix, this isn't an ASP.NET web form)

3. View it in your browser and click on the button:

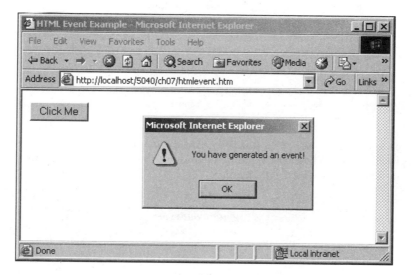

How It Works

This is an example of a built-in HTML event, known as an **intrinsic event**. These events are supported by nearly every HTML tag you care to mention, from `<body>` to `<img>` and of course, as in this example `<input>`. Below is a list of some of the events that it is possible for your browser to react to:

❑ `onmouseup` – occurs when a mouse button is released while hovering over an element

❑ `onmousedown` – occurs when a mouse button is pressed and held while hovering over an element

❑ `onmouseover` – occurs when a mouse is moved over an element

❑ `onmousemove` – occurs when a mouse button is first pressed and held down while over an element

237

- ❏ onclick – occurs when a mouse is clicked over an element

- ❏ ondblclick – occurs when a mouse is double-clicked while hovering over an element

- ❏ onkeyup – occurs when a key is released over an element

- ❏ onkeypress – occurs when a key is pressed and released over an element

- ❏ onkeydown – occurs when a key is pressed and held down while hovering over an element

In our extremely simplistic program, we have just created a form with a single button:

```
<form>
<input type="button" value="Click Me" onclick=
                                      "alert('You have raised an event!')">
</form>
```

The <input> tag is set to have a type of button, so when the button is clicked it isn't automatically submitted. Next, we use onclick. Inside this event attribute there is a little bit of JavaScript code that brings up a dialog box with a message (**alert**) in it. The code inside the onclick attribute is known as an **event handler**. An event handler is simply a section of code that manages a suitable response to the event, just like the Sub Page_Load() subroutine does.

We could change the code so that our button reacts to a different event; here we've changed it to the onmouseover event:

```
<form>
<input type="button" value="Click Me" onmouseover=
                                      "alert('You have generated an event!')">
</form>
```

If you go back and change your code, it will now react if you move your mouse over the button, rather than having to click on it. The event handling code is just the same. You could also amend your code so that your button can respond to several events:

```
<form>
<input type="button" value="Click Me" onclick=
                                      "alert('You have generated an event!')"
                                      onmouseover=
                                      "alert('You have generated an event!')">
</form>
```

The reason we're talking about how HTML does this, is because the ASP.NET way is very similar, and it provides a good introduction. We'll go on to look at ASP.NET now.

Server Control Events in ASP.NET

ASP.NET, like HTML, allows you to use events, such as onclick and onload within your server-side controls, and then write ASP.NET code that "reacts" to them in any .NET language. One of the main advantages is that you don't have to rely on a modern browser to get these events to work. However the browser used to deal with the events in HTML in ASP.NET the web server deals with them and sends pure HTML back to the browser.

You can add events to ASP.NET controls, in exactly the same way that you would add them in HTML to client-side controls. In ASP.NET an `onclick` event for a button control, might look like this:

```
<asp:button id="button1" text="Click me" onclick=
                                    "ClickEventHandler" runat="server" />
```

Here we supply the name of a subroutine in the `onclick` event attribute. This subroutine name will be mapped directly onto a subroutine with the same name found in your script code:

```
<script language="vb" runat="server">
Sub ClickEventHandler(Sender As Object, E As EventArgs)
   ... ASP.NET code here...
End Sub
</script>
```

If you haven't provided a subroutine with the same name, then nothing will happen when the event is triggered. The code will only be run when the name of the subroutine in the server control attribute matches the name of a subroutine in your code. You can call the subroutine whatever name you want, as long as you are consistent in using the same name in the server control and within the `<script>` tags.

The arguments we provide for this event handler are used to let the calling event pass information to the handler. The first of these – `Sender` – provides a reference to the object that raised the event, while the second – `E` – is an event class that captures information regarding the state of the event being handled and passes an object that's specific to that event.

ASP.NET server controls have a reduced set (compared to HTML) of events that can be added to controls as extra attributes. These are as follows (note that these event names aren't case sensitive):

Event name	Description
onload	Occurs when the control has loaded into the window or frame
onunload	Occurs when a control has been removed from a window or frame
Onclick	Occurs when a mouse button (or similar) is clicked when hovering over the `<asp: button>` control
Oninit	Occurs when the web page is first initialized
onprerender	Occurs just before the control is rendered

In addition to this, we also have the following events that can't be handled by the user in an event handler, but that occur in ASP.NET and cause actions within ASP.NET:

selectindexchanged checkchanged	Occur when the contents of a control have been altered, such as a checkbox being clicked, or a list item being selected. These only apply to the appropriate controls, such as list items and checkboxes.

The large difference between HTML controls and ASP.NET server controls, is the way they're dealt with. With HTML form controls, when the event is raised, the browser deals with it. It will sit around waiting for a user to click on the page or move their mouse. But, with server-side controls, the event is raised by the browser, but instead of being dealt with by it, the client raises a trigger telling the server to handle the event. In fact the server only generates a single form postback event, which occurs when you click on the ASP.NET button control. Anything else that might have been done in the page is packaged up within this single event. If you've checked a radio button and chosen an item from a listbox, this information is recorded when you send the form.

It doesn't matter what kind of event was raised, the client will always return this single postback event to the server. Some events are impossible to deal with on the server, however, such as key presses or mouseovers, so there are no equivalent ASP.NET events for these. They will not be passed onto the server and have to be handled by the client. The reasons for this are simple.

With HTML, your browser will wait for you to click on a control. It can sit around all day waiting for you, if you keep the same page open. This does not happen in ASP.NET. As mentioned previously, HTTP only allows you to open a connection, get a page, and close that connection. Similarly, the server cannot keep a copy of page object open on the server, on the off chance that you might submit details to the page at a later point. No, the whole set of events, corresponding to the changes you have made to the page, have to be dealt with in a single discrete action.

The page object is initialized, the page loaded, then the control events are all bundled up into a single postback event and dealt with, then the page is unloaded. This happens in a matter of seconds or milliseconds. And explains why only a select few events can be dealt with by your server-side code.

The advantage of passing events to the server is that it adds better structure to your code, because you can separate out your event handling code in your ASP.NET applications entirely. There are some disadvantages too – wherever possible it's a good idea to do client processing, to offload work from central CPUs to improve performance.

Now, let's look at an example of how events work with the ASP.NET server controls. Before we do this we need to introduce another new server control.

The ASP.NET Button server control

There is one ASP.NET server control in particular that can be used to react to events. It performs the equivalent functionality of setting the `<input>` tag to type "Button" in HTML. This is the button control, and the reason we haven't mentioned it before is that you need to understand events to be able to make any decent use of it.

The button control has the following format:

```
<asp:button  id="id_name" event="event_handler_name" runat="server"/>
```

To get it to work you need to specify an event. The ASP.NET button control supports the following events:

- oninit
- onprerender
- onload
- onclick
- onunload

If we're going to get our page to respond dynamically, we need to use the only event capable of doing this, the `onclick` one. Let's take a look at an example now.

This example contains three ASP.NET server controls. The first is a check box to register a user's choice, the second is a button which will raise the event and the third is a label control. You can't render dialog boxes directly in ASP.NET, but to display information dynamically you can use the label control.

The example asks the user for some information about whether they wish to receive further information from a company. It will display a message appropriate to the user's response depending on whether they checked the checkbox or not.

Try It Out – Using the ASP.NET Button Server Control

1. Open up your text editor and type in the following code:

```vb
<script language="vb" runat="server">
  Sub ClickHandler(Sender As Object, E As EventArgs)
    If Request.Form("ExtraInfoBox") = "on" then
      Message.Text = "<br /><br />You will hear from us shortly"
    Else
      Message.Text = "<br /><br />You will not receive any further" & _
                                                " information from us"

    End If
  End Sub
</script>
<html>
  <head>
    <title>Server-side event processing example</title>
  </head>
  <body>
    <form runat="server">
      <asp:CheckBox id="ExtraInfoBox" Text=
                "Click here to receive extra information" Runat="server" />
      <br /><br />
      <asp:Button id="Button1" Text="Click Here to Submit"
                                    onclick="ClickHandler" runat="server"/>
      <asp:Label id="Message" runat="server"/>
    </form>
  </body>
</html>
```

2. Save this as `event.aspx`

3. Run the code in your browser:

4. Check the box and click on the "Click here to Submit" button. An appropriate message is displayed:

How It Works

We're simply taking the event raised when a user clicks on the button and running a short passage of ASP.NET code. Our subroutine `ClickHandler` is the event handler specified in the `onclick` event attribute. This event handler examines the check box in the example and displays a different message in the `label` control depending on whether or not the check box has been selected. This is our event handler/subroutine code:

```
<script language="vb" runat="server">
  Sub ClickHandler(Sender As Object, E As EventArgs)
    If Request.Form("ExtraInfoBox") = "on" then
      Message.Text = "<br /><br />You will hear from us shortly"
    Else
      Message.Text = "<br /><br />You will not receive any further " & _
                                         " information from us"

    End If
  End Sub
</script>
```

This code will display an appropriate message depending on whether the contents of the `ExtraInfobox` check box control has been activated or not. The crucial difference from all of the other examples we have looked at so far is that, instead of the automatically-generated `Page_Load` event, we are using our own customized event. This means, our code is only run when the click event happens. If nobody clicks on the button then nothing happens.

Another important point to notice about the click event handler code placed at the top of the page, is that it requires two parameters. Up to now our `Page_Init` and `Page_Load` events have required no parameters, because we didn't need to pass information between them. You can use parameters here in just the same way as you would with normal subroutines, but you should be aware that there are special reasons why events require parameters.

Each event that is generated also generates information about itself, such as which control it was generated by. To be able to use this information within your subroutine you have to pass in two parameters. The first of these has type `Object` and is named `Sender`, the second is of type `EventArgs` and is named `E`. Both of these parameters are passed to any server-side event that can be raised by ASP.NET. They're standard parameters, which all event procedures are passed. If you don't specify them when using server control events, then you will cause an error.

Now we're going to move on and consider this in more detail.

Event-Driven Programming and Postback

A big issue throughout this book so far has been the Postback architecture. You may not have noticed this, as we've not focused on it or explained it until now. Postback is the process by which the browser posts information back to the server telling the server to handle the event, the server does so and sends the resulting HTML back to the browser again. Postback only occurs with web forms, and it is only server controls that post back information to the server.

ASP.NET doesn't look after the processing of all events as it is still necessary that we handle some events (such as `onmouseover`) on the client-side, due to the fact that the server couldn't possibly react in time to such events.

The great advantage of processing some events on the server however is that you don't have to rely on a particular browser to recognize your client-side script, and you can send back extra information, for example the state of a particular control, to help influence you decision. This is something fundamentally different to what happens in HTML. Let's just demonstrate this now with an example:

Try It Out – Demonstrating HTML's lack of Postback

1. Open your web page editor and type in the following:

```
<html>
<head>
  <title>HTML Event Example</title>
</head>
<body>
<form method="get">
Select either A, B or C and click the button at the bottom<br/>
```

```
<br/>
A<input type="radio" value="a" name="test"><br />
B<input type="radio" value="b" name="test"><br />
C<input type="radio" value="c" name="test"><br /><br />
<input type="submit" value="Click Me" onclick="
                                    alert('You have generated an event!')">

</form>
</body>
</html>
```

2. Save this as `htmlevent2.htm`, making sure you remember the HTM suffix again

3. View this in your browser and click on a choice:

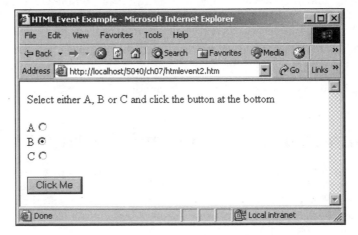

4. Now click on the click me button – after receiving a dialog saying that you have generated an event you will see the following:

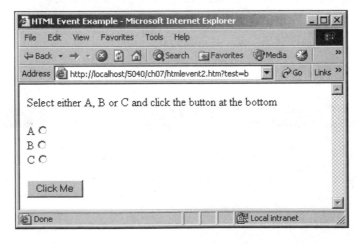

Your selection has disappeared!

How It Works

There isn't anything unusual happening in our HTML form. Though you should note that, as we've omitted the action attribute of the form, it will post the data to back to itself:

```
<form method="get">
Select either A, B or C and click the button at the bottom<br/>
<br/>
A<input type="radio" value="a" name="test"><br />
B<input type="radio" value="b" name="test"><br />
C<input type="radio" value="c" name="test"><br /><br />
<input type="submit" value="Click Me" onclick="alert('You have generated an
event!')">
</form>
```

As you can see from the URL, a querystring has been appended to submit the information:

`http://localhost/5040/ch07/htmlevent2.htm?test=b`

When we go back to the page however, our selection has disappeared. This is the normal behavior for HTML. ASP.NET can improve upon this however, as we shall see. Let's adapt our previous example to use as ASP.NET server control instead:

Try It Out – Using Postback

1. Type the following into your page editor:

```
<html>
<head>
  <title>Postback Event Example</title>
</head>
<body>
<form runat="server">
Select either A, B or C and click the button at the bottom<br/>
<br/>
<asp:radiobuttonlist id="test" runat="server">
<asp:listitem id="option1" value="a" runat="server" />
<asp:listitem id="option2" value="b" runat="server" />
<asp:listitem id="option3" value="b" runat="server" />
</asp:radiobuttonlist>
<br /><br />
<input type="submit" value="Click Me" onclick=
                              "alert('You have generated an event!')">
</form>
</body>
</html>
```

2. Save this as postback.aspx

3. View this in your browser and select a choice and click on the button:

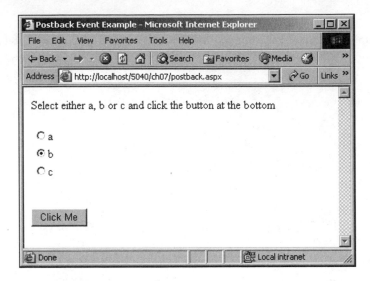

This time your choice is remembered.

How It Works

This is an example of the concept of postback in action. Click on View Source in your browser to view your code – because of differences between machines and browsers your code won't look exactly like this, but it will be pretty similar:

```html
<html>
<head>
  <title>Postback Event Example</title>
</head>
<body>
<form name="ctrl0" method="post" action="postback.aspx" id="ctrl0">
<input type="hidden" name="__VIEWSTATE" value="dDw0MDk5MTgxNTU7Oz4=" />

Select either a, b or c and click the button at the bottom<br/>
<br/>
<table id="test" border="0">
  <tr>
    <td>
      <span value="a">
        <input id="test_0" type="radio" name="test" value="a" />
        <label for="test_0">a</label>
        </span>
    </td>
  </tr><tr>
    <td>
      <span value="b">
        <input id="test_1" type="radio" name="test" value="b"
                                            checked="checked" />
        <label for="test_1">b</label>
        </span>
    </td>
  </tr><tr>
```

```
            <td>
              <span value="c">
                <input id="test_2" type="radio" name="test" value="c" />
                <label for="test_2">c</label>
              </span>
            </td>
          </tr>
        </table>
        <br /><br />
        <input type="submit" value="Click Me" onclick=
                                    "alert('You have generated an event!')">
      </form>
    </body>
  </html>
```

The `<asp:radiobuttonlist>` control has been turned into its equivalent `<input>` controls and has been formatted as part of a table. Also the event attribute is no longer specified in the input tag. The largest change however, is the addition of the hidden **VIEWSTATE** control:

```
<input type="hidden" name="__VIEWSTATE" value="dDwOMDk5MTgxNTU7Oz4=" />
```

Information about the state of the form is sent back in an associated hidden control, called _VIEWSTATE. This information is generated by ASP.NET. In fact, the information contained within _VIEWSTATE control in the value attribute is actually an encrypted version of the old version of the form. ASP.NET is able to look at the old version and compare it to the current version. From this it knows how to persist the state of ASP.NET server controls between page submissions. If there are differences, such as a different radio button being selected, then internal events are generated by ASP.NET in response to this and it deals with it appropriately, to create a "current" version of the form. This _VIEWSTATE control is crucial to ASP.NET being able to remember the state of controls between page submissions, without actually maintaining a page object or HTTP connection throughout.

ASP.NET, has used this postback information about the state of the page, to create a new version of it, with the state of the corresponding controls being remembered. This can be used by the browser in future iterations of the page, but is never displayed again. Postback works therefore by using only HTML tags and controls, which contain information that can be interpreted by ASP.NET.

Now, we're going to move on to see that information about the state of controls isn't the only thing that ASP.NET posts back.

Changing the way we program on the Web

Throughout this chapter, we've been referring to `Sub Page_Load()` as just another subroutine, and indeed this is all it is. But it is slightly different in that ASP.NET automatically calls this subroutine for us. As virtually all ASP.NET code is placed in subroutines or functions, we rely on the event associated with this code to kick-start our applications.

In order for ASP.NET to handle other events, you'll need to create your own event handlers, using your own subroutines. These subroutines will be called by event attributes of the HTML server controls, such as `onclick`. When you call these subroutines you are able to pass information about the event within which they are calledusing the event parameters we discussed earlier.

For clarification, let's look back for a moment to the example that we used earlier in this chapter. We created a web form called `event.aspx` that reacted when the user clicked a button and ran a subroutine called `Sub ClickHandler()`:

```vb
<script language="vb" runat="server">
Sub ClickHandler(Sender As Object, E As EventArgs)
   If Request.Form("ExtraInfoBox") = "on" then
     Message.text = "<br><br>You will hear from us shortly"
   Else
     Message.text = "<br><br>You will not receive any further information" & _
                                                   " from us"
   End If
End Sub
</script>
```

We provided two parameters to the click-handler subroutine. The first thing that happens when an event is generated, is that a corresponding object is passed as a parameter. This contains information about which object is sending the information about the event. The second parameter contains a set of related information – such as data about which class the event is a member of. It's still too early to deal completely with what is happening here, as you won't understand it without a thorough understanding of objects (which we cover in Chapter 8), but it should be a little clearer when we come to talk about it again in the next couple of chapters. All you need to know is that parameters pass details to a subroutine about the specific event that has been generated. Every subroutine/event handler works in the same way, whether raised by ASP.NET or by the programmer, and must be passed these "generic" parameters.

This isn't however the only information that is passed. The data contained within the form is also passed by ASP.NET, at the same time, Up until now we've accessed this information using this format: `Request.Form("variable_name")`:

```vb
Sub ClickHandler(Sender As Object, E As EventArgs)
   If Request.Form("ExtraInfoBox") = "on" then
     Message.Text = "<br><br>You will hear from us shortly"
     ...
```

The way in which we have been referencing information passed by forms can now been completely changed. The `Request.Form("variable_name")` syntax is perfectly valid, but it is superceded by a better way to reference data captured by the server controls that'll we consider now.

We've not been able to introduce this method until now, as you need an understanding of how events work in VB.NET and how procedures (both functions and subroutines) work, to be able to take advantage of it. Instead of using the `Request.Form()` syntax, we can use a completely separate object with the identifier name:

```vb
If ExtraInfoBox = "on" then
```

Here, we don't have to make any reference to the HTTP request as we've done in previous chapters, as it's handled "invisibly" by ASP.NET for us. Indeed **all** of the HTML server controls are created as separate objects, which you can access locally in the subroutine you have called. These objects exist the whole time, but you can only alter their properties in the event-handling subroutines and nowhere else, as their scope only applies to the subroutine. These objects allow you to reference any of the attributes of the server control as follows:

```
[ServerControl].[ServerControlAttribute]
```

In our previous example, the ExtraInfoBox was a checked box. Looking it up the class browser, you can see that the checkbox control has a check **property** (properties correspond directly with attributes). We could reference this attribute as follows in the ASP.NET code:

```
ExtraInfoBox.Checked
```

We could therefore, change out example to read as follows:

```
<script language="vb" runat="server">
Sub ClickHandler(Sender As Object, E As EventArgs)
  If ExtraInfoBox.Checked then
    Message.Text = "<br><br>You will hear from us shortly"
  Else
    Message.Text = "<br><br>You will not receive any further information" & _
                                              " from us"

  End If
End Sub
</script>
```

Now we're checking the contents of the attribute directly, rather than worrying about what value we have set the server control to. We then perform a test for a Boolean value, if there is anything in the ExtraInfoBox checkbox property we execute the contents of the if...then structure, if there isn't we don't.

The great thing about this format, is that we don't have to worry about initializing or declaring ExtraInfoBox, we just assign the ID in our server control:

```
<asp:CheckBox id="ExtraInfoBox" Text=
                  "Click here to receive extra information" Runat="server" />
```

Then call an event subroutine with the ASP button control:

```
asp:Button id="Button1" Text="Click Here to Submit" onclick="ClickHandler()"
                                              runat="server"/>
```

In this model, when the user submits the form. The form data is sent, not using the <Input type="submit">, but by the ASP Button server control. This control generates an event which calls our subroutine as an event, and by passing two parameters (Sender As Object, E As EventArgs) you are able to use all of the form data directly on your page.

Another advantage of doing things this way, is that you don't need to worry about whether your data has already been declared in the page, as you do with Request.Form(), as the object will automatically be declared for us by ASP.NET.

In fact all programming in VB.NET is event-driven and object-oriented, it's just a case of whether:

❑   ASP.NET raises the event, such as Page_Load() or Page_Init()

❑   The user of the web page raises it by clicking on a button and raising an associated handler

Whichever is the case, they both operate in the same way, causing the program to break from whatever it was doing and move to the requested function or subroutine.

We're going to look at an example that utilizes this new way of doing things. It contains two text boxes to take information from the user, and will perform a calculation depending on whether the user selects an add, subtract, divide, or multiply button.

Try It Out – Event-driven Example

1. Open up your web page editor and type in the following:

```
<script runat="server" language="vb">

  Sub Add(sender as object, e As EventArgs)
    lblAnswer.Text = CDbl(tbxInput1.text) + CDbl(tbxInput2.text)
  End Sub

  Sub Subtract(sender as object, e As EventArgs)
    lblAnswer.Text = CDbl(tbxInput1.text) - CDbl(tbxInput2.text)
  End Sub

  Sub Factor(sender as object, e As EventArgs)
    lblAnswer.Text = CDbl(tbxInput1.text) * CDbl(tbxInput2.text)
  End Sub

  Sub Ratio(sender as object, e As EventArgs)
    lblAnswer.Text = CDbl(tbxInput1.text) / CDbl(tbxInput2.text)
  End Sub

</script>
<html>
  <form runat="server">
    <asp:textbox id="tbxInput1" runat="server" />
    <asp:button id="btnAdd" runat="server" text=" + " Onclick="Add" />
    <asp:button id="btnSubtract" runat="server" text=" - "
                                               Onclick="Subtract" />
    <br/>
    <asp:textbox id="tbxInput2" runat="server" />
    <asp:button id="btnFactor" runat="server" text=" x " Onclick="Factor" />
    <asp:button id="btnRatio" runat="server" text=" ÷ " Onclick="Ratio" />
    <br/>
    <b>Answer = <asp:Label id="lblAnswer" runat="server" /></b>
  </form>
</html>
```

2. Save this as `eventdriven.aspx`

3. View it in your browser:

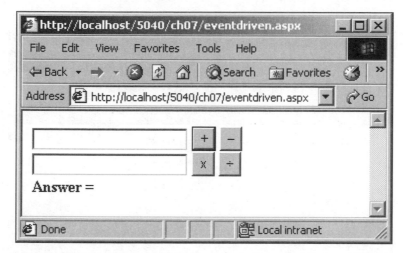

4. Enter two numbers into the text fields, and select the multiply button to perform a calculation:

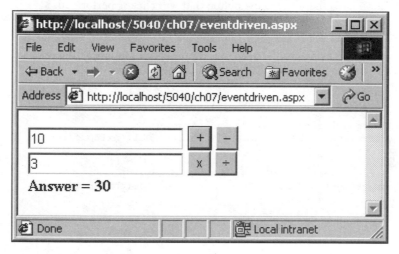

5. You will see the answer displayed for you particular operation. Go back alter the numbers, and click a different button, such as subtract:

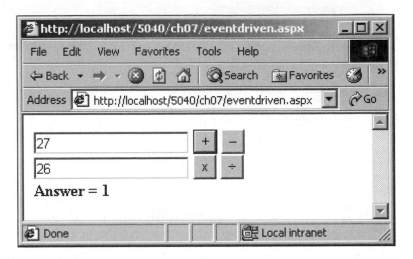

Only the operation corresponding to the button that was click is performed.

How It Works

This example works by using event-driven programming, as we outlined previously. We have created four separate subroutines, Add, Subtract, Factor, and Ratio.

```vb
<script runat="server" language="vb">

  Sub Add(sender as object, e As EventArgs)
    lblAnswer.Text = CDbl(tbxInput1.text) + CDbl(tbxInput2.text)
  End Sub

  Sub Subtract(sender as object, e As EventArgs)
    lblAnswer.Text = CDbl(tbxInput1.text) - CDbl(tbxInput2.text)
  End Sub

  Sub Factor(sender as object, e As EventArgs)
    lblAnswer.Text = CDbl(tbxInput1.text) * CDbl(tbxInput2.text)
  End Sub

  Sub Ratio(sender as object, e As EventArgs)
    lblAnswer.Text = CDbl(tbxInput1.text) / CDbl(tbxInput2.text)
  End Sub

</script>
```

These subroutines are called by the four ASP.NET button controls we have created:

```
...
<asp:button id="btnAdd" runat="server" text=" + " Onclick="Add" />
<asp:button id="btnSubtract" runat="server" text=" - " Onclick="Subtract" />
...
<asp:button id="btnFactor" runat="server" text=" x " Onclick="Factor" />
<asp:button id="btnRatio" runat="server" text=" ÷ " Onclick="Ratio" />
```

Each button has a symbol corresponding to its equivalent mathematical operation, and it calls that relevant subroutine. All four subroutines work in an identical way. Let's look at Sub Add more closely:

```
Sub Add(sender as object, e As EventArgs)
  lblAnswer.Text = CDbl(tbxInput1.text) + CDbl(tbxInput2.text)
End Sub
```

This is called by the onclick attribute of btnAdd, and is passed the two generic parameters. These parameters allow it to access the two textboxes, which contain the numbers the user entered:

```
<asp:textbox id="tbxInput1" runat="server" />
  ...
<asp:textbox id="tbxInput2" runat="server" />
  ...
```

The first text box is called tbxInput1, so we can reference it as tbxInput1, and reference its contents by referring to its text attribute. The second text box is tbxInput2 and can be reference by referring to its text attribute also.

As the text attribute returns its information as a string, we have to use CDbl, which converts the data type from a string to a double. Then we can perform a mathematical operation on our two pieces of data, effectively saying:

```
tbxInput1 + tbxInput2
```

Then we store our data in the <asp:label> control, lblanswer. Once again, we can access its text attribute, but instead of getting the information, here we are setting it. So we are effectively saying:

```
lblAnswer.text = tbxInput1 + tbxInput2
```

This information is displayed on our screen. The other three subroutines work in the same way, and will only be executed in the event that the particular button associated with them is pressed.

Summary

We've kept this chapter short, as we want to focus on the main points that are central to the event-driven way in which ASP.NET works. It generates a set of events which occur whenever a web page is initialized, loaded and unloaded on the server. In the duration of this sequence, ASP.NET can also react to other events that may have been generated by the server controls. The code needed to react to these events is placed in event handlers. By passing two generic parameters to these event handlers, you are able to use all of the form data

Event-driven programming is something utilized in ASP.NET and something that fundamentally alters the way in which pages/web forms are created. You might create a web form with several sections of code, some of which are never executed, while others will be executed constantly. When web forms are created you now need to think, which events will occur, and how do I make my pages react to them?

In the next chapter, we move on the concept of objects and see how everything in ASP.NET, including events, are in fact just objects. This will fundamentally alter, yet again, the way in which we create our ASP.NET web forms.

Exercises

1. Explain why event-driven programming is such a good way of programming for the Web.

2. Run the following HTML code in your browser (remember to save the page with a `.htm` extension). Now translate the HTML into a set of ASP.NET server controls so that the information entered into the form is maintained when the submit button is clicked. Add a subroutine to the button to confirm that the details entered were received:

```
<html>
<head>
  <title>HTML</title>
</head>
<body>
  <form>
    <h4>Please enter your name:<h4>
    <input type="text"><br /><br />
    <h4>What would you like for breakfast?<h4>
    <h4>Cereal<input type="checkbox"><h4>
    <h4>Eggs<input type="checkbox"><h4>
    <h4>Pancakes<input type="checkbox"><h4><br />
    <h4>Feed me:<h4>
    <h4>Now<input type="radio" name="test"><h4>
    <h4>Later<input type="radio" name="test"><h4>
    <input type="submit" value="Thank you!">
  </form>
</body>
</html>
```

3. Add a `Page_Load` event handler to the ASPX code you have just created which confirms the selections made in the following format:

Thank you very much _____ .

You have chosen _____ for breakfast. I will prepare it for you _____ .

4. Create a very basic virtual telephone using an ASPX file that displays a textbox and a button named "Call". Configure your ASPX file so that when you type a telephone number into your textbox and press "Call", you are:

❑ presented with a message confirming the number you are calling

❑ presented with another button called "Disconnect" that, when pressed, returns you to your opening page, leaving you ready to type another number

5. Using the `Select Case` construct, associate three particular telephone numbers with three names, so that when you press the "Call" button, your confirmation message contains the name of the person you are 'calling' rather than just the telephone number.

Introduction to Objects

"Computers only become something when given a special application. Ditto Lego. Lego's discrete modular bricks are indestructible and fully intended to be nothing except themselves."

    – excerpt from "Microserfs" by Douglas Coupland (HarperCollins, 1995)

In previous chapters, we've seen how we can hook up various statements and control structures in ASP.NET and use them to generate individual dynamic web pages. As your web pages (and ultimately web applications) become more complicated however, your code will gradually become more difficult to understand; consequently it will become more difficult to maintain, and you'll wonder whether it was worth all that hard work in the first place.

What's more, all the functionality we've implement in our pages so far is tied to a specific page, which make it difficult to reuse this logic elsewhere without going to the trouble of cutting and pasting (and making any subsequent modifications) in every separate file you want to support it.

In this chapter, we're going to start learning how we can get round these problems, by writing more modular code. We're going to look at one of the core concepts of .NET – **objects** – and here are some of the questions we'll answer:

- ❑   How and why you should organize your code

- ❑   How to use components to organize your code

- ❑   What **objects** and **classes** are, and how to use them as components

- ❑   How to use objects

The entire .NET Framework (including ASP.NET, ADO.NET, Windows Forms and everything else you're likely to come across) is based on objects. Whenever you write any sort of program for .NET, you're actually working with objects – whether or not you realize it. We're going to be seeing a lot of these objects in the course of the book, therefore it's absolutely critical that you have solid understanding of the topics we discuss in this chapter.

Organizing Your Code

In very simple applications (as we've seen in the opening chapters of this book), any given task may only ever be performed once – larger applications may require the same task be performed many times over by different parts of the application. Instead of rewriting that code over and over, it's much more efficient to identify such tasks, and reuse code as much as possible:

❑   If we reuse code, there is less to write overall, so we can develop our application more quickly.

❑   If we reuse code, the final application will be smaller, and therefore, will probably have fewer bugs. Indeed, debugging the application should be easier anyway, because there will be fewer lines of code to wade through.

Consider an ASP.NET web application that stores data in a database. Connecting to the database and retrieving data are tasks that the application performs. Using techniques we've learnt so far, we'd need to repeat every line of the code required to perform these tasks in every page that required database access. As soon as we wanted to change the application's database system, we would have to change the database access code in every single page. In a large application, this could amount to hundreds or even thousands of pages that we'd have to update.

There are two reasons why such a change is a problem. Firstly, the changes are tedious and time consuming to make. We all know that "time is money", and the developer's time could be better spent improving the application. Secondly, the more code the developer changes, the more risk there is of introducing new errors.

Both these problems can be avoided if, instead of repeating the same code in many different parts of an application, the code is written once and accessed by the different parts of the application as and when they need it.

Of course, there is some extra work involved in making your code reusable: each block of code must be designed to meet the requirements of each part of the application that will use it. You therefore need to design applications with this in mind, so that you don't wind up asking your recycled code to do something slightly different each time it's called.

> Efficient reusability stems from good planning, and while this may entail a little more **work initially, it can pay enormous dividends as your application grows.**

If we now consider a typical web site that uses dynamically generated pages, maintenance often falls to two specific people to undertake:

❑   the **designer**, whose role is to maintain the **presentation** (graphics, layout, interface – commonly summarized as "look and feel") of the site

❑   the **developer**, who is responsible for the **functionality** or **logic** of the application, providing code to manage database access and business rules for example

Some situations may see a clear separation between these roles – others may entail some overlap between them. The key point is that when you're thinking about the design of the page you don't want to have to worry about the .NET code that provides its functionality. Designers typically want to treat a task like database access as a "black box" – that is, you put something simple in and get something simple out, but don't need to know what happens in between. Likewise, as a developer, you probably don't want to worry about the details of how your data is going to be displayed.

This separation of roles leads us to a practical organization of an application into **layers** or **tiers**, and as we progress through the book we'll see this arrangement made more and more explicit.

We've already been structuring our code to separate logic (`<script>` blocks) and presentation (`<html>` blocks). Fortunately, ASP.NET makes it very easy for us to do this, thanks to its use of objects. We're now going to take a proper look at the notion of objects, and see how we can use them to organize our code to the best possible extent.

So, What is an Object?

A **software object** is simply a bundle of code that describes some sort of real-world object. It might be a physical object (such as a book or a person), or a conceptual object (like a schedule or a CD track listing). Anything that exists in the real world can be represented in some fashion as a software object.

> Typically we don't use the term "software object", but simply talk about an "object". We call the idea of using objects in software "object orientation", sometimes known as "OO", or "OOP" for "object-oriented programming".

It's human nature to think about the world in terms of objects – in other words, we break it down into smaller units, each of which is a self-contained entity to which we can assign a name. Each has its own particular attributes, and can engage in various activities with other objects around it.

We can consider a car as one example of an real-world object – we can name it ("this is a car"), we can clearly separate it from other entities in the real world ("a fish is not a car"), we can list its attributes ("this car is blue"), and list the actions it can perform ("this car can start, stop, change gear"). We can even describe relationships between it and other objects ("a person can drive the car", "the car has four wheels", "the car is an automobile").

> Objects can be physical **(like a car, which we can touch)** or conceptual **(like a specific route between two points, which exists as a well-defined entity, but has no physical element).**

Let's start out by taking a close look at our car example. Many of the samples in this chapter are going to see us developing a software object that represents a car – this could be used in an application that simulates traffic flow – and it doesn't take too much imagination to think of a few related examples of real-world objects that we might also consider modelling as objects:

- the **car** itself
- the **factory** that produced it
- the **wheels** on the car
- the **brake** pedal
- the **engine**

Of course, these are all physical objects. We might also want to consider conceptual objects, such as the car **manufacturer**. (While it's hard to get a physical grip on something like General Motors or Ford, it still exists as a well-defined legal entity.) All of these real-world objects are well defined and self-contained, with state (what they *are*) and behavior (what they *do*). For example:

❏ the **car** is *blue* and can *accelerate*

❏ the **factory** is *in Germany* and *makes cars*

❏ the **wheels** are *fully inflated* and can *turn round*

When we talk about a **software object**, we're referring to a special sort of software construct that bundles together data and functions in a self-contained unit. By doing so, we can represent these real-world objects as software objects, with state represented by the object's **properties** (data stored in the object) and behavior represented by its **methods** (object-specific functions). In the next few sections, we'll take a look at how we might settle on a suitable representation, what we can do with an object once we've defined it, and why it makes our lives so much easier.

Perhaps we want to write a program that simulates traffic in city – it's natural to think about modelling it in terms of objects. For example, we'll frequently want to reuse code that describes "a car", "a route", "a traffic light" and establish interactive relationships between these blocks of code.

Object-Oriented Programming (OOP) gives us a very elegant and powerful way to reuse code, and in the course of the chapter, you'll see that it also has the following benefits:

❏ It appeals to the way humans think

❏ It helps us write code more efficiently

❏ It helps us write simpler code

❏ It helps us write code that's easier to change later

❏ It helps us write more reliable code

❏ It helps us write more comprehensible code

The Microsoft developers who built the .NET Framework have defined a massive collection of objects, and the Framework's entire set of functionality is built around these in one way or another. Whenever we write a program in .NET, we're actually just hooking together various objects so that they can do something useful for us. In fact, objects lurk quietly behind every one of the elements we've seen so far – amongst hundreds of different ready-built object types are form `buttons`, labels, basic variable types `Integer`, `Boolean`, and `String`; even the web page itself has an object to describe it.

Abstraction – Modeling the Real World

When we write code using objects, we do it by breaking our large complex program down into lots of smaller easily understandable pieces. Then we can spend more time thinking about how each of these objects talks to each of the others. If we are thinking on this slightly higher level we can forget the details of how any particular object works. The benefit of this is that our program is much easier to understand, because we do not need to keep the whole thing in our heads at once.

For example, think about a car. A car is a complex beast with many hundreds or even thousands of parts. If you considered every single part, and tried to take in the detailed nature of how each one interacted with all the others, you'd probably find yourself with quite a headache – even if you'd spent the last 30 years designing cars, there would probably be plenty of elements (the CD player or the GPS system, for example) that you'd simply not worry about, as long as they did their specific job properly.

On a high level, we know what a car is for, we know what to expect of it, and we know what it can do for us. We can name the most important parts of a car: the engine, the wheels, the pedals, and so on. Once we can get away from the 'nuts and bolts' level and consider the car in terms of these large pieces, most of the problem of complexity just vanishes. In practice, you don't need to know the precise mechanics of the braking system in order to bring the car to a halt – you simply press the pedal and the car slows down:

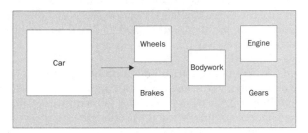

Breaking programs up in this manner has a similar effect – we can make use of each piece in an application without worrying too much about the details of how that piece works. It also means that if we have a problem in one part of the system, we don't need to worry about the details in any other part of the system, since each one can be treated as a discrete unit. Again, in practice, you don't need to know how the drive shaft works in order to fix a flat tire.

When we design an object, we are generally looking to implement some complex or frequently used functionality, and expose the simplest possible useful interface. Developers who then use the object should have just enough control to do what they need to do with it – but beyond that, we want to hide as many operational details from them as possible. This is a process known as **abstraction**.

The details that we abstract away can be separated into to main categories:

❑ Details that **aren't relevant** or **appropriate** to the particular situation we're modelling – if we designed a 'person' object to represent someone registered on our web site, we'd want it to incorporate details that were relevant to our particular line of business. It's unlikely that a bookshop site would require this object to describe 'hair color', whereas a dating service might well want it to. Likewise, we might incorporate 'shift up a gear' and 'shift down a gear' functionality into our car object – we *don't* want to let it 'change to 5th gear', as there's no telling what that might do to the gearbox (particularly if we'd just come out of 1st).

❑ Details that are **implicit**, either to the specific situation, or in the functionality that *is* exposed – if the person object can tell you about 'date of birth', there's little point in having it tell you about 'age' as well, since you can deduce one from the other. Perhaps we're just considering cars that are being driven on the freeway – we don't need to specify whether or not the car has wheels, since it's a safe bet that we won't be considering any flying cars (not for a while at least...).

261

Ultimately, we need to be able to make an informed decision as to what features each object needs to describe. As we'll see in a moment, these 'features' break down as things that the object *is*, and things that the object can *do*. The important thing is that once we've established the main blocks that make up our model, we can treat each one as a black box. Provided it's been well designed (as appropriate to the needs of our situation), we only need to give it a valid input to receive a valid output – we don't need to worry about exactly what processing has occurred.

Encapsulation – The Black Box

Once we have a model of the main objects we want to use in our program, we need to know about their most important characteristics. When we do this we treat each one as a black box, and simply consider what we want the object to do for us – we can largely ignore *how* it will do that. This helps us to focus on the most important aspects of the problem, rather than getting dragged into every minute part of the overall functionality right from the very start.

As an analogy, consider this. You're taking a friend out for lunch, but when you get to the parking lot where you've left your car, you find a rogue engineer stood in front of pile of several thousand pieces of metal and plastic – he helpfully points out that you'll have to reconstruct your automobile before you can drive it anywhere. The chances are that (once you'd called the police) you'd try and get a ride from your friend, whose own car is nearby and still in one piece.

If the same engineer handed you a set of keys and pointed to a nearby Z3, however you might well jump in, and more than likely be able to pop the key in the ignition, start the engine, and put it in gear before driving off for an afternoon on the road. The point is, you don't need to understand how the raw components of your car fit together in order to drive it.

When we're using objects, their essential characteristics are what matter, not how they work underneath, which means we have a great deal less to think about. .NET provides hundreds of ready-built objects for us to use, therefore there's less work for us to do too.

There's just one question we haven't answered: how do we actually apply this to software objects?

Object Properties

Let's look more closely at our car example. If we were going to specify a car as an object, we'd expect it to be able to be able to tell us about itself:

- ❏ How fast is the car moving?
- ❏ What color is it?
- ❏ Is the engine running?
- ❏ How long is the car?
- ❏ What's the number/license plate?
- ❏ How many doors are open?

Attributes like these (by which an object exposes itself to the outside world) are called **properties**.

Object Methods

It's also important to look at the things our object ought to *do* for us:

❑   Change gear
❑   Steer right/left
❑   Accelerate
❑   Brake
❑   Start engine
❑   Stop engine

Actions like these that we expect an object to perform are called **methods**. You can think of them as being similar to verbs – "doing" words. Methods should always correspond to things that the object can *do to* or *do with* its properties. For instance, a 'change gear' method is only useful if our car object has a 'gear number' property for it to modify. Likewise, well-chosen methods should relate specifically to the object that contains them. For example a 'take off' method would not fit in terribly well with our Car object, as it clearly doesn't fit in with what a car does.

The process of packaging up functionality in an object by specifying these essential characteristics and behaviors is called **encapsulation** – this is the fundamental feature of an object-oriented system that supports the process of abstraction. Once we encapsulate functionality within an object, we can treat it as a perfectly self-contained whole and only consider its most important properties (data held within the object) and methods (blocks of code that can use and/or modify that data). We can then focus on how our object interacts with other code and forget about how it works inside; never again will we need to hold the entire application in mind at once.

So, once we have a car object, we can ask it to do things for us without needing to know how it does it. Since .NET provides us with so many useful, ready-built objects, we can pick and choose from them according to what we want them to *do* for us; as long as we know what methods and properties they expose, we don't need to worry about how they work underneath. Effectively, Microsoft has built half our web site for us already, and in the next chapter we'll specifically look at each of the main objects that underpin all our ASP.NET web pages. Before that though, we're going to introduce you to the basic mechanics of defining, creating, and using objects.

Using Objects

So, now that we have some idea why objects can be useful to us, how are we going to work with them in the context of a web page? First, we need to consider where they come from.

"Mommy, where do objects come from?"

Before we ask .NET to create an object, it has to find out what how that object works, and what it is supposed to look like. If we want to create a brand new type of object, we need to start out by defining a blueprint for that object, which we call an **object class definition** (or more usually, just a **class**). This must describe *everything* there is to know about how any object of that type works, both internally and externally.

When we actually create an object – a specific **instance** of the class – the .NET Framework takes this blueprint and uses it as a template for the new object. For example, if we'd defined a class called Car, we could then use it to create several Car type objects:

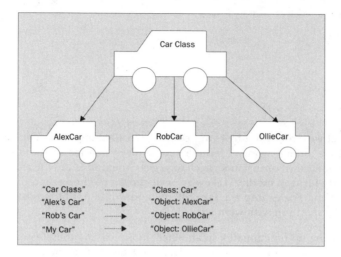

The diagram above shows how we might create (the technical term is actually **instantiate**) three separate objects from a single class. In this case, we call them AlexCar, RobCar, and OllieCar, denoting the fact that they represent three different cars belonging to three different people. We might choose to set the color property on Alex's car object to "red" – even if we then set the same property on Rob's car object to "yellow", Alex's car would stay red.

Just to give you an idea of precisely how simple it is to do this, here's a snippet of code that instantiates all three objects and assigns properties as described. We'll assume for now that we've already defined the Car object, and we'll see how we can do that in a moment:

```
Dim AlexCar, RobCar, OllieCar As Car

AlexCar = New Car()
RobCar = New Car()
OllieCar = New Car()

AlexCar.Color = "red"
RobCar.Color = "yellow"
```

Defining a class

It's very easy to define a class in ASP.NET, and it's not dissimilar to how we declared variables and subroutines in the last couple of chapters. In fact, variables and subroutines play a crucial role in our class definitions, since we use them both in defining methods and properties. Let's take a look at how we might define our Car class – for now, we'll consider just two properties Color and Gear, and one method ChangeGear().

We start out by declaring that we want to define a public class called Car:

```
Public Class Car
```

The fact that we specify the **visibility** of this class as Public, means that we'll be able to use it from anywhere in our code. There are other options available (Private and Protected), which can be used to restrict use of the class to specific parts of an application – this doesn't really become an issue until we look at defining classes within classes, so we'll leave further discussion until the next chapter, when we look at that topic.

Our next step is to declare a couple of variables: a string to denote the color of the car object, and an integer denoting the gear it's currently in:

```
Private _Color As String
Private _Gear As Integer
```

Now, it's important to note that these variables do *not* comprise the class properties – there's more to properties than that. These are simply private variables that will be held within each instance of a Car type object; they will only visible to code that's part of *that particular object*.

Elements within a class or object are generically referred to as **members,** and the full technical name for these particular variables is **private instance data members**: they represent *data*, and are *private* within each *instance* of the class. It's common practice to name private members with an underscore at the beginning, so that it's clear throughout our code which members are for internal use only.

> We can define the overall state of an object by considering the values of all its data members. If the data members within two instances of the same class all have identical values, we can say that the objects have identical state.

We're now ready to expose our first property. This is also declared with Public visibility, which means that we'll be able to access this property (called Color) from outside the object:

```
Public Property Color() As String
  Get
    Return _Color
  End Get
  Set(value As String)
    _Color = value
  End Set
End Property
```

As you can see, we're now using the private data member _Color (which, as we know, holds a string describing the color of each Car instance) and specifying two sub-blocks: Get and Set. These are actually special methods that let us define the code that's used to respectively retrieve values from the private member and set values on it. They're known technically as **accessor methods**, since they grant us *access* to the object's private members.

Accessors are a much better way to expose an object's data members than letting users manipulate them directly. Apart from helping us specify certain properties as providing only read (or write) access, they give us the ability to write custom code that is executed whenever the property is accessed.

265

So, whenever we try to retrieve (that is, 'get') the property value, the code we've defined between `Get` and `End Get` will be executed, and the value specified in the final `Return` statement is the value our calling code gets back. In this case, we simply return whatever value happens to be stored in `_Color` at the time.

In this case, we just want to get and set the contents directly, so we use the `Return` statement to Get the private value:

```
Get
   Return _Color
End Get
```

Likewise, when we try to assign (that is, 'set') a new value to the property, we run the code defined between `Set` and `End Set`. In this case, the parameter value is assigned to the local string value, and we use value to assign this data to the private member:

```
Set(value As String)
  _Color = value
End Set
```

In fact, even if we don't specify `(value As String)` ASP.NET will automatically put the assigned data in a variable called value, which is defined with the same type as we've used for the property. In other words, although it's not such good practice, we could actually get away with saying:

```
Set
  _Color = value
End Set
```

When we talk about a property, we're actually referring to the object-specific data that's exposed by these two accessor methods. In this case, that's the *value* of the private member _Color – take note: that's not the variable itself, but just the data it contains.

Our next property, `Gear()` gives a clearer example of this important distinction, as we only define a `Get` method to give us access to the private member _Gear. This requires us to specify the keyword `ReadOnly` within the property declaration header:

```
Public ReadOnly Property Gear() As Integer
   Get
     Return _Gear
   End Get
End Property
```

What's the point of this then? Now we can only *look* at a `Car` object's `Gear` property, and have no way to change it. Well, as we mentioned earlier on, one of the advantages of using objects is that we can hide away any functionality that we deem inappropriate. If we simply exposed the _Gear integer to the outside world as a property, we could easily set it to any integer value; however, that would break our model, insofar as there's not much we can usefully say about a car that's supposedly in 1739th gear (apart from expressing a little scepticism). What's more, we'd like to protect the gearbox from too much wear and tear, so we're restricting our drivers to incremental gear changes – that is, one gear up (or down) at a time.

This is where our method definition makes an appearance. It's literally just a subroutine that takes a single parameter and uses it as the basis for performing operations on the private member _Gear. What's more, it can take a look at the modified value of _Gear, and ensure that it's maintained within certain constraints. We've decided to model a 5-gear car, so (assuming that 'neutral' is represented by a zero value, and 'reverse' by negative one) we constrain it between values of -1 and +5:

```
Public Sub ChangeGear(direction As Integer)
   If direction < 0 Then _Gear -= 1
   If direction > 0 Then _Gear += 1
   If _Gear > 5 Then _Gear = 5
   If _Gear < -1 Then _Gear = -1
End Sub
```

When we call this method, we'll need to specify a single integer parameter – if that's positive, we move up one gear; if it's negative we move down one gear. If either of our constraints is breached, the gear number is set to the constraining value.

All we then have to do is mark the end of our class definition:

```
End Class
```

In order to use this class definition in an ASPX file, we simply need to place it in a declarative code block (that is, inside the body of a `<script runat="server">` element). However, before we do that, let's take a quick look at how we're going to use our new class. We need to start out by creating an **instance** of the class – that is, we have a blueprint for our Car; now we need to find out how to use it to make an *actual* Car object.

Creating Objects

The process of creating an object from a class definition is called **instantiation**, and we do it in much the same way as we do with variables of the built-in types (String, Integer, and so on). We can break the process down into two stages: declaration and initialization.

We declare an object in exactly the same way as we declare a variable. For example, to declare a Car type object called AlexCar, we can do it like this:

```
Dim AlexCar As Car
```

If we were now to try to use it, however, we'd find ourselves in a spot of bother – let's consider why.

Simple data types don't take up very much memory, so there's little or no harm in setting aside memory for them as soon as they've been declared: once you say `Dim number As Integer`, you can use the label number straight away in your code to refer to a section of memory that's been set aside to hold an Integer type value.

Although we've now established that the label 'AlexCar' should refer to an object of type 'Car', the .NET Framework won't actually set aside any memory for that object until you specifically ask it to. As we know, good coding practice requires us to declare all our variables upfront, so that we don't fall prey to subtle typos at every turn – just the same goes for objects. An object may take up a relatively large block of memory, however and since we might not need to use it straight away, it's crucial that we have the option to delay the allocation of memory, so as not to consume great swathes of system resources unnecessarily.

267

We therefore need a second line of code to actually create a slot in memory for our object. We use the New keyword to actually *initialize* the Car object:

```
Dim AlexCar As Car
AlexCar = New Car()
```

So, the first line specifies a label that we'll use to point to the Car object, while the second actually creates the Car object for us. As luck would have it, we can squash the two statements into one:

```
Dim AlexCar As New Car()
```

You'll see this style of Dim statement used whenever we create an object from a class. We now have the means to instantiate a fully functional (if rather simple) Car object.

Using Methods and Properties

We use an object's methods to tell it to do things, and its properties expose information about its state, or what it *is*. It's very easy to make a method call – simply state the name of the object whose method you want to call, add a period, add the name of the method, and add a pair of brackets. If the method requires you to specify any parameters, you can add them inside the brackets, separated by commas.

If we want our to make our AlexCar object change up a gear, we should be able to forget about the gearbox and all its inner workings, and simply tell it to do what we want in the form of a very simple command. In this case, we'd call the ChangeGear() method with a positive parameter as follows:

```
AlexCar.ChangeGear(+1)
```

The syntax used to make a method call is just like we used in the last chapter to call a subroutine or function, except that we need to specify a particular object name before the method name, so that it's clear which object's method we wish to call.

In fact, all the calls we looked at in the last chapter were actually method calls themselves. All those subs and functions were defined as part of the declarative code block (between <script> tags), but not within an explicit class declaration therefore, they were incorporated as methods on the underlying Page object. All our page code also resides in this object, we can call these local methods without specifying an object beforehand.

As well as asking the object to perform actions for us, we can find out about its current state by means of its properties. These allow us to access and modify the data within the object – we access them using the same dot notation as we did to make method calls – but don't require us to use brackets after their names. For example, we could set the color of the car using this statement:

```
MyCar.Color = "Turquoise"
```

Alternatively, if we wanted to assign the color of Alex's car to a string variable, we could write some code like this:

```
Dim strCarColor As String
strCarColor = AlexCar.Color
```

> Remember, an object's properties don't necessarily map one-to-one with the data stored inside it. In some cases, our accessor methods (by which means the properties are exposed) may expose data that's based on the information held in several different private members. It may even be that the information exposed originates in an external data source, such as a file or database.

Try It Out – Working with a Car Object

In this example, we'll place our Car class definition within an ASP.NET page and use it to create an object called MyCar. We'll then set the object's Color property to Yellow, and display that color on the page by reading it back out of the object.

1. Create a file called car_object1.aspx, and type in the following code:

```
<%@ page language="vb" runat="server" %>

<script runat="server">

Public Class Car

   Private _Color As String
   Private _Gear As Integer

   Public Property Color As String
     Get
        Return _Color
     End Get
     Set
        _Color = value
     End Set
   End Property

   Public ReadOnly Property Gear As Integer
     Get
        Return _Gear
     End Get
   End Property

   Public Sub ChangeGear(direction As Integer)
     If direction < 0 Then _Gear -= 1
     If direction > 0 Then _Gear += 1
     If _Gear > 5 Then _Gear = 5
     If _Gear < -1 Then _Gear = -1
   End Sub

End Class

Sub Page_Load()
   Dim MyCar As New Car()
   Response.Write("<b>New object 'MyCar' created.</b>")

   Response.Write("<br/>Color: " & MyCar.Color)
   Response.Write("<br/>Gear: " & MyCar.Gear)
```

```
    MyCar.Color = "Black"
    MyCar.ChangeGear(+1)
    Response.Write("<br/><b>Properties updated.</b>")

    Response.Write("<br/>New color: " & MyCar.Color)
    Response.Write("<br/>New gear: " & MyCar.Gear)

End Sub

</script>
```

2. Save the file and call it up in your browser – here's what it looks like:

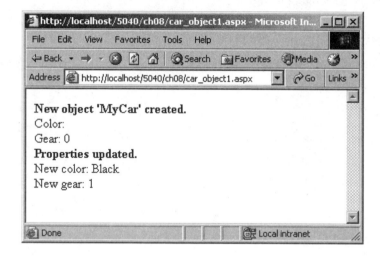

How It Works

Our first block of code defines our public car class, as we described earlier. The first thing we do in here is to declare our private members, variables `_Color` and `_Gear` that will store each of our `Car` objects' internal data:

```
<%@ page language="vb" runat="server" %>

<script runat="server">

Public Class Car

   Private _Color As String
   Private _Gear As Integer
```

Next, we define the public property `Color()`, so that when we come to use a `Car` object, we can read values straight from its private member `_Color` (courtesy of `Get`) and assign values to it (thanks to `Set`):

```
Public Property Color As String
   Get
      Return _Color
   End Get
   Set
      _Color = value
   End Set
End Property
```

Our next property Gear is specified as ReadOnly; it therefore has just one accessor method Get, so that we can read the value of _Gear, but can't assign values to it directly:

```
Public ReadOnly Property Gear As Integer
   Get
      Return _Gear
   End Get
End Property
```

The method ChangeGear() however lets us modify _Gear by increments – we specify an integer parameter called direction, and depending on whether it's positive or negative, we move the car up or down a gear. We don't want it getting carried away, so we check to see if _Gear is too high or low to make sense in the context of our model; if it's out of range, we simply pull it back into range again:

```
Public Sub ChangeGear(direction As Integer)
   If direction < 0 Then _Gear -= 1
   If direction > 0 Then _Gear += 1
   If _Gear > 5 Then _Gear = 5
   If _Gear < -1 Then _Gear = -1
End Sub

End Class
```

That's our class defined; now to make use of it. We want to demonstrate how the object's properties change over time, therefore we've put all our code into the Page_Load sub, where we know it will be executed in sequence. As we know, using Response.Write() like this isn't really the best way to write ASP.NET pages; in this case though, it helps us to demonstrate what's happening to the object as we progress through the code.

We start off by creating a Car type object called MyCar, and generating a message to that effect:

```
Sub Page_Load()
   Dim MyCar As New Car()
   Response.Write("<b>New object 'MyCar' created.</b>")
```

Next, we use properties Color and Gear to access information from the object, and then write it out to the browser along with appropriate captions:

```
   Response.Write("<br/>Color: " & MyCar.Color)
   Response.Write("<br/>Gear: " & MyCar.Gear)
```

We now assign the string "Black" to the Color property; and use the ChangeGear() method with a positive parameter to move up a gear. Note that even if we'd specified ChangeGear(+10), the gear number would still only have gone up by one:

271

```
MyCar.Color = "Black"
MyCar.ChangeGear(+1)
Response.Write("<br/><b>Properties updated.</b>")
```

Finally, we write out the new property values, so that we can see how they've changed:

```
Response.Write("<br/>New color: " & MyCar.Color)
Response.Write("<br/>New gear: " & MyCar.Gear)

End Sub

</script>
```

We've now seen a very simple demonstration of how we can define a class, create an object, and then use and manipulate its public members (that is, the object's properties and methods).

> You may have spotted that the Response.Write() mechanism we've been using to send text to the browser actually takes the form of an object method call. Response is actually the name of an object used by ASP.NET to work with the HTTP response stream – the stream of data that's sent from the web server to a client browser, carrying all the page information (including all the HTML source) that's used to make up the web page you end up seeing displayed.
>
> Response is actually an instance of the HttpResponse class, and Write() is one of the methods defined by this class. We're going to take a much more detailed look at Response (and other important ASP.NET objects) in the next chapter.

That's all well and good as a demonstration, but we haven't really seen much practical benefit so far. It seems like an awful lot of trouble to go to just to bundle a few values together. That's partly because we don't have a specific use in mind for our Car object; we selected it simply because it's a familiar real-world object that has lots of complex functionality to model – as such it's great for making a conceptual start, but not really terribly useful until we perhaps decide to build some kind of a driving simulator.

Let's look at another example, which might be a little more useful in the context of a simple web application – a calculator.

Try It Out – Creating a Calculator Class

In this section, we're going to start building a class called Calculator that will allow us to perform simple operations on user-supplied values. Just like a real calculator, one of our Calculator objects should be able to maintain a 'working value', and let us perform sequences of operations (add, subtract, multiply, divide) on that as required. We therefore need the following public members:

❑ Properties – CurrentValue

❑ Methods – Add, Subtract, Multiply, Divide, Clear

We therefore need a private data member, which we'll call _current, to hold the data we'll expose via the CurrentValue property.

1. Create a new file in your test directory. The first thing we need to do is define the `Calculator` class, so add the following code:

```
<%@ page language="vb" runat="server" %>

<script runat="server">

  Public Class Calculator

    Private _current As Double

    Public ReadOnly Property CurrentValue As Double
      Get
        Return _current
      End Get
    End Property

    Public Sub Add(addValue As Double)
      _current += addValue
    End Sub

    Public Sub Subtract(addValue As Double)
      _current -= addValue
    End Sub

    Public Sub Multiply(addValue As Double)
      _current *= addValue
    End Sub

    Public Sub Divide(addValue As Double)
      _current /= addValue
    End Sub

    Public Sub Clear()
      _current = 0
    End Sub

  End Class
```

2. Now we add some operations to be executed when the page is loaded:

```
  Sub Page_Load()
    Dim MyCalc As New Calculator()
    Response.Write("<b>Created a new Calculator object.</b><br/>")
    Response.Write("Current Value = " & MyCalc.CurrentValue)

    MyCalc.Add(23)
    Response.Write("<br/><b>Added 23 - MyCalc.Add(23)</b><br/>")
    Response.Write("Current Value = " & MyCalc.CurrentValue)

    MyCalc.Subtract(7)
    Response.Write("<br/><b>Subtracted 7 - MyCalc.Subtract(7)</b><br/>")
    Response.Write("Current Value = " & MyCalc.CurrentValue)

    MyCalc.Multiply(3)
    Response.Write("<br/><b>Multiplied by 3 - MyCalc.Multiply(3)</b><br/>")
    Response.Write("Current Value = " & MyCalc.CurrentValue)
```

```
      MyCalc.Divide(4)
      Response.Write("<br/><b>Divided by 4 - MyCalc.Divide(4)</b><br/>")
      Response.Write("Current Value = " & MyCalc.CurrentValue)

      MyCalc.Clear()
      Response.Write("<br/><b>Cleared - MyCalc.Clear()</b><br/>")
      Response.Write("Current Value = " & MyCalc.CurrentValue)
   End Sub

</script>
```

3. Finally, save the page as `calculator_object.aspx` and point your browser to it. You'll see something like this:

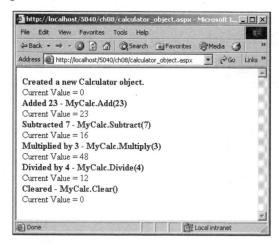

How it Works

What we've done here is conceptually very similar to what we did when with the Car class: we started off by defining a class, and used it to instantiate an object, which we then manipulated in a number of different ways via its public members. In this case, we only have access to the object's innards via five methods – the only property on a `Calculator` object is specified as `ReadOnly`:

```
<%@ page language="vb" runat="server" %>

<script runat="server">

   Public Class Calculator

     Private _current As Double

     Public ReadOnly Property CurrentValue As Double
       Get
         Return _current
       End Get
     End Property
```

Notice that we've used the `Public` keyword again – this tells .NET that anyone with an instance of Calculator is allowed access to the `CurrentValue` property (even if it is limited to read-only). If we were to replace `Public` with `Private`, `CurrentValue` would only be available to other properties and methods within the same object.

Our first method `Add()` will add a specified `Double` to the current value held in `_current`. The next three perform various other operations in the same way:

```
Public Sub Add(addValue As Double)
  _current += addValue
End Sub

Public Sub Subtract(addValue As Double)
  _current -= addValue
End Sub

Public Sub Multiply(addValue As Double)
  _current *= addValue
End Sub

Public Sub Divide(addValue As Double)
  _current /= addValue
End Sub
```

The final method `Clear()` simply resets our `_current` data member back to zero:

```
Public Sub Clear()
  _current = 0
End Sub

End Class
```

Now we define the usual `Page_Load()` subroutine, in which we instantiate an object based on our Calculator class:

```
Sub Page_Load()
  Dim MyCalc As New Calculator()
  Response.Write("<b>Created a new Calculator object.</b><br/>")
  Response.Write("Current Value = " & MyCalc.CurrentValue)
```

Each of the next few blocks of code calls one of the object's (rather self-explanatory) methods, and writes out the current value once the method call's completed:

```
MyCalc.Add(23)
Response.Write("<br/><b>Added 23 - MyCalc.Add(23)</b><br/>")
Response.Write("Current Value = " & MyCalc.CurrentValue)

MyCalc.Subtract(7)
Response.Write("<br/><b>Subtracted 7 - MyCalc.Subtract(7)</b><br/>")
Response.Write("Current Value = " & MyCalc.CurrentValue)

MyCalc.Multiply(3)
Response.Write("<br/><b>Multiplied by 3 - MyCalc.Multiply(3)</b><br/>")
Response.Write("Current Value = " & MyCalc.CurrentValue)
```

```
      MyCalc.Divide(4)
      Response.Write("<br/><b>Divided by 4 - MyCalc.Divide(4)</b><br/>")
      Response.Write("Current Value = " & MyCalc.CurrentValue)

      MyCalc.Clear()
      Response.Write("<br/><b>Cleared - MyCalc.Clear()</b><br/>")
      Response.Write("Current Value = " & MyCalc.CurrentValue)
   End Sub

</script>
```

Once again, we've used Response.Write() to display a running tally, so that we can see how each of our operations affects the MyCalc.CurrentValue property. In practice though, we'd endeavour to find a cleaner way to present the data, probably using a variety of ASP.NET controls to separate our code (responsible for dynamic content generation) from the presentation structure (using pure HTML and control elements to mark where we want our dynamic content placed).

Initializing Objects with Constructors

So far we've glossed over a few technicalities that arise when we're creating objects. One of these is the matter of initialization: we'll often define object properties that need to have well-defined values at all times. Perhaps we're modeling a bookstore – each Book object we create will need to have a well-defined Title property, as well as an ISBN property.

We *could* just leave it to trust that every time someone using our class made a new Book(), they'd follow it up with statements like:

```
Book.Title = "Beginning ASP.NET"
Book.ISBN = 1861005040
```

In fact, trusting the user should be the very last thing we want to do. Most of the advantages of using objects stem from the fact that they let us prevent users getting so much as a chance to break their functionality. The other problem we might face is that properties such as these are likely to be defined as ReadOnly – after all, we shouldn't allow users to rename a Book object when the physical book it represents doesn't let us do so.

As far as our bookstore is concerned, a book without a name and ISBN is useless. Consequently, a Book object that doesn't have well-defined properties Title and ISBN is a *broken* book object. So how do we get round this? We follow the example of our real life book: we make sure that the relevant internal members are given appropriate values when the object is created – that is, we initialize these private members as part of the instantiation process.

We can do this by defining a special class method that will be called whenever we construct an object. As you'll recall from our earlier discussion, we can break the process of instantiation down into two stages:

```
Dim AlexCar As Car          'declaration
AlexCar = New Car()         'initialization
```

The second of these stages is responsible for setting up the object in memory, and will call on a **constructor** method for that object to do the necessary work. Constructors normally just work behind the scenes, and we don't need to know what they're doing – we just trust them to get our objects ready for use, and to set their data members to sensible values.

However, we can also make use of constructors explicitly – when we specifically want to initialize an object's data members (that is, specify how we want the object to be set up). We can tap into this process by simply defining a class method called New(). Whenever we construct an object using the New keyword, .NET will look out for a definition of this method within the class; if one exists, it will automatically execute any code we've placed inside it as a part of the construction process.

Try it out – Initializing Book Properties

In this example, we're going to create an object called MyBook from a brand new Book class, within which we'll define a constructor method so that it's automatically initialized with values for _Title and _Isbn.

1. Open up your editor and type in this code:

```
<%@ page language="vb" runat="server" %>

<script runat="server">
Public Class Book
    Private _Title As String
    Private _Isbn As Integer
    Private _Price As Decimal

    Public Sub New()
      _Title = "Beginning ASP.NET"
      _Isbn = 1861005040
    End Sub

    Public ReadOnly Property TitleInfo As String
       Get
          Return _Title & " <i>(ISBN: " & _Isbn & ")</i>"
       End Get
    End Property

    Public ReadOnly Property Title As String
       Get
          Return _Title
       End Get
    End Property

    Public ReadOnly Property Isbn As Integer
       Get
          Return _Isbn
       End Get
    End Property

    Public Property Price As Decimal
       Get
          Return _Price
       End Get
       Set(value As Decimal)
          _Price = value
       End Set
    End Property
End Class
```

2. We now add some code that will create and use the object when the page is loaded:

```
Sub Page_Load()
  Dim MyBook As New Book()
  Response.Write("<b>New book 'MyBook' created.</b>")

  MyBook.Price = "39.99"
  Response.Write("<br/>Title info: " & MyBook.TitleInfo)
  Response.Write("<br/>Price: $" & MyBook.Price & "<br/>")
End Sub

</script>
```

3. Now save the file in your test directory as `book_object.aspx`, and call it up from your browser – you should see this:

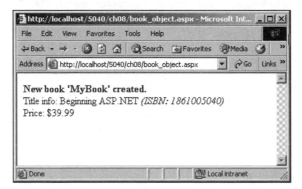

All well and good – that is, until we want to create an object that represents a different book. Due to the way we've defined our constructor, we've effectively hard-wired this specific book information into our class definition, and in doing so, radically reduced the potential usefulness of the class. Unless the bookstore's business plan relies solely on the runaway success of this one book, they are going to need a little more flexibility.

In fact, this isn't an enormous problem.

4. Update the constructor method as follows:

```
Public Sub New(newTitle As String, newIsbn As Integer)
  _Title = newTitle
  _Isbn = newIsbn
End Sub
```

5. Now add appropriate parameters to the end of the `Dim` statement in `Page_Load()`:

```
Sub Page_Load()
  Dim MyBook As New Book("Beginning ASP.NET", 1861005040)
  Response.Write("<b>New book 'MyBook' created.</b>")
  ...
End Sub
```

6. If you run the sample again, you'll see exactly the same results. However, if you now add the following lines to Page_Load(), you'll see that we now have much more flexibility:

```
Sub Page_Load()
  Dim MyBook As New Book("Beginning ASP.NET", 1861005040)
  Response.Write("<b>New book 'MyBook' created.</b>")
  MyBook.Price = "39.99"
  Response.Write("<br/>Title info: " & MyBook.TitleInfo)
  Response.Write("<br/>Price: $" & MyBook.Price & "<br/>")

  Dim AnotherBook As New Book("Professional ASP.NET", 1861004885)
  Response.Write("<b>New book 'AnotherBook' created.</b>")
  AnotherBook.Price = "59.99"
  Response.Write("<br/>Title info: " & AnotherBook.TitleInfo)
  Response.Write("<br/>Price: $" & AnotherBook.Price & "<br/>")
End Sub

</script>
```

7. Call up the page one last time, and you should see information displayed on both books:

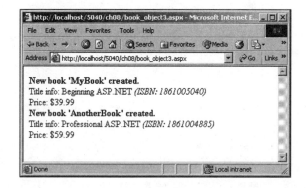

How It Works

The most important sections in this example are the New() method we define on our Book class, and the Dim statement we use to instantiate an object from that class. Any code we place inside the New() constructor method gets executed as and when each new Book type object is created:

```
Public Sub New(newTitle As String, newIsbn As Integer)
  _Title = newTitle
  _Isbn = newIsbn
End Sub
```

By using parameters as part of the constructor method call, we can specify how we want each object to be initialized as a part of the Dim statement we use to instantiate it:

```
Dim MyBook As New Book("Beginning ASP.NET", 1861005040)
```

Now that these values are set for the new object, they can only be accessed via ReadOnly properties, such as MyBook.Title, MyBook.Isbn, or MyBook.TitleInfo (which returns an HTML string containing both the title and ISBN for the appropriate book in a standard format).

Overloaded Methods

When we write methods and subroutines that take parameters, it's important to account for all the different combinations of parameters we might want them to accept. If we consider the constructor method that we defined in the last example, perhaps we need the option to specify a subtitle for the book as part of the instantiation. We want to keep it separate from the main title (since the subtitle may be long and too unwieldy to display comfortably on the web site), but can't guarantee that we'll need to specify it for every book. In fact, most books won't require its use at all. The obvious solution is to add it to the class as follows:

```
Public Class Book
    Private _Title As String
    Private _Isbn As Integer
    Private _Price As Decimal
    Private _Subtitle As String

    Public Sub New(newTitle As String, newIsbn As Integer, _
                              newSubtitle As String)
        _Title = newTitle
        _Isbn = newIsbn
        _Subtitle = newSubtitle
    End Sub

    Public ReadOnly Property Subtitle As String
        Get
            Return _Subtitle
        End Get
    End Property
    ...
```

That's absolutely fine, assuming we have a subtitle to assign:

```
Dim ABigBook As New Book("Professional Linux Programming", 1861003013, _
        "Databases, PostgreSQL, MySQL, LDAP, security, device drivers, "& _
        "GTK+, GNOME, Glade, GUI, KDE, Qt, Python, PHP, RPC, "& _
        "diskless systems, multimedia, internationalization, CORBA, PAM, "& _
        "RPM, CVS, Flex, Bison, Beowulf, Clustering, ORBit, MPI, PVM, "& _
        "and XML")
```

Even if we don't, we can always just specify an empty string:

```
Dim AnotherBigBook As New Book("Professional C#", 1861004990, "")
```

This opens us up however, to another 'can break, will break' situation. Since most of the books aren't going to require users to specify the last parameter, it's quite possible that sooner or later someone will forget to put it in – the class will have all the information it needs to fully instantiate an object, but the method call's **signature** will be incorrect, so it won't work.

> When we talk about a method's signature, we're referring to the specific combination of parameter types that the method definition is designed to accept. If two methods both accept parameters (String, Integer, String) then we can say that they have the same signature. If we then call one of them, but only specify a single parameter, then our method call has an incorrect signature. If we've specified `Strict=True` as part of the `Page` directive, we can't rely on implicit type conversion. Therefore, a method call that specifies parameters of the incorrect type –(String, Integer, Integer) for example – would also be considered as having an invalid signature.

Fortunately, there's a quick way out. We simply define *another* constructor method – one that takes just two parameters (as this one did in the first place). We then have:

```
Public Sub New(newTitle As String, newIsbn As Integer)
  _Title = newTitle
  _Isbn = newIsbn
End Sub

Public Sub New(newTitle As String, newIsbn As Integer, _
                            newSubtitle As String)
  _Title = newTitle
  _Isbn = newIsbn
  _Subtitle = newSubtitle
End Sub
```

Basically, we now have two constructor methods with the same name on our Book class – the only difference lies in their signatures. Fortunately, this is enough for .NET to distinguish between them, and we can safely use either form.

It's actually very common to find objects with several constructors, each having a different signature. For example, if you use the Class Browser (which we looked at briefly in Chapter 2) to take a look at the methods available on the System.DateTime class, you'll see that it actually contains *seven different* constructor methods:

Class System.DateTime

Constructors

Visibility	Constructor	Parameters
public	DateTime	(Int64 ticks)
public	DateTime	(Int32 year , Int32 month , Int32 day)
public	DateTime	(Int32 year , Int32 month , Int32 day , Calendar calendar)
public	DateTime	(Int32 year , Int32 month , Int32 day , Int32 hour , Int32 minute , Int32 second)
public	DateTime	(Int32 year , Int32 month , Int32 day , Int32 hour , Int32 minute , Int32 second , Calendar calendar)
public	DateTime	(Int32 year , Int32 month , Int32 day , Int32 hour , Int32 minute , Int32 second , Int32 millisecond)
public	DateTime	(Int32 year , Int32 month , Int32 day , Int32 hour , Int32 minute , Int32 second , Int32 millisecond , Calendar calendar)

In this case, the different signatures reflect different ways (and different levels of accuracy) in which we may want to specify a date and time. We can use a single Int64 value (a long type of Integer) to specify the number of ticks (100 nanosecond units – that is, 10000000 ticks make one second) between midnight on January 1st in the year 1AD and the time we wish to specify. This helps us if we need to make very accurate measurements over short periods of time, as we might want to do when examining the performance of the server. For more pedestrian use of the DateTime object, we can opt to specify three Int32 values (Int32 is what .NET calls standard Integers internally) for the year, month, and day. Or, if we want the time as well, we can specify that down to the second, or even down to the millisecond. There's also the option to specify a Calendar object

Calendar objects are designed to help account for various different implementations of the calendar – for instance, leap years and BC/AD distinctions are accounted for when using the Gregorian calendar, whereas the Japanese calendar recognizes an era corresponding to the reign of each Emperor.

Effectively, Microsoft has defined seven *different* constructors that happen to share the same name. Depending on how we want to use the `DateTime` object we're instantiating, we can choose the most appropriate one, without having to remember seven different constructor method names. We describe this process as **overloading** the constructor.

> When we overload an object method, the main proviso is that each version of that method should have a different signature.

In fact, we can apply this principle to any method calls we define on an object. If we have a class that defines two methods that basically do the same thing, but use different parameters to do so, we might want to consider using just one name for all three. Consider our `Car` class for a moment. It already features a `ChangeGear()` method, whose signature is of the form:

```
ChangeGear(direction As Integer)
```

Perhaps we now decide to offer users the opportunity to specify "up" or "down" as parameters, which will move the gear incrementally up or down respectively. Our initial approach might be to define a brand new method – `ChangeGearUsingWords(direction As String)`. That should work just fine, but it's going to be a pain for a developer using it to have to remember to use the new method name. It's surely far better to overload the original method, so that it's simply a matter of choosing between a string and an integer for the parameter. We can do this as follows:

```
Overloads Public Sub ChangeGear(direction As Integer)
  ...
End Sub

Overloads Public Sub ChangeGear(direction As String)
  ...
End Sub
```

Note that we use the keyword `Overloads` in defining both methods. Now that we're not working with constructors we need to be a little more explicit, and specify this keyword before defining each method we're going to overload.

> *While it's quite possible for ASP.NET to figure out what's going on here without the keyword (as with type conversion, it won't actually complain at all unless you have the 'Strict' option turned on) it's worth including nevertheless, simply so that it's clear to anyone looking at your code – including yourself – that these methods have been overloaded.*

We can now call the method as `MyCar.ChangeGear("up")` or `MyCar.ChangeGear("down")`, and it will do exactly what we'd expect. What's more, the old technique `MyCar.ChangeGear(+55)` still works as well, so we don't break any code we've already written to use *that* form.

Using one name for several similar actions is often far more convenient to programmer than having five very similar methods with different names. Overloading can therefore make life a great deal easier for developers.

Try it out – Using an Overloaded Constructor

In this example we're going to use some of the constructors defined on the Framework class System.DateTime. We'll create four separate objects from the same class, using a different constructor each time. Each time, we'll display the resultant setting. First, we'll create a DateTime object using its default constructor; next we'll use a constructor that lets us specify a particular date; third, we'll use a constructor that lets us specify the time as well, and finally, we'll just specify a few million ticks, to see how they work in practice.

1. Open up your editor and type in this code:

```
<%@ Page Language="VB" %>

<script runat="server">
  sub Page_Load()
    Dim myDateTime1 As New DateTime()
    Response.Write(myDateTime1)
    Response.Write("<br />")

    Dim myDateTime2 As New DateTime(1972,11,4)
    Response.Write(myDateTime2)
    Response.Write("<br />")
    Dim myDateTime3 As New DateTime(1972,11,4,14,5,0)
    Response.Write(myDateTime3)
    Response.Write("<br />")

    Dim myDateTime4 As New DateTime(260000000)
    Response.Write(myDateTime4)
    Response.Write("<br />")
  end sub
</script>
```

2. Save the file in your test directory as datetime_constructor.aspx

3. Open up your browser and view the file; you should see something like this:

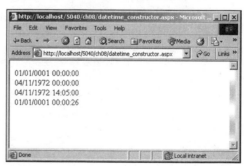

Note that the first line shows "1/1/0001 12:00:00 AM", which is the default 'zero' date and time that the object uses if we do not specify anything else.

How It Works

First time around, we simply instantiate the object using its default constructor. Since it's a basic system object, we don't *need* to specify brackets after the class name, but we do so here for clarity:

```
Dim myDateTime1 As New DateTime()
```

With the second `DateTime` object we pass three parameters to the constructor: integers representing year, month, and day respectively:

```
Dim myDateTime2 As New DateTime(1972,11,4)
```

We now create our third `DateTime` object and pass it six parameters, specifying not only the date, but also the time. The last three parameters are integers representing hour, minutes, and seconds:

```
Dim myDateTime3 As New DateTime(1972,11,4,14,5,0)
```

Finally, we specify 260 million ticks, which equate to 'zero' plus twenty-six seconds:

```
Dim myDateTime4 As New DateTime(260000000)
```

As we'd expect, the time shows up as 12:00:26 AM on January 1st in the year 1AD.

Try it out – Using an Overloaded Method

Let's look at a worked example of overloading one of our own methods. While we're at it, we're going to give our `Car` class a single constructor method, so that `Car` objects can be defined with a specific color.

1. Open up our earlier sample `car_object1.aspx`, and modify it as follows:

```
<%@ page language="vb" runat="server" %>

<script runat="server">
Public Class Car
  ...
  Overloads Public Sub ChangeGear(direction As Integer)
    If direction < 0 Then _Gear -= 1
    If direction > 0 Then _Gear += 1
    If _Gear > 5 Then _Gear = 5
    If _Gear < -1 Then _Gear = -1
  End Sub

  Overloads Public Sub ChangeGear(direction As String)
    If direction = "down" Then ChangeGear(-1)
    If direction = "up" Then ChangeGear(+1)
  End Sub

  Sub New()
    _color = "cold grey steel"
  End Sub

End Class

Sub Page_Load()
  ...
  Response.Write("<br/>New color: " & MyCar.Color)
  Response.Write("<br/>New gear: " & MyCar.Gear)
```

```
    MyCar.ChangeGear("up")
    Response.Write("<br/><b>Shifted 'up' one gear.</b>")

    Response.Write("<br/>New gear: " & MyCar.Gear)

End Sub

</script>
```

2. Now save this in your test directory as `car_object_overload.aspx`, and call it up in your browser:

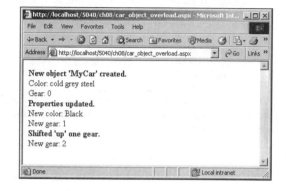

How It Works

We'll start by taking a look at the class definition, where we can see the original version of the method, which takes an integer parameter:

```
Overloads Public Sub ChangeGear(direction As Integer)
    If direction < 0 Then _Gear -= 1
    If direction > 0 Then _Gear += 1
    If _Gear > 5 Then _Gear = 5
    If _Gear < -1 Then _Gear = -1
End Sub
```

Now comes the clever part – we define a new subroutine that gives us a new way to do the same thing. Note that we *might* have just done it as follow, using a near copy of the code in our original method, with just three differences:

```
Overloads Public Sub ChangeGear(direction As String)
    If direction = "down" Then _Gear -= 1
    If direction = "up" Then _Gear += 1
    If _Gear > 5 Then _Gear = 5
    If _Gear < -1 Then _Gear = -1
End Sub
```

However, it should be quite obvious that this is unnecessary – what's more, it opens up a whole new set of potential problems. Just imagine what would happen if we decided to change the top gear specified, but only remembered to update it in the first method. Perhaps ChangeGear(string) would now max out at 6, while ChangeGear(int) still stopped at 5. The two overloaded methods would behave differently, when they clearly should not.

For these reasons, you're encouraged to do all you can reuse code at every level, and that's what we've actually done:

```
Overloads Public Sub ChangeGear(direction As String)
  If direction = "down" Then ChangeGear(+1)
  If direction = "up" Then ChangeGear(-1)
End Sub
```

This clearly requires less original code, and keeps all our bounds checking in one place.

We now add a very simple constructor, so that _color is never left undefined:

```
Sub New()
  _color = "cold grey steel"
End Sub
```

Finally, we add a call to our new version of the MyCar.ChangeGear() method: the first one still passes an integer parameter (moving the gear up from 0 to 1), while the second passes the string "up" which moves it into second gear:

```
MyCar.ChangeGear("up")
Response.Write("<br/><b>Shifted 'up' one gear.</b>")

Response.Write("<br/>New gear: " & MyCar.Gear)
```

Summary

In this chapter, we've covered quite a few subject areas and many of those have involved new concepts and definitions of words. Here are the core object-oriented concepts we looked at:

- ❑ **Abstraction** – when we're traveling through an ASP.NET project, think about what objects you'll need and what their most important characteristics and behaviors are
- ❑ **Encapsulation** – every object is a magic black box that is supremely good at one thing. .NET provides literally hundreds of ready-built objects for us to use
- ❑ **Classes** – we create objects from classes, which we can think of as templates for making objects

Then we looked at practical examples using different features of objects and using them in different ways. Here are the areas where we looked at example ASP.NET pages:

- ❑ **Instantiating objects** – creating objects from classes, just like using a cookie cutter to cut out cookies. We saw how we create, instantiate, objects using an expression like this: Dim myCar As New Car(),
- ❑ **Methods** – we ask objects to perform actions for us by calling their methods. We call methods like this: myCar.StartEngine()
- ❑ **Properties** – we can look at and change information inside objects using their properties. We use properties like this: color = myCar.Color
- ❑ **Constructors** – when an object is created its constructor method initializes it. This is particularly useful to us when we want to initialize an object with specific values; we pass parameters to the object when it is created.
- ❑ **Overloading** – methods are often overloaded so that they can be called using different parameters according to what we want to use them for. We saw how to create a DateTime object by passing its

constructor various different combinations of parameters. We also saw how to overload the `ChangeGear()` method on our `Car` class so that it could take either a string or an integer parameter.

Exercises

1. Explain the following terms in your own words, and give an example of how each one might be applied in the context of a simple object-oriented holiday booking application:

- ❑ Object
- ❑ Class
- ❑ Property
- ❑ Method

2. Explain what classes we might want to define in order to model each of the following real-world scenarios, along with the members we'd expect them to have. If there is more than one possible solution, explain what additional information we require to establish which one will be most suitable:

- ❑ Purchasing items at a supermarket checkout
- ❑ Enrolling on a college course
- ❑ Maintaining an inventory of office equipment

3. Extend our `Car` class example to demonstrate on the browser that the value of the object's `Gear` property is restricted to a range of values between -1 and +5. Explain in your own words why it's a good idea to define functionality in method overloads that relies on calling an existing version of the same method.

4. We may want to display the `Price` property of a `Book` object in some currency other than US dollars. Define a new property `ConvPrice`, whose accessor method `Get` takes two parameters denoting a currency symbol and a conversion rate, and returns the book price in the appropriate currency.

5. Of course, this isn't quite how book prices are calculated for an international market, with additional factors such as local taxation playing a part in the total cost. Normally, separate prices are listed for the main countries in which a particular book will be sold. Update the book class again, so that we can specify three different prices for each object – you might want to use the values on the back of this book.

Define additional data members for these extra prices, and a property called `LocalPrice` that lets us specify a country code parameter ("US", "UK", "Can", for example) to denote which country's pricing value we want to Get or Set. Prices should still be stored internally as Decimal variables. Overload the `Get accessor` method so that we can optionally specify a currency symbol for display with the price.

Shared Members and Class Relationships

Now that we've introduced the basic concepts behind objects and how to use them in isolation, we can start considering some of the ways in which they might be associated as part of a bigger picture – that is, how objects can relate to one another.

The most obvious relationship between two objects, originates in something we *do* with one object in the process of dealing with another – that is, a behavioral relationship. For example, if we specify one object as a parameter in a method call on another object – the second object *uses* the first in order to execute that method. Integral it is though, the relationship is a temporary one however– as soon as the method call is complete, the objects have nothing more to do with each other.

We must also consider some more lasting relationships – structural relationships that play a permanent role in defining both an object's internal architecture and its behavior. Perhaps we define a member that applies to all objects in a particular class, and not to any one in particular. Alternatively, we might consider a class data member whose type is defined by a different object class, or a new class that duplicates the functionality of an existing one but then expands upon it.

There's also the issue of functionality that can't be applied to any specific object – for example, a property that exposed the total number of Car objects we'd instantiated, or performed an operation on them all at once.

In this chapter, we're going to look at three particular relationships between objects:

- ❑ Member sharing – members defined on the class as a whole, and not on any specific object
- ❑ Object containment – one object type used as a data member inside another
- ❑ Object inheritance – one class based on another

Shared Members

So far, all the properties and methods we've looked at only have any meaning when applied to a specific object instance. In the last chapter, we demonstrated how separate objects were typically independent of one another, and that a method called on one would leave another totally unaffected – this is technically referred to as an **object instance member** (thereby, giving us **object instance properties** and **object instance methods**).

There may be occasions however when we want to share functionality between objects of a particular type. We may want to define methods and properties that apply to the class as whole, and aren't tied to a specific object: **shared members** (sometimes also referred to as **static members**) let us do just this.

Perhaps we want to keep track of how many `Car` objects we've created – we want a shared property called `Count` that can return this value, which is going to be independent of any particular object. Alternatively, we might want to implement a shared method called `Ford()`, which can be called once to set all our car objects' color properties to "Black".

Shared Properties

As we've seen, we use the following syntax to access an object instance property:

```
<object>.<instanceproperty>
```

We can use exactly the same syntax to access a shared property:

```
<object>.<sharedproperty>
```

The property applies to all objects of that class however, therefore, we don't need to specify any particular instance; rather we can specify the relevant class name like this:

```
<class>.<sharedproperty>
```

> A shared (or static) **member is one that operates across all instances of a class. It can be accessed via the object class itself as well as any specific instance of that class.**

We specify that we want to share a class member by using the keyword `Shared`. This must also be applied to any variables, properties, or methods that our shared member makes use of – we obviously can't use instance members without having specified a particular object.

Try It Out – Using a Shared Property

Let's make a new class called `User`, which we might use to represent registered visitors to our site. We won't define any functionality except for a shared property called `Count`, which we can use to keep track of how many `User` objects we've created. In this example, we'll create three instances of the `User` class and display the value of the shared property as we go.

This is just a demonstration, and we want to look at how our page settings evolve over time, therefore we're going to use `Response.Write` to output data directly to the HTTP Response stream.

6. Create a file called `counting.aspx` in your test directory, and add the following code:

```
<%@ page language="vb" runat="server" %>

<script runat="server">

Public Class User
  Private Shared _Count = 0

  Public ReadOnly Shared Property Count As Integer
    Get
      Return _Count
    End Get
  End Property

  Sub New()
    _Count += 1
  End Sub

End Class

Sub Page_Load()

  Response.Write("User.Count = " & User.Count)
  Response.Write("<hr/>Creating User Alex.")
  Dim Alex As New User()
  Response.Write("<br/>Alex.Count = " & Alex.Count)
  Response.Write("<hr/>Creating User Rob.")
  Dim Rob As New User()
  Response.Write("<br/>Rob.Count = " & Rob.Count)
  Response.Write("<hr/>Creating User Jake.")
  Dim Jake As New User()
  Response.Write("<br/>Jake.Count = " & Jake.Count)
  Response.Write("<hr/>User.Count = " & User.Count)
End Sub

</script>
```

7. Open up your browser and view the file. Here's what it looks like:

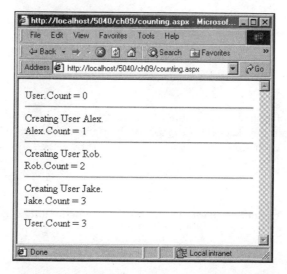

How It Works

We start off by defining our class `User`, with a private shared member called `_Count`. Note the naming convention we use – an underscore at the beginning of the name of a private member, which serves to helps us remember that this variable won't actually be visible from outside a `User` object. This particular variable is what we shall use to keep track of the total number of `User` objects we've created:

```
Public Class User
   Private Shared _Count = 0
```

We now expose the private variable via the shared property `Count`. We don't need to edit the object count therefore, we also define the property as `ReadOnly`:

```
Public ReadOnly Shared Property Count As Integer
   Get
      Return _Count
   End Get
End Property
```

The custom constructor method `New()` simply increments the `_Count` variable:

```
Sub New()
   _Count += 1
End Sub
```

We use `Page_Load` to generate some output for the browser to display, and track the status of our shared property as we create a number of `User` objects:

```
Sub Page_Load()
   Response.Write("User.Count = " & User.Count)
   Response.Write("<hr/>Creating User Alex.")
   Dim Alex As New User()
   Response.Write("<br/>Alex.Count = " & Alex.Count)
   Response.Write("<hr/>Creating User Rob.")
   Dim Rob As New User()
   Response.Write("<br/>Rob.Count = " & Rob.Count)
   Response.Write("<hr/>Creating User Jake.")
   Dim Jake As New User()
   Response.Write("<br/>Jake.Count = " & Jake.Count)
   Response.Write("<hr/>User.Count = " & User.Count)
End Sub
```

Take special note of the first line – we're able to use the `Count` property even before we've instantiated any `User` objects. We can then access it from any of the `User` objects we subsequently make, but the value stays independent of the source; we get the same `Count` value, no matter where we look at it from.

Shared Methods

In just the same way we can define shared methods, whose functionality is common to all objects of the same type.

We use a shared method in just the way you'd expect (that is, just like a normal 'object instance' property), only once again we have the option to call it on the class as a whole, rather than on one specific object:

```
<classname>.<methodname>(...)
```

As with our shared properties, we don't even need to create an instance of the class to make use of the method call. There are plenty of useful examples of shared methods in .NET, some of which we've been using already. For example, all constructor methods are shared by definition – they can't be object instance methods, since you don't actually *have* an object on which to make a object instance method call *until* you've called New().

One very good example of a .NET class that makes use of shared methods is System.Math. In fact, it doesn't feature any public instance members at all – even its constructor is private, so it's impossible (and indeed quite pointless) to instantiate an object of type Math. However, the methods it does expose allow us to perform all sorts of useful mathematical operations, as well as providing us with a couple of useful constants (the exponential constant E and the 'circumference/diameter of a circle' ratio PI). Let's take a look at a few things we can do with this class.

Try it out – Using Shared Members on the System.Math Class

Let's look at another example using some more shared methods of the Math class. In the example we're going to use the methods of the Math class to find the square, absolute value and logarithm of a number entered into a textbox.

1. Open up your editor and type in the following code:

```
<%@ page language="vb" runat="server" %>

<script runat="server">
  Sub Page_Load()
    pi.text = Math.PI
    exp.text = Math.E
  End Sub

  Sub Update(Sender As Object, E As EventArgs)
    Dim dblInput As Double = CDbl(input.text)

    sqrt_input.text = dblInput
    sqrt_result.text = Math.Sqrt(dblInput)

    abs_input.text = dblInput
    abs_result.text = Math.Abs(dblInput)

    log_input.text = dblInput
    log_result.text = Math.Log10(dblInput)
  End Sub
</script>

<html>
  <body>
    <hr />
    Pi = <asp:label id="pi" runat="server" /><br />
    Exponential Constant = <asp:label id="exp" runat="server" />
```

```
    <hr />

    <form runat="server">
    Input = <asp:textbox id="input" runat="server" />
    <asp:button text="Submit" runat="server" onclick="update" />
    </form><hr />

    Square root of <asp:label id="sqrt_input" runat="server"/>
    = <asp:label id="sqrt_result" runat="server" /><br />

    Absolute Value of <asp:label id="abs_input" runat="server"/>
    = <asp:label id="abs_result" runat="server" /><br />

    Logarithm of <asp:label id="log_input" runat="server"/>
    = <asp:label id="log_result" runat="server" /><br />

  </body>
</html>
```

2. Save the file in your test directory as `math.aspx`.

3. Open up your browser and enter a positive value in the textbox. Hit the `Submit` button, and you should see something like this:

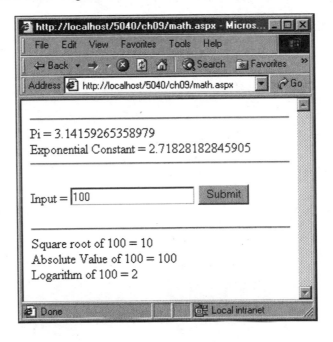

4. Now try this again, but using a negative value for input:

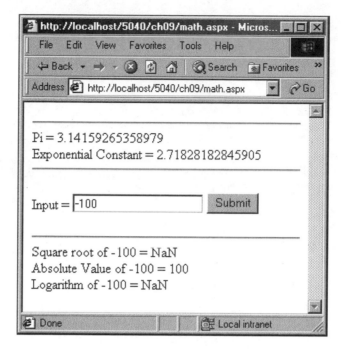

How It Works

We start off by setting up label text for the two constants exposed by the `Math` object:

```
<script runat="server">
  Sub Page_Load()
    pi.text = Math.PI
    exp.text = Math.E
  End Sub
```

Now, we define a subroutine with which to update various other labels according to what's been entered in the textbox called `input`. We convert that from a `String` to a `Double`, and use it as a parameter in each of three calls to shared methods on the Math class; the results are assigned as text on the appropriate labels:

```
  Sub Update(Sender As Object, E As EventArgs)
    Dim dblInput As Double = CDbl(input.text)

    sqrt_input.text = dblInput
    sqrt_result.text = Math.Sqrt(dblInput)

    abs_input.text = dblInput
    abs_result.text = Math.Abs(dblInput)

    log_input.text = dblInput
```

```
        log_result.text = Math.Log10(dblInput)
    End Sub
</script>
```

We define the presentation code, starting off by presenting our two constants:

```
<html>
  <body>
    <hr />
    Pi = <asp:label id="pi" runat="server" /><br />
    Exponential Constant = <asp:label id="exp" runat="server" />
    <hr />
```

We specify a form control, in which we place the textbox (for user input) and button (with which we can raise an Update event, and call the corresponding subroutine):

```
    <form runat="server">
    Input = <asp:textbox id="input" runat="server" />
    <asp:button text="Submit" runat="server" onclick="update" />
    </form><hr />
```

Finally, we use some more label controls to display the results of our efforts:

```
    Square root of <asp:label id="sqrt_input" runat="server"/>
    = <asp:label id="sqrt_result" runat="server" /><br />

    Absolute Value of <asp:label id="abs_input" runat="server"/>
    = <asp:label id="abs_result" runat="server" /><br />

    Logarithm of <asp:label id="log_input" runat="server"/>
    = <asp:label id="log_result" runat="server" /><br />
  </body>
</html>
```

Now that we've looked at how useful an individual class can be on its own, without any pesky objects stealing the limelight, let's start thinking about some of the ways in which different classes be used to work together.

Class Relationships

Let's consider our car model again, and some of the objects we might associate with it. We might identify the following relationships:

❑   A Key *enables* a Car.

❑   An Engine *powers* a Car.

❑   A Person *drives* a Car.

❑   A Driving Test *requires* a Car.

For the rest of this chapter, we're going to explore three types of relationship that each play very significant roles in an object-oriented system:

❑   *One class* using *another*

❑   One class *containing* another – for example, a Car contains an Engine

❑   One class *inheriting* functionality from another – for example, FlyingCar might inherit from Car

We already know that objects are designed to make our lives easier – as we're going to see, these relationships enable objects to permeate every level of a program, and even form the basis of the programming environment in which we write it.

Association – "Uses a"

Let's start out by considering the simplest and most fleeting relationship between object classes – one class *using* another. An object of the former class (A) might use the latter class (B) in either one of the following ways:

❑   A member defined on class A receives, creates, and/or returns an object of class B

❑   Class A defines an data member as an object of class B

It's possibly a little clearer to define the relationship in terms of what it isn't:

> **If an object of class A can perform its full set of functionality while having absolutely no awareness of class B, we can safely say that class A *does not use* class B.**

Let's start by looking at some ways in which we might want to use one object in a method call on another.

Let's imagine a lending library whose inventory/membership system features one object type to represent individual account-holders at the library (class Account), and another to represent individual books, magazines, CDs and so on. that may be borrowed (class Item). Supposing the Account class defines a method called Borrow() – when a visitor borrows a book (or whatever), we simply call this method on the relevant Account object.

Of course, we want to uniquely identify the book that this person has borrowed, and store this data inside their Account object (so that we can keep track of how much they currently have on loan). We don't need to store every bit of information we have on the book, perhaps just an ISBN and a copy number. Instead of submitting these values (or finding suitable equivalents if they're borrowing a magazine or CD), we can simply pass in the appropriate Item object, and code the Borrow() method to get whatever information it needs from that Item's public properties.

As another example, let's return to our Car object from the last chapter: suppose we extend it to support methods Start() and Stop().We don't just want anyone to be able to start the car, so we could design the former method to accept a single parameter – an object of class Key. We could compare a property on this object against a new private Car member representing the ignition, and assuming they matched, start up the engine. If there is no match, we've clearly specified the wrong key, so the car won't start for us.

297

Let's take a look at how we could code this.

Try It Out – Using a Key object to Start() up a Car object

We're going to base this example on the code we developed in the last chapter, which we last saved in a file called `car_object_overload.aspx`. Make a copy of this file, and rename it as `car_object3.aspx`.

1. Open `car_object3.aspx` and add the following Key class definition to the `<script>` block:

```vb
<%@ page language="vb" runat="server" Debug="true"%>

<script runat="server">

Public Class Key
  Private _Shape As Integer

  Public Sub New(newshape As Integer)
    _Shape = newshape
  End Sub

  Public ReadOnly Property Shape As Integer
    Get
      Return _Shape
    End Get
  End Property
End Class
```

Now, add the following new Car class definition:

```vb
Public Class Car
  Private _Color As String
  Private _Gear As Integer
  Private _Ignition As Integer
  Private _EngineRunning As Boolean
  Private Shared _Count = 0

  Public Shared ReadOnly Property Count As Integer
    Get
      Return _Count
    End Get
  End Property

  Public Property Color As String
    Get
      Return _Color
    End Get
    Set(value As String)
      _Color = value
    End Set
  End Property
```

```
      Public ReadOnly Property Gear As Integer
         Get
            Return _Gear
         End Get
      End Property

      Public ReadOnly Property IsRunning As String
         Get
            If _EngineRunning Then
               Return "The engine is running."
            Else
               Return "The engine is not running."
            End If
         End Get
      End Property

      Overloads Public Sub ChangeGear(direction As Integer)
         If direction < 0 Then _Gear -= 1
         If direction > 0 Then _Gear += 1
         If _Gear > 5 Then _gear = 5
         If _Gear < -1 Then _gear = -1
      End Sub

      Overloads Public Sub ChangeGear(direction As String)
         If direction = "down" Then ChangeGear(-1)
         If direction = "up" Then ChangeGear(+1)
      End Sub

      Public Sub Ignition(IgnitionKey as Key)
         If IgnitionKey.Shape = _Ignition Then _EngineRunning = True
      End Sub

      Public Sub EngineOff()
         _EngineRunning = False
      End Sub

      Sub New(IgnitionShape as Integer)
         _Color = "cold grey steel"
         _Ignition = IgnitionShape
         _Count += 1
      End Sub

End Class
```

2. Finally, we have the new `Page_Load` block as follows:

```
Sub Page_Load()
   Dim AlexKey As New Key(0987654321)
   Dim RobKey As New Key(1861005040)
   Dim MyKey As New Key(1234567890)

   Dim MyCar As New Car(1234567890)
   Response.Write("<b>New object 'MyCar' created.</b>")


   Response.Write("<br/>Color: " & MyCar.Color)
   Response.Write("<br/>Gear: " & MyCar.Gear)

   MyCar.Color = "Black"
```

```
    MyCar.ChangeGear(+1)
    Response.Write("<br/><b>Properties updated.</b>")

    Response.Write("<br/>New color: " & MyCar.Color)
    Response.Write("<br/>New gear: " & MyCar.Gear)

    MyCar.ChangeGear("up")
    Response.Write("<br/><b>Shifted 'up' one gear.</b>")

    Response.Write("<br/>New gear: " & MyCar.Gear)

    Response.Write("<hr/>Attempting to start MyCar with AlexKey: ")
    MyCar.Ignition(AlexKey)
    Response.Write(MyCar.IsRunning)

    Response.Write("<hr/>Attempting to start MyCar with RobKey: ")
    MyCar.Ignition(RobKey)
    Response.Write(MyCar.IsRunning)

    Response.Write("<hr/>Attempting to start MyCar with MyKey: ")
    MyCar.Ignition(MyKey)
    Response.Write(MyCar.IsRunning)
    Response.Write("<br/>Attempting to stop MyCar: ")
    MyCar.EngineOff()
    Response.Write(MyCar.IsRunning)

End Sub
</script>
```

3. Save the file in your test directory, and call it up from your browser. You should see this:

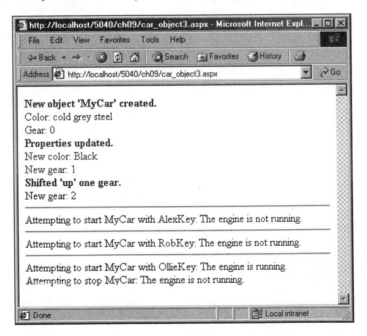

How It Works

We start off by adding a new class definition to our web form. This provides a template for our Key objects, and exposes a single read-only property called Shape; this is an integer value that we use to represent the precise shape of the car key we're modelling. Since a key works by applying one of many possible shapes to some kind of lock mechanism (in this case, the ignition) therefore, we're modeling it as an integer value in the range defined by the Integer data type (-2,147,483,648 to 2,147,483,647), representing any one of 4,294,967,296 unique key shapes:

```
Public Class Key
   Private _Shape As Integer

   Public Sub New(newshape As Integer)
     _Shape = newshape
   End Sub

   Public ReadOnly Property Shape As Integer
      Get
         Return _Shape
      End Get
   End Property
End Class
```

We now declare a private integer variable _Ignition on the Car class. We'll use this to hold a value that represents the unique key shape required to start the engine. We can then compare the two to discover whether the right key has been used. We also declare a private Boolean variable called _EngineRunning, which we'll use to represent the state of the engine:

```
Public Class Car
   Private _Color As String
   Private _Gear As Integer
   Private _Ignition As Integer
   Private _EngineRunning As Boolean
```

We add a new read-only property called IsRunning, which will tell us whether or not the engine is running or not. Rather than directly exposing the private data member _IsRunning, we use it as a condition in the property's Get method to determine an appropriate message as a return value:

```
Public ReadOnly Property IsRunning As String
   Get
      If _EngineRunning Then
        Return "The engine is running."
      Else
        Return "The engine is not running."
      End If
   End Get
End Property
```

Now for the crux of the example: an Ignition() method on the Car class, which takes a Key object as its one parameter. We use IgnitionKey as a label to refer to this object, and read its Shape property in the usual way. As we've noted, the particular shape of a car key is represented as an Integer (effectively representing any one of 4,294,967,296 possible shapes), and the car's ignition is represented likewise. If the two match up, then _EngineRunning is set to True, and the car has been started successfully. Otherwise, nothing happens at all:

```
Public Sub Ignition(IgnitionKey as Key)
   If IgnitionKey.Shape = _Ignition Then _EngineRunning = True
End Sub
```

There's no such condition attached to switching off the engine, so we use the method EngineOff() to unset _EngineRunning no matter what:

```
Public Sub EngineOff()
   _EngineRunning = False
End Sub
```

Finally, we amend our Car class constructor, so that each new object is defined with a specific _Ignition setting, submitted as an Integer parameter:

```
Sub New(IgnitionShape as Integer)
   _Color = "cold grey steel"
   _Ignition = IgnitionShape
End Sub

End Class
```

Now we add some code to Page_Load that will make use of this new functionality. We start by instantiating three Key objects, each with different shapes:

```
Sub Page_Load()
   Dim AlexKey As New Key(0987654321)
   Dim RobKey As New Key(1861005040)
   Dim MyKey As New Key(1234567890)
```

We instantiate a Car object (called MyCar), whose ignition is set with the same value used to describe the shape of MyKey:

```
   Dim MyCar As New Car(1234567890)
   Response.Write("<b>New object 'MyCar' created.</b>")
   ...
```

We apply each of the Key objects to MyCar.Ignition(), and find (predictably enough), that only one of them works:

```
   Response.Write("<hr/>Attempting to start MyCar with AlexKey: ")
   MyCar.Ignition(AlexKey)
   Response.Write(MyCar.IsRunning)

   Response.Write("<hr/>Attempting to start MyCar with RobKey: ")
   MyCar.Ignition(RobKey)
   Response.Write(MyCar.IsRunning)

   Response.Write("<hr/>Attempting to start MyCar with MyKey: ")
   MyCar.Ignition(MyKey)
   Response.Write(MyCar.IsRunning)
   Response.Write("<br/>Attempting to stop MyCar: ")
   MyCar.EngineOff()
   Response.Write(MyCar.IsRunning)
End Sub
```

Note that when call the `Ignition()` method, we can't simply submit an Integer like this:

```
Ignition(1234567890)
```

The parameter *must* be a `Key` object, and its `Shape` property is always what's used to test against the ignition.

Of course, this is quite a trivial example, and still some way off perfection: for example, we'd ideally automate the key instantiation process, so we don't have to explicitly create two objects for each `Car` we make. What's more, it doesn't really show off all the advantages of passing objects rather than standard data types.

If you consider the reasons we looked at in the last chapter for using objects in the first place however, you should get an idea of why this approach is a good thing. Classes `Key` and `Car` both *encapsulate* the `Shape` functionality, so that any code using a `Key` to call the `Car.Ignition()` method **doesn't need to know anything about how either works**. So, for example, if we decided to change the way we represent key shape (perhaps use a `Long` instead), any code that used the `Key` object to start the car would remain unaffected.

Containment – a "has a" relationship

Earlier on, we identified two possible ways for one object to be *used* by another; the first involved submitting one object as a method parameter in a call on the other object, and we've just looked at one way in which that might be used. The association between objects is brief, lasting only as long as the method call.

The second describes a somewhat more involved association, often referred to as **containment** (also known as *composition* or *aggregation*). This is a very powerful object-oriented technique, by which we can define the data members of one class as objects derived from another class. For example, our `Car` class might define a private member of type `Engine` (another new class, designed to represent the car's engine). We could then say that the `Car` class (and every `Car` type object we instantiate from it) contains an `Engine` object.

Why is it great to have one object within another? The answer's quite simple: it helps us to define complex classes using simpler, existing ones, and therefore provides us with a frequently useful way to reuse code.

> **When some class A defines a data member of class B, we can say that an object of class A contains an object of class B.**

Containment is often described as a "has a" relationship – in many cases, we can take the names of a class and object that's contained within it, place the words "has a" between them, and find that it's a valid statement.

In fact, it's often worth trying out a few others as well, such as 'contains', 'is composed of', 'comprises', and 'consists of'. If any of these fit the bill, then you're probably looking at a sensible use of containment.

When you establish your overall object model, this should prove helpful in identifying which objects should contain which other objects. If we apply this to our car example we might get:

❑   A car has an engine

It's reasonable to use an engine object as a data member within the car class. On the other hand:

❑   An engine has a car

Doesn't really make any sense.

Let's assume we've defined an Engine class, whose properties include SerialNo, Rpm, Name (which is set by the constructor), and IsRunning, whose methods include SwitchOn and SwitchOff. We might use an Engine object like this to replace our private Boolean _EngineRunning, so that our Car class becomes a little richer in useful detail.

> We won't show you how to define the Engine class here, as its particular implementation details really aren't important to the present discussion. If you want to test the code below, a simple class definition featuring a single constructor method should be quite adequate.

Here's some new code for the Car class that could expose an engine object like the one we've described as a property called MyEngine:

```
Public Class Car
   Private _Color As String
   Private _Gear As Integer
   Private _Ignition As Integer
   Private _Engine As Engine
   ...
   Public Property MyEngine As Engine
     Get
       Return _Engine
     End Get
     Set
       _Engine = value
     End Set
   End Property

   Sub New()
     _color = "cold grey steel"
     _Ignition = IgnitionShape
   End Sub

End Class
```

We can now create a new Car object, and set this property with a new Engine object:

```
Dim SchumaCar As New Car()
ShumaCar.MyEngine = New Engine("Ferrari 050 V10")
```

The `SchumaCar` object now contains an actual object of type `Engine` (whose Name property is the string "Ferrari 050 V10") and we can access this directly via the property `ShumaCar.MyEngine`. This exposes the contained `Engine` object in its entirety, therefore we might examine the engine's `Name` property using the expression:

```
Engine_Name = SchumaCar.MyEngine.Name
```

We can make method calls on the Engine object in a similar fashion:

```
Engine_Name = SchumaCar.MyEngine.SwitchOn()
```

Of course, this gives us all the functionality we'd expect from the `Ignition()` method on the `Car` object itself. In fact, it exposes rather more than we'd like, since we now have direct access to the engine, we're in a position to start it up without a key – effectively 'hotwiring' the car!

What we ought to have done in this case, is to make the `Engine` object a private member of the `Car` class (as we did with the original `_EngineRunning` Boolean) and access its functionality via `Car` methods and properties. However, what this example has shown us is that when we do want direct access to objects inside objects, it's really not hard at all.

Containment in .NET

As we've noted already, the .NET Framework features many, many objects, and we're going to take a look at some of the most intrinsically important ones (in the context of working with ASP.NET pages, that is) in the next chapter. As you'll see, using objects as class properties is an extremely widespread practice, strictly speaking, just about *everything* we see in .NET is an object (including all our data types: `Integer`, `String`, `Boolean`, and so on), so it's actually fair to say that it's fundamental to object-oriented programming in .NET.

Before we try and take on *all* of these important .NET objects, let's consider just one of them, and see how it exposes information to us via a contained object.

In the next example we're going to look at some of the properties of the `Browser` object that ASP.NET provides for us – this is exposed as a property of the intrinsic object `Request`, which we'll look at in much more detail in the next chapter. For now, suffice it to say that `Request` is a `System.Web.HttpRequest` type object (that is, based on a class called `HttpRequest`, as defined in the .NET namespace `System.Web`). This object is instantiated as a standard part of the web form execution process, and is used to hold all the information from the HTTP Request that our browser submitted to the server. You might like to take a look at the members of this class, using the Class Browser application:

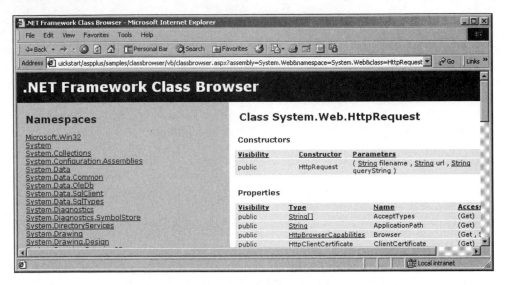

The `Request` object's properties are used to expose the data submitted in the current HTTP Request. One of the public members this class supports is a property called `Browser`, and this exposes an object of type `HttpBrowserCapabilities`, which is also defined in the `System.Web` namespace. This object is used specifically to expose data in the HTTP Request pertaining to the client browser – it supports properties that include Browser (the type of browser being used), Version (the browser version), Frames (whether or not the browser supports frames), and plenty more besides.

Try It Out – Using Contained Objects

We're now going to use `Request` and `Request.Browser` to tell us a few things about our browser software:

1. Open up your editor and type in this code:

```
<%@ Page Language="VB" %>

<script runat="server">
  sub Page_Load()
    lblRequestType.Text =     Request.RequestType
    lblAOL.Text =             Request.Browser.AOL
    lblJavaScript.Text =      Request.Browser.JavaScript
    lblBrowserType.Text =     Request.Browser.Type
    lblTableSupport.Text =    Request.Browser.Tables
  end sub
</script>

<html>
  <body>
    Request type : <asp:label id=lblRequestType runat="server" /><br />
    AOL : <asp:label id=lblAOL runat="server" /><br />
    JavaScript : <asp:label id=lblJavaScript runat="server" /><br />
    Browser : <asp:label id=lblBrowserType runat="server" /><br />
    Tables : <asp:label id=lblTableSupport runat="server" />
  </body>
</html>
```

2. Save the file as `containment.aspx`

3. Call up your browser and view the file. Here's what it looks like in Internet Explorer 6:

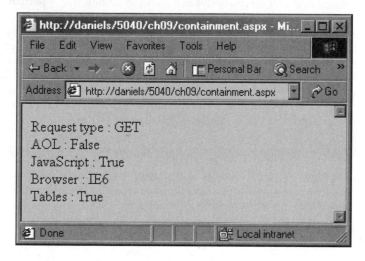

How It Works

One of the first lines in the page is a statement that accesses a property called `RequestType` on the `Request` object; this tells us whether the page was requested using a `GET` or `POST` method. The value it sends back is assigned to the label control `lblRequestType`:

```
lblRequestType.Text =    Request.RequestType
```

Subsequent information comes from one level deeper, from within the Browser object, which is contained by the `Request` object:

```
lblAOL.Text =            Request.Browser.AOL
lblJavaScript.Text =     Request.Browser.JavaScript
lblBrowserType.Text =    Request.Browser.Type
lblTableSupport.Text =   Request.Browser.Tables
```

Notice, how we reference the `Request` object, and then use a period to specify the `Browser` property on that object. This `Browser` property returns an `HttpBrowser` type object, and this is usually referred to as the `Browser` object. This object exposes its own properties, which we access in the same way: simply add a period, followed by the name of the property.

For example, we can see that the `Request.Browser.Type` property returns a string denoting what browser we're using – in this case, it's Internet Explorer 6, so it returns `"IE6"`.

There's one more type of class relationship we need to look at before properly delving into all the .NET classes and how they work. What if we have an existing class that defines a set of fantastically useful functionality, but seems to be missing one or two little features that we need to make use of it...?

Inheritance – "is a"

Let's assume that we have accurately and thoroughly modeled all of the essential features of our Car class; we've implemented it, tested it rigorously, and found to be bug free – perhaps it's now being used in a number of different applications.

A new scientific breakthrough however, has made the long-touted "flying car" a practical reality, and we wish to model these beautiful airborne machines as well. Now it turns out that the only feature of a flying car that we need to model (above and beyond those we've already modeled for a normal car) is its altitude, as well as providing methods to let us control its vertical motion. All the other features we need to describe a car are the same as those that we've already programmed for the Car class; although the flying car is a wonder to behold, it's fundamentally *still* a car.

This new FlyingCar class is going to need some methods that the Car class simply doesn't implement:

❑   Ascend()

❑   Descend()

We're also going to need an extra property:

❑   Altitude

How might we approach this new requirement for a FlyingCar class? If we didn't know anything about object-oriented programming, we might try one of the following approaches:

Add redundancy to the original class

Simply add an altitude property and vertical steering methods to our Car definition, and simply leave these attributes empty when they aren't applicable. We could also track whether these attributes were applicable to a given Car object, by adding a Boolean data member denoting whether a specific car can fly:

```
Public Class Car
   Private _Color As String
   Private _Gear As Integer
   Private _Ignition As Integer
   Private _Engine As Engine
   Private _Altitude As Boolean
   Private _CanFly As Boolean
   ...
```

Of course, any new methods we wrote for this class would need to take account of its value, and this results in convoluted code, which is difficult to debug and maintain.

Define a near duplicate class

We could create a new FlyingCar class by duplicating the contents of class Car class and adding the extra features we require to this copy. Of course, this would be terribly inefficient, as most of our code would then be identically defined in two places. What's more, if we wanted to modify the internal functionality of the Car at some later date, then we'd have to make the same changes in both classes.

Strictly speaking, either of these two approaches would work, but either way, the inherent redundancy in the code would make them far more difficult to maintain. What's more, they really break down quite horribly when you consider adding a third, fourth, or even a fifth type of 'special' Car.

Define a new class that inherits functionality from the original class

Fortunately, we have another alternative – we can solve this problem by taking advantage of **inheritance**, a powerful object-oriented mechanism, by which we can define a new class solely in terms of the differences (in terms of the functionality it supports) between it and another existing class.

We can, therefore, define a `FlyingCar` as a special type of `Car` with three extra members that normal `Car`s have no need for:

```
Public Class FlyingCar : Inherits Car
  Private _Pressure As Integer

  Public ReadOnly Property Altitude As Integer
    Get
      Return PressureToAltitude(_Pressure)
    End Get
  End Property

  Private Function PressureToAltitude(pressure As Integer) As Integer
    ...
[0]  End Funtion

  Sub Ascend()
    ...
  End Sub

  Sub Descend()
    ...
  End Sub

  Sub New(IgnitionShape as Integer)
    MyBase.New(IgnitionShape)
  End Sub

End Class
```

Note that we need to add an explicit constructor method for this new class – if we don't do this, we're likely to see the following error message on compiling the code:

> Cannot implicitly create a constructor for 'Class FlyingCar' because its base class 'Car' doesn't declare a public constructor that has no parameters. Either define a constructor on 'Class FlyingCar' or a parameterless constructor on base 'Class Car'.

By defining the constructor `Sub New(ignition As Integer)` on the `Car` class, we actually overrode the default constructor `New()`, which (having no parameters, and therefore, assuming no specific functionality) is the only variety of constructor that .NET can safely reuse for an inheriting object. Since there isn't one, we need to either provide one (allowing a Car object to be created without an ignition setting – not what we want) or define a new one for the `FlyingCar` class. We use `MyBase` to refer to the inherited object, and simply call the original one-parameter constructor.

Apart from that, all we've defined are two methods, one property, and a private data member. When we come to instantiate a `FlyingCar` object, we'll find that all these members are implemented, along with all the functionality we defined in the original `Car` class.

Terminology for Inheritance

The `Car` class from which we've derived `FlyingCar` is usually referred to as the **base class** (or sometimes as the **parent class**, **superclass**, or **supertype**), whereas `FlyingCar` can be referred to as a **subclass** of `Car` (or alternatively as a **child class**, **derived class,** or **subtype**).

Inheritance is often referred to as establishing an 'is a' relationship between two classes: if we can say that class A (in this case the `FlyingCar`) 'is a' particular variety of class B (the `Car`), then it makes sense to model A by deriving from B.

Note that anything that we can say about a base class must also be true about all of its subclasses – that is:

❑   A Car has an engine, so a FlyingCar has an engine.

❑   A Car has a gearbox, so a FlyingCar has a gearbox.

❑   A Car steers left and right, so a FlyingCar steers lefts and right.

One simple, but effective test for the legitimacy of inheriting from a class, is as follows:

> **If you can say anything about a base class A that cannot be said about a proposed subclass B, then B is not really a valid subclass of A.**

Of course, the converse is not true. A subclass is a special case of its base class, so it is quite legitimate to say something like "a `FlyingCar` can fly up and down, whereas a `Car` cannot" without compromising the model.

When we want a class that has the features and functionality of an existing class, but with some additional features, we can use **Inheritance** to create a new object type that supports both. When an object of type A can be treated as a specialized version of another object of type B, we can say that class A is derived – or **inherits** – from class B. Objects of type A will support all the methods and properties supported by objects of type B, as well as any additional members that have been defined in A.

Some object-oriented systems allow you to inherit from more than one class (a process known as multiple inheritance). This is not the case here however: a .NET class can only directly inherit functionality from one other class. The inheritance may have many layers however – that is, the ancestor class may itself be inherited from another class, which may inherit from yet another, and so on.

The Pros and Cons of Inheritance

Inheritance is one of the most powerful features of an object-oriented system, because:

❑   **Derived classes are much more succinct than they would be without inheritance**. Derived classes only define what it is that makes them different from their ancestor class. A flying car is simply a car that can also move vertically.

❑ **We can reuse and extend tested code without modifying it.** We make our new class FlyingCar without disturbing the original Car class definition in any way. Any other code that relies on Car objects will be unaffected by the existence of FlyingCar, so we avoid having to retest existing sections of our application.

❑ **You don't need the source code for a class in order to derive a new class from it.** As long as you have the compiled version of a class, the inheritance mechanism works just fine; you therefore don't require the original class definition in order to extend it. You can often save a lot of time and effort by finding an existing class (a system class, or third-party offering) that does much of what you need, and then deriving a subclass from it. You simply need to add the features you want for your own purposes.

❑ **Classification is the natural way for humans to organize information.** As we've already noted, it makes sense to organize our software along the same lines as those along which we think. Our code is therefore much more intuitive, and consequently easier to maintain and extend.

Bear in mind though: overusing inheritance can make programs more complex than they need to be. It's just as important to know when *not* to use inheritance as it is to know when and how to use it in the first place. If you use it inappropriately, and your program breaks down as a consequence, you may well find yourself having to rewrite large quantities of code just to get back to where you started. Use it sparingly, and use it wisely.

Inheritance in .NET

Every class (and therefore every object) in .NET ultimately inherits from a class called Object, defined in the System namespace, which provides us with a small set of standard properties and methods that it's useful for all objects to support, regardless of what type they are:

Class System.Object

Constructors

Visibility	Constructor	Parameters
public	Object	( )

Methods

Visibility	Return	Name	Parameters
public static	Boolean	Equals	(Object objA , Object objB)
public	Boolean	Equals	(Object obj)
public	Int32	GetHashCode	( )
public	Type	GetType	( )
public static	Boolean	ReferenceEquals	(Object objA , Object objB)
public	String	ToString	( )

Hierarchy
System.Object

For example, one of the properties it supports is called GetType. This exposes an object of class Type, whose FullName property is a string naming the class (or type) of the object on which we're calling it. The simplest way to see this in action, is to take a look at the string returned for an Object type object:

```
Dim obj As New Object
Response.Write(obj.GetType.FullName)
```

If you add this code to the logic in a web form, you'll see the following result:

System.Object

That's all well and good. Now, let's try the same with another type of object:

```
Dim value As New Integer
Response.Write(value.GetType.FullName)
```

If you use this code in your web form, you'll see the following result:

System.Int32

This is the system class that .NET uses internally to work with `Integer` variables. In fact, whenever you're working with an `Integer`, you're effectively working with an `Int32` type object.

Let's try this one more time, using an object based on our `Car` class:

```
Dim MyCar As New Car(1234)
Response.Write(MyCar.GetType.FullName)
```

If you put this code into a web form (along with the `Car` class definition of course), and save it in a file called `car_gettype.aspx`, you should see something like this:

ASP.car_gettype_aspx+Car

There are some important things to note here:

❑ We've successfully used a property called `GetType` on the `MyCar` object, even though it's not specified in the class definition

❑ The full name of the type we get back consists of three parts, denoting:

  ❑ The ASP namespace – this is the standard namespace used to hold the page classes that are generated automatically from ASPX files

  ❑ The name of the page class – this is based on the name of the actual ASPX file being used; in this case, my web form was saved as `car_gettype.aspx`

  ❑ The name of the user-defined class – in this case, `Car`

In fact, only the first point is of immediate concern to us: we've demonstrated one of the features that the `Car` class has *automatically* inherited from the `Object` class. We don't need to define a `GetType` property; it's simply there, ready and waiting, no matter how little code we've put in our own class.

The second point is less relevant to our present discussion, but interesting nevertheless, as it digs a little further into how ASP.NET works under the covers. As we know, all the code we're writing in our pages is actually VB.NET code; it's only when we put it together with HTML and server controls (and expose all this from an ASPX file on the web server) that we get a proper web form. This reveals a little of the structure of the page class, which makes substantial use all of these class relationships, and some more besides.

Try It Out – Using Inheritance to Create a Scientific Calculator Class

To round off our discussion of inheritance, we're going to look at using it to beef up the functionality of the simple calculator class we defined in the last chapter. We're going to define a `ScientificCalculator` class, which will support all the functionality of `Calculator`, but with an additional method `SquareRoot`.

This is a fairly typical example of inheritance – we take the base behavior of something we already have and roll in our own functionality without much effort at all.

1. Make a copy of `calculator_object.aspx` and call it `sci_calculator_object.aspx`.

2. Now open up the file, and add the following code to the `<script>` block:

```
<%@ page language="vb" runat="server" %>
<script runat="server">

    Public Class ScientificCalculator : Inherits Calculator

      Public Sub SquareRoot()
        Dim root As Double
        Dim current As Double = MyBase.CurrentValue

        root = Math.Sqrt(current)
        MyBase.Clear()
        MyBase.Add(root)
      End Sub

    End Class

    Public Class Calculator

      Private _current As Double
      ...
    End Class
</script>
```

3. Modify/add the following highlighted code in the `Page_Load` sub:

```
Sub Page_Load()
    Dim MyCalc As New ScientificCalculator()
    Response.Write("<b>Created a new ScientificCalculator object.</b><br/>")
    Response.Write("Current Value = " & MyCalc.CurrentValue)
    ...
```

```
    MyCalc.Divide(4)
    Response.Write("<br/><b>Divided by 4 - MyCalc.Divide(4)</b><br/>")
    Response.Write("Current Value = " & MyCalc.CurrentValue)

    MyCalc.SquareRoot()
    Response.Write("<br/><b>Square root - MyCalc.SquareRoot()</b><br/>")
    Response.Write("Current Value = " & MyCalc.CurrentValue)

    MyCalc.Clear()
    Response.Write("<br/><b>Cleared - MyCalc.Clear()</b><br/>")
    Response.Write("Current Value = " & MyCalc.CurrentValue)
End Sub
```

4. Save the file, and check your browser – you should see this:

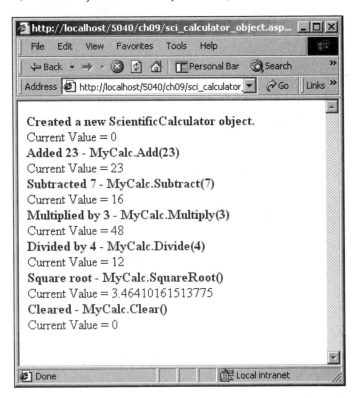

How it Works

We start off by defining our new class `ScientificCalculator`. To tell .NET that we want it to inherit functionality from another class, we simply add a colon to the end of the opening statement, followed by the keyword Inherits and name of the base class – in this case, `Calculator`. We then define our new method, in the normal way:

```
Public Class ScientificCalculator : Inherits Calculator

    Public Sub SquareRoot()
```

```
        Dim root As Double
        Dim current As Double = MyBase.CurrentValue

        root = Math.Sqrt(current)
        MyBase.Clear()
        MyBase.Add(root)
    End Sub

End Class
```

You might be wondering why we don't just assign _current with the result of the Math.Sqrt() operation that we use to calculate the square root. The answer's actually quite simple: _current is defined as a private member of the Calculator class, and is therefore, invisible to any code outside that class – and that includes the ScientificCalculator subclass. There'd be little point in hiding private object members from the outside world if we could simply hack in by way of inheritance.

We must therefore apply any results via the public methods already exposed by the Calculator class. This isn't too tricky – we can simply Clear() the existing value and Add() our own result.

We start this Sub by setting up two variables: current to hold the current value of the calculator (accessed via the property CurrentValue, on the Calculator object that we're using as MyBase), and root to hold the result of our operation. We then use Math.Sqrt() to calculate the square root of the current value, and assign this to calculator's private value setting as described above.

Note that we don't have to worry about defining a constructor method: .NET can safely use the default constructor New() based on the one that's automatically defined for the Calculator class.

When we create the MyCalc object, we want an instance of the new class, so we need to change our original specification of the class name Calculator to that of ScientificCalculator:

```
Sub Page_Load()
    Dim MyCalc As New ScientificCalculator()
    Response.Write("<b>Created a new ScientificCalculator object.</b><br/>")
    Response.Write("Current Value = " & MyCalc.CurrentValue)
```

SquareRoot is not a member of Calculator, so if we forget to make this change we'll get an error when we come to call that method.

ScientificCalculator inherits from Calculator, so all the methods and properties that we defined on Calculator are also available to ScientificCalculator. We demonstrate this by calling each of those methods again, before we call the new SquareRoot method:

```
    MyCalc.SquareRoot()
    Response.Write("<br/><b>Square root - MyCalc.SquareRoot()</b><br/>")
    Response.Write("Current Value = " & MyCalc.CurrentValue)
```

Summary

In this chapter we've looked at some of the relationships it's possible to establish between object classes, and considered both the principles behind them and how we use them in our ASP.NET pages. While objects are by no means a universal panacea for all our problems, they can help us enormously in our endeavours to write robust, organized code, and to do so quickly and efficiently.

- ❑ **They appeal to the way humans think**. It's quite intuitive to build pages using objects with names such as DateTime, Page, Button, Label, and Browser. These words describe concepts we're already familiar with, and we can work with them in a way that is natural to us.

- ❑ **They help us write simpler, more efficient code**. Once we have broken a complex application into units of encapsulated functionality, we can more readily focus on specific problems, rather than trying to take on board the application as a whole. This increased focus helps us to write code faster, since there's less for us to think about at any given time. Furthermore, each unit is likely to consist of simpler program code than it would otherwise.

- ❑ **They make it easier to reuse code**. By building an application up from self-contained, task-specific pieces, we are more likely to be able to reuse these pieces in other contexts. The .NET Framework is a great example of reusing objects – we can write robust, efficient web forms faster, since the Framework provides us with so much ready-built functionality.

- ❑ **They help us write code that's easier to change later**. We find that when an application has grown, although it becomes more complex, the fact that it still consists of a set of objects that work together, we can more easily locate the objects that need changing.

- ❑ **They help us write more reliable code**. Objects are both self-contained and well defined therefore, it's relatively easy to write code to test them thoroughly. Once an object has been thoroughly tested, we can reuse it many times without having to worry about its robustness.

- ❑ **They help us write more comprehensible code**. If you break down your program's functionality in a logical, systematic fashion, and model it on identifiable real-world entities, other users should find it relatively easy to figure out what each object does. In an ideal situation, a newcomer to your application can establish a simple understanding of how it works based on just a brief exposure to the code.

It's often useful to create methods or properties that are shared between all the objects created from a specific class. These are called shared methods or shared properties and we use them by referencing the class name instead of the object name – for example: numberOfUsers = User.Count

It's very common in .NET for an object to contain another object. This happens because a property on one object returns another type of object. When this happens, we can use a special syntax to keep code tidier: ObjectA.ObjectB.ObjectC.SomeMethod()

Every class defined in .NET inherits from Object, whose properties and methods are therefore available on all objects. Each class has its own methods and properties, but also gets a few for free, courtesy of the Object class. These include the GetType property, which tells us what type the object is. This can be used on objects of any class, even those we define ourselves for which we have not defined a GetType member.

Now we have looked at object-oriented programming in general, and a few specific classes that .NET provides, the next chapter will explore some of the useful objects that ASP.NET makes available to our web forms.

Exercises

1. Name three different types of class relationship, and give examples of when it would be appropriate to use each one.

2. Create an ASP.NET page that displays the current date and time using the shared property Now of the DateTime class

3. Define an Account class for library users that has a Borrow() method, and an Item class that represents a library book with properties Title and ISBN. Code the Borrow() method so that it gets the title and ISBN of the borrowed book from the Item object.

4. Define an Engine class, whose properties include SerialNo, Rpm, and Name (to be set by the class constructor), and whose methods include SwitchOn and SwitchOff. Now integrate it with the Car class so that you can access these properties and methods from instances of the Car class.

5. Using inheritance, define a FlyingCar class that has an Ascend() method, a Descend() method and read-only property that returns the altitude of the flying car.

Objects in ASP.NET

The bulk of the .NET framework consists of a huge library of object classes, and just about anything we do in ASP.NET will make substantial use of objects, which have been defined by these classes. One of the dominant characteristics of .NET is that it defines everything – from intrinsic variables, right up to full-blown applications – as explicit objects.

The framework includes literally hundreds of classes, which is great for us, as it means we have a tremendous amount of ready-made functionality on tap. That means we have less code to write, and can do things quicker and more easily. Don't be put off by the number of classes there are to learn, some may already be familiar to you and the rest will just take a little time, but it's worth it!

The classes provided help us out with a whole host of different tasks: working with files, XML data, databases, web pages, monitoring web site performance, generating random numbers – in fact it's almost a case of "you name it, there's a class for it". We're going to be spending most of the rest of the book getting to know the objects you're most likely to use with ASP.NET, what they are and what we can do with them.

For now, we're going to focus specifically on objects that are central to how ASP.NET functions. In doing so, we should start to crystallize your understanding of how ASP.NET hangs together, and how you're going to get the most out of it when developing web applications. In the course of the chapter, you'll learn about:

- ❏ Namespaces and finding classes in .NET
- ❏ The Page class, and some of the useful things it enables us to do – such as redirecting visitors to other pages, and finding out about the browser your visitor is using
- ❏ ASP.NET applications and application state– what web applications are, and how to store commonly used pieces of information centrally in a web site
- ❏ ASP.NET sessions and session state – looking at how a shopping basket system might work, and saving visitor's preferences

Namespaces

Some of the many classes that .NET includes, provide the fundamental building blocks of .NET programming (basic data types like `System.String` and `System.Bool`, classes that let the user manipulate files, and so on.), while some relate specifically to web development, and others to developing Windows applications. Many more are potentially useful in any number of situations (supporting features such as security and localization).

> **Localization is the process of "translating" the language used in the user interface of a computer program to different languages and dialects.**

Before we start looking at the most important web development objects, let's consider how we go about finding the classes we need. The .NET framework uses a rather neat naming scheme to organize all its classes: **namespaces**. A namespace is a group of similar classes. For example, if you wanted to find classes that let you connect to a database, you'd look for classes that are listed as being in the `System.Data namespace`. If you want to look for classes that let you build web pages, look for classes listed as being in the `System.Web` namespace. Both of these namespaces are contained within the general `System` namespace. These particular namespaces contain classes that can be used to implement input/output processes (`.IO`) and web (`.Web`) development respectively.

> *The names of namespaces are usually quite short, but always very accurate in describing what classes they contain. For example, the System.XML namespace contains classes to do almost anything you can think of with XML data.*

Namespaces are arranged hierarchically, with `System` at the root; `System` contains all the classes that define the fundamental building blocks. For example, the definition of `Boolean` and `String` types are in the `System` namespace, as they can be used within all namespaces. The `System.Web` namespace contains generic classes for building web sites, while `System.Web.UI` has classes for building pages from user interface components like buttons. When we want to program HTML buttons, we'll use a much less widely used class, way down in `System.Web.UI.HtmlControls`. You can see how the hierarchy flows.

> **As a rule, classes at the top of the tree are highly generic, while those towards the bottom are highly specialized.**

Think about how postal addresses work across the world, and how they relate to individual houses or offices. In our case, the things we're trying to locate are classes (houses), and we work out where they are by using namespaces that describe their location (postal addresses).

When we reference a class in a namespace, we use this syntax:

```
<namespace name>.<class name>
```

For example, the class we use to work with files is called `File`, and it lives in the `System.IO` namespace, so we reference it like this:

```
System.IO.File
```

We can then extend that to reference methods, or properties, of the class (the following code is a simplified version of how to open a file, but for now, let's just get hold of the concept):

```
System.IO.File.Open("filename.txt")
```

In some places, you'll see the VB.NET keyword `Imports` used to import a namespace to a file, so that we can reference the class name directly. For example, if a page imports the `System.IO` namespace, it can reference the `File` class without explicitly prefixing it with the namespace:

```
File.Open("filename.txt")
```

There three main reasons why Microsoft have arranged the .NET classes into namespaces in this way:

❑ **Organization** – There are far too many classes to usefully put in a list. The namespaces are organized hierarchically, therefore it's quite easy (and intuitive) to browse through them and find out what's available (in the .NET documentation or on the Microsoft Developer Network web site at http://msdn.microsoft.com). If we know about a class that resides in a particular namespace, we can be pretty sure that similar classes are also held in that namespace. This means we can easily find classes related to one we're already using, as well as seeing what other functionality .NET provides in that area.

❑ **Universality** – One of the biggest hazards of object-oriented programming on a large scale is the possibility that two different classes of a type of object will be mistaken for one another. As you might recall from the last chapter, we had to import the 'Cars' namespace before using the 'Car' class. Supposing there was already a base class called 'Car' in the `System.Web.Util` namespace; as long as we don't import that namespace as well, there is no room for ambiguity when we come to say `Dim MyCar As New Car()`. Sooner or later, we may well want to start creating our own – so .NET doesn't just have to manage Microsoft's classes, but ours too.

❑ **Ease of use** – By default, we must reference classes using a full namespace hierarchy. As we said above, however once we import a namespace, the classes within it can be referenced simply by name. Since the classes are arranged in logical function-specific groups, therefore we can usually get away with importing a few namespaces, and then referencing all the classes by name only. You only have to *try* working with the classes in `System.Security.Cryptography` (for example) to appreciate how much typing this can save you!

Use of namespaces in .NET stems from their use in XML schemas: many situations require the structure of an XML document to be well-defined (in the same way that we need to know the methods and properties of an object) in order for software to usefully interact with it. See www.w3.org/TR/REC-xml-names for more details.

Namespaces for ASP.NET

All the web-related classes (forming the backbone of everything we do in ASP.NET) are grouped together in (and below) the `System.Web` namespace. While the most important ASP.NET classes are held in the `System.Web` namespace, we're going to be using plenty of classes from other namespaces in the course of the book. These, then, are the namespaces that we'll make most use of when building web sites with ASP.NET:

- ❑ `System.Web` – This provides a large range of classes that help us build web sites. `System.Web` is imported automatically into any ASPX file you run, and the classes it holds are responsible for virtually all of the web-based functionality we've seen so far – more on these shortly.

- ❑ `System.Web.UI`– This provides classes that represent the controls we use to build web pages, for example HTML elements, buttons, labels, calendars, and dropdown lists. We were actually using some of the `System.Web.UI` classes in Chapter 3, when we looked at web forms. We'll see more about them in Chapter 14, when we look at server controls.

- ❑ `System.IO` – As we saw earlier, this namespace provides classes we can use to work with files.

- ❑ `System.Collections` – Holds various collections classes. Collections are objects that contain lists of other objects; we'll take a look at them more closely in the next chapter.

- ❑ `System.Diagnostics` – This namespace holds classes that can help us diagnose problems when things go wrong. We'll see more of this in Chapter 14.

- ❑ `System.Data` – We use classes in this namespace to work with data and databases. We'll come across these classes in Chapter 12 and Chapter 13.

- ❑ `System.Globalization` – Classes in this namespace help us to create globalized web sites that can work in different parts of world.

- ❑ `System.Drawing` – The classes in this namespace offer us graphical functions, so that we can dynamically generate images.

- ❑ `System.XML` – This namespace is home to a number of classes for working with XML data.

These are still just a small proportion of the overall set of base classes in the .NET framework – to fully document them all would be a mammoth undertaking. You can get an idea of how many different classes there are by running the **Class Browser** sample in the ASP.NET **QuickStart** tutorial. This allows you to browse through the full set of namespaces, and look at the members of the classes in each. Once you've installed the **QuickStart**, you can find the sample at http://localhost/quickstart/aspplus/samples/classbrowser/vb/classbrowser.aspx.

Meanwhile, the focus of this chapter is specifically on the classes within the `System.Web` and `System.Web.UI` namespaces. We're going to start off by looking at the class used to help define the 'magic object' that lurks quietly behind every ASP.NET page we see...

The Page Class

To understand the role of the Page class, it's important to have a picture of what's going on when we request an ASP.NET page from the web server. As we know, IIS hands over most of the hard work involved to the .NET framework.

When a browser initially calls up an ASP.NET page, IIS recognizes that this is an ASPX file request, and lets the ASP.NET module (aspnet_isapi.dll) deal with it. The aspnet_isapi.dll places the ASPX file we request into a new class definition. This new class is defined in a namespace called ASP; so the contents of a file called mypage.aspx end up in a class called ASP.mypage_aspx.

> The easiest way to see this class definition is to actually break the code in your ASPX file. By default, the error message presented will give you the option to *View Compilation Source*, and this compilation source, in our example above, would be a file called ASP.mypage_aspx.

The new ASP class is then instantiated as an object in the CLR. A render method is then called on our new object, that returns appropriate HTML via the aspnet_isapi.dll to IIS, which then sends the HTML to the client that originally made the request. We can see this process taking place in the diagram below:

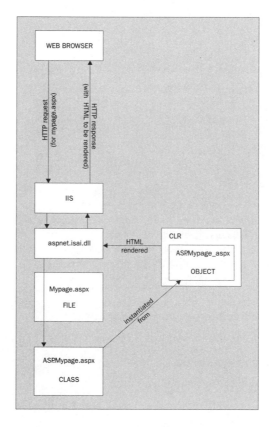

So that's how .NET gets us from an ASPX file on the server to an HTTP response full of useful HTML. What we haven't mentioned is the fact that our ASP class inherits from the Page class. This means that our ASP.NET page has access to the useful functionality that the Page class provides.

The Page class lives in the System.Web.UI namespace, (UI refers to 'User Interface', which is what users of our web site see on the page constructed from HTML). Let's update our diagram to incorporate this important aspect:

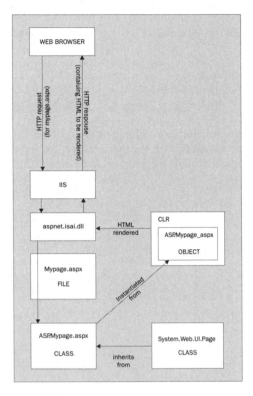

The Page class is like a fairy godmother, as it brings us a wealth of useful properties and methods that we can use on our ASP.NET pages. It also gives us access to a range of other objects created from classes in the System.Web namespace, and we'll be looking at these later on in this chapter. To whet your appetite, here is just a small selection of the things it enables us to do:

- ❏ Redirecting people to another page
- ❏ Find out about the web browser our visitor is using
- ❏ Find out what web site the person was on before they came to ours
- ❏ Personalize pages for our visitors
- ❏ Store commonly used information centrally
- ❏ Find out exactly what web address the person typed in to get to our web page

So the ASP class that all our ASPX files are placed within inherits from the Page class when it is called , now let's look at the first item on the above list in more detail.

Redirecting the User to Another Page

Sometimes when we build a web page, we want to automatically send the user to another pageFor example, if an unauthenticated user tried to access a password protected page on a web site, we'd want them to be redirected to a page where they are asked to sign in and provide a password.

The `Page` object has a property called `Response`. We have come across the `Response` property a few times in the book, but in this chapter, we'll learn a little more about how it actually works. When called, the `Response` property returns an object of the type `HttpResponse`. This features a method called `Redirect` that we can use to send the user off to another page; we just pass it a string representing the web address of the new page.

For example, we could create a very simple ASP.NET page (`redirect.aspx`) that automatically redirects us to the Wrox web site:

```
<%@ Page Language="VB" %>
<%
  Response.Redirect("http://www.wrox.com/")
%>
```

At the moment, we're focusing on the `Redirect` method, but we will look at the `Response` object in more detail shortly.

Let's look at a slightly more useful example.

Try It Out – Navigating with a Dropdown List

In this example, we're going to display a dropdown list that shows some web sites and a button, both of which will be created using server controls. When we select one and click the Go button, we'll be taken to the web site we have chosen.

1. Open up your editor and type in the following code:

```
<%@ Page Language="VB" %>
<html>
  <body>
    <form id="WebForm1" method="post" runat="server">
      <asp:DropDownList id=MyDropDownList runat="server"/>
      <asp:button id=MyButton runat="server" Text=""/>
    </form>
  </body>
</html>
```

2. Save this file as `navigator.aspx`. If you call up the file from your browser at this stage, you'll see this:

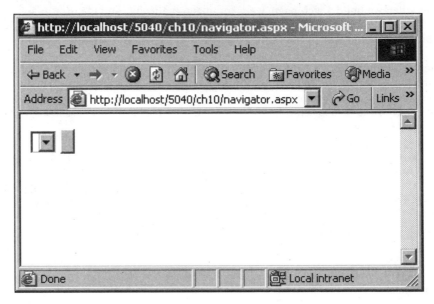

We can see that both the dropdown list and the button are shown, although both are rather small, as we haven't added any items yet!

3. Let's add some code to do that – update the code as marked:

```vb
<%@ Page Language="VB" %>
<script language="vb" runat="server">

    Sub Page_Load(Source As Object, E as EventArgs)
      If Not IsPostBack Then
        MyButton.Text = "OK"
        MyDropDownList.Items.Add("http://www.microsoft.com")
        MyDropDownList.Items.Add("http://www.wrox.com")
        MyDropDownList.Items.Add("http://msdn.microsoft.com")
      End If
    End Sub
  </script>
<html>
 <body>
  <form id="WebForm1" method="post" runat="server">
    <asp:DropDownList id=MyDropDownList runat="server"/>
    <asp:button id=MyButton runat="server" Text=""/>
  </form>
 </body>
</html>
```

View the file again in your browser, and you'll see that the button now says **OK** and the dropdown list contains three items describing three web site addresses:

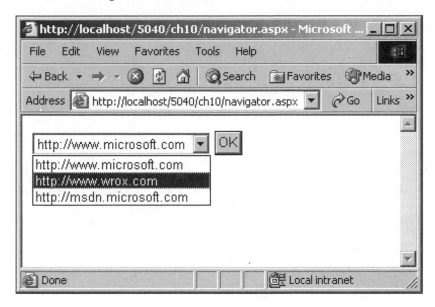

4. Now we have a page that looks the way we want, but if we select a web site from the list and click **OK**, nothing happens. Let's fix that now, add the marked code:

```vb
<%@ Page Language="VB" %>
<script language="vb" runat="server">
    Sub Page_Load(Source As Object, E as EventArgs)
      If Not IsPostBack Then
        MyButton.Text = "OK"
        MyDropDownList.Items.Add("http://www.microsoft.com")
        MyDropDownList.Items.Add("http://www.wrox.com")
        MyDropDownList.Items.Add("http://msdn.microsoft.com")
      End If
    End Sub

    Public Sub Click (ByVal sender As Object, ByVal e As System.EventArgs)
      Response.Redirect(MyDropDownList.SelectedItem.Text)
    End Sub
</script>
<html>
  <body>
    <form id="WebForm1" method="post" runat="server">
      <asp:DropDownList id=MyDropDownList runat="server"/>
      <asp:button id=MyButton runat="server" OnClick="Click" Text=""/>
    </form>
  </body>
</html>
```

327

5. Save the page, and open it in your browser again, and you'll find that when you select an item and click OK, you'll be taken to the web site you selected.

How It Works

Let's take a quick look through the code we've just added. First of all, we create a dropdown list and a button:

```
<asp:DropDownList id=MyDropDownList runat="server"/>
<asp:button id=MyButton runat="server" OnClick="Click" Text=""/>
```

Next, in step 3, we made sure this is the first time the page has been viewed:

```
If Not IsPostBack Then
```

We added this check because the page is reloaded every time the OK button is clicked, to carry out our Redirect method. In effect, this means that each time we press the button, another three duplicate items would appear in the dropdown list, as they would be reloaded. After this, we have a statement that adds the text OK to the button:

```
MyButton.Text = "OK"
```

In fact, we could just as easily do this by including a value attribute (Text="OK") in the <asp:Button> line. In this case, I chose to use a line of code to do it, as it's a nice simple demonstration of how we can manipulate a button using code.

Then we add three items to the dropdown list using the Add method, which takes a string as a parameter:

```
MyDropDownList.Items.Add("www.microsoft.com")
MyDropDownList.Items.Add("www.wrox.com")
MyDropDownList.Items.Add("msdn.microsoft.com")
```

Moving on to Step 4, the first change we made was to add an **event handler** to the button definition. What we're saying is "when someone clicks here (which causes an event), execute the specified subroutine (handle the event)":

```
<asp:button id=MyButton runat="server" OnClick="Click" Text="">
```

Next, we added the event handler itself, the Click() subroutine which starts off like this:

```
Public Sub Click(ByVal sender As Object, ByVal e As System.EventArgs
```

The important things to notice here are that firstly this is a subroutine, and secondly, that it is called Click(). Of secondary importance are the parameters that are passed to the subroutine. Nearly all event handlers in the .NET framework take these two parameters. The first parameter is a reference to the control or object that actually fired the event. The second parameter is a reference to an object that gives extra information about the event itself. In our case, sender will be the button object that the user clicked and e will be blank, because no extra information is passed through with this event.

Next you can see the `Response.Redirect()` method call, just like we used in the last example, except this time, we're passing it a string parameter that we obtain by using the `Text` property on the selected `MyDropDownList` item:

```
Response.Redirect(MyDropDownList.SelectedItem.Text)
```

This example is a pretty good demonstration of ASP.NET pages that use some objects and work with events; we'll be doing a lot more of this throughout the rest of the book.

Now we've seen the .NET framework from a high level, and we've seen how to use the `Redirect()` method of the `HttpResponse` class.

The HttpResponse class provides a way for the page to communicate with the browser. It is commonly used to send HTML code back to the browser and, as in this case, tell the browser to load a different page. We can get hold of an instance of `HttpResponse` through the `Response` property of the `Page` class.

Let's look at the `Response` object and its cousins in the `System.Web` namespace in a little more detail.

ASP.NET Core Objects

In this section, we'll look at what are perhaps the most important objects in ASP.NET:

- ❏ `Request` – gives us access to information about the person or process requesting the web page
- ❏ `Response` – provides a way for us to accurately control how the response is sent back to the person who made the request
- ❏ `Server` – provides a range of useful web-related utilities.
- ❏ `Application` – implements a useful site-wide storage location for frequently used information
- ❏ `Session` – makes it possible for us to store information for each user's session, for example, a shopping cart

These objects are fundamental to how ASP.NET operates, and also to how we make use of ASP.NET's features. Before we look at the objects themselves and the facilities they provide, let's see how ASP.NET makes these objects available to us.

Each of the objects (`Request`, `Response`, and so on) is created from a class. For example, although we refer to the `Response` object, it is created from the `System.Web.HttpResponse` class. The reason we call it the `Response` object is because the specific instance of the `HttpResponse` class that we're interested in is accessible using a property of our `Page` object called `Response`.

Remember the diagram we looked at when we were seeing how the `Page` object fitted into the process of retrieving an `ASPX` page? Let's look at the lower part of that diagram again to see exactly how the `Response` object is called. Say our file, `mypage.aspx`, contains a `Response.Redirect` command – this is how it would be accessed:

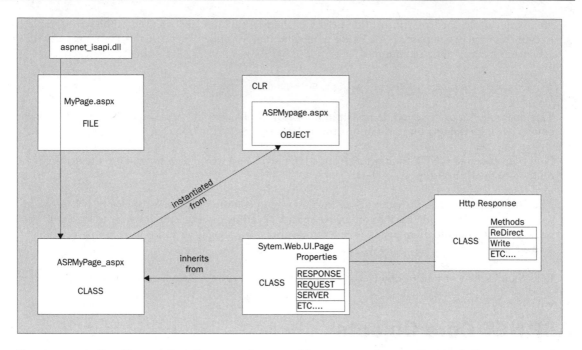

You can see in the diagram that the Page class provides a range of properties, including Response, Request, and Server. When we access the Response property, it returns an object of the type HttpResponse. We can then use methods from that object, such as Redirect().

What this means is that, because there's no work to do in locating the relevant object, we can use a very simple statement to access methods and properties on an HttpResponse object (or any of the others) directly from our ASP.NET page.
Now we know how to get at these objects, let's find out what they can do for us.

Request Object

When someone opens a web browser and requests a web page from our site, our web server receives an HTTP request that contains a whole load of information about the user, their PC, the page and their browser. As we noted in the last chapter, all that information is neatly packaged up and made available to us in the Request object.

This means that, rather than being concerned with finding bits of information from all over the place, everything related to that single HTTP request is provided in a single object which contains a series of methods and properties we can use to find out what we need to know. The Request object is effectively passing a message to us from the person's web browser saying, "here's who I am, and here's what I want":

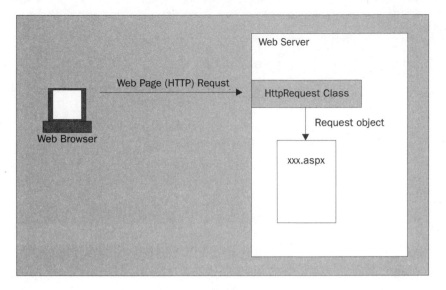

We've already looked briefly at this object and its Browser property – let's take a look at the rest of the properties that are returned as part of the HttpRequest class:

Property	Description
ApplicationPath	Tells us which folder of our web application the requested page lives in.
Path	Is the same as ApplicationPath in that it returns the full web address path to where our page is, but also includes the page's filename.
PhysicalApplicationPath	Returns the full path to our page, but on our physical disc, not as a web address.
Browser	Provides access to the Browser object that is hugely useful in finding out about the visitor's web browser software and its capabilities.
Cookies	This property lets us see the cookies that the visitor may have from previous visits to our site. We'll look at cookies later in the chapter.
IsSecureConnection	Whether the HTTP connection is using encryption (in most cases it won't be).
RequestType	Whether the request was a GET or POST request.
QueryString	Returns any parameters that have been passed to the page using GET.

Table continued on following page

Property	Description
Url	Returns the complete address as submitted by the browser.
	To display the web address held by the Url object as a string, we use its method ToString().
RawUrl	Like Url, but the protocol and domain name are missed off of the beginning.
	(so if http://www.wrox.com/article.aspx is returned by Url, RawUrl returns /article.aspx.)
UserHostName	Returns the name of the machine requesting the page from our web server. (In some cases, knowing the name of the user's computer can be useful in identifying the user for security purposes.)
UserHostAddress	Returns the IP address of the machine requesting our page.
UserLanguages	Tells us what language settings the browser has configured.

As usual, the syntax we use to access these commands is:

```
Request.PropertyName
```

Now let's put a couple of these properties to use.

Try It Out – Checking the Browser

In this example, we'll create a variation on our containment.aspx example from the last chapter. This web form will look at what version of Internet Explorer we're using, and suggest we upgrade if we're not using version 6 or later.

1. Open up your editor and type in the following code:

```
<%@ Page Language="VB" %>
<script language="vb" runat="server">
  Sub Page_Load(Source As Object, E as EventArgs)
    If Not IsPostBack Then
      If Request.Browser.Browser = "IE" Then
        If Request.Browser.MajorVersion < 6 Then
          MyLabel.Text = "Time to upgrade Internet Explorer!"
      Else
          MyLabel.Text = "Your copy of Internet Explorer is up to date."
      End If
      Else
        MyLabel.Text = "You're not using Internet Explorer"
      End If
    End If
```

```
   End Sub
</script>

<html>
  <body>
    <asp:Label id=MyLabel runat="server" Text=""/>
  </body>
</html>
```

2. Save this file as `browsercheck.aspx`

3. Open up your browser and view the file. If you're using Internet Explorer 6, you'll see this:

If you're using a version of Internet Explorer prior to version 6, you'll see something like this:

333

How it Works

The first thing we do on the page is to add a label control `MyLabel`.

```
<%@ Page Language="VB" %>
<html>
  <body>
    <asp:Label id=MyLabel runat="server" Text=""/>
  </body>
</html>
```

When ASP.NET runs the page, it will fire the load event on the page. This will cause the `Page_Load` event handler we added in the script block to be executed:

```
<script language="vb" runat="server">
Sub Page_Load(Source As Object, E as EventArgs)
```

Once the page is loaded, the first thing we want to do, is check to see if the page has been posted back, or whether it's the first time it has been accessed. We use the `IsPostBack` method here to check that, just as we did when we created `navigator.aspx`, above:

```
If Not IsPostBack Then
```

We've already discussed the `Browser` property, but here we're using two objects within the Browser property: `Browser` and `MajorVersion`. `Browser` is used to return the name of the browser, and `MajorVersion` returns the version number of the browser being used. So, then, firstly, we check to see if the name of the browser is given as IE:

```
If Request.Browser.Browser = "IE" Then
```

and, if it is, we check to see what the version number is:

```
If Request.Browser.MajorVersion < 6 Then
```

If the version number is less than 6 (the latest version at the time of writing), we politely suggest to the user that they upgrade. If not, we tell the user that it's up to date. In both cases, we tell the user by setting the `Text` property of the `MyLabel` control that we created at the start of the page:

```
        MyLabel.Text = "Time to upgrade Internet Explorer!"
    Else
        MyLabel.Text = "Your copy of Internet Explorer is up to date."
    End If
```

On the other hand, the user might not be using Internet Explorer, in which case, we tell them that!

```
    Else
      MyLabel.Text = "You're not using Internet Explorer"
```

Response Object

Just as the `Request` object lets us see the incoming HTTP request, the `Response` object provides access to the HTTP response that is going to be sent back to the requesting web browser. This response includes the HTML for the requested page.

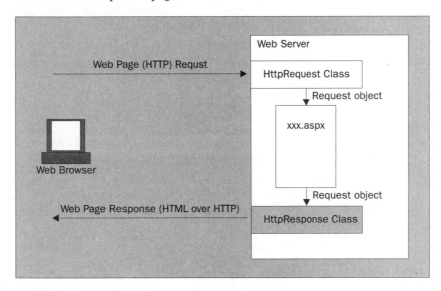

The `Response` object is of the type `HttpResponse`. The `HttpResponse` class provides a range of properties and methods for us to use, including the `Write()` and `Redirect()` methods that we've used in previous examples.

When ASP.NET is running the code in our pages, it gradually builds up the HTML that will be sent back to the browser. ASP.NET has what's called a **buffer**; as the HTML is generated, it is placed in the buffer. Normally, the HTML is held in the buffer so that it isn't sent to the browser until the page finishes executing, however we can change that behavior if we want. (In most cases, it's *not* useful to change this behavior, but we're going to do it here in order to illustrate an important point about ASP.NET performance.) The `Response` object is where we tell the page buffer what we want it to do; it's our way of managing what gets sent back to the web browser and how and when it is sent.

Here are some of the most useful properties and methods on the `HttpResponse` class:

Property	Description
Buffer	The default value of this property is `True`, which means the page is buffered and sent in one block. If we set it to `False`, the response will be sent piecemeal along the wires as and when each piece is generated. Sending the HTML in pieces like this is much slower than using the buffer, but it means the site visitor has the chance to see some HTML before the page has finished executing (which is useful if your user might be left waiting for a long piece of code to be compiled)

Table continued on following page

Property	Description
ContentType	With this property, we can set the type of data we're sending back. This setting specifies what's called a **MIME type**. (MIME, or Multipurpose Internet Mail Extensions is a way of identifying the different kinds of resources that Internet services like the Web and e-mail can transfer. An HTML page is represented with the MIME type text/html. A GIF image with image/gif, and so on). The details of how this works aren't important for most browsers, however.
Cookies	The use of this property is how we save visitors' settings to their hard drive. We'll look at cookies in detail later in the chapter.
Clear()	If we call this method, the buffer will be emptied and the contents discarded, but we can continue and add more HTML to it if we want to.
Flush()	When we call this method, all the HTML in the buffer is sent to the web browser, but we can continue creating HTML.
End()	This command is terminal; it sends all the HTML from the buffer and our page stops executing. It's useful if we want to end page execution and ensure we don't send anything else across to the web browser.
Redirect()	We've seen this method in action already; it redirects the user to another page. Note that one important rule with Redirect is that no HTML is allowed to already have been sent to the browser. You can ensure that this is the case by explicitly not outputting any HTML, or by turning on buffering and not sending the contents of the buffer (don't use Flush or End!). ASP.NET will produce an error if you attempt to use Redirect when HTML has already been sent to the browser.
Write()	We've seen this method in action too; it just writes a string to the HTML stream, if buffering is turned on, it'll write to the buffer and wait to be sent later.
WriteFile()	This method is exactly the same as Write, except it writes the contents of a file to the HTML output stream.

Let's look at an example page that uses some of these methods and properties so we can see, in more concrete terms, what the Response object lets us do.

Try It Out – HTML Buffering

In this example, we'll create a page that we can use to see what effect buffering has on our pages. By default, buffering is turned on, but we'll see what happens when we turn it off.

1. Open up your editor and type in the following code:

```
<%@ Page Language="VB" %>
<html>
  <body>
    <%
    Dim i As Integer
    For i = 1 to 50
      Response.Write(" X")
```

```
      Next
      %>
   </body>
</html>
```

2. Save this file as `buffer.aspx` in your web site.

3. Open up your browser and view the file. You'll see this:

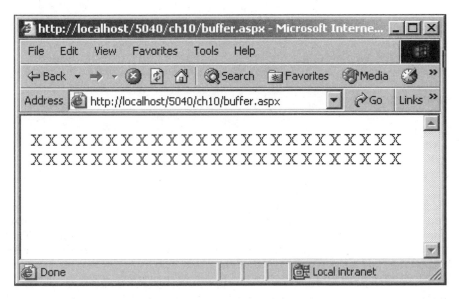

Notice that the page contents appear quickly, and in one go.

4. Now add the marked line of code to turn off buffering:

```
<%@ Page Language="VB" %>
<html>
   <body>
      <%
      Response.Buffer = False
      Dim i As Integer
      For i = 1 to 50
        Response.Write(" X")
      Next
      %>
   </body>
</html>
```

5. Now reload the page in your web browser. You'll find that the page no longer appears in one burst, but as a trickle of HTML as each of the Xs appears. You'll also see that it is much, much slower.

If you find that your machine doesn't seem much slower the second time, try increasing the "50" in the code sample.

How it Works

To start with, we created a for loop which loops our integer variable i 50 times:

```
<%@ Page Language="VB" %>
<html>
  <body>
    <%
    Dim i As Integer
    For i = 1 to 50
      Response.Write(" X")
    Next
    %>
  </body>
</html>
```

Then we turned buffering off by setting the Response.Buffer object to false:

```
Response.Buffer = False
```

With buffering switched on, ASP.NET will collect the entire HTML document that makes up the page, before sending it back to the server. The advantage of this approach is that the performance of building the page up using the code we write on the page remains relatively constant. ASP.NET asks for the HTML that makes up page, it gets the HTML, then it passes the HTML back to IIS, and tells IIS to send it back to the browser. When first tried out buffer.aspx, we saw it loaded quickly.

> **With buffering switched off, ASP.NET passes the text to IIS character-by-character. What this means is that it will take longer to physically process the page from top to bottom. On most web sites, you get better performance with buffering switched on, as it takes more processing power and system resources to build the page incrementally than it does to send it all back down to the client at once.**

Let's look at another example that uses the Response object.

In this example, we'll create a page that displays the contents of a text file that's located in the same folder as our ASP.NET page.

Try It Out – Writing a file to the screen

1. Open up your editor and type in the following code:

```
<%@ Page Language="VB" %>
<html>
  <body>
    <H2>Response.WriteFile()</H2>
<%
```

```
    Dim filename As String
        filename = Request.PhysicalApplicationPath + "file.txt"
        Response.WriteFile(filename)
        %>
    </body>
</html>
```

2. Save this file as `writefile.aspx` in your web site.

3. Create a file called `file.txt` in the root folder of the application that `writefile.aspx` is in (if you are using the physical directory we set up in Chapter 1, we're talking about the `BegASPNET` folder), and type this code into it:

```
<B>this text has come from file.txt</B>
```

4. Open up your browser and view the `writefile.aspx` file. You'll see this:

We can see that the text from `file.txt` has appeared in our page.

How it Works

The `PhysicalApplicationPath` property of `Request` returns the path that the web site is actually installed it. We take this path, and tack the name of our file onto the end of it, in this case. `"file.txt"`:

```
    <%
    Dim filename As String
    filename = Request.PhysicalApplicationPath + "file.txt"
```

Once we have a filename, we pass it over to the `WriteFile` method.

```
Response.WriteFile(filename)
%>
```

This method opens the file, reads its contents, and inserts the contents of the file into the HTML that makes up the page.

Server Object

The `Page` class also gives us access to a property called `Server` that returns an object of the type `HttpServerUtility`. This class defines a general-purpose web-related toolbox that includes some very useful bits of functionality.

Here are some of the most useful methods and properties:

Member	Description
MachineName	This read-only property returns the Windows name of the machine that ASP.NET is running on.
ScriptTimeO ut	This property gets, and sets, the amount of time before an ASP.NET page times out; this will happen if the code takes an extraordinary amount of time to execute. The default setting for the `ScriptTimeOut` property is 90 seconds. It's generally not necessary to change this value, but if your web site is generating huge pages, or ones that take an enormous amount of time to generate, you may need to extend it.
HtmlEncode( )	This method takes a string, and encodes it, so it can be displayed in a browser. Browsers can display most text without conversion, but there are some characters, particularly '<' and '>' which, because they are used in HTML code, will be interpreted as HTML, and not shown correctly. In HTML, if we want to display a '<' we use `&lt;` and to display '>' we use `&gt;`. If we wrote the string <EEEK!>, it would appear blank in a browser, because it would read it as an <EEEK> HTML tag, which doesn't exist. If we pass that string through `HtmlEncode()`, it will return `&lt;EEEK!&gt;` which will be displayed as <EEEK!> in a browser.
HtmlDecode( ) -	This method is the exact opposite of the `HtmlEncode()` method. It takes HTML encoded characters like `&gt;` and converts them to normal characters like '>'.
MapPath()	This method takes a **virtual path** (in other words a web address without the server name) like `/webapp/myfile.aspx`, and returns the exact location of that file on the physical disc, which in this case might be `C:\InetPub\wwwroot\webapp\myfile.aspx`.

Member	Description
UrlEncode()	This method is used when we want to pass a string in a web address (URL). For example, if we wanted to use the URL, `page.aspx?command=stand & stare`, we'd get into difficulties, because URLs cannot include spaces, and characters like '?' and '&' have special meanings. URLs expect these characters to be encoded, for example spaces are converted to '+'s. If we pass our parameter `stand & stare` through `UrlEncode`, it returns `stand+%26+stare`, which has converted the spaces to '+'s and the '&' to '%26'.
UrlDecode()	We use this method to take parameters passed to us across URLs, and convert them to normal strings again. For example, the string `stand+%26+stare` would be `UrlDecoded` as `stand & stare`.

These encode and decode methods can be quite hard to grasp, so let's look at an example that uses them both. This example is a good demonstration of how **not** to build web sites using ASP.NET, but it'll demonstrate admirably how these methods work!

You'll probably find in day-to-day work that the objects we use to build ASP.NET applications automatically deal with encoding issues to the degree that we physically won't need to call these methods ourselves.

Try It Out – Using Server.UrlEncode()

In this example, we'll create a pair of pages, the second of which generates a birthday card using the name and age passed from the first. The first page just shows an HTML link that passes the name and age parameters on the URL to the second page.

1. Open up your editor and type in the following code for our first page:

```
<%@ Page Language="VB" %>
<html>
  <body>
    <%
    Dim Name As string
    Dim Age As string
    Age = 23
    Name = "Sniff"
    %>
    <a href="birthday2.aspx?age=<% Response.Write(Age) %>&name=<%
    Response.Write(Name)%>">click here</a>
  </body>
</html>
```

Notice how the page uses an `<a>` tag, into which we squirt the values for `Age` and `Name` using `Response.Write()`. (The `<a>`, or "anchor" tag places a link on the browser that we can click to visit a different page). The `href` property is an HTML control used to specify or receive a URL. So here, we use the `href` property to specify that the following is a URL, which also tells us that we're passing the two parameters as a `GET` request. Effectively, the URL that IE will go to when we click on the link is: birthday2.aspx?age=23&name=Sniff.

2. Save this file as `birthday1.aspx`.

3. Open up your editor again, and type in the following for our second page. Notice how we create two variables called `Name` and `Age`, and then set them to the two parameters passed as part of the `GET` request with the `QueryString` property on the `Request` object:

```
<%@ Page Language="VB" %>
<html>
  <body>
    <center>
      <%
      Dim Name As string
      Dim Age as string
      Name = Request.QueryString("Name")
      Age = Request.QueryString("Age")
      %>
      <h1>Happy Birthday <% Response.Write(Name) %></h1>
      <h3>May the next
      <% Response.Write(Age) %>
      years be as good!</h3>
    </center>
  </body>
</html>
```

4. Now save this page as `birthday2.aspx`.

5. Call up the `birthday1.aspx` page – you'll see a single link that says click here. If you roll over the link, you'll see that it points to …/birthday2.aspx?age=23&name=Sniff.

6. Click on the link to navigate to `birthday2.aspx` and you'll see this:

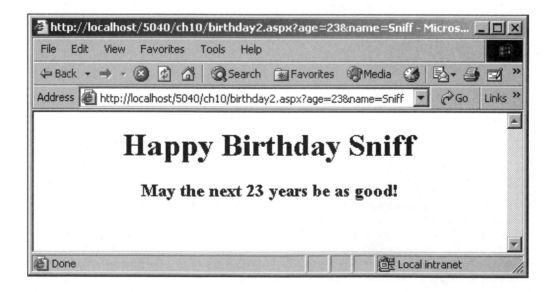

7. The screenshot demonstrates that we have successfully passed our two parameters (Name and Age) across to the second page, using the QueryString property of the Request object to access the parameters' values ('23' and 'Sniff'). It looks like the application works fine – or does it?

Open up birthday1.aspx again, and change the name from "Sniff" to "Sniff & Jack", like this:

```
<%@ Page Language="VB" %>
<html>
  <body>
    <%
    Dim Name As string
    Dim Age As string
    Age = "23"
    Name = "Sniff & Jack"
    %>
    <a href="birthday2.aspx?age=<% Response.Write(Age) %>&name=<%
    Response.Write(Name)%>">click here</a>
  </body>
</html>
```

8. Open up birthday1.aspx in your browser again and refresh the page so the HTML link reflects the change we have made. If you click the link now, you'll see this:

9. This is the same as we had before! What's going on? The reason relates to the bit of our HTML link that looks like this:

```
.../birthday2.aspx?age=23&name=Sniff & Jack
```

Our second page is interpreting that as `age=23`, `name="Sniff"`, `Jack=""` and there's also a risk of further confusion, as our URL includes spacing – which is not allowed. This isn't what we want at all; we don't want spaces, and we want the final `&` to be sent as part of the `Name` parameter, not interpreted as a divider between parameters. The solution to this is to 'URL encode' the `Name` and `Age` values using the `UrlEncode()` method before we create the HTML link.

10. Change the code by adding the two marked lines below, and let's also change the age to use another illegal character, to make sure that's encoded correctly too:

```
<%@ Page Language="VB" %>
<html>
  <body>
    <%
    Dim Name As string
    Dim Age As string
    Age = "twenty three??"
    Name = "Sniff & Jack"
    Age = Server.UrlEncode(Age)
    Name = Server.UrlEncode(Name)
    %>
    <a href="birthday2.aspx?age=<% Response.Write(Age) %>&name=<%
    Response.Write(Name)%>">click here</a>
  </body>
</html>
```

Open `birthday1.aspx` in your browser again, and refresh the page. If you roll over the link you'll find it has changed:

```
/birthday2.aspx?age=twenty+three%3f%3f&name=Sniff+%26+Jack
```

Notice how the query '?' has been converted to %3f, while the ampersand '&' has been converted to %26. These character codes are directly supported by URLs, so this link will now work. Let's try it; click the link, you should see this:

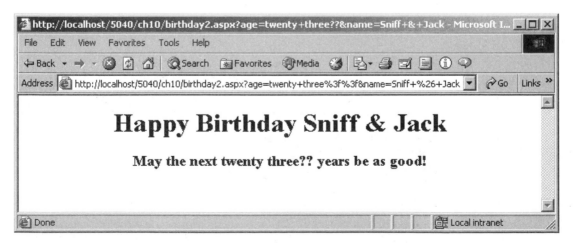

How it Works

We've kind of explained the code as we've gone along this time, but to sum up, the `UrlEncode()` method will examine each character in a string to ensure it is in a form that can be correctly transmitted as part of a URL. As a bonus, ASP.NET automatically decodes the URL string at the other end, so we don't need to explicitly use `UrlDecode()` in `birthday2.asp`.

Let's continue this example, and look at the `HtmlEncode()` method of the `HttpServerUtility` class – as accessible through the `Server` object – to display characters used in HTML code in the browser.

Try It Out – Using Server.HtmlEncode()

1. Open up `birthday1.aspx`, and make the change shown:

```
<%@ Page Language="VB" %>
<html>
  <body>
    <%
    Dim Name As string
    Dim Age As string
    Age = "twenty three??"
    Name = "<Sniff> & <Jack>"
    Age = Server.UrlEncode(Age)
    Name = Server.UrlEncode(Name)
    %>
    <a href="birthday2.aspx?age=<% Response.Write(Age) %>&name=<%
    Response.Write(Name)%>">click here</a>
  </body>
</html>
```

2. Now open `birthday1.aspx` up in your browser again, and hit **Refresh**.

3. Now click on the link, here's what you'll see:

4. As you can see, we have a new problem: the `Name` parameter isn't appearing correctly, and only the '&' is visible.

5. Open up `birthday2.aspx` and make the changes marked:

```
<%@ Page Language="VB" %>
<html>
  <body>
    <center>
      <%
      Dim Name As string
      Dim Age as string
      Name = Request.QueryString("Name")
      Age = Request.QueryString("Age")
      Name = Server.HtmlEncode(Name)
      Age = Server.HtmlEncode(Age)
      %>
      <h1>Happy Birthday <% Response.Write(Name) %></h1>
      <h3>May the next
      <% Response.Write(Age) %>
      years be as good!</h3>
    </center>
  </body>
</html>
```

6. Now refresh `birthday2.aspx` in your browser; you'll see this:

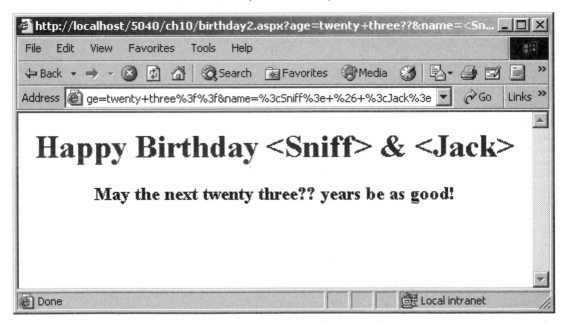

How it Works

We altered the code we created in `birthday1.aspx`, by changing our name values to:

```
Name = "<Sniff> & <Jack>"
```

When we clicked on our link however, the names didn't appear. The reason for this is that the browser attempted to treat `<Sniff>` and `<Jack>` as HTML tags, rather than text. As a rule, when a browser doesn't understand a tag it will ignore it – the principle behind this being that the browser believes some new HTML tag has been introduced that it doesn't know about, so it decides to display the page as best it can.

In HTML, if we want to display a "less than" symbol '<' on the page, we have to use a special syntax, and type `&lt;`. As luck would have it, `HtmlEncode()` can do all this for us. So we added the following lines to `birthday2.aspx`:

```
Name = Server.HtmlEncode(Name)
Age = Server.HtmlEncode(Age)
```

and our new name values were printed on the screen.

Let's see what has happened as a result of our tinkering. If we use our browser and select View Source, we can see that the HTML for the first line of our page looks like this:

```
<h1>Happy Birthday &lt;Sniff&gt; &amp; &lt;Jack&gt;</h1>
```

Each of the '<' and '>' characters have been encoded in such a way that they are properly displayed by the browser, rather than interpreted as HTML tags.

`HtmlEncode()` is especially useful if visitors to your web site are typing text into forms, and you want to display it on a page. For example, if you had a guestbook on your site where people can leave messages, you probably want any '<' and '>' characters displayed rather than interpreted as HTML to prevent people messing with your site, and putting pictures and their own HTML code into your guestbook.

State Handling

One of the ways that web servers manage to handle thousands of users each minute is by implementing what's known as "stateless connections". Whenever you ask a browser to return a page, image, or other resource, the following happens:

1. you connect to the server

2. you tell it what page, image, or other item you want

3. it sends you the resource you ask for

4. the server disconnects you and forgets everything about you

It's this "forgets everything" bit that's important. If a web server tried to watch you for twenty minutes as you moved from page to page on a popular web site, like Amazon or MSN, you'd need a server the size of a house to store the information. Instead, web servers treat every request they get in an unassociated manner, in other words two consecutive requests from you are treated as two, separate, unassociated requests.

State management is a trick that allows the web server to make some determinations about who you are, where you have already been on the site and what you've done. Simply, the server and browser work together and use a tiny piece of memory or disk space that gives the ASP.NET pages running on the server enough information to go away and find out who you are, if it needs to.

ASP.NET provides a range of features to help us manage the **state** (persistence) of various elements of our web applications. What do we mean by state? Let's have a look at some examples of where we see states used in web sites:

❑   If our web site uses our company telephone number quite a lot, it would be very useful to be able to store it somewhere so that it's easily accessible to all the pages in our web site. It would also be handy to store it centrally so that if (when!) the number changes, we can update it in one place and be confident the change will be reflected across the web site.

❑   When we use a web site and add items to our shopping basket, we expect the contents of the basket to be retained as we shop. The state of our basket needs to be stored during our visit to the web site as we move around the site.

❑   When we log onto most web sites, we expect not to have to log on each time we come back. The fact that we have logged in before and should be allowed in without being asked to log in again has been stored to achieve this.

❑   When we fill in a form on a web site, we expect the web site to keep the information we entered so we don't have to enter it again.

As you can see, states are widely used, but there are a variety of different types of state that are being used. Do note that although there are quite a few, they're not hard to work with and all the difficult stuff has been done for us, even more so with ASP.NET than previous versions of ASP.

Some of the questions we'll look at in the following sections are:

❑   What is the scope of each type of state? Does it apply to each user, across the whole web site, or is it just for one visit to the web site by one person?

❑   Where is the state stored? Is it in the user's browser, or in our web server's memory, or in a file or database somewhere?

❑   How do we change states? If we wanted to empty a shopping basket, how do we do that?

Application State

Sometimes we want to store a piece of information in a way that it's always easily accessible by any page of the web site. This is what Application state is for; a central, site-wide store of variables that we can get at from any page.

We make use of it by using an object instantiated from the HttpApplicationState class. We get at the object using another property of the Page class (just like Response and Request). The property is called Application; in terms of the code we write to use application state, it's pretty minimal.

Words can make the `Application` object sound complex, so let's look at an example that will show you that in practice it's pretty straightforward.

Try It Out – Using Application State

Let's look at an example web site where we have a company telephone number (555 1234), that we want to store centrally, and in such a way that any page viewed by any visitor can access it and display it.

1. Open up your editor and type the following:

```
<%@ Page Language="VB" %>
<html>
  <body>
    <%
    Application("CompanyTelephone") = "555 1234"
    %>
    <b>Application state changed successfully</b>
  </body>
</html>
```

2. Save the file as `application1.aspx` in your web site

3. Open your editor again and type the following into a new page:

```
<%@ Page Language="VB" %>
<html>
  <body>
    <b>Company Telephone = <% Response.Write(Application("CompanyTelephone")) %>
    </b>
  </body>
</html>
```

4. Save this page as `application2.aspx`

5. Call up `application1.aspx` in your browser and you'll see this:

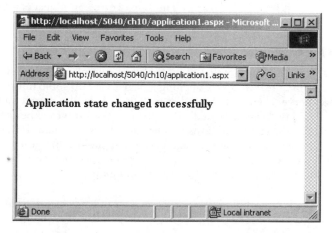

6. Now open `application2.aspx` in your browser:

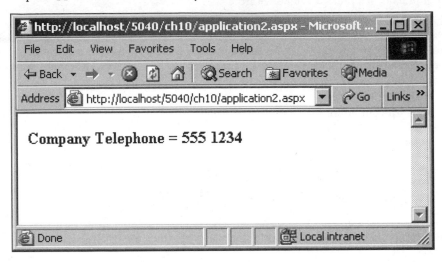

How It Works

As you can see, we were able to view the company telephone number from our browser window, even when the code that generated the window didn't contain the information. We were able to do this using this statement:

```
<% Response.Write(Application("CompanyTelephone")) %>
```

This statement is saying, "Tell me the value of the 'CompanyTelephone' application state".

Now, initially we set the telephone number in the application state using this statement:

```
Application("CompanyTelephone") = "555 1234"
```

Here, we are referencing the `Application` property of the `Page` object, and passing the parameter, `CompanyTelephone`. What this command is saying is "please create me a new state variable called `CompanyTelephone` and set it to 555 1234". The `Application` object is a container for all the application state variables we set; it is a collection object.

Initial Configuration for Application State

You may be wondering about the fact that to set the company telephone number to "555 1234" we had to open a page. Surely on a real web site, opening a page to set up some information every time we start Internet Information Server is going to be rather irritating! Actually, there's a more realistic problem with this approach than just "being irritated". Imagine our Web server experiences a power failure in the middle of the night – the computer turns off and turns back on again. IIS automatically starts when the computer starts, but unless we visit the page part of our site (in this case the phone number), it won't work properly. We'd have to remember to check the site periodically, and if the information appeared to be missing, we'd have to open the page to set everything up.

A much better approach is to configure the application state when our web site starts up, which is where the `global.asax` file comes in. This file contains code which is executed in response to certain events, in this case the most useful event is one that's fired when the web application starts (i.e. when the first visitor hits the site). Let's continue our example:

7. Open up your editor and type the following:

```
<script language="VB" runat="server">
Sub Application_OnStart()
  Application("CompanyTelephone") = "555 4321"
End Sub
</script>
```

8. Save the file as `global.asax` in your application folder. The file must be in the root of a web application, which in this case means the topmost folder (`5040`).

Because we have created a new `global.asax` file, the web application restarts behind the scenes to take our changes into effect. When a web application starts up, ASP.NET looks for a `global.asax` file, and if it finds one, it looks for a subroutine called `Application_OnStart()`. If it exists, the code inside the procedure is executed. In our case, this means that when our web site starts up, the company telephone number is set to our new number, "555 4321".

9. Open `application2.aspx` in your browser, and you'll see that without using `application1.aspx`, our `CompanyTelephone` application state has been set correctly to the new phone number, "555 4321":

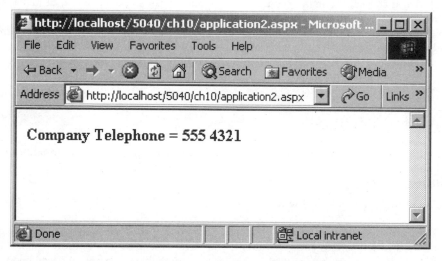

With the `Application` object, making changes to small pieces of information like this is much easier; the data is centralized and easily accessible by any of our ASP.NET pages using the `Application` object.

As you can see in the diagram below, the `Application` state is accessible from all the pages within a web application, and it is initially configured using the `global.asax` file:

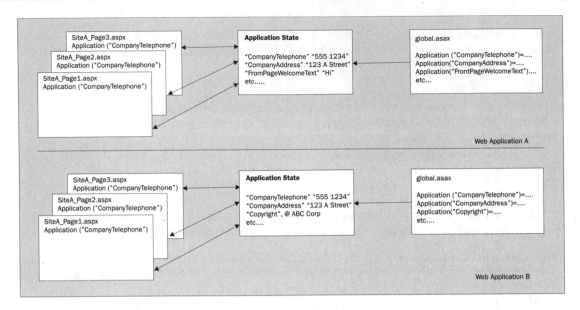

Note that if your web server contains more than one web application, each one has its own application state store and its own `global.asax` file.

If we find ourselves needing to alter the application state from within an ASP.NET page, we need to consider what happens if two pages attempt to make a change at the same time. (The nature of a web site is such that it can handle many requests at once and, as the chances of two or more pages being requests at a given moment is not zero, we have to accommodate this eventuality). It's possible that one will overwrite the changes made by the other in a way that we do not expect, or that cannot be predicted. Because of this, when we alter application state from an ASP.NET page, we use a pair of methods on the `Application` object called `Lock()` and `Unlock()` like this:

```
Application.Lock()
Application("SomeGlobalCounter") = <value>
Application.UnLock()
```

This structure ensures that no two pages can alter the application state at the same time.

Using Application State

Here are a few suggestions for using `application` state.

❑ Use it for frequently used data. The `application` state is designed for information that will be used widely across your web site. If you have a piece of information which is only used occasionally, you're better storing that in a file on disk, which you access when you need to. There's a file called `web.config` that will fulfill this purpose admirably in most cases and you'll see more about that in chapter 19.

❑ Don't go overboard with the number of pieces of information you put in the application state. Be aware that information in the application state is held in memory, so your web server will use up more memory for each state you add.

❑ The `Application` object is a collection object; this means it is an object that contains a group of other objects, like the `QueryString` property. The upshot of this is that you can, if you need to, store objects within the `Application` object, not just simple textual information.

❑ If you're making heavy use of the `application` object, keep a list somewhere of the items you have stored in it, so when you're writing pages, you know what information you already have easy access to.

❑ If your site starts getting high traffic volumes, you'll generally find fewer performance problems if you use the `web.config` file instead of the `application` state (again, see Chapter 19 for more information).

Session State

When a web site uses a shopping basket, where is that data stored? The shopping basket is a great example for how we use `Session state`. A session is a single visit to a web site, and normally includes visits to a number of pages. A session ends when the person has not viewed a page on the site for a certain period of time. The default "timeout" is twenty minutes, in other words, if the user hasn't visited a page on the site within twenty minutes, the session ends. We use session state to manage information that we want to be available while someone is using our web site, and which is specific to that particular person. Each session usually represents an individual user, but some people may have two browsers open, and so have two sessions running.

Here are some examples of where we might use session state:

❑ Shopping basket – a list of items the web site visitor has decided to buy. The list is maintained throughout their visit to the web site.

❑ Visitor name – many sites personalize pages on the basis of the current user's identity. If we have a database of users, and we know who our visitor is, we can add details we hold about the person to the session, so that our pages can easily access it. A common candidate for this is the person's name.

❑ Visitor settings – if someone visits our site and specifies a preference that affects how pages are displayed, it often makes sense to keep this type of information in the session.

In the diagram below, we can see that there are multiple session states, one for each active session:

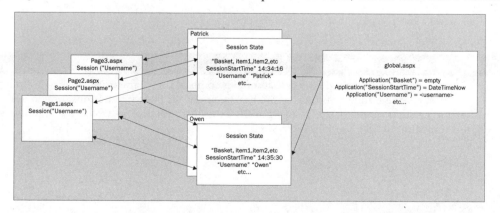

We can see that every page in the site has access to the session for the current user, which holds details specific to that session including, for example, the name of the person, the contents of their shopping basket, and the time the session started. We can also see that when a session starts (that is, when someone first opens a web page on our site) the `global.asax` file sets up the session, just like with the `Application` state. In this example, we set the shopping basket to be empty, we use the current time (`DateTime.Now`) to set the start of the session time, and we set up the username (probably from a database).

We work with session state in much the same way as we do with application state. The session is accessible through a property of the `Page` object called `Session` that returns an object of type `HttpSessionState`.

Here are some of the more commonly used methods and properties of the `HttpSessionState` class:

- ❏ `Abandon()` – this method ends the current session. All information in the session is cleared, and if the person visits a page subsequently, a new session will be created for them. (This is useful for "resetting" things so that the user is effectively given a brand-new session).

- ❏ `Clear()` – this method removes all the information from the session state, but does not end the session.

- ❏ `IsNewSession` – this property returns `True` if the session was created when the user accessed the current page. This might be useful in cases when a session needs to be initialized with some data before it can be used.

- ❏ `TimeOut` – this property gets and sets the period of idle time in minutes before a session expires. By default this value is set to twenty minutes; that is after twenty minutes during which the person has not accessed a page their session will end.

In addition to these properties, we can also use the `Session` object just like the `Application` object. For example, to store a person's name in our session, we use a statement like this:

```
Session("Name") = "Owen Blacker"
```

To read information out of the session, we use a statement like this:

```
Dim VisitorsName As string
VisitorsName = Session("Name")
```

Let's look at an example page that uses session state.

Try It Out – Using Session State

In this example, we'll build a simple page that mimics some of the characteristics of a shopping basket. Our page will show the number of items in the basket, and we'll have two buttons; one to add an item to the basket and another to empty the basket. For the sake of simplicity, we won't track the items in the basket, just the count of the number of items.

1. Open up your editor and type the following:

```
<%@ Page language="VB"%>
<html>
  <body>
    <form id="BasketForm" method="post" runat="server">
      <asp:Button id="Empty" OnClick="EmptyClick" runat="server" Text="Empty"/>
      <br />
      <asp:Button id="Add" OnClick="AddClick" runat="server" Text="Add"/>
      <br />
      Basket items : <%=Session("BasketCount")%>
      <br />
    </form>
  </body>
</html>
```

2. Add the following code to the start of the page:

```
<%@ Page language="VB"%>
<script language="vb" runat="server">
  Sub EmptyClick(sender As System.Object, e As System.EventArgs)
    Session("BasketCount") = 0
  End Sub

  Sub AddClick(sender As System.Object, e As System.EventArgs)
    Session("BasketCount") += 1
  End Sub
</script>
<html>
  <body>
    <form id="BasketForm" method="post" runat="server">
      <asp:Button id="Empty" OnClick="EmptyClick" runat="server"_ Text="Empty"/>
      <br />
      <asp:Button id="Add" OnClick="AddClick" runat="server" Text="Add"/>
      <br />
      Basket items : <%=Session("BasketCount")%>
      <br />
    </form>
  </body>
</html>
```

When the `EmptyClick` subroutine executes, it uses the highlighted statement to set the `BasketCount` session variable to zero. When the `AddClick` subroutine executes, it increments the number of items in our basket by one.

3. Save the file as `session.aspx` in your web site.

4. Open your browser, and view `session.aspx`; you'll see this:

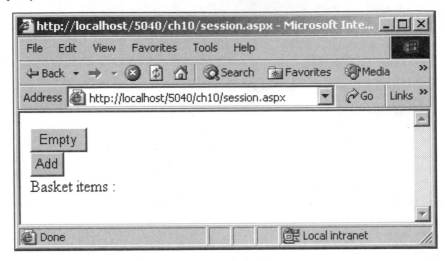

Click the **Add** button; the page will reload and you'll see this:

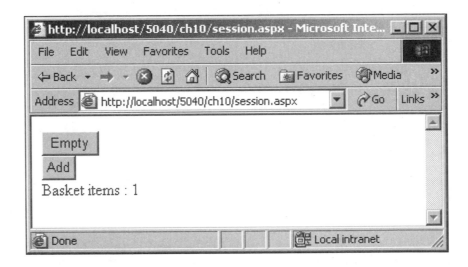

5. Click the **Add** button again, and you'll see that the number of items in the basket has increased. You'll also notice that if you refresh the page, the count of the number of items in the basket will remain the same; the information is stored in the session, and will persist between refreshes. The session information is only lost if you close the browser, or leave it inactive for more than twenty minutes.

6. Now click the Empty button so we can see the EmptyClick subroutine functioning. Once EmptyClick has executed, the page looks like this:

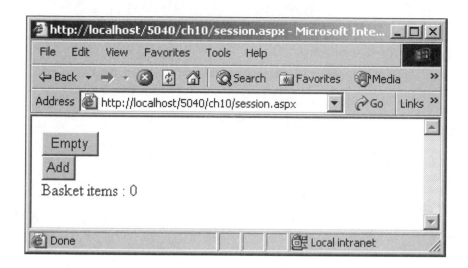

How it Works

In this page, we have a button to add an item to our basket (Add), we have a button to empty our basket (Empty), and a Response.Write() statement, `<%=Session("BasketCount")%>`, that displays the number of items in our basket. Both the buttons have defined OnClick attributes, that specify the subroutines that are called when we click the buttons:

```
<script language="vb" runat="server">
Sub EmptyClick(sender As System.Object, e As System.EventArgs)
   Session("BasketCount") = 0
End Sub

Sub AddClick(sender As System.Object, e As System.EventArgs)
   Session("BasketCount") += 1
End Sub
</script>
```

The EmptyClick subroutine resets the session variable BasketCount to zero. We could have used Session.Abandon() or Session.Clear() to empty the basket, although both of these methods would clear every other session variable which, may not be what we want. It's better to identify the session variables you want to clear, and clear them explicitly, rather than deleting the whole lot. (Use a scalpel, not a broadsword!)

The AddClick subroutine increments the BasketCount by one. Whichever button is pressed, the results are rendered to the page by retrieving the session value:

```
<form id="BasketForm" method="post" runat="server">
  <asp:Button id="Empty" OnClick="EmptyClick" runat="server" Text="Empty"/>
  <br />
```

```
        <asp:Button id="Add" OnClick="AddClick" runat="server" Text="Add"/>
        <br />
        Basket items : <%=Session("BasketCount")%>
        <br />
    </form>
```

Initial Configuration for Session State

Just as with application state, we can configure our web site to add information to the session when it begins, to do this we use the global.asax file again. So, for example, if we wanted to add a message to the session when it first starts, we do it by adding code like this to global.asax:

```
<script language="VB" runat="server">
Sub Session_OnStart()
  Session("Message") = "Buy some of our products, Bill!"
End Sub
</script>
```

On any page, we can then use a statement like this to coax our visitors into spending their hard earned cash:

```
<%=Session("Message")%>
```

This statement produces the following output:

```
Buy some of our products, Bill!
```

Using Session State

The session store is designed for storing information about each session, which, in real terms, usually relates to each web site visitor. As with the application store, use the **session store** for regularly accessed information. Each session uses up memory, so it's a bad place to store information that you're not making good use of. Just as with the Application object, you can, if you wish, store objects inside the Session object.

By default each session usually lasts twenty minutes after a period of no activity, and there's roughly one session for each person at your site; this means sessions can create heavy memory demands if there are a lot of people visiting your site. As a general rule, don't put large amounts of information in the session, because your web server will grind to a halt when it gets busier.

Remember that if you extend the timeout duration for a session, your web server is likely to need more memory, as it will be storing each session for longer.

Cookies

A **cookie** is a small piece of information that relates to a specific user, and usually also relates to a specific web site. Cookies are a way of storing information relating to a user and a web site for longer periods of time than with a session. Cookies are also different in that the state is stored on the user's hard drive (usually with the web browser software in a folder called Cookies). Remember that with session state, the information is stored on the web server.

Here are some examples of where cookies are used:

❑ User preferences – if a user specifies a preference on a web site, it often makes sense to store that preference using a cookie on the user's hard drive. If we store it in a session, it'll be lost when their session times out, and they will be forced to specify the preference again when they return. Alternatively, we could store the preference in a database, and load it into the session when the user comes to the site, but cookies are often easier, especially for smaller web sites.

❑ Sign in & "remember me" – you've almost certainly been to a web site where you've had to sign in, and it had a checkbox labeled something like remember me. If you check the box, next time you come to the site you won't have to sign in. What happens here is the web site places a cookie on the user's hard drive, which includes enough information so that the next time they come back in, they are signed in behind the scenes and don't have to do it manually.

❑ Pop-up windows – many web sites open a small window when you visit their site showing an advert or promotion. Most companies are aware of the irritation these can cause, so the more responsible ones tend to display the window once and write a cookie to the user's hard drive. When the visitor returns to the site it checks for the cookie; if the cookie exists it does not show the advert again.

How Do Cookies Work?

On your PC, there is a set of cookie files that have been placed there by your web browser software at the request of web sites that you have visited. On Windows 2000, Internet Explorer cookies are stored in `C:\Documents and Settings\<username>\Cookies\`. Look in this folder now. You'll find hundreds! But how did they get there?

When your web browser sends an HTTP request to the web server, it replies with an HTTP response, including the HTML for the page. In addition to that content, we can add cookie data to the HTTP response, which the browser software will dutifully save to disk for us. You can see this process in the upper half of the diagram, Request 1:

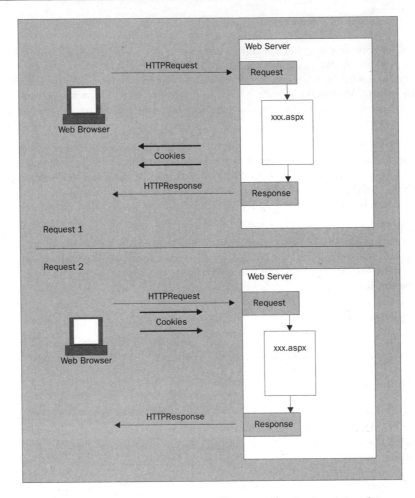

When we request another page from the web server (Request 2), whether it is a few seconds later or a few days later, the cookie data will be loaded from our hard drive by the web browser into the HTTP request. The result of this is that if we save cookie data to a visitor's hard drive, we get sent that data each time they come back to our web site. This is an important point – cookies persist outside of the timeout period for the session, or even when the browser is closed. To get rid of them, we as web site owners have to tell the browser to delete them or, as a user, we can delete them manually.

You probably won't be surprised to hear that we set the cookie state using the Response object, and we read the existing cookie state using the Request object. Let's look at an example and see these objects working their magic.

Try It Out – Using Cookies

In this example, we're going to put together a page, for which the visitor can specify the background color. Once they have chosen a background color, the color is stored as a cookie, and so our page will use that setting for all future visits.

1. Open up your editor and type the following:

```
<%@ Page Language="VB" %>
<html>
  <body>
    <form id="CookieForm" method="post" runat="server">
      <asp:DropDownList id=MyDropDownList runat="server"/>
      <asp:button id=MyButton runat="server" OnClick="Click"/>
    </form>
  </body>
</html>
```

In this page, we've created a form that holds a dropdown list and a button. We'll configure the list so that it will display a series of colors for us to choose for the page background, and the button will save a cookie containing our choice. We can see that the button is wired up with an `OnClick` attribute, so when it's clicked, the `Click()` subroutine will be called. We'll see that in a moment.

2. Add the following code to the page; it sets the name of the button, and also adds three colors to the dropdown list:

```
<%@ Page Language="VB" %>
  <script language="vb" runat="server">
    Sub Page_Load(Source As Object, E as EventArgs)
      If Not IsPostBack Then
        MyButton.Text = "Save Cookie"
        MyDropDownList.Items.Add("Blue")
        MyDropDownList.Items.Add("Red")
        MyDropDownList.Items.Add("Gray")
      End If
    End Sub
```

```
<html>
  <body>
    <form id="CookieForm" method="post" runat="server">
      <asp:DropDownList id=MyDropDownList runat="server"/>
      <asp:button id=MyButton runat="server" OnClick="Click"/>
    </form>
  </body>
</html>
```

3. Now we add the interesting code, the code that saves our cookie:

```
<%@ Page Language="VB" %>
  <script language="vb" runat="server">
    Sub Page_Load(Source As Object, E as EventArgs)
      If Not IsPostBack Then
        MyButton.Text = "Save Cookie"
        MyDropDownList.Items.Add("Blue")
        MyDropDownList.Items.Add("Red")
        MyDropDownList.Items.Add("Gray")
      End If
    End Sub
```

```
    Public Sub Click(ByVal sender As Object, ByVal e As System.EventArgs)
      Dim MyCookie As New HttpCookie("Background")
      MyCookie.Value = MyDropDownList.SelectedItem.Text
      Response.Cookies.Add(MyCookie)      End Sub
  </script>
<html>
  <body>
    <form id="CookieForm" method="post" runat="server">
      <asp:DropDownList id=MyDropDownList runat="server"/>
      <asp:button id=MyButton runat="server" OnClick="Click"/>
    </form>
  </body>
</html>
```

4. Save the file as `cookie1.aspx` in your web site.

5. Open `cookie1.aspx` in your browser, you'll see this:

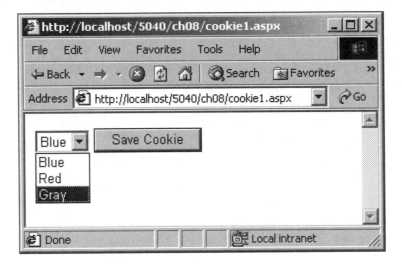

6. Now let's create a page that uses the cookie we've safely stored away on the user's machine. Create a new page in your editor, and type the following:

```
<%@ Page Language="VB" %>
  <script language="vb" runat="server">
    Sub Page_Load(Source As Object, E as EventArgs)
      Response.Cache.SetExpires(DateTime.Now)
    End Sub
  </script>
  <html>
    <body bgcolor="<%=Request.Cookies("Background").Value%>">
    </body>
  </html>
```

7. Save the second page as `cookie2.aspx`.

8. Open `cookie1.aspx` in your browser, select a color, and then open `cookies2.aspx`.

You'll find that whatever color you choose on `cookie1.aspx` is reflected by the background color of `cookie2.aspx`. The `cookie2.aspx` file is making use of the `Background` cookie, which is being sent to it by the web browser every time it sends an HTTP request.

9. Now close down your web browser. Restart it, and go to `cookie2.aspx`; you'll find that the background color has successfully been read from the cookie. This is where cookies differ from sessions, they're designed to store information for a much longer period.

How It Works

Saving the cookie is done by the first ASPX page. The code for the `Click` subroutine that gets called when the user clicks the **Save Cookie** button is:

```
Public Sub Click(ByVal sender As Object, ByVal e As System.EventArgs)
    Dim MyCookie As New HttpCookie("Background")
    MyCookie.Valuc = MyDropDownList.SelectedItem.Text
    Response.Cookies.Add(MyCookie)
End Sub
```

The subroutine does three things. Firstly, it creates an object from the `HttpCookie` class, and passes a name for the cookie as a parameter; it is effectively saying, "create me a cookie and call it 'Background'". In the next line, we use the `Value` property of the `cookie` object to specify the value for the `Background` cookie. Finally, in the last line of the subroutine, we add the new cookie to the HTTP response using the `Response` object, and its `Cookies` property. When the web browser receives our HTTP response, it will write the cookie information to the hard disk.

The second ASPX page is where we actually read the cookie. In this page, we have added a statement to the `<body>` tag that squirts the color setting from the `Background` cookie into the `bgcolor` attribute of the `<body>` tag. To get the background color from the cookie, we used the `Cookies` property on the `Request` object that returns an object of the type `HttpCookieCollection`. This class represents a set of cookies, and we access a single cookie with this syntax: `Request.Cookies("cookie name")`. This returns the cookie with that name, and then to retrieve its value, we use the `Value` property on the end of the statement:

```
<%@ Page Language="VB" %>
<html>
  <body bgcolor="<%=Request.Cookies("Background").Value%>">
  </body>
</html>
```

We have also added a `Page_Load()` subroutine, which has a single function; it uses the `SetExpires` method on the `Cache` object, which is returned by `Response`. The `SetExpires` method takes a `DateTime` as a parameter, and ensures that the web browser does not cache the page after that time. What this statement is doing is ensuring that our browser does not keep a copy of the page so that when we select different background colors using `cookies1.aspx`, the changes are reflected when we open up `cookies2.aspx`. If you have pages in a web site that you do not want the browser to cache, this is how you do it:

```
<script language="vb" runat="server">
  Sub Page_Load(Source As Object, E as EventArgs)
    Response.Cache.SetExpires(DateTime.Now)
  End Sub
</script>
```

"Shelf Life" – How Long Do Cookies Last?

You may be wondering how long cookies last for; well, they last for as long as we like. For example, if we wanted to set our background configuration up so it lasted for thirty days, we'd create a `TimeSpan` object to represent the period of thirty days. When we pass four parameters to `TimeSpan`'s constructor, it interprets that as days, hours, minutes and seconds, hence why we're using 30,0,0,0:

```
Dim dt As DateTime = DateTime.Now()
Dim ts As New TimeSpan(30,0,0,0)
```

Then we create our cookie just as before:

```
Dim MyCookie As New HttpCookie("Background")
MyCookie.Value = MyDropDownList.SelectedItem.Text
MyCookie.Expires = dt.Add(ts)
Response.Cookies.Add(MyCookie)
```

Sessions and Cookies

In Chapter 3, we looked at persistence, and you saw how HTTP is a stateless protocol, which means state information is not preserved between pages. This means, for example, that if we request a page and then straight away request another, the web server has no way of knowing that the two requests are from the same person. It could try using the machine (IP) address of the computer, but these tend to change, so that method is pretty unreliable.

The stateless nature of HTTP doesn't affect application state, because the state information is the same for all the people using the site, and it doesn't affect cookies, because we save information to the visitor's hard drive. However, this statelessness does affect sessions; in fact on the basis of HTTP being stateless, sessions shouldn't be possible at all. So how does the web server know that the first request and the second request came from the same person?

The answer is that even though session information, such as a visitor's name, is stored in the web server, every session also has a **Session ID** that is stored as a cookie on the visitor's machine. A session ID is a unique code that identifies the session on the server. This is what allows sessions to be maintained across multiple pages; cookies allow us to store state, and use it, even with the stateless HTTP protocol.

When we create a session using our web browser, each request we make for a page includes the cookie containing our session ID. When the web server sees the session ID, it hooks up all our session variables because it knows who we are. When our session expires, the web server simply ignores the incoming session ID.

One final point about the difference between session state and cookies is that we can only store simple text information in a cookie, whereas, we can store any type of information (including objects) within the `Session` object.

Summary

We started off this chapter with a look at the .NET framework from a high level, including a brief overview of some of the most commonly-used namespaces before directing our focus towards the namespaces most specific to Internet development, `System.Web` and `System.Web.UI`.

We saw how the `Response` and `Request` objects represent HTTP requests and responses, and how those objects are accessible from the `Page` object, whose properties and methods are accessible to all our pages automatically. We also looked briefly at how the `Browser` object helps us find out about the web browser our web site visitor is using, as well as looking at using methods like `UrlEncode()` and `HtmlEncode()` that are provided by the `Server` object.

Finally, we covered state management in .NET – how, and where, we can store state. We looked at application state, which is available to our whole web application and we looked at session state, which is provided for each person's visit to our web site. We also learnt about cookies; how to explicitly save them to a visitor's computer, and how they are used to implement sessions.

Exercises

1. Explain the role of the Page class in ASP.NET and describe what sort of things we can do with it.

2. Write an ASP.NET page that returns the Windows name of your computer and the URL of the page that you are visiting.

3. (a) Write one ASP.NET page that prompts a user to enter a value for the radius of a circle then calculates its area (Area = Pi *(radius)^2)and another ASP.NET page that prompts the user to enter the length of the radius and then calculates the circumference (circumference = 2*Pi*radius). Both pages should access the value of Pi (3.142) stored in application state.

(b) Repeat the above example storing the value of PI in `global.asax`.

4. Using session variables implement a shopping cart that lets you add up to five items from a dropdown listbox and displays:

(a) The total number of items selected

(b) A list of all the items in the cart

There should also be a means of emptying all the items contained in the cart.

5. Create an ASP.NET page that contains textboxes in which a user can enter his name, address and telephone number. Using cookies, display this information on a separate ASP.NET page.

Objects and Structured Data

The last couple of chapters will have started to give you a pretty good idea of how objects make it easier to write large modular programs, and use chunks of predefined functionality from a completely separate block of code, which may even be in a different file. We're now going to link up this discussion of objects to our understanding of data types (from Chapter 4) by considering some of the more structured forms of data that objects help us to work with.

In the course of this chapter, we're going to look at **collections**. In simple terms, these are objects designed to hold collections of other objects (hence the name) together in a single unit; they also implement a number of standard methods that we can use to work with those contained objects. The .NET Framework features a number of very useful collection objects, and we'll be taking a look at some of them shortly.

What is a Collection?

The term **collection** refers to a special sort of object that lets us bundle other objects inside it and work on them individually, or as a group. Of course, we can do this already to some extent – we have already used objects as class properties – so what's new? The most noticeable difference, is in flexibility: when we're defining class properties, we have to specify exactly what properties we're going to call (and, implicitly, how many of them there are) within in the class definition. That's generally not the case with a collection – in fact, we can start off with a completely empty collection object, and subsequently add to, or delete as many records as we need to from the collection.

The other difference is one of internal organization. When we use objects as properties, we lock ourselves into a very rigidly defined structure, effectively hard-wiring everything into the class definition. Objects contained within collections (which we refer to as **elements** of the collection) are far more loosely associated, and need only be connected by the fact that they're all held within the same unit. Therefore, they're much more flexible and able to meet your own particular needs.

Different types of Collection

The organization (if there is any) of the contained objects, depends on the particular variety of collection you're using.

The simplest type of collection is just a bunch of objects grouped together in no particular order – this is often referred to as a **set**. A set that consists of {object1, object2, object3, object4} is functionally equivalent to a set consisting of {object3, object2, object4, object1} – order is not important here.

> *Note that each object in a set must be unique – since there is no built-in structure, we'd have no way to tell the difference between two identical objects.*

A collection in which objects are stored in a particular sequence is known as a **list**. We can specify positions at which to add or remove new objects within the sequence, and the list is free to expand or decrease in size. The list has a well-defined order, therefore the elements do not need to be unique. Here's an example of a list, in this case a list of author names:

Author Name	Index Value
Ollie	0
John	1
Juan	2
Chris	3

Let's say that we wanted to add another author called Chris to this list. By default, it will be added to the end of the list. We can specify that we want it added as the second element (index = 1) however, in which case the list becomes:

Employee Name	Index Value
Ollie	0
Chris	1
John	2
Juan	3
Chris	4

As you can see, the index values of all subsequent names in the list have changed automatically.

A **map** collection stores objects in **key/value** pairs: one of these objects uniquely identifies the pair (the **key**), while the other object contains the information we wish to store (the **value**). The role of the key is much the same as the index in a list or array, in that it uniquely identifies a particular element. Unlike an index, however a key does not need to be an integer, but can be any type of object at all.

Obviously, since we use the key to uniquely identify an object pair within the map collection, you cannot duplicate any key/values within the map.

When we want to retrieve information from a map, we locate the relevant pair by looking up the appropriate key/value. Consider the directory of books shown below:

ISBN	Book Title
1861005040	Beginning ASP.NET
1861004885	Professional ASP.NET
1861004966	Beginning VB.NET

Every book has a unique ISBN, so it would be most convenient if we could get the book title by using its ISBN. In this case we would use the ISBN as a key to retrieve the book title.

Other types of lists include:

❑ **stacks** – lists in which new objects are always added to the end of the list, and removed from the end of the list (a "last in, first out" system). This is analogous to a pile of papers – the first one you put down remains at the bottom of the stack, and isn't exposed until you've moved all your other papers off it again.

❑ **queues** – lists in which new objects are always added to the end of the list, and removed from the beginning of the list (a "first in, first out" mechanism).

Arrays as Collections

Much of our discussion of collections may sound strangely familiar – elements, indexes, objects grouped together as a single unit; these are all characteristics of the arrays we looked at back in Chapter 4. In fact, arrays represent another variety of collection object, albeit quite a rigidly structured one.

We might think of a one-dimensional array (an array containing just one value per index) as a pre-populated fixed list, since it has all of the properties of a list collection described above, except that its elements are initialized when we create it, and its size is fixed – once we have defined it we cannot add new elements to it. Like lists, we use a unique index value to reference a particular element within an array. The value of a particular element in an array however, does not change unless we've manipulated that element directly. With lists, adding or removing objects can affect the placement (and index value) of other objects. This is a consequence of the ability of lists to fluctuate in size.

All the examples we worked through in Chapter 4 were quietly making use of the three main methods defined by the `System.Array` class:

❑ `CreateInstance` – Initialize a new instance of the `System.Array` class

❑ `SetValue` – Set the value of an element at a specified index

❑ `GetValue` – Get the value of an element at a specified index

Let's consider a very simple use of an array:

```
Dim AnimalArray(4) as string
Dim strAnimal as string

AnimalArray(0) = "Dog"
AnimalArray(1) = "Cat"
AnimalArray(2) = "Elephant"
AnimalArray(3) = "Lion"
AnimalArray(4) = "Cat"


strAnimal = AnimalArray(2)
```

We start off by instantiating a one-dimensional array of type string, with a dimension length of 4 (remember that as the first element in our dimension is of index 0, defining a length of 4 actually gives us 5 elements). As we'd expect, this calls the class constructor (which instantiates an empty `Array` object called `AnimalArray`); it also calls the `Array.CreateInstance` method, which *initializes* the array by instantiating each of the elements in it. We could rewrite the first line as:

```
Dim AnimalArray As Array = Array.CreateInstance(GetType(String), 4)
```

Note that `CreateInstance` is a shared method (see Chapter 9 for more on shared methods), so we call it on the `Array` class rather than on our `AnimalArray` object. The first parameter we specify corresponds to the object type we wish to use for each element in the array. In this case, it should be an array of strings, so using `GetType()`, we specify the string type as the parameter.

The second parameter is the length of the 0th order index – the fact that we don't specify any more parameters indicates that we only require an array with one dimension.

When we assign values to elements in the array, we're implicitly using the `SetValue` method on the array. We could rewrite our first assignment as:

```
AnimalArray.SetValue("Dog", 0)
```

Likewise, we retrieve the third element (index = 2) for assignment to the `strAnimal` string variable by using the `GetValue` method:

```
strAnimal = AnimalArray.GetValue(2)
```

So, having said all this, we could rewrite our whole sample as follows:

```
Dim AnimalArray As Array = Array.CreateInstance(GetType(String), 4)
Dim strAnimal as string

AnimalArray.SetValue("Dog", 0)
AnimalArray.SetValue("Cat", 1)
AnimalArray.SetValue("Elephant", 2)
AnimalArray.SetValue("Lion", 3)
AnimalArray.SetValue("Cat", 4)

strAnimal = AnimalArray.GetValue(2)
```

It certainly doesn't make our code any more concise, but it does help to illustrate that we're working with a collection object, and making well-defined method calls on that object throughout. In the course of this section, we're going to take a look at some of the other methods implemented by the Array class, and see how they can make our lives easier.

Try It Out – A Simple Array Example

First though, we're going to turn our code snippet into an ASP.NET page. Note that we've reverted to using shorthand, indexed notation when declaring the array and assigning element values, as we're not going to modify these in subsequent examples. We've left GetValue as an explicit method call however, so that it's easier to compare with the other calls we're going to make:

1. Create a file called animal_array.aspx in your test directory, and enter the following code:

```
<%@Page language="vb" %>

<script runat="server" language="vb">
  Sub Page_Load(Source As Object, E as EventArgs)
    Dim AnimalArray(4) as string
    AnimalArray(0) = "Dog"
    AnimalArray(1) = "Cat"
    AnimalArray(2) = "Elephant"
    AnimalArray(3) = "Lion"
    AnimalArray(4) = "Cat"
    MyLabel.Text = AnimalArray.GetValue(2)

  End Sub
</script>

<html>
<asp:label id="MyLabel" runat="server" />
</html>
```

2. Call up animal_array.aspx from your web browser, and predictably enough, you'll see this:

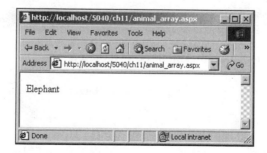

How It Works

Most of this code should be quite familiar to you. As usual, we include a Page directive, open a <script> block and specify a Page_Load procedure containing code to be called when the page is called up and loaded into memory. Inside this procedure, we place the array code we discussed earlier on; the only difference is that we assign the array element to MyLabel.Text, the Text property of a the MyLabel control, which we specify in the presentation block at the end of the listing.

When we call up the page, the code in `Page_Load` is executed, the third element in `AnimalArray` is assigned to `MyLabel.Text`:

```
MyLabel.Text = AnimalArray.GetValue(2)
```

As well as the presentation code (that is, the label control) is rendered on the browser.

Let's use this simple example to look at a few of the other things we can do with arrays.

Searching an Array

Say we wanted to find out which element in our array contains a specific value. The `Array` class provides us with another shared method called `IndexOf`, which returns the first occurence of a value in a specified array. For example, to find out which element contains the first occurrence of the string `"Cat"`, we might use the expression:

```
Array.IndexOf(AnimalArray, "Cat")
```

In our example, this would return the integer value 1. We can extend this slightly by adding an extra integer parameter, which specifies an index from which to start searching. For example, if we said:

```
Array.IndexOf(AnimalArray, "Cat", 2)
```

The search would commence at array index number 2, and return the index of the *next* `"Cat"` element in the array, namely 4. Finally, note that the shared method `LastIndexOf` will return the index of the *final* occurrence of the specified string. We might therefore use the expression:

```
Array.LastIndexOf(AnimalArray, "Cat")
```

To return the value 4.

We can use these features together to step through each occurrence of `"Cat"` elements in an array as follows:

Try it out –Searching an array

We're going to extend our `animal_array.aspx` page so that it lists all the occurrences in our array of the specific element that we want to find, in this case the string `"Cat"`:

1. Open up your editor and modify the code as highlighted below:

```
<%@Page language="vb" %>

<script runat="server" language="vb">
  Sub Page_Load()
    Dim intCounter As Integer = -1
    Dim AnimalArray(4) As string
    AnimalArray(0) = "Dog"
    AnimalArray(1) = "Cat"
    AnimalArray(2) = "Elephant"
    AnimalArray(3) = "Lion"
```

```
    AnimalArray(4) = "Cat"

    Do
       intCounter = Array.IndexOf(AnimalArray, "Cat", intCounter+1)
       MyText.InnerHtml += "AnimalArray(" & intCounter & ")<br/>"
    Loop Until intCounter = Array.LastIndexOf(AnimalArray, "Cat")
  End Sub
</script>

<html>
  The string "Cat" occurs in the following elements:
  <br/>
  <div id="MyText" runat="server" />
</html>
```

2. Save the file and call it up from your browser:

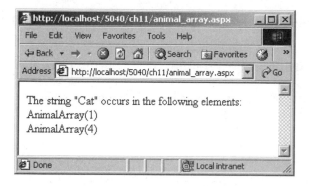

How It Works

The first line we add to our last sample declares an integer that we're going to use to keep track of our search progress through the array. We initialize its value as -1, for reasons that will become apparent shortly:

```
    Dim intCounter As Integer = -1
```

Once we've set up the array, we start a Do...Until loop to search for elements and output their indexes. The first line of code within this loop uses the Array.IndexOf method to search for an instance of "Cat" on our animal array, starting at index intCounter+1. We've initialized intCounter to -1, so the search begins at AnimalArray(0) as we require – but why use -1 and intCounter+1 in the first place? Bear with me just a moment more, and all will be explained:

```
    Do
  intCounter = Array.IndexOf(AnimalArray, "Cat", intCounter+1)
```

We've assigned the result of our search (which, as we already know, is the integer '1') to our intCounter variable (so intCounter now equals 1), which we now use to generate a message in the MyText HTML control:

```
    MyText.InnerHtml += "AnimalArray(" & intCounter & ")<br/>"
```

Assuming this isn't the final instance of a "Cat" element in the array, we want to execute the last two lines of code again. At last it's time to explain the `intCounter+1` issue – this time, we want to search from `AnimalArray(2)` onwards, otherwise we're simply going to find `AnimalArray(1)` all over again. If you *don't* add 1 here, you'll find that your program loops round indefinitely (or at least until the process times out) finding exactly the same element, each every time, and never getting any further.

Our new search proceeds from `AnimalArray(2)` and ought to find another "Cat" at `AnimalArray(4)`, thus returning the value 4 for assignment to `intCounter`:

```
intCounter = Array.IndexOf(AnimalArray, "Cat", intCounter+1)
```

Once again, we add the information to our presentation control:

```
MyText.InnerHtml += "AnimalArray(" & intCounter & ")<br/>"
```

The last line of the loop specifies that when `intCounter` is equal to the last index of "Cat", the loop should stop:

```
Loop Until intCounter = Array.LastIndexOf(AnimalArray, "Cat")
```

Of course, now that `intCounter` is 4, it's equal to the last index value, and the loop ends. We then use the same presentation code to display our results:

```
<html>
  The string "Cat" occurs in the following elements:
  <br/>
  <div id="MyText" runat="server" />
</html>
```

Working on Multiple Elements in an Array

There are various other `Array` methods that we can use to work on several elements at once. In particular, we can rearrange the order of elements in an array using the methods `Reverse` and `Sort`. To reverse the order of the elements in our `AnimalArray`, we'd simply use:

```
Array.Reverse(AnimalArray)
```

Likewise, to sort the elements into order, we'd just say:

```
Array.Sort(AnimalArray)
```

Now, wait just a moment. We're currently dealing with an array of strings, and it's not too hard to see how we can arrange them into some kind of order – given that all characters correspond to a specific numerical code (as defined by the Unicode standard) a case-sensitive alphabetical sort is the obvious one.

> In fact, the precise manner in which .NET sorts strings will depend on factors such as the language you're using and the alphabetical conventions of your culture. It is possible to specify both of these attributes, but a full discussion of this is beyond the scope of the book. In our examples, we assume that the language and culture conventions in place are EN-US.

Likewise, there's not much of an issue if we're sorting Integers, DateTimes, or other numerically based types. It gets a little murkier however if you start considering arrays of other objects. How do we sort an array of arrays, for example? At this point, we could go into the details of how .NET determines how a specific type of object should be sorted, but it's a little beyond the scope of the book. Suffice to say, you can sort Enum, String, and Version type objects, along with any objects that are inherently numeric, but not much else.

If you want to make your own objects sortable in this way, you'll need to employ some relatively advanced techniques, and you may want to check out 'Professional ASP.NET' (Wrox Press, ISBN 1861004885)

Try It Out – A Simple Array List Example

In order to demonstrate our new ability to rearrange array elements, we're going to update our last example so that it displays the full array in a dropdown list. In order to populate it, we're going to use the for each technique that was introduced in Chapter 6:

1. Copy the last sample into a file called sorted_array.aspx in your test directory, and enter the following code:

```
<%@Page language="vb" %>

<script runat="server" language="vb">
  Sub Page_Load()
    Dim AnimalArray(4) As String
    Dim strAnimal As String
    AnimalArray(0) = "Dog"
    AnimalArray(1) = "Cat"
    AnimalArray(2) = "Elephant"
    AnimalArray(3) = "Lion"
    AnimalArray(4) = "Cat"

    For Each strAnimal In AnimalArray
      MyDropDownList.Items.Add(strAnimal)
    Next
  End Sub
</script>

<html>
<asp:dropdownlist id="MyDropDownList" runat="server" />
</html>
```

2. Call up sorted_array.aspx from your web browser, and you should see this:

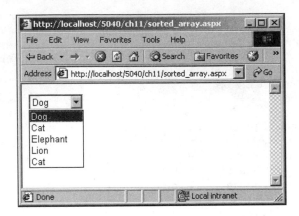

3. Now we'll update our code so that our dropdown list shows all the animals sorted in reverse order. Open up your editor and add a single line as shown below:

```
...
AnimalArray(0) = "Dog"
AnimalArray(1) = "Cat"
AnimalArray(2) = "Elephant"
AnimalArray(3) = "Lion"
AnimalArray(4) = "Cat"
Array.Reverse(AnimalArray)

For Each strAnimal In AnimalArray()
  MyDropDownList.Items.Add(strAnimal)
Next
...
```

4. Save the file again, and call it up from your browser – you should now see this:

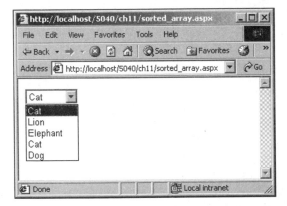

5. Now we'll update our code, so that our dropdown list shows all the animals sorted in alphabetical order. Open up your editor and modify the same line, as shown below:

```
...
AnimalArray(0) = "Dog"
AnimalArray(1) = "Cat"
AnimalArray(2) = "Elephant"
AnimalArray(3) = "Lion"
AnimalArray(4) = "Cat"
Array.Sort(AnimalArray)

For Each strAnimal In AnimalArray()
  MyDropDownList.Items.Add(strAnimal)
Next
...
```

6. Save the file again, and call it up from your browser – you should now see this:

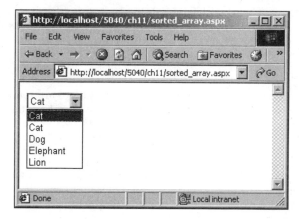

How It Works

Basically, we use a `for each...next` statement to cycle through our array's elements and use the string they contain (that we defined as `strAnimal` in the first piece of new code we added) to populate a dropdown list:

```
For Each strAnimal In AnimalArray
  MyDropDownList.Items.Add(strAnimal)
Next
```

Remember that we were introduced to the `For Each...Next` statement in Chapter 6, where we saw how it could be used to iterate through the elements in an array. As we're going to see later on, it can be used on all other collection objects in precisely the same way.

The order in which the elements appear in the dropdown list depends upon the order in which they're stored. So before the dropdown list is populated, we call the shared method `Reverse()` on the `Array` class to reverse the order in which the elements are stored, and, later, `Sort()` to arrange them alphabetically.

Data Binding

Another feature of all collections, is that we can specify them as data sources by just adding a pair of statements. If you make the following changes to the code in the sample file `sorted_array.aspx`, for example, you'll see that the page looks the same as it did in our earlier examples:

```
      . . .
        AnimalArray(0)  =  "Dog"
        AnimalArray(1)  =  "Cat"
        AnimalArray(2)  =  "Elephant"
        AnimalArray(3)  =  "Lion"
        AnimalArray(4)  =  "Cat"

        MyDropDownList.DataSource = AnimalArray
        MyDropDownList.DataBind()
      End Sub
    </script>
      . . .
```

The first new line that we have added simply instructs the dropdown server control where to get its data from – in this case, the array. The second line binds the control to (that is, configures it so as to actually make use of) the specified data source. In this case, it simply applies the array elements to the items in the dropdown list.

Pros and cons of working with arrays

Arrays are a very popular way to group elements together and there are some good reasons for that. As we noted earlier, however arrays also have some distinct limitations. Let's take a look at how arrays measure up:

Benefits of arrays

❑ **Easy to use.** Arrays really are very easy to use, and are present in almost every programming language – if you have done any programming before you will almost certainly have come across them. One of the reasons arrays are so widespread is that they are used to implement simple linear lists.

❑ **Fast to alter elements.** Arrays are just a consecutive list of items so altering one of the items is extremely fast and pretty easy, as we can easily locate any element.

❑ **Fast to move through elements.** An array is stored contiguously in memory, therefore it's quick and easy to cycle through the elements one by one from start to finish.

❑ **We specify the type of the elements.** You'll notice that when we create an array, we can define it as a string array, or an integer array, or whatever. In fact, you can create an array to hold any type of object, and .NET will ensure that you only add objects of that type to the array. This benefit is not present with many other types of collection where you can add a mixture of objects of different types to the same collection.

Limitations of arrays

❑ **Fixed size.** Once you have created an array, it will not automatically resize if you try to add more items onto the end of it. Although you can use the ReDim statement to change the size of an array's dimension, it is slow for large dimensions, and the fact that you have to perform the operation explicitly is far from ideal. Sometimes it's useful to have a list that just resizes, as we need it to.

❑ **Inserting elements is difficult.** If we wanted to add an element between two existing elements, it can be quite challenging. Firstly, we may have to increase the size of the array to make space, but we then have to move all the elements up one so we have a gap for our new element. Arrays are just not designed to have new elements inserted in the middle.

Getting more from Collections

All in all, arrays are quite simple to understand, and very easy to use. We often need to find different ways to group items together however – it all depends on what we need to do with them. The examples we've seen so far only really hint at the flexibility that collections can offer us – there's a lot more to come:

❑   A collection can contain an *unspecified* number of related objects (the **elements** in that collection)

❑   Elements of a collection need only be *related* by the fact that they exist in the collection

❑   Elements of a collection do not have to share the same *data type*

❑   An object's *position* in the collection can change whenever a change occurs in the collection as a whole; therefore, the position of any specific object in the collection can vary.

Given the number of different features that collections offer, you probably won't be surprised to discover that .NET provides a namespace called `System.Collections`, which contains quite a few collection classes that we can use in our applications; some of these are frequently used, others less often. In the next section of the chapter, we're going to spend some time looking at a few of the most useful ones:

❑   `ArrayList`

❑   `Hashtable`

❑   `SortedList`

> *Although the .NET* `Array` *type is not defined within the* `System.Collections` *namepace, it is nevertheless a bona fide collection. Arrays are so widely used (playing an integral part in virtually all .NET code) therefore the* `Array` *class sits in the first-level namespace,* `System.Array`.

ArrayList

The `System.Collections.ArrayList` class is a special array that provides us with some functionality over and above that of the standard `System.Array`. Most importantly, we can dynamically resize it by simply adding and removing elements. Let's see how an `ArrayList` measures up:

Benefits of ArrayList

❑   **Supports automatic resizing**. When we create an `ArrayList`, we do not need to specify the array bounds; that is, we do not need to know at the start how big the collection is going to be. As we add elements, the array automatically ensures there's enough space for the new element. If there isn't enough space, .NET doubles the size of the `ArrayList` before adding the new element.

❑   **Flexibility when inserting elements**. With an array, we have a blank set of element spaces (we define the number of elements the list will contain at the beginning), and we can set each one to contain our chosen values. With `ArrayList`, we start with a collection with no elements, and we add them as we choose. In addition to this, we can do something that is pretty hard with arrays, we can insert elements at any chosen position in the collection.

❑   **Flexibility when removing elements**. In an array we can set any item to be blank (for example 0 or ""), but we can't remove it entirely unless we shift all the elements above it down a place. With `ArrayList`, we can completely remove elements very easily.

❏ **Easy to use.** How easy `ArrayList` is to use is depends on your point of view, but given that it has some pretty intuitively named methods and properties, and they represent something we are all familiar with (items in a list), I think it's fair to say they are easy to use. You'll see later that there's a little bit more to creating an `ArrayList` object than an array, and the way we add elements is a little different as well, but that doesn't make it more difficult to work with.

Limitations of ArrayLists

❏ **Performance & Speed.** Given that the `ArrayList` control seems to offer so much more than arrays, you may be wondering why we bother using arrays at all – the reason is simply a matter of speed. The flexibility of an `ArrayList` comes at a cost, and since memory allocation is a very expensive business (in performance terms at least), the fixed structure of the array makes it a lot faster to work with.

We create objects from the `ArrayList` class in the usual way:

```
Dim myArrayList as new ArrayList()
```

We're using the new keyword since we are creating a new instance of the `ArrayList` object. As you can see, we don't need to specify how large it should be. Once we have an empty `ArrayList` object, we can use the `Add()` method to add elements to it. Note that each new item is added to the end of the collection:

```
myArrayList.Add("Dog")
myArrayList.Add("Cat")
myArrayList.Add("Elephant")
myArrayList.Add("Lion")
myArrayList.Add("Cat")
```

Although the syntax for using `ArrayLists` is a little different from arrays, they're really quite similar to use.

Try it out – Using an ArrayList

Let's update our animals dropdown list so it uses an `ArrayList` instead of an array as its data source.

1. Open up your editor, and enter the following code, much of which is similar to our previous examples:

```
<%@Page language="vb" %>

<script runat="server" language="vb">
Sub Page_Load()
    Dim AnimalArrayList as new ArrayList()
    AnimalArrayList.Add("Dog")
    AnimalArrayList.Add("Cat")
    AnimalArrayList.Add("Elephant")
    AnimalArrayList.Add("Lion")
    AnimalArrayList.Add("Cat")
    MyDropDownList.DataSource = AnimalArrayList
    MyDropDownList.DataBind()
End Sub
</script>
```

```
<html>
<asp:dropdownlist id="MyDropDownList" runat="server" />
</html>
```

2. Save the file as `arraylist1.aspx` in your test folder, and call it up in your browser:

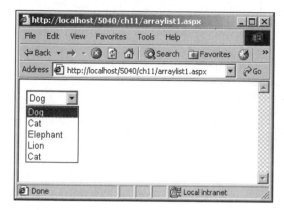

3. Now add a single line to the code as highlighted below:

```
Dim AnimalArrayList as new ArrayList
AnimalArrayList.Add("Dog")
AnimalArrayList.Add("Cat")
AnimalArrayList.Add("Elephant")
AnimalArrayList.Add("Lion")
AnimalArrayList.Add("Cat")
AnimalArrayList.Add("Platypus")
MyDropDownList.DataSource = AnimalArrayList
MyDropDownList.DataBind()
```

4. Open up the page again, and you'll see that the new item has been added to the dropdown list:

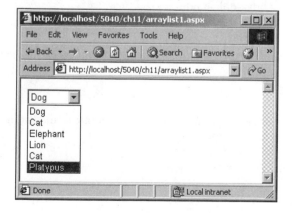

How It Works

All we're doing that's new here, is to use an `ArrayList` to hold our list of animals instead of using a standard array, as we've done before. We begin by instantiating it as `AnimalArrayList`:

```
Dim AnimalArrayList as new ArrayList
```

Note that we don't specify a length for the new `ArrayList`, and nor do we specify an element object type. This is because the elements will be assigned dynamically (as and when we need them), and can be of any type.

Next we use the object's `Add` method to add strings as elements:

```
AnimalArrayList.Add("Dog")
AnimalArrayList.Add("Cat")
AnimalArrayList.Add("Elephant")
AnimalArrayList.Add("Lion")
AnimalArrayList.Add("Cat")
```

Finally, we specify `AnimalArrayList` as a data source for the dropdown list, and bind the data:

```
MyDropDownList.DataSource = AnimalArrayList
MyDropDownList.DataBind()
```

This is enough to get our sample up and running. When we add an extra element in step 3:

```
AnimalArrayList.Add("Platypus")
```

We see the effect of the dynamic sizing – we have an additional element in the `ArrayList` without having to have made the collection any longer. If we did this with an array and it was not long enough to hold the additional item, we'd see an error.

Some more ArrayList techniques

Just like a standard array object, `ArrayList` provides the methods: `IndexOf()`, `Reverse()`, and `Sort()`. It also provides a property called `Count` (which is equivalent to the `Array` objects `Length` property; it lists the number of elements in the collection) and a few more very useful methods, some of which we're going to take a brief look at now.

Inserting Elements into an ArrayList

As we've seen, it's very simple to use the `Add()` method to add an item to the end of an `ArrayList`:

```
AnimalArrayList.Add("Platypus")
```

If, on the other hand, we want to insert the item into the middle of the list (in the example below, this is location 2), we can use `Insert()` as follows:

```
AnimalArrayList.Insert(2,"Platypus")
```

Using this in place of `Add()` in our last example, our list would wind up looking like this:

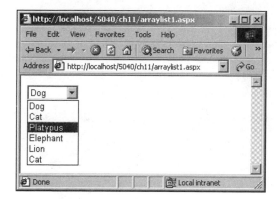

Removing Elements from an ArrayList

As an `ArrayList` makes it possible to insert items anywhere in the collection, it will probably come as no surprise that we can remove any element as well. Notice that when we talk about removing an element from an `ArrayList`, we're not just emptying an element (as we would if we set an array element equal to `nothing`) – we're literally destroying the element, and shortening the length of the array list.

To remove our Platypus element, we have two choices:

❑　We can either remove the element by specifying its index:

```
AnimalArrayList.RemoveAt(2)
```

❑　Or we can remove it using its content:

```
AnimalArrayList.Remove("Platypus")
```

Note that if a collection contains more than one matching element, only the first one (sequentially) will be removed.

Try It Out – Inserting and Removing Elements in an ArrayList

1. Make a copy of our previous sample and name it `arraylist2.aspx`

2. Make the alterations highlighted below:

```
...
Sub Page_Load()
    Dim AnimalArrayList as new ArrayList
    AnimalArrayList.Add("Dog")
    AnimalArrayList.Add("Cat")
    AnimalArrayList.Add("Elephant")
    AnimalArrayList.Add("Lion")
    AnimalArrayList.Add("Cat")
    AnimalArrayList.Add("Platypus")
    AnimalArrayList.Insert(1,"Chicken")
    AnimalArrayList.Remove("Cat")
    AnimalArrayList.RemoveAt(0)
```

```
        MyDropDownList.DataSource = AnimalArrayList
        MyDropDownList.DataBind()
End Sub
...
```

3. Call up the page in your browser, and you'll see this:

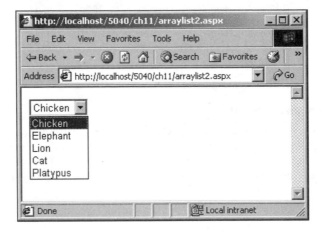

How It Works

All we've done here is to perform three additional operations on the `AnimalArrayList` object. We start by inserting the string "Chicken" as the second element (index = 1):

```
        AnimalArrayList.Insert(1,"Chicken")
```

All subsequent elements now move along one place. We then remove the first instance of the string "Cat":

```
        AnimalArrayList.Remove("Cat")
```

All subsequent elements now move back down an index. Finally, we remove the element with index = 0:

```
    AnimalArrayList.RemoveAt(0)
```

The dog is banished, and the chicken takes pride of place at the top of the list. We've added one item and removed two, so we've ultimately shortened our list by one.

Hashtable

Earlier in the chapter, we described how map collections operate by bundling up objects as key/value pairs; the `System.Collections.Hashtable` class provides us with precisely this functionality. In some respects, the `Hashtable` object is quite similar to `ArrayList`, except that we don't have to use a numerical index – in fact we can use a variety of object types for the key (or index), and virtually any kind of object at all for the value.

For example, if we wanted to use country codes (such as US and UK) as settings in our page, we might want to discover the actual name of the relevant country, perhaps to display as text on the page. Here's an example of a `Hashtable` object that stores country codes and the full name of the country, in which we're using a string as both the key (country code) for the elements and also the element values (country name).

```
UK    United Kingdom
US    United States
DE    Germany
```

Let's take a look at the pros and cons of using the `Hashtable` object.

Benefits of Hashtable

❑ **Key/Value elements**. Each element in a `Hashtable` contains more information than an element in an `Array` or an `ArrayList`; it's smarter. The `Hashtable` object is less about storing information in a list, and more about doing lookups from one piece of data to another (as in our country code example above).

❑ **Inserting elements**. When we use a `Hashtable`, we're free to add as many pairs of key/value elements as we want. You'll remember we found that with plain old arrays, we specify how large they are upfront, and it's hard to extend beyond that size, but with the `Hashtable` object (as with `ArrayList` objects) there's no limitation like that, we just keep on adding items.

❑ **Removing elements**. Just as we can add items, we can remove items from `Hashtable` objects very easily too. Like an `ArrayList`, the `Hashtable` does the work of storing the key/value pairs in memory for us.

❑ **Fast Lookup**. The `Hashtable` collection provides very fast look-up.

Limitations of Hashtables

❑ **Performance & Speed**. Although the lookup speed is very quick, each time we add and remove items from a `Hashtable`, .NET has to do quite a bit of work in order to keep its lookup mechanism optimized. This work ultimately makes `Hashtable` objects rather slower to update than `ArrayList` objects.

❑ **Keys must be unique**. Generally this isn't a problem. For example, with our country name lookup, there's only one country name for US, but if we had a `Hashtable` object full of names matched to email addresses, we might find that some people have more than one email address. We can't add more items to the collection, because we're only allowed one key for the person's name. There is a solution to this though. There are collections in .NET where we can store one key and several values, generally the most useful of which is `NameValueCollection`, which we'll look at briefly later in the chapter.

❑ **No useful sorting**. The items in a `Hashtable` are actually sorted internally, to make it easy for the `Hashtable` to find objects very quickly, but it's not done by using the keys or the values, so for our purposes, the items may as well not be sorted at all.

Using a Hashtable

We create a `Hashtable` object from the `Hashtable` class, just like an `ArrayList` or any other Framework object:

```
Dim myHashtable As New Hashtable()
```

Once we've created it, we can then add the key/value pairs. Remember that the key is like an index for the entry, and the value is the data we're storing. We store each element using the Add() method:

```
myHashtable.Add("UK", "United Kingdom")
myHashtable.Add("US", "United States")
myHashtable.Add("DE", "Germany")
```

This syntax works fine, but it's often tidier to use this simplified way of writing the same thing:

```
myHashtable("UK") = "United Kingdom"
myHashtable("US") = "United States"
myHashtable("DE") = "Germany"
```

This syntax is much easier to read and makes use of a shortcut that .NET has built in. It does exactly the same thing, but there's much less typing, and it's a lot easier to read too. To read an element out, we just specify the key, and the value is returned:

```
Dim CountryName As string
CountryName = myHashtable("DE")
```

This will output the value **Germany**. Be aware that the keys are *case-sensitive*, so if we had written the following, we would have seen a blank result:

```
CountryName = myHashtable("de")    ' blank result, incorrect case
```

Sometimes, it's useful to be able to wander through our Hashtable object looking at each item and using the key and value data that it contains. Perhaps we want to display all the key/value pairs, or we want to run through some checks on them. It's a collection, therefore we're able to use a for each...next loop to do just this.

Let's look at an example page that cycles through the elements in our country codes Hashtable.

Try it out – Moving through a Hashtable

In this example, we're going to build a page that displays a list of countries in a dropdown list. We're going to do it in such a way that when the page is submitted, the result we get back is a country code, and not the country name. What we're doing here is presenting user-friendly names, while behind the scenes we're using standard ISO country codes that are more efficient for our application to process.

1. Open up your editor and enter the following code:

```
<%@Page language="vb" debug="true"  %>

<script runat="server" language="vb">
  Sub Page_Load(Source As Object, E as EventArgs)
    Dim myHashTable as new Hashtable
    Dim Item As DictionaryEntry

    myHashTable("UK") = "United Kingdom"
    myHashTable("US") = "United States"
```

```
      myHashTable("DE") = "Germany"

    If Not Page.IsPostback Then
      For Each Item In myHashtable
        Dim newListItem As new ListItem()
        newListItem.Text = Item.Value
        newListItem.Value = Item.Key
        myDropDownList.Items.Add(newListItem)
      Next
    End If
  End Sub

  Sub Click(Source As Object, E as EventArgs)
    myLabel.Text = myDropDownList.SelectedItem.Value
  End Sub
</script>

<html>
  <form runat="server">
    <asp:dropdownlist id="myDropDownList" runat="server" />
    <asp:button id="myButton" runat="server" text="OK" Onclick="Click" />
    <br /><br />
    <asp:Label id="myLabel" runat="server" text="" />
  </form>
</html>
```

2. Save it as `hashtable1.aspx` in your test directory, call up the page in your browser, and select a country from the dropdown list. Hit OK, and the page will refresh to show you the corresponding country code. Assuming we selected **Germany**, we'll see this:

How It Works

When the page is loaded for the first time, we declare our `Hashtable` object, along with a `DictionaryEntry` object that we shall use shortly to hold key/value pairs:

```
<script runat="server" language="vb">
  Sub Page_Load(Source As Object, E as EventArgs)
```

```
Dim myHashTable as new Hashtable
Dim Item As DictionaryEntry
```

We define specific elements in the `Hashtable` using country codes as keys, and corresponding country names as values:

```
myHashTable("UK") = "United Kingdom"
myHashTable("US") = "United States"
myHashTable("DE") = "Germany"
```

As long as we're not making a `Postback` request, we then use `for each...next` to cycle through the key/value pairs in `myHashtable`, using the `Item` variable as our placeholder. For each item, we create a new `ListItem` object to hold the pair of objects, and assign them as an entry in the dropdown control:

```
If Not Page.IsPostback
  For Each Item In myHashtable
    Dim newListItem As new ListItem()
    newListItem.Text = Item.Value
    newListItem.Value = Item.Key
    myDropDownList.Items.Add(newListItem)
  Next
  End If
End Sub
```

Notice that we assign each item value (the country name) to the `Text` property of the list item (so as to be displayed on the list) while the item key is assigned to the corresponding `Value` property.

Next, we define an event handler to assign the `Value` property (of whichever item is currently selected in the dropdown list) to the `Text` property of the label control `myLabel`. This is how we'll present it on the browser:

```
Sub Click(Source As Object, E as EventArgs)
  myLabel.Text = myDropDownList.SelectedItem.Value
  End Sub
</script>
```

Finally, we have our presentation code – we create a form, in which we place a dropdown list, a button control (which we can use to trigger a call on `Click`), and the label `myLabel` to display the selected item value:

```
<html>
  <form runat="server">
    <asp:dropdownlist id="myDropDownList" runat="server" />
    <asp:button id="myButton" runat="server" text="OK" Onclick="Click" />
    <br /><br />
    <asp:Label id="myLabel" runat="server" text="" />
  </form>
</html>
```

When we click the button, we initiate a postback, and the button's `Onclick` event triggers the `Click` procedure, which assigns the appropriate country code to the label control. The refreshed page then shows the selected country code.

Note that if our `Hashtable` *population code wasn't inside the* `If...Then` *conditional block (the first part of which checks to see if the page has been posted to itself, it would be executed every time we triggered a postback,, and the dropdown list would grow by three entries every time.*

SortedList

A `SortedList` is another collection that stores key/value pairs, in which we can not only insert and remove items at will, but also rely on the items being usefully ordered. In fact, it's really just like a `Hashtable` object whose elements are automatically sorted according to key/value. Just like `ArrayList` and `Hashtable`, the `SortedList` class lives in the `System.Collections` namespace.

The items in a `SortedList` are always stored in a well-defined order, therefore we can reference elements using an index – in effect we get the best aspects of a `Hashtable` object (the ability to use key/value pairs) along with the best aspects of an `ArrayList` (the ability to sort the items). Remember, however, that the items in a `SortedList` are sorted on the *key*, and not on the value.

`SortedList`, then, is most useful when we have to sort a list of key/value pairs for which the ordering of the key is what matters, rather than the order of the values. For example, we might use a sorted list to hold entries in a dictionary:

key	value
aardvark	a large burrowing nocturnal ungulate mammal (*Orycteropus afer*) of sub-Saharan Africa that has a long snout, extensile tongue, powerful claws, large ears, and heavy tail and feeds especially on termites and ants.
amaryllis	an autumn-flowering. So South African bulbous herb (*Amaryllis belladonna* of the family Amaryllidaceae, the amaryllis family) widely grown for its deep red to whitish umbellate flowers; *also* : a plant of any of several related genera (as *Hippeastrum* or *Sprekelia*).
armadillo	any of a family (Dasypodidae) of burrowing edentate mammals found from the southern U.S. to Argentina and having the body and head encased in an armor of small bony plates.
artichoke	a tall composite herb (*Cynara scolymus*) like a thistle with coarse pinnately incised leaves; *also* : it has an edible immature flower head which is cooked as a vegetable.

Source: Merriam-Webster Online, Collegiate Dictionary (www.m-w.com/cgi-bin/dictionary)

We create and use a `SortedList` collection just like we do a `HashTable`. Remember, we have to use the new keyword when we create the object. Adding items to a sorted list is exactly the same as with a `Hashtable`, the only difference being that each item is automatically inserted in the correct position in the list, according to the key-based sort order.

Try It Out – Using a SortedList

We're now going to modify our last example to present a list of words in alphabetical order, and display their definitions on request.

1. Create a new file called `sortedlist.aspx` in your test directory, and enter the following code:

```vb
<%@Page language="vb" debug="true"  %>

<script runat="server" language="vb">
  Sub Page_Load(Source As Object, E as EventArgs)
    Dim mySortedList as new SortedList
    Dim Item As DictionaryEntry

    mySortedList("armadillo")="any of a family ... small bony plates"
    mySortedList("amaryllis")="an autumn-flowering ... Hippeastrum or Sprekelia)"
    mySortedList("zebra")="any of several fleet ... white or buff"
    mySortedList("artichoke")="a tall composite herb ... cooked as a vegetable"
    mySortedList("aardvark")="a large burrowing ... termites and ants"

    If Not Page.IsPostback
      For Each Item In mySortedList
        Dim newListItem As new ListItem()
        newListItem.Text = Item.Key
        newListItem.Value = Item.Value
        myDropDownList.Items.Add(newListItem)
      Next
    End If
  End Sub

  Sub Click(Source As Object, E as EventArgs)
    myLabel.Text = myDropDownList.SelectedItem.Value
  End Sub
</script>

<html>
  <form runat="server">
    Pick a word from the list:
    <asp:dropdownlist id="myDropDownList" runat="server" />
    <asp:button id="myButton" runat="server" text="OK" Onclick="Click" />
    <br /><br />
    <b>Definition: </b>
    <asp:Label id="myLabel" runat="server" text="" />
  </form>
</html>
```

2. Now call up the page from your browser, and expand the dropdown list. Note that the words are listed in alphabetical order, even though we didn't add the in alphabetical order in the code:

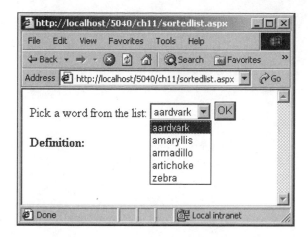

3. Select one of the words from the list, and hit **OK**. You'll now see a screen like this (with an abbreviated dictionary definition):

How It Works

We simply substitute a SortedList collection for the HashTable used in our previous example, and assign some new 'dictionary entry' elements, using word-definition pairs as key/value elements:

```
Dim mySortedList as new SortedList
Dim Item As DictionaryEntry

mySortedList("armadillo")="any of a family ... small bony plates"
mySortedList("amaryllis")="an autumn-flowering ... Hippeastrum or Sprekelia)"
mySortedList("zebra")="any of several fleet ... white or buff"
mySortedList("artichoke")="a tall composite herb ... cooked as a vegetable"
mySortedList("aardvark")="a large burrowing ... termites and ants"
```

We cycle through elements in the SortedList – which are already in alphabetical order – and for each one, we assign the key (word) to the Text property of a dropdown list element, and the associated value (definition) to the corresponding Value property:

```
If Not Page.IsPostback
  For Each Item In mySortedList
    Dim newListItem As new ListItem()
    newListItem.Text = Item.Key
    newListItem.Value = Item.Value
    myDropDownList.Items.Add(newListItem)
  Next
End If
```

Besides a couple of additions to the presentation code, that's pretty much all the new code we added here. We display the text, dropdown list, button and label, and once again, use the button's OnClick event to trigger the Click procedure.

Summary

Collections are objects that are specifically designed to hold collections of other objects together as a unit. They feature standard methods with which to manipulate and organize their bundled elements, which may be worked on individually or as a group. These elements are only loosely associated by the fact that they're held in the same collection – consequently they're far more flexible than most other data structures.

Arrays are in fact a very rigidly structured type of collection. It's therefore quite straightforward to perform relatively complex operations – such as searching and sorting on element values (by means of shared method calls on the System.Array class). We can use collections as data sources for server controls, we can therefore bind arrays to such controls and show the contents of their elements on a web page without much effort at all.

The array class is defined in System.Array.

An ArrayList is a flexible variation on the standard array, which we can dynamically resize by simply adding and removing elements at any position. Its flexibility comes at the cost of slightly higher system overheads than those incurred by a standard array, and reduced performance.

A Hashtable is similar to the ArrayList, but doesn't require the use of a numerical index. Rather it bundles up elements as key/value pairs, and sorts them internally based on their keys – it's therefore very efficient to do key-based lookups on elements in a HashTable. It also means however that HashTables are less efficient than other collections when it comes to adding and removing elements.

A SortedList is another collection that stores elements as key/value pairs. In this case, we can also rely on the items being usefully ordered by key, and can therefore reference its elements using a numerical index.

All these other collections are defined in the System.Collections namespace.

Exercises

1. Describe a situation in which you would use each of the following and state why that choice is the best:

- ❑ arrays
- ❑ arraylists
- ❑ hashes
- ❑ sorted lists?

2. Create an array with the following items:

Dog, Cat, Elephant, Lion, Frog.

Display it in a dropdown list alongside another dropdown list that gives options on how the array is sorted.

3. Bind a dropdown list to an array containing five colors, then create a submit button that displays a line of text in the selected color when clicked.

4. Using a hashtable, display a list of user names in a dropdown list with a submit button that displays the corresponding user ID when pressed. On the same page add two textboxes in which a user can enter new user names and IDs into the hashtable.

The newly created user name should appear in the dropdown list box, and the corresponding user ID should be displayed when the submit button is clicked.

5. Create an ASPX page that takes value entered via a textbox and searches for it in this sorted list:

```
mySortedList("armadillo")="any of a family ... small bony plates"
mySortedList("amaryllis")="an autumn-flowering ... Hippeastrum or Sprekelia)"
mySortedList("zebra")="any of several fleet ... white or buff"
mySortedList("artichoke")="a tall composite herb ... cooked as a vegetable"
mySortedList("aardvark")="a large burrowing ... termites and ants"
```

The results of the search should be displayed on the page.

Reading from Data Sources

Data is the lifeblood of business, and being able to write ASP.NET pages that can access, display, manipulate, and modify information from external sources is an essential skill for an ASP.NET developer. So far we have learnt how to create dynamic pages that come alive with interaction, but when it comes time to deploy pages that are actually useful for a business we will need to be able to work with data. Just about any practical work on the Web will involve reading from and writing to various data stores. It may be as simple as providing a list of retail outlets or as complex as processing an online order, but the common thread is the ability to use a web client – usually a browser – as an interface to data.

The .NET Framework includes a set of data access technologies, called ADO.NET that make it easy for us to connect to data sources, access their data, display it, and even alter it. In this chapter, we will introduce the main objects that make up ADO.NET, and look at how and when we might want to use them. You will see that it is not necessary to study ADO.NET data connections in great depth to start getting results.

By the end of this chapter you will be able to create pages with several different methods of accessing information from a database and then displaying it. In the following chapter, we will see how to modify that data – add, change and delete records, and we will see the important role played by XML in data access with .NET.

Understanding Modern Databases

Almost all useful applications need to be able to store and retrieve data. We have already discussed one way to manage data – using files – and while this approach is perfectly adequate for many simple applications, it has certain inherent limits in terms of design, performance, and scalability, which we will cover below.

Another option is to use databases, and in the following section we're going to consider the following:

- ❑   The advantages of databases over ordinary file systems
- ❑   What a relational database is, and introduce the core concepts associated with it

As a programmer, one of the first decisions you'll have to make when creating even the simplest real-world application is the correct **data storage model** to use in other words:

> **How is your application going to store data?**

Let's look in detail at the problems of storing information in a file. A file contains only the data, there is no **metadata**, that is information about how the data is organized. So it is more difficult to create rules to speed up tasks that use the file. If you're looking for a specific entry in a long list, you must search through the entire list until you find it; in other words, to find one specific entry, you must check the value of all the other entries in the file. Even if you find a something that matches your search near the top of the file, you will still need to check all the other entries just in case there are any duplicates.

A **database** is a collection of data that's been organized in such a way that its contents can easily be accessed and manipulated. Using a few well-established rules, you can determine how best to organize your data, and make it much easier to work with. A **database management system** (**DBMS**) provides software that's used to store, retrieve, and modify data in a database. In this section, we're going to take a look at how we can optimize database performance by choosing the right data model.

Data Models

At its simplest, a database arranges data in **tables**, each divided into **rows** and **columns**. Each row of each table comprises a data **record**, which may contain several **fields** of information.

> **For all practical purposes, the term 'row' is synonymous with 'record', while 'column' is synonymous with 'field'. This is useful to bear in mind when visualizing tables.**

Suppose you record users of your site. The simplest (and most primitive) method of achieving this would be to create a single table that records both user information and log data. It might look something like this, consisting of five columns (or fields) and five rows (or records):

User ID	User Name	User Country	Page	Last Access
John	John Kauffman	Republic of China	`/index.html`	2001-02-28
Ewan	Ewan Buckingham	United Kingdom	`/info/contact.html`	2001-06-20
Jake	Jake Manning	United States	`/aspx/index.aspx`	2001-04-12
Ewan	Ewan Buckingham	United Kingdom	`/quake/index.html`	2001-04-21
Alessandro	Alessandro Ansa	Italy	`/index.html`	2001-06-21

Normalization and Relational Databases

Take a closer look at the table above. The structure of the table is inefficient, because a visitor's information is recorded into the table *every* time he makes a visit. Because of this duplication, a lot of the data in the table is *redundant*.

Such redundancy is undesirable in a database. Why? Let's have an example. Say user "ewan" decides to move to the United States. In order to update the table, *every one* of his records would have to be modified to include his address country. This is on top of the fact that every copy of his details takes up precious space on our hard drive. Redundancy is terribly inefficient, potentially wasting a great deal of time and space.

The notion of database **normalization** was developed to reduce data redundancy as much as possible. Normalization is the process of breaking up the data into several tables, so as to minimize the number of times we have to repeat the same data. For example, we could split the table above into a user information table and an access log table:

User ID	User Name	User Country
John	John Kauffman	Republic of China
Ewan	Ewan Buckingham	United Kingdom
Jake	Jake Manning	United States
Alessandro	Alessandro Ansa	Italy

User ID	Page	Last Access
John	`/index.html`	2001-02-28
Ewan	`/info/contact.html`	2001-06-20
Jake	`/aspx/index.aspx`	2001-04-12
Ewan	`/quake/index.html`	2001-04-21
Alessandro	`/index.html`	2001-06-21

Notice how the original table splits naturally into these two new tables. This is because the original table provided data about two distinct things (or **entities**): users and access logs. Each new table contains data concerning just one entity. The split into entity tables is an important principle of the normalization process.

Having split our table up into entities, we can now take another step in the normalization process. Each entity must have (at least) one **unique** field, in other words no entries in the field are repeated. Because of the unique nature of this field, each entry in it uniquely identifies ('IDs') each record in the table. This is important, because the ID can then be used to refer to a specific record in the table. The field used to ID records is often known as the **primary key**. Note that only one primary key is permitted per table.

For example, in the user table we could use the User ID field as a primary key because it contains unique values. However, the User Name field also contains unique values. Which field should we pick to be the primary key? Well, there are other considerations. User names can often change if a user gets married for instance. Also, users might withhold their names for security reasons, so the corresponding entries in the User Name field would be NULL. Since we don't expect IDs to be changed very often or withheld, it would seem best to use this field as the primary key in this case.

Let's review the benefits of normalization. Because we have moved the user information to one table and the access log entries to another, the process of modifying a user's details becomes much more simple we only have to modify one record in the user table. You should note that since these tables are related (they both contain the field User ID, and the values in this field correspond between tables), the database is now termed **relational**. This means that we can **join** information from the related tables in order to find answers to complex **queries**, which otherwise couldn't be answered by either table on its own. For example:

❑   "What's the nationality of our resident Quake fan?"

We know that it's "ewan" – that is, Ewan Buckingham from the UK. This is illustrated in the figure below:

ID	USER NAME	USER COUNTRY
john	John Kauffman	Republic of China
jake	Jake Manning	United States
alessandro	Alessandro Ansa	Italy
ewan	Ewan Buckingham	United Kingdom

USER TABLE

ID	PAGE	LAST ACCESS
john	/index.html	2000-02-28
ewan	/Info/contact.html	2000-06-20
jake	/aspx/index.html	2000-04-21
ewan	/quake/index.html	2000-04-21
alessandro	/Index.html	2001-06-21

ACCESS LOG TABLE

To summarize the basic rules of normalization:

❑   Minimize redundant data in individual tables

❑   Create a separate entity table for each set of related data

❑   Specify a unique field in each table to act as the primary key

Rule number three can be extended to use two or more fields as a primary key to further eliminate redundancy. For example, the user "john" might access the "/index.html" page many times. The only piece of information that needs to be changed in these access log records, is his last access time to the page. Therefore, the User ID and Last Access fields could also be combined into a primary key to uniquely identify an access record.

Examples of so-called **Relational Database Management Systems** (**RDBMS**) include commercial products such as Microsoft SQL Server, Access, Oracle, Informix, as well as freely available systems such as MySQL and PostgreSQL.

For more information about Relational Databases see "Beginning SQL Programming" (ISBN 1861001800 published by Wrox Press).

Now that we have some idea what a database is and how it works, we are going to take a look at the technology that comes with the .NET Framework for accessing data from ASP.NET pages – ADO.NET.

ADO.NET

ADO.NET is a name for the group of object classes provided by the .NET framework for interacting with data from data stores. As we know, one of the main advantages of object-oriented programming is that it lets us wrap up all sorts of complex functionality in a self-contained, encapsulated unit. All we then have to deal with is a well-defined interface, consisting of methods and properties.

ADO.NET can interact with many types of data – not only data stored in databases, but also data stored in email servers, text files, application documents like Excel and XML data. Here is a list of the kind of data sources we can connect up to:

❑ Enterprise-strength RDBMS such as Oracle, Microsoft SQL Server, IBM DB2

❑ Desk-top RDBMS such as Access

❑ File and directory systems, such Windows FAT32

❑ Comma-delimited or fixed-length text files

❑ Non-database files, such as Excel

❑ Microsoft Exchange Server 2000 data, such as Email (with some limitations)

❑ XML-based data

The beauty is that the above list is not fixed. The structure of ADO.NET connections is such that providers, drivers and adapters can be written for data source formats that we haven't even imagined yet. ADO.NET allows you the option of being relatively abstracted from the source. Your database administrator only has to grant permission to use a single view of the data. Even without having access to the rest of the data source, you can still use ADO.NET to bring data into your ASP.NET page.

ASP.NET also offers easier formatting of data on the page then Classic ASP. The `DataGrid`, which we will meet later on in the chapter, creates most of the HTML tags for you. Furthermore, ADO.NET provides tools to work with data in an XML format.

When working with ADO.NET, we actually work with a **disconnected** set of data. When a web site visitor requests data, a connection is made and the data is transferred, after which the connection is closed. The visitor can then make changes to the data, but they will not be immediately updated in the source – we have to reopen the connection before updating the database with the changes made by the visitor. The benefits of this are efficiency and scalability. If we didn't use this disconnected model, then it would mean that we would have to keep connections open until the end of the session for each user. On the Web, where there may be thousands of concurrent users, keeping a connection open for each user is very expensive. Using disconnected data can makes our applications a lot more efficient and able to handle greater workloads; that is, they will be more scalable.

In summary, ADO.NET gives you the power to pull in data from diverse sources and reduces the amount of code needed to do so. On the other hand, you must still learn how to work with the ADO.NET Objects and SQL as well as have a firm understanding of the data source with which you are working. Let's take a closer look now at how ADO.NET communicates with the data store.

Managed Providers

To be able to get data from a data store you need some way to talk to the data store. It's a bit like talking to someone from another country when you both speak different languages – you need some form of translator. The data provider does that translation job for us. In the current version of ADO you use OLEDB Providers and ODBC Drivers, which are generic languages for talking to databases. In ADO.NET we have Managed Data Providers to do this job for us (so named since they run within the managed environment of the Common Language Runtime).

Supplied with .NET are two managed providers:

❑　Managed Provider for SQL Server, which only talks to SQL Server. Since this provider only needs to talk to one database it's optimized and extremely fast.

❑　Managed Provider for OLEDB, which sits on top of OLEDB, allowing us to talk to data stores for which there is an OLEDB Provider, but not a specify Managed Provider.

This gives us a structure like so:

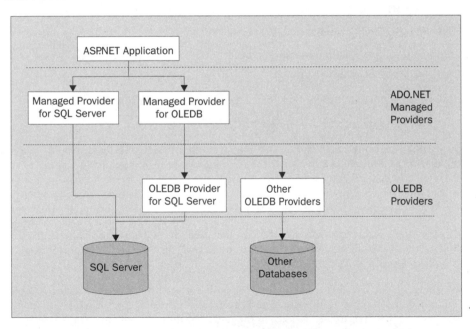

Here you can clearly see the division between the various components. What's also clear is that using the Managed Provider for OLEDB has the extra OLEDB layer to go through, making it slightly less fast than a managed provider that can access the data store directly. So, while you can access SQL Server through the OLEDB method it's always best to go direct.

As well as these two managed providers, there is a Managed Provider for ODBC, which allows access to ODBC data stores (that is, those that don't even have OLEDB Providers). This provider isn't part of the standard installation, but is freely available on the Microsoft web site.

In the future we can expect to see managed providers for other databases (such as Oracle) as well as other stores of data (such as Microsoft Exchange Server). These will further enhance our ability to use ADO.NET as a central mechanism for accessing data.

OLEDB Providers and ODBC Drivers are part of the Microsoft Data Access Components (MDAC), and come supplied with ADO. Windows 2000 ships with ADO 2.5, and later versions (2.6 and 2.7) are available from http://www.Microsoft.com/data). Other database vendors also supply OLEDB Providers and ODBC Drivers, and you should consult your vendor if you have a database that is not supported by the standard providers or drivers. For more details on ADO and OLEDB Providers consult the ADO Programmer's Reference (also from Wrox Press). There are versions for ADO 2.0, 2.1, and 2.6.

Data providers are made up of four core objects, the `Connection` object, the `Command` object, the `DataReader` and the `DataAdapter`. We will now take a look at how they work together.

ADO.NET Objects

The ADO.NET `Connection` object acts as a pointer to the desired Managed Data Provider. It is with the `Connection` object that we specify the location of the database. The ADO.NET connection then allows data to flow through to the `Command` object, which describes what data to read or write, and how to do so. At the command level you can specify, for example, that you want only records from year 2003 or you want your records to be ordered from smallest to largest. Data is then inserted into a `DataSet` or a `DataReader`. To display the data on the ASP.NET page, the `DataSet` or `DataReader` object can then be set (bound) as the source for a `DataGrid` or `<div>` on your ASP page. You think of the flow of information from data source to ASP.NET page, as effected by the ADO.NET objects working with each other to manipulate and access the underlying data, as shown below:

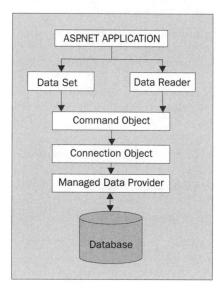

To work with data on your web page you need to have in place six elements, there are some exceptions and alternatives, but for now try to remember these:

❑ Source of Data – most commonly a relational database like SQL Server, Oracle or Access. You will need to understand the basic structure of the data such as table and field names.

❑ Managed Data Provider, which provides the facilities for conversing with our data stores.

❑ ADO.NET `Connection` Object – a conduit for your ASP.NET page to talk with a Provider or Driver.

❑ ADO.NET `Command` Object – a tool that contains instructions about what to read from or say to your data.

❑ ADO.NET `DataReader` or `DataSet` object – a place to hold data that has been read or is to be written.

❑ ASP.NET controls – objects run at the server to format and display the data on the page – primarily the `<asp:DataGrid>` control, but sometimes also the `<div>`, `<span>` elements.

Let's now take at look at these objects in detail with examples showing how they are used.

The Connection Object

The ADO.NET `Connection` object is used to connect to a data source – it represents the actual connection between the data source and the data consumer. To open up a connection, the `Connection` object has an `Open()` method which opens up the connection specified in the **connection string**. The connection string contains the information we need to connect to the actual store of data; it is made up of three parts, although there are differences among the different Providers and Drivers:

❑ The first specifies the kind of Provider or Driver that we want to use.

❑ The second specifies which database to use.

❑ The last section usually contains security information such as the user's name and password. These can come from the web page's visitor, or may simply be an ID representing the web server and therefore not specific for any one visitor.

The three most common strings you will come across are those for Access, SQL Server and the Managed SQL-Server direct connection. For Access, use the Jet Provider (*Jet* refers to the date engine within Access):

```
"provider=Microsoft.Jet.OLEDB.4.0;data source=MyDrive:MyPath/MyFile.MDB"
```

The standard OLEDB string for a database in a Microsoft SQL Server (all on one line):

```
"provider=SQLOLEDB.1;server=MyServerName;database=MyDatabase;uid=MyUserID;pwd=MyPassword"
```

The Managed Provider for Microsoft SQL Server has a similar syntax (note that there is no specification of a provider):

```
"server=MyServerName;database=MyDatabase;uid=MyUserID;pwd=MyPassword"
```

The syntax of the connection string is slightly different from some of other strings that we have come across:

❑ The arguments are separated by semicolons

❑ Some argument names have a space in them (for example, initial catalog), which looks odd, but is correct

❑ Quotes are not used around each argument value, rather a pair of double quotes goes around the entire string

We will be connecting to the Northwind data source that comes as a sample database of a small company with Access. In this chapter we will restrict ourselves to reading and displaying data, and in the next chapter we will be modifying it.

Connecting to Northwind

You will first need to make sure that Northwind is installed. You can usually find it in C:\Program Files\Microsoft Office\Office\Samples. Once you've found the Northwind.mdb file (also sometimes named NWind.mdb), make a copy of it for use in our examples; the code samples in this chapter assume that it has been placed at:

```
C:\BegASPNET\ch12\Northwind.mdb
```

Alternatively, you could use Northwind with another RDBMS such as Microsoft SQL Server. Northwind installs automatically with both SQL Servers 7.0 and 2000. If you are using SQL Server you can explore the database with the following steps:

❑ Start | Microsoft SQL Server | Query Analyzer

❑ Use SQL Server authentication to connect to a desired database. Specify a server name and appropriate login details (by default, name = 'sa' and password is blank).

❑ Use the dropdown listbox on the toolbar to set the current database to Northwind.

❑ Press *Ctrl-D* to display the results in a grid.

❑ Type in the query Select * from Employees, and hit *F5* to run the query.

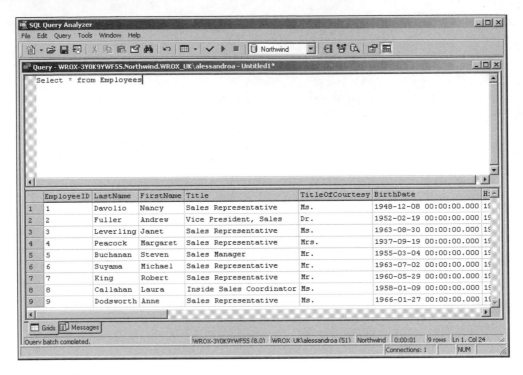

You should see this:

You can get more information by running the following statements:

```
SELECT Table_Name FROM Information_Schema.Columns GROUP BY Table_Name ORDER BY
Table_Name
```

```
SELECT * FROM Information_Schema.Columns ORDER BY Table_Name, Column_Name
```

Another option for SQL Server users is to open your Enterprise Manager, expand Microsoft SQL Servers, expand SQL Server Group and expand your server. Then expand Databases and Northwind and you will be able to see the list and properties of tables and other objects.

> *It might be a good idea to repeat the Try It Outs in this chapter with your own set of data. Once you have set the connection string your main changes will be how to use your own table and field names.*

Try It Out – Connecting to the Northwind database in Access 2000

We're going to start our practical samples small, since there's a lot of ground to cover, and many ADO.NET objects to introduce. Here, we're only going to work with one of them, and focus on the simple mechanics of establishing a connection to a database:

1. Make sure you've got a copy of the Northwind.mdb file in C:\BegASPNET\ch12

2. Save the following code as `oledb_connection.aspx`. You can type it or download from Wrox at **www.wrox.com**

```
<%@ import Namespace="System.Data" %>
<%@ import Namespace="System.Data.Oledb" %>

<script language="VB" runat="server">
  Sub Page_Load()
    Dim strConnection as String = "Provider=Microsoft.Jet.OLEDB.4.0;"
    strConnection += "Data Source=C:\BegASPNET\ch12\Northwind.mdb"
    data_src.text = strConnection

    Dim objConnection as New OledbConnection(strConnection)

    try
      objConnection.Open()
      con_open.text="Connection opened successfully.<br />"
      objConnection.Close()
      con_close.text="Connection closed.<br />"
    catch e as Exception
      con_open.text="Connection failed to open.<br />"
      con_close.text=e.ToString()
    end try
  end Sub
</script>

<html>
  <body>
  <h4>Testing the data connection
  <asp:label id="data_src" runat="server"/></h4>
  <asp:label id="con_open" runat="server"/><br />
  <asp:label id="con_close" runat="server"/><br />
  </body>
</html>
```

3. Call up the page in your browser, and you should see the following result:

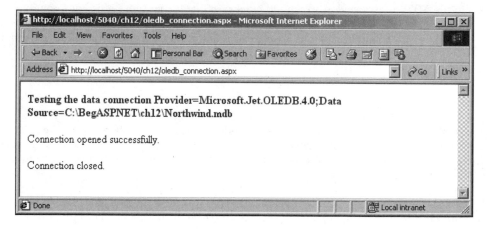

4. Now modify the connection string as follows:

```
Dim strConnection as String = "Provider=Microsoft.Jet.OLEDB.4.0;"
strConnection += "Data Source=C:\BegASPNET\ch12\NonExistent.mdb"
data_src.text = strConnection
```

5. Call up the page again, to see how it handles the invalid file reference in the connection string:

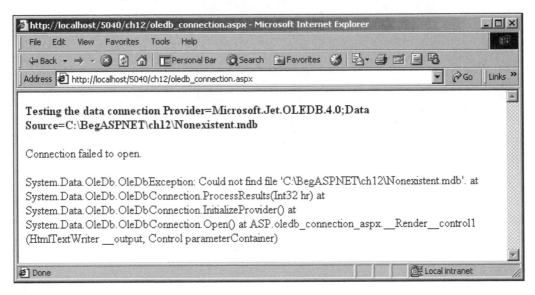

How It Works

The MDB file is used by Access to store all the information required to fully define the Northwind database, including both structure and data. The difference between this and a simple flat data, is that the data in the MDB is arranged in structured blocks, so that it's far more efficient to query.

Our code begins with a couple of declaratives, which import all the extra namespaces we require:

```
<%@ import Namespace="System.Data" %>
<%@ import Namespace="System.Data.Oledb" %>
```

The System.Data.Oledb namespace contains a class definition for OledbConnection, which we used to create a connection object for linking our code to the specific data source we're interested in. While we don't explicitly use any of the classes in the System.Data namespace at this stage, they underlie pretty much all of the data access functionality we will use, so it's good practice to import it nevertheless.

We define a connection string, strConnection, which specifies the data provider we want to use (in this case the Microsoft JET engine), and the actual source we want to connect to (the Northwind.mdb file we copied earlier).

```
<script language="VB" runat="server">
  Sub Page_Load()
    Dim strConnection as String = "Provider=Microsoft.Jet.OLEDB.4.0;"
    strConnection += "Data Source=C:\BegASPNET\ch12\Northwind.mdb"
```

You can type the `strConnection` text all on one line, but it has been concatenated here to accommodate the size of paper in the book.

Next we assign the connection string to the `data_src` label's `text` property (so that we can show it on the finished page), and then use it to create an `OledbConnection` object:

```
    data_src.text = strConnection

    Dim objConnection as New OledbConnection(strConnection)
```

Note that we can use this syntax to instantiate the connection object, because the `OledbConnection` class supports a constructor method that assigns a specified string parameter to its `ConnectionString` property. We could just as well have said:

```
    Dim objConnection as New OledbConnection()
    objConnection.ConnectionString = strConnection
```

*Be careful not to confuse a string and an object with similar names. The **Connection** is an ADO.NET Object, while the **connection string** is a variable containing the object's arguments. The string is quite long, so we've built it into a variable called* `strConnection`. *We then created the Connection object and named it* `objConnection`. *The connection string (*`strConnection`*) is used to provide the information for the making the connection with the connection object (*`objConnection`*).*

The next block of code sits inside a `try...catch` block, so that we can catch any exceptions that occur as a result of attempting to connect to the database. For now, we simply open the connection and close it again. If an exception is thrown in the course of the process, the catch clause picks it up, and uses the `con_open` and `con_close` labels to tell us what went wrong:

```
    try
      objConnection.Open()
      con_open.text="Connection opened successfully.<br/>"
      objConnection.Close()
      con_close.text="Connection closed.<br/>"
    catch e as Exception
      con_open.text="Connection failed to open successfully.<br/>"
      con_close.text=e.ToString()
    end try
  end Sub
</script>
```

The final step in the Try It Out, demonstrates the sort of information we can expect to get in the event that an exception occurs. We off by specify some HTML with which to render the page, and include the three label controls that we referenced above:

```
<html>
  <body>
  <h4>Testing the data connection
  <asp:label id="data_src" runat="server"/></h4>
  <asp:label id="con_open" runat="server"/><br/>
  <asp:label id="con_close" runat="server"/><br/>
  </body>
</html>
```

So, that's pretty straightforward – there's not much to show for it yet, but we have at least established a connection. Before we move on, let's take a quick look at what changes we need to make in order to access the same Northwind example in a SQL Server database.

Try It Out – Connecting to the Northwind database in SQL Server 2000

As we've established, the mechanics of connecting to a SQL Server database aren't that different to those we saw above. We simply need to use a different class of connection object, and a different construction for the connection string:

1. Make a copy of the previous ASPX sample and rename it `sql_connection.aspx`.

2. Make the following amendments to the connection specification – of course, you'll need to use appropriate values of your own for the server name (and possibly the user id and password):

```
<%@ import Namespace="System.Data" %>
<%@ import Namespace="System.Data.SqlClient" %>
<script language="VB" runat="server">
  Sub Page_Load()
    Dim strConnection as String = "user id=sa;password=;"
    strConnection += "database=northwind;server=Your_SQLServer;"
    strConnection += "Connect Timeout=30"
    data_src.text = strConnection

    Dim objConnection as New SqlConnection(strConnection)

    try
    ...
    catch e as Exception
    ...
    end try
  end Sub
</script>

<html>
  ...
</html>
```

Note that this code will not work if your instance of SQL Server has been setup to only use Integrated Login. In that case, you'll need to replace user id and password parameters with `Integrated Security=SSPI`:

3. Call up the page in your browser, and you should see the following result:

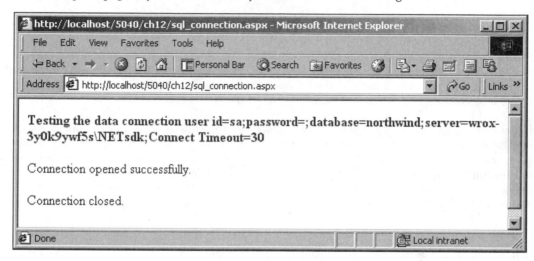

4. Once again, we break the connection string by providing an invalid password:

```
Sub Page_Load()
    Dim strConnection as String = "user id=sa;password=WrongPassWord;"
    strConnection += "database=northwind;server=your_SQLserver;"
    strConnection += "Connect Timeout=30"
```

5. Call up the page again, to see how it handles the invalid password in the connection string:

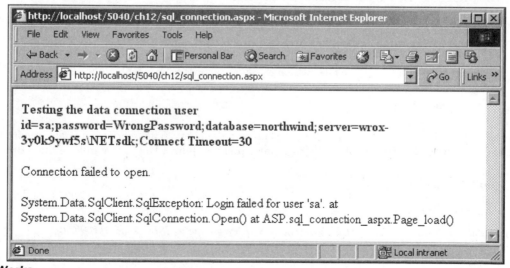

How It Works

This example demonstrates the flexibility of ADO.NET. We have connected to a completely different data source, SQL server, yet very little of our code has had to change. The only real differences between this Try It Out and the last, is that we used a `SqlConnection` object, instead of an `OledbConnection` object and the connection string has to point to a different database. We will see more of `SqlConnection` later in the chapter. Let's now take a look at some more ADO.NET objects.

The Command Object and DataReader

Simply connecting to a data source is not enough, we also need to be able to read it and make modifications to it. This is where the ADO.NET `Command` object comes in handy – it contains all the instructions that we want to apply to the database, and we can use its `ExecuteReader()` method to create a `DataReader` that displays the results of our query in a table.

But even before we begin using the `Command` object we need to learn how to communicate with a relational database management system so that we can do things like create databases and tables, and save, retrieve or update data. All of these tasks can be achieved using a standard language called **SQL**, or **Structured Query Language**. There is a SQL standard called ANSI SQL, which defines the syntax that any database understands, although there are some modifications and extensions to ANSI SQL that are used by each RDBMS vendor; however, the basic concepts and commands are always the same.

SQL Queries

SQL statements or **commands,** are sent to a database engine, which returns the records that meet the request in the statement. Some statements return a set of all the records meeting the conditions we've specified – for example, we might ask the engine to retrieve records containing "John" as the first name. Other SQL statements don't return a result set – instead, they are commands that tell the database engine to do something, for example: "Delete all records that contain John as the first name".

There are four important commands from which SQL statements can be constructed:

- ❑ SELECT: used to **retrieve** data from one or more tables
- ❑ DELETE: used to **delete** data from a table
- ❑ INSERT: used to **add a new record** into a table
- ❑ UPDATE: used to change data in an existing record of a table

The typical form of a SELECT query, which retrieves records from a table, looks like this:

```
SELECT LastName, FirstName FROM User WHERE FirstName = 'John'
```

Take a closer look at the FROM and WHERE clauses in the query. The query returns any record **FROM** the user table **WHERE** the value of the First_Name field is "John". Here's a sample of the output:

```
Simpleton John
Smith John
Thomas John
```

You can learn more about SQL in Beginning SQL Programming ISBN 1-861001-80-0.

After we have written our SQL query, we need to pass it to the `Command` object as a string, so that we can apply it to the database. All we have to do, is set the SQL query string as a parameter to the `Command` object when we create it; we also need to pass it the `Connection` object as a parameter so that it knows how to find the database:

```
Dim strSQL as String = "SELECT LastName, FirstName FROM User..."
Dim objConnection as New OledbConnection(...

Dim ObjCommand as New OledbCommand(strSQL, ObjConnection)
```

After our connection has been made and the command object has applied the query on the database, we need a way of displaying the results. Fortunately, the `Command` object has an `ExecuteReader` method that creates an object called the `DataReader` – an ADO.NET tool for displaying data on pages. The `DataReader` is simple to use, it accepts data from the `ExecuteReader` method and then allows you to loop through its contents and put the information onto the page.

Try It Out – Reading Data with the DataReader

Our first try at using data in an ASP.NET page will be very simple. We will read the names of the employees from Northwind and display them in a list on the page:

1. Create a file called `datareader.aspx` in your `C:\BegASPNET\ch12` test directory, and enter the following code. The shaded code is different from our last Try It Out, so you can start with a copy of the file and modify as follows:

```
<%@ import Namespace="System.Data" %>
<%@ import Namespace="System.Data.Oledb" %>

<script language="vb" runat="server">
Sub Page_Load()
  Dim strConnection as String = "Provider=Microsoft.Jet.OLEDB.4.0;"
    strConnection += "Data Source=C:\BegASPNET\ch12\Northwind.mdb"
    data_src.text = strConnection
  Dim strSQL as string = "SELECT FirstName, LastName FROM Employees"
  Dim strResultsHolder as string

  Dim objConnection as New OledbConnection(strConnection)
  Dim objCommand as New OledbCommand(strSQL, objConnection)
  Dim objDataReader as OledbDataReader

  try
    objConnection.Open()
    con_open.text="Connection opened successfully.<br />"
  objDataReader = objCommand.ExecuteREader()

  Do While objDataReader.Read()=True
    strResultsHolder +=objDataREader("FirstName")
    strResultsHolder +=" "
    strResultsHolder +=objDataREader("LastName")
    strResultsHolder +="<br>"
  Loop

  objDataReader.Close()
```

```
    objConnection.Close()
    con_close.text="Connection closed.<br>"
  divListEmployees.innerHTML = strResultsHolder
  catch e as Exception
    con_open.text="Connection failed to open successfully.<br>"
    con_close.text=e.ToString()
  end try
end Sub
</script>

<html>
  <body>
  <h4>Reading data from the connection
  <asp:label id="data_src" runat="server"/> with the DataReader object.</h4>
  <asp:label id="con_open" runat="server"/><br>
  <div id="divListEmployees" runat="server">list will go here</div>
  <asp:label id="con_close" runat="server"/><br>
  </body>
</html>
```

2. Call up the file in your browser, and you should see the following:

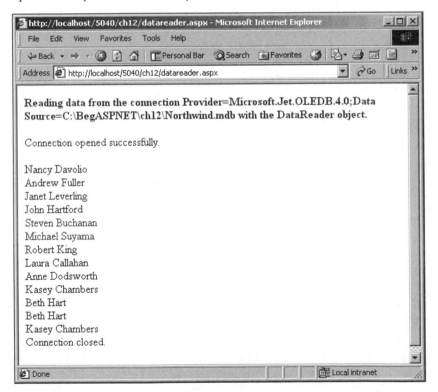

How It Works

As usual, we start by importing the name spaces that will allow us to use the objects we need:

```
<%@ import Namespace="System.Data" %>
<%@ import Namespace="System.Data.Oledb" %>
```

Instead of making our statements very long and confusing (especially on the limited confines of the printed page), we put several strings into variables, namely:

❑   A connection string describing the provider we want to use and where to find the required database

❑   A description of the data we want from the database

❑   A list of employees names extracted from the database

So, we set up three string variables to hold the connection string, the query string, and the results we're going to get back from the query:

```
Sub Page_Load()
  Dim strConnection as String = "Provider=Microsoft.Jet.OLEDB.4.0;"
    strConnection += "Data Source=C:\BegASPNET\ch12\Northwind.mdb"
    data_src.text = strConnection
  Dim strSQL as string = "SELECT FirstName,LastName FROM Employees"
  Dim strResultsHolder as string
```

We now need three ADO.NET objects with which to query the database:

❑   A `Connection` object: This links our code to the data source specified in the connection string by means of an OLEDB provider

❑   A `Command` object: This holds and issues the SQL query against that data source

❑   A `DataReader` object: This holds and exposes the structured data records that it returns

Here's how we instantiate them:

```
Dim objConnection as New OledbConnection(strConnection)
Dim objCommand as New OledbCommand(strSQL, objConnection)
Dim objDataReader as OledbDataReader
```

Now that we've done our preparation, we are ready to fly into action. We open up a connection, and use the `ExecuteReader` method on our command object to execute the `strSQL` query – the results are then stored in the `DataReader` object:

```
try
  objConnection.Open()
  con_open.text="Connection opened successfully.<br />"
objDataReader = objCommand.ExecuteReader()
```

Once the data is in the `DataReader`, we use a loop to walk through each of the records, and read the names of each employee into our results string. We read data from the `DataReader` into our results string, and apply some basic formatting along the way:

```
Do While objDataReader.Read()=True
  strResultsHolder +=objDataREader("FirstName")
  strResultsHolder +=" "
  strResultsHolder +=objDataREader("LastName")
  strResultsHolder +="<br />"
Loop
```

Now that we are done with using our ADO.NET objects, we close them. This frees up memory and improves the scalability of the site (that is, its ability to handle more simultaneous users). Notice however, that we don't close the `Command` object, it has no `Close` method:

```
objDataReader.Close()
objConnection.Close()
```

> *Note that in ASP.NET we do not have to set the `object=nothing` like we did in older ASP versions. This 'garbage collection' is done automatically. However, in some scenarios setting the object to nothing will free up resources sooner than waiting for the automatic clean-up.*

Now we have a full list of names in the variable `strResultsHolder`, and we are trim and clean with all our ADO.NET objects closed. Our final step is to apply the string built in `strResultsHolder` to the text of the `<div>` control. Note that since the string includes HMTL (albeit just ` ` and `<br />`) we must apply it to the `InnerHTML` property rather than the `InnerText` property:

```
divListEmployees.innerHTML = strResultsHolder
```

Finally, we take care of any exceptions that may have been thrown, and specify the required presentation elements – these include a `<div>` element that we've called `divListEmployees`, which is where the results of our database query are shown, notice that its `runat` attribute is `"server"`:

```
  catch e as Exception
    con_open.text="Connection failed to open successfully.<br />"
    con_close.text=e.ToString()
  end try
end Sub
</script>

<html>
  <body>
  <h4>Reading data from the connection
  <asp:label id="data_src" runat="server"/> with the DataReader object.</h4>
  <asp:label id="con_open" runat="server"/><br>
  <div id="divListEmployees" runat="server">list will go here</div>
  <asp:label id="con_close" runat="server"/><br>
  </body>
</html>
```

Simple Data Binding

Data binding refers to the process in which we create a link between the data source and the data consumer; if we want to display data from a database using a server control, for instance, then we have to bind it to the database first. So far, we've learnt how to connect to a database, send a command to it, and retrieve the data, when we get the data out of the database, we know how to loop through the records and display them as simple text. Unfortunately, if we want to do anything more sophisticated with the data, like displaying it in a table, formatting it and sorting it, then we're stuck. With ASP.NET, there are ways in which we can handle this data and do fancy things to it using the `<asp:datagrid>` server control. All we need to do is bind it to the data source, and we can use it to do the following:

❑ Automatically format the output into a table for presentation on the page without having to loop through the records

❑ Format the table, we can do things like add a hyperlinks column, format headers and footers, alternate the colors of each row

❑ Sort the data in the table

We will see more of the `DataGrid` and Data Binding in Chapter 14, but for now let's take a look at how we can use it along with the Command object to extracted from a database and displaying in a pleasing way, and with less code.

Try It Out – Using the DataGrid

In this example we will use the `Command` object's `ExecuteReader` method to make a page that shows the `Lastname`, `City`, and `Country` for each employee of Northwind. However, unlike the previous example where we had to manually loop through the rows, this example uses the `DataGrid` control and data binding.

1. Create a new file called `execute_reader.aspx`, and enter the following code:

```
<%@ Import Namespace="System.Data" %>
<%@ Import Namespace="System.Data.OleDb" %>

<script language="vb" runat="server">
  Sub Page_Load()
    dim strConnection as string = "Provider=Microsoft.Jet.OLEDB.4.0;"
      strConnection += "Data source=C:\BegASPNET\ch12\northwind.mdb;"
    dim strSQL as string = "Select LastName, City, Country from employees;"

    dim objConnection as new OLEDBConnection(strConnection)
    dim objCommand as new OLEDBCommand(strSQL,objConnection)

    objConnection.Open()
    dgEmps.DataSource = objCommand.ExecuteReader(CommandBehavior.CloseConnection)
    dgEmps.DataBind()
  end sub
</script>

<html>
  <body>
    <h2>Using ExecuteReader to create a table</h2>
```

```
    <asp:datagrid id="dgEmps"
        runat="server"
        CellPadding="3"
        Font-Name="arial"
        Font-Size="8pt"
        HeaderStyle-BackColor="#dcdcdc"
        HeaderStyle-ForeColor="blue"
    />
  </body>
</html>
```

2. Test the page in your browser.

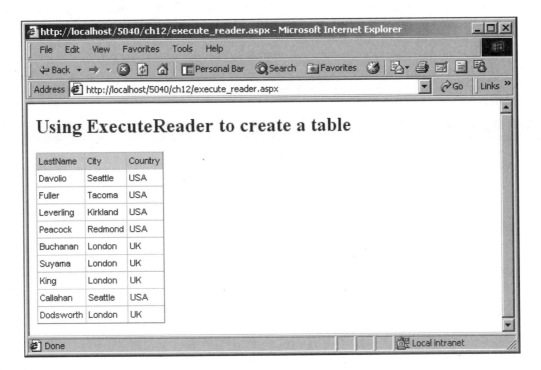

How It Works

The code starts no differently to our previous page. We begin by importing namespaces so we can find and use our ADO.NET objects, and there's no difference in connection or SQL strings, or in the creation of our Connection and Command objects. Note however, that we don't create a `DataReader` object directly:

```
<%@ Import Namespace="System.Data" %>
<%@ Import Namespace="System.Data.OLEDB" %>

script language="vb" runat="server">
  Sub Page_Load()
```

```
dim strConnection as string = "Provider=Microsoft.Jet.OLEDB.4.0;"
  strConnection += "Data source=C:\BegASPNET\ch12\northwind.mdb;"

dim strSQL as string = "Select LastName, City, Country from employees;"

dim objConnection as new OLEDBConnection(strConnection)
dim objCommand as new OLEDBCommand(strSQL, objConnection)
```

Now though, we encounter a change. Once we've taken care to explicitly open a connection we fill the `DataGrid` control with the results returned by the `Command`'s `ExecuteReader` method, and then we perform the binding:

```
  objConnection.Open()
  dgEmps.DataSource = objCommand.ExecuteReader(CommandBehavior.CloseConnection)
  dgEmpls.DataBind()
end Sub
<\script>
```

Finally, we have the `<html>` section that contains the `DataGrid` server control where we apply a bit of formatting to make our table look a little pretty:

```
<html>
  <body>
    <h2>Using ExecuteReader to create a table</h2>
    <asp:datagrid id="dgEmps"
        runat="server"
        CellPadding="3"
        Font-Name="arial"
        Font-Size="8pt"
        HeaderStyle-BackColor="#dcdcdc"
        HeaderStyle-ForeColor="blue"
    />
  </body>
</html>
```

You can see that not only do you have to write less code to get the data, but that you don't even have to loop through the rows either. That's because the `DataGrid` takes care of this for you, creating an HTML table, and the row elements for each row in the data.

The `DataReader` is an extremely efficient way of extracting and displaying data from a database, it has been optimized for this task. However, it pays for this efficiency by cutting back on other functionality. There are several limitations:

❑ It provides read-only access – you cannot change data using a `DataReader`

❑ It is forward-only – you can only loop forwards through the data

❑ It can only work with data from a single table

If you need to change the data, then other objects need to be used. We'll look at changing data in the next chapter, but we will use these other objects to display data without altering it.

The DataSet and DataTable Objects

ADO.NET works with disconnected data, it makes a copy of the data in the database for us to work with, and then updates the database after we have finished. The `DataSet` represents the data in the database, unlike the `DataReader` it can hold several tables and the relationships between them. There are four ADO.NET objects at our disposal when working with `tables`:

❑ `DataTable`: This is the actual table itself.

❑ `DataSet`: The central object we deal with is the `DataSet`, which can contain multiple tables and establish ad hoc relationships between them. These relationships associate a row in one table with another row in a different table.

❑ `DataAdapter`: This is used to pass results `from the Connection` into the `DataSet` The `Fill` method copies the data into the `DataSet,` and the `Update` method copies the data in the `DataSet` back into the data source.

❑ `DataView`: `This` represents a specific view of the `DataTables` held in the `DataSet`. This is a description of the records and columns you want to read from the entire `DataSet`.

Let's look at these diagrammatically:

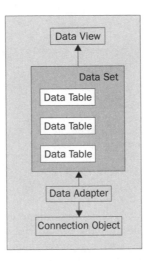

The flow of data is just the same as for the data reader. We get our data from a RDBMS or other data source by using Managed Data Provider (see the section above on Connections for more details).

Try It Out – Reading Data into a Table

We're now going to modify our last example, so that the First and Last names of the Northwind employees are presented neatly in an HTML table, using a `DataSet` object and a `DataGrid` control to save us from having to loop through the records:

1. Start off by creating a file called `datagrid.aspx`, and add the following code:

```
<%@ import Namespace="System.Data" %>
<%@ import Namespace="System.Data.Oledb" %>
```

```vb
<script language="vb" runat="server">
  Sub Page_Load()
    Dim strConnection as String = "Provider=Microsoft.Jet.OLEDB.4.0;"
      strConnection += "Data Source=C:\begASPNET\ch12\Northwind.mdb"
      data_src.text = strConnection
    Dim strSQL as string = "SELECT FirstName, LastName FROM Employees;"
    Dim objDataSet as new DataSet()

    Dim objConnection as new OledbConnection(strConnection)
    Dim objAdapter as new OledbDataAdapter(strSQL, objConnection)

    objAdapter.Fill(objDataSet, "Employees")

    Dim objDataView as New DataView(objDataSet.Tables("Employees"))

    dgNameList.DataSource=objDataView
    dgNameList.DataBind()
  end Sub
</script>
<html>
  <body>
  <h4>Reading data from the connection
  <asp:label id="data_src" runat="server"/> to the DataGrid control.</h4>
  <asp:datagrid id="dgNameList" runat="server" /><br />
  </body>
</html>
```

2. Use your browser to call up the file, and you should see the following:

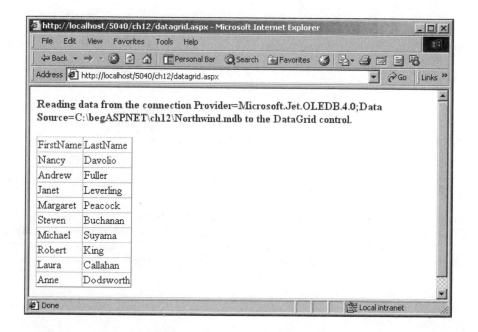

How It Works

This page starts out just the same as our previous `DataReader` example – the two strings that we create and fill serve the same functions as before. The first is the connection string that specifies the provider and database we want to work with. The second holds the description (in SQL syntax) of the data we want to read from the database:

```
Dim strConnection as String = "Provider=Microsoft.Jet.OLEDB.4.0;"
    strConnection += "Data Source=C:\BegASPNET\ch12\Northwind.mdb"
Dim strSQL as string = "SELECT FirstName, LastName FROM Employees;"
```

We now start creating our ADO.NET objects, and begin to depart from our `DataReader` example. The first difference appears when we create a `DataSet` object in place of the string we used previously to store our result set. This is so that we can retain the full structure of the data returned from the database:

```
Dim objDataSet as new DataSet()
```

We must also create a `DataAdapter` which will allow the data from our database to be modified for our result set:

```
Dim objConn as new OledbConnection(strConnection)
Dim objAdapter as new OledbDataAdapter(strSQL, objConnection)
```

Note that when the `DataAdapter` is created it takes two arguments:

- ❑ The query string that will define the exact set of data we want from the database (described by the variable `strSQL`)

- ❑ The `Connection` object (`objConnection`)

We now instruct the `DataAdapter` to output all its data to the `DataSet` object, and to give the newly created table the name "Employees". It is important for this table to have a well-defined name, since `DataSet` objects can contain multiple tables and create ad hoc relationships between them:

```
objAdapter.Fill(objDataSet, "Employees")
```

ADO.NET lets us create various **views** of the information within a `DataSet`. This allows us, for example, to add several tables to a page, giving each its own set of columns and records as determined by various views. In our case, we just want to view the entire `Employees` table as created in the last line:

```
Dim objDataView as New DataView(objDataSet.Tables("Employees"))
```

Now that we have the desired view of our data tucked away safely in our `DataSet` within the ASP.NET code, we can focus on displaying that on the page. The next line establishes that the `DataGrid` control should get its data from the `DataView` object; we then call the `Bind` method, which is actually responsible for assigning data to the 'name list' grid control, and results in its actually being displayed on the page:

```
dgNameList.DataSource = objDataView
dgNameList.DataBind()
```

Whereas in the `DataReader` we created a `<div>` HTML control in the presentation block to hold our output, we now use a `datagrid` server control to create an HTML table:

```
<html>
  <body>
  <h4>Writing data from the connection
  <asp:label id="data_src" runat="server"/> to the DataGrid control.</h4>
  <asp:datagrid id="dgNameList" runat="server" /><br>
  </body>
</html>
```

Note that ASP.NET actually sends out a grid appropriate to the requesting device. So if the visitor was using a WAP phone or PDA, the result may not actually be an HTML table.

To summarize our Basic Data Table Try It Out, we want to keep in mind six points:

3. To display a table, we use a `DataGrid` control rather then a `<div>`

4. We need to create four ADO.NET objects: `Connection`, `DataSet`, `DataAdapter`, and `DataView`

5. The `DataSet` holds structured data, and can store multiple tables and relationships between them

6. The `DataAdapter` conducts data through the `Connection` object and into a `DataSet`

7. The `DataView` brings together a set of columns and records from the `DataSet`

8. After the `DataView` is created we have to set the `DataGrid`'s source to the `DataView` and bind the data

We'll look at data grids again when we take a thorough look at ASP.NET's server controls in Chapter 18.

Microsoft SQL Server and ADO.NET

Microsoft has paved the way to optimize ADO.NET objects for various data sources, and we've seen that we can use the Managed Provider for OLEDB to talk to an Access database. In addition to three of the objects used in the previous examples (`OleDbConnection`, `OleDbCommand`, and `OleDbDataAdapter`), Microsoft has also produced sisters to each of these objects that are optimized for the Microsoft SQL Server, which use the Managed Provider for SQL Server. They are named, logically, `SQLConnection`, `SQLCommand`, and `SQLDataAdapter`. These objects are optimized for the Microsoft SQL Server, they do not need to contain code to accommodate the differences among various other data sources. The SQL- set of objects is both faster and less consuming of resources. In the future, we might see additional ADO.NET objects that are optimized for data sources of other vendors.

> **Only use the SQL objects when your data source is Microsoft SQL Server version 7.0 and later.**

In order to use the SQL-objects you must first import the namespace containing them. So your page must begin with:

```
<%@Page Language="VB"%>
<%@ import Namespace="System.Data" %>
<%@ import Namespace="System.Data.SqlClient" %>
<html>
```

Also note the different syntax in the connection string. You do not use a provider, so there is no "Provider=" clause, instead we use "Server=".

You can obtain a trial version of SQL Server 2000, which is valid for 120 days, as a download from Microsoft or on the CD included with the *Beginning SQL Programming* text mentioned earlier in the chapter. Another option, is to use just the data engine for SQL server. If you have a licensed copy of a Microsoft development tool, such as VB, Access or Visual Studio, you can get MSDE free from Microsoft. An equivalent product is available with the same restrictions for SQL Server 2000 called SSDE. Both can be downloaded from the Microsoft site, search for MSDE or SSDE. Alternatively, you can learn the ideas by studying this code without actually running it.

Try It Out – ADO.NET SqlClient Objects

We will use the SQL Server version of ADO.NET objects to create a list of Names and Hire dates of the Northwind Employees. Start by creating a new page named `DataTableBasicUsingSQLObjects.aspx` in your BegAspNet application:

1. Type or download, copy and paste, the following code. Note that when you specify `strConnection` you should use the name of your own Microsoft SQL server:

```
<%@Page Language="VB"%>

<%@Import Namespace="System.Data" %>
<%@Import Namespace="System.Data.SqlClient" %>

<html>
<head><title> WROX Beginning ASP.NET - Data - Data Table <br/>
Using Microsoft SQL Objects</title></head>

<body>
<h2>Display of Data in a Table (Grid) Using SQL Objects</h2>

Northwind Employees:
<asp:datagrid   id="dgrEmployees" runat="server" />

<script language="vb" runat="server">
Sub Page_Load()

' First we will set up variables to hold two strings
Dim strSQL as string = "SELECT FirstName,LastName FROM Employees;"
```

```
Dim strConnection as String =
"server=your_SQLServer;database=Northwind;uid=sa;password=;"

Dim objDataSet As New DataSet()
Dim objConnection As New SqlConnection(strConnection)

'create a new DataAdapter using the connection object and select statement
Dim objDataAdapter As New SqlDataAdapter(strSQL, objConnection)

'fill the dataset with data from the DataAdapter object
objDataAdapter.Fill(objDataSet, "Employees")

'create a DataView object for the Employees table in the DataSet
Dim objDataView As New DataView(objDataSet.Tables("Employees"))

'assign the DataView object to the DataGrid control
dgrEmployees.DataSource = objDataView
dgrEmployees.DataBind()    'and bind (display) the data

End Sub
</script> </body> </html>
```

2. Save the page and open it your browser. You should see the same list of employees as you did when using Northwind data in Access:

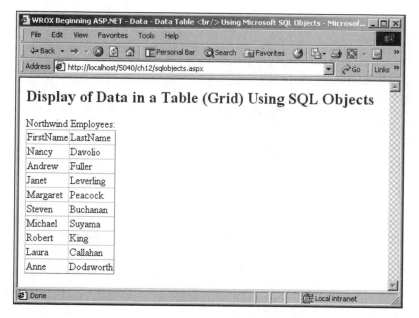

How It Works –

Remember that our objective here is to list the employees from Northwind in Microsoft SQL Server. We could make the connection using OLEDB, but in this Try It Out, we will use the more efficient ADO SQL objects.

We start by importing a different namespace, the one holding the names of ADO's SQL- objects:

```
<%@Page Language="VB"%>
<%@Import Namespace="System.Data" %>
<%@Import Namespace="System.Data.SqlClient" %>
```

There is no change from the OLEDB technique we studied earlier, until we have to create the string that will provide the connection details. Instead of using a driver or provider, we just identify our server and database:

```
' First we will set up variables to hold two strings
Dim strSQL as string = "SELECT FirstName,LastName FROM Employees;"
Dim strConnection as String =
"server=your_SQLServer;database=Northwind;uid=sa;pwd=;"
```

When we create our connection, we instantiate a SQLConnection and SQLDataAdapter, rather then their OLEDB equivalents, as below:

```
Dim objDataSet As New DataSet()
Dim objConnection As New SqlConnection(strConnection)
Dim objDataAdapter As New SqlDataAdapter(strSQL, objConnection)
```

The remainder of the code is no different then when using the OLEDB flavor of the objects.

The take-home message is simple. If your data is stored in Microsoft SQL Server version 7 or later (including 2000) then your ASP.NET data pages will be more efficient by using the SQL version of the ADO objects.

Catching Errors

As we've already seen, the .NET languages we can use in ASP.NET provide us with a useful Try...Catch mechanism for effective catching exceptions. Potentially problematic sections of code can be put in a guarded Try block, and are executed until they are complete, or until an exception is raised.

Let's consider how we can get the most out of this mechanism in the context of reading data. First, consider a few things that might go wrong:

❑   Code contains references to an ADO.NET object that does not exist

❑   Code (or user) asks for data that does not exist, like a person with last name "zzz"

❑   Code tries to connect with an improper connection string

❑ Code contains references to columns or tables that do not exist

❑ Code (or user) does not supply the correct User ID or Password

❑ Code uses a SQL statement of incorrect syntax

❑ The Web Server can not communicate to the data source because of a network problem

The key to using the VB.NET error-catching, is to understand which of these errors will be caught, and which will have to be resolved using other tools. You might be surprised at what is not caught. Internal errors, such as mistyping an ADO.NET object's name (#1 above), will cause an error in the compilation to CLR and thus, not get to deployment. Situations such as a WHERE clause that does not find a matching record (#2) are not caught – you just get no records returned. The `Try...Catch` does throw an error for an incorrect connection string.

Try It Out – Reading Data into a Table With Error-Trapping

In this exercise, we will add a simple error-catching routine. Then we will make some specific errors to see what is and is not trapped.

1. Create a new file called `datatable_errorcheck.aspx` and enter the following code:

```vb
<%@ import Namespace="System.Data" %>
<%@ import Namespace="System.Data.Oledb" %>

<script language="vb" runat="server">
Sub Page_Load()
  Dim strConnection as String = "Provider=Microsoft.Jet.OLEDB.4.0;"
    strConnection += "Data Source=C:\BegASPNET\ch12\Northwind.mdb"
    data_src.text = strConnection
  Dim strSQL as string = "SELECT FirstName, LastName FROM Employees;"
  Dim objDataSet as new DataSet()

  Dim objConnection as new OledbConnection(strConnection)
  Dim objAdapter as new OledbDataAdapter(strSQL, objConnection)

  Try
    objAdapter.Fill(objDataSet, "Employees")

    Dim objDataView as New DataView(objDataSet.Tables("Employees"))

    dgNameList.DataSource=objDataView
    dgNameList.DataBind()
  Catch objError as OledbException
    If Left(objError.Message,21)="Login failed for user" Then
      divErrorReport.InnerHTML = "Problem with Log-in"
    ElseIf Left(objError.Message,19)="Could not find file" Then
      divErrorReport.InnerHTML = "We could not find the MDB file that you asked for"
    Else
      divErrorReport.InnerHTML =  "<br />message - " & objError.Message
      divErrorReport.InnerHTML += "<br />source - " & objError.Source
    End If
  End Try
end Sub
```

```
  </script>

<html>
  <body>
  <h4>Writing data from the connection
    <asp:label id="data_src" runat="server"/>
    to the DataGrid control with error checking.</h4>
  <div id="divErrorReport" runat="server"> </div>
  <asp:datagrid id="dgNameList" runat="server" /><br />
  </body>
</html>
```

2. Save the page, and take a look at it in your browser. Assuming there are no errors in the code, it should look almost exactly as it did before.

3. Now let's try introducing some deliberate errors – we might add a request for the employees' middle names:

```
Dim strSQL as string = "SELECT FirstName,LastName,MiddleName FROM Employees;"
```

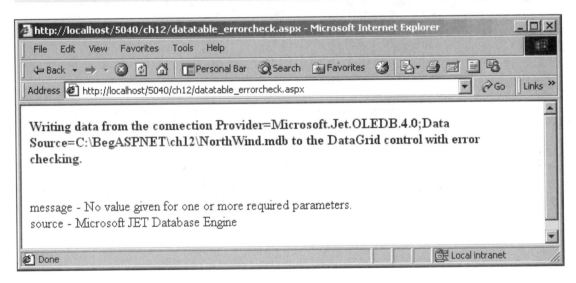

4. Or we might specify a non-existent database:

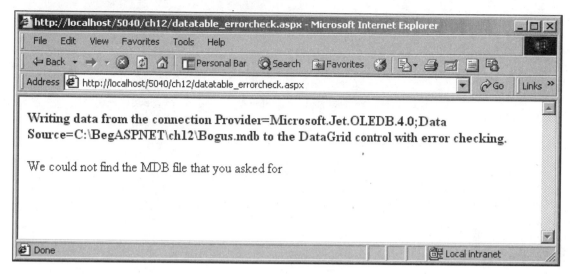

How It Works –

The code starts the same as the last few pages, so lets skip down to where we start to declare our objects. Note that we keep the dim of most objects outside the TRY block, since we are using the TRY block to catch specific connection-related problems:

```
Sub Page_Load()
  Dim strConnection as String = "Provider=Microsoft.Jet.OLEDB.4.0;"
    strConnection += "Data Source=C:\BegASPNET\ch12\Northwind.mdb"
    data_src.text = strConnection
  Dim strSQL as string = "SELECT FirstName, LastName FROM Employees;"
  Dim objDataSet as new DataSet()

  Dim objConnection as new OledbConnection(strConnection)
  Dim objAdapter as new OledbDataAdapter(strSQL, objConnection)
```

Now we start a section of code that will either fully execute all lines without problems or execute none of them and give us the CATCH code instead..

```
Try
    objAdapter.Fill(objDataSet, "Employees")

    Dim objDataView as New DataView(objDataSet.Tables("Employees"))

    dgNameList.DataSource=objDataView
    dgNameList.DataBind()
```

Now we write code that will be executed if there is a problem in any of the TRY section lines:

```
Catch objError as OledbException
    If Left(objError.Message,21) ="Login failed for user" Then
        divErrorReport.InnerHTML = "Problem with Log-in"
    ElseIf Left(objError.Message,19)="Could not find file" Then
        divErrorReport.InnerHTML = "We could not find the MDB file that you asked for"
    Else
        divErrorReport.InnerHTML =  "<br />message - " & objError.Message
        divErrorReport.InnerHTML += "<br />source - " & objError.Source
    End If
```

Don't forget to end the whole try...catch structure with an End Try:

```
    End Try
```

The remainder of the page simply displays our results (or error).

Summary

Having learned the basics of ASP.NET theory and the techniques to interact with users, the next most important skill tool for web sites is the ability to work with data. ASP.NET uses ADO.NET, a suite of objects which allow a language such as VB.NET or C++ to interact with data. ADO.NET is compatible with almost any kind of data through a long list of available providers and drivers, however, generally we are working with relational data.

The basic ADO.NET tools are a Connection object, a Command object, and either a DataSet or a DataReader.

Connection Strings provide information to the Connection object on which data source and how to work with that source. Connections strings have an odd syntax for their argument, so be careful to enter them exactly as provided.

Command objects inform ADO.NET how to connect and read information from the data store. The data then actually resides in a DataSet. Alternatively, the data can be passed through a DataReader, which works more quickly by not actually holding the data.

Although SQL statements are not required by ADO.NET for many operations on data, they are generally used as the fastest and most efficient way to get the job done. If you are using Microsoft SQL Server as your data source, then you can then use a special set of ADO.NET objects that are optimized for that brand of RDBMS. Don't forget to import the namespace and be mindful of the connection string.

If you only need to read (not write) data, and you can get it in its final form with your SQL statement (no further sorting or filtering), then you can improve your page's performance by using the ExecuteReader. This method of the ADO.NET Command Object fills your DataGrid without taking the time or memory space to create, stock, and read a DataSet.

In this chapter, we covered the theory of ADO .NET and the techniques to read data. In the next chapter, we learn to take user input and write that to our data store.

Exercises

1. Explain how the process of normalization helps us optimize databases.

2. Rewrite this section of code using the relevant connection object and Namespace so that it can be used to connect to a SQL Server database, and modify the connection string accordingly:

```
Dim strConnection as String = "Provider=Microsoft.Jet.OLEDB.4.0;"
    strConnection += "Data Source=C:\begASPNET\ch12\Northwind.mdb"

Dim objConnection as New OledbConnection(strConnection)
```

3. Write an ASP.NET page that uses the connection object to connect to the Northwind database and displays the following information using a `datagrid`:

a) The address, City, contact name and telephone number of all suppliers

b) The names and addresses of all the German customers

4. (a) Connect to Northwind and fill a `DataSet` with the Company Name and Contact Name fields of the suppliers table, create a `DataView` of the suppliers table and bind it to an `<asp:datagrid>` server control to display the results.

(b) Repeat the above exercise, but this time bind the `DataGrid` to the `DataSet` instead.

(c) Now fill the same `DataSet` with the First names and Last Names of the Employees table as well and create another `<asp:datagrid>` to display the results so that both tables appear on one page.

5. Connect to a SQL Server database using the `SqlConnection` object including a `Try ...` `Catch` block that traps login failures and incorrect connection strings.

Manipulating Data Sources

In the last chapter, we focused on the underlying theory of ADO.NET and on reading data. This is the place to start, because it's what we do the most of in ASP.NET pages – display data. We saw the use of the `DataSet`, `DataReader`, and `DataView` objects, as well as how data binding can enable the ASP.NET server controls to easily display data.

Of course, showing the data isn't the end of the story, as we often have to update it too. So, in this chapter, we talk about how to change data in the data store by creating, editing, and deleting information. In particular we'll be covering:

- ❑ The idea that there are two basic techniques of writing to a data store (using SQL statements and using methods of ADO.NET objects)

- ❑ Creating new records

- ❑ Changing existing records

- ❑ Deleting records

- ❑ Working with XML in ADO.NET pages, namely reading from an XML file into a `DataSet` object and writing from a `DataSet` object into an XML file.

You may think the latter of these doesn't quite fit into this chapter, but one of the underlying principles of ADO.NET is the tight integration with XML. We won't be covering XML in detail, but we'll be focusing on the methods of updating an XML file using the ADO.NET objects, just to show you how easy it is.

Disconnected Data

In the previous chapter, we mentioned that ADO.NET is based on a disconnected architecture; once we've read the data, we disconnect from the source. This happens for two main reasons:

- ❑ Database connections are resource hungry. Keeping a database connection open means it uses more resources (such as memory) on the database server. Database connections are also often limited in number, so keeping the connection open means one less connection available for someone else. The idea is to use the resource for the least amount of time – so, get in, get the data, and get out.

❑ Application architecture. In previous versions of ASP we've sometimes built applications utilizing component technologies such as Microsoft Transaction Server (or COM+ Services as it's called in Windows 2000). This has meant we often have to pass data around the various components, and in these cases the data is disconnected from the data source. For the loosely coupled architectures that .NET brings to the world, the disconnected model is perfect.

This whole idea of disconnected data is that it's not only more efficient for the database, but it also allows us to build better applications using components. This sort of architecture is usually quicker to implement, more robust, and more maintainable. However, it doesn't come without problems:

❑ How do we actually update the data? Any changes we make will be made to the disconnected data, and not to the original data source, so how do we get those changes back to the original data source?

❑ What happens if someone else updates the same data? It's not unusual for two people to want to update the same data at the same time, and if they are both disconnected, what happens when one person updates the data source, followed by the other? Does the edit for the first person get overwritten?

We'll be concentrating on the first of these two problems, discussing the various ways in which data can be updated. The second topic is far more complex, and beyond the scope of the book – if you're interested in finding out about how ADO.NET can help us deal with this problem, you may like to refer to *"Professional ASP.NET"* (Wrox Press, ISBN 1861004885).

Methods of Updating Data

ADO.NET offers two main methods for writing to your data store. By writing, here, we mean creating new records, changing data in existing records and deleting records:

❑ In the first technique you use methods of ADO.NET objects to update the data, usually after finding the correct record first.

❑ In the second technique you create a SQL statement that fully describes the writing operation that you want to perform. Then you direct ADO.NET to action that statement on the data source.

The latter of these requires knowledge of the SQL language itself. We'll discuss this later in the chapter, but let's concentrate on the ADO.NET features first.

DataSets and DataTables

So far our use of data has been limited to the `DataReader` and the `DataSet`. While the `DataReader` gives the best performance, it is limited to retrieving data based upon a single table, query or stored procedure. The `DataSet` however, has the advantage of being able to deal with multiple sets of data. Let's now take a quick look at a `DataSet` in action; consider the following code used to display the employees in a data grid:

```
<%@ Import Namespace="System.Data" %>
<%@ Import Namespace="System.Data.OleDb" %>

script language="VB" runat="server">
```

```
    Sub Page_Load(Sender As Object, E As EventArgs)

      Dim strConnection As String
      Dim strSQL         As String
      Dim objDataSet     As New DataSet()
      Dim objConnection As OleDbConnection
      Dim objAdapter     As OleDbDataAdapter

      ' set the connection and query details
      strConnection = "Provider=Microsoft.Jet.OLEDB.4.0; " & _
                      "Data Source=C:\BegASPNET\ch13\Northwind.mdb"
      strSQL = "SELECT FirstName, LastName FROM Employees;"

      ' open the connection and set the command
      objConnection = New OledbConnection(strConnection)
      objAdapter = New OledbDataAdapter(strSQL, objConnection)

      ' fill the dataset with the data
      objAdapter.Fill(objDataSet, "Employees")

      ' bind the data grid to the data
      dgNameList.DataSource = objDataSet.Tables("Employees").DefaultView
      dgNameList.DataBind()

      ' now do another one
      strSQL = "SELECT CategoryName, Description FROM Categories"
      objAdapter = New OleDbDataAdapter(strSQL, objConnection)
      objAdapter.Fill(objDataSet, "Categories")
      dgCategoryList.DataSource = objDataSet.Tables("Categories").DefaultView
      dgCategoryList.DataBind()
    End Sub

</script>

<html>
  <body>
  <asp:DataGrid id="dgNameList" runat="server" />
  <br /><br />
  <asp:Datagrid id="dgCategoryList" runat="server" />
  </body>
</html>
```

The important point here is these lines:

```
      objAdapter.Fill(objDataSet, "Employees")
      objAdapter.Fill(objDataSet, "Categories")
```

This is where we place the data from the command into the DataSet. The second argument is the name we want this data to have when it is stored in the DataSet. If this isn't supplied (it's optional), then the name used will be that of the source table (in our case this is the same). The reason we give it a name, is that a DataSet can contain one or more DataTables:

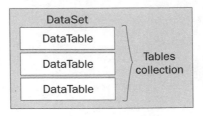

Each `DataTable` is held as part of the `Tables` collection. So, this allows us to store multiple sets of data within a `DataSet`. We're only going to use a single `DataTable` in this chapter, but the techniques work the same no matter how many tables you have.

To access an individual table in a `DataSet` you use the `Tables` collection. For example, assuming we have a `DataSet` populated with data (as in our previous code sample):

```
Dim objEmps As DataTable
Dim objCats As DataTable

objEmps = objDataSet.Tables("Employees")
objCats = objDataSet.Tables("Categories")
```

This is why we name the data when we add it to the `DataSet`, as it allows us to easily reference it when we want it later. The name is also used when mapping tables within the `DataSet` to each other, but we're not going to be looking at this here.

The DataRow Object

In the same way that a `DataSet` can consist of many tables, a `DataTable` can consist of many rows, one for each row of data retrieved from the original data source. Each of these rows is represented by a `DataRow` object and is held within the `Rows` collection:

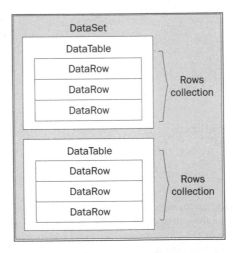

So, the actual data is accessed through the `DataRow`. We could use the following code to extract a single value from the first row:

```
    Dim objTable   As DataTable
    Dim strFirstName As String

    objTable = objDataSet.Tables("Employees")

    strFirstName = objTable.Rows(0).Item("FirstName")
```

Notice that the Rows collection is zero based – so index 0 refers to the first row, index 1 refers to the second row, and so on. The name we pass into the Item collection is the name of the column containing the data we want to extract. If we wanted to extract a single value for another field in the same row, we'd use the following code:

```
    strLastName = objTable.Rows(0).Item("LastName")
```

Let's now look at an example that allows us to modify data within a DataTable.

Try It Out – Adding, Changing and Deleting Rows

We'll be doing this Try It Out in stages, showing you three simple ways to manipulate the data held in a table. You will need to copy the Northwind database into your C:\BegASPNET\ch13 directory for this example.

1. Create a new file called EditingData.aspx (or download it from the sample site), with the following code in it:

```
<%@ Import Namespace="System.Data" %>
<%@ Import Namespace="System.Data.OleDb" %>

<script language="VB" runat="server">

  Sub Page_Load(Sender As Object, E As EventArgs)

    Dim strConnection As String
    Dim strSQL        As String
    Dim objDataSet    As New DataSet()
    Dim objConnection As OleDbConnection
    Dim objAdapter    As OleDbDataAdapter

    strConnection = "Provider=Microsoft.Jet.OLEDB.4.0; " & _
                    "Data Source=C:\BegASPNET\ch13\Northwind.mdb"
    strSQL = "SELECT FirstName, LastName FROM Employees;"

    objConnection = New OledbConnection(strConnection)
    objAdapter = New OledbDataAdapter(strSQL, objConnection)

    objAdapter.Fill(objDataSet, "Employees")

    dgNameList1.DataSource = objDataSet.Tables("Employees").DefaultView
    dgNameList1.DataBind()

    ' --------------------------------------------------------------
    ' Marker 1
```

```
    ' -----------------------------------------------------------
    ' Marker 2

    ' -----------------------------------------------------------
    ' Marker 3

  End Sub

</script>

<html>
 <body>
  <table width="100%">
   <tr>
    <td>Original Data</td>
    <td>Data with new Row</td>
    <td>Data with edited Row</td>
    <td>Data with deleted Row</td>
   </tr>
   <tr>
    <td valign="top"><asp:DataGrid id="dgNameList1" runat="server" /></td>
    <td valign="top"><asp:DataGrid id="dgNameList2" runat="server" /></td>
    <td valign="top"><asp:DataGrid id="dgNameList3" runat="server" /></td>
    <td valign="top"><asp:DataGrid id="dgNameList4" runat="server" /></td>
   </tr>
  </table>
 </body>
</html>
```

The Marker 1, 2, and 3 comments will help us add code as we expand this example.

2. Now browse to the newly created file:

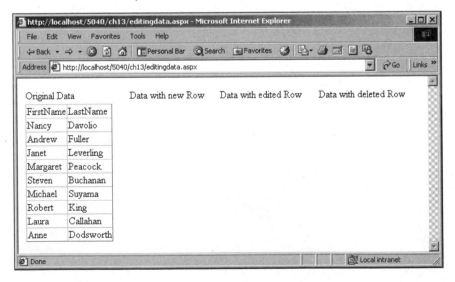

This is no different from some of the examples you saw in the previous chapter, but it's the foundation for showing the changes we'll be making.

3. Now switch back to your editor, and add the following code at Marker 1. This will add a row to the table and display it in another grid:

```
Dim objTable  As DataTable
Dim objNewRow As DataRow

objTable = objDataSet.Tables("Employees")
objNewRow = objTable.NewRow()
objNewRow.Item("FirstName") = "Norman"
objNewRow.Item("LastName") = "Blake"
objTable.Rows.Add(objNewRow)


' bind the data grid to the new data
dgNameList2.DataSource = objTable.DefaultView
dgNameList2.DataBind()
```

4. Back in the browser, hit the **Refresh** button (or *F5*) to see the new page:

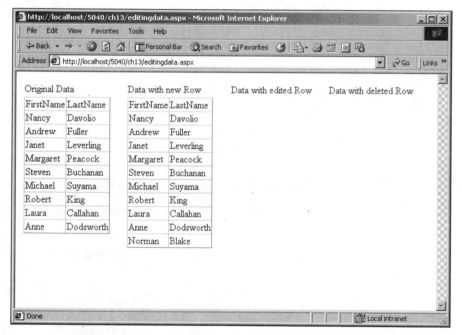

Here you can see than another row has been added to the end of the table.

5. Let's look at editing a row now. Switch back to the code and add the following at Marker 2:

```
Dim objRows() As DataRow

' Find the row to change
objRows = objTable.Select("FirstName='Margaret' AND LastName='Peacock'")
objRows(0).Item("FirstName") = "John"
objRows(0).Item("LastName") = "Hartford"
' bind the data grid to the new data
dgNameList3.DataSource = objTable.DefaultView
dgNameList3.DataBind()
```

6. Back in the browser, hit the **Refresh** button (or *F5*) to see the new page:

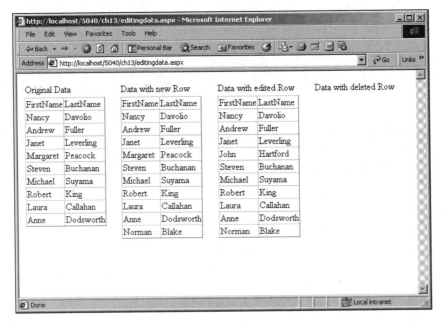

You can see that the row for **Margaret Peacock** has been changed to **John Hartford**.

7. Let's make the last addition to the code, by adding the following at Marker 3:

```
' ---------------------------------------------------------------
' delete a row from the table

' The Rows collection is 0 indexed, so this removes the sixth row
objTable.Rows(5).Delete()

' bind the data grid to the new data
dgNameList4.DataSource = objTable.DefaultView
dgNameList4.DataBind()
```

8. Back in the browser, hit the **Refresh** button (or *F5*) to see the new page:

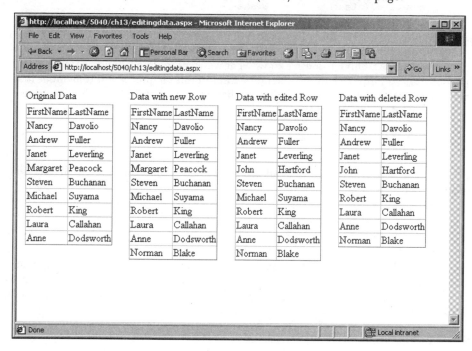

Here you can see that the row for **Michael Suyama** has been deleted, and doesn't appear in the fourth table.

Let's see how all of this code works. We don't need to examine the code that gets the data from the database or binds it to the grid, as it's the same as the code we used in the previous chapter. What we need to concentrate on here, is how we changed the data, and that was done by the code fragments we put in the markers.

How It Works – adding rows

The first section of code adds a new row to the tale. The first thing we do, is to declare two variables – one to point to the `DataTable` containing the data, and one to hold the data for the new row:

```
Dim objTable   As DataTable
Dim objNewRow As DataRow
```

Now we use the table variable to point to the `Employees` table:

```
objTable = objDataSet.Tables("Employees")
```

Next we use the `NewRow()` method of the `DataTable` object to create a new row:

```
objNewRow = objTable.NewRow()
```

At this stage the row is empty, so we need to add some details. The rows in our table only hold first and last name information, but if you have tables with more columns then you can just fill in their values too:

```
objNewRow.Item("FirstName") = "Norman"
objNewRow.Item("LastName") = "Blake"
```

Now that we've filled in the details, we need to add the new row to the existing table. Using the NewRow() method only creates a new row for us, and we have to add it to the table ourselves. This isn't done automatically as ADO.NET doesn't know what we want to do with the new row, so it leaves us to make the choice. If you flip back to the diagram earlier in this chapter you'll remember that each DataTable has a Rows collection. The collection has an Add method, into which we pass the DataRow we want adding to the table:

```
objTable.Rows.Add(objNewRow)
```

Now we have the new row in the table, so all that's left to do is bind the table to the second DataGrid on the page, allowing us to see the results:

```
dgNameList2.DataSource = objTable.DefaultView
dgNameList2.DataBind()
```

One thing to remember is that we are still disconnected from the database. This means that if your database has constraints (such as forcing the first and last names to have values), these constraints won't be enforced when adding the data to the DataSet. It's only when you update the original data store (which we'll see how to do later) that this becomes an issue.

How It Works – editing rows

The first thing we do in this code section is to declare a variable that can hold the rows we want to edit.

```
Dim objRows() As DataRow
```

Notice that this is an array, because the method we use to find selected rows returns an array of DataRow objects.

Next, we use the Select method of the table to find the row we want.

```
objRows = objTable.Select("FirstName='Margaret' AND LastName='Peacock'")
```

The string we pass is the same as a SQL WHERE clause.

Finally, we update the data for the selected row. There could be many rows returned by the Select method, so we index into the array. In our case we know there is only one row returned.

```
objRows(0).Item("FirstName") = "John"
objRows(0).Item("LastName") = "Hartford"
```

It isn't necessary to use the Select method, since you can edit the data directly, but using this method here makes it clear which row we are editing. What you can also do is just index into the Rows collection, using this code:

```
        Dim objRow As DataRow

        objRow = objTable.Rows(3)

        objRow("FirstName") = "John"
        objRow("LastName") = "Hartford"
```

First we declare a variable to hold the row to be edited.

```
        Dim objRow As DataRow
```

Now we can point this variable at the row we are going to edit, by indexing into the `Rows` collection. It's important to note that the `Rows` collection (like other collections) is zero-based, so the following line of code refers to the fourth row:

```
        objRow = objTable.Rows(3)
```

Once the row variable is pointing to the correct row, we can just update the values for the appropriate columns:

```
        objRow("FirstName") = "John"
        objRow("LastName") = "Hartford"
```

Now that the data has been changed, we bind the data to a new grid so we can see the results:

```
        dgNameList3.DataSource = objTable.DefaultView
        dgNameList3.DataBind()
```

Another method of finding rows is to use the `Find` method on the `Rows` collection. This method does require that primary keys are present.

How It Works – deleting rows

Deleting a row from a table is simple, because we just use the `Delete` method of the `DataRow`. In the code below, we index into the `Rows` collection (each member of which is a `DataRow`), specifying the row number as the index. Remember that the `Rows` collection is zero-based, so this removes the sixth row:

```
        objTable.Rows(5).Delete()
```

Once again we bind the data to a new grid:

```
        dgNameList4.DataSource = objTable.DefaultView
        dgNameList4.DataBind()
```

Like the editing code, we could have used the `Select` method of the table to return the rows to delete.

Updating the Original Data Source

You can see from the code shown above how simple changing data is. The one thing you have to remember though, is that we are dealing with disconnected data. The `DataSet` has not retained a connection to the original database, so any changes we have made are only reflected in our `DataSet` (you can easily see this by hitting the Refresh button on the browser – on subsequent refreshes the original data is always the same). Other people using the database will not be able to see those changes.

This situation is one of the big problems of disconnected data, but it's not a problem you have to worry about too much. ADO.NET was designed with disconnected data in mind, and provides simple ways for us to push our data back to the original data store. Part of this mechanism is the `Command` object, which was briefly introduced in the previous chapter. To understand about how the `DataSet` and the original data store are synchronized we need to look at the `Command` objects in more detail. We need to see how we can generate the commands that will perform the update of the data store. There's a lot to get through before we can actually perform this update, but it's not complex. It's important to go through this stage so that you understand exactly what's happening, so bear with me for a while.

The Command Object

In the previous chapter, we used a `Command` object to provide a link between the `Connection` and the `DataAdapter`, allowing SQL commands to be run. To perform many simple actions with ADO.NET you don't need to know much about the command objects, but there are some properties that will be required if you want to customize the update process. These properties are:

Property	Description
Connection	A Connection object containing the details of the connection to the data store.
CommandText	The text of the command to be run.
CommandType	The type of command, such as a SQL string or the name of a stored procedure. This can be one of: Text, to indicate a text string (this is the default). TableDirect, to indicate the name of a table. StoredProcdure, to indicate the name of a stored procedure.
Parameters	A collection of Parameter objects, for use with commands that require parameters to be passed to the data store.

Like some of the other objects in ADO.NET, the command object comes in two flavors:

❑   `OleDbCommand`, for use with OLEDB DataStores.

❑   `SqlCommand`, for use only with SQL Server

A third flavor, for ODBC is also planned, for dealing with ODBC data sources.

In the previous chapter we showed a command being used like this:

```
Dim objCommand as New OleDbCommand(strSQL, objConnection)
```

This created a new `Command` object, passing in a SQL String and a Connection object. This has the effect of setting the `CommandText` property to the SQL string passed in, and the `Connection` property to the Connection object passed in.

The DataAdapter Object

Having explained the `Command` object in a little more detail it's now time to see where this fits into the `DataAdapter`. Let's first look at a line of code we used earlier the chapter:

```
Dim objAdapter As New OledbDataAdapter(strSQL, objConnection)
```

Here we create a new `OleDbDataAdapter`, passing in a SQL string and a `Connection` object, much the same as we did for the `Command` object example. So what's the difference between the Data Command and the Data Adapter? The Command is designed to run a command, and the Adapter is designed to provide a storage space for multiple commands, which provide two-way interaction between the actual data store and the `DataSet`. Firstly, we have to have a command to fetch the data from the data store. Then we need a separate one to update the data, another to insert new data, and finally one to delete data. It's not possible to use the same command because the syntax is different. Remember how in the previous chapter we mentioned the following SQL statements:

❑ SELECT: used to **retrieve** data from a database

❑ DELETE: used to **delete** data from a database

❑ INSERT: used to **insert** data into a database

❑ UPDATE: used to **update** data in a table

To run any of these types of SQL queries we would use a `Command` object, but since there are four possible types of command we need a way to store those multiple commands.

The DataAdapter Command Objects

The `DataAdapter` has four properties that hold `Command` objects for just this purpose – the storing of commands to perform the different types of fetch and update operations to be run against the data store. The diagram below should make this clear:

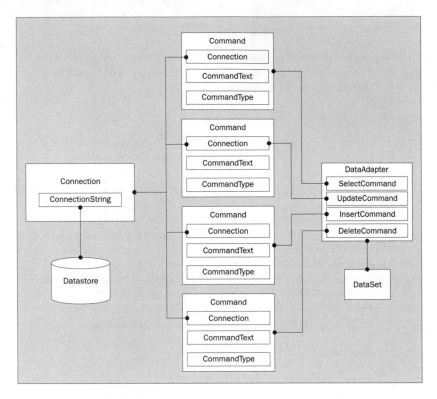

Here you can see four properties of the `DataAdapter`:

Property	Description
`SelectCommand`	The Command used when data is fetched from the data store.
`UpdateCommand`	The Command used when the data store is to be updated.
`InsertCommand`	The Command used when data is to be inserted into the data store.
`DeleteCommand`	The Command used when data is to be deleted from the data store.

Each of these properties is a full `Command` object, and therefore contains the properties of the `Command` object, such as `CommandText` and `CommandType`.

This is important, because it's these `Command` objects that are used whenever data is transferred to and from the data store. The great news is that you don't always have to create these yourself. For example, let's consider the `DataAdapter` line of code again:

```
Dim objAdapter As New OledbDataAdapter(strSQL, objConnection)
```

We didn't explicitly create a `Command` object for this, but the command still worked. Here's what happens:

1. A `Command` object is automatically created for us

2. The command text (`strSQL`) is assigned to the `CommandText` property of the `Command` object

3. The `Connection` object (`objConnection`) is assigned to the `Connection` property of the `Command` object

4. The `CommandType` property of the `Command` object is set to `Text`

5. The `Command` object is assigned to the `SelectCommand` of the `DataAdapter`

So, under the covers ADO.NET is doing a lot of work for us. Where this gets really clever is that the other commands can be generated too.

The CommandBuilder Object

To allow ADO.NET to generate the commands for updates, insertions, and deletions we have to use a `CommandBuilder` object. This object uses details from the `SelectCommand` property to work out what the SQL statements should be for the other commands, and creates a command object for us. It's pretty simple to use, so let's give it a go, and then we'll look at the code in more detail later.

Try It Out – Auto-Generated Commands

1. In your editor, create a new file called `CommandObjects.aspx`, and add the following code:

```
<%@ Import Namespace="System.Data" %>
<%@ Import Namespace="System.Data.OleDb" %>

<script language="VB" runat="server">

  Sub Page_Load(Sender As Object, E As EventArgs)

    Dim strConnection As String
    Dim strSQL        As String
    Dim objDataSet    As New DataSet()
    Dim objConnection As OleDbConnection
    Dim objAdapter    As OleDbDataAdapter
    Dim objCommand    As OleDbCommand
    Dim objBuilder    As OleDbCommandBuilder

    ' set the connection and query details
    strConnection = "Provider=Microsoft.Jet.OLEDB.4.0; " & _
                    "Data Source=C:\BegASPNET\ch13\Northwind.mdb"
    strSQL = "SELECT EmployeeID, FirstName, LastName FROM Employees"

    ' open the connection and set the command
    objConnection = New OledbConnection(strConnection)
    objAdapter = New OledbDataAdapter(strSQL, objConnection)

    ' create the other commands
    objBuilder = New OleDbCommandBuilder(objAdapter)
    objAdapter.UpdateCommand = objBuilder.GetUpdateCommand()
```

445

```
      objAdapter.InsertCommand = objBuilder.GetInsertCommand()
      objAdapter.DeleteCommand = objBuilder.GetDeleteCommand()

      ' now display the CommandText property from each command
      lblSelectCommand.Text = objAdapter.SelectCommand.CommandText
      lblUpdateCommand.Text = objAdapter.UpdateCommand.CommandText
      lblInsertCommand.Text = objAdapter.InsertCommand.CommandText
      lblDeleteCommand.Text = objAdapter.DeleteCommand.CommandText

   End Sub

</script>

<html>
 <body>
  <table border="1">
   <tr>
    <td>Command</td>
    <td>CommandText</td>
   </tr>
   <tr>
    <td>SelectCommand</td>
    <td><asp:Label id="lblSelectCommand" runat="server" />
   </tr>
   <tr>
    <td>UpdateCommand</td>
    <td><asp:Label id="lblUpdateCommand" runat="server" />
   </tr>
   <tr>
    <td>InsertCommand </td>
    <td><asp:Label id="lblInsertCommand" runat="server" />
   </tr>
   <tr>
    <td>DeleteCommand</td>
    <td><asp:Label id="lblDeleteCommand" runat="server" />
   </tr>
  </table>
 </body>
</html>
```

2. Save the file and view it in your browser:

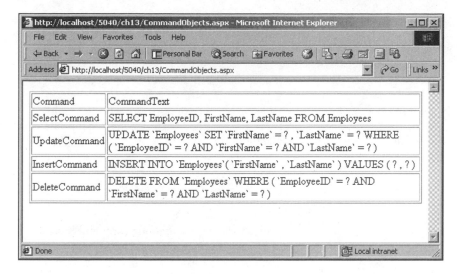

Here you can see that the SQL statements to perform updates, inserts, and deletions have been created for us. Let's see how this works:

How It Works

The first thing, as usual, is the variable declarations. You've seen most of these before, but notice the new one at the end, for the `OleDbCommandBuilder` – it's this object that will build the SQL commands for us:

```
Dim strConnection As String
Dim strSQL        As String
Dim objDataSet    As New DataSet()
Dim objConnection As OleDbConnection
Dim objAdapter    As OleDbDataAdapter
Dim objCommand    As OleDbCommand
Dim objBuilder    As OleDbCommandBuilder
```

Next comes the connection string:

```
strConnection = "Provider=Microsoft.Jet.OLEDB.4.0; " & _
                "Data Source=C:\BegASPNET\ch13\Northwind.mdb"
```

Now the SQL string to select the data. One important thing to notice is that we have now included the `EmployeeID` column. This is a requirement for the `CommandBuilder`, since commands cannot be auto-generated unless a key field is available:

```
strSQL = "SELECT EmployeeID, FirstName, LastName FROM Employees"
```

Now we create the connection and data adapter, the same as we have done previously:

```
objConnection = New OledbConnection(strConnection)
objAdapter = New OledbDataAdapter(strSQL, objConnection)
```

Now comes the clever bit. We create a new `OleDbCommandBuilder` object, and pass into it the `DataAdapter` we are using. This tells the command builder where to get the `SelectCommand`, from which it will build the other commands:

```
objBuilder = New OleDbCommandBuilder(objAdapter)
```

Once the Command Builder has been created we can use the `GetUpdateCommand`, `GetInsertCommand`, and `GetDeleteCommand` methods to build the appropriate commands. These we set to the associated property of the adapter:

```
objAdapter.UpdateCommand = objBuilder.GetUpdateCommand()
objAdapter.InsertCommand = objBuilder.GetInsertCommand()
objAdapter.DeleteCommand = objBuilder.GetDeleteCommand()
```

Now we just display the `CommandText` property of each of the four command objects:

```
lblSelectCommand.Text = objAdapter.SelectCommand.CommandText
lblUpdateCommand.Text = objAdapter.UpdateCommand.CommandText
lblInsertCommand.Text = objAdapter.InsertCommand.CommandText
lblDeleteCommand.Text = objAdapter.DeleteCommand.CommandText
```

Let's look at these statements in a little more detail, just so you can understand what they are doing.

The SelectCommand

This doesn't need much explanation, but it's worth reiterating the point that for the command builder to generate the other commands you need a key field. That's why we've included the `EmployeeID`. It needs this because key fields help us to uniquely identify rows:

```
SELECT EmployeeID, FirstName, LastName FROM Employees
```

The UpdateCommand

The `UpdateCommand` uses the SQL `UPDATE` statement. This comprises three main parts:

❑ The `UPDATE` keyword, which is followed by the table name

❑ The `SET` keyword, which identifies the fields to be updated. It's similar to setting variables, only we use the name of the field and the value it is to be set to. The question marks are placeholders, which ADO.NET automatically replaces with the value to be updated.

❑ The `WHERE` clause, which filters the rowset. This allows us to make sure that the correct row is updated.

```
UPDATE `Employees`
SET `FirstName` = ? , `LastName` = ?
WHERE ( `EmployeeID` = ? AND `FirstName` = ? AND `LastName` = ? )
```

The InsertCommand

The `InsertCommand` uses the SQL `INSERT` statement. This comprises three main parts:

❑ The `INSERT INTO` keywords, which is followed by the table name

❑ The field names to be inserted. These are surrounded by parenthesis

❑ The `VALUES` keyword, followed by the placeholders for the values to be inserted

```
INSERT INTO `Employees`
( `FirstName` , `LastName` )
VALUES ( ? , ? )
```

The DeleteCommand

The `DeleteCommand` uses the SQL `DELETE` statement, which comprises two main parts:

❑ The `DELETE FROM` keywords, followed by the table name

❑ The `WHERE` clause, which filters the rowset. This allows us to make sure that the correct row is deleted

```
DELETE FROM `Employees`
WHERE ( `EmployeeID` = ? AND `FirstName` = ? AND `LastName` = ? )
```

The DataAdapter.Update Method

At this stage, we've been through two examples that show how to change the data within a `DataSet`, and how to generate the commands that will update the data store. What we need to do now is combine the two, and add the command that actually updates the data store with our changes. For this we use the `Update` method of the `DataAdapter`.

Try It Out – Synchronizing the Data Store

1. Create a new file called `Synchronize.aspx`, with the following code. There's quite a bit of code here, so you might prefer to download the sample from the Wrox site. This section fills a DataSet and binds it to a DataGrid:

```vbnet
<%@ Import Namespace="System.Data" %>
<%@ Import Namespace="System.Data.OleDb" %>

<script language="VB" runat="server">

  Sub Page_Load(Sender As Object, E As EventArgs)

    Dim strConnection As String
    Dim strSQL        As String
    Dim objDataSet    As New DataSet()
    Dim objConnection As OleDbConnection
    Dim objAdapter    As OleDbDataAdapter

    ' set the connection and query details
    strConnection = "Provider=Microsoft.Jet.OLEDB.4.0; " & _
                    "Data Source=C:\BegASPNET\ch13\Northwind.mdb"
```

```
strSQL = "SELECT EmployeeID, FirstName, LastName FROM Employees;"

' open the connection and set the command
objConnection = New OledbConnection(strConnection)
objAdapter = New OledbDataAdapter(strSQL, objConnection)

' fill the dataset with the data
objAdapter.Fill(objDataSet, "Employees")

' bind the data grid to the data
dgNameList1.DataSource = objDataSet.Tables("Employees").DefaultView
dgNameList1.DataBind()
```

2. Add the rest of the `<script>` block to synchronize.aspx:

```
' --------------------------------------------------------------
' add a new row to the table
Dim objTable  As DataTable
Dim objNewRow As DataRow

objTable = objDataSet.Tables("Employees")
objNewRow = objTable.NewRow()
objNewRow("FirstName") = "Norman"
objNewRow("LastName") = "Blake"
objTable.Rows.Add(objNewRow)

' add another new row. We'll be deleting the one above later.
' we can't delete existing rows from the database because of
' referential integrity (every employee also has Orders)
objNewRow = objTable.NewRow()
objNewRow("FirstName") = "Kasey"
objNewRow("LastName") = "Chambers"
objTable.Rows.Add(objNewRow)


' bind the data grid to the new data
dgNameList2.DataSource = objTable.DefaultView
dgNameList2.DataBind()


' --------------------------------------------------------------
' edit an existing row in the table
Dim objRow As DataRow

' The Rows collection is 0 indexed, so this changes the fourth row
objRow = objTable.Rows(3)
objRow("FirstName") = "John"
objRow("LastName") = "Hartford"

' bind the data grid to the new data
dgNameList3.DataSource = objTable.DefaultView
dgNameList3.DataBind()
```

```
    ' ----------------------------------------------------------------
    ' delete a row from the table

    ' The Rows collection is 0 indexed, so this removes the sixth row
    objTable.Rows(objTable.Rows.Count - 2).Delete()

    ' bind the data grid to the new data
    dgNameList4.DataSource = objTable.DefaultView
    dgNameList4.DataBind()


    ' ================================================================
    ' generate the update commands
    Dim objBuilder      As OleDbCommandBuilder

    objBuilder = New OleDbCommandBuilder(objAdapter)
    objAdapter.UpdateCommand = objBuilder.GetUpdateCommand()
    objAdapter.InsertCommand = objBuilder.GetInsertCommand()
    objAdapter.DeleteCommand = objBuilder.GetDeleteCommand()


    ' ================================================================
    ' update the data store
    objAdapter.Update(objDataSet, "Employees")


    ' ================================================================
    ' refresh the data in the DataReader and bind it to a new grid
    ' to prove that the data store has been updated

    strSQL = "SELECT EmployeeID, FirstName, LastName FROM Employees"
    objConnection.Open()
    Dim objCmd As New OleDbCommand(strSQL, objConnection)
    dgUpd.DataSource = objCmd.ExecuteReader(CommandBehavior.CloseConnection)
    dgUpd.DataBind()

  End Sub

</script>
```

3. Now finish off `synchronize.aspx` with the `<html>` code:

```
<html>
 <body>
  <table width="100%">
   <tr>
    <td>Original Data</td>
    <td>Data with new Row</td>
    <td>Data with edited Row</td>
    <td>Data with deleted Row</td>
   </tr>
   <tr>
```

```
      <td valign="top"><asp:DataGrid id="dgNameList1" runat="server" /></td>
      <td valign="top"><asp:DataGrid id="dgNameList2" runat="server" /></td>
      <td valign="top"><asp:DataGrid id="dgNameList3" runat="server" /></td>
      <td valign="top"><asp:DataGrid id="dgNameList4" runat="server" /></td>
    </tr>
  </table>

  <hr />

  Data fetched from database after the update:<br/>

  <asp:DataGrid id="dgUpd" runat="server"/>

  </body>
</html>
```

4. Save the code and view the page in your browser:

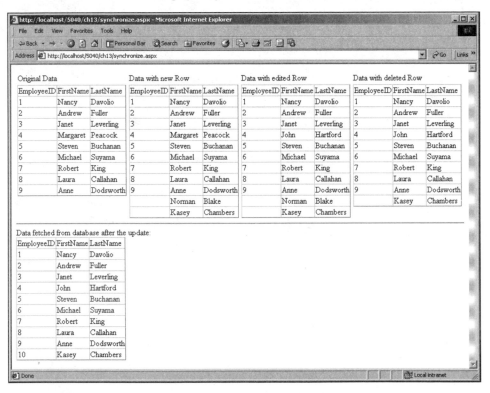

The top half of the screen shows the changes within the DataSet, before these changes are sent back to the data store. This is slightly different from our previous example. For new data we've actually added two rows, which allows us to delete one of them. If we delete any of the existing rows, we'll get an error when we try to update the data store, because the Northwind database has rules to stop certain deletes. One of these is if Employees have any Orders (otherwise if the Employees were deleted, their orders wouldn't have an Employee associated with them). In the Northwind database all employees have orders, therefore we have to add our own row to show deletion.

What you also notice is that there is no number in the `EmployeeID` field for these new rows. This is because this field is an `AutoNumber` field in the database, and it's the database that generates the number. We haven't yet updated the database there's no number; therefore in other words we are looking at our proposed data changes before they are applied.

Once we've done the updates to the `DataSet` we update the database, and the bottom table shows the data retrieved from the database. You can see that the changes we've done are now reflected in the data. The new row now has an `EmployeeID`, and the row we added and then deleted never made it to the database. Let's see how all of this works. If you click the Refresh button on your browser, you'll see the ID for the new record.

How It Works

We don't need to go through all of the code as much if it is the same as the previous examples. Let's first look at the addition of the two rows. The code is the same for adding the second row as it is for the first row – you just use the `NewRow` method of the table to create a new row and then you `Add` it to the `Rows` collection:

```
objTable = objDataSet.Tables("Employees")
objNewRow = objTable.NewRow()
objNewRow("FirstName") = "Norman"
objNewRow("LastName") = "Blake"
objTable.Rows.Add(objNewRow)

objNewRow = objTable.NewRow()
objNewRow("FirstName") = "Kasey"
objNewRow("LastName") = "Chambers"
objTable.Rows.Add(objNewRow)
```

For the deletion we've stated that we can't delete existing rows, so we decide to delete the first new row we added:

```
objTable.Rows(objTable.Rows.Count - 2).Delete()
```

This line of code shows another property of the `Rows` collection – `Count`. This identifies the number of items in the collection – in our case it's the number of rows in the table. We want to delete the second from last one so we subtract two from the count (remember that the collection is zero-based, so the last item is `Count - 1`).

Finally, we can synchronize the database with our changes, using the `Update` method of the `DataAdapter`:

```
objAdapter.Update(objDataSet, "Employees")
```

This method takes two arguments. The first is the `DataSet` that contains the changes to be sent back to the database, and the second is the name of the `DataTable` within the `DataSet` that contains the changes. Remember that a `DataSet` can contain more than one Table, so it's important we get the right one.

Updating Data – Summary

At this stage, we've covered the basics of updating data, so let's just recap a few important points before we continue:

- ❑ The `DataSet` uses disconnected data, so changes are only made to the local `DataSet`.

- ❑ A `DataSet` can contain many `DataTables`, held in the `Tables` collection.

- ❑ Each `DataTable` has a `Rows` Collection containing `DataRow` objects, one for each row in the table.

- ❑ To edit values you just change the fields directly. There is no need to use methods to start and stop editing.

- ❑ To insert rows into the `DataSet` you use the `Add` method of the `Tables` collection. To generate the new row to be added you use `NewRow` method of the `DataTable`.

- ❑ To delete rows from the `DataSet` you use the `Delete` method of the Rows collection.

- ❑ To synchronize the database you must create the `UpdateCommand`, `InsertCommand` and `DeleteCommand` objects. You can do this manually or use the `CommandBuilder` object to do this for you.

- ❑ If you use the `CommandBuilder` object, the `SelectCommand` it uses as a template must contain a key field.

- ❑ You use the `Update` method of the `DataAdapter` to synchronize the `DataSet` and the database.

Let's now take a brief look at using SQL directly.

Using SQL

You've already used SQL directly, to fetch data from a database using the SELECT statement. We're not going to talk about SQL in detail, since that's really outside the scope of this book, but what we need to do is look at how SQL can be used to update databases, either directly, or by the use of stored procedures.

The DataAdapter Commands

In the previous example, we used the `CommandBuilder` to generate `Command` objects and their associated SQL commands. You've seen that this is an extremely easy technique, but what you may not realize is that you can either change what that `CommandBuilder` generates, or even create it yourself.

For example, consider this code:

```
Dim objBuilder     As OleDbCommandBuilder

objBuilder = New OleDbCommandBuilder(objAdapter)
objAdapter.UpdateCommand = objBuilder.GetUpdateCommand()
objAdapter.InsertCommand = objBuilder.GetInsertCommand()
objAdapter.DeleteCommand = objBuilder.GetDeleteCommand()
```

It's the same code we used previously. If you want to change the SQL for a particular command you can do:

```
objAdapter.InsertCommand.CommandText = "INSERT INTO . . ."
```

Or, if you don't want to use the `CommandBuilder`, you can create the `Command` objects directly:

```
Dim objCommand As New OleDbCommand
objCommand.Connection = objConnection
objCommand.CommandText = "INSERT INTO . . ."

objAdapter.InsertCommand = objCommand
```

There's nothing to stop you doing this, although the `CommandBuilder` does save some typing. However since it has to generate the SQL commands however, therefore while the program is running, there's a slight performance hit over manually creating the commands.

Using Stored Procedures

Another option is to use stored procedures instead of SQL statements. A stored procedure is a batch of SQL statements that is stored on the database server and given a name. You can then call this stored procedure just by its name (similar to the way we use subroutines in code), rather than having to retype the SQL. Another advantage is that most databases compile stored procedures, so they are generally more efficient than written SQL statements. In Microsoft Access, the **Query** is equivalent to a stored procedure.

Let's consider the Northwind query called **Sales By Category**. The SQL for this is:

```
SELECT DISTINCTROW Categories.CategoryID, Categories.CategoryName,
                   Products.ProductName,
                   Sum([Order Details Extended].ExtendedPrice) AS ProductSales
FROM Categories INNER JOIN
          (Products INNER JOIN
              (Orders INNER JOIN [Order Details Extended]
                  ON Orders.OrderID = [Order Details Extended].OrderID)
                  ON Products.ProductID = [Order Details Extended].ProductID)
              ON Categories.CategoryID = Products.CategoryID
WHERE (((Orders.OrderDate) Between #1/1/1997# And #12/31/1997#))
GROUP BY Categories.CategoryID, Categories.CategoryName, Products.ProductName
ORDER BY Products.ProductName;
```

Don't worry about the SQL – you don't need to know how it works, just that it's rather complex. Having this in your ASP.NET page not only makes the page harder to read, but it's also not a great design choice. After all, this is SQL, and the database is best at handling SQL so why not store it in the database. This is where stored procedures of queries come in, as they store long and complex SQL statements, allowing us to refer to them just by name. Stored procedures are also more efficient because the database server compiles them, so they are quicker than the equivalent SQL statement being run directly.

To use this stored procedure in place of a normal SQL statement you have to set the `CommandText` and `CommandType` properties. Let's give this a go:

Try It Out – Using Stored Procedures

1. Create a new file called StoredProcedure.aspx, and add the following code:

```
<%@ Import Namespace="System.Data" %>
<%@ Import Namespace="System.Data.OleDb" %>

<script language="VB" runat="server">

  Sub Page_Load(Sender As Object, E As EventArgs)

    Dim objConnection As OleDbConnection
    Dim objCmd        As OleDbCommand
    Dim strConnection As String

    strConnection = "Provider=Microsoft.Jet.OLEDB.4.0;" & _
                    "Data Source=C:\BegASPNET\ch13\Northwind.mdb"


    ' Create and open the connection object
    objConnection = New OleDbConnection(strConnection)
    objConnection.Open()

    ' Create the Command and set its properties
    objCmd = New OleDbCommand()
    objCmd.Connection = objConnection
    objCmd.CommandText = "[Sales by Category]"
    objCmd.CommandType = CommandType.StoredProcedure

    dgSales.DataSource = objCmd.ExecuteReader(CommandBehavior.CloseConnection)
    dgSales.DataBind()

  End Sub

</script>

<html>
  <body>
    <h2>Using a stored procedure</h2>
    <asp:datagrid id="dgSales" runat="server" />
  </body>
</html>
```

2. Now save the changes, and view the file from your browser:

How It Works

Let's just look at the bit of code that's new:

```
objCmd = New OleDbCommand()
objCmd.Connection = objConnection
objCmd.CommandText = "[Sales by Category]"
objCmd.CommandType = CommandType.StoredProcedure
```

Here we create a Command object and then set the properties directly. We use the name of the stored procedure as the CommandText property (putting the square brackets around the name, which Access requires if the name has spaces in it), and setting the CommandType to StoredProcedure. You don't have to do anything else to use stored procedures.

Direct SQL Commands

Using the DataSet is a great way of dealing with disconnected data, but there are times when you don't need it. For example, consider a registration form on a web site to allow you to register for access to the site. This might offer you the chance to add a user name and password. In this case you wouldn't need a DataSet, since all you are doing is adding one row. It makes more sense to run a SQL command directly.

Try It Out – Direct SQL Commands

1. Create a new file called DirectSQL.aspx and add the following code:

```
<%@ Import Namespace="System.Data" %>
<%@ Import Namespace="System.Data.OleDb" %>

<script language="VB" runat="server">
```

```
Sub Page_Load(Sender As Object, E As EventArgs)

    Dim objConnection As OleDbConnection
    Dim objCmd        As OleDbCommand
    Dim strConnection As String
    Dim strSQL        As String

    strConnection = "Provider=Microsoft.Jet.OLEDB.4.0;" & _
                    "Data Source=C:\BegASPNET\ch13\Northwind.mdb"

    ' Create and open the connection object
    objConnection = New OleDbConnection(strConnection)
    objConnection.Open()

    ' set the SQL string
    strSQL = "INSERT INTO `Employees` ( `FirstName` , `LastName` )" & _
                    " VALUES ( 'Beth' , 'Hart' )"

    ' Create the Command and set its properties
    objCmd = New OleDbCommand(strSQL, objConnection)

    ' execute the command
    objCmd.ExecuteNonQuery()

    lblStatus.Text = "Command run"

    End Sub

</script>

<html>
  <body>
    <h2>Using SQL directly</h2>
    <asp:Label id="lblStatus" runat="server"/>
  </body>
</html>
```

2. Now save the changes and open this page from your browser window. All you'll see is some text saying that the command has been run, and the new row has been added. Open the database to prove this:

Let's see exactly what the code does:

How It Works

Some of the code we've already seen before, such as setting the connection details. This is the important bit, starting with the SQL statement. This is a SQL INSERT statement, which inserts a new row into the database (not the DataSet – remember we're not using a DataSet here). We're going to insert the name **Beth Hart** (I just happen to be listening to her CD as I write!):

```
strSQL = "INSERT INTO `Employees` ( `FirstName` , `LastName` )" & _
              " VALUES ( 'Beth' , 'Hart' )"
```

Next, we create the Command object using this SQL string and the Connection object:

```
objCmd = New OleDbCommand(strSQL, objConnection)
```

Finally we use the ExecuteNonQuery method of the Command. This method is designed especially for this type of SQL statement, where no results are returned. We are telling the database directly that we want to add the new row, and that there is no data to return. This saves ADO.NET having to build any objects to hold data:

```
objCmd.ExecuteNonQuery()
```

You can also run UPDATE and DELETE statements this way.

Using SQL – Summary

We've come to the end of our short discussion of using SQL directly. This is a topic which has far more to offer, but is really outside the scope of this book. We've shown that you can use the CommandBuilder object to have the SQL statements generated for you automatically however, so you don't need to learn SQL in depth to use these great ADO.NET features.

If you wish to learn more about SQL then there are plenty of books covering this subject. For example, Wrox Press has a *Beginning SQL* (ISBN *1861001800*) book for just this purpose.

It's now time to turn our eyes to a short look at XML and how it's used within ADO.NET.

XML

We're not going to delve too much into XML here (it was first introduced in Chapter 5), as what we want to cover is the interaction between the ADO.NET objects and XML. Previous incarnations of ADO have allowed some interaction with XML, but it always felt as though it was a feature added on due to public demand. The ADO.NET objects on the other hand have been designed with XML in mind, and you've got the opportunity to deal with XML data as though it came from a database. This means that you don't have to learn the complex ways of handling XML – you can use the methods you've already learnt in this chapter.

Try It Out – Writing out to XML files

In this example we'll extract the Employees from the database and save the details as an XML file.

1. Create a new file called `WritingXML.aspx` and add the following code:

```
<%@ Import Namespace="System.Data" %>
<%@ Import Namespace="System.Data.OleDb" %>

<script language="VB" runat="server">

  Sub Page_Load(Sender As Object, E As EventArgs)

    Dim strConnection As String
    Dim strSQL       As String
    Dim objDataSet    As New DataSet()
    Dim objConnection As OleDbConnection
    Dim objAdapter    As OleDbDataAdapter

    ' set the connection and query details
    strConnection = "Provider=Microsoft.Jet.OLEDB.4.0; " & _
                    "Data Source=C:\BegASPNET\ch13\Northwind.mdb"
    strSQL = "SELECT FirstName, LastName FROM Employees;"

    ' open the connection and set the command
    objConnection = New OledbConnection(strConnection)
    objAdapter = New OledbDataAdapter(strSQL, objConnection)

    ' fill the dataset with the data
    objAdapter.Fill(objDataSet, "Employees")

    objDataSet.WriteXml(Server.MapPath("Employees.xml"))

    Response.Write("XML File Generated")

  End Sub

</script>
```

Notice that there's no HTML in this page – just ASP.NET code.

2. Now save the changes and view the page from your browser. All you'll see is the text stating that the file has been generated.

3. Now have a look in the directory that you have set up as your ASP.NET application and you'll see a file called `Employees.xml`.

4. Double click on this file to view it:

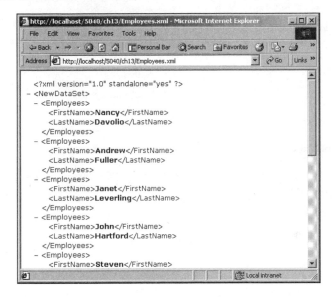

Here you can see that a standard XML file has been produced. Let's see just how easy it is.

How It Works

The only line we need to concern ourselves with here is the one that writes the file. All of the others we've seen several times before:

```
objDataSet.WriteXml(Server.MapPath("Employees.xml"))
```

There are two things to note here. The first is that we use the `WriteXml` method of the `DataSet`, which extracts the information from the `DataSet`, formats it into XML, and writes it to the specified location. The second point is the use of `Server.MapPath`, which produces a file path pointing at the current application directory. This means that the XML file will be written into the directory that is configured as the application root directory. You could easily substitute a fixed path here.

That's all you have to do – just one line of code. Note that there's a corresponding method `WriteXmlSchema` that writes out the XML Schema.

Try It Out – Reading from XML files

Reading from XML files is just as easy as creating them – let's give it a go:

1. Create a new file called `ReadingXML.aspx`, and add the following code:

```
<%@ Import Namespace="System.Data" %>
<%@ Import Namespace="System.Data.OleDb" %>

<script language="VB" runat="server">

  Sub Page_Load(Sender As Object, E As EventArgs)

    Dim objDataSet    As New DataSet()

    objDataSet.ReadXml(Server.MapPath("Employees.xml"))

    dgEmployees.DataSource = objDataSet.Tables(0).DefaultView
    dgEmployees.DataBind()

  End Sub

</script>

<html>
  <body>
  <asp:DataGrid id="dgEmployees" runat="server" />
  </body>
</html>
```

2. Make sure you have viewed the `WritingXML.aspx` file. This ensures that the XML file we want to read in has been created. If you don't do this an error will occur as the file will not be found.

3. Open `ReadingXML.aspx` from your browser:

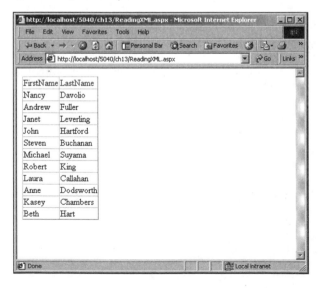

How It Works

There's even less to this code since we're not dealing with a database. First, we define a new `DataSet`, into which we'll put the XML:

```
Dim objDataSet     As New DataSet()
```

Then we use the `ReadXml` method of the `DataSet` to read in the specified XML file. We use `Server.MapPath` again to ensure that the file is picked up from the application directory:

```
objDataSet.ReadXml(Server.MapPath("Employees.xml"))
```

The XML file is well-formed, therefore the `DataSet` can infer the column names when it creates a `DataTable` in the `DataSet`.

Finally, we bind the data to a `DataGrid`. In previous examples we indexed into the Tables collection using the name of the table. That was because we specified the name when we filled the `DataSet`. Here we are not specifying the name however, so we just pick the first entry.

```
dgEmployees.DataSource = objDataSet.Tables(0).DefaultView
dgEmployees.DataBind()
```

Like with `WritingXML`, there is a corresponding `ReadXmlSchema` method to read in an XML Schema. It's important to note that this schema isn't used for validation – it's used purely to infer the structure of the fields created.

XML into Strings

The `DataSet` also has two methods that allow you to extract the XML information into a string. For example:

```
Dim strXML As String
Dim strSchema As String

strXML = objDataSet.GetXml()
strSchema = objDataSet.GetXmlSchema()
```

This allows you to pass the XML data to components that only support XML in string format.

XML in a DataSet

One thing that's important to note is that once you load XML into a `DataSet` you can use any of the examples we have shown earlier in this chapter. A `DataSet` is a `DataSet`, no matter where the data originated. You can modify the data as though it were relational (in other words as though it came from a database), and then save it back to an XML file. The great thing about this is that you only have one set of techniques to learn, which means you can be much more productive. If you are suddenly handed an XML file and told to integrate that into your application, you don't have to learn all of the specifics (and there are lots of them) for handling XML documents. You can just use the `DataSet`.

Try It Out – Editing XML Data

1. Create a new file called `EditingXML.aspx`, and add the following code:

```
<%@ Import Namespace="System.Data" %>
<%@ Import Namespace="System.Data.OleDb" %>

<script language="VB" runat="server">

  Sub Page_Load(Sender As Object, E As EventArgs)

    Dim objDataSet    As New DataSet()

    ' read in the XML file
    objDataSet.ReadXml(Server.MapPath("Employees.xml"))

    ' show it in a grid
    dgEmployees1.DataSource = objDataSet.Tables(0).DefaultView
    dgEmployees1.DataBind()

    ' modify a row
    objDataSet.Tables("Employees").Rows(0).Item("FirstName") = "Bob"
    objDataSet.Tables("Employees").Rows(0).Item("LastName") = "Dylan"

    ' add a new row to the table
    Dim objTable  As DataTable
    Dim objNewRow As DataRow

    objTable = objDataSet.Tables("Employees")
    objNewRow = objTable.NewRow()
    objNewRow.Item("FirstName") = "Norman"
    objNewRow.Item("LastName") = "Blake"
    objTable.Rows.Add(objNewRow)

    ' save it to a new file
    objDataSet.WriteXml(Server.MapPath("Employees2.xml"))

    ' read in the new file
    Dim objDataSet2    As New DataSet()
    objDataSet2.ReadXml(Server.MapPath("Employees2.xml"))

    ' show it in another grid
    dgEmployees2.DataSource = objDataSet2.Tables(0).DefaultView
    dgEmployees2.DataBind()

  End Sub

</script>

<html>
 <body>
  <table>
   <tr>
    <td valign="top"><asp:DataGrid id="dgEmployees1" runat="server" /></td>
```

```
        <td valign="top"><asp:DataGrid id="dgEmployees2" runat="server" /></td>
    </tr>
    </table>
  </body>
</html>
```

2. Save the file, and browse to it in your browser:

Notice that the first row has changed, and that a new row has been added.

How It Works

Let's look at the code for this to see what we've done. First, we create a `DataSet` and load an XML file into it.

```
Dim objDataSet    As New DataSet()

objDataSet.ReadXml(Server.MapPath("Employees.xml"))
```

We use the `Server.MapPath` technique to ensure that the XML file comes from the same location as the Web page.

Now we display the file in a data grid:

```
dgEmployees1.DataSource = objDataSet.Tables(0).DefaultView
dgEmployees1.DataBind()
```

Once displayed in the grid, we start to modify data. First, we edit the first row, changing both columns.

```
objDataSet.Tables("Employees").Rows(0).Item("FirstName") = "Bob"
objDataSet.Tables("Employees").Rows(0).Item("LastName") = "Dylan"
```

Now we add a new row – this is the same technique we used before.

```
Dim objTable  As DataTable
Dim objNewRow As DataRow

objTable = objDataSet.Tables("Employees")
objNewRow = objTable.NewRow()
objNewRow.Item("FirstName") = "Norman"
objNewRow.Item("LastName") = "Blake"
objTable.Rows.Add(objNewRow)
```

Once the data has been changed we save it to a new XML file. We could save it to the same file, but using a different file allows us to compare the two if we want to.

```
objDataSet.WriteXml(Server.MapPath("Employees2.xml"))
```

Finally, we read in the new file and display it in a new grid.

```
Dim objDataSet2     As New DataSet()
objDataSet2.ReadXml(Server.MapPath("Employees2.xml"))

dgEmployees2.DataSource = objDataSet2.Tables(0).DefaultView
dgEmployees2.DataBind()
```

This really reinforces the point that you can use the `DataSet` to manipulate XML files. This method may not be perfect for every XML file, but for many cases it works fine.

What to study next

ADO.NET is a huge topic, and we clearly cannot cover it all here. Luckily, there is plenty of information available on Web Sites and in books. The documentation supplied with the .NET Framework has a great set of samples covering ADO.NET and its use, so make sure you read them. Sure you're a developer, and developers don't do documentation, but believe me it is worth it. The Wrox book *"Professional ASP.NET"* *(ISBN 1-861004-88-5)* also has several chapters devoted to ADO.NET.

In particular, topics that are worth learning more about are:

❑   The SQL Language. Even if you don't use it a great deal it's worth getting a good understanding, as it makes developing data sites far easier. I recommend *Beginning SQL* from Wrox Press (ISBN *1861001800)*.

❑   Data binding and templating, to show how the `DataGrid` control can be customized to provide a better look. There's a section on this in the next chapter.

❑   Concurrency, so you can deal with update errors when you synchronize your `DataSet` with the database.

Summary

This chapter has continued the ADO.NET story, looking into changing data. We've seen that disconnected data raises problems, but that these problems can be overcome. Changing data within a `DataSet` is extremely easy, and synchronizing these changes with the database only requires one line of code. We've also looked at this synchronization process, seeing how there are four commands to manage the changes. You have the opportunity to let ADO.NET manage these commands for you, as well as the ability to customize them using your own SQL statements. This gives you the best of both worlds: the simple approach that's also flexible.

We've also looked at running SQL commands directly, and not using the `DataSet`. It's important to remember that however great the `DataSet` is for handling disconnected data, there are times when it simply isn't required.

Finally, we looked at the simple ways in which XML files can interact with `DataSets`, provide us with a single set of objects for dealing with both relational and XML data.

Now it's time to look at the ASP.NET server controls in detail, to see how they can make the creation of web pages easier, and with a lot less code than we've been used to.

Exercises

1. What do we mean by 'disconnected data' and why is it so important?

2. Load a `DataSet` with the Shippers table from Northwind and add the following data into the `DataSet` using a `DataTable`:

❑ Company Name: FastShippers
❑ Phone: (503) 555-9384

3. Using the `CommandBuilder` object, update the Northwind Shippers table with the new information held in the `DataSet`.

4. Using direct SQL commands, change the phone number of FastShippers to (503) 555-0000 and display the updated table in a `DataGrid`.

    a. Generate a dataset from this XML file, bind it to a `DataGrid` to display it:

```xml
<?xml version="1.0" standalone="yes" ?>
 <NewDataSet>
   <books>
     <bookName>Beginning ASP.NET programming</BookName>
     <ISBN>1861005040</ISBN>
   </books>
   <books>
     <BookName>Professional ASP.NET programming</BookName>
     <ISBN>1861004885</ISBN>
   </books>
   <books>
     <BookName>Beginning VB.NET programming</BookName>
     <ISBN>1861004966</ISBN>
   </books>
 </NewDataSet>
```

    b. Add a new book to this `DataSet`, Beginning C# programming, ISBN 1861004982

    c. Delete the entry for Beginning ASP.NET programming and display the DataSet in a DataGrid.

ASP.NET Server Controls

By now, you should be fairly comfortable with the object-oriented approach used by the .NET Framework to create ASPX pages. You gained some experience (in Chapter 3) of using ASP.NET server controls (also known as web controls). This chapter will continue the discussion of ASP.NET server controls and provide numerous details and samples illustrating their usage. HTML server controls and User controls are not covered in this chapter. Throughout this chapter, the phrase "ASP.NET server controls" will refer to that specific group of controls derived from the `System.Web.UI.WebControls` base class, which includes, for example, `<asp:button>`, `<asp:textbox>`, `<asp:listbox>`, and `<asp:datagrid>`.

ASP.NET server controls are reusable components that can perform the same work as traditional HTML controls, but have the additional benefit of being "programmable objects". In other words, they can be programmatically accessed, just like any other .NET object or class, respond to events, get/set properties, and do all the other things objects do.

ASP.NET server controls use a tag-like syntax for declaring the various controls used on a web page – for example:

```
<asp:button id="SampleButton" runat="server" text="I'm A Sample Button!"/>
```

One of the unique qualities of ASP.NET server controls is that, even though their tag syntax is different from HTML's, every ASP.NET server control is rendered to standard HTML after being processed on the server, thus abstracting the functionality of the entire HTML control set. Additional ASP.NET server controls, provide the ability to render rich web content – for example, a `Calendar` control for displaying dates, a `DataGrid` control for displaying data, as well as other controls, which we will explore throughout this chapter.

Here's a summary of the topics we will cover in this chapter:

❑ A review of the syntax and benefits of ASP.NET server controls

❑ A brief recap of the `System.Web.UI.Page` lifecycle

❑ Using a variety of ASP.NET server controls on a web form.

❑ Using validation controls – you'll learn some techniques for validating user input in a web form

❑ Introducing data rendering controls – a brief introduction to this very powerful group of controls for displaying data

❑ Presenting a complete application that allows you to incorporate your own schedule of events within the context of an ASP.NET calendar control

In the past, the way we would create a web page might vary, but it would almost always involve the embedding of various HTML tags in our pages – perhaps some client-side scripting to handle event processing, or validate form input, and some text to make up the overall content of the page. Additionally, the advanced developer would often be required to write pages in a manner that supported a variety of browser types and capabilities, thus mixing in special-case code, and even client-side validation, which added an additional layer of development complexity that was often difficult to maintain.

In this chapter, we're going explore ASP.NET server controls in detail – specifically, what they are, how to create them, and how to programmatically manipulate them within ASP.NET web forms (ASPX files). We will explore the various types of ASP.NET server controls, which can be broken down into four broad categories:

❑ **Intrinsic controls** – these controls correspond to their HTML counterparts, or simulate one if none exists. Examples include the Button, ListBox, and TextBox controls.

❑ **Data-centric controls** – controls used for binding and displaying data from a data source, such as the DataGrid control.

❑ **Rich controls** – these controls have no direct HTML counterparts. Rich controls, like the Calendar control, are made up of multiple components, and the HTML generated will typically consist of numerous HTML tags (as well as client-side script), to render the control in the browser.

❑ **Validation controls** – like, for example, the RequiredFieldValidator, which can be used to ensure proper data input within a web form.

By the end of this chapter, you will be able to create your own web forms that utilize a variety of the ASP.NET server controls available. You will be exposed to the variety of ASP.NET control properties available to you as a web developer, which can be used to tailor the look or functionality of the various controls. You will also learn to write event handlers for the various events raised by ASP.NET server controls.

Other Types Of Controls

The thrust of this chapter is primarily to describe and demonstrate the various aspects of ASP.NET server controls. There are, however, two additional types of controls that you should be aware of:

❑ HTML Server Controls

❑ User Controls

HTML Server Controls

HTML server controls correspond directly to various HTML tags, and are defined within the `System.Web.UI.HtmlControls` namespace. These controls derive their functionality from the `System.Web.UI.HtmlControls.HtmlControl` base class. Microsoft provides this suite of HTML server controls for a couple of reasons:

❑ Some web developers may prefer to work with the HTML-style of control that they're used to

❑ Developers can convert existing HTML tags to HTML server controls fairly easily, and thus gain some server-side programmatic access to the control

The following HTML tag declaration is, believe it or not, a fully qualified HTML server control that can be accessed programmatically on the server within your web form's code:

```
<INPUT id="MyHTMLTextBox" type="text" name="MyHTMLTextBox" runat="server">
```

What makes this a programmable HTML server control? Simply the reference to `runat="server`. In this example, using `runat="server"` ensures that the .NET Framework will convert the HTML tag into a corresponding `HtmlInputText` object (there is an HTML server control object for every corresponding HTML tag). We also add `id="MyHTMLTextBox"`, to provide a unique name of the object so that we can reference it in our server-side code.

Like ASP.NET server controls, HTML server controls offer a variety of features, which include:

❑ **Programmatic Object Model** – you can access HTML server controls programmatically on the server using all the familiar object oriented techniques. Each HTML server control is an object and, as such, you can access its various properties and get/set them programmatically.

❑ **Event Processing** – HTML server controls provide a mechanism to write event handlers in much the same way you would for a client-based form. The only difference is that the event is handled in the server code.

❑ **Automatic Value Caching** – when form data is posted to the server, the values that the user entered into the HTML server controls are automatically maintained when the page is sent back to the browser.

❑ **Data Binding** – it's possible to bind data to one or more properties of an HTML server control.

❑ **Custom Attributes** – You can add any attributes you need to an HTML server control. The .NET Framework will render them to the client browser without any changes. This enables you to add browser-specific attributes to your controls.

❑ **Validation** – you can actually assign an ASP.NET validation control to do the work of validating an HTML server control. Validation controls are covered in detail later in this chapter.

One reason you might consider using HTML server controls in your own web form pages, is to leverage an existing HTML page's HTML tag or code base. For example, let's say you have an existing HMTL page that you would rather not re-write from scratch, but still would like to write some server-side code to access various properties of the various controls on the page. Converting an existing HTML page's controls to HTML server controls is simple: you just add the `runat="server"` attribute within the tag declaration of the HTML control. You might also need to add an `id="MyControl"` reference, where "MyControl" is your unique naming identifier for this object so that you can reference the object in your server-side code.

HTML Server Controls vs. ASP.NET Server Controls

Given that Microsoft has provided two distinct categories of server controls (HTML and ASP.NET server controls), with both sets of controls sharing some degree of overlapping functionality, you may be a bit confused as to which set of controls you should use within your web forms. The short answer is simply this: **you can use both**! It's perfectly okay to mix the usage of HTML server controls and ASP.NET server controls within your web forms – using one set of controls does not restrict you to that control type. Depending on your preferences and web page requirements, there may, however, be reasons to choose one set over the other. Despite the overlap in functionality, there are some clear distinctions between these controls that you should be aware of when developing your ASP.NET web form pages (we'll be covering the ASP.NET behaviors listed below throughout this chapter):

Control Feature	HTML Server Control Behavior	ASP.NET Server Control Behavior
Control Abstraction	HTML server controls provide a one-to-one mapping with a corresponding HTML tag and offer no real abstraction.	ASP.NET server controls, on the other hand, offer a high level of abstraction – in other words, they don't necessarily map to any existing HTML control. For example, an ASP.NET Calendar server control has no single HTML control equivalent – it's actually made up from a collection of several controls. As such, you will often hear the phrase "rich control" associated with many ASP.NET server controls, since their functionality is typically the result of a combination of several other controls.
Object Model	HTML server controls utilize a very HTML-centric object model. Additionally, the HTML attribute convention is not strongly typed.	ASP.NET server controls provide a consistent and type-safe programming model. All ASP.NET server controls inherit a set of base properties and methods (such as `ForeColor`, `BackColor`, `Font`, and so on)
Target Browser	HTML server controls do not automatically detect the capabilities of the browser loading the page. It's up to the you to make sure the HTML controls you use are compatible with the browsers that might be consuming your page!	ASP.NET server controls automatically detect the client browser requesting the page and render the controls based the browser's capabilities.

Control Feature	HTML Server Control Behavior	ASP.NET Server Control Behavior
How The Control Renders	HTML server controls provide you with complete control over what gets rendered and sent to the client browser. This is primarily due to the fact that however you declare the HTML control is how it will render. The only exception to this is the associated client-side script that gets automatically generated.	ASP.NET server controls provide a higher level of abstraction in terms of how the controls are rendered. In other words, when you use ASP.NET server controls, you leave the details of rendering up to the object. Naturally, the properties you choose to set for the control may play a roll in controlling how and what is actually rendered. But the bottom line here is that you don't have as much control over the rendered output. Most developers will conclude, however, that the delegation of the messy rendering details is a welcome relief!

User Controls

User controls, as you might guess, are controls that you write yourself. You create these controls with any text editor, or with the assistance of an IDE like Visual Studio.NET. A user control can consist of text, HTML tags, HTML server controls, and ASP.NET server controls, along with any additional server-side code to handle events and perform server-side processing. The purpose of a user control is to provide the ability to reuse common user interface functionality across your ASP.NET web applications. For example, consider a typical logon page. You might have one textbox control for the logon name, another for the password, and a button control to submit the form logon data to the server. You might additionally have some validation controls to validate the user's input, and various server-side code to perform the actual logon authentication. If this was a common set of functionality that was going to be used by several pages in your web application, you might consider creating a user control to facilitate this functionality so that you only need write it once. You can think of a user control as being very similar to an ASP.NET web form. However, unlike a web form, a user control must always be included into an existing web form in order to work. A user control cannot load independently from a web form. User controls are covered in more detail in Chapter 13.

Now let's get into the substance of this chapter – ASP.NET Server Controls.

ASP.NET Server Controls

ASP.NET server controls serve as the building blocks for creating ASP.NET web forms. Like their HTML counterparts, ASP.NET server controls provide all the basic controls necessary for building web forms (`Button`, `ListBox`, `CheckBox`, `TextBox`, et al.), as well as a collection of rich controls (controls with several functions – we'll look at them later on), like the `Calendar` and `DataGrid` controls. The various control families are categorized and discussed later in this section, along with many mini-examples to demonstrate syntax and other features. At this point though, you might be wondering what benefits there are, if any, to using ASP.NET server controls instead of standard HTML controls. Here's a listing of some of the benefits ASP.NET server controls offer us:

- ❑ Rich Object Model
- ❑ Automatic Browser Detection
- ❑ Properties
- ❑ Events

Rich Object Model

ASP.NET server controls draw from the rich features of the .NET Framework. As such, each of the ASP.NET controls inherits base methods, properties and events from the `System.Web.UI.WebControls` base class. As you may recall from previous chapters, inheritance is a key feature of object oriented design and programming. When instantiating an ASP.NET server control, you're really creating an instance of an object that gives you access to the properties, methods, and events of its base class.

Automatic Browser Detection

ASP.NET server controls detect client browser capabilities, and create the appropriate HTML and client-side script for the client browser. In other words, ASP.NET pages, and the controls within them, are compiled and "served up," meaning they're not merely static text files. For example, consider the following ASP.NET button control declaration:

```
<asp:Button id="SampleButton" runat="server" Text="My Button"/>
```

When this control is processed on the server, the resultant HTML generated for both Netscape and Internet Explorer will be pretty much the same:

```
<input type="submit" name="SampleButton" value="My Button" id="SampleButton" />
```

Depending on the type of browser and its limitations and capabilities, as well as the type of ASP.NET control being rendered, however, there may in fact be a difference in the HTML generated. In the case of a simple button control, the significance is not immediately apparent – just about any browser today will be able to render a standard button. The benefits for the developer are substantial once **events**, **properties** and **validation** come into play, however, as these are all factors which affect how the ASP.NET control is generated for the client browser. The bottom line here is that the HTML/script rendered for the different browsers (IE, Netscape, Opera) is all handled by the ASP.NET server control and, by and large, the developer is freed from having to worry too much about client browser capabilities and/or limitations.

Properties

All ASP.NET controls share a common set of base properties, as well as their own class-specific properties. These properties allow you to change the look and even the behavior of the control. Throughout this chapter, you will be exposed to a variety of properties for the various ASP.NET server controls. Some of the more common base class properties shared by all ASP.NET server controls include:

❑ BackColor – the background color of the control. The possible values for all color properties can be ascertained by referencing the .NET Framework's Color structure properties in the SDK Documentation (or by using ILDasm or the class browser sample). For example, AliceBlue, AntiqueWhite, or even a hexadecimal value like #C8C8C8.

❑ ForeColor – the foreground color of the control.

❑ BorderWidth – the width of the border of the control, in pixels.

❑ Visible – if set to True (the default for all controls) the control will be displayed. If set to False, the control will be hidden. This property is useful for when you want to hide a particular control on the web form. For example, if you were obtaining details from a user, and in one box, they had declared their nationality as English, then you might want to hide another box that asks them for their Social Security Number.

❑ Enabled – whether on not the control is enabled. If set to False, the control will appear grayed out, and will not process or respond to events until its Enabled property is set to True.

❑ Height – the height of the control in pixels.

❑ Width – the width of the control in pixels.

❑ ToolTip – hover text displayed dynamically on mouse roll-over. Typically, used to supply additional help without taking up space on the form.

❑ Font-Size – the size of the control's font.

The above properties are merely an abbreviated listing; many more common properties are available. To see these, have a look at the SDK Documentation. An important thing to note is that not all browsers support all the possible property settings. You needn't worry too much about this however, because, when ASP.NET server controls are rendered, the output generated for the target browser will generally be suitable for that browser, whatever its capabilities or limitations are.

The following is an example of an ASP.NET Button server control with several of the common base class properties assigned, to give the it a rather distinctive look:

```
<asp:Button id="MyButton" runat="server" Text="I'm an ASP.NET server control
Button!"
  BackColor="purple"
  ForeColor="white"
  BorderWidth="4"
  BorderStyle="Ridge"
  ToolTip="Common Properties Example!"
  Font-Name="Tahoma"
  Font-Size="16"
  Font-Bold="True"
/>
```

When rendered and displayed in the client browser, this ASP.NET Button server control will look something like this:

I'm an ASP.NET server control Button!

The HTML generated for this control (for Internet Explorer 6.0) looks like this:

```
<input type="submit" name="MyButton" value="I'm an ASP.NET server control Button!"
id="MyButton" title="Common Properties Example!" style="color:White;background-
color:Purple;border-width:4px;border-style:Ridge;font-family:Tahoma;font-
size:16pt;font-weight:bold;" />
```

Have a go yourself – to look at the HTML, just select View > Source.

Events

ASP.NET server controls support the ability to assign event handlers in order to execute programmatic logic in response to whatever events a given ASP.NET server control may raise. As we saw in Chapter 3, an event handler is essentially the code you write to respond to a particular event. For example, a Button control raises an OnClick event after being clicked; a ListBox control raises an OnSelectedIndexChanged event when its list selection changes; a TextBox control raises an OnTextChanged event whenever its text changes, and so on.

Events and event handlers are extremely useful to us as web developers, because they provide a mechanism for responding dynamically to events in our forms, in that we can write our own event handlers to perform any special logic or processing that the form or control calls for. For example, let's say we were asked to write a page that contained a button that listed the current date and time to the latest second. For demonstration purposes, when the user clicks on the button, we would like the date and time to be displayed as the button's new text.

Try It Out – Creating an event handler

1. The first step would be to declare the ASP.NET button control. To do this, type the following text into our code editor:

```
<form id=SampleEvent method=post runat="server">
  <asp:Button id="CurrentTimeButton" runat="server"
      Text="Click for current time..." OnClick="UpdateTime" />
</form>
```

2. Save this file as eventhandler.aspx.

If you run this code in your browser right now, you'll see the following error message:

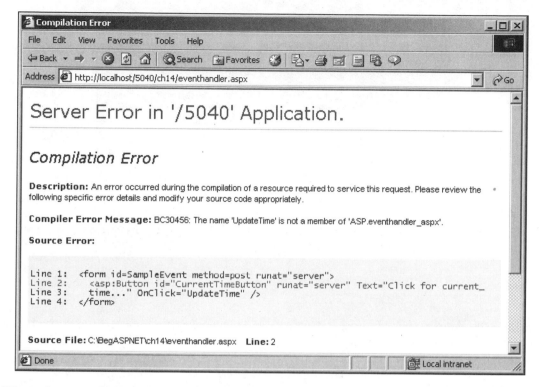

We get this error, because we have not yet defined our UpdateTime event handler. Let's do this now.

3. Open up eventhandler.aspx, and amend the code by adding the following opening section:

```
<script language="VB" runat="server">
  Public Sub UpdateTime (ByVal sender As Object, ByVal e As system.EventArgs)
    ' Perform custom logic here - update the button text with current time
    CurrentTimeButton.Text = DateTime.Now.ToShortTimeString()
  End Sub
</script>

<form id=SampleEvent method=post runat="server">
  <asp:Button id="CurrentTimeButton" runat="server"
      Text="Click for current time..." OnClick="UpdateTime" />
</form>
```

To find out all the properties, methods and events pertaining to the controls such as the ASP.NET
Button control, take a look at the class browser.

4. Now if you run the code in your browser, you'll see the button we created, and when you click on it, you'll see the current time:

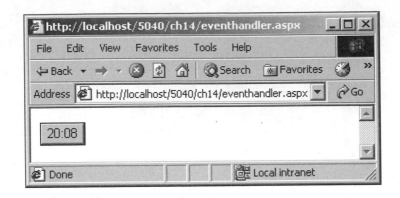

How It Works

In this example, a CurrentTimeButton server control is declared, and its corresponding Text property is set to "Click for current time...":

```
<asp:Button id="CurrentTimeButton" runat="server"
    Text="Click for current time..." OnClick="UpdateTime" />
```

Additionally, we've assigned the name of our custom event handler, UpdateTime, to the OnClick event method for this button control.

The OnClick event method for the Button control is essentially a placeholder, which can be assigned the name of a method (which we write, and in this case is UpdateTime) to perform the processing when that particular event is raised. The method name we assign to the OnClick handler must conform to the required "method syntax" (same number or arguments, same types, same return value) defined by the event method.

We then defined our custom UpdateTime event handler to update the button text with the current time as follows:

```
Public Sub UpdateTime (ByVal sender As Object, _
                       ByVal e As system.EventArgs)
    ' Perform custom logic here – update the button text with current time
   CurrentTimeButton.Text = DateTime.Now.ToShortTimeString()
   End Sub
```

All we are doing here is firstly establishing the UpdateTime subroutine, and then assigning to the Text property of our CurrentTimeButton, the values DateTime.Now.ToShortTimeString(). This is basically saying, "when the UpdateTime sub routine is triggered, display the current time in the text property of CurrentTimeButton, which is a string data type".

Page Lifecycle

Although this topic is covered elsewhere in this book, it's worthwhile to review the
`System.Web.UI.Page` object's lifecycle, in the context of ASP.NET server controls. Specifically, we
will briefly review how the ASP.NET `Page` class loads, processes events, and closes down. When
designing a web form, you are really referencing the base functionality of the ASP.NET `Page` class. As
such, the `Page` class offers its own methods, properties, and events to the form. When loading a web
form for the first time, you might, for example, want to preload the `Page` object's server controls with
values from a database, or set property values to various server controls on the page dynamically. The
following listings provide an overview of the various methods that are commonly overridden in your
ASPX `Page` object implementation, that allow you to perform processing during the various stages of
the `Page` object's lifetime.

Page_Load

The `Page_Load` method is a virtual method (recall that a virtual method of an object is one which you
can override) of the `Page` class, which means it can be (and often is) overridden in the `Page` class
implementation. The `Page_Load` method is invoked when the ASPX page is loaded for the first time,
or refreshed. The following is an example implementation of the `Page_Load` method:

```
Sub Page_Load(ByVal Sender As System.Object, ByVal e As System.EventArgs)
    If Not Page.IsPostback Then
        ' First time page loads –
        ' perform initialization here!
    End If
End Sub
```

The most interesting part of the above listing is the reference to the `Page` class's `IsPostback` property.
The `IsPostback` property is significant because this property can be used to distinguish whether or
not a page is being loaded for the very first time, or if it's being loaded as the result of what is
commonly referred to as a "Postback" – in other words, if a `Button` server control was clicked, an
`OnClick` event would be raised and the form data would be posted back to the server – hence the term
Postback. We have seen this method several times in the past few chapters

The most common uses for implementing the `Page_Load` method in your ASPX pages are to:

❑ check whether this is the first time the page is being processed, or to perform processing after
being refreshed

❑ perform data binding the first time the page is processed, or re-evaluate data binding
expressions on subsequent round trips, to display the data sorted differently, for example.

❑ Read and update control properties.

Event Handling

The second part of a page's lifecycle, is the event handling stage. After an ASPX page is loaded and
displayed, additional event handlers will be invoked when control events are raised. For example, after
a user clicks an ASP.NET `Button` control, the `OnClick` event will be raised, thus posting the event to
the server. If an event handler is written and assigned to process the `OnClick` event for that particular
control, it will be invoked whenever the `Button` control is clicked.

Not all controls perform this type of automatic "posting back" to the server when an event is raised. For example, the TextBox control does not, by default, post back notification to the server when its text changes. Similarly, the ListBox and CheckBox server controls do not, by default, post back event notifications to the server every time their selection state changes. For these particular controls, their AutoPostBack property (which can be set to either True or False) would need to explicitly be set to True in the control's declaration (or set programmatically within the code) to enable automatic post back of event/state changes to the server for processing.

If you create an ASP.NET server control that performs server-side processing whenever the control's state changes (like when a CheckBox is checked), and you don't seem to be getting the results you expect, check if the control has an AutoPostBack property, and if so, set it to True. This property typically defaults to False if not explicitly declared when the control was defined. We'll take a closer look at the AutoPostBack property in action in the Try It Out section that follows.

Page_Unload

Page_Unload serves the opposite purpose of the Page_Load method. The Page_Unload method is used to perform any cleanup just prior to the page being unloaded. It is a virtual method of the Page class, which can be implemented. You would want to implement the Page_Unload method in cases where any of the following actions needed to be performed:

❑   Closing files

❑   Closing database connections

❑   Any other cleanup or discarding of server-side objects and/or resources

The following is an example implementation of the Page_Unload method:

```
Sub Page_Unload(ByVal Sender As System.Object, ByVal e As System.EventArgs)
    ' Perform any cleanup here!
End Sub
```

One thing to note is that the unloading of a page doesn't happen when you close the browser or move to another page. The Page_Unload event happens when the page has finished being processed by ASP.NET, and before it's sent to the browser.

Try It Out – "Oh To Travel, Travel, Travel"

Okay, let's get right into this, and do something neat with ASP.NET server controls. In this section, we'll put together a single web form, travel.aspx, that allows us to book a flight from New York to London with only a couple clicks of the mouse! Okay, so it will only be a demo – we won't actually "book" anything (sigh). We will, however, get some experience building a web form that uses a variety of ASP.NET server controls.

1.   Open your code editor and add the following starter lines to layout the Framework for this ASPX page, and save it as travel.aspx:

```
<%@ Page Language="VB" %>
<%@ Import Namespace="System.Drawing" %>
```

```
      <script language="VB" runat="server">

      </script>

<html>
<head></head>
  <body>
    <h1>Travel: New York to London</h1>
      <form id="TravelForm" method="post" runat="server">

        <!-- Flight Info -->

        <!-- BOOK IT BUTTON SECTION & FEEDBACK -->

      </form>
  </body>
</html>
```

We'll be referencing the .NET Framework's Color structure in our code, therefore we needed to add an Import directive referencing the System.Drawing namespace at the top of this page. The remainder of the code consists of the <script></script> tag sections (where we will insert our code for this page), and the two HTML tags to setup our page.

2. In this step, we're going to add some flight date boxes to the page. We're using the ASP.NET panel control to serve as our container for the various controls on our simulated tab. The panel control is a visual tool to display a box, within which other controls can be rendered. Add the following lines:

```
<!-- Flight Info -->
<asp:panel id="Panel" runat="server" Width="504px" Height="89px"
          BackColor="Wheat">
Departure Date:
<asp:TextBox id="flightDepartureDateTextBox" runat="server"
            Width="80px" Height="22px"/>
Return Date:
<asp:TextBox id="flightReturnDateTextBox" runat="server"
            Width="80px" Height="22px"/></br>

<asp:RequiredFieldValidator id="validateFlightDepartureDate" runat="server"
     ErrorMessage="Please enter a valid Departure Date.  "
     ControlToValidate="flightDepartureDateTextBox" />
<asp:RequiredFieldValidator id="validateFlightReturnDate" runat="server"
     ErrorMessage="Please enter a valid Return Date."
     ControlToValidate="flightReturnDateTextBox" />
<asp:CustomValidator id="validateFlightDates" runat="server"
     ControlToValidate="flightDepartureDateTextBox"
     OnServerValidate="ValidateTravelData" />

</asp:panel>
```

Note here that we added three validation controls: two `RequiredFieldValidator` controls, and a `CustomValidator` control. These controls will serve to force the user to enter a value into the `Departure Date` and `Return Date` `TextBox` controls. The `CustomValidator` control will raise an `OnServerValidate` event, and call our `ValidateTravelData` method, which will perform the work of validating that the date entries make sense logically (for example, the departure date can't be later than the return date). The `RequiredFieldValidator` control ensures that something is entered into the field, so the user can't skip an entry.

3. The next control we'll add to this form is the `bookTheTripButton`, which will serve to post the form data to the server, and the `feedbackLabel` label control will serve to provide instructions, and offer feedback in the event of an invalid data entry. Add the following lines:

```
<!-- BOOK IT BUTTON SECTION & FEEDBACK -->
<p>
<asp:Button id="bookTheTripButton" runat="server" Text="Book This Trip"
        OnClick="bookTheTripButton_Click" />
</p>

<p>
<asp:Label id="feedbackLabel" runat="server" BackColor="Wheat" Font-Bold="True"
        Text="Select your options, then click the 'Book This Trip' button!" />
</p>
```

4. Recall from step 2 that we added two `RequiredFieldValidator` controls and the `CustomValidator` control. In this section, we'll write the event handler for the `OnServerValidate` event, the `ValidateTravelData` method, to validate our dates and their logic. Add the following lines between the script tags:

```
<script language="VB" runat="server">
Protected Sub ValidateTravelData (source As Object, _
                    args As System.Web.UI.WebControls.ServerValidateEventArgs)

    ' Since we have a bit to validate
    ' assume that the entry is invalid....
    args.IsValid = False

    Dim departDate, returnDate As Date
    feedbackLabel.ForeColor = Color.Red

    Try
        departDate = Date.Parse(flightDepartureDateTextBox.Text)
    Catch ex As Exception
        feedbackLabel.Text = "Invalid data entry: Departure Date is invalid.  " _
                        + "Enter a valid date, for example:  2001/07/04"
        Return
    End Try

    Try
        returnDate = Date.Parse(flightReturnDateTextBox.Text)
    Catch ex As Exception
        feedbackLabel.Text = "Invalid data entry: Return Date is invalid.  " _
                        + "Enter a valid date, for example:  2001/07/04"
        Return
```

```
        End Try

        ' Verify that the departure date is less than the
        ' return date - no same day trips in this system!
        If (departDate >= returnDate) Then
            feedbackLabel.Text = "Invalid data entry: The Departure Date must be " _
                                + "earlier than the Return Date and no same-day " _
                                + "returns for this travel package!"
            Return
        End If

        ' Verify that the departure date is not in the past or today!
        If (departDate < Date.Now) Then
            feedbackLabel.Text = "Invalid data entry:  The Departure Date cannot " _
                                + "be in the past or today!"
            Return
        End If

        ' Everthing is valid - set the IsValid flag...
        args.IsValid = True

    End Sub
```

```
</script>
```

5. The final step in this `travel.aspx` example, is to write an event handler for the `bookTheTripButton`'s `OnClick` event. Add the following lines to your <script> block, after the lines we just added:

```
<script language="VB" runat="server">
...
```

```
Private Sub bookTheTripButton_Click(ByVal sender As System.Object, _
                                    ByVal e As System.EventArgs)

    ' Has the page been validated for all data entry?
    If (Not Page.IsValid) Then
        Return
    End if

    ' We're all set - book the flight!
    Dim departDate, returnDate As Date
    departDate = Date.Parse(flightDepartureDateTextBox.Text)
    returnDate = Date.Parse(flightReturnDateTextBox.Text)

    feedbackLabel.ForeColor = Color.Black
    feedbackLabel.Text = "Success!  Your trip from New York to London " _
                        + "will depart on the " _
                        + departDate.ToLongDateString() _
                        + " and return on the " _
                        + returnDate.ToLongDateString()

End Sub
```

```
</script>
```

How It Works – travel.aspx

If you load `travel.aspx` in your browser, you should see something like the following page:

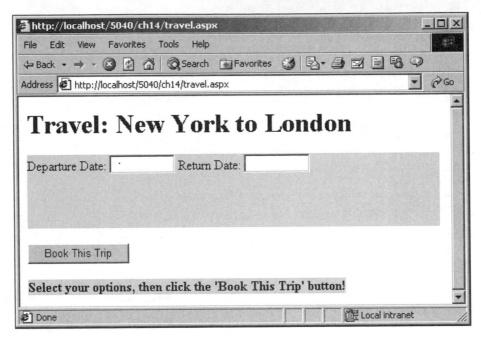

In the `<!-- Flight Info -->` section of `travel.aspx`, we begin by creating the `panel`, in which we will contain our text boxes, and set its colour, width and height (in pixels). We then create our `Departure Date`, and `Return Date` text boxes, again specifying their size.

```
<asp:panel id="Panel" runat="server" Width="504px" Height="89px"
BackColor="Wheat">
Departure Date:
<asp:TextBox id="flightDepartureDateTextBox" runat="server"
            Width="80px" Height="22px"/>
Return Date:
<asp:TextBox id="flightReturnDateTextBox" runat="server"
            Width="80px" Height="22px"/></br>
```

Then we go on to validate the **Departure Date** and **Return Date** `TextBox` entries. After we established our `RequiredFieldValidator` controls, we added a `CustomValidator` control to our page – the event handler we assigned to the `OnServerValidate` event property was `ValidateTravelData`:

```
<asp:CustomValidator id="validateFlightDates" runat="server"
                    ControlToValidate="flightDepartureDateTextBox"
                    OnServerValidate="ValidateTravelData" />
```

This method is invoked when the form is posted back to the server. In this example, we're concerned about the data entries in the **Departure Date** and **Return Date** `TextBox` controls. We already know that the user entered something – the `RequiredFieldValidator` controls handled that task. We still don't know if the dates the user entered were valid however, – this will be the work of our `CustomValidator` method handler, `ValidateTravelData`. Let's review the pertinent sections from step 4:

```
Protected Sub ValidateTravelData (source As Object, _
                    args As System.Web.UI.WebControls.ServerValidateEventArgs)

    ' Since we have a bit to validate
    ' assume that the entry is invalid....
    args.IsValid = False

    Dim departDate, returnDate As Date
    feedbackLabel.ForeColor = Color.Red

    Try
        departDate = Date.Parse(flightDepartureDateTextBox.Text)
    Catch ex As Exception
        feedbackLabel.Text = "Invalid data entry: Departure Date is invalid.  " _
                    + "Enter a valid date, for example:  2001/07/04"
        Return
    End Try

    Try
```

The first thing we do, is to set the `IsValid` property of the `args` argument (a `ServerValidateEventArgs` object) to `False`:

```
    args.IsValid = False
```

We're being pessimistic here, but until we validate everything, we want to be sure that nothing passes our validation test until the very end of the method. Next, we declare two variables of type Date:

```
    Dim departDate, returnDate As Date
```

We perform the work of getting the user's date input within a `Try ... Catch` block, so we can catch exceptions:

```
    Try
        departDate = Date.Parse(flightDepartureDateTextBox.Text)
    Catch ex As Exception
        feedbackLabel.Text = "Invalid data entry: Departure Date is invalid.  " _
                    + "Enter a valid date, for example:  2001/07/04"
        Return
    End Try
```

The `Date` object's static `Parse` method is called to pass the user's **Departure Date** entry. An exception will be thrown under two conditions: a null date (no date entered), or a malformed, or incorrect date entered; one that doesn't meet the criteria of the `Date` datatype. The `flightReturnDateTextBox` is similarly validated:

```
Try
    returnDate = Date.Parse(flightReturnDateTextBox.Text)
Catch ex As Exception
    feedbackLabel.Text = "Invalid data entry: Return Date is invalid.  " _
                    + "Enter a valid date, for example:  2001/07/04"

    Return
End Try
```

If an exception is thrown, we provide the user with some feedback text, via the `feedbackLabel` that we created in the `<!-- BOOK IT BUTTON SECTION & FEEDBACK -->` part of our code file. We then promptly return the execution to the program that called this subroutine, so it is ready for the user to have another go. Try entering **Today** as your departure date, and **Tomorrow** as your return date, for example, and you'll see this:

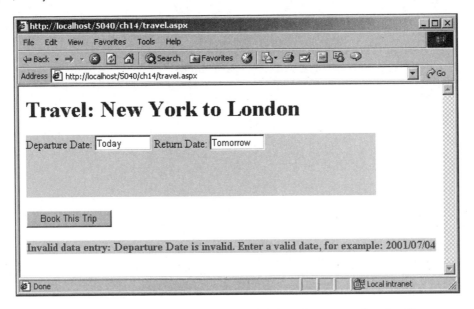

Even after it's confirmed that the user entered two valid dates however, there's still some more work to do. The next validation ensures that the departure date entered is earlier than the return date:

```
' Verify that the departure date is less than the
' return date - no same day trips in this system!
If (departDate >= returnDate) Then
    feedbackLabel.Text = "Invalid data entry:  The Departure Date must be " _
                    + "earlier than the Return Date and no same-day " _
                    + "returns for this travel package!"

    Return
End If
```

The code for this section is pretty straightforward, using just an `if` statement, which sends a feedback message if the departure date is greater then the return date. The code then returns to the state it was in before the validation control was called. Just to make things even more robust, we validate that the departure date is not in the past, using the same technique:

486

```
' Verify that the departure date is not in the past or today!
If (departDate < Date.Now) Then
    feedbackLabel.Text = "Invalid data entry:  The Departure Date cannot " _
                    + "be in the past or today!"
    Return
End If
```

If we were to attempt to book our trip from New York to London without entering anything into the **Departure Date** and **Return Date** boxes, the assigned `RequiredFieldValidator` controls would kick into action and display a message to the user:

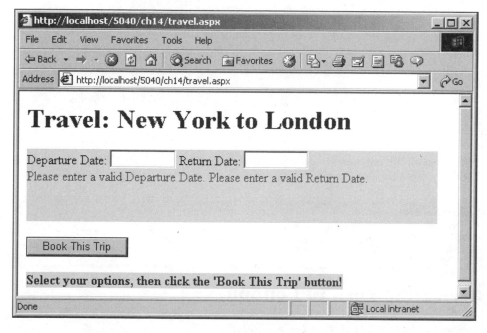

As you may have noticed, date validation can be a bit tedious – but it's worth the effort! The nice thing about this implementation is that we didn't need to restrict the user to a particular date format for their data entry. Yes, we suggested a format like YYYY/mm/dd, but the user could have entered "10/31/2001" or even "October 31, 2001" – this is because we called the `Date.Parse` method, which did the work of parsing the user's date entry.

Let's have a quick look at the button function of the web form. The button itself is very simple – we just give it some text and define its `OnClick` event as `bookTheTripButton_Click`:

```
<p>
<asp:Button id="bookTheTripButton" runat="server" Text="Book This Trip"
        OnClick="bookTheTripButton_Click" />
</p>
```

When the button is clicked, it sends the form information back to the server, which then processes all the server controls we have used. If our page validates correctly (if `args.IsValid = True`) our `bookTheTripButton` `OnClick` event is triggered:

```
Private Sub bookTheTripButton_Click(ByVal sender As System.Object, _
                                    ByVal e As System.EventArgs)

    ' Has the page been validated for all data entry?
    If (Not Page.IsValid) Then
        Return
    End if

    ' We're all set - book the flight!
    Dim departDate, returnDate As Date
    departDate = Date.Parse(flightDepartureDateTextBox.Text)
    returnDate = Date.Parse(flightReturnDateTextBox.Text)

    feedbackLabel.ForeColor = Color.Black
    feedbackLabel.Text = "Success!  Your trip from New York to London " _
                    + "will depart on the " _
                    + departDate.ToLongDateString() _
                    + " and return on the " _
                    + returnDate.ToLongDateString()

End Sub
```

In the end, when all the dates and logic are validated, our trip from New York to London will be booked with a simple click of the mouse:

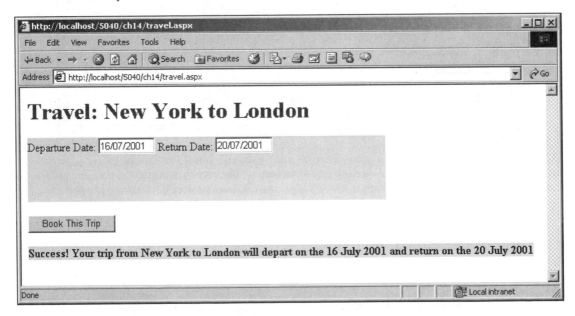

Control Families

ASP.NET server controls can be grouped into four basic family types: **Intrinsic**, **Validation**, **Rich**, and **Data Rendering** controls. These control families are fairly broad and are based primarily on the function or purpose of the control.

When designing a web form, you'll often need to ask yourself two questions: "What do I need to display?" and "How am I going to display it?". Once you're familiar with the various controls and what they do, it's relatively easy to know which ASP.NET server controls you'll need to get the job done. When you create ASP.NET pages, you are free to mix and match all kinds of different controls within your pages, including standard HTML controls.

Intrinsic Controls

These are controls that correspond directly to HTML commands, such as `Button`, `Checkbox`, `DropDownList` and `TextBox`. We are familiar with these controls now, as we've been using them throughout the book, so we won't spend any more time explaining how they all work, but here is a list to remind you of which controls fall into this group:

Control	Purpose
Button	General-purpose button – you typically write an `OnClick` event handler
CheckBox	Single checkbox
DropDownList	Drop-down listbox – a.k.a. "combo box", for selecting from a list of items
Hyperlink	Corresponds to the HTML `<a></a>` tag for displaying a hyperlink.
Image	Display an image file, GIF, JPG other image file.
Label	Provides a way to display text on a page. Corresponds to the HTML `<span>` tag
ListBox	Provide a scrollable list of items, single or multiple selection
Panel	Corresponds to the HTML `<DIV>` tag – typically serves as a container for other controls
RadioButton	Single radio button, similar to a checkbox, except you must handle deselect programmatically
Table	An HTML table
TableCell	Cell within a table
TableRow	Row within a table
TextBox	TextBox – single or multiple lines

Validation Controls

The worth of any given web form could be measured by the accuracy of the data it was designed to collect. If the data is bogus, with values that are missing, out of range, or simply meaningless, your clients will probably complain pretty quick!

To help alleviate the problem of invalid data entry, and to ease some of the development burden, Microsoft has provided a family of ASP.NET server controls that specialize in validating input and, if necessary, provide feedback to the user.

Validation controls are good examples of how ASP.NET server controls, in general, serve to abstract common tasks that would typically involve manual client-side validation scripting. By using ASP.NET validation controls within ASP.NET web forms, developers are relieved of the work of writing custom client-side validation for their web pages. Validating a user's data entry is important in a variety of scenarios. For example, if we wrote a logon form that collects a user's name and password, we would want to validate that these fields were entered before passing the data on to the server.

We've already seen some validation controls in action in `travel.aspx`, so we won't spend long looking at them here. Just take a look through the list of controls below, to get an idea of what is possible:

Control	Purpose
CompareValidator	Compares a user's entry against a constant value (less than, equal, greater than, and so on).
CustomValidator	Checks the user's data entry using validation logic from a custom method that you write – processed on the server or the client.
RangeValidator	Checks that a user's entry is between specified lower and upper boundaries. Check ranges within pairs of numbers, alphabetic characters, and dates. Boundaries can be expressed as constants, or as values derived from another control.
RegularExpressionValidator	Checks that the entry matches a pattern defined by a regular expression. This type of validation allows you to check for predictable sequences of characters, such as those in social security numbers, e-mail addresses, telephone numbers, postal codes and IP addresses.
RequiredFieldValidator	Ensures that the user does not skip an entry

Rich Controls

Rich controls are controls are compound in nature, and provide extended functionality. In other words, these controls are typically combinations of two or more intrinsic controls that provide similar, but distinct functionality in one single control. Another distinguishing trait of these controls is that they don't have any direct correlation to any HTML controls, although they do in fact render to HTML when displayed in the client browser.

Control	Purpose
AdRotator	Displays advertisement banners on a web form. The displayed ad is randomly changed each time the form is loaded or refreshed.
Calendar	Displays a one-month calendar for viewing/selecting a date, month or year.

Control	Purpose
CheckBoxList	Multiple-selection check box group. Can be dynamically generated with data binding (we'll come to this shortly).
ImageButton	Provides a clickable image with (optional) access to the clicked coordinates for support image-map functionality.
LinkButton	Hyperlink-style button that posts back to the page of origin.
RadioButtonList	Mutually exclusive radio button group. Can be dynamically generated with data binding.

The nice thing about this family of "Rich Controls" is that they are just as easy to use as the other ASP.NET server controls. They may boast more features and properties, but the basic way to define them and interact with them programmatically is exactly the same as all ASP.NET server controls. We haven't seen much of these yet, so let's look at a couple to see how they're used (to find out what properties any other controls have, consult the documentation).

Calendar

One of the simplest and most practical uses for this control is to allow a user to select a particular date. It's even possible, via the `SelectionMode` property, to configure the control to allow the user to select a range of dates. The `Calendar` control has many properties, and we'll list a few here, that are of particular interest:

```
<asp:Calendar id="Calendar1" runat="server"
    FirstDayOfWeek="Default|Monday|Tuesday|Wednesday|
    Thursday|Friday|Saturday|Sunday"
```

Notable here is the `FirstDayOfWeek` property – this enables you to choose which day of the week your calendar starts from, and we will use this property in the example at the end of this chapter. Some calendars default to Sunday as the first day of the week – for business purposes, however, it's typically more practical to view the week starting from Monday. A nice feature!

```
SelectionMode="None|Day|DayWeek|DayWeekMonth"
```

By default, the `Calendar` control's `SelectionMode` defaults to `Day`. This is useful when you want your user to select a single day. You can select multiple days by setting the `SelectionMode` property to either `DayWeek`, however, which will allow you to select a single day or an entire week, or `DayWeekMonth`, which will allow you to select a single day, an entire week, or the entire month:

```
SelectMonthText="HTML text"
SelectWeekText="HTML text"
```

The Calendar control's `SelectMonthText` and `SelectWeekText` allow you to customize the HTML – use these properties if you're really going for a customized look.

You need not define all of the properties of the ASP.NET `Calendar` control to display the control. In fact, the following declaration will create an ASP.NET `Calendar` server control that looks and displays, depending on your tastes and needs, very nicely:

```
<asp:Calendar id="MyCalendarControl" runat="server" />
```

When delivered to the client browser, the result is an HTML calendar display that provides links which, when defined, enable you to navigate through the various days, months and years. Try it for yourself:

≤	July 2001					≥
Mon	Tue	Wed	Thu	Fri	Sat	Sun
25	26	27	28	29	30	1
2	3	4	5	6	7	8
9	10	11	12	13	14	15
16	17	18	19	20	21	22
23	24	25	26	27	28	29
30	31	1	2	3	4	5

Have a look at the HTML that your ASP.NET produced to create this page – over 100 lines of code, consisting of HTML and JavaScript, were generated to produce this and you wrote only a single line!

The ASP.NET Calendar control is extremely feature-rich. Refer to the ASP.NET documentation for complete details on this control.

LinkButton

The LinkButton control is functionally very much the Button control. What distinguishes this control, though, is that when rendered in the client browser, it looks like a traditional hyperlink. The LinkButton object's functionality is dependent upon how the OnClick event handler is implemented. The following is an example of a LinkButton declaration:

```
<html>
  <body>
    <form runat="server">
      <asp:LinkButton id="WroxLinkButton" runat="server"
        Text="Visit the Wrox Press Home Page"
      />
    </form>
  </body>
</html>
```

In this example, the Text property is set, and the OnClick event is assigned the name of the method handler, OnWroxLinkButtonClick. When displayed in the browser, this particular LinkButton will look like this:

Visit the Wrox Press Home Page

If we added the following event handler an OnClick event to our link button:

```
<script language="VB" runat="server">
  Public Sub OnWroxLinkButtonClick(sender As Object , e As System.EventArgs)
    Response.Redirect("http://www.wrox.com")
  End Sub
</script>
```

An `OnClick` event to our link button:

```
<html>
  <body>
    <form runat="server">
      <asp:LinkButton id="WroxLinkButton" runat="server"
        Text="Visit the Wrox Press Home Page"
        OnClick="OnWroxLinkButtonClick"
      />
    </form>
  </body>
</html>
```

We end up at the Wrox website! Try it for yourself.

This is a button rather than a straightforward hyperlink, therefore we can use it to perform server-side processing, such as logging entries to a database in order to track our web site's URL usage.

Data Rendering Controls

These controls are extremely feature-rich (they have numerous properties to choose from) and greatly simplify the work of displaying a variety of data, particularly database-related data. The definition of "data" in the context of these controls is very broad. It could include database records, an `ArrayList`, an XML data source and so on.

Before we look at the controls themselves, we need to get hold of two important concepts:

❑ **Data Binding.** This is the term used to describe the process of associating information in a data store (which could be anything from a database table, to an `ArrayList` object) with a server control. Data binding is established by setting the server control's `DataSource` property to reference a particular set of data (with a line similar to `DataSource = set of data`). All data referenced will come from this data source. Once this link has been established, the set of data is then referenced by the `DataSet` object.

❑ **Templates.** This is a way to define the various layout elements of a particular control; to describe how the data is displayed in the browser. The `DataGrid` and `DataList` have default templates, so you only need to create templates if you want to change the default look.

Now let's look at those controls:

Control	Purpose
DataGrid	Creates a multi-column, data-bound grid. This control allows you to define various types of columns, both to layout the contents of the grid and to add specific functionality (edit button columns, hyperlink columns, and so on).
DataList	Displays items from a data source using templates. You can customize the appearance and contents of the control by manipulating the templates that make up its different components.
Repeater	The Repeater control is a data-bound list that renders a row for every row in the data source. You define the appearance of the Repeater rows using templates. The Repeater control does not have any built-in selection or editing support.

There is a great deal to these controls. Each is very powerful, and, unfortunately, it is beyond the scope of this book to examine them thoroughly (each one deserves an entire chapter at least). Let's take a bit of a closer look however, at how each one functions.

DataGrid

As well as allowing you to create a grid, the DataGrid control also lets you format its columns and rows to control the layout of your grid, using templates (see the DataList control for a list of some of the templates). For example, you could alternate the colors for the rows of data being displayed. As well as templates, this control supports several interesting properties, which include:

❑ AllowSorting: enables you dynamically sort and re-display the data based on a selected column. For example, if you had a table containing your employees surnames and salaries, enabling sorting would allow you to sort your table according to either column.

❑ AllowPaging: the ability to view subsets of the data called by the DataGrid control on different pages. The number of items displayed on the page is determined by the PageSize property.

❑ AlternatingItemStyle: the style (such as background colour) of every other item listed.

❑ FooterStyle: the style of the footer at the end of the list (if any).

❑ HeaderStyle: the style of the header at the beginning of the list (if any) .

❑ ItemStyle: the style of individual items.

To use the DataGrid control, you have to specify it within tags, set the relevant properties, define the columns in your table, and then apply the relevant template for those columns. Within the template tags, you include the information the template must be applied to:

```
<asp:DataGrid id="EventData"
  AllowSorting="true"
    <Columns>
      <asp:TemplateColumn HeaderText="Column1">
        <ItemTemplate>
          <%# Container.DataItem("ShortDesc") %>
        </ItemTemplate>
      </asp:TemplateColumn>
```

```
        <asp:TemplateColumn HeaderText="Column2">
          <ItemTemplate>
            <%# Container.DataItem("DetailDesc") %>
          </ItemTemplate>
        </asp:TemplateColumn>
      </Columns>
  </asp:DataGrid>
```

We'll see the `DataGrid` control in action in the last Try It Out of this chapter.

DataList

The `DataList` control is useful for displaying rows of database information (which can become columns in `DataGrid` tables) in a format that you can control very precisely using **templates** and **styles**. Manipulating various template controls changes the way your data is presented. The DataList control enables you to select and edit the data that is presented. The following is a listing of some supported templates:

❑ `ItemTemplate`: required template that provides the content and layout for items referenced by `DataList`.

❑ `AlternatingItemTemplate`: if defined, this template provides the content and layout for alternating items in the `DataList`. If not defined, `ItemTemplate` is used.

❑ `EditItemTemplate`: if defined, this template provides editing controls, such as text boxes, for items set to 'edit' in the `DataList`. If not defined, ItemTemplate is used.

❑ `FooterTemplate`: if defined, the `FooterTemplate` provides the content and layout for the footer section of the `DataList`. If not defined, a footer section will not be displayed.

❑ `HeaderTemplate`: if defined, this provides the content and layout for the header section of the `DataList`. If not defined, a header section will not be displayed.

❑ `SelectedItemTemplate`: if defined, this template provides the content and layout for the currently selected item in the `DataList`. If not defined, `ItemTemplate` is used.

❑ `SeparatorTemplate`: if defined, this provides the content and layout for the separator between items in the `DataList`. If not defined, a separator will not be displayed.

To use the `DataList` control and its templates, you have to specify it in tags, and then specify your templates within tags as well. Unlike the DataGrid, items to be affected by the template occur within the template tags. Each template has its own set of properties, which you can find in the .NET documentation (and remember to be sure to have defined your `DataSource`):

```
<asp:DataList id="DataList1" runat="server">
    <FooterTemplate>
      'Items to be affected by this template
    </FooterTemplate>
    <SeparatorTemplate>
      'Items to be affected by this template
    </SeparatorTemplate>
</asp:DataList>
```

If you use the `DataList` control to set up a column in a grid, you can set additional templates within that column by using the `DataGrid` control. Refer to the ASP.NET documentation for more information.

Repeater

The `Repeater` control is very similar to the `DataList` control with one very important distinction: the data displayed is always **read only** – you cannot edit the data being presented. It is particularly useful for displaying repeating rows of data. Like the `DataGrid` and `DataList` controls, it utilizes templates to render its various sections. The templates it uses are generally the same as the ones used with the DataList control, and the syntax is also the same. We'll see an example of the `Repeater` control in action in the next Try It Out.

We've now looked at almost everything we're going to in this chapter. All that is left to do is to bring everything together in two exercises, the first of which creates a dynamic calendar, and the second one uses the `EditItemTemplate` to create an editable able of information.

Try It Out – MyCalendar

In the previous sections of this chapter, you were exposed to many of the most common ASP.NET server controls, including the `Calendar` control. Many web sites, particularly personal home pages, share information regarding upcoming events. For example, a local soccer team might have a web site that displays the team's game schedule for the players, parents, coaches, and so on; or a band might display an on-line calendar that shows all upcoming gigs for their fans. In either case, the ability to render intuitive and familiar calendar-related events or appointments on a web page is crucial.

Due tothe centrality of the calendar to many situations, we've decided to base this Try It Out around the Calendar control. We're not going to try to replicate the advanced features of a desktop calendaring tool, such as Microsoft Outlook though. The object of our application will be to share some key dates and appointments on the Web, in the context of a familiar calendar.

To flesh this out a little, here's a mini-specification of some of the features we'll be implementing for the `MyCalendar` application:

❑ The `Calendar` control should read our calendar data from an XML file (we'll be using the XML file as a data source). This will make it easy to update and change the calendar data, without ever having to change the ASPX file. Due to this, none of our appointments or events will be hard-coded within the ASPX page itself.

❑ We'd like to be able to see several events within a day.

❑ While we obviously want to see the title of an event or appointment on the calendar, we also want to see some additional information (for example, a detailed description of the event and the start/end time). To enable this, when we click on the event link, a listing of all details should appear.

❑ Although the `Calendar` control defaults to Sunday as the first day of the month, we want the first day of the month to be Monday.

❑ Weekends should display in a slightly different shade (so we know they're coming!), as should days that are part of the previous or next month.

Since we're taking all our information from an XML file, let's begin by looking at the XML that we're going to use.

The XML Source – MyCalendar.xml

The source XML file we shall use will just contain the basic information we want display in the Calendar control. The MyCalendar.xml file, as with all the listings throughout this book, is available for download on www.wrox.com. The following excerpt of the MyCalendar.xml file is provided, just to show you the XML syntax used, as well as some of the sample data:

```
<MyCalendar>
  <Event>
    <ShortDesc>Concert at the Riverfront</ShortDesc>
    <DetailDesc>4th of July celebration. Bring stand and a jacket.</DetailDesc>
    <EventDate>2001/07/04</EventDate>
    <StartTime>9:30PM</StartTime>
    <EndTime>11:00PM</EndTime>
  </Event>
  <Event>
    <ShortDesc>CCT Rehearsal - Brigadoon</ShortDesc>
    <DetailDesc>Community Theatre orchestra rehearsal - bring mutes.</DetailDesc>
    <EventDate>2001/07/14</EventDate>
    <StartTime>3:30PM</StartTime>
    <EndTime>6:30PM</EndTime>
  </Event>
</MyCalendar>
```

The elements of this XML file are fairly straightforward:

- ❑ MyCalendar – the root element. XML requires a single root element to contain the child elements.

- ❑ Event – basically serves as the main parent for each group of elements.

- ❑ ShortDesc – a short description of the event.

- ❑ DetailDesc – a detailed description of the event – could be random notes, comments, or thoughts.

- ❑ EventDate – the date on which the event occurs. In the sample data, the format used is yyyy/mm/dd, which should serve to eliminate any ambiguity between various local date discrepancies. In fact, because we will use the DateTime object to reference this information, any valid format that the DateTime object can parse will be acceptable. Having said that, you might prefer to use your local date format – it's certainly easier to read because that's what you are used to.

- ❑ StartTime – the time the event starts.

- ❑ EndTime – the time the event ends.

The rest of the XML file is very similar to this excerpt – it merely contains information that we are going to reference in our MyCalendar.aspx file. Let's take a look at this now.

The Web Form – MyCalendar.aspx

The following is the complete listing of the MyCalendar.aspx web form implementation. You'll declare the various ASP.NET server controls used in this web form, as well as the corresponding code and event handlers, in a series of incremental steps. The example is quite a long one, therefore we'll discuss much of what is going on as we go through it. At the end, further analysis and discussion will be provided in the subsequent "How It Works" section.

1. Download `MyCalendar.xml` from www.wrox.com, and save it in the Chapter 14 folder of your BegASPNET virtual directory.

2. Create a new file, called `MyCalendar.aspx`, save it in the same folder as `MyCalendar.xml`, and add the following lines, which will serve as a starting point for creating the page's ASP.NET server control objects, as well as the corresponding code and event handlers:

```
<%@ Page Language="VB" %>
<%@ Import Namespace="System.Data"%>
<%@ Import Namespace="System.IO" %>

<html>
<head>
<script language="VB" runat="server">

</script>

</head>
<body>

</body>
</html>
```

3. Add the following code between the <body> tags:

```
<body>
  <h1>My Calendar</h1>

    <form id="MyCalendarForm" method="post" runat="server">
      <p align="center">
      <asp:Calendar id="MyCalendar" runat="server"
        SelectedDate="2001/07/17"
        VisibleDate="2001/07/01"
        FirstDayOfWeek="Monday"
        DayNameFormat="Full"
        ShowDayHeader="True"
        ShowGridLines="True"
        ShowNextPrevMonth="True"
        ShowTitle="True"
        nextprevstyle-backcolor="DodgerBlue"
        nextprevstyle-forecolor="White"
        nextprevstyle-font-bold="True"
        nextprevstyle-font-size="Large"
        TitleFormat="MonthYear"
        TitleStyle-BackColor="DodgerBlue"
        TitleStyle-ForeColor="White"
        TitleStyle-Font-Size="Large"
        TitleStyle-Font-Bold="True"
        dayheaderstyle-backcolor="DodgerBlue"
        dayheaderstyle-forecolor="White"
        daystyle-horizontalalign="Left"
```

```
                daystyle-verticalalign="Top"
                daystyle-font-size="Small"
                SelectedDayStyle-Font-Bold="True"
                selecteddaystyle-horizontalalign="Left"
                selecteddaystyle-verticalalign="Top"
                selecteddaystyle-font-size="Small"
                selecteddaystyle-forecolor="Red"
                TodayDayStyle-HorizontalAlign="Left"
                TodayDayStyle-VerticalAlign="Top"
                todaydaystyle-backcolor="White"
            </asp:Calendar>
            </p>
        </form>
    </body>
```

In this step, we're adding the main visual component of the page – the ASP.NET `Calendar` control. The `Calendar` control will be responding to events, it's declared within the context of a `<form>` tag. The numerous properties defined here will serve, not only to give the `Calendar` control a unique look, but will also affect its behavior. The `FirstDayOfWeek` property is set to "Monday", for example. If you have a look through the other properties we're defining here, you'll find they're pretty self-explanatory.

A couple things to note so far: the `SelectedDate` and `VisibleDate` properties are hard coded for demonstration purposes only – this is discussed in more detail in the How It Works section to follow.

To conclude the definition of this `Calendar` control, assign event handlers for the `OnDayRender` and `OnSelectionChanged` events just before the closing `</asp:Calendar>` tag. These will be explained in detail later in this section:

```
<body>
...
                OnDayRender="MyCalendar_DayRender"
                OnSelectionChanged="MyCalendar_SelectionChanged">
            </asp:Calendar>
            </p>
        </form>
    </body>
```

4. You'll now add a `Label` control to the page, which will later serve to provide some date selection feedback to the user, regarding the currently selected date. Add these lines after the declaration of the `Calendar` control, and just before the `</form>` end tag:

```
<body>
...
            <p align="center">
            <asp:label id="SelectedDate" runat="server" font-size="Large" />
            </p>
        </form>
    </body>
```

499

5. The final visual components used in this example consist of two controls: the `Panel` and `Repeater` controls. When a user selects a date from the calendar, the `OnSelectionChanged` event (for which we assigned the handler in step 2) will be raised by the `Calendar` control. This will enable us to gather an `ArrayList` of all daily events and bind them to the `Repeater` control. The ASP.NET `Panel` control serves as a container for the `Repeater` control, and will be used to control the visibility state of the displayed `Repeater` elements (when the `Panel` control's `Visible` property is set to `false`, all corresponding child controls, like the `Repeater` control, are also hidden).

The code we're adding here, just sets up the Repeater control (within the panel control) and establishes the properties of the templates, which will be used to display our information. Insert the following ASP.NET `Panel` and `Repeater` control declarations before the final `</form>` end tag:

```
<body>
...
      <asp:panel id="DailyDetailsPanel" runat="server">
        <asp:Repeater id="DailyEventDetailRepeater" runat="server">
          <HeaderTemplate>
          <p align="center">
          <table border="1" width="100%">
          <table style="color:Black;border collapse:collapse;">
            <tr style="color:White;background-color:DodgerBlue;font-weight:bold;">
              <td><b>Event</b></td>
              <td><b>Description</b></td>
              <td><b>Start Time</b></td>
              <td><b>End Time</b></td>
            </tr>
          </HeaderTemplate>
          <ItemTemplate>
            <tr style="background-color:White;">
              <td> <%# DataBinder.Eval(Container.DataItem, "ShortDesc") %> </td>
              <td> <%# DataBinder.Eval(Container.DataItem, "DetailDesc")%> </td>
              <td> <%# DataBinder.Eval(Container.DataItem, "StartTime") %> </td>
              <td> <%# DataBinder.Eval(Container.DataItem, "EndTime") %> </td>
            </tr>
          </ItemTemplate >
          <AlternatingItemTemplate>
            <tr style="background-color:Gainsboro;">
              <td> <%# DataBinder.Eval(Container.DataItem, "ShortDesc") %> </td>
              <td> <%# DataBinder.Eval(Container.DataItem, "DetailDesc")%> </td>
              <td> <%# DataBinder.Eval(Container.DataItem, "StartTime") %> </td>
              <td> <%# DataBinder.Eval(Container.DataItem, "EndTime") %> </td>
            </tr>
          </AlternatingItemTemplate>
          <FooterTemplate>
          </table>
          </p>
          </FooterTemplate>

        </asp:Repeater>
      </asp:panel>
    </form>
</body>
```

6. At this point, all the visual components used in `MyCalendar.aspx` have been declared and set up. Over the next few steps, we will add the method and event handler code implementations between the `<script>` `</script>` tags of the page. Add the following code for the `Page_Load` method implementation:

```
<script language="VB" runat="server">

    Protected Sub Page_Load(ByVal Sender As System.Object, _
                            ByVal e As System.EventArgs)
      If Not IsPostback Then
        ShowDailyEvents()
      End If
    End Sub

</script>
```

In this listing, the `IsPostback` property is checked to see if this is the first time the page has been loaded – if so, a method, `ShowDailyEvents`, is called, which will perform the work of binding and displaying the daily event data in the `Repeater` control. We'll define `ShowDailyEvents` shortly.

7. The `Calendar` control in this page declares an event handler for the `OnSelectionChanged` event that we added in step 2. Remember that in step 2 the name of the event handler we assigned was `MyCalendar_SelectionChanged`. The implementation for this event handler should be added within the `<script>` `</script>` tags, and below the `Page_Load` method we just added, as follows:

```
<script language="VB" runat="server">
...
    Public Sub MyCalendar_SelectionChanged(ByVal sender As Object, _
                                           ByVal e As System.EventArgs)
      ShowDailyEvents()
    End Sub

</script>
```

When the user clicks a new date on the calendar control (thus triggering the `OnSelectionChanged` event), the `MyCalendar_SelectionChanged` event handler will call the `ShowDailyEvents` method. So this is almost functionally identical to our `Page_Load` implementation, above.

8. In order to display our custom calendar events within the `Calendar` control, we must write a method that loads the data from `MyCalendar.xml` into a `DataSet` object. This is implemented as follows (again, add this code in your `<script>` `</script>` tags, below the event handler we just added):

```
<script language="VB" runat="server">
...
    Protected Function LoadMyCalendarData() As DataSet

    Dim sourceXML as String = Server.MapPath("MyCalendar.xml")
      If ( Not File.Exists ( sourceXML ) ) Then
        Return Nothing
```

```
        End if

    Dim cachedDataSet as DataSet = Session("MyCalendarData")
      if ( Not cachedDataSet Is Nothing ) Then
        Return cachedDataSet
      End if
    Dim dataSet As DataSet = New DataSet()


    Try

      dataSet.ReadXml(sourceXML)

      Session("MyCalendarData") = dataSet

    Catch e As Exception
      SelectedDate.Text = e.Message
      dataSet = Nothing
    End Try


    Return dataSet

  End Function
</script>
```

The key points to observe from this listing are that we first check to see if the file, MyCalendar.xml (that we defined, along with the location of the file, in the first line, as sourceXML) exists. If it doesn't exist on the server file system, we won't be able to display any of our custom calendar data in the Calendar or Repeater controls. Note also that we use the Session object to determine if we've already loaded (or cached) this DataSet object – if so, we can use it and optimize our code slightly. We'll discuss this more in the How It Works section. The part of the code in the Try block loads the XML data into a DataSet object via the ReadXml method (which enables the XML in the file to be read). The Catch block checks that LoadMyCalendarData does return something when it is called, as it is possible that nothing could be returned, particularly if MyCalendar.xml contains any malformed data:

9. We are able to display our own data within the calendar by implementing an event handler for the Calendar control's OnDayRender event, which is raised each time a visible day in the calendar is being rendered. The MyCalendar_DayRender method (remember we introduced this in step 2) renders the Calendar control's Cell display by iterating through each record in the DataSet to determine if there is an event to display for the particular day being rendered. This method will also perform the work of setting various Cell.BackColor properties based on if the day being rendered is a weekend, weekday, or a day from a next or previous month. It is implemented as follows, and is to be placed, once again, within the <script> </script> tags:

```
<script language="VB" runat="server">
...
  Protected Sub MyCalendar_DayRender(ByVal Sender As System.Object, _
                              ByVal e As DayRenderEventArgs )
```

```
     if ( e.Day.IsOtherMonth )
       e.Cell.BackColor=System.Drawing.Color.FromName("Gainsboro")
     Else If ( e.Day.IsWeekend )
       e.Cell.BackColor=System.Drawing.Color.FromName("PaleGoldenrod")
     Else
       e.Cell.BackColor=System.Drawing.Color.FromName("LightGoldenrodYellow")
     End if

  Dim dataSet as DataSet = LoadMyCalendarData()
     if dataSet is Nothing
       Exit Sub
     End if

  Dim zRow as DataRow

     For Each zRow in dataSet.Tables(0).Rows
       Dim compareDate as DateTime
       compareDate = GetSafeDate ( zRow.Item("EventDate") )

       If ( compareDate = e.Day.Date ) Then

         ' Event matches date criteria - display it...
         Dim myEventData as New MyCalendarEventData
         myEventData.ShortDesc = zRow.Item("ShortDesc")
         myEventData.DetailDesc = zRow.Item("DetailDesc")
         myEventData.StartTime = zRow.Item("StartTime")
         myEventData.EndTime = zRow.Item("EndTime")

         Dim dailyEventLabel as New Label
         dailyEventLabel.Text = "<br />" + myEventData.ShortDesc
         e.Cell.Controls.Add ( dailyEventLabel )
       End if
     Next

  End Sub
```

```
</script>
```

10. The next section implements the method, `ShowDailyEvents`, that we referenced in steps 5 and 6. This method's task is to display the detailed information for all events (the detailed event description, the start time, the end time, and so on), based on the currently selected day in the calendar. This detailed display of calendar data will actually be rendered via a `Repeater` control, and will be displayed below the Calendar. In this way, we'll have a bit more real estate to display the detailed information about the selected day's events, which would normally be too verbose to display in within the Calendar control itself. Add the following lines in the `<script> </script>` tags:

```
<script language="VB" runat="server">
...

  Protected Sub ShowDailyEvents()

    Dim d As Date = MyCalendar.SelectedDate()
```

```
    Dim dataSet as DataSet = LoadMyCalendarData()
    if dataSet is Nothing
      Exit Sub
    End if

    Dim zRow as DataRow
    Dim aEvents as new ArrayList()

    For Each zRow in dataSet.Tables(0).Rows
      Dim compareDate as DateTime
      compareDate = GetSafeDate ( zRow.Item("EventDate") )

      If ( compareDate = d ) Then

        ' Event matches date criteria - display it...
        Dim myEventData as New MyCalendarEventData
        myEventData.EventDate = d
        myEventData.ShortDesc = zRow.Item("ShortDesc")
        myEventData.DetailDesc = zRow.Item("DetailDesc")
        myEventData.StartTime = zRow.Item("StartTime")
        myEventData.EndTime = zRow.Item("EndTime")

        aEvents.Add ( myEventData )

      End If
    Next

    ' Bind to the Repeater control...
    DailyEventDetailRepeater.DataSource = aEvents
    DailyEventDetailRepeater.DataBind()

    If ( aEvents.Count > 0 ) Then
      DailyDetailsPanel.Visible = True
      SelectedDate.Text = "Events For " + d.ToLongDateString()
    Else
      DailyDetailsPanel.Visible = False
      SelectedDate.Text = "No Events Scheduled For " + d.ToLongDateString()
    End if

  End Sub
```

```
</script>
```

11. The `MyCalendar.xml` data source file could conceivably contain an invalid date entry in its `EventDate` XML element tag therefore, we'll add the following helper method to our page to guarantee that a non-null `DateTime` object is always returned, regardless of the date value obtained from the source XML:

```
<script language="VB" runat="server">
...

  Private Function GetSafeDate ( ByVal proposedDate as String ) As DateTime
```

```
    ' returns a non-null DateTime even if proposed date can't be parsed
    Dim safeDate as DateTime = DateTime.MinValue
    Try
      safeDate = DateTime.Parse ( proposedDate )
    Catch e As Exception
      Response.Write ( "<!-- Failed to parse date: " + e.Message + " -->" )
    End Try

    GetSafeDate = safeDate

  End Function
```
</script>

12. In this step, we add a `MyCalendarEventData` class implementation. This class serves as a container for the various data elements that make up our own custom calendar event data:

```
<script language="VB" runat="server">
...

  Public Class MyCalendarEventData

    Private m_ShortDesc As String
    Private m_DetailDesc As String
    Private m_EventDate As DateTime
    Private m_StartTime As String
    Private m_EndTime As String

    Public Property ShortDesc() As String
      Get
        Return m_ShortDesc
      End Get
      Set
       m_ShortDesc = value
      End Set
    End Property

    Public Property DetailDesc() As String
      Get
       Return m_DetailDesc
      End Get
      Set
       m_DetailDesc = value
      End Set
    End Property

    Public Property EventDate As DateTime
      Get
        Return m_EventDate
      End Get
      Set
       m_EventDate = Value
      End Set
    End Property
```

```
   Public Property StartTime() As String
     Get
      Return m_StartTime
     End Get
     Set
      m_StartTime = value
     End Set
   End Property

   Public Property EndTime() As String
     Get
      Return m_EndTime
     End Get
     Set
      m_EndTime = value
     End Set
   End Property

 End Class
```

```
</script>
```

Once you've completed all the steps for entering the controls and code, you should be able to load the `MyCalendar.aspx` file into your browser. You should see the following display served up after the page loads:

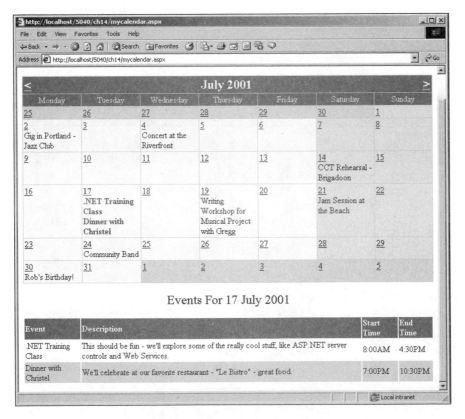

How It Works

The first step in creating the `MyCalendar.aspx` web form was to define what we wanted it to do, which was this: given a custom XML file with various calendar event data (`MyCalendar.xml`), load each of the event items in an ASP.NET Calendar control. In steps 1 through 4, above, we basically created an ASPX page that defined three different ASP.NET server controls: `Calendar`, `Repeater` and `Panel`.

Calendar Implementation Details

The `Calendar` control serves as the primary visual interface for the user. We set a host of properties to customize the look of the control – see step 2 for details. The first question you might be wondering is, why does the `Calendar` control default to July 2001, and why is the date July 17, 2001 selected by default? It comes down to the following code:

```
<asp:Calendar id="MyCalendar" runat="server"
   SelectedDate="2001/07/17"
   VisibleDate="2001/07/01"
```

The `SelectedDate` property is used to set the date that the calendar will default to when first opened. The `VisibleDate` property sets the month of the calendar that is visible, for example, defining the date `"2001/08/01"` will make the month August of 2001 visible.

As previously mentioned, the `SelectedDate` and `VisibleDate` properties were set this way for demonstration purposes only, since the entries in the `MyCalendar.xml` file only have calendar data for this particular time span.

When we declared the `Calendar` control, we assigned event handlers for two of the `Calendar` controls events:

```
<asp:Calendar id="MyCalendar" runat="server"
...
   OnDayRender="MyCalendar_DayRender"
   OnSelectionChanged="MyCalendar_SelectionChanged">
...
```

The `MyCalendar_DayRender` event is invoked whenever the `Calendar` control begins to display a day that will be visible, and the `MyCalendar_SelectionChanged` event is invoked when a new date is selected.

Our `Calendar` control displays six weeks worth of data – the days representing the month being displayed, as well as a share of days from the previous and next months. In order to give our `Calendar` control a unique look, we implemented a bit of logic to determine if the day being rendered was part of another month (`IsOtherMonth`), a weekend day (`IsWeekEnd`), or if the day was part of the month being displayed. The logic for displaying the various `Calendar` `Cell` color formatting is demonstrated in this code fragment (from step 8):

```
Protected Sub MyCalendar_DayRender(ByVal Sender As System.Object, _
                        ByVal e As DayRenderEventArgs )

   if ( e.Day.IsOtherMonth )
      e.Cell.BackColor=System.Drawing.Color.FromName("Gainsboro")
```

507

```
    Else If ( e.Day.IsWeekend )
       e.Cell.BackColor=System.Drawing.Color.FromName("PaleGoldenrod")
    Else
       e.Cell.BackColor=System.Drawing.Color.FromName("LightGoldenrodYellow")
    End if
    ...
End Sub
```

The way this code works is that we use an `if` statement to determine whether the day being called is a month, for example, `if ( e.Day.IsOtherMonth )`. If this statement is true, we define the backcolour of that `Cell` by importing the `System.Drawing` namespace, and requesting the color we want. The variable `e` is automatically passed into this event procedure by ASP.NET. It contains additional information about the control that might be useful to a programmer. In our case we use it to set the color of the `Cell` (which represents a day).

The next step in rendering the `MyCalendar.xml` data to a given `Calendar Cell` involved loading the XML data source into a `DataSet`. What might not be obvious is the use of the `Session` object to store a cached instance of the loaded `DataSet`. The reason for caching the `DataSet` object, is so that we can reduce the number of times the calendar data (stored in the `MyCalendar.xml` file) is loaded from scratch. The `DataSet` object will be cached for the lifetime of the session.

In step 7, before we attempted to load the file, we first checked the `Session` object for an instance of a `MyCalendarData` object, which is a `DataSet` object. If there's already one declared, there's no need to perform the work of loading in the XML file again – the `cachedData` object is returned. If `Session("MyCalendarData")` returns `Nothing`, then we perform the work of loading the XML source, but once we're done loading it, we assign the dataset to the `Session("MyCalendarData")` object:

```
Protected Function LoadMyCalendarData() As DataSet
  ...
Dim cachedDataSet as DataSet = Session("MyCalendarData")
if ( Not cachedDataSet Is Nothing ) Then
   Return cachedDataSet
End if
  ...
Try
   fileStream = New FileStream(sourceXML, FileMode.Open)
   dataSet.ReadXml(fileStream)
   fileStream.Close()

   Session("MyCalendarData") = dataSet
  ...
End Function
```

In using the `DataSet` from the `Session` object, we don't need to load the `MyCalendar.xml` file from scratch each time the `Calendar` control renders a day item. Keep in mind that the `Calendar` control renders 6 weeks worth of days, which amounts to 42 calls (6 weeks times 7 days in a week) to the `LoadMyCalendarData` method on a single page load – so even though the `LoadMyCalendar` method is being invoked numerous times, it's **optimized** to use the cached `DataSet` stored in `Session("MyCalendarData")`.

The code to render the `MyCalendar.xml` data to a specific `Cell` within the `Calendar` control is fairly straightforward. We loop through all the rows in our `DataSet` object's default `Table` and compare with the date the `Calendar` control is currently rendering – if the dates are the same, we have some work to do. Remember that each row represents a single event, and each time a day is rendered we have to see if that day matches one of the events. Otherwise, we loop through to the next item. When we encounter a match, we actually add the content to the `Calendar` object's `Cell` property, by creating a new `Label` object, setting its display properties, and adding it to the `Cell` object's `Controls` container:

```
Protected Sub MyCalendar_DayRender(ByVal Sender As System.Object, _
                                   ByVal e As DayRenderEventArgs )
...
Dim zRow as DataRow

For Each zRow in dataSet.Tables(0).Rows
  Dim compareDate as DateTime
  compareDate = GetSafeDate ( zRow.Item("EventDate") )

    If ( compareDate e.Day.Date ) Then

      ' Event matches date criteria - display it...
      ...
      Dim dailyEventLabel as New Label
      dailyEventLabel.Text = "<br />" + myEventData.ShortDesc
      e.Cell.Controls.Add ( dailyEventLabel )
    End If
Next

End Sub
```

Repeater Control Implementation Details

The sole reason for implementing a `Repeater` control is to display the specific `MyCalendar.xml` event details that correspond to the currently selected day in the calendar. The details of an event or an appointment could contain quite a bit of information, therefore trying to put it all into a single `Cell` object of the `Calendar` control probably wouldn't look all that great. Displaying a short description (`ShortDesc`) in the `Calendar` control's `Cell`, however, and relegating the detailed description (`DetailDesc`), and any additional information to the `Repeater` is prudent.

The mapping of the `MyCalendar.xml` data to the `Repeater` control is handled by the `ShowDailyEvents` method, which is invoked when the page first loads, and also as a result of an `OnSelectionChanged` event posted by the `Calendar` control. This event is automatically reaised when the day (or month) selected is changed by the user. Recall from step 10 that we declared a class, `MyCalendarEventData`. This contained various `Private` members and corresponding `Public` properties, which served as a container for the data extracted from the `MyCalendar.xml` file:

```
Public Class MyCalendarEventData

    Private m_ShortDesc As String
    Private m_DetailDesc As String
    Private m_EventDate As DateTime
    Private m_StartTime As String
```

```
      Private m_EndTime As String

      Public Property ShortDesc() As String
        Get
          Return m_ShortDesc
        End Get
        Set
         m_ShortDesc = value
        End Set
      End Property
      ...
```

There are at least two reasons for going through the effort of creating this class. The first is purely related to object oriented design. In the event that the MyCalendar.xml file changes, or if new elements are added, it's good practice to have an object, like MyCalendarEventData, to map the new values to. This way, we would only have to make the changes under the relevant sections of our XML file – the method that calls these sections would still work.

The second reason is interrelated with the first, but is actually more practical: we can bind MyCalendarEventData objects to any data rendering control, like a Repeater control (which we did in steps 8 and 9).

This brings us back to the ShowDailyEvents method. When invoked, this method performs a similar set of tasks to the MyCalendar_DayRender method, with a key difference: it renders all the matching events for a given day to the Repeater control, not the Calendar control. The ShowDailyEvents method proceeds to loop through all the DataRow objects in the DataSet object's default table in order to build an ArrayList of MyCalendarEventData objects. We need to do this because the DataSet contains all events, and not just those for the selected day. So, we build an ArrayList containing just those events for the selected day. As you can see in the code we added in step 9:

```
   Protected Sub ShowDailyEvents()
     ...

     Dim aEvents as new ArrayList()

     For Each zRow in dataSet.Tables(0).Rows
       Dim compareDate as DateTime
       compareDate = GetSafeDate ( zRow.Item("EventDate") )

       If ( compareDate = d ) Then

         ' Event matches date criteria - display it...
         Dim myEventData as New MyCalendarEventData
     ...
         aEvents.Add ( myEventData )
       End If
     Next

     ' Bind to the Repeater control...
     DailyEventDetailRepeater.DataSource = aEvents
     DailyEventDetailRepeater.DataBind()
   ...

     End Sub
```

The significance of storing the matching MyCalendarEventData objects in the aEvents variable (an ArrayList containing just those events for the selected day) is that we can bind this sub-set of records to the DailyEventDetailRepeater object to generate a detailed listing of the events for the selected day.

The final details concerning the Repeater control implementation deal with display issues. For some days, there may be no specific events. As such, when the user clicks on a particular day Cell link of the Calendar control that has no related events, we implement the following code to toggle the visibility of the Panel control (which contains the DailyEventDetailRepeater object):

```
Protected Sub ShowDailyEvents()
    ...

    if ( aEvents.Count > 0 ) then
      DailyDetailsPanel.Visible = True
      SelectedDate.Text = "Events For " + d.ToLongDateString()
    else
      DailyDetailsPanel.Visible = False
      SelectedDate.Text = "No Events Scheduled For " + d.ToLongDateString()
    End if

    End Sub
```

The SelectedDate object is a Label control that is not declared within the DailyDetailsPanel declaration, and therefore will not be affected when the DailyDetailsPanel.Visible property is changed. The DailyEventDetailRepeater control's visibility status, however, this will correspond to whatever the DailyDetailsPanel.Visible property is. This is a nice feature to use, especially when you want to control the visibility state of a group of controls with one single property change.

Editing the Data Using Templates

In Chapter 13, we looked at updating data in DataSets, and in this chapter we've looked at using the grids and templates. One of the most powerful features behind ASP.NET is the templating architecture, which allows us to define a different set of controls depending upon the actions of the user. For the DataGrid and DataList we can use the EditItem template we saw earlier to automatically display different controls when the user wishes to edit some data.

Let's look at a simple example to see how this works.

Try It Out – Using the EditItem Template

1. Create a new file called EditTemplate.aspx, and add the following HTML elements and ASP.NET server controls. Don't worry about it looking long and complex – we'll explain it after we've seen what it does:

```
<html>
  <body>
    <form runat="server">

      <asp:Label id="ErrorMessage" runat="server" /><br/>

      <asp:LinkButton OnClick="DEDR_Add" Text="Add new event"
```

```
                    runat="server"/><br/>

    <asp:DataGrid id="EventData"
        AutoGenerateColumns="false" width="100%" runat="server"
        OnEditCommand="DEDR_Edit"
        OnUpdateCommand="DEDR_Update"
        OnCancelCommand="DEDR_Cancel"
        OnDeleteCommand="DEDR_Delete">

      <HeaderStyle ForeColor="White" BackColor="DodgerBlue"
                   Font-Bold="true"/>
      <ItemStyle BackColor="White"/>
      <AlternatingItemStyle BackColor="Gainsboro"/>

      <Columns>
        <asp:TemplateColumn HeaderText="Event">
          <ItemTemplate>
            <%# Container.DataItem("ShortDesc") %>
          </ItemTemplate>
          <EditItemTemplate>
            <asp:TextBox id="txtShortDesc" Size="25"
                 Text='<%# Container.DataItem("ShortDesc") %>'
                 runat="server"/>
          </EditItemTemplate>
        </asp:TemplateColumn>

        <asp:TemplateColumn HeaderText="Description">
          <ItemTemplate>
            <%# Container.DataItem("DetailDesc") %>
          </ItemTemplate>
          <EditItemTemplate>
            <asp:TextBox id="txtDetailDesc" Size="50"
                 Text='<%# Container.DataItem("DetailDesc") %>'
                 runat="server"/>
          </EditItemTemplate>
        </asp:TemplateColumn>

        <asp:TemplateColumn HeaderText="Start Time">
          <ItemTemplate>
            <%# Container.DataItem("StartTime") %>
          </ItemTemplate>
          <EditItemTemplate>
            <asp:TextBox id="txtStartTime" Size="7"
                 Text='<%# Container.DataItem("StartTime") %>'
                 runat="server"/>
          </EditItemTemplate>
        </asp:TemplateColumn>

        <asp:TemplateColumn HeaderText="EndTime">
          <ItemTemplate>
            <%# Container.DataItem("EndTime") %>
          </ItemTemplate>
          <EditItemTemplate>
            <asp:TextBox id="txtEndTime" Size="7"
```

```
                        Text='<%# Container.DataItem("EndTime") %>'
                        runat="server"/>
              </EditItemTemplate>
            </asp:TemplateColumn>

            <asp:TemplateColumn>
              <ItemTemplate>
                <asp:LinkButton CommandName="Edit"    Text="Edit"
                        runat="server"/>
                <asp:LinkButton CommandName="Delete" Text="Delete"
                        runat="server"/>
              </ItemTemplate>
              <EditItemTemplate>
                <asp:LinkButton CommandName="Cancel" Text="Cancel"
                        runat="server"/>
                <asp:LinkButton CommandName="Update" Text="Update"
                        runat="server"/>
              </EditItemTemplate>
            </asp:TemplateColumn>

          </Columns>

      </asp:DataGrid>

    </form>

  </body>
</html>
```

2. Now add the following to the top of this page:

```
<%@ Import Namespace="System.Data" %>
<%@ Import Namespace="System.IO" %>

<script language="VB" runat="server">

  Sub Page_Load(Sender As Object, E As EventArgs)

    If Not Page.IsPostBack Then
      EventData.DataSource = LoadMyCalendarData
      EventData.DataBind()
    End If

  End Sub


  Protected Function LoadMyCalendarData() As DataSet

    Dim sourceXML as String = Server.MapPath("MyCalendar.xml")
      If ( Not File.Exists ( sourceXML ) ) Then
        Return Nothing
      End if
```

```
    Dim cachedDataSet as DataSet = Session("MyCalendarData")
      If ( Not cachedDataSet Is Nothing ) Then
        Return cachedDataSet
      End if
    Dim dataSet As DataSet = New DataSet()

    Try
      dataSet.ReadXml(sourceXML)

      Session("MyCalendarData") = dataSet

    Catch e As Exception
      ErrorMessage.Text = e.Message
      dataSet = Nothing
    End Try

    Return dataSet

End Function



Sub DEDR_Edit(Sender As Object, E As DataGridCommandEventArgs)

  EventData.EditItemIndex = CInt(e.Item.ItemIndex)
  EventData.DataSource = LoadMyCalendarData
  EventData.DataBind()

End Sub


Sub DEDR_Update(Sender As Object, E As DataGridCommandEventArgs)

  Dim dataSet  As DataSet = LoadMyCalendarData
  Dim row      As Integer = CInt(e.Item.ItemIndex)
  Dim EditText As TextBox

  EditText = E.Item.FindControl("txtShortDesc")
  dataSet.Tables(0).Rows(row).Item("ShortDesc") = EditText.Text
  EditText = E.Item.FindControl("txtDetailDesc")
  dataSet.Tables(0).Rows(row).Item("DetaiLDesc") = EditText.Text
  EditText = E.Item.FindControl("txtStartTime")
  dataSet.Tables(0).Rows(row).Item("StartTime") = EditText.Text
  EditText = E.Item.FindControl("txtEndTime")
  dataSet.Tables(0).Rows(row).Item("EndTime") = EditText.Text

  dataSet.WriteXml(Server.MapPath("MyCalendar.xml"))

  Session("MyCalendarData") = Nothing

  EventData.EditItemIndex = -1

  EventData.DataSource = LoadMyCalendarData
  EventData.DataBind()
```

```
    End Sub


  Sub DEDR_Cancel(Sender As Object, E As DataGridCommandEventArgs)

    EventData.EditItemIndex = -1

    Session("MyCalendarData") = Nothing

    EventData.DataSource = LoadMyCalendarData
    EventData.DataBind()

  End Sub

  Sub DEDR_Delete(Sender As Object, E As DataGridCommandEventArgs)

    Dim dataSet As DataSet = LoadMyCalendarData
    Dim row      As Integer = CInt(e.Item.ItemIndex)

    dataSet.Tables(0).Rows(row).Delete

    dataSet.WriteXml(Server.MapPath("MyCalendar.xml"))

    Session("MyCalendarData") = Nothing

    EventData.EditItemIndex = -1

    EventData.DataSource = LoadMyCalendarData
    EventData.DataBind()

  End Sub


  Sub DEDR_Add(Sender As Object, E As EventArgs)

    Dim dataSet As DataSet = LoadMyCalendarData

    Dim newRow As DataRow
    newRow = dataSet.Tables(0).NewRow()
    newRow.Item("EventDate") = "15/07/2001"
    newRow.Item("ShortDesc") = ""
    newRow.Item("DetailDesc") = ""
    newRow.Item("StartTime") = ""
    newRow.Item("EndTime") = ""
    dataSet.Tables(0).Rows.Add(newRow)

    dataSet.WriteXml(Server.MapPath("MyCalendar.xml"))

    Session("MyCalendarData") = Nothing

    EventData.DataSource = LoadMyCalendarData
    EventData.DataBind()
```

```
      EventData.EditItemIndex = EventData.Items.Count - 1
      EventData.DataSource = LoadMyCalendarData
      EventData.DataBind()

   End Sub

</script>
```

3. Now view the page from your browser:

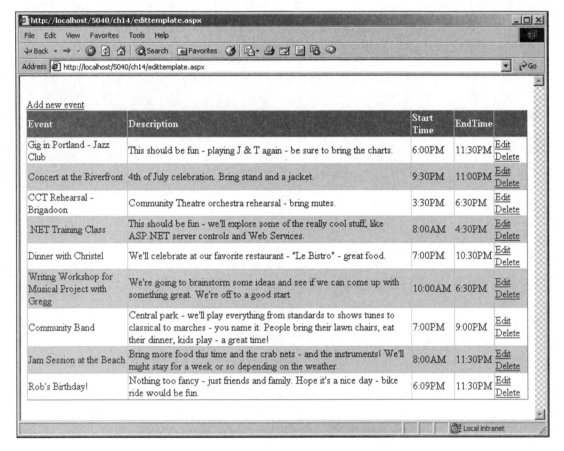

There's nothing very special about this – it's a standard looking grid, with options to add and edit data.

4. Now hit the Edit link for the first row:

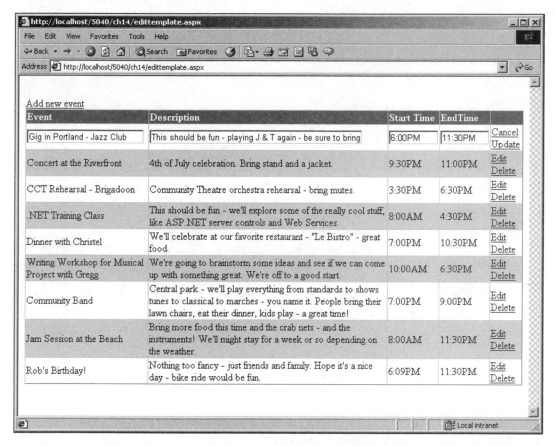

Notice how the row has changed – instead of just text, we now have text boxes allowing us to edit the text. The links in the last column have also changed, now indicating we can either cancel the changes, or update the data with our changes.

5. Try making some changes to the text and hitting the Cancel button. Notice how the changes you typed in are ignored. Try the Edit link again, and this time the Update link – the changes are now saved.

6. Now try the Add new event link:

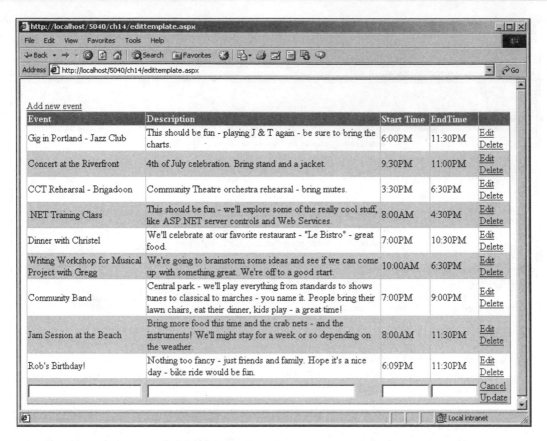

Notice how an extra row has been added, with empty values for you to type in the new data. Try pressing Cancel, and you see that the empty row disappears. Add another row and this time press Update to save the changes.

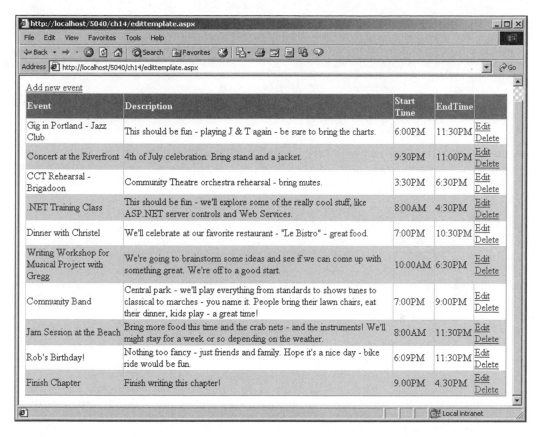

7. For the row you have just added, press the Delete link to test this function out.

Let's see how all of this works.

How It Works– Using the EditItem Template

Let's first look at the controls. We start with the server form, and a label to be used for displaying any error messages that might occur:

```
<html>
  <body>
    <form runat="server">

      <asp:Label id="ErrorMessage" runat="server" /><br/>
```

Next, we add a LinkButton which is used as the link that adds new rows to the data. You could use an ordinary button here, but I think this looks neater:

```
<asp:LinkButton OnClick="DEDR_Add" Text="Add new event"
    runat="server"/><br/>
```

Now we start on the `DataGrid`. The first thing to note, is that we have set the `AutoGenerateColumns` attribute to false, telling the `DataGrid` not to generate any columns automatically. One of the great features of the `DataGrid` is that when you bind data to it, it cycles through the rows and columns of the data and generates the HTML table accordingly. In this example, we don't want that, as we want to create the columns ourself:

```
<asp:DataGrid id="EventData"
     AutoGenerateColumns="false" width="100%" runat="server"
```

Also, on the `DataGrid`, are some command properties. The `DataGrid` understands the concept of editing data, and has some special properties that allow us to tell it which event procedures are to be run when a set command is selected. You'll see how these commands are defined a little later:

```
OnEditCommand="DEDR_Edit"
OnUpdateCommand="DEDR_Update"
OnCancelCommand="DEDR_Cancel"
OnDeleteCommand="DEDR_Delete">
```

Next, we define some style properties of the `DataGrid` object. We could have done this using the attributes of the grid itself, but I thought it would be worthwhile showing a different way to do it. For example, we could do this:

```
<asp:DataGrid id="EventData"
     HeaderStyle-ForeColor="White" HeaderStyle-BackColor="DodgerBlue"/>
```

There's no difference in the way the two methods of declaring these attributes work, so you can pick a style that you prefer. All we are doing here is defining the style properties for the various templates (the `Header`, `Item` and `AlternatingItem`).

```
<HeaderStyle ForeColor="White" BackColor="DodgerBlue"
            Font-Bold="true"/>
<ItemStyle BackColor="White"/>
<AlternatingItemStyle BackColor="Gainsboro"/>
```

Now comes the bit where we define our columns. Remember, that it's us that's defining them, not the grid. For each column we are going to use a `TemplateColumn` (this is just a column type that allows you to customize the layout of controls in the column), denoting that the column is to have a template applied. Earlier in the chapter you saw some code like this:

```
<asp:DataList id="DataList1" runat="server">
   <FooterTemplate>
     'Items to be affected by this template
   </FooterTemplate>
   <SeparatorTemplate>
     'Items to be affected by this template
   </SeparatorTemplate>
</asp:DataList>
```

This defined a template and then, within the template, the columns. The `DataGrid` works the other way round, defining the columns first, and then the templates within each column. This is sensible because the grid is inherently columnar. So, we have our first template column, with some text to be placed in the header:

```
<Columns>
  <asp:TemplateColumn HeaderText="Event">
```

Now, for this new column, we define the templates, the first being the `ItemTemplate`, which just shows the data:

```
<ItemTemplate>
  <%# Container.DataItem("ShortDesc") %>
</ItemTemplate>
```

The line in the template is an advanced form of data binding. You've seen how we use the `DataSource` property of a server control (such as a `DataGrid` or `Repeater`) to identify where the data comes from. When you are defining the columns yourself, you need to specify which fields in the data are shown. To do this we have to refer to the `Container`, since this is where the data is stored. In our case the `Container` is the `DataSet` that the grid is bound to. We use the `DataItem` collection to point to a specific item – it's `ShortDesc` in the example above, but could be the name of any field. ASP.NET knows this is advanced databinding because we have surrounded the binding details with `<%# %>`. This is very similar to the `<% %>` ASP tags, but it's the # which is the important bit – it's that that switches on the binding features.

The grid will automatically put the HTML table tags (the TR and TD tags) in for us, so all we have to do is output the data using the databinding syntax described above. For the `EditItemTemplate`, which comes into effect when we are editing this row, we need some way to type in text, so we use a `TextBox`. In this case, we set the `Text` property of the text box to contain the data that we showed in the `ItemTempate`:

```
<EditItemTemplate>
  <asp:TextBox id="txtShortDesc" Size="25"
       Text='<%# Container.DataItem("ShortDesc") %>'
       runat="server"/>
</EditItemTemplate>
</asp:TemplateColumn>
```

So that's the definition of one column. It's a `TemplateColumn` with two templates: one for just displaying the data, and one for editing the data. The `ItemTemplate` is normally used, until the row is put into edit mode (you'll see how in a while). When this happens ASP.NET automatically displays the `EditItemTemplate` for the selected row.

The other columns are exactly the same as this, just getting their data from different columns in the data set. The final column is different however, as it's here that we have out edit links. Again, there are two templates. For the `ItemTemplate` we have a link to **Edit** and a link to **Delete**. When we are in edit mode (the `EditItemTemplate`) we want different buttons – to **Update** and **Cancel**. I've again used `LinkButtons` as I think they look nicer in this sample, but you could easily use standard buttons:

```
<asp:TemplateColumn>
  <ItemTemplate>
    <asp:LinkButton CommandName="Edit"   Text="Edit"
         runat="server"/>
    <asp:LinkButton CommandName="Delete" Text="Delete"
         runat="server"/>
  </ItemTemplate>
```

```
<EditItemTemplate>
  <asp:LinkButton CommandName="Cancel" Text="Cancel"
       runat="server"/>
  <asp:LinkButton CommandName="Update" Text="Update"
       runat="server"/>
</EditItemTemplate>
</asp:TemplateColumn>
```

The key thing about this is the `CommandName` property, which identifies which command this button is associated with. Remember how when we defined the grid we identified event procedures with commands – well it's these commands that we were defining the procedures for. So the button with `CommandName="Edit"` will call the event procedure defined by `OnEditCommand="DEDR_Edit"`.

Now let's look at the code. When the page is first loaded, we use the `LoadMyCalendarData` routine to load the calendar details from the XML file. This is exactly the same routine as we used earlier in the MyCalendar.aspx example, so we won't look at that again here.

Now let's look at the event procedures for editing, starting with the one for directly editing an entry. This is run when we select the **Edit** link, and its job is to tell the grid which row is being edited. It does this by setting the `EditItemIndex` property on the grid. Whenever this is set to a row, the `EditItemTemplate` for that row is displayed instead of the `ItemTemplate`. To identify the correct row, we use the arguments of the event procedure – these arguments are defined by ASP.NET, and provide information on which object called the event, along with various other sorts of information. In this case, the other information is the index number of the row that we are editing, as defined by the `ItemIndex` property. This is provided automatically by ASP.NET, because we have the link button in a row on the grid, whenever that link button is pressed the index number is supplied to the event procedure, thus allowing us to identify the correct row. As soon as the `EditItemTemplate` appears, we can make our changes:

```
Sub DEDR_Edit(Sender As Object, E As DataGridCommandEventArgs)

  EventData.EditItemIndex = CInt(e.Item.ItemIndex)
  EventData.DataSource = LoadMyCalendarData
  EventData.DataBind()

End Sub
```

To update a row, we have to extract the data we have inserted into the text boxes on the row. We once again obtain the current row number, and this will be used to index into the rows in the `DataSet`:

```
Sub DEDR_Update(Sender As Object, E As DataGridCommandEventArgs)

  Dim dataSet As DataSet = LoadMyCalendarData
  Dim row As Integer = CInt(e.Item.ItemIndex)
```

To find the information in the `DataSet` text boxes, we have to use the `FindControl` method. Although we have given our text boxes names, because they are used within a grid, these names could be ambiguous. So, when generating a grid, ASP.NET uses this name as part of a unique name for the controls on the grid. We don't know what the rest of this unique name is, therefore we have to use `FindControl` to find the correct control. Once we have found the row, we then update the data in the `DataSet`:

```
Dim EditText As TextBox

EditText = E.Item.FindControl("txtShortDesc")
dataSet.Tables(0).Rows(row).Item("ShortDesc") = EditText.Text
EditText = E.Item.FindControl("txtDetailDesc")
dataSet.Tables(0).Rows(row).Item("DetaiLDesc") = EditText.Text
EditText = E.Item.FindControl("txtStartTime")
dataSet.Tables(0).Rows(row).Item("StartTime") = EditText.Text
EditText = E.Item.FindControl("txtEndTime")
dataSet.Tables(0).Rows(row).Item("EndTime") = EditText.Text
```

At this stage the `DataSet` has been updated, but the data hasn't been written back to the XML file, so we use `WriteXml` to write the file out to disk:

```
dataSet.WriteXml(Server.MapPath("MyCalendar.xml"))
```

When we initially read the XML we placed it in `Session` state, to save having to read it again. Now that the data has changed it needs to be reloaded into the `Session`, however, so we remove the copy currently in the `Session`:

```
Session("MyCalendarData") = Nothing
```

We then set the `EditItemIndex` of the grid to −1, which takes the grid out of edit mode. When this happens the `EditItemTemplate` is no longer used, and the row reverts back to using the `ItemTemplate`:

```
EventData.EditItemIndex = -1
```

Finally, we reload the data into the grid:

```
EventData.DataSource = LoadMyCalendarData
EventData.DataBind()

    End Sub
```

That takes care of changing existing data, but what about canceling changes? When in edit mode, we have the **Cancel** link, which calls the following procedure. This is quite simple, first setting the `EditItemIndex` to −1, to take the grid out of edit mode. We then invalidate the `Session` state, and reload the data. Strictly speaking we don't always need to invalidate the `Session` variable here. For example, when editing a row, the changes are only available as part of the form – it's the **Update** procedure that updates the `DataSet`. So, we could just rebind to the cached data, which hasn't changed. When we add a row, however, we do update the `DataSet` – in this case just rebinding wouldn't work – we actually have to invalidate the `Session` state, and reload the data from the file:

```
Sub DEDR_Cancel(Sender As Object, E As DataGridCommandEventArgs)

    EventData.EditItemIndex = -1

    Session("MyCalendarData") = Nothing
```

```
        EventData.DataSource = LoadMyCalendarData
        EventData.DataBind()

    End Sub
```

To delete a row, we just have to identify the row number selected (using the ItemIndex), and then use this to delete the selected row in the DataSet. Once deleted, we write the data to the XML file and invalidate the Session data because, the data has changed:

```
    Sub DEDR_Delete(Sender As Object, E As DataGridCommandEventArgs)

        Dim dataSet As DataSet = LoadMyCalendarData
        Dim row      As Integer = CInt(e.Item.ItemIndex)

        dataSet.Tables(0).Rows(row).Delete

        dataSet.WriteXml(Server.MapPath("MyCalendar.xml"))

        Session("MyCalendarData") = Nothing
```

We then take the grid out of edit mode, and rebind the data:

```
        EventData.EditItemIndex = -1

        EventData.DataSource = LoadMyCalendarData
        EventData.DataBind()

    End Sub
```

Adding data is slightly different to the other methods of changing data, because there is no specific Add command. What we have to do is add the row to the dataset, and then rebind the data. First, we load the data from the Session:

```
    Sub DEDR_Add(Sender As Object, E As EventArgs)

        Dim dataSet As DataSet = LoadMyCalendarData
```

Then we use the NewRow method of the table to create a new row object.

```
        Dim newRow As DataRow
        newRow = dataSet.Tables(0).NewRow()
```

Now we have the new row, we can set the data for it. You can use any date here (perhaps the date selected from a Calendar), but I used similar dates to the previous entries. The other data is set to empty strings:

```
        newRow.Item("EventDate") = "2001/07/15"
        newRow.Item("ShortDesc") = ""
        newRow.Item("DetailDesc") = ""
        newRow.Item("StartTime") = ""
        newRow.Item("EndTime") = ""
```

Once the data is set, we add the new row the to the table.

```
dataSet.Tables(0).Rows.Add(newRow)
```

Now we save the data to its file , invalidate the Session, and reload it:

```
dataSet.WriteXml(Server.MapPath("MyCalendar.xml"))

Session("MyCalendarData") = Nothing


EventData.DataSource = LoadMyCalendarData
EventData.DataBind()
```

Now the data is reloaded, we set the EditItemIndex of the new row, so that the row is put into edit mode. You don't have to do this, but it saves the user from having to click the Edit link on the new row. We use the Items collection of the Datagrid to identify how many rows it has. The Count property tells us how many rows, and since the rows are indexed from 0, we subtract 1 from this count, and then rebind the data (thus forcing the switch of templates):

```
EventData.EditItemIndex = EventData.Items.Count - 1
EventData.DataSource = LoadMyCalendarData
EventData.DataBind()

    End Sub

  </script>
```

That's all there is to it. It seems a lot, but there's not actually much code. The key things to remember are:

- Use Button or LinkButton controls to provide the edit commands
- Link these edit command buttons with event procedures using the On...Command attributes of the DataGrid
- Set the EditItemIndex to the required row and rebind the data to put the grid into edit mode
- Set the EditItemIndex to –1 to cancel from edit mode

This example used an XML file, but in each of the event procedures that updated data you could easily update a database. This could be done by either using the built in commands of the DataSet, or by issuing SQL commands directly. There are several examples in the ASP.NET QuickStart that show this.

AutoGenerating the Columns

As an alternative solution to writing the column information yourself, you can let the DataGrid do most of the layout for you. In our code above we used the AutoGenerateColumns attribute to tell the grid **not** to automatically create columns from the bound data. That enabled us to provide the exact layout we required. If you let the grid generate the columns, however, you can also add columns using the Columns tag. The following code shows how this is done – it lets the grid handle the columns for the data, while we add the extra columns for the edit links:

525

```
<asp:DataGrid id="EventData"
      width="100%" runat="server"
      OnEditCommand="DEDR_Edit"
      OnUpdateCommand="DEDR_Update"
      OnCancelCommand="DEDR_Cancel"
      OnDeleteCommand="DEDR_Delete">

    <HeaderStyle ForeColor="White" BackColor="DodgerBlue"
               Font-Bold="true"/>
    <ItemStyle BackColor="White"/>
    <AlternatingItemStyle BackColor="Gainsboro"/>

    <Columns>

      <asp:TemplateColumn>
        <ItemTemplate>
          <asp:LinkButton CommandName="Edit"    Text="Edit"
               runat="server"/>
          <asp:LinkButton CommandName="Delete" Text="Delete"
               runat="server"/>
        </ItemTemplate>
        <EditItemTemplate>
          <asp:LinkButton CommandName="Cancel" Text="Cancel"
               runat="server"/>
          <asp:LinkButton CommandName="Update" Text="Update"
               runat="server"/>
        </EditItemTemplate>
      </asp:TemplateColumn>

    </Columns>

</asp:DataGrid>
```

This would create a grid like so:

	ShortDesc	DetailDesc	EventDate	StartTime	EndTime
Add new event					
Edit Delete	Concert at the Riverfront	4th of July celebration. Bring stand and a jacket.	04/07/2001	9:30PM	11:00PM
Edit Delete	CCT Rehearsal - Brigadoon	Community Theatre orchestra rehearsal - bring mutes.	14/07/2001	3:30PM	6:30PM
Edit Delete	Finish Chapter	Finish writing this chapter	15/07/2001	9:00AM	4:30PM

Having the edit links in the first column isn't a big issue, although I personally prefer them at the end. What's more of a problem is that the headings now reflect the names of the columns, rather than some neat text. In the long run, I think defining your own templates is better, as you have finer control over what your data will look like.

The EditItemTemplate technique is also available with the DataList, which is particularly useful when you require a more free-form approach to your layout, as opposed to the more columnar layout of the grid. Whichever way you choose to display your data, templating makes it really easy.

Summary

This chapter introduced a variety of ASP.NET server controls available to use within any web form. Numerous examples were provided to illustrate how to use ASP.NET server controls within an ASPX page, as well as specific examples for working with these controls programmatically. By now you should have a good basic understanding of ASP.NET server controls, including:

❑ The syntax for declaring an ASP.NET server control

❑ The benefits of ASP.NET server controls, such as the rich object model, automatic browser detection, a variety of properties, events, and re-usability

❑ The various ASP.NET server control families (intrinsic, validation, rich, and data rendering controls)

ASP.NET server controls derive their methods, properties and events from the various classes and objects that make up the .NET Framework and provide an object-oriented way to write dynamic web forms. All ASP.NET server controls are declared using same tag element naming conventions, similar to well-formed XML, and provide a uniform way to declare properties, and assign event handler methods.

Some insight into the ASP.NET page lifecycle, in relation to ASP.NET server controls was provided. The `Page` object's `Page_Load` and `Page_Unload` methods were explained to provide a context for when and why these methods are implemented. We also covered the basics of event handling as related to the `Page` object's `IsPostback` property.

The ASP.NET validation controls covered in this chapter, and the examples herein, should serve to open a gateway to understanding the tools you have at your disposal for creating web forms that are capable of validating data. Although we only scratched the surface of the possibilities of the various data rendering controls, such as the `DataGrid`, `DataList` and `Repeater`, you should be able to see their advantages in rendering a variety of types of data.

Reusable Code for ASP.NET

So far, most of the ASP.NET pages we've built have been quite specialized and self-contained. We've put a lot of functionality into each one, and only really retained the benefits of our hard work from one page to another, by copying the entire contents into a new .ASPX file.

It should come as no surprise to discover that this isn't really a viable way to write functionality-rich web sites – particularly not if you're on a salary and expected to deliver results before the next millennium. For that reason, we're now going to spend a little time discussing how to write reusable code for ASP.NET. Note that we're not just talking about objects here (although, yet again, objects play a crucial role in the story), but about code **components**: totally independent files that encapsulate groups of useful functionality.

In the course of this chapter, we're going to look at two specific ways to use components in ASP.NET:

- ❏ User controls – a Web Form that is encapsulated in a re-usable Server Control
- ❏ Code Behind – used for separating HTML user interface design (color, aesthetics and so on) from any page code

First though, we're going to take a careful look at what we mean when we talk about components, and consider the various advantages they offer us.

From Objects to Components

When we first met objects in Chapter 8, we discussed how they are essentially a software construct that bundles together data and functionality. We define a few very specific interfaces on an object so that we can use the functionality it contains, for example, by creating methods and properties that we can access programmatically. Let's have a brief example.

We can have a class that describes a car, as represented below:

```
The Car Class
Methods:       Move
               StartEngine
               OpenDoor
Properties:    Color
               Make
               Model
```

As you can see – our car isn't particularly exciting, but we're only interested in a brief example. Our class defines a set of specific methods and properties, and these will exist in any object derived from this class. If I was to instantiate a new object, based on this class, I could call methods – for example, my car can move, I can start the engine, and I can open my door, just like any other car. However, the properties of my own car define it as a black Ford Puma – and not every car is a black Ford Puma. Other cars, represented by other instances of our class, could be different colors, makes, and models.

We can set properties and call methods on our object programmatically. These methods are probably quite complex under the covers. If I want to start the engine, I have to check that my car is in neutral, that the handbrake is on, and that all of my passengers are wearing seatbelts before I turn the key – yet all the programmer needs to do is say "Start the engine". I could change the order of the pre-engine start sequence under the covers, or I could even include a verbal warning for the passengers of my car, but the programmer would still only have to say exactly the same thing to start that engine. In programming terms, we're talking about **encapsulation**, where we hide away the behind-the-scenes action, to only expose a limited set of functionality to our programmer. In this way, if the structure of the object changes internally, we're still able to use it in conjunction with our other objects seamlessly.

By hiding away absolutely everything that doesn't concern task-specific usage of that object, thereby hiding implementation details from the consumer, we make it a lot easier to plug it together robustly with other objects. This makes it far easier for large teams of developers to build complex applications that don't fall prey to lots of low-level weaknesses. Another developer could work on a driver class, which could interact both with the car, and with a passenger class, as developed by someone else. As long as the interfaces available in each class don't change, they're still able to interact.

The crucial information we need to make an object, is held in the class definition, and any code with access to this class should be able to instantiate an instance of our class, and store this in an object. The way in which the object works is encapsulated, so that only the public methods and properties are available to the programmer.

In a similar way, a component is a set of re-usable code that is stored in such a location that it is accessible by many applications. Like an object, it encapsulates functionality, but the difference, is that an object is an implementation unit; a component is a deployment or packaging unit. A component could be a single class, or it could hold multiple class definitions.

All the code we've written so far has been held in specific .aspx pages. So, what's the point in having all this wonderful reusable code if we can only get at it from within a single page?

> **We need to break out our re-useable code into a separate component that we can reference from our .aspx pages.**

A component packages up a set of classes and interfaces, in order to isolate and encapsulate a specific set of functionality, and can provide a well-specified set of publicly available services. It is designed for a specific purpose rather than for a specific application.

Components

Technically speaking, a component is a self-contained unit of functionality, with external interfaces that are independent of its internal architecture. In other words, it's a bunch of code that's been packaged up as a black box, so that it can be used in any number of different applications as required.

If you spend a lot of time working with Microsoft Windows, you're almost certain to have come across (or at least heard of) DLL files – Dynamic Link Libraries. Many of these files contain components that define most of the functionality you're likely to come across in Windows, including that of any applications you've installed.

> *Note that DLLs are classified as system files, which are hidden by default. They can only be seen in Windows Explorer if your Folder Options are set to 'Show hidden files and folders'.*

For example, every time you fire up an instance of Internet Explorer, you're actually running a small program called iexplore.exe, which accesses numerous DLLs that reside in your system directory (if you have Windows 2000 running on your C drive, this will probably be C:\WinNT), and most of the browser's functionality is defined inside these files. This directory also contains the file explorer.exe, which is the executable for Windows Explorer. You might note that both these applications feature an identical **Address** bar, where you type in the URL of a website, or the path to a local directory – this user interface element has been implemented once, packaged inside a component, and is now being used by both programs.

What's more, if you enter the URL for a web page in the Windows Explorer address bar, you can view that page and even browse the Web in the main pane, without having to use iexplore.exe at all. Likewise, you can use iexplore.exe to view and browse your files, simply by entering a file path in the address bar.

What we can deduce from this is that either there's a lot of duplication between the two EXE files, or that the two sets of browser functionality are actually implemented as standalone components that can be accessed by both applications! In fact, it is down to the components.

Another case to consider is the Microsoft Office suite, which features many components that are shared amongst the individual Office applications, and throughout Windows itself. For example, there is one component that handles the Save As dialog as used by Word, Excel, Outlook, and the rest – this is why the Save dialog looks the same, no matter which application you run it from. This component is actually a Windows component, but the Office package makes use of this whenever you save or load a file. You can also use this from any other application that will let you save or load files, for example, Internet Explorer, or even Notepad. In this component, there's probably some code that has the presentation code for all of the buttons, some logic that understands what to do when you click on those buttons (for example, show the contents of a different directory in the main window in the middle of the dialog).

Throughout this book, we've been using the `aspnet_isapi.dll`, which has been working away behind IIS to process all of our ASP.NET pages. When IIS spots that someone is requesting a page with the extension `.aspx`, it uses this component to process them and communicate with the .NET framework.

Why use Components?

You should be starting to build up a picture of components as small, self-contained nuggets of functionality that can potentially make life a lot simpler when it comes to building any sort of non-trivial application. In this respect, they are similar to objects, but a component is re-useable code whose behind-the-scenes functionality is encapsulated away, so that only certain interfaces are available to the programmer. It can contain one or more class definitions, from which objects can be created, and which can be used for behind-the-scenes code. So, what are the benefits of using components?

❑   An individual component is a lot more simplistic than a full-blown application. It is restricted to a set of pre-defined functionality.

❑   Since components are self-contained, we can seamlessly upgrade (or fix) them simply by replacing one component with another that supports the same interfaces (methods, properties, and so on)

❑   Since using components is a good way of dividing our application into serviceable chunks, sometimes the functionality a component contains may be reusable elsewhere. We might even make it available to other programmers, or incorporate some of their components in our own applications.

Ultimately, components reduce the amount of code you write and make the code easier to maintain – once you've written one, you can re-use it over and over again within as many different applications as you like. Moreover, you can even obtain components from third party component vendors, which is a very popular way to enhance the functionality of your ASP.NET sites. You may need components that use the drawing capabilities of .NET to their limit, and your existing knowledge may not cover this – which is the time when you may consider looking for a third party solution.

Applying Component Theory to our Applications

Let's look at how componentization relates to our application models. So far in this book, we've created ASP.NET pages that do all sorts of things, from working with information input via a form, through to connecting to a database and working with data. Throughout, we've encouraged you to keep your code separated into distinct blocks – namely dynamically generated content (ASP.NET code) and presentation (HTML and various controls) – so that it's easier to change the way a page *looks* without affecting what it *does* too much, and vice versa. Also consider, that our raw content is most likely to be stored in a database, and that most of our code serves to provide a framework of logical operations between that and the presentation code.

Let's look at an example. Image that a team of developers was creating a website that sold books. One set of developers would probably be concerned with the look and feel of the site, and whether it was easy to use. They'd be responsible for the public image of the company via the Web, so they'd be more concerned with design, color, usability, and so on These are our designers, and they're probably using HTML and perhaps some graphics tools like Flash for fancy loading screens. You would probably also have another set of developers whose main interests lay in providing nifty blocks of code that did cool things when you clicked a button, or that validates the information entered into a form by the customers. These developers might also be responsible for generating the code required for connecting to the database of different books, and preparing the information on individual titles for display on the site. The designers would then make use of that information and display it in an aesthetically pleasing fashion.

If we were to constantly use ASP.NET pages that had all of the code and HTML on the same page, it would be awkward for both sets of people to work on the site at once. Simple mistakes could easily be made that could break part of the site, because someone deleted a character. Also, every page would have to be hand-made, and code would have to be copied, pasted, and amended as appropriate. If you made one change to the functionality of your site, you'd have to remember to make that change to all the appropriate pages. However, if you could separate out the HTML and design-focused code from the ASP.NET code blocks, and then re-use bits of that code, it would be much easier to update a single bit of code to change the functionality – every page that used it would be automatically updated. Web Designers get to play with color and layout as much as they like, and the ASP.NET developers can fine-tune their code without altering the look and feel of the site.

In this chapter, we'll look at two ways of dividing code into re-usable sections, User controls and Code Behind. In the next chapter, we'll take this one step further, and look at compiled components and custom server controls.

We're now going to move on to look at User controls, which is the first application of this code-separation concept that we'll be meeting.

User Controls

When the ASP.NET team first devised the concept of user controls, they were called pagelets. A term that many people disliked. Sadly, they were renamed, but I feel that the term pagelet, which implies a mini-page, was a good descriptive term for these controls.

User controls are web forms encapsulated into a reusable control. They are used to hold repetitive blocks of code that many of the pages in a web site need. For example, consider the Microsoft web site: each page has the same header style – a menu bar and a logo. This is a very common feature for a lot of websites; even our own www.wrox.com has this kind of style:

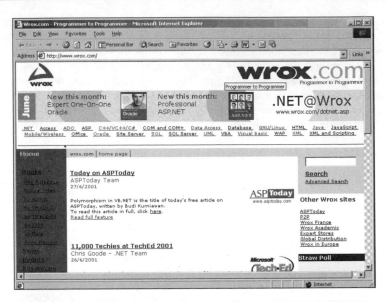

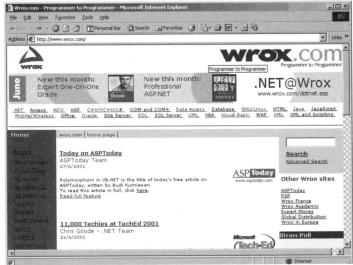

The Wrox site has the same kinds of menu bars at the top, left-hand side, and right-hand side of the screen at all times. These panes, panels or frames, depending on what you call them, and how you code them, are just one example of the types of things that user controls can provide programmatically.

Instead of having to copy and paste over chunks of repeated code to provide the header on all of our pages, we can create a simple **user control** that will have these chunks of code inside it, ready to be used. It's a way of accessing the same functionality over and over again.

> *If you ever programmed with ASP3.0, you'll probably be familiar with **include files**. User controls are similar to include files, but because ASP.NET is so different from ASP3.0, these controls are also created and used in a different manner.*

User controls can also do a lot more than simply produce headers and footers. We can give these User controls the ability to look and behave a bit like ASP.NET server controls. We can code properties so that our control can adapt depending on which attributes have been set on it. Anywhere on a site where many pages have similar blocks of functionality, we can use a user control to provide a repository for these repetitive code blocks. They are similar to custom-made rich server controls, but they don't quite go as far as full custom controls. True custom controls derive from the `System.Web.UI.Control` class, which we'll look at in more detail in the next chapter. Take, for example, a user login control. A user login control could be created as a user control, using a couple of text boxes and labels. This control is saved with a `.ascx` file extension, and can be called from any of the ASP.NET pages in our application using just two lines of code. The main principle of user controls, is that we could essentially cut out a portion of code from our ASP.NET page and paste it into a user control, where it would probably work just fine – as long as the ASP.NET page knows where to find the code, and where to put it.

Pros and Cons of User Controls

User controls are ideal for:

- ❑ Repetitive elements on pages like headers, menus, login controls, and so on
- ❑ Reducing the amount of code per page by encapsulating those repetitive elements into user controls

User controls are not ideal for:

- ❑ Separating presentation HTML from the code blocks (ideal for using Code Behind, which we'll meet later in this chapter)
- ❑ Encapsulating business logic in a re-usable package (ideal for pre-compiled assemblies, which we'll meet in the next chapter)
- ❑ Creating a control that can be re-used more widely than in just your application (ideal for custom server controls, which we'll meet in the next chapter)

We're going to look at two examples in this section. The first example shows how we can create a very simple user control that provides a common header for a web site. The second example will show off more of the capabilities of user controls, by creating a user login control.

Let's take a look at an example and see user controls in action, to help demonstrate their usefulness.

Try-It-Out – our first user control

We're going to have a go at creating a simple user control that forms a header for our web site. In our example, we've used an image, called `logo.gif`. This file is available for download, along with the rest of the code for the book, from **www.wrox.com**, but you could substitute any small image of your choice.

1. Open up your editor and enter the following code:

```
<script language="VB" runat="server">

  Public BackColor as String = "darkblue"

</script>
```

```
<table style="background-color:<%=BackColor%>" width="100%" cellpadding="10"
cellspacing="0">
  <tr>
    <td width="10%">
      <img src="logo.gif" align="left" />
    </td>
    <td width="60%">
      <font face="verdana,arial" size="4" color="lightyellow">
      Welcome to the shop!
      </font>
    </td>
    <td width="30%">
      <font face="verdana,arial" size="2" color="lightyellow">
      Stuff to buy...
      </font>
    </td>
  </tr>
</table>
```

2. Save this file as `header.ascx`

3. Now open up your editor again, and enter the following code into a new file, which will form our ASP.NET web form:

```
<%@ Register TagPrefix="UserControl" TagName="Header" Src="header.ascx" %>

<html>
<body>

<form runat="server" method="post">

  <UserControl:Header id="MyHeader" runat="Server" />

  <h3>A simple control for playing with header color</h3>

  <asp:DropDownList id="ColorList" runat="Server" />
  <asp:button text="Apply Color" OnClick="SubmitBtn_Click" runat="server" />
  <br /><br />
  <asp:label id="SelectedColor" runat="Server" />

</form>
</body>

<script language="VB" runat="Server">

  Public Sub Page_Load()

  If Not Page.IsPostback

    Dim arrColors As New ArrayList(5)
    arrColors.Add("Red")
    arrColors.Add("Green")
    arrColors.Add("Blue")
```

```
        arrColors.Add("Orange")
        arrColors.Add("Purple")

        Colorlist.Datasource = arrColors

        Page.DataBind()

      End If

   End Sub

   Public Sub SubmitBtn_Click(Sender As Object, E As EventArgs)

      Dim NewColor as String
      NewColor = Colorlist.SelectedItem.Text
      selectedcolor.text= "You selected " & NewColor
      MyHeader.BackColor= NewColor

   End Sub

</script>

</html>
```

4. Save this file as `main.aspx` and view it in your browser:

How it works

The majority of our user control is static HTML, but we've added the ability to change the background color of our header. Our main ASP.NET page takes the user input of the color and applies it to the header control. Let's start going through the code step by step by looking at our user control:

```
<script language="VB" runat="server">

   Public BackColor as String = "darkblue"

</script>
```

The beginning of our user control is where all the excitement happens. We declare a small script block and declare a public variable, which will hold a string for setting the background color of our header control. The default value is darkblue, but the user input from our ASP.NET page can change this (all the user has to do is select the required color in the drop-down listbox and hit the **Apply Color** button, and the color is changed):

```
<table style="background-color:<%=BackColor%>" width="100%" cellpadding="10"
cellspacing="0">
```

The next line creates a table. You'll notice that the background-color style attribute has a shortcut to the BackColor variable that we just declared. This is where the actual color applying takes place:

```
   <tr>
   <td width="10%"">
   <img src="logo.gif" align="left" />
   </td>
   <td width="60%">
     <font face="verdana,arial" size="4" color="lightyellow">
     Welcome to the shop!
     </font>
   </td>
   <td width="30%">
     <font face="verdana,arial" size="2" color="lightyellow">
     Stuff to buy...
     </font>
   </td>
  </tr>
</table>
```

There's not a lot to say about the rest of our code – it's simply an HTML table with three cells. The first contains an image, the second is the title of our page, and the third contains some text. In a real web site, the third option could well hold links, or whatever we like – but we're just interested in ASP.NET in this book, not website design.

Let's take a look at the **consumer** of our .ascx user control, our main.aspx ASP.NET file:

```
<%@ Register TagPrefix="UserControl" TagName="Header" Src="header.ascx" %>
```

The first line is where we declare that we're using a user control. This tag must appear at the top of your page, before any HTML code, in order for it to work. We set two attributes of the Register tag:

❑   The TagPrefix attribute
❑   The TagName attribute

The `TagPrefix` is the collective name for our group of controls. The `TagName` is the name of this specific control. For example, if we were using an ASP.NET textbox control on our page, we use the syntax `<asp:textbox />`. The `TagPrefix` in this case is the bit before the colon; for an ASP.NET textbox, this is **`<asp:...>`**, and the `TagName` in this case follows the colon, and is `<...:`**`textbox`**`>`. In our example, we are defining our `TagPrefix` as `UserControl`, and our `TagName` as `Header`, so that when we come to use our control, we call it using `<UserControl:Header />` as we'll see below. We could have a whole library of `UserControl` tags, each identified by different `TagNames` in our code. The final part of our line is where we specify the source file of our user control. ASP.NET expects this to be in the same place as our ASP.NET file. If this is not the case, then the relative or absolute path must be entered here:

```
<html>
<body>

<form runat="server" method="post">
```

We start off the bulk of the page with pretty straightforward HTML as usual, then we move on to applying our user control to our page:

```
<UserControl:Header id="MyHeader" runat="Server" />
```

The syntax used here is identical to the syntax we're used to with ASP.NET controls, as we saw above. In this line, we create a new instance of our control, and assign it a name or ID; in this case, we'll refer to this control as `MyHeader`. The `MyHeader` control will have access to the public variable that we declared in our user control code. We'll see how this is useful to us in just a few moments:

```
<h3>A simple control for playing with header color</h3>

<asp:DropDownList id="ColorList" runat="Server" />
<asp:button text="Apply Color" OnClick="SubmitBtn_Click" runat="server" />
<br /><br />
<asp:label id="SelectedColor" runat="Server" />
```

These lines of code create some ASP.NET server controls in the remainder of our page. We create a drop-down listbox, a button, and a label, and we assign IDs to them, so that we'll be able to work with them programmatically later on in our code:

```
</form>
</body>
```

We now finish off the HTML part of our page, and move on to the `<script>` block, where we'll work with our controls:

```
<script language="VB" runat="server">

  Public Sub Page_Load()
```

The first part of our script block contains a subroutine that runs whenever the page load event is fired:

```
If Not Page.IsPostback

    Dim arrColors As New ArrayList(5)
    arrColors.Add("Red")
    arrColors.Add("Green")
    arrColors.Add("Blue")
    arrColors.Add("Orange")
    arrColors.Add("Purple")

    Colorlist.Datasource = arrColors

    Page.DataBind()

End If

End Sub
```

We are creating an array, called `arrColors`, which contains a list of 5 different colors, which is bound to the `Datasource` attribute of the `ColorList` control when the page loads. Finally, this code is contained in an `If Not Page.IsPostback` structure, which means that we only do the data binding the first time the page is accessed. We're not changing the list of values in our array at any point, so we're saving ourselves a small amount of work by only binding the array to the control the first time the page is loaded:

```
Public Sub SubmitBtn_Click(Sender As Object, E As EventArgs)
```

We're creating a subroutine to react to the clicking of the button. Next comes the fun part:

```
Dim NewColor as String
NewColor = Colorlist.SelectedItem.Text
selectedcolor.text= "You selected " & NewColor
MyHeader.BackColor= NewColor
```

We create a new variable, called `NewColor`, as a string to hold the text that's entered in the textbox. The second line assigns the text property of the selected item in our drop-down listbox to the `NewColor` variable. We then change the value of the text in our label control to produce a confirmation message for the user. We're changing this to read: "You selected " followed by the color we typed in, which is stored in the `NewColor` variable. Finally, we access the `BackColor` attribute of our control, and we change the value of this attribute to be the same as the color we typed in:

```
    End Sub

</script>

</html>
```

At the end of our example, we simply close up the remainder of our code, and that's it.

Although this example was fairly simple, I hope it will have given you a good insight into how user controls work, and the principles behind them.

Let's take a look at a slightly different type of control now. This is a control that shows a list of books on promotion.

Try It Out: Creating a Featured Items List Control

This example will create another re-useable user control for showing a list of books from a WroxShop database. This database is available for download from www.wrox.com.

1. Open up your editor and type in the following code:

```
<%@ import Namespace="System.Data" %>
<%@ import Namespace="System.Data.Oledb" %>

<%

  Dim strConnection as String
  strConnection = "Provider=Microsoft.Jet.OLEDB.4.0;" & _
                    "Data Source=c:\BegASPNET\Ch15\WroxShop.mdb"

  Dim strSQL as String
  strSQL = "SELECT * FROM Books"

  Dim objConnection as New OledbConnection(strConnection)
  Dim objCommand as new OledbCommand (strSQL, objConnection)
  Dim objDataReader as OledbDataReader
  Dim strResult as String

  objConnection.Open()
  objDataReader = objCommand.ExecuteReader()

  strResult = "<table><tr><td class='datatablehead'>ISBN</td>"
  strResult += "<td class='datatablehead'>Title</td>"
  strResult += "<td class='datatablehead'>Price</td>"
  strResult += "<td class='datatablehead'>Description</td></tr>"

  Do While objDataReader.Read()
    strResult += "<tr><td class='datatable'>" & objDataReader("ISBN")
    strResult += "</td><td class='datatable'>" & objDataReader("Title")
    strResult += "</td><td class='datatable'>" & objDataReader("Price")
    strResult += "</td><td class='datatable'>" & objDataReader("Description") & _
                                                  "</td></tr>"
  Loop

    strResult += "</table>"

  BookList.Text = strResult

  objDataReader.Close()
  objConnection.Close()

%>

<ASP:Label ID="BookList" Runat="Server" />
```

❏ Save this file as `featuredbooks.ascx`. Next, open up your `main.aspx` file and add the following highlighted lines of code:

```
<%@ Page Language="VB" Debug="true" %>
<%@ Register TagPrefix="UserControl" TagName="Header" Src="header.ascx" %>
<%@ Register TagPrefix="UserControl" TagName="FeaturedBooks"
Src="featuredbooks.ascx" %>

<html>
<head>
<link rel="stylesheet" type="text/css" href="http://localhost/5040/ch15/style.css"
title="style">
</head>
<body>

<form runat="server" method="post">

  <UserControl:Header id="MyHeader" runat="Server" />

  <h3>A simple control for playing with header color</h3>

  <asp:DropDownList id="ColorList" runat="Server" />
  <asp:button text="Apply Color" OnClick="SubmitBtn_Click" runat="server" />
  <br /><br />
  <asp:label id="SelectedColor" runat="Server" />

    <br /><hr /><br />

    Today's Selected Books:
    <UserControl:FeaturedBooks id="BookList" runat="Server" />

</form>
</body>

<script language="VB" runat="Server">

  Public Sub Page_Load()

    If Not Page.IsPostback

      Dim arrColors As New ArrayList(5)
      arrColors.Add("Red")
      arrColors.Add("Green")
      arrColors.Add("Blue")
      arrColors.Add("Orange")
      arrColors.Add("Purple")

      Colorlist.Datasource = arrColors

      Page.DataBind()

    End If

  End Sub
```

```
Public Sub SubmitBtn_Click(Sender As Object, E As EventArgs)

    Dim NewColor as String
    NewColor = Colorlist.SelectedItem.Text
    selectedcolor.text= "You selected " & NewColor
    MyHeader.BackColor= NewColor

End Sub

</script>

</html>
```

2. Save this as `main2.aspx`. You may have noticed we referred to a CSS file in our code – for completeness, we've included the code for this file here, but we're not going to be examining it in detail, because it's outside the scope of this book:

```css
body {
font-family:verdana;
}

td.datatablehead {
Background:#b0c4de;
font-family:Verdana,arial;
font-size:x-small;
font-weight:bold;
text-align:left;
}

td.datatable {
Background:#f0f8ff;
font-family:Verdana,arial;
font-size:x-small;
}
```

❑ Save this file as `style.css` in the same directory as your other files, and open `main.aspx` in your browser:

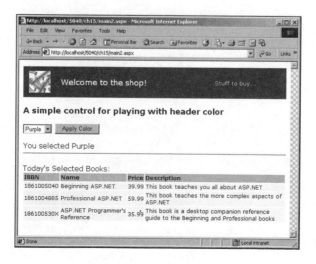

How It Works

In this example, we created a second control and added this to our front page in a similar way to before. Let's start by looking at our new control:

```
<%@ import Namespace="System.Data" %>
<%@ import Namespace="System.Data.Oledb" %>
```

Our first two statements should be relatively familiar from our work in the data access chapters earlier in the book. We are importing the namespaces that are necessary for working with data from an Access database, using the Oledb connection method:

```
<%

    Dim strConnection as String
    strConnection = "Provider=Microsoft.Jet.OLEDB.4.0;" & _
                        "Data Source=c:\BegASPNET\Ch15\WroxShop.mdb"

    Dim strSQL as String
    strSQL = "SELECT * FROM Books"
```

Our first few lines of code, specify a connection string to our database, which in our case is a small Access database (available for download from www.wrox.com). We then enter the details of the SQL statement for obtaining the required data from our database:

```
    Dim objConnection as New OledbConnection(strConnection)
    Dim objCommand as new OledbCommand (strSQL, objConnection)
    Dim objDataReader as OledbDataReader
    Dim strResult as String

    objConnection.Open()
    objDataReader = objCommand.ExecuteReader()
```

We're using a DataReader in our code to obtain data from the database. We create a new connection using the connection string, before executing the SQL statement. We create a new OledbDataReader object, called objDataReader, and a string called strResult, which will be used for holding the output of our reader. We open the connection, and connect the objDataReader object to the resulting rowset:

```
    strResult = "<table><tr><td class='datatablehead'>ISBN</td>"
    strResult += "<td class='datatablehead'>Title</td>"
    strResult += "<td class='datatablehead'>Price</td>"
    strResult += "<td class='datatablehead'>Description</td></tr>"
```

To start work on our table we simply add HTML table information to the strResult string:

```
    Do While objDataReader.Read()
       strResult += "<tr><td class='datatable'>" & objDataReader("ISBN")
       strResult += "</td><td class='datatable'>" & objDataReader("Title")
       strResult += "</td><td class='datatable'>" & objDataReader("Price")
       strResult += "</td><td class='datatable'>" & objDataReader("Description") & _
                                                    "</td></tr>"
    Loop
```

We then loop through the contents of the `objDataReader` and enter the values obtained from each row and column of the table into the `strResult` string using the concatenation `+=` syntax:

```
    strResult += "</table>"

  BookList.Text = strResult

  objDataReader.Close()
  objConnection.Close()

%>
```

The remainder of our script block closes up the HTML table, and populates the `BookList` label control's text property with the contents of the `strResult` string. We then close up the `objDataReader`, and the `objConnection` objects to free up resources:

```
  <ASP:Label ID="BookList" Runat="Server" />
```

The last thing we do is create a basic ASP.NET Label control to hold the output of our processing, which in our case, is a table of data.

Let's look at the new lines of code in our `.aspx` page:

```
  <%@ Register TagPrefix="UserControl" TagName="FeaturedBooks"
  Src="featuredbooks.ascx" %>
```

Our first line of code references our second control in exactly the same way as before, and assigns it the same `TagPrefix`, but a different `TagName`:

```
  <link rel="stylesheet" type="text/css" href="http://localhost/5040/ch15/style.css"
  title="style">
```

The next line is a simple line of code to import the stylesheet for our page to help display the page's output more clearly:

```
  <br /><hr /><br />

  Today's Selected Books:
  <UserControl:FeaturedBooks id="BookList" runat="Server" />
```

The only other code we need, is a single line to add the new control in the same way as before. We give this control the ID of `BookList`. We also added a little bit of HTML to help with the presentation.

We're not going to look at how the CSS works in detail, but there are many more books you can look at if you want to know more about CSS. You could try Wrox Press's *HTML 4.01 Programmer's Reference, ISBN 1-861005-33-4.*

Next, we're going to move on to look at Code Behind, and how we can better divide up our code into manageable sections.

Code Behind

When we were creating simple forms in Chapter 3, we simply created textboxes and worked with buttons that sent data on a round trip to the server. We later enhanced these forms by adding code that handles validating our input, etc. We had to put all of the extra code to enable validation in small functions at the bottom of our pages to avoid cluttering up our presentation code. There is a cleaner way of doing this, however, which is to move all of this code into a **Code Behind** file.

A Code Behind file can be used to store all of the script blocks of an ASP.NET page. While it's perfectly possible to include this in the same page as the presentation HTML code, separating out the script blocks is a good way to cleanly separate presentation from the code. The presentation code remains all in one .aspx file (or, if you've got a couple of user controls for repetitive presentation elements, it can reside in part in .ascx files), and the Code Behind code lives in a language-specific file, for example, .vb for a Visual Basic.NET Code Behind file, or .cs for a C# Code Behind file. The .aspx file is the central point for the application, and it is from here that we reference the Code Behind file, and any user controls.

A Code Behind file can be written in any .NET-compatible language, so we could write out code in VB.NET (as we have been throughout this book so far) or we could use C#, or JScript, for example. We'll take a brief look at this concept in the next chapter, when we talk about .NET Assemblies – don't worry if you haven't got any experience with the other languages, as we'll stick with VB.NET for this chapter, and the majority of the next.

Let's take a look at a simple example of a Code Behind file.

Try It Out:-Our First Code Behind file

In this example we're going to create a very simple Web Form with a textbox and a button, and we'll give this simple arrangement some extra functionality by adding a Code Behind file.

1. Create a file called CodeBehind1.vb, save it in your BegASPNET\Ch15 directory, and enter the following code:

```vb
Imports System
Imports System.Web.UI
Imports System.Web.UI.WebControls

Public Class MyCodeBehind : Inherits Page

  Public name as Textbox
  Public message as Label

  Public Sub SubmitBtn_Click(Sender As Object, E As EventArgs)

    Dim user as String
    user = name.text
    message.text="Hello " & User

  End Sub

End Class
```

2. Next, save the following code as `CodeBehind1.aspx` in the same directory:

```
<%@ Page Inherits="MyCodeBehind" Src="CodeBehind1.vb" %>

<html>
<body>

  Please enter your name then click the button below:<br /> <br />

<form action="CodeBehind1.aspx" Method="Post" Runat="Server">
  <asp:textbox id="name" runat="Server" /> <br />
  <asp:button text="ClickMe!" OnClick="SubmitBtn_Click" runat="server" /> <br
/><br />
  <asp:label id="message" runat="Server" />
</form>
</body>
</html>
```

3. Call up the `.aspx` in your browser, and follow the instructions provided. You should then see a result like the one shown below:

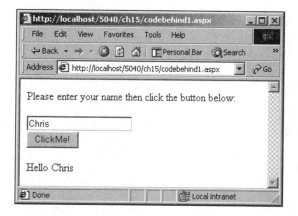

How It Works

This example did a very basic job of passing information from the `.aspx` page to the `.vb` page and back again. We input a name into a textbox on the `.aspx` page, the `.vb` Code Behind file took this name and passed it into a string along with some text, and then outputted this string to a label control that was sitting almost invisibly on our page. Let's look at the stages step by step so that we can fully-understand this process:

```
<%@ Page Inherits="MyCodeBehind" Src="CodeBehind1.vb" %>
```

This line of code is essential when working with Code Behind. The first part of the statement tells us that we want to inherit from the `MyCodeBehind` class. We briefly met inheritance in Chapter 9, but to quickly recap, this effectively says "find me the `MyCodeBehind` class and use its functionality in the page". The second part of this statement tells us where to find the class – in this case, we've stored this class in our `CodeBehind1.vb` file. It's worth noting that we can only use one of these declarations per `.aspx` page:

```
<html>
<body>

  Please enter your name then click the button below:<br /> <br />

<form action="CodeBehind1.aspx" Method="Post" Runat="Server">
  <asp:textbox id="name" runat="Server" /> <br />
  <asp:button text="ClickMe!" OnClick="SubmitBtn_Click" runat="server" /> <br
/><br />
  <asp:label id="message" runat="Server" />
</form>
</body>
</html>
```

The rest of this ASP.NET page is a simple Web Form with a textbox, a button, and a label control. These controls are exactly the same as the controls we first met in Chapter 3 – there's nothing particularly special about them. Let's move on to our Code Behind file and see how this works. You'll notice that the syntax in this file looks different from the sort of code we've been using so far – this is because this is a VB file, not an ASP.NET Web Form. This code doesn't necessarily have to be used in a Web Form – we could even use this code as part of a Windows Form:

```
Imports System
Imports System.Web.UI
Imports System.Web.UI.WebControls
```

This first block of code lays the foundation for our Code Behind file. These three lines of code import important namespaces from the .NET Class Library. These namespaces are used to access all of the functionality of ASP.NET pages. These are actually loaded by default in any ASP.NET page, though we never get to see this ourselves, because it's all done behind the scenes. As we saw in Chapter 2, these namespaces provide us with easy access to the classes that they contain. When we wish to make use of one of their classes, we can simply refer to the class by name, instead of having to type out the full path including all of the namespace:

```
Public Class MyCodeBehind : Inherits Page
```

The next line of code assigns a name to the class in the Code Behind file. If you remember, the first line in our ASP.NET page mentioned MyCodeBehind – well, this is what the ASP.NET page is looking for. The second part of this line means that we are Inheriting from our ASP.NET page. We'll look at inheritance in more detail shortly, but all we need to know now is that this means "take the Page class, combine it with the one defined below, and call it MyCodeBehind". Essentially, both of the Inherits statements in the two files are like a kind of glue – they make the two files stick together as if they were one single file:

```
Public name as Textbox
Public message as Label
```

These two lines are simply variable declarations, and they mimic the names of the controls on the ASP.NET page:

```
Public Sub SubmitBtn_Click(Sender As Object, E As EventArgs)

   Dim user as String
   user = name.text
   message.text="Hello " & User

End Sub
```

We then move on to the nitty-gritty of our Code Behind file. This block of code is where the action happens. We are creating a subroutine to react to a Click event of our **Click Me!** button. We are declaring a variable called user, and we're giving this new variable the value that is held in the textbox that has been entered by the user, then we change the text attribute of our label control to our welcome message, thus displaying our message on the screen:

```
End Class
```

We then close our class with a simple statement.

This example was very simple, and it doesn't show off the capabilities of the Code Behind style of coding to its fullest. We can use this technique to encapsulate a lot of logic to deal with user input, thereby separating out the jobs of the designer and the programmer, which is one of the goals of ASP.NET.

Code Behind and User Controls

We can apply the principle of Code Behind to our User Controls in exactly the same way as we can to .aspx pages. Let's look at our FeaturedBooks user control, and break the code contained in this into a separate Code Behind file.

Try-It-Out – Separating Presentation from Code in a User Control

For this example, we'll be working with the main2.aspx, style.css, and featuredbooks.ascx files that we used earlier in the chapter.

1. Open up your editor and enter the following code (note that a lot of this code is based on the content of featuredbooks.ascx, so you can copy and paste the un-highlighted lines if you prefer):

```
Imports System
Imports System.Web.UI
Imports System.Web.UI.WebControls
Imports System.Data
Imports System.Data.Oledb

Public Class DisplayBooksClass : Inherits UserControl

   Public BookList as Label
```

```
Sub Page_Load()

If Not Page.IsPostback

   Dim strConnection as String
   strConnection = "Provider=Microsoft.Jet.OLEDB.4.0;" & _
                   "Data Source=c:\BegASPNET\Ch15\WroxShop.mdb"

   Dim strSQL as String
   strSQL = "SELECT * FROM Books"

   Dim objConnection as New OledbConnection(strConnection)
   Dim objCommand as new OledbCommand (strSQL, objConnection)
   Dim objDataReader as OledbDataReader
   Dim strResult as String

   objConnection.Open()
   objDataReader = objCommand.ExecuteReader()

   strResult = "<table><tr><td class='datatablehead'>ISBN</td>"
   strResult += "<td class='datatablehead'>Title</td>"
   strResult += "<td class='datatablehead'>Price</td>"
   strResult += "<td class='datatablehead'>Description</td></tr>"

   Do While objDataReader.Read()
      strResult += "<tr><td class='datatable'>" & objDataReader("ISBN")
      strResult += "</td><td class='datatable'>" & objDataReader("Title")
      strResult += "</td><td class='datatable'>" & objDataReader("Price")
      strResult += "</td><td class='datatable'>" & objDataReader("Description") &_
                                                 "</td></tr>"

   Loop

   strResult += "</table>"

   BookList.Text = strResult

   objDataReader.Close()
   objConnection.Close()

 End If

 End Sub

End Class
```

2. Save this file as `featuredbooks_CB.vb`. This is our Code Behind file for our user control. Now, open up your editor, and enter the following code:

```
<%@ Control inherits="DisplayBooksClass" src="featuredbooks_CB.vb"
                                        ClassName="FeaturedBooks" %>

<ASP:Label ID="BookList" Runat="Server" />
```

3. Save this file as `featuredbooks_CB.ascx`. Now open up `main2.aspx`, and enter the following highlighted lines of code:

```
<%@ Page Language="VB" Debug="true" %>
<%@ Register TagPrefix="UserControl" TagName="Header" Src="header.ascx" %>
<%@ Register TagPrefix="UserControl" TagName="FeaturedBooks"
Src="featuredbooks.ascx" %>
<%@ Register TagPrefix="UserControl" TagName="FeaturedBooks_CB"
Src="featuredbooks_CB.ascx" %>

<html>
<head>
<link rel="stylesheet" type="text/css" href="http://localhost/5040/ch15/style.css"
title="style">
</head>
<body>

<form runat="server" method="post">

  <UserControl:Header id="MyHeader" runat="server" />

  <h3>A simple control for playing with header color</h3>

  <asp:DropDownList id="ColorList" runat="server" />
  <asp:button text="Apply Color" OnClick="SubmitBtn_Click" runat="server" /> <br
/><br />
  <asp:label id="SelectedColor" runat="server" />

  <br /><hr /><br />

  Today's Selected Books:
  <UserControl:FeaturedBooks id="BookList" runat="server" />

  <br /><hr /><br />

  Tomorrow's Selected Books:
  <UserControl:FeaturedBooks_CB id="BookList2" runat="server" />

</form>
</body>

<script language="VB" runat="server">

  Public Sub Page_Load()

   If Not Page.IsPostback

     Dim arrColors As New ArrayList(5)
     arrColors.Add("Red")
     arrColors.Add("Green")
     arrColors.Add("Blue")
     arrColors.Add("Orange")
     arrColors.Add("Purple")

     Colorlist.Datasource = arrColors
```

```
      Page.DataBind()

   End If

 End Sub


 Public Sub SubmitBtn_Click(Sender As Object, E As EventArgs)

   Dim NewColor as String
   NewColor = Colorlist.SelectedItem.Text
   selectedcolor.text= "You selected " & NewColor
   MyHeader.BackColor= NewColor

 End Sub

</script>

</html>
```

4. Save this as main3.aspx. Now, open up main3.aspx in your browser, and you should see the following:

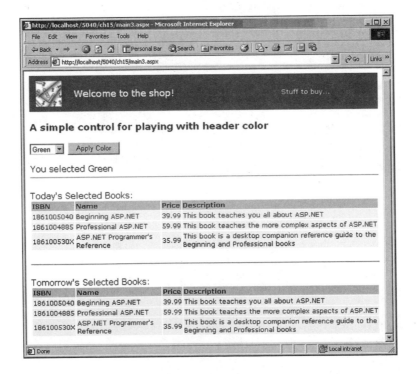

How It Works

All we've done in this example is effectively copy out all of the code from our user control and paste it into a Code Behind file, tweaking a few bits along the way. We ended up with two nearly identical parts on our `main3.aspx` page, and in reality, you'd only need one of these. However, we kept both controls on this page, in this case, to highlight the fact that the output is identical.

Let's start our discussion with our Code Behind file, `featuredbooks_CB.vb`:

```
Imports System
Imports System.Web.UI
Imports System.Web.UI.WebControls
Imports System.Data
Imports System.Data.Oledb


Public Class DisplayBooksClass : Inherits UserControl
```

This first block of code is different from the beginning of our original control `featuredbooks.ascx`. This block of code is now in VB, not in script blocks. We start off by importing all of the namespaces we need. The last two of these are for the data access we'll be doing later in the chapter. We then have to declare a class to contain our code – we've called ours `DisplayBooksClass`, and it inherits from the `UserControl` class. This statement must be included for all Code Behind files for user controls:

```
Public BookList as Label

Sub Page_Load()

If Not Page.IsPostback
```

The next thing we must do is to declare a public variable related to our `label` control. If we don't explicitly state that this is a public variable, our control has nothing to display, because no data is returned to it. Finally, we declare the beginning of a `Page_Load` subroutine, which runs as soon as the page is instantiated. In this, we have the `If Not Page.IsPostback` statement that means that this code only gets run once, when the page is first loaded. It's unlikely that code like this would change so frequently that it would need to be refreshed every time the page is loaded.

We'll not look at the bulk of the code on this page again, because we went through it in detail when we first used it in our original User control:

```
End If

End Sub

End Class
```

Finally, we close up the `If` statement, the `Page_Load` subroutine, and the Class. Our Code Behind file is now complete.

Let's take a quick look at the changes to the `.ascx` file:

```
<%@ Control inherits="DisplayBooksClass" src="featuredbooks_CB.vb"
                                         ClassName="FeaturedBooks" %>

<ASP:Label ID="BookList" Runat="Server" />
```

Our `featuredbooks_CB.ascx` file is much smaller than our original `.ascx` file. We have two lines of code. The `@ Control` directive in the first line of code is where we attach the Code Behind file to our control. We have three parameters to set here: the first is the `inherits` statement, with which we identify which class we're using. The next parameter describes where our Code Behind code resides, and the final parameter gives our control a class name. This is needed in case we dynamically create the control on a page. The last line of code in our control creates the label that contains the output of the data code in the Code Behind.

Finally, let's look at the two new lines in our `.aspx` file:

```
<%@ Register TagPrefix="UserControl" TagName="FeaturedBooks_CB"
Src="featuredbooks_CB.ascx" %>
```

The first line is almost identical to the previous lines we encountered. We've simply adapted it to find the new control, and we've given it a different name to differentiate it from the other controls:

```
<br /><hr /><br />

Tomorrow's Selected Books:
<UserControl:FeaturedBooks_CB id="BookList2" runat="Server" />
```

Finally, the last lines of new code simply add another horizontal HTML line to our page, output some slightly amended text, and then add our new control to the page. This control will look completely identical to the previous control, which is the intended effect.

In a real system, we'd only use one of these two controls, but we included both so that you could compare and contrast the output.

Let's return to the concept of Inheritance one more time, so as to explain more about this concept before we move on any further.

Inheritance

Inheritance is a feature of Object-Oriented Programming that has been lacking from the Visual Basic programmer's feature set until its introduction in Visual Basic.NET. It's a really useful feature which saves time and hassle, and is pretty simple and logical to grasp, so you should grow to love it.

In our examples above, we created two files, and told them both to inherit from each other. In basic terms, this means "make use of the functionality in both files as if they were one". However, we can make use of inheritance in even better ways than this.

Imagine we define a class for a generic car. This class could have the following characteristics, as we saw earlier:

The Car Class	
Methods:	Move
	StartEngine
	OpenDoor
Properties:	Color
	Make
	Model

Our car is very simplistic, but the general concepts that it embodies are common to all cars. Every car can move, every car has an engine that starts, and every car has a door that can be opened (except if you live in Hazard County). On top of this, all cars have a color, make, and model. But what if we were to have a class for off-road vehicles or sports cars? Let's take a look at the sort of characteristics we could define here:

The Off-Road Car Class	
Methods:	Move
	StartEngine
	OpenDoor
	EngageFourWheelDrive
	DisengageFourWheelDrive
Properties:	Color
	Make
	Model
	FourWheelDriveEngaged

The Sports Car Class	
Methods:	Move
	StartEngine
	OpenDoor
	RaiseTop
	LowerTop
Properties:	Color
	Make
	Model
	TopDown

In our off-road class, we've introduced a `FourWheelDriveEngaged` property, which is a boolean. This property reflects the status of the four-wheel drive feature of the car, which we can either engage or disengage using the two new methods. In our sports car class, we have a similar situation, except that we're raising or lowering the top depending on the weather.

If we were coding these kinds of class, we could copy and paste from our original definition into two new classes. However, this isn't very efficient, and tends to be error-prone. Instead, since our car class contains characteristics common to all kinds of cars, including off-road and sports cars, we are able to **inherit** from this **base class**, which contains the common characteristics, and **extend** this class by adding the appropriate methods and properties to form two new classes in a minimum of effort. Our new classes benefit from having less code, and they also benefit from re-using code that has been thoroughly tested elsewhere. You don't actually need to see what the code for the base class does under the covers – someone else could code the base car class, and you could go off and extend this functionality to cover your specific implementations.

The only limitation to inheritance, is that you can only inherit from one class at a time. You cannot, therefore, define a Sports Utility Vehicle (SUV) class that inherits both from the Off-Road Car class and the Sports class. You need to create a separate class specifically for this class of car. This is designed to reduce errors and simplify coding. For example, our sports car may move in a totally different way from our off-road car – it may have a manual gear change lever, instead of being an automatic, so you'd have to worry about a clutch somewhere in the equation. If our SUV tried to move, and it had somehow managed to inherit from both classes, it could get very confused. Fortunately, this situation doesn't happen because of the fact that we're prevented from doing this. If you do try, you'll probably end up with an error message.

> *Note that this applies only to implementation inheritance. There is another form of inheritance called interface inheritance, but we'll not be covering this here. This is handled differently when it comes to multiple inheritance. If you're interested in getting knee-deep in inheritance, and OO concepts in general, then you might want to read Beginning Java Objects ISBN 1-861004-17-6. Although this book is based on Java, the concepts discussed apply to anyone interested in Object Oriented Programming. Plus, you'll notice that Java is very similar to C#, which is handy.*

The concept of inheritance applies well to the concepts we'll be meeting in the next chapter.

Summary

In this chapter, we have introduced two methods of encapsulating sections of code into separate files, to keep our code as maintainable as possible:

❑ User Controls, which are designed for sections of `.aspx` files that are repeated on numerous pages in a site

❑ Code Behind, which is for containing all of the script code in our page in one file, leaving the `.aspx` file purely for the HTML and control placement to be done by designers

These two methods are relatively straightforward, and are simply methods of moving code into different areas to improve readability, reduce complexity, and reduce errors caused by mixing presentation and script.

In this chapter, we also discussed inheritance from an implementation perspective, and talked about inheriting and extending from a class.

In the next chapter, we'll move on to looking at more advanced methods of encapsulating code functionality into re-usable components, namely .NET Assemblies and Custom Server Controls.

Exercises

1. Explain what a User Control is, and under what circumstances you'd use User Controls in your pages.

2. Think of a scenario where using a User Control is beneficial, and explain what kind of controls you might have in that situation. Explain which parts of your code could be separated out into a Code Behind file, and why you would do this.

3. Create a User Control that produces a user login control. You'll need to ask the users for a User ID, which will be an email address, and they'll need to enter their password.

4. Add some very basic validation to the control to check that they've entered a value in the email address box, and to check that the password field has a value in it too, also checking that the email is a valid email, and the password is exactly eight characters, no spaces. Next, create a simple web form that displays this control on the page. Test your code to see if the validation is being performed correctly.

5. As an additional exercise, you may want to write some code that connects to a database, and retrieves the user's details, provided the email address and password that are entered match up with the records in the database. This would be useful for retrieving information on a customer's previous orders, etc.

.NET Assemblies and Custom Controls

In the previous chapter, we met User Controls and Code Behind as two different ways to break up our code into manageable sections. These sections could be used for encapsulating commonly used chunks of ASP.NET code, and for separating out the script sections of our page into separate files. In this chapter, we'll be concentrating on some more advanced techniques of componentization, namely, creating .NET Assemblies and Custom Server Controls.

.NET Assemblies are components containing a collection of classes, encapsulated into a compiled assembly. They can be written in any .NET-compliant language, and are pre-compiled into a `.dll` file. The `.aspx` page then references this file to gain access to the functionality contained in it. These assemblies differ from Code Behind and User Controls in the following ways:

- ❑ They are easily re-distributable, and can be deployed with ease on any other system

- ❑ You can reference multiple assemblies from an `.aspx` page, but you can only reference one Code Behind file

- ❑ User Controls are a much better way to store repeated presentation code, leaving assemblies ideally positioned for containing application logic

> .NET Assemblies are groups of functionally-associated class and interface definitions encapsulated in a compiled file.

Three Tier Application Design

Let's take the concept of separation of content from presentation one step further. Once we've separated the elements of an application into distinct purpose-specific categories, often referred to as layers, it becomes much easier to structure them efficiently. In many respects, everything we've said in the book so far about structured code has served as a preparation for what we're about to do – breaking out this 'application logic' code into separate components that we can use both here and elsewhere. So, in traditional application design terms, we ultimately have our ASP.NET pages to deal with the top **presentation layer**, a database to store our content in a bottom **data layer**, and components that sit in between to marshal the flow of data between them – these provide the core logic of our application, and are usually referred to collectively as the **application logic layer**:

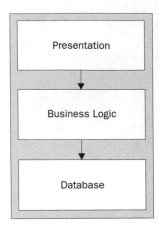

The diagram above represents the three layers we've just described– in fact, an application built using this sort of architecture is known technically as a **3-tierapplication**. So, how do these fit together? Our user might click a button on a travel-related web site that says "Show me all available hotels in Gran Canaria", and this would call a class in one of our application logic components that connected to the database and queried it for all hotels matching the criterion – in this case, we're looking for hotels in Gran Canaria, but we could expand this to match hotels available on a certain date, hotels of a certain style.

If we look at these actions, the button on the site may well be generated by a designer, while the code that connects to the data store and performs the query is application logic, and the data store itself is part of the data tier.

The three tiers in three-tier applications can be broken down as follows:

❑ Data – This could be any type of data store, for example, a database, an XML file, an Excel work sheet, or even a text file containing data

❑ Application Logic – This contains all the code that we use to query the database, manipulate retrieved data, pass data to the user interface, and handle any input from the UI as well

❑ Presentation – This comprises all our user interface code, containing a mixture of static HTML, User Controls and server controls

So how does this relate to the concepts we've met so far, and how do assemblies and server controls fit into the mixture?

ASP.NET Application Design

User Controls were used to encapsulate frequently-used sections of ASP.NET code into separate files, to improve manageability, and make it easier to re-use code. We even placed some data logic into a user control. In the first of our Code Behind examples, we didn't exactly encapsulate any business logic into our Code Behind file: instead, we chose to use our Code Behind file to hide the code that processed our Web Form. In the next example of using Code Behind, we took the data-processing logic of the User Control and split that out into another Code Behind file. Taking this a bit further, we could have the following situation:

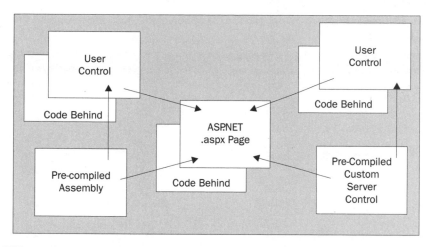

Each ASP.NET `.aspx` page can have a Code Behind file. Each User control `.ascx` can have a Code Behind file. These User Controls can be used by any of our ASP.NET pages. We can create assemblies that can be used by any of our User Controls, ASP.NET pages or Server controls. We can also create custom server controls that can be used again by any of our User Controls or ASP.NET pages. Our application logic can reside in our assemblies, Code Behind files, ASP.NET pages, Server controls, or User Controls, so traditional three tier application design is a little more tricky. Once you decide how you're going to structure your application, however, this process is clearer.

You need to decide what part of your code does what. One scenario is that you keep your `.aspx` files purely for HTML and control elements. You then use Code Behind to handle `On Click` events for any buttons, or `On Change` events for selections, and so on. You can then apply exactly the same process to the User Controls, separating presentation and code as appropriate. You can then create assemblies that will plug in to your Code Behind files to contain all of your data connectivity code, and the code to process your data. Finally, Server controls could also inherit from a class in an assembly, so you're left with a very neat model. This process is entirely up to you. You could, theoretically, keep all of your code in `.aspx` pages, however, this isn't recommended, given the benefits that encapsulating functionality into different components can bring to your applications.

Since we've looked at the User Interface design, and we've just seen how we can encapsulate application logic into a Code Behind file, let's now move on to looking at how we can create a component, then we'll look at encapsulating some of our application logic into a .NET component.

.NET Assemblies

An assembly is a logical grouping of functionality into a physical file. One or many custom controls and business logic components can reside in an assembly. This collection of components is compiled into a `.dll` file, forming our assembly, which can be used in our ASP.NET pages. We can create classes with functionality related to connecting to databases, qualify these in a namespace, then compile them into a `.dll` and import the functionality from our `.aspx` pages in a syntactically similar way to how we imported the functionality in User Controls or Code Behind files.

For our first ASP.NET Assembly, we'll create a component with just one method – the SayHello method.

Try It Out – Our First ASP.NET Component

Let's have a go at creating our first ASP.NET component. Firstly, open up your editor and type in the following code:

```
Namespace HelloWorld

   Public Class HelloVB

     Public Function SayHello() As String

        Return "Hello World - I'm a component!"

     End Function

   End Class

End Namespace
```

Save this file as `Component1.vb` in your `C:\BegASPNET\Ch16` directory.

How it works

This is a very simplistic component; so let's take a brief look at what it does:

```
Namespace HelloWorld
```

The first line qualifies all of the following classes into a namespace, similar to the .NET namespaces that we encountered in the previous chapter. Once our component is compiled, this namespace can be imported by other pages and applications, and the classes it contains can be easily accessed, just like the `System` namespaces in our Code Behind example:

```
Public Class HelloVB
```

The next line declares the solitary class in our namespace, which we're calling `HelloVB`. Once we have imported our `HelloWorld` namespace in an `.aspx` page, for example, we will be able to access the `HelloVB` class from within our ASP.NET page:

```
Public Function SayHello() As String

   Return "Hello World - I'm a component!"

End Function
```

The next few lines are where our method is coded. We declare our function, in this case called `SayHello()`, and we say that it will return a string. By declaring this function as `Public`, we're making this available to the outside work as an interface. We'll be able to call a `SayHello()` method on any object derived from this class once we're in our `.aspx` page. We're going to be really simplistic and explicitly tell our function to return the text "Hello World – I'm a component!" whenever the method is called, but in a more-complex component, you can obviously do a lot more than this, as we shall see later:

```
    End Class

  End Namespace
```

The last lines of code in our component simply close up the class declaration and the namespace declaration.

This component must now be **compiled**, and the compiled version of the component must be saved to the /bin directory of your web application. If there's not one there already, you'll need to create one yourself. Previously, when using COM, any components created had to be registered with the system registry. With .NET, all we need to do is save our files in the right place, compile them, and away we go.

> **Note that in our case, our Web application is called** 5040**, and it is linked to the** C:\BegASPNET **directory, not to the individual chapter folder. You need to create your \bin directory as a sub-directory of** C:\BegASPNET **(our application root) for these examples to work.**

But hang on – what do we mean by compiled, and what's so special about compiled components?

What is Compilation?

When we create an ASP.NET page, we write code using some form of editor, and save our code somewhere on our system. When that page is requested, the code is compiled into **Intermediate Language (IL)** behind the scenes when the page is first run, and stored in a cache until the web server is restarted, or until the page, the .aspx file, has been changed in some way, for example, if you added some code and re-saved the file. The cached Intermediate Language code is then **Just-In-Time (JIT)** compiled into native machine code at runtime.

When we use an ASP.NET page, or a Code Behind file, we suffer a performance hit the first time the page is accessed because the page and the Code Behind file would have to be compiled to IL, then JIT compiled. Once the page has been accessed once, the process of accessing the page is much quicker because all that needs to be done then is for the JIT compiler to run. However, when we create a .NET assembly, we do the compilation to IL in advance, saving us from even more of this performance hit. This means that components are much faster than an .aspx page the first time a page is run. On subsequent hits, the page will be a lot quicker because the output of the compiled page is cached for a specified duration, or until the page is altered in some fashion by the developer. Our compiled assembly is then more discrete – it's much harder now to look through how the classes are structured exactly, although methods are available for seeing how the rough structure of the assembly is put together. (We'll not be looking into this in detail here because this is outside the scope of this book).

Before we compile our component, we have to do a quick bit of setting up to make sure our system is configured correctly so that it can locate all the files needed.

Try-It-Out – Configuring your Environment Variables

Before you can compile any .NET components, you need to configure your system to locate some files. These files are vbc.exe, and the System.dll files that are required by the compiler. This is a one-off process, and needs to be done before you attempt to compile any assemblies. There's no harm done if you forget to do this, but these examples will not work correctly without going through this process.

1. Right-click on the My Computer icon on the desktop, and select Properties. In the dialog that appears, select the Advanced tab from the top, then click on the Environment Variables button. A new dialog will appear:

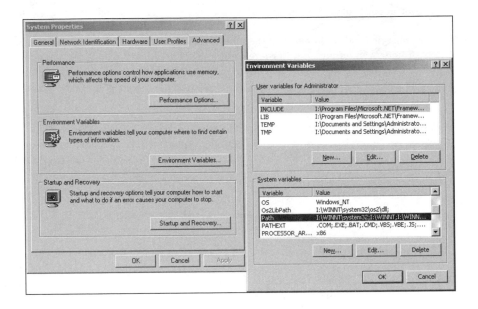

2. You need to highlight the Path statement in the bottom window of the Environment Variables dialog, and then click on the Edit button. Your path may look something like this:

```
%SystemRoot%\system32;%SystemRoot%;%SystemRoot%\System32\Wbem
```

You need to add to this the following text:

```
;%SystemRoot%\Microsoft.NET\Framework\v1.0.2914
```

So that the path now reads:

```
%SystemRoot%\system32;%SystemRoot%;%SystemRoot%\System32\Wbem;%SystemRoot%\Microso
ft.NET\Framework\v1.0.2914
```

> **You'll need to substitute the number at the end of the path to correspond to the build number of the .NET Framework running on your system (beta 2 of .NET is 2914, but the final released product number will be a different number – this chapter was written based on beta 2 of the .NET Framework).**

Once you've done this, close the three windows in turn by clicking on their respective **OK** buttons. You will now be able to use command-line compilers without a problem.

How it works

This command should tell the computer exactly where to look when you compile your applications using the `vbc.exe` file, or any of the other compilers for other languages. Once this has been done, you shouldn't have to do this again. By entering this information, our operating system will know where to look if we simply type `vbc` to compile a file:

```
;%SystemRoot%\Microsoft.NET\Framework\v1.0.2914
```

The first part of the additional information we entered is the semi-colon, which simply indicates that there is another item to be stored in the path declaration of the environment variables. The `%SystemRoot%` declaration is a short-hand notation that corresponds to the location of the WinNT directory on your hard drive. If your copy of windows is installed on your C drive, this will be `C:\WinNT`. The remainder of the path is simply the path to the location of your .NET system files. If you browse to this directory using Windows Explorer, you'll see something like the following:

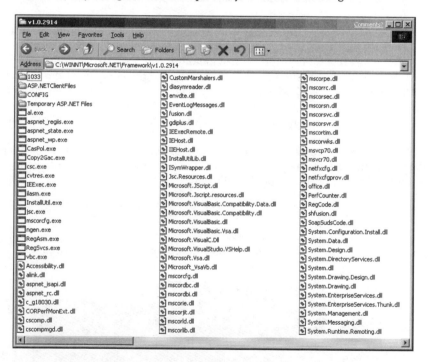

You may be able to see files such as `csc.exe`, `jsc.exe`, and `vbc.exe`, as well as some important `.dll` files, such as `System.dll`, etc. We'll be using these later in the chapter.

Now let's move on to compiling our first component.

Try It Out – Compiling our first ASP.NET Component

1. Firstly, we need to open up a command prompt. The easiest way to do this is to go to the **Start** menu and click on **Run...**, then in the dialog box that appears, type cmd and click **OK**. If you've got Windows 95, 98, or ME you need to go to the **Start** menu and click on **Run...**, then in the dialog box that appears, type command and click **OK**. You should see the following window appear:

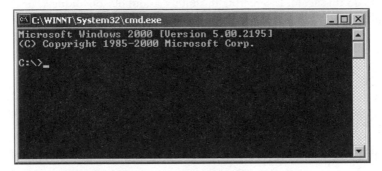

For the sake of all those unfamiliar with working from a command line interface (those who grew up in a post-DOS world), this window can be used to work with our operating system on a textual basis. Instead of using **My Computer** or **Windows Explorer** to see what's on your hard drive, you can simply type **Dir**, press *Enter*, and the contents of the root directory of your C drive will be displayed. We're not going to go into this in too much detail here, but if you want to know more about using the command line, there's a list of useful commands in Appendix C. Now, let's move on to actually working with a command prompt.

2. We need to be looking at the correct directory before we can perform any operations on the files it contains. Assuming you've followed the same procedure as we have for storing our files, in this window we need to type the following:

```
cd c:\BegASPNET
```

Then press *Enter* and you should see something similar to the following:

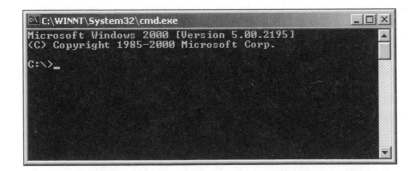

The text on your screen might be slightly different from mine, but the important thing is that typing in this command gives us a `C:\BegASPNET>` prompt.

3. Next, we need to create a new directory. Type the following into your command prompt window:

```
md bin
```

This will create a new folder called `bin` as a subdirectory of our main directory. You can take a look at our system by typing `dir /w` to display a list of all of the folders and files within the `C:\BegASPNET` folder. You should see the following:

```
C:\WINNT\System32\cmd.exe

Microsoft Windows 2000 [Version 5.00.2195]
(C) Copyright 1985-2000 Microsoft Corp.

C:\>cd c:\BegASPNET

C:\BegASPNET>md bin

C:\BegASPNET>dir /w
 Volume in drive C has no label.
 Volume Serial Number is 80FB-4B32

 Directory of C:\BegASPNET

[.]          [..]         [bin]        [ch01]       [ch02]       [ch03]
[ch04]       [ch05]       [ch06]       [ch07]       [ch08]       [ch09]
[ch10]       [ch11]       [ch12]       [ch13]       [ch14]       [ch15]
[ch16]       [ch18]       [ch20]       web.config
              1 File(s)            224 bytes
             21 Dir(s)   5,776,715,776 bytes free

C:\BegASPNET>
```

As you can see, it's pretty barren of files, except for a `Web.config` file, however it contains folders of all of the other chapters in the book so far, along with the new `\bin` directory, represented by `[bin]`. This directory is where we will store all of the components we need for our ASP.NET pages.

4. Now we need to compile `Component1.vb` into a `.dll`. Firstly, leave this command prompt window running, and switch back to Notepad, where you need to create a new file. Type the following into a new file called `MakeComponent1VB.bat`, and save this in our `c:\BegASPNET` folder:

```
set indir=C:\BegASPNET\Ch16\Component1.vb
set outdir=c:\BegASPNET\bin\Component1VB.dll

vbc /t:library /out:%outdir% %indir%
```

Save the file and return to your command prompt window, where you should now type the following:

```
MakeComponent1VB
```

This is shorthand for `MakeComponent1VB.bat` – the operating system treats .bat files as executable files, and runs the code inside them. You should see the following text appear on your screen:

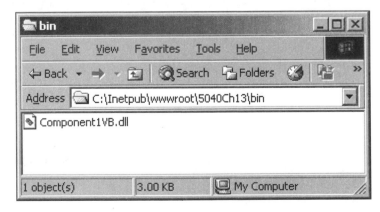

We'll examine how this works in just a moment. However, if you received any kind of error messages when you ran this command, and the output looked different to what we can see above, double check your code to make sure it's typed in correctly (especially the spacing in the `.bat` file because DOS is very picky about this). If this doesn't solve your problem, then check that your environment variables are configured correctly.

How it works

So, what did this do? Well, let's take a look at what's been created, then we'll look at the compilation batch file in more detail – it's not at complicated as it looks, honest!

If you browse your hard drive in the normal way and look at the `c:\begaspnet\bin` directory, you'll notice that there's a new file in here – `Component1VB.dll`. This is our compiled assembly, ready for use:

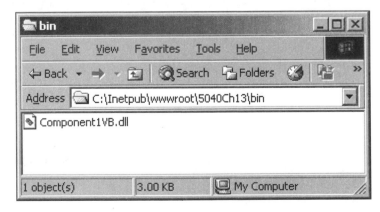

Let's take a look at the compilation batch file that we created, and go through it step by step. Firstly, here's the code we entered:

```
set indir=C:\BegASPNET\Ch16\Component1.vb
set outdir=c:\BegASPNET\bin\Component1VB.dll

vbc /t:library /out:%outdir% %indir%
```

Let's start at the beginning:

```
set indir=C:\BegASPNET\Ch16\Component1.vb
```

This first part of the file creates an alias for the path to the Visual Basic.NET file that we created earlier – our source file:

```
set outdir=c:\BegASPNET\bin\Component1VB.dll
```

The next part of our file creates an alias for the path to the file we're creating in the compilation process. We include the name that the file will assume once it's compiled:

```
vbc /t:library /out:%outdir% %indir%
```

Finally, we get to the actual compile command. The first part of the command is the name of the Visual Basic.NET compiler vbc.exe file. Essentially, typing vbc on its own is similar to double-clicking on a shortcut, except that in this case we need to pass in additional information for the compiler to work. The next part of our command is providing some of that information:

```
vbc /t:library /out:%outdir% %indir%
```

This is what's known as a **switch** or an **option**. We're telling the VB compiler that when it compiles, we want to produce a **library** file, or assembly, and not an executable. If we'd not included this switch, a default value would have been used instead – the default value would have produced an executable.

Then we come to the last two parts of our statement. Firstly:

```
vbc /t:library /out:%outdir% %indir%
```

The first part of this is another option that we're passing in to the compiler, telling it where to put our compiled file. This is where we use the alias we created earlier that pointed to the path where we're creating the component, and include the name of the component itself. We're telling our compiler to go to the bin directory, and call the output of our compilation Component1VB.dll:

```
vbc /t:library /out:%outdir% %indir%
```

The last option in this section refers to our other alias, which simply told the compiler where to get the source code that we're going to compile from.

More about Command Line Compilation

It's worth noting that we could have simply typed in the complete command manually, like this:

```
vbc /t:library /out:c:\BegASPNET\bin\Component1VB.dll C:\BegASPNET\Ch16\Component1.vb
```

The reason we created a batch file to run this command is simplification. By manually creating aliases for each of the paths and splitting these out from the main compile command, it helps to simplify the compilation process. This is particularly useful for more complex compilations.

When we're working from the command line, there are several other options available to us other than those we've already met. When we compiled our component, we used the /t parameter to specify the type of output the compiler would create – in our case, we used /t:library switch to produce a DLL library file. This option, a shortened form of /target, can also take the following arguments:

Option	Effect
/target:exe	Tells the compiler to create a command-line executable program. This is the default value, so if the /target parameter is not included, an .exe file will be created.
/target:library	Tells the compiler to create a DLL file that will contain an assembly that consists of all of the source files passed to the compiler. The compiler will also automatically create the manifest for this assembly. We'll not be looking at manifests in this chapter, since it's outside the scope of this book, but suffice to say that a manifest is a description of the contents of the assembly.
/target:module	Tells the compiler to create a DLL, but not to create a manifest for it. This means that in order for the module to be used by the .NET Framework, it will need to be manually added to an assembly using the Assembly Generation tool (AL.EXE). This tool allows you to create the assembly manifest information manually, and then add modules to it. Again, we'll not be looking at this in any more detail.
/target:winexe	This tells the compiler to create a Windows Forms application, which is not covered in this book. (For more information about Windows Forms, you can refer to *Professional Windows Forms, ISBN 1-861005-54-7*, or *Professional C#, ISBN 1-861004-99-0.*)

There are two other compilers supplied by default with the .NET Framework, which are used to compile C# and JScript components. These compilers are in the same directory as the vbc.exe compiler, and are called csc.exe and jsc.exe respectively.

Accessing a Component from within an ASP.NET Page

There's one more thing we need to learn about before we can use our component: we need to specify some configuration information to our ASP.NET application. We do this in a file called Web.config.

Configuring an ASP.NET Application with Web.config

Web.config is an XML-based file that specifies important configuration that every ASP.NET application will need. It can store everything from information on session state timeout values, to references to ASP.NET components. Being based on XML it's human-readable, and this makes it very easy to add, remove, or change settings. Any changes to configuration that we make are instantaneous; they take effect as soon as the file is saved.

Let's take a quick look at an example of a Web.config file:

```
<configuration>
  <system.web>
    <sessionState timeout="10" />
    <compilation>
      <assemblies>
        <add assembly="AssemblyName" />
      </assemblies>
    </compilation>
  </system.web>
</configuration>
```

> *A quick word of warning – Web.config files are case-sensitive, so all the tag names must be typed in with care. For example, the camel-casing of the sessionState tag is an example of one of these tags.*

This simple configuration file sets the session state timeout of a page to be 10 minutes, and it references an assembly called AssemblyName. We'll be meeting Web.config again in Chapter 20, so we're not going to look into this in much more detail, but it's important to get a general understanding here, because we'll be needing to use this when we utilize our components.

Speaking of which, we've still got a component that contains code that simply says "Hello World – I'm a component!" and we've not used it yet. Let's access this component from a simple ASP.NET page and display that text.

Try It Out – Using a Compiled Component

There's one stage we need to perform before we can actually enter the code into our ASP.NET page and get moving: we need to create a reference to our assembly from our web.config file in our c:\BegASPNET directory (our Application root). This means that any ASP.NET page within this application will be able to talk to our component.

1. If it doesn't yet exist, create a blank file called web.config, enter the following lines of code and save it in the C:\BegASPNET\ch16 folder:

```
<configuration>
  <system.web>
    <compilation>
      <assemblies>
        <add assembly="Component1VB" />
      </assemblies>
    </compilation>
  </system.web>
</configuration>
```

Now we can start to work on our ASP.NET page. Fire up your editor and type the following code:

```
<%@ Import Namespace="HelloWorld" %>

<html>
<body>

Our component says: <br /> <br />

<asp:Label id="label1" runat="server" />

<script language="vb" runat="server">

Sub Page_Load(Source As Object, E As EventArgs)

  Dim Component as new HelloVB()

  label1.text=Component.SayHello()

End Sub

</script>

</body>
</html>
```

2. Save this as `Component1.aspx` in your `c:\BegASPNET\Ch16` folder, and view it in your browser:

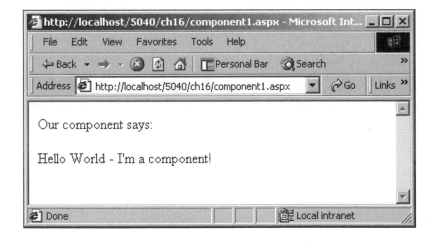

How it works

Let's start by looking at the `web.config` file:

```
<configuration>
  <system.web>
    <compilation>
      <assemblies>
        <add assembly="Component1VB"/>
      </assemblies>
    </compilation>
  </system.web>
</configuration>
```

We mentioned `web.config` files shortly before we completed our example. This file contains a directive, surrounded by the `<assemblies>` tag, that references our assembly:

```
<add assembly="Component1VB"/>
```

This line simply tells our application to use the `Component1VB.dll` file that we created earlier. Without this directive, our `.aspx` file wouldn't know where to look to find our component.

Let's move on to take a look at out ASP.NET page:

```
<%@ Import Namespace="HelloWorld" %>
```

Our first line refers to the name of the Namespace that we declared in our component. If you refer back to our component, you'll remember that we had the following lines of code:

```
Namespace HelloWorld

...

End Namespace
```

This is what we are referring to here. The namespace declaration is different from the class declarations in that a namespace can contain more than one class. These classes can then be referenced with the notation `namespace.class`, but if you use the `Import Namespace` command, you can simply refer to the `class` by name. It's a form of shorthand, and is exactly the same as the syntax we used in our Code Behind file earlier on when we imported the `System.Web.UI` and similar namespaces. They act as shortcuts to commonly used classes.

So, going back to our ASP.NET page:

```
<html>
<body>

Our component says: <br /> <br />
```

We use plain and simple HTML to put some text on the screen directly so that we can compare this with the output of our component:

```
<asp:Label id="label1" runat="server" />
```

Our next line of code creates a label, which we will use to display the output of our component logic. In our case, we know that we're expecting some text, and the label control is a great placeholder for text.

```
<script language="vb" runat="server">

Sub Page_Load(Source As Object, E As EventArgs)
```

We open a script block (we're using VB), and we want to run this block on the server. We then declare a subroutine that will run when the page loads:

```
Dim Component as new HelloVB()

label1.text=Component.SayHello()
```

We instantiate a new instance of our `HelloVB` class by creating an object, in this case called `Component`. This object now has all the functionality of our class available to it as its own methods and properties. In our case, it has only one method – the `SayHello()` method. The second line of code shown above changes the value of the `text` property of the `label1` control to display the output of our `SayHello()` method of the `Component` object:

```
End Sub
</script>n

</body>
</html>
```

The remainder of our code finishes off our example nice and neatly. We close our subroutine, then we close our script block. All that remains then is to close the web page correctly with closing `</body>` and `</html>` tags.

No doubt some of you will be using Visual Studio. Creating an assembly in Visual Studio is a little different from the command line method. However, since Visual Studio is such a vast product, and since we've already discussed how we can compile components from the command line, we'll not be looking at compiling components from Visual Studio.NET in here. If you'd like to know more about Visual Studio, you might want to look at Beginning Visual Basic.NET, ISBN 1-861004-96-6, or Beginning C#, ISBN 1-861004-98-2, which cover development in Visual Studio in detail.

XCopy Deployment

If you've ever played around with Windows in detail, you've probably heard of the **Registry**. The Registry is a database that holds all the information about your computer, hardware, setup, and software. It provides Windows with a way of locating DLL files, or components. In this sense, it's a bit like the yellow pages of your computer. Any traditional DLL that is created has to have an entry in the registry, so that the computer can locate it when it's needed. This process was called **Registration**. With basic ASP.NET components, there's no longer any need to do this (although the process can be a little more complex for global and shared components – we'll discuss this later in this chapter). All we need to do is have the right directory in the right place, and ASP.NET will know where to look and what to do with it.

When we created our DLL, we had to place our compiled component into a /bin directory. This is a subdirectory of our Web application, or virtual directory.

> **Every time you need to use a component with .NET Web applications, you need to place your components in a /bin directory, and tell your ASP.NET pages where to find it by adding a short line of code into your web.config file.**

This is the equivalent to the old-style method of registration, except that you don't need to type any relatively complicated commands to get the computer to locate the component – ASP.NET knows exactly where to look, because we've told it in the web.config file. This means that if you want to deploy your application on another server, all you have to do is copy over the component, the web.config file, and any ASP.NET pages, Code Behind files, or User Controls that form the application. In the good old days of DOS, this sort of thing was done with a command called **xcopy**, hence the term xcopy deployment.

When your component is created, it can be accessed by any of your web pages in that application space. All you need to do is add a short line to your code to import the functionality in the component and you're away. If, however, you need to alter the functionality in the component in any way, all you need to do is go back to your original source file, alter the code, and recompile it. Once that process is complete, the new component will be used by any web site hits that require it. This is totally different to the scenario faced by old ASP developers, who had to stop and start the web application to update their components, thereby losing uptime for the duration of the process. When a change is made to a component, ASP.NET allows any requests that are currently executing to complete, and directs all new incoming requests to the new component, so the users of a site barely notice any change.

Writing code in other languages

Since the .NET Framework is happily language-agnostic, we can write our components in any language we like. For the most part of this book, we've been writing code in Visual Basic.NET. Our first component was written in Visual Basic, so now we'll look at that first component again, but this time written in C#, and show how easy it is to work with any language to create your components.

Try It Out – Writing a Component in C#

Although this example is written in C#, don't panic if you've never looked at C# code. As we'll see, there are a lot of similarities between the two languages since they have to follow the same sorts of rules in order to both be .NET compliant.

1. Start by opening up your editor and enter the following code:

```
namespace HelloWorldCS {

  public class HelloCS {

    public string SayHello() {

      return "Hello World - I'm a component in C#!";

    }

  }

}
```

> Note that because C# is case sensitive, you must take particular care to copy this example letter by letter.

2. Save this file as `Component2.cs`

3. Open up your editor, and enter the following code:

```
set indir=C:\BegASPNET\Ch16\Component2.cs
set outdir=c:\BegASPNET\bin\Component2cs.dll

csc /t:library /out:%outdir% %indir%
```

Save this file as `MakeComponent2CS.bat` in your `C:\BegASPNET` folder.

4. Next, open up a command prompt and in the same way as before, type the following:

```
cd c:\BegASPNET
```

5. Next, type in the following command to compile our component:

```
MakeComponent2CS
```

You should see the following:

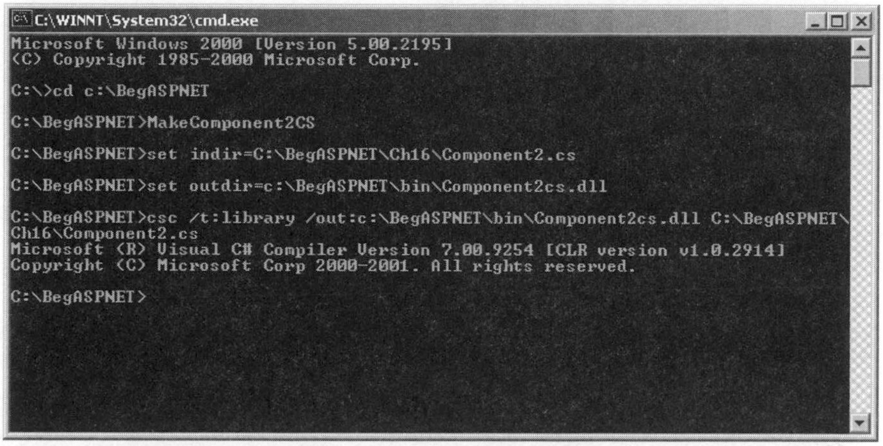

6. We've now compiled our component. We need to make one last alteration to our `Web.config` file. Open it up and add the following highlighted line:

```
<configuration>
  <system.web>
    <compilation>
      <assemblies>
        <add assembly="Component1VB" />
        <add assembly="Component2CS" />
      </assemblies>
    </compilation>
  </system.web>
</configuration>
```

7. Next, open up your editor, and open up `Component1.aspx`. Amend the file by inserting the highlighted lines as shown below, and save it as `Component2.aspx`:

```
<%@ Import Namespace="HelloWorld" %>
<%@ Import Namespace="HelloWorldCS" %>
<html>
<body>

Our component says: <br /> <br />

<asp:Label id="label1" runat="server" />
<br /><asp:Label id="label2" runat="server" />

<script language="vb" runat="server">

Sub Page_Load(Source As Object, E As EventArgs)

  Dim Component as new HelloVB()
```

```
label1.text=Component.SayHello()

Dim Component2 as new HelloCS()

label2.text=Component2.SayHello()

End Sub

</script>

</body>
</html>
```

8. Now, open up `Component2.aspx` in your browser:

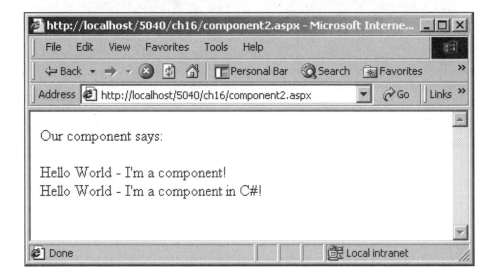

How it Works

Although the syntax was somewhat unfamiliar in this example, it's not too hard to put the two files side by side to compare them:

```
namespace HelloWorldCS {
```

Our namespace declaration is now case sensitive (since C# is case sensitive), and there's a curly bracket at the end of the line:

```
public class HelloCS {
```

Our class definition is also case sensitive, and it also has a curly bracket at the end of the line,

```
    public string SayHello() {
```

We don't actually need to tell C# what kind of procedure we're creating, so we can omit the word
Function from our declaration. Instead of saying As String, we simply include the word string
before the name of our method – this implies that the method must return a string. Again, there's a curly
bracket at the end of this line:

```
    return "Hello World - I'm a component in C#!";
```

Our return statement has barely changed, except for the content of the message. You'll notice a semi
colon at the end of the line – where VB automatically assumes each line takes up only one line, and you
have to use an underscore to continue a line on a new line, C# doesn't end a line until it sees a semi-
colon. There is, therefore, no need for a continuation character:

```
      }

    }

  }
```

We finish with a rather alien bit of bracket-frenzy – this is simply C# closing up our method, our class,
and finally our namespace, in exactly the same way as we did in VB. The difference is that the VB
syntax is End Function, End Class, and End Namespace. In C#, because of the use of brackets, the
compiler knows that everything between each nested set of brackets is a separate block. It's a kind of
programming shorthand.

Let's briefly look at the new lines we encountered in our ASP.NET page:

```
  <%@ Import Namespace="HelloWorldCS" %>
```

We add an extra Import statement at the top of our ASP.NET page to reference our new component,
in a very similar way to the previous examples.

```
  <br /><asp:Label id="label2" runat="server" />
```

We need to add a line break and another label, which we'll use to store the output of our component,
just as we did with the VB component

```
    Dim Component2 as new HelloCS()

    label2.text=Component2.SayHello()
```

Finally, we call out to the component in exactly the same way as we did before, and output the message
to our new label control.

As you'll see, our ASP.NET page hardly looks any different – there's no curly brackets or semi-colons in here, because that's all held in our C# component. We have referenced two components, one originally written in VB, one originally written in C#, and they've both been integrated seamlessly into our page. We could have written other 'Hello World' components in other languages, and the results would be the same. This is one of the coolest features of .NET, and it's one that many developers will grow to love. Imagine, if you're a VB developer, working on a project with a C# developer, and a Perl developer – you could all write components to be used in ASP.NET pages, with no need to worry about which language the original component code was written in, as long as it has been compiled into Intermediate Language code. The only way this is possible is to have a compiler that is supported by the Common Language Runtime. The .NET Framework only includes a handful of compilers by default (VB, C#, and JScript), but there are likely to be compilers available for a lot more languages appearing over time. Perl is one of those languages for which we expect to see a compiler in the near future, as well as languages like Python, Fortran, Pascal, and even Cobol.

Introducing Business Objects

Business objects are components that contain code for accessing data, or application logic. Our previous example of using an assembly didn't exactly push the boundaries of components, so in this next example, we're going to be slightly more adventurous and include some business logic.

In the following example, we will create a component that connects to the `Authors` table in the `WroxShop` Access database we used in the previous chapter. We will create a namespace with one class, the `WroxAuthors` class, which has the following methods and properties:

Methods	`GetAuthorsByBook`	Queries the database for a list of authors on each book
	`GetBooks`	Queries the database to find a list of available books
Properties	`DatabaseConnection`	Creates a connection to the database

Again, we've limited the functionality in the component for reasons of simplicity, but you extend this much further and include methods that add and delete records from the database, and so on.

Try It Out: Encapsulating Business Logic into a Component

In this example, we will be connecting to a database, running a query against that database, then displaying selected records in a data grid on an ASP.NET page.

1. Copy the `WroxShop` database that we used in Chapter 15 into your Chapter 16 directory

2. Time to start up your favorite editor again, and enter the following code:

```
Option Explicit
Option Strict

Imports System
Imports System.Data
```

```
Imports System.Data.OleDB

Namespace BusinessObjectVB

  Public Class WroxAuthors

    private m_DSN as String

    public Sub New(DSN as string)
      m_DSN = DSN
    end sub

 public function  GetAuthorsByBook ( ISBN as String)  as DataSet

   dim myConnection as new OleDbConnection(m_DSN)
   dim myDataAdapter as new OleDbDataAdapter("SELECT Authors.AuthorFirstName, " & _
"Authors.AuthorSurname, Books.Title FROM Authors LEFT JOIN Books ON " & _
"Authors.Book = Books.Title WHERE (((Books.ISBN)='" & ISBN & "'));", myConnection)

   dim authorsByBook as new DataSet()
   myDataAdapter.Fill(authorsByBook)

   return authorsByBook
 end function

   public function  GetBooks ()  as DataSet

     dim myConnection as new OleDbConnection(m_DSN)
     dim myDataAdapter as new OleDbDataAdapter("SELECT * FROM Books", myConnection)

     dim Books as new DataSet()
     myDataAdapter.Fill(Books)

     return Books
   end function

   end class
end namespace
```

3. Save this file as `WroxAuthors.vb`. Next, open up your editor, and enter the following code, which will form our Make file. Save this as `C:\BegASPNET\MakeAuthorsVB.bat`:

```
set indir=C:\BegASPNET\Ch16\WroxAuthors.vb
set outdir=C:\BegASPNET\bin\WroxAuthorsVB.dll
set assemblies=System.dll,System.Data.dll,System.XML.dll

vbc /t:library /out:%outdir% %indir% /r:%assemblies%
```

4. Once you've saved this file, open up a command prompt and type the following:

```
cd c:\begaspnet
```

Press *Enter*, then type the following:

```
MakeAuthorsVB
```

This should produce the following output:

5. We're going to use an `.aspx` page with a Code Behind file. Close down the command prompt window, then open up your editor again, and enter the following code, which will form the `.aspx` page:

```
<%@ Import Namespace="BusinessObjectVB" %>
<%@ Page Language="vb" debug="true" src="wroxauthorscb.vb"
Inherits="WroxAuthorsCodebehind"%>
<html>
<body>

Please select a book: <br /> <br />

<form Method="Post" runat="Server">

  <P>
    <asp:DropDownList id="DropDownList1" runat="server"></asp:DropDownList>
    <asp:Button id="Button1" runat="server" Text="Submit"></asp:Button>
  </P>
  <P>
    <asp:DataGrid id="DataGrid1" runat="server"></asp:DataGrid>
  </P>
</form>

</body>
</html>
```

6. Save this file as `WroxAuthors.aspx`.

7. Now, fire up your editor again and enter the following code. This will form our Code Behind file:

```
Imports System
Imports System.Web.UI
Imports System.Web.UI.WebControls
Imports BusinessObjectVB

Public Class WroxAuthorsCodebehind : Inherits Page

    Public DropDownList1 As DropDownList
    Public Button1 As Button
    Public DataGrid1 As DataGrid

  Public Sub Page_Load(Source As Object, E As EventArgs)
     Dim objWroxAuthors as new WroxAuthors _
  ("provider=Microsoft.Jet.OLEDB.4.0;data source=C:\BegASPNET\Ch16\WroxShop.mdb")

    If Not Page.IsPostback

      DropDownList1.DataSource = objWroxAuthors.GetBooks()
      DropDownList1.DataValueField="ISBN"
      DropDownList1.DataTextField="Title"
      DropDownList1.DataBind()

    Else

      DataGrid1.DataSource=objWroxAuthors.GetAuthorsByBook _
                                    (DropDownList1.SelectedItem.Value)
      DataGrid1.DataBind()

    End If

  End Sub

End Class
```

8. Save this file as `WroxAuthorsCB.vb`.

9. We need to set the reference in our `Web.config` file, so open that back up in your editor, and change it to appear as follows:

```
<configuration>
  <system.web>
    <compilation>
      <assemblies>
        <add assembly="Component1VB"/>
        <add assembly="WroxAuthorsVB" />
      </assemblies>
    </compilation>
  </system.web>
</configuration>
```

10. Finally, fire up your browser, and view `WroxAuthors.aspx`. Select a book from the drop down list, hit **Submit**, and you should see something like this:

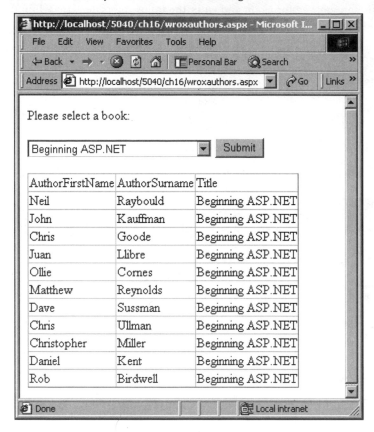

How it works

We've got a lot to get through here, so let's start off with our component:

```
Option Explicit
Option Strict
```

We didn't include these first two lines of code in our first example to keep our code to a minimum but, for the sake of completeness and accuracy, we've included them here. The first line will be familiar to anyone with any previous VB or ASP knowledge, as it's the standard way of forcing us developers to declare every variable before we use it. This encourages good coding practice, and it's really useful for beginners, because it helps to trap errors at an earlier stage. The second statement shown above, `Option Strict`, is used to prevent implicit type conversions, which helps to avoid a lot of type-related errors in your code. This basically helps during the debugging process because errors will get thrown up if you try to perform a multiply operation on a string, for example:

```
Imports System
Imports System.Data
Imports System.Data.OleDB
```

Our next three lines of code import all the standard namespaces that are used when working with data from a non-SQL Server data source in ASP.NET. We met these previously in Chapters 12 and 13:

```
Namespace BusinessObjectVB
```

We declare that in this example, we are creating a namespace called `BusinessObjectVB`. If we want to shortcut access to the classes in this namespace, we need to use the `Imports` statement in our ASP.NET page:

```
Public Class WroxAuthors
```

Our class in this example is called `WroxAuthors`, and this is the template from which we'll create an object:

```
private m_DSN as String
```

The next line creates a private variable, which is a variable that our ASP.NET pages can't access, but anything within this component can access. This variable is used inside of the component to pass in the value of the DSN, the data source information, when called by the main ASP.NET page:

```
public Sub New(DSN as string)
    m_DSN = DSN
end sub
```

We create a subroutine that will form our public property. This property accepts the value of a DSN, and when we set this property from our ASP.NET page, we must pass in the DSN for our database. This DSN is handled here, where the value of our DSN is passed to our private variable m_DSN. This is essential when we connect to our database:

```
public function  GetAuthorsByBook ( ISBN as String)  as DataSet

    dim myConnection as new OleDbConnection(m_DSN)
    dim myDataAdapter as new OleDbDataAdapter("SELECT Authors.AuthorFirstName, " & _
"Authors.AuthorSurname, Books.Title FROM Authors LEFT JOIN Books ON " & _
"Authors.Book = Books.Title WHERE (((Books.ISBN)='" & ISBN & "'));", myConnection)
```

Our next section of code is where we code our method, `GetAuthorsByBook`. This method is used to query the database to find out which of the authors have written on a specific book, identified by the parameter ISBN, which is implicitly selected by the user at run-time using a drop-down box control. (The drop-down box lists book names, but our function has the corresponding ISBN passed to it because the ISBN for a book will always be strictly unique.) Our next two lines of code are where we create our `SQLConnection` object, as we saw in the previous chapters, and our `DataAdapter`. The `DataAdapter` is where we enter the details of our query, which we will execute on the database once we try to fill our `DataAdapter`:

```
        dim authorsByBook as new DataSet()
        myDataAdapter.Fill(authorsByBook)

        return authorsByBook
    end function
```

These two lines populate our new `DataSet` with information via the `SqlAdapter`; we then finish this method by setting the return value:

```
    public function  GetBooks ()  as DataSet

        dim myConnection as new OleDbConnection(m_DSN)
        dim myDataAdapter as new OleDbDataAdapter("SELECT * FROM Books", myConnection)
```

The next section is similar to the previous section. We are creating a function that obtains a list of books from the `Books` table of our `Wroxshop` database, so that the user can choose one of them. The selected book is then passed into the `GetStates` method when it's called, and the query is run:

```
        dim Books as new DataSet()
        myDataAdapter.Fill(Books)

        return Books
    end function

    end class
end namespace
```

The final pieces of code start off by creating a `DataSet` and filling it with the output of the `OleDbDataAdapter` – the output of the `MyDataAdapter` is the results of our query. We then set our return value to be a list of books, before closing the function, the class, and finally, the namespace.

Next to be explained is our ASP.NET page:

```
    <%@ Import Namespace="BusinessObjectVB" %>
```

Our first line imports our namespace to make it easier to work with our class:

```
    <%@ Page Language="vb" debug="true" src="wroxauthorscb.vb"
    Inherits="WroxAuthorsCodebehind"%>
```

The next line of code references the Code Behind file that we'll be using for this page:

```
    <html>
    <body>

    Please select a book: <br /> <br />
```

The next lines of code are fairly simple and are completely HTML-based:

```
<form Method="Post" runat="Server">

  <P>
    <asp:DropDownList id="DropDownList1" runat="server"></asp:DropDownList>
    <asp:Button id="Button1" runat="server" Text="Submit"></asp:Button>
  </P>
  <P>
    <asp:DataGrid id="DataGrid1" runat="server"></asp:DataGrid>
  </P>
</form>

</body>
</html>
```

This block of code is where our form is laid out. Encapsulating these controls in one form binds them together, so that the compiler knows that hitting the Submit button will post back the values of any controls with a `runat="server"` tag on them. The first two controls are our drop-down box and button. The box will display the list of books from which a user can choose. The button fires the postback. The last control in this section is an ASP.NET `DataGrid` control, like we met in Chapter 14. This control will be used to store the results of our query.

Let's move on to the Code Behind file:

```
Imports System
Imports System.Web.UI
Imports System.Web.UI.WebControls
Imports BusinessObjectVB
```

The first lines of code import all the necessary namespaces, along with one extra namespace – this is the namespace containing our components, so we need to reference it here by name:

```
Public Class WroxAuthorsCodebehind : Inherits Page

    Public DropDownList1 As DropDownList
    Public Button1 As Button
    Public DataGrid1 As DataGrid
```

We declare our class here, inherit from the `Page` object, and create three public variables corresponding to the three controls on our Web Form:

```
Public Sub Page_Load(Source As Object, E As EventArgs)
    Dim objWroxAuthors as new WroxAuthors _
 ("provider=Microsoft.Jet.OLEDB.4.0;data source=C:\BegASPNET\Ch16\WroxShop.mdb")
```

The next few lines are where it starts to get really interesting. We have a script block with a `Page_Load` event handler. In this event handler, the first thing we do is instantiate a new instance of our class into the `objWroxAuthors` object, and we pass in the connection string as a parameter. Note that this connection string applies to the database we used in Chapter 15, so you'll either have to copy the same database file into your Chapter 16 directory, or alter the path to look at the copy in the Chapter 15 folder:

```
If Not Page.IsPostback

    DropDownList1.DataSource = objWroxAuthors.GetBooks()
    DropDownList1.DataValueField="ISBN"
    DropDownList1.DataTextField="Title"
    DropDownList1.DataBind()
```

This `If ... Then ... Else` statement is very useful to us. When we first load the page, when we're *not* posting back to the server, we only need to concern ourselves with the first part – this part populates our drop-down list with a list of books, using the parameters specified in the component. We identify the `DataSource` as being our `DataSet` that we obtained from our component, then we set two values on our `DropDown` box. We are binding to the `ISBN` field of our table, but we're displaying the `Title` field, so we're binding to unique data, and displaying data in a more human-readable form. We don't expect everyone else to memorize ISBNs. Finally, we bind our data to the drop-down list:

```
Else

    DataGrid1.DataSource=objWroxAuthors.GetAuthorsByBook _
                                        (DropDownList1.SelectedItem.Value)
    DataGrid1.DataBind()
```

In the second part of our `Datagrid` control, we react to a postback by a user, and we pass in the `DataSource` attribute for our `DataGrid`. We finally bind this data source to our grid, and hey presto, a table of authors and their book appears:

```
    End If

  End Sub

End Class
```

We close up our file in the usual way.

Finally, let's take a quick look at that new line in our `Web.config` file:

```
    <add assembly="WroxAuthorsVB" />
```

We added a line to reference our new assembly in exactly the same way as we did previously.

This example wasn't meant to be a tutorial in ADO.NET – you should refer back to Chapters 12 and 13 for more information on ADO.NET. This example was simply one implementation of using an encapsulated business object.

Custom Server Controls

ASP.NET pages revolve around the concept of Server controls. Control-based development is the new 'Big Thing', as you may have gathered by now. Earlier in the book, we learnt how to use the built-in HTML Server Controls, the ASP.NET Server Controls, and we learnt how to create our own User Controls for re-use in our Web Forms. Now we're going to look at what ASP.NET Custom controls are, how they differ from User Controls and Business Objects, and how these are created.

What are Custom Controls?

Custom controls are very similar to business logic components in their design – they contain classes and are compiled. However, the main difference between a custom control and a business logic component is that a custom control generates an interface, while a business logic component doesn't. When we place a server control on our page, we have a visible interface.

How are Custom Controls different from User Controls?

Custom controls inherit from the `System.Web.UI.Control` namespace, and are compiled. User Controls are simply partial ASP.NET pages that link to our main ASP.NET page. Custom controls are meant to be more easily re-useable. You'll probably find Custom control vendors appearing in the usual influx of marketing e-mail, in exactly the same way as traditional Component vendors.

How are Custom Controls different from Business Objects?

While a Business Object is designed to hold application logic, such as database connection information, or the code to produce a dataset based on a query, custom controls are designed to produce viewable output. They are both compiled to make it easier to deploy components on other systems or applications. They can also inherit from other assemblies and business objects themselves.

Let's have a go at creating a simple Custom control, and displaying it in a very simple ASP.NET page.

Try It Out – our first ASP.NET Custom Control

We're going to create a very simple custom control that will output some text to our ASP.NET Web Form.

1. Fire up your editor and enter the following code:

```
Imports System
Imports System.Web.UI

Namespace WroxControls

  Public Class WelcomeControl : Inherits Control

    Overrides Protected Sub Render (writer as HtmlTextWriter)

      writer.write("<h2>Welcome to the Wrox Shop - we cater for all your " & _
                                        "ASP.NET needs</h2>")

    End Sub

  End Class

End Namespace
```

Save this as `CustomControl.vb`

2. Open your editor once again, and enter the following code:

```
set outdir=c:\begaspnet\bin\CustomControlVB.dll
set indir=C:\begaspnet\ch16\CustomControl.vb
Set assemblies=System.dll,System.Web.dll

vbc /t:library /out:%outdir% %indir% /r:%assemblies%
```

Save this file as `MakeCustomControlVB.bat` in your `C:\BegASPNET` directory.

3. Open up a command prompt and type the following:

```
cd C:\BegASPNET
```

Then run the batch file:

```
MakeCustomControlVB
```

You should see the following:

4. Open up your `Web.config` file and add the following line:

```
<configuration>
  <system.web>
    <compilation>
      <assemblies>
        <add assembly="Component1VB" />
        <add assembly="CustomControlVB" />
      </assemblies>
    </compilation>
  </system.web>
</configuration>
```

5. Finally, open up your editor once more, and enter the following code:

```
<%@ Register TagPrefix="CustomControl" Namespace="WroxControls"
Assembly="CustomControlVB" %>

<html>
<body>

  <CustomControl:WelcomeControl runat="server" />

</body>
</html>
```

6. Save this file as `CustomControl.aspx`, then view it in your browser:

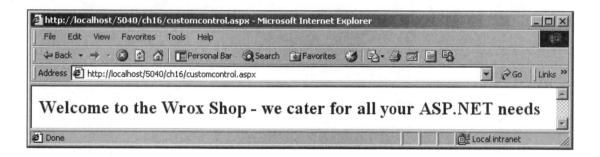

How it works

We created a very simple control with very limited output to demonstrate a very simple custom control. Let's take a look at how we put it together:

```
Imports System
Imports System.Web.UI
```

Our `Imports` statements have to be included at the beginning of our file as usual:

```
Namespace WroxControls
```

Our namespace declaration comes next, and we're calling our namespace `WroxControls`:

```
    Public Class WelcomeControl : Inherits Control
```

Our next line creates a class called `WelcomeControl`. We are then inheriting from the `Control` class of the `System.Web.UI` namespace. This is an important part of custom control development, because all custom controls must inherit from this namespace. This class provides a lot of basic functionality behind the scenes that any control needs in order to work:

```
Overrides Protected Sub Render (writer as HtmlTextWriter)
```

We're creating one method in our class. There are a couple of new terms in here, which you're probably unfamiliar with. There is likely to be a standard method in the `Control` class called `Render`, and what we're doing here is altering how that method works by **overriding** its functionality with our own functionality. While we don't want to go too far into the world of VB programming here, you need to know that this statement is required to provide the output we specify, instead of the default output from the `Control` class. We will be using an `HtmlTextWriter` to display the output of our control:

```
writer.write("<h2>Welcome to the Wrox Shop - we cater for all your " & _
                                        "ASP.NET needs</h2>")
```

We call the `write` method of our `HtmlTextWriter` to produce some output on our page. This is a simple piece of H2-style text:

```
   End Sub

  End Class

 End Namespace
```

We finish off our control by closing the subroutine, the class, and the namespace.

Next, we created a make file:

```
set outdir=c:\begaspnet\bin\CustomControlVB.dll
set indir=C:\begaspnet\ch16\CustomControl.vb
Set assemblies=System.dll,System.Web.dll

vbc /t:library /out:%outdir% %indir% /r:%assemblies%
```

In a similar way to the previous make files, we set aliases for our input and output directories, as well as for the assemblies we need to reference to complete the compilation. We compile the file in the same way as before using the `vbc` command:

```
<add assembly="CustomControlVB" />
```

We added a line to our `Web.config` file to reference our new control.

Let's move on to the ASP.NET page now:

```
<%@ Register TagPrefix="CustomControl" Namespace="WroxControls"
Assembly="CustomControlVB" %>
```

Our first line is where we reference our control so that our page knows where to look. We set a `TagPrefix` like we did with our User Controls, however, we do not set a `TagName` – we'll see why in a moment. We specify that the namespace we're using is the `WroxControls` namespace, and that we're using the `CustomControlsVB` namespace:

```
<html>
<body>

  <CustomControl:WelcomeControl runat="server" />

</body>
</html>
```

The last bits on our page include one line of interest. This is where we place our control on the page. We call it by the `TagPrefix` we set earlier, followed by the Class name we specified in the control. We specify a `runat="server"` attribute and close the tag, and hey presto! – we've just used our first custom control.

How it all fits together

We're going to have one last example to incorporate the concepts we've learnt over the course of these two chapters. We'll be using quite a few files from Chapter 15 in here, so make sure you copy the following files over to your Chapter 16 directory too:

```
featuredbooks_CB.ascx
featuredbooks_CB.vb
header.ascx
logo.gif
style.css
```

All we'll be working on here is an `.aspx` page. Let's take a look at the code, before moving on to look at the output.

Try It Out: Putting it all Together

This example incorporates some User Controls, some Code Behind, a business object and a custom control – quite a handful, but not terribly complicated - as we'll see.

1. Enter the following code and save it as `main.aspx` in your `C:\BegASPNET\Ch16` directory:

```
<%@ Page Language="vb" debug="true" src="main_cb.vb"
Inherits="MainAppCodebehind"%>
<%@ Register TagPrefix="UserControl" TagName="Header" Src="header.ascx" %>
<%@ Register TagPrefix="UserControl" TagName="FeaturedBooks_CB"
Src="featuredbooks_CB.ascx" %>
<%@ Register TagPrefix="CustomControl" Namespace="WroxControls"
Assembly="CustomControlVB" %>

<html>
<head>
<link rel="stylesheet" type="text/css" href="http://localhost:5040/ch16/style.css"
title="style">
</head>
<body>
```

```
<form runat="server" method="post">

  <UserControl:Header id="MyHeader" runat="Server" />

  <CustomControl:WelcomeControl runat="server" />

  <h3>A simple control for playing with header color</h3>

  <asp:DropDownList id="ColorList" runat="Server" />
  <asp:button text="Apply Color" OnClick="SubmitBtn_Click" runat="server" />
  <br /><br />
  <asp:label id="SelectedColor" runat="Server" />

  <br /><hr /><br />

  Today's Selected Books:
  <UserControl:FeaturedBooks_CB id="BookList" runat="Server" />

  <br /><hr /><br />
  Please select a book: <br /> <br />
  <P>
    <asp:DropDownList id="SelectBook" runat="server"></asp:DropDownList>
    <asp:Button id="SelectBookSubmit" runat="server" Text="Submit"></asp:Button>
  </P>
  <P>
    <asp:DataGrid id="AuthorGrid" runat="server"></asp:DataGrid>
  </P>

</form>

<script language="VB" runat="Server">

  Public Sub SubmitBtn_Click(Sender As Object, E As EventArgs)

    Dim NewColor as String
    NewColor = Colorlist.SelectedItem.Text
    selectedcolor.text= "You selected " & NewColor
    MyHeader.BackColor= NewColor

  End Sub

</script>

</body>

</html>
```

2. Save the file, then open up your editor one last time, and enter the following code:

```
Imports System
Imports System.Collections
Imports System.Web.UI
Imports System.Web.UI.WebControls
```

```
Imports BusinessObjectVB

Public Class MainAppCodebehind : Inherits Page

    Public ColorList As DropDownList
    Public SelectedColor As Label
    Public SelectBook As DropDownList
    Public SelectBookSubmit As Button
    Public AuthorGrid As DataGrid

  Public Sub Page_Load(Source As Object, E As EventArgs)
      Dim objWroxAuthors as new WroxAuthors
("provider=Microsoft.Jet.OLEDB.4.0;data source=C:\BegASPNET\Ch16\WroxShop.mdb")

    If Not Page.IsPostback

      SelectBook.DataSource = objWroxAuthors.GetBooks()
      SelectBook.DataValueField="ISBN"
      SelectBook.DataTextField="Title"
      SelectBook.DataBind()

      Dim arrColors As New ArrayList(5)
      arrColors.Add("Red")
      arrColors.Add("Green")
      arrColors.Add("Blue")
      arrColors.Add("Orange")
      arrColors.Add("Purple")

      Colorlist.Datasource = arrColors
      Colorlist.DataBind()

    Else

      AuthorGrid.DataSource=objWroxAuthors.GetAuthorsByBook
(SelectBook.SelectedItem.Value)
      AuthorGrid.DataBind()

    End If

  End Sub

End Class
```

3. Save this file as `Main_CB.vb` in the same directory, then view `main.aspx` in your browser:

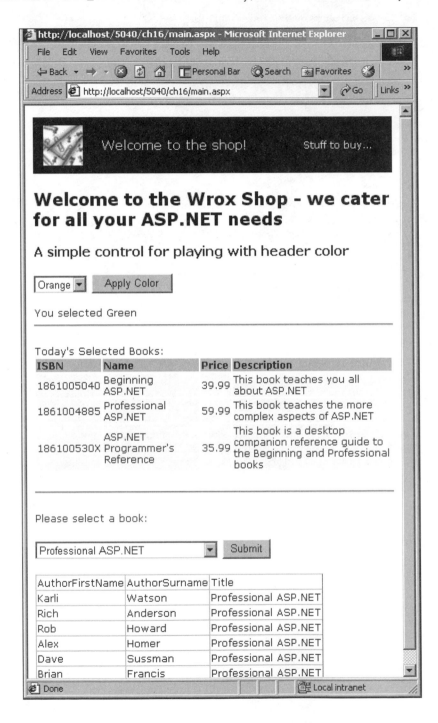

How it Works

We've basically combined a lot of the components we've developed over the course of these two chapters and displayed them on one page. Since we've already looked at how these components worked, we'll not be going into too much detail here. Let's dive in quickly:

```
<%@ Page Language="vb" debug="true" src="main_cb.vb"
Inherits="MainAppCodebehind"%>
<%@ Register TagPrefix="UserControl" TagName="Header" Src="header.ascx" %>
<%@ Register TagPrefix="UserControl" TagName="FeaturedBooks_CB"
Src="featuredbooks_CB.ascx" %>
<%@ Register TagPrefix="CustomControl" Namespace="WroxControls"
Assembly="CustomControlVB" %>
```

The top of our file references our Code Behind file, our header control, our featured books control, and our custom welcome message control:

```
<html>
<head>
<link rel="stylesheet" type="text/css" href="http://localhost/5040/ch16/style.css"
title="style">
</head>
<body>
```

We have some HTML that references a style sheet to provide some consistency in presentation:

```
<form runat="server" method="post">

  <UserControl:Header id="MyHeader" runat="Server" />

  <CustomControl:WelcomeControl runat="server" />
```

We include two controls – our header control, and our welcome message custom control, at the top of our page.

```
<h3>A simple control for playing with header color</h3>

<asp:DropDownList id="ColorList" runat="Server" />
<asp:button text="Apply Color" OnClick="SubmitBtn_Click" runat="server" />
<br /><br />
<asp:label id="SelectedColor" runat="Server" />
```

We include the code to change the color of our header:

```
<br /><hr /><br />

Today's Selected Books:
<UserControl:FeaturedBooks_CB id="BookList" runat="Server" />
```

We include our featured books control:

```
<br /><hr /><br />
Please select a book: <br /> <br />
<P>
  <asp:DropDownList id="SelectBook" runat="server"></asp:DropDownList>
  <asp:Button id="SelectBookSubmit" runat="server" Text="Submit"></asp:Button>
</P>
<P>
  <asp:DataGrid id="AuthorGrid" runat="server"></asp:DataGrid>
</P>
</form>
```

Finally we include the control for selecting a book and displaying the list of authors who worked on that book:

```
<script language="VB" runat="Server">

  Public Sub SubmitBtn_Click(Sender As Object, E As EventArgs)

    Dim NewColor as String
    NewColor = Colorlist.SelectedItem.Text
    selectedcolor.text= "You selected " & NewColor
    MyHeader.BackColor= NewColor

  End Sub

</script>
```

We have a small script block that handles the changing of the color of the header control:

```
</body>

</html>
```

Finally, we finish off our ASP.NET page.

A very quick look through the Code Behind again doesn't reveal anything too new:

```
Imports System
Imports System.Collections
Imports System.Web.UI
Imports System.Web.UI.WebControls
Imports BusinessObjectVB
```

We import all of our namespaces:

```
Public Class MainAppCodebehind : Inherits Page

    Public ColorList As DropDownList
    Public SelectedColor As Label
```

```
Public SelectBook As DropDownList
Public SelectBookSubmit As Button
Public AuthorGrid As DataGrid
```

We create our class, and declare some public variables:

```
Public Sub Page_Load(Source As Object, E As EventArgs)
    Dim objWroxAuthors as new WroxAuthors
("provider=Microsoft.Jet.OLEDB.4.0;data source=C:\BegASPNET\Ch16\WroxShop.mdb")
```

We create a `Page_Load` event handler which connects to our datastore:

```
If Not Page.IsPostback

    SelectBook.DataSource = objWroxAuthors.GetBooks()
    SelectBook.DataValueField="ISBN"
    SelectBook.DataTextField="Title"
    SelectBook.DataBind()
```

We populate the book list drop-down box with data:

```
    Dim arrColors As New ArrayList(5)
    arrColors.Add("Red")
    arrColors.Add("Green")
    arrColors.Add("Blue")
    arrColors.Add("Orange")
    arrColors.Add("Purple")

    Colorlist.Datasource = arrColors
    Colorlist.DataBind()
```

We then populate the color drop-down list with data:

```
Else

    AuthorGrid.DataSource=objWroxAuthors.GetAuthorsByBook
(SelectBook.SelectedItem.Value)
    AuthorGrid.DataBind()

End If
```

We then bind the data on our authors to the data grid:

```
End Sub

End Class
```

Finally, we close up the class, and we're done.

Summary

In this chapter we have continued the thread started in Chapter 15 and discussed creating .NET Business Object, Assemblies, and Custom Server Controls. We learnt:

❑   How to compile a .NET assembly

❑   How to use a compiled assembly in a page

❑   How to encapsulate business logic into a component

❑   How to use User Controls, Code Behind, Components, and Custom controls on the same page

We've not gone into too much detail with regard to custom controls, since this is a vast and complex area – one that is covered in more detail in *Professional ASP.NET ISBN: 1-861004-88-5*.

Exercises

1.   Explain the benefits of using Components, and what sorts of things we should encapsulate in a .NET assembly. When should we use compiled `.dlls` instead of Code Behind files and User Controls?

2.   What is business logic? Give an example of the sort of code that can be described as business logic, and talk about how this code can be reused elsewhere.

3.   Create a new component that converts from imperial units to metric and back again. You'll need four methods: Celsius to Fahrenheit temperatures, Fahrenheit to Celsius, Kilometers to Miles, and Miles to Kilometers. You'll need the following data:

❑   Fahrenheit temperature = Celsius temperature * (9/5) + 32

❑   Celsius temperature = (Fahrenheit temperature – 32) * (5/9)

❑   1 Mile = 1.6039 Kilometers (to 4 decimal places)

❑   1 Kilometer = 0.6214 Miles (to 4 decimal places)

4.   Create an ASP.NET page that uses this functionality. One example might be a page about holiday destinations. Users in other countries might want to know distances in metric instead of imperial, or temperatures in Celsius, rather than Fahrenheit.

5.   Additionally, you might want to access this functionality from a completely different type of site, for example, one that has some scientific purpose that requires unit conversion, a route planner that will provide results in both miles or kilometers, or a weather site that needs to provide today's temperatures in both Celsius and Fahrenheit. A completely different situation would be a cookery site that displayed instructions for cooking a meal in an oven set to either Celsius or Fahrenheit temperatures.

Debugging & Error Handling

One of the fundamental truths of organized systems is that the more complex they become, the more likely they are to go wrong. While most of the examples we've looked at so far in this book have been quite simple, the principles behind OOP and the .NET framework are aimed at making it easier for you to build larger, more complex applications – after all, this is where you're most likely to make your money as a developer.

Once you have planned and created your program, the steps involved in ensuring that your code runs smoothly at all times can be broken down into two main categories:

- ❑ **Debugging** – However hard we try to write flawless code, mistakes are always going to creep in. We can minimize their effect by identifying those areas of our solution that are most error prone, and adhering to good coding practices to make the errors more obvious.

- ❑ **Error Handling** – Even if the code itself is flawless, there's no guarantee that everything will go according to plan when we come to use it. We have to anticipate all kinds of runtime errors, and know what to look out for when things go wrong, so we can set about putting them right. On top of this, we also have to be aware of errors that can stem from the environment in which our application is run – such as the network connection or power supply failing, and anticipate how we will handle these conditions.

This chapter will provide information to help you to identify problems, fix them, and prevent them occurring in future. We'll look specifically at the following topics:

- ❑ Different types of errors that can occur
- ❑ Good coding practice
- ❑ Identifying potential errors
- ❑ Locating errors in the page
- ❑ Tracing
- ❑ Exceptions
- ❑ Handling Exceptions
- ❑ Handling errors
- ❑ Notifying and logging any errors that have occurred

A Few Good Habits

Whether you're an expert developer, or a beginner developing your first application, it's important to realize that you can significantly reduce the probability of an error occurring, by adopting some very straightforward habits. Finding an error in your application shouldn't be a cue to panic – it should be your cue to plan a way to fix the problem. This chapter covers information that will help you to define a plan of action when an error occurs.

Before we go into detail about the different kinds of errors that might occur in your page, let's talk about the preparations you can make to reduce the time it takes to identify and fix an error:

- ❑ **Understand** your code – The most important factor in finding a cause for an error, is to understand the code. You should be able to identify the various sections of the code, such as presentation logic containing different controls, business logic containing various functions, and so on, and be able to say whether they are executed either client-side or server-side. A good understanding of the various sections of the code in your page will help you locate the cause of an error. Internal comments and documentation can be invaluable when doing this.

- ❑ **Identify** where it might break – Before even loading the page and testing its functionality, identify the potential problem areas. For instance, say you have developed a page that communicates with a database and pulls a set of records with specific information. To do this, you first create a connection to the database, and then execute a query to retrieve the records. A potential trouble spot for errors is in the lines where you create the connection, or in which you create the query. We will discuss different kind of errors later in this chapter, which will assist you in looking out for potential problems at an early stage.

- ❑ **Amend** identified error conditions – Once you have identified areas that could break within your page, the next step is to make sure the conditions under which your error might occur are as stable as possible. Remember the old adage, "prevention is better than cure".

So what can we learn from the above three steps? Mistakes in your code are not the end of the world. What matters is how quickly you can identify them and provide a fix. With that in mind, let's start with a look at the different kinds of errors that can occur.

Syntax errors

As the name suggests, this type of error occurs when there is a problem in the syntax of the code. This will, most likely, be the first type of error that you'll encounter when developing ASP.NET pages. It might occur for one of the following reasons:

- ❑ A typo or bad grammar in the code syntax. For example, instead of typing `<asp:textbox>` for creating a text box control in your page, you type `<asp:textbx>`. The browser shows an error.

- ❑ Incorrect code syntax. For instance, when creating a text box control, we might forget to close the tag as shown below:

```
<asp:TextBox id="txtName" runat="server">
```

When it should actually be:

```
<asp:TextBox id="txtName" runat="server" />
```

❑   Combining or splitting keywords between languages. This is an error that I make quite a lot. If you switch coding between JScript.NET and VB.NET, you encounter it even more often. A good example is the `elseif` keyword. So what is that correct syntax? It depends on the language you are using. In VB.NET, the correct syntax is `elseif`, whereas in JScript.NET the correct syntax is `else if`.

❑   Not closing a construct properly. This error occurs if we forget to close a construct, such as a `for...next`, or a nested `if...then...else...end if` statement. Take a look at this, for example:

```
If condition1 then
   'do this
else if conidtion2 then
   'do this
if condition2a then
   'do this
else
   'do this
end if
```

Did you catch the error in the above code? An `end if` is missing. Imagine how difficult it would be to spot this if we had the above code block set amongst hundreds of other lines of code.

These are just a few common examples of syntax errors. There is no way we could provide a list of all possible syntax errors that you might encounter, but the good news is that syntax errors are usually easy to find and fix.

The error page, which is the page that will be returned to you when you try to access an ASPX page with syntax errors using your browser, will provide information about the suspected error and the line number the error has occurred in. Let's have a look at an example of this error message.

Try It Out – Syntax error

1. Use your favorite editor to type the following lines of code. Let's make a spelling mistake (or typo) when creating the textbox control, as shown below:

```html
<html>
  <head>
    <title>Syntax Error Example </title>
  </head>
  <body>
    <form method="post" action="sytntaxerror.aspx" runat="server">
      <asp:TetBox id="txtQuantity" runat="server" />
    </form>
  </body>
</html>
```

2. Save this file as `syntaxerror.aspx` and load the file using a browser. We're expecting to see a textbox in the browser, as shown in the figure below:

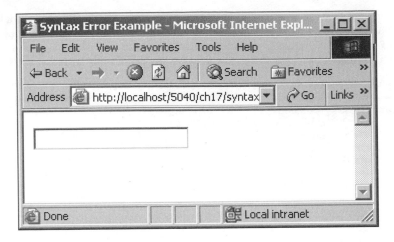

What we actually see however is:

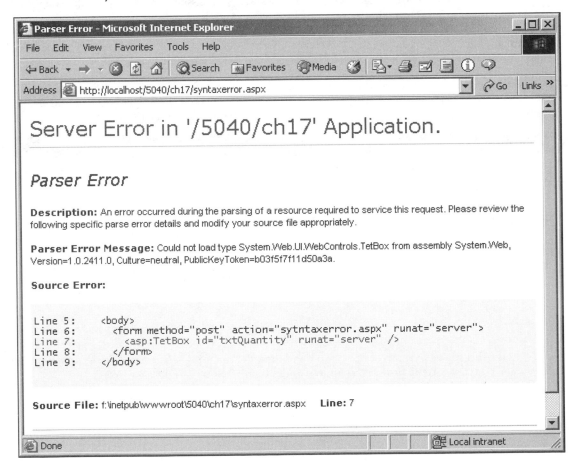

How It Works

As the error message clearly states, the ASP.NET parser points to line 7, and asks us to check the details. When we look through the line, we can see that we have a spelling mistake: `Tetbox`, which should, of course, be `TextBox`. If you correct the spelling mistake, and re-run the code, you will see the results as shown in the first figure.

Errors of this kind are very common, and are usually quick and easy to fix, since the error message provides a detailed breakdown of the error and the line on which it occurs.

Logical errors

The second type of error is the "Logical Error", and unfortunately, they are relatively difficult to find and fix. As the name implies, this kind of error occurs due to a mistake in the programming logic. The following are some of the more common reasons for this type of error:

❑ **Division by zero** – This is an infamous error that has been around since the days of valve-based computers. This error occurs when your program ends up dividing a number by zero. But why in the world are we going to divide a number by zero? In most cases, this occurs because the program divides a number by an integer that should contain a non-zero number, but for some reason, the integer contains a zero. For instance, this could happen if you do not use the `Explicit` setting in your program and make a spelling mistake in the variable name that is in the denominator. This results in a logical error.

❑ **Type mismatch** – Type mismatch errors occur when you try to work with incompatible data types, and inadvertently try to add a string with a number, or store a string to a variable of date datatype. It is possible to avoid this error by explicitly converting the data type of a value before operating on it. We will talk about variable data type conversion later in this chapter.

❑ **Incorrect output** – This type of error occurs when you use a function, or a subroutine, that returns a different output to what you are expecting in your program.

❑ **Use of a non-existent object** – This type of error occurs when you try to use an object that was never created, or an attempt to create the object failed.

❑ **Mistaken assumptions** – This is another common mistake that we make, which could be corrected during the testing phase (if one exists). This type of error occurs when the programmer uses an incorrect assumption in the program. For instance, a program that adds withdrawal amounts to a current balance, instead of subtracting them.

❑ **Processing invalid data** – This is type of error occurs when the program is accepting invalid data. An example of this, would be a library checkout program that accepts a book's return date as February 29th, 2001, in which case, you may not have to return the book for a while!

While this is far from being an exhaustive list of possible logical errors, it should give you an feel for what to look out for when testing your code.

System errors

These are errors that are generated by ASP.NET itself. They may be due to malfunctioning code, a bug in ASP.NET, or even one in the Common Language Runtime. Although you could find this type of error, it is usually not possible to fix the problem – particularly if it is an ASP.NET or CLR error.

Other errors that can be placed in this category are those that arise due to the failure of a web server or component, a hardware failure, or a lack of server memory.

Good Coding Practice

Now that we have an overview of the different kind of errors we're likely to encounter, let's consider some of the ways in which we can help to prevent them happening. It may not be feasible to expect perfect, totally error-free programs, but there are some precautions we can take to reduce or avoid the most common mistakes.

Indent your code

This is quite an obvious and straightforward step. Although it won't ensure an error free program, this will really help to improve the readability of your code, either for yourself or for others. Remember, the syntax error that occurred because of a missing end if in a nested if...then...end if block? Indenting your code will help you in finding those kinds of errors quickly. The following example lays out the code we used in our Syntax error Try It Out, above, in two different ways. See the difference for yourself:

```
<html>
<head>
<title>Syntax Error Example </title>
</head>
<body>
<form method="post" action="sytntaxerror.aspx" runat="server">
<asp:TetBox id="txtQuantity" runat="server" />
</form>
</body>
</html>

<html>
  <head>
    <title>Syntax Error Example </title>
  </head>
  <body>
    <form method="post" action="sytntaxerror.aspx" runat="server">
      <asp:TetBox id="txtQuantity" runat="server" />
    </form>
  </body>
</html>
```

Use sensible naming conventions – and stick to them

Naming conventions are useful, but only when applied consistently. Identify a suitable convention, and stick to it throughout your application. A common practice is to use first three letters of the name to denote the data type, followed by the actual variable name. Try to avoid using variables like i, j, tmp, or temp, as they are not very descriptive. For instance, in the following code block, we use the two variables, i and j:

```
Dim i,j
For i= 1 to 10
  For j= 1 to 20
    'do this
  next
next
```

In the following code block, we call our variables `intClassCounter` and `intStudentCounter` respectively. The name you give a variable should explain what it's used for; in this example, they are clearly identifiable as counters for classes and students:

```
Dim intClassCounter as integer, intStudentCounter as integer

For intClassCounter= 1 to 10 'loop through 10 different class
  For intStudentCounter = 1 to 20
    'do something
  next
next
```

Comment your code

Here's another good, and easy, technique. This task also aids readability of the code. Commenting code goes hand in hand with the variable naming convention. Believe me, code you have written will look extremely confusing, even to you, after a period of time (maybe a few weeks or months). Writing comments with your code will help you remember exactly what your code is doing, which will be invaluable when you try to debug the code after a period of time.

Structure your code

Use subroutines and functions in your code to implement specific tasks. This is even more important for tasks that are used several times in your applications. For instance, consider a situation when you need to format the display of a date. The database might store a date in the form "CCYYMMDD", whereas you need to display it on the screen as "MM/DD/CCYY". We could then create a subroutine, such as the one shown below:

```
Public Sub FormatDate(CCYYMMDD)
  Dim intYear, intMonth, intDay
  intYear = left(CCYYMMDD,4)
  intMonth = mid(CCYYMMDD,5,2)
  intDay = right(CCYYMMDD,2)
  response.write (Cstr(intMonth) &"/"& Cstr(intDay) &"/"& Cstr(intYear))
End Sub
```

If you need to format the display of your date at different places in your program, you can simply call this sub to format the display, rather than writing in the whole process over and over again. Not only does this saves us time; if there's an error in the code (or we need to change it), we only need to change our sub code once.

Use the Page Explicit setting

One of the options we can set in the `Page` directive at the top of an ASPX is as follows:

```
<%@ Page language="VB" runat="server" explicit="True" %>
```

If you set `explicit` to `True` and try using a variable that hasn't been defined, you'll find that your code raises an error. This can actually save you falling foul of a various logical errors that might have occurred because of a typo in the variable name – otherwise, these are very hard to find. For instance, take a look at the following code:

```
Dim DepositAmount, AccountBalance
AccountBalance = 5000 ' the initial balance is $5000
DepositAmount = 2000 ' Customer deposits $2000
'adding the deposit to the balance to get the new balance
AccountBalance = AccountBalance + DepostAmount
```

You expect to see the new account balance as $7000, but actually the balance will still be $5000. This is because the variable DepositAmount is misspelt in the line it is added to the AccountBalance. This will raise an error if explicit is used, since DepositAmount variable is not defined.

Use the Page Strict setting

This is another level of protection that you can opt for, also set from the Page directive:

```
<%@ Page language="VB" runat="server" strict="True" %>
```

Use of this setting will prevent any implicit type conversion that results in a data loss.

Convert variables to the correct data types

Converting the values provided in your web page to an appropriate data type before using them in your program will prevent **Type Mismatch** errors when we're using the Strict setting. For example, if the user provides "12.23" for a numeric field for which you're expecting an integer, assigning this value to the integer variable will result in an error. To prevent this error, convert the value entered to an integer before assigning it to a variable of integer datatype. We could use one of the following conversion functions provided by VB.NET:

Conversion Function	Return Datatype
Cbool	Boolean
Cbyte	Byte
Cchar	Char
Cdate	Date
CDbl	Double
Cdec	Decimal
Cint	Integer
CLng	Long
Cobj	Object
Cshort	Short
CSng	Single
CStr	String

The following line shows the syntax for using this conversion function:

```
blnCondtion = CBool(varSomeVariable) ' Converts to a Boolean
intNumber = CInt(varAnotherVariable) ' Converts to an Integer
```

Or, we could use the Convert class in the System namespace provided by the .NET framework. The following shows the syntax of using the ToString method of the Convert class.

```
StrSomeVariable = Convert.ToString(intSomeInteger)
'Convert Integer to String
```

All these techniques can be used to help standardize and improve the readability of your code. A great many basic errors can thus be avoided. However, even if you do apply all these suggestions, your code still can't be guaranteed bug-free. In the next section, we're going to look at how to thoroughly test your code and (if necessary) fix it before it goes into a production environment.

Try to break your code

So, we've developed an application, and done our best to minimize the occurrence of the bugs we've described above. What's next? The next step is to test your code, in order to isolate and fix any errors that might occur once it's in the public domain.

We can break down our testing strategy into two main approaches:

❑ Being nice to your program – Supply your program with legal values, or values that your program is designed to expect and handle. For instance, if your program contains an age field, supply only numbers, not letters. Watch how your program behaves – does it respond as your expect it to with the legal values you're supplying it?

❑ Try to break your program – This is the fun part. Supply your program with illegal values. For instance, in our age field example above, you could provide AF as the value. This ensures that your program handles all illegal values appropriately. Depending upon the kind of data you are expecting in your program, you might have to do anything from a simple numeric, or alphabetic, check to a validity check (such as inserting invalid dates into a date field).

Trapping invalid data

Testing your code by supplying both legal, and illegal, values is necessary for the proper functioning of your program. Your program should return expected results when providing legal values, and handle errors when supplied with illegal values. In this section, we'll talk about ways to handle the illegal values supplied to your program. We have two objectives here:

❑ Prevent the occurrence of errors that may leave you with many disgruntled users

❑ Prevent your program accepting and using illegal values, such as .10 for the age field

There are two main techniques that we can use to fulfill these objectives: manual trapping and validation.

Manual trapping

When building our application, we could create error traps to catch illegal values before they get into the page processing, where they might halt the execution of the page, or provide invalid results. How do we block illegal values from sneaking in to page processing? Let's develop a page that accepts order quantity from the user.

Try It Out – Catching illegal values

1. Type the following code into your editor:

```
<%@ Page language="VB" Debug="true" %>

<script language="vb" runat="server">
```

```
Sub CompleteOrder(sender As Object, e As EventArgs)
  if txtQuantity.Text = "" then
    lblOrderConfirm.Text = "Please provide an Order Quantity."
  else if not IsNumeric(txtQuantity.Text) then
    lblOrderConfirm.Text = "Please provide only numbers in Quantity field."
  else if CInt(txtQuantity.Text) <= 0 then
    lblOrderConfirm.Text = "Please provide a Quantity greater than 0."
  else if CInt(txtQuantity.Text) > 0 then
    lblOrderConfirm.Text = "Order Successfully placed."
  else
    lblOrderConfirm.Text = "Please provide a valid Order Quantity."
  end if
End Sub
</script>

<html>
  <head>
    <title>Manual Trapping Example</title>
  </head>
  <body>
    <form method="post" action="manualtrapping.aspx" runat="server">
      <asp:Label text="Order Quantity" runat="server" />
      <asp:TextBox id="txtQuantity" runat="server" />
      <br />
      <asp:Button id="btnComplete_Order" Text="Complete Order"
                                          onclick="CompleteOrder"
                                          runat="server"/>
      <br />
    <asp:Label id="lblOrderConfirm" runat="server"/>
    </form>
  </body>
</html>
```

2. Save this file as `manualtrapping.aspx`.

3. Now load this file using your browser. The following figure shows the result of providing an order quantity of 10:

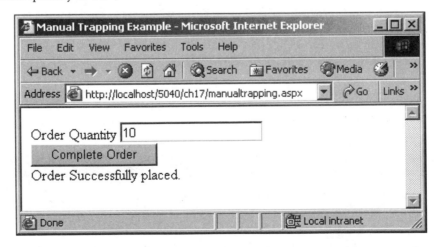

Try supplying different values to the order quantity text box and verify if the page behaves as expected.

How It Works

First point to notice is that we have added an extra directive to our page calls:

```
<%@ Page language="VB" Debug="true" %>
```

This will enable us to view detailed error messages throughout the course of the chapter. We will discuss how it works within the course of this chapter.

We are using two label controls, one textbox control, and one button control. The first label control is the label for the order quantity textbox:

```
<asp:Label text="Order Quantity" runat="server" />
```

The second label control is to display the message, "lblOrderConfirm" after processing the order:

```
<asp:Label id="lblOrderConfirm" runat="server"/>
```

The textbox accepts an entry from the user for the order quantity:

```
<asp:TextBox id="txtQuantity" runat="server" />
```

The button calls the CompleteOrder procedure when clicked:

```
<asp:Button id="btnComplete_Order" Text="Complete Order"
                              onclick="CompleteOrder"
                              runat="server"/>
```

Within the CompleteOrder sub, we create a series of checks to avoid illegal values. First we check for no entry to the text box:

```
if txtQuantity.Text = "" then
     lblOrderConfirm.Text = "Please provide an Order Quantity."
```

which is followed by the numeric check:

```
else if not IsNumeric(txtQuantity.Text) then
   lblOrderConfirm.Text = "Please provide only numbers in Quantity field."
```

This is followed by the check for a negative number or zero:

```
else if CInt(txtQuantity.Text) <= 0 then
       lblOrderConfirm.Text = "Please provide a Quantity greater than 0."
```

Finally, we check if the number is greater than zero, and if it did not match any of the checks so far, we display a message to enter a valid value:

```
else if CInt(txtQuantity.Text) > 0 then
       lblOrderConfirm.Text = "Order Successfully placed."
     else
       lblOrderConfirm.Text = "Please provide a valid Order Quantity."
     end if
```

Using validation controls

The second technique is to use one, or several, of the different validation controls provided by ASP.NET. Refer to Chapter 14 for a detailed discussion about using validation controls.

Validation controls are used to validate user input. For instance, you could use the RequiredFieldValidator control to ensure that users enter a value to a text box. By doing this, you could avoid runtime errors that occur because of your program using a null, while it is expecting an entry from the user.

By using one of the many validation controls provided by ASP.NET, which are listed below, you could present the users with a message informing them about the incorrect value supplied, and the value your program is expecting. This prevents the program from processing an illegal value, and developing an error.

The following table lists the various validation controls provided by ASP.NET:

Name of the Validation Control	Description
RequiredFieldValidator	Ensures that users enter a value to a field.
CompareValidator	Compares the value entered by the users with an entry to another control or to a constant value. For instance, comparing value entered to the password and re-enter your password text boxes.
RangeValidator	Ensures that the users entry is within the range specified.
RegularExpressionValidator	Ensures that user entry matches a pattern. For instance, this validator could be used to validate email address, phone numbers.
CustomValidator	Lets you create your own logic to validate the user entry.
ValidationSummary	Displays the error messages from all the validation controls used in your page in a summary.

Let's look at an example to demonstrate how to use these controls. In the following Try It Out, we'll use the RequiredFieldValidator to ensure that the user provides a value for the Order Quantity field.

Try It Out – Using RequiredFieldValidator

1. Open manualtrapping.aspx from the previous exercise, and make the following changes to second half of it:

```
<form method="post" action="usingvalidationcontrol.aspx" runat="server">
    <asp:Label text="Order Quantity" runat="server" />
    <asp:TextBox id="txtQuantity" runat="server" />
<asp:RequiredFieldValidator ControlToValidate="txtQuantity" runat="server"
ErrorMessage="Please enter a value in the Order Quantity
Field"></asp:RequiredFieldValidator>
    <br />
<asp:Button id="btnComplete_Order" Text="Complete Order" onclick="CompleteOrder"
runat="server"/><br>
    <asp:Label id="lblOrderConfirm" runat="server"/>
</form>
```

2. Save this file as `usingvalidationcontrol.aspx`.

3. Use your browser to open `usingvalidationcontrol.aspx`. When you try to complete the order without entering anything, you're presented with the following request:

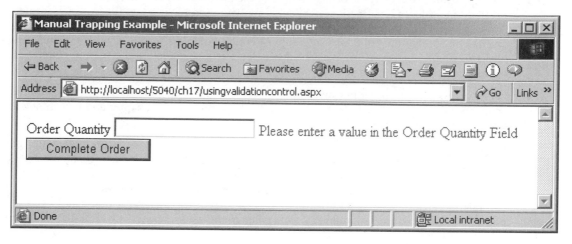

How It Works

In this example, we have used a `RequiredFieldValidator` control. The `ControlToValidate` property is used to specify the control we are validating:

```
<asp:RequiredFieldValidator ControlToValidate="txtQuantity" runat="server"
```

In this case, we are validating the order quantity text box. The `ErrorMessage` property is used to provide an error message when the user does not enter a value to the order quantity field:

```
ErrorMessage="Please enter a value in the Order Quantity Field">
```

Finding Errors

Okay, so we adopted the good coding practices listed earlier in our program, and used different techniques to trap the invalid data, now why are we still talking about finding errors? Even after taking the above precautions, our program might still end up in an error page. It could be, because we did not cover all possible error scenarios in our testing, (point the fingers at the testers), or another program did not behave as expected (refer it to the other team) or worse, the server administrators did not set up the server right (blame it on the network administrators.). However well you plan ahead, it is always difficult, if not impossible, to catch every bug in advance. So what do we do if our well-constructed code still doesn't work?

There are different kinds of errors that could occur in your page as discussed earlier in this chapter. So the first step is to identify the error type. Once we find that, then we can develop an appropriate fix for it. In this section we'll talk about the different categories of error.

How and from where do errors arise?

The errors that occur in an ASP.NET page can be grouped into four categories, as given below:

❑ Configuration Errors – These occur because of the incorrect syntax, or structure, of a configuration file. In a nutshell, an ASP.NET configuration file is a text file, in XML format, that contains a hierarchical structure to store application-wide configuration settings. There can be one configuration file for every application on your web server. The web configuration files are named web.config. We'll be discussing web.config files, and errors, in chapter 16, so we won't discuss these further until then.

❑ Parser errors – These occur because of incorrect syntax, or bad grammar, within the ASP.NET page. Sound familiar? If not, then go back to the beginning of this chapter and take a look at the "Syntax error" section.

❑ Compilation errors – These are also syntax errors, but they occur when using statements that are not recognized by the language compiler, rather than ASP.NET itself. For example, using endif (one word) to close an if block in VB.NET, or not providing Next to close a For loop, will result in a compilation error. The difference between the parser error and compilation error is that parser error occurs when there is a syntax error in the ASP.NET page, whereas the compilation error occurs when there is a syntax error within the VB.NET or JScript.NET code block.

❑ Runtime errors – As the name implies, these are errors that are not detected during compilation or parsing, but are caught during execution. For example, when the user enter letters into a field expecting numbers, and your program assigns the user entry to an integer variable, you will get a runtime error when the code tries to execute.

Let's modify our manualtrapping.aspx file to generate a compilation error.

Try It Out – Generate a compiler error

1. Open manualtrapping.aspx, and make the following change:

```
Sub CompleteOrder(sender As Object, e As EventArgs)
    if txtQuantity.Text = "" then
        lblOrderConfirm.Text = "Please provide an Order Quantity."
    else if not IsNumeric(txtQuantity.Text) then
lblOrderConfirm.Text = "Please provide only numbers in Quantity field."
    else if CInt(txtQuantity.Text) <= 0 then
lblOrderConfirm.Text = "Please provide a Quantity greater than 0."
    else if CInt(txtQuantity.Text) > 0 then
        lblOrderConfirm.Text = "Order Successfully placed."
    else
lblOrderConfirm.Text = "Please provide a valid Order Quantity."
    endif
End Sub
```

2. Save the file as compilationerror.aspx

3. Run compilationerror.aspx in your browser window, and you should see the following:

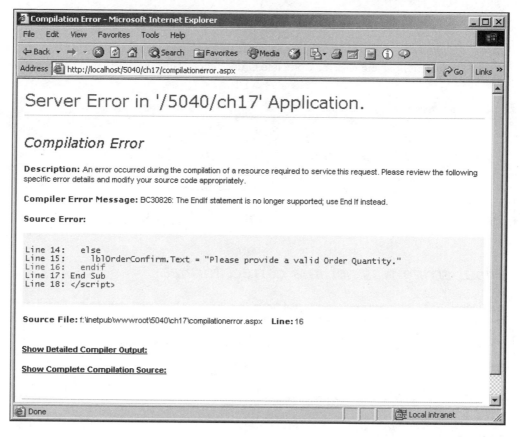

How It Works

All we have done here is changed the end if of our manualtrapping.aspx to endif. As we would expect, when we try to run the new compilationerror.aspx file in the browser, it tells us we have a compiler error in line 16, and even tells us how to fix it.

Let's modify the manualtrapping.aspx file, once again, to generate a runtime error, so we can get a clearer understanding of this.

Try It Out – Generate a runtime error

1. Open manualtrapping.aspx, and modify the code as follows:

```
Sub CompleteOrder(sender As Object, e As EventArgs)
    if txtQuantity.Text = "" then
        lblOrderConfirm.Text = "Please provide an Order Quantity."
    else if CInt(txtQuantity.Text) <= 0 then
lblOrderConfirm.Text = "Please provide a Quantity greater than 0."
    else if CInt(txtQuantity.Text) > 0 then
        lblOrderConfirm.Text = "Order Successfully placed."
    else
        lblOrderConfirm.Text = "Please provide a valid Order Quantity."
    end if
End Sub
```

617

2. Save the new file as `runtimeerror.aspx`.

3. View the `runtimeerror.aspx` file using the browser. Provide a non-numeric value to the order quantity text box, and click the **Complete Order** button. The following figure shows the result:

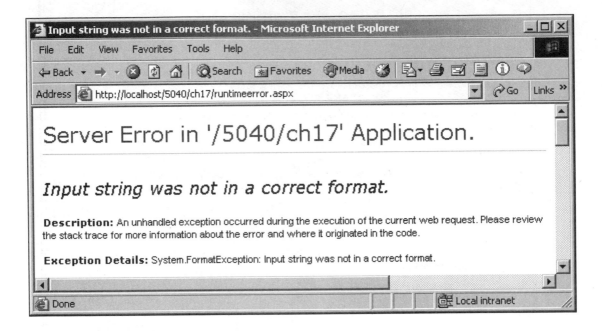

How It Works

In this example, we removed the numeric check performed within the `CompleteOrder` function:

```
else if not IsNumeric(txtQuantity.Text) then
        lblOrderConfirm.Text = "Please provide only numbers in Quantity _
                                              field."
```

By doing this, the code generated a runtime error when the `CInt` function tried to convert a non-numeric entry, provided by the user, to an integer field.

Now we know the different categories of error that could occur in an ASP.NET page. When an error does occur in an ASP.NET page, the details about the error are sent to the client. Don't worry, though, SP.NET, by default, shows detailed error information only to a **local client**.

A local client is a client running on the same machine as the web server. For instance, if you create the ASP.NET examples from this book on a machine running a web server, and access them using a browser on the same machine, then the browser is a local client.

So, the fact that ASP.NET sends detailed information about errors to local clients, is actually very helpful to the developer during the development phase.

Customized Error Messages

The next question is, what if the development server is on a different machine? Well, ASP.NET allows you to specify whether you want the detailed message to be displayed on the local client, or a remote client, or both. You can specify this information using the <customErrors> section in the web configuration file, web.config. As I said earlier, we'll discuss web.config later in the book, for now, just create a new file in your application folder (which should be 5040) called web.config, so that you can get used to using it in this chapter. The following example shows a sample setting for the <customErrors> section:

```
<configuration>
    <system.web>
        <customErrors defaultRedirect="userError.aspx" mode="On">
            <error statusCode="404" redirect="PagenotFound.aspx" />
        </customErrors>
    </system.web>
</configuration>
```

Notice that all settings in web.config have to be enclosed with <configuration> and <system.web> tags. Also make sure that you copy of the upper and lower case of this code exactly as is shown, because web.config is case-sensitive, and even writing On as on will break the code!

As shown above, the <customErrors> configuration section has two attributes. The first attribute is the defaultdirect attribute, and this specifies the URL for the page to be redirected to when an error occurs. The above configuration setting will redirect the user to a default error page, userError.aspx when an error occurs.

The second attribute is the mode attribute, which takes three values: On, Off and RemoteOnly. The value, On, specifies that the custom error is enabled, so the users will be redirected to the custom error page specified in defaultdirect attribute. The value Off specifies that the custom error is disabled, so the users will not be redirected to a friendly error page. The value RemoteOnly specifies that only remote clients should be redirected to the custom error page, not local clients, which is the default setting.

The <customError> configuration section contains a sub tag, <error>, and this is used to specify error pages for different errors. In the above example, I have specified PagenotFound.aspx page as the error page when error 404 occurs. You could provide multiple <error> subtags for different error codes.

Let's create the two friendly error pages, userError.aspx and PagenotFound.aspx, specified in the configuration file.

Try It Out – Creating error pages

1. First of all, make sure the <customErrors> section in your web configuration file matches the code example above and is saved in the application root.

2. Now we'll create the userError.aspx page. Open up your editor, and enter the following code:

```
<html>
  <head>
  <title> Friendly Error Page</title>
  </head>
  <body>
  <h2> An error has occurred in executing this page. Sorry for the inconvenience.
The site administrator is aware of this error occurrence.</h2>
  </body>
</html>
```

3. Next we'll create the `PagenotFound.aspx` page. Enter the following code:

```
<html>
  <head>
  <title> Friendly Error Page</title>
  </head>
  <body>
  <h2> Sorry, the resource you are requesting is not available. Please verify the
address. </h2>
  </body>
</html>
```

4. Before testing this page, if you are using a local client to view the pages, then change the `mode` setting in the `<customErrors>` section of your `web.config` file to `On` from `RemoteOnly`. Otherwise, you will still see the detailed error message, instead of the friendly error message page. Don't forget to change the `mode` setting before moving the files to production environment.

5. Now, load the `runtimeerror.aspx` file, using your browser. The following figure shows the result in a browser:

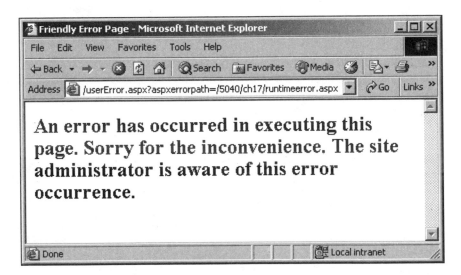

What we see in this figure is the `userError.aspx` file and not the detailed error message showing the runtime error.

6. Now, try to access a file that is not existing in your application folder. Something like `iknowthispageisnotfound.aspx`. The following figure shows the result of accessing a file that is not found in the application:

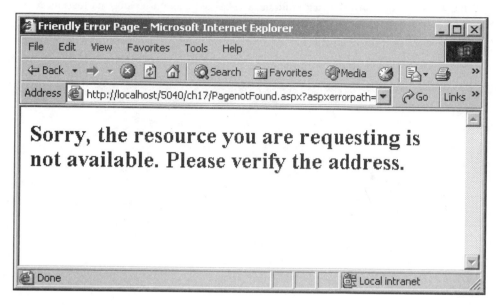

What we see is the `pagenotfound.aspx` file, with the friendly error message and not the default page not found message from the web server.

How It Works

We began by making sure that the `<customErrors>` section in the web configuration file pointed to the correct file. Specifically, that the default error page displayed was `"userError.aspx"`, and the error page for status code 404 was `"PagenotFound.aspx"`:

```
<customErrors defaultRedirect="userError.aspx" mode="RemoteOnly">
  <error statusCode="404" redirect="PagenotFound.aspx" />
</customErrors>
```

Once we had done this, we inserted our own text into the `"userError.aspx"` and `"PagenotFound.aspx"` files. Then we checked that `<customErrors>` was set to On, so that our new error pages were sent to the local browser, enabling us to view them when we triggered them by using files containing mistakes.

In the above example, we saw how we could redirect users to a friendly error page using the different attributes in the `<customErrors>` section of `web.config`. By doing this, the users are redirected the same friendly error page when an error occurs in any page in the application. There is a way to redirect users to different friendly error pages based on which page the error has occurred, though. Using the `ErrorPage` property in the `Page` directive, as shown below, does this:

```
<% @ Page ErrorPage="ErrorPage.aspx" %>
```

For instance, if you have this directive in `runtimeerror.aspx`, then the users will be redirected to `ErrorPage.aspx` when an error occurs in `runtimeerror.aspx`.

Now let's go back to the local client scenario. ASP.NET displays a **call-stack** when a runtime error occurs. What is a call-stack? A call-stack contains a series of procedure calls that lead up to an error. Before you do this, we suggest you delete the web.config file as otherwise, all errors generated will be handled by this file.

Let's create a page that leads up to a runtime error.

Try It Out – Viewing the call-stack

1. *Type in the following code:*

```
<%@ Page Language="VB" Debug="true" %>
<script language="VB" runat="server">
  Sub CreateRunTimeError
    dim intCounter as integer
    intCounter = "Test"
    response.write ("The value of counter is :" & intCounter)
  End sub
</script>

<%
  CreateRunTimeError()
%>
```

2. Save this file as `callstack.aspx`.

3. Open this file in your browser. You should see something like the following (as long as you have deleted `web.config`):

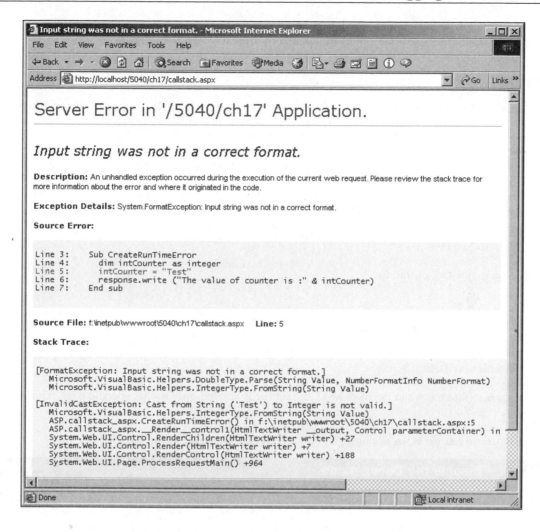

How It Works

In the block of code we entered, we created a variable called intCounter, of integer datatype, and then we assigned a string to this variable:

```
dim intCounter as integer
    intCounter = "Test"
```

When we ran this code, an error was generated when the program tried to execute an integer datatype containing a string. We were presented with the error page above. The error page contains different sections, such as **Exception Details** (we'll discuss exceptions shortly), **Source Error**, **Stack Trace** and so on. The **Stack Trace** contains the call-stack, which says that the value we are trying to assign to an integer variable is not valid. If you look through the call-stack, you can see the series of procedures that led to the exception.

Try the same example with just one change. Change the value assigned to intCounter from "Test" to "123". Executing this page will not generate an error because "123" could be cast to an integer data type.

The information provided under the Source Error section is useful in locating the line in which the error occurred. The display of this information is controlled by the **Debug mode**.

Debug mode

If the Debug mode is enabled, then the Source Error section of the error message is displayed as part of the error message, which pinpoints the location in the code that created the error. If the Debug mode is disabled, then the Source Error section is not displayed.

Now the question is: where and how can I set the value to the Debug mode?

The Debug mode can be set at two different places. The first place should be familiar, as we have used it twice already within this chapter. You can set it at every page within the Page directive, as shown below:

```
<%@ Page Debug="true" %>
```

This enables the Debug mode.

Or

```
<%@ Page Debug="false" %>
```

This disables the Debug mode.

If the Debug mode is set at the page level, the setting is applied only to that specific page. That was easy.

Let's return to our previous example, and disable the Debug mode at the page level.

Try It Out – Disable the Debug mode

1. Open the callstack.aspx file, and insert the following line at the top of the page:

```
<%@ Page Language="VB" Debug="false" %>
```

2. Save the file as debugmode.aspx, and access the page using the browser. You will see an error page that looks like the one below:

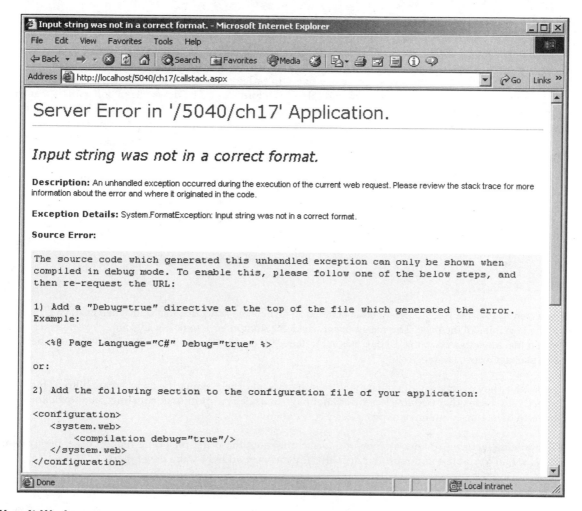

How It Works

We disabled the Debug mode in our callstack.aspx by adding the line:

```
<%@ Page Debug="false" %>
```

At the top of the page. Then when we run our new file in the browser, we saw a new error message. In this error message, under the **Source Error** section, there are instructions to enable the Debug mode for displaying the source code that generated the exception, but the actual source code is not there.

As mentioned a moment ago, there are two ways to set the Debug mode. The second way is to set it at the application level, using the <compilation> configuration section in the configuration file (see Chapter 16).

Setting the debug mode at the application level will display the **Source Error** section in the error message for all the files under the application. This has a performance overhead though, so before moving your application to a production environment, make sure you disable the Debug mode.

Tracing

When developing an application, we execute the page at different levels of that development, and for effective debugging we always need to see the values assigned to variables and the state of different conditional constructs at different stages of execution. In earlier versions of ASP, developers used the ubiquitous `response.write` statement to display this information. The downside of doing this is that when completing the application development, the developer has to go to every page, and either comment, or remove, the `response.write` statements they created for testing purposes. To get around this, programmers used a conditional construct before using the `response.write` statement, as shown below:

```
If Debug = true then
   response.write "Value of Application Date variable is:" & dtAPPL_DATE & "<br>"
End if

If Debug = true then
   Do while not adoRs.EOF
      response.write "Name:" & adoRs.Fields("NAME") & "; Telephone:" & _
                        adoRs.Fields("TELE_NO") & "<br>"
   loop
End if
```

The `Debug` variable is set to true or false, either in an include file (a file that that is included in all your pages), or at the beginning of the page. This meant that if you didn't want to have to delete all your `response.writes`, you'd just have to make sure Debug was set to false. Of course, this still meant a lot of changes before the package was customer-ready.

ASP.NET, however, provides a new feature to bypass all of this, using the `Trace` capability. This effectively means that the developer does not have to use any conditional construct, as shown above, or have to delete or comment `response.write` statements.

The tracing feature provides a range of information about the page, including request time, performance data, server variables, and most importantly, any message added by the developers.

The following figure shows a sample of some trace information displayed in the browser:

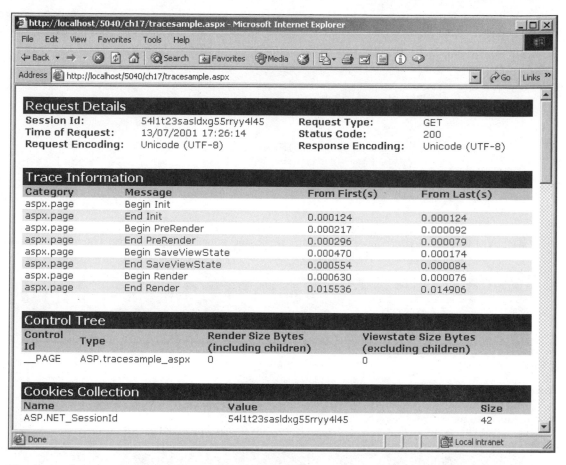

The tracing feature is disabled by default. Similar to the debug mode, tracing can be either enabled, or disabled at either the page, or application level. We'll now discuss these levels, and tracing itself, in more detail.

Page-Level Tracing

Tracing can be enabled at the page level to display trace information using the Page directive's Trace attribute, as shown below:

```
<%@ Page Trace = "true" %>
```

Or:

```
<%@ Page Trace = "false" %>
```

When tracing is enabled, the trace information is displayed after the page's contents. Let's create a simple ASP.NET page with a text box and a label control, and enable tracing at the page level.

Try It Out – Enabling Trace at the page level

1. Open your code editor and type in the following code:

```
<%@ Page Trace="true"%>
<html>
  <head>
    <title>Page Level Tracing</title>
  </head>
  <body>
    <form method="post" action="pageleveltracing.aspx" runat="server">
      <asp:label text="Name" runat="server" />
      <asp:textbox name="txtName" runat="server" />
    </form>
  </body>
</html>
```

2. Save this file as `pageleveltracing.aspx`, and view it using browser. The following figure shows how this file should look:

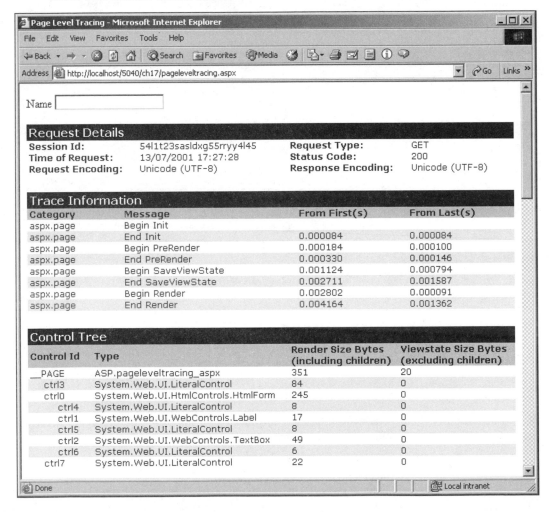

How It Works

First of all we enabled the page trace with the line:

```
<%@ Page Trace="true"%>
```

We then created a textbox with some text beside it. What we got was the textbox, plus a whole load of tracing!

We're now going to look at each section of the trace output to get a fuller understanding of what we're looking at here:

❑ Request Details – This section contains information pertaining to the page request, such as the Session ID for the current session, the request type (whether it is GET or POST), the time at which the request was made, the encoding type of the request among others as shown in below:

Request Details			
Session Id:	eyouok55ijut2jbxwdbahu55	**Request Type:**	GET
Time of Request:	6/17/2001 12:34:25 AM	**Status Code:**	200
Request Encoding:	Unicode (UTF-8)	**Response Encoding:**	Unicode (UTF-8)

❑ Trace Information – This is the section in which the actual trace information is displayed. It is also the section were the messages written by developers are displayed. As shown below, this section displays the category, the message and the time since the first message was displayed and the most recent message was displayed:

Trace Information			
Category	**Message**	**From First(s)**	**From Last(s)**
aspx.page	Begin Init		
aspx.page	End Init	0.006500	0.006500
aspx.page	Begin PreRender	0.006642	0.000142
aspx.page	End PreRender	0.006764	0.000122
aspx.page	Begin SaveViewState	0.007932	0.001168
aspx.page	End SaveViewState	0.009137	0.001205
aspx.page	Begin Render	0.009264	0.000128
aspx.page	End Render	0.010613	0.001349

❑ Control Tree – This section displays details about the different controls used in the page. The details include the ID provided for the control, the type of control used among others as shown in the figure below:

Control Tree			
Control Id	**Type**	**Render Size Bytes (including children)**	**Viewstate Size Bytes (excluding children)**
__PAGE	ASP.pageleveltracing_aspx	341	20
ctrl3	System.Web.UI.LiteralControl	87	0
ctrl0	System.Web.UI.HtmlControls.HtmlForm	233	0
ctrl4	System.Web.UI.LiteralControl	3	0
ctrl1	System.Web.UI.WebControls.Label	17	0
ctrl5	System.Web.UI.LiteralControl	3	0
ctrl2	System.Web.UI.WebControls.TextBox	49	0
ctrl6	System.Web.UI.LiteralControl	4	0
ctrl7	System.Web.UI.LiteralControl	21	0

❑   Cookies Collection – This section displays all cookies used in the page. The figure below shows only the `SessionID` since it is the only member of the cookie used in our page:

Cookies Collection

Name	Value	Size
ASP.NET_SessionId	eyouok55ijut2jbxwdbahu55	42

❑   Headers Collection – This section displays the various HTTP headers sent by the client to the server, along with the request as show below:

Headers Collection

Name	Value
Connection	Keep-Alive
Accept	image/gif, image/x-xbitmap, image/jpeg, image/pjpeg, application/msword, */*
Accept-Encoding	gzip, deflate
Accept-Language	en-us
Host	ajoys-mobile
User-Agent	Mozilla/4.0 (compatible; MSIE 6.0b; Windows NT 5.0; .NET CLR 1.0.2728; .NET CLR 1.0.2901)

❑   Server Variables – This section displays all the members of the Server Variables collection as shown below:

Server Variables

Name	Value
ALL_HTTP	HTTP_CONNECTION:Keep-Alive HTTP_ACCEPT:image/gif, image/x-xbitmap, image/jpeg, image/pjpeg, application/msword, */* HTTP_ACCEPT_ENCODING:gzip, deflate HTTP_ACCEPT_LANGUAGE:en-us HTTP_HOST:ajoys-mobile HTTP_USER_AGENT:Mozilla/4.0 (compatible; MSIE 6.0b; Windows NT 5.0; .NET CLR 1.0.2728; .NET CLR 1.0.2901)
ALL_RAW	Connection: Keep-Alive Accept: image/gif, image/x-xbitmap, image/jpeg, image/pjpeg, application/msword, */* Accept-Encoding: gzip, deflate Accept-Language: en-us Host: ajoys-mobile User-Agent: Mozilla/4.0 (compatible; MSIE 6.0b; Windows NT 5.0; .NET CLR 1.0.2728; .NET CLR 1.0.2901)
APPL_MD_PATH	/LM/w3svc/1/root/Chapter9
APPL_PHYSICAL_PATH	d:\inetpub\wwwroot\Chapter9\
AUTH_TYPE	
AUTH_USER	
AUTH_PASSWORD	
LOGON_USER	
REMOTE_USER	
CERT_COOKIE	
CERT_FLAGS	
CERT_ISSUER	

Now that we've introduced the information displayed in the trace page, let's talk about techniques you can use to write your own message to the Trace Information section, and get updates on what's going on behind the scenes as your code is executed.

Writing to the trace log

Each ASP.NET page provides an object called `Trace` that can be used to write messages to the trace log. Note, though, that the messages are only displayed when tracing is enabled. There are two methods that can be used to write messages to the trace log:

❑   `Trace.Write`

❑   `Trace.Warn`

Both of these methods are used to write messages to the trace log, but when using the `Trace.Warn` method, the messages are displayed in red. You may want to use `Trace.Warn` for writing unexpected results, or incorrect values, for variables in your program, to highlight them. Let's create an example that shows the usage of these two methods.

Try It Out – Writing to the trace log

1. Type the following code into your code editor:

```vb
<%@ Page Trace="true"%>
<script language="VB" runat="server">
  Sub WriteToTrace()
    ' This is where messages are written to Trace Log
    ' Syntax as follows:
    ' Trace.Write ("Category", "Message to be displayed")
    ' Trace.Warn ("Category", "Message to be displayed")
    Dim intCounter as integer
    intCounter=1
  Trace.Write ("FirstCategory", "Variable is initialized")
    do while intCounter > 10
    intCounter = intCounter + 1
    loop
  if intCounter < 10 then
  Trace.Warn("ErrorCategory", "Value of intCounter is not incrementing")
    end if
  end Sub
</script>
<%
  WriteToTrace()
%>
```

2. Save this file as `writetotrace.aspx`, and then open it in your browser. Note that the message we wrote using the `Trace.Warn` method is displayed in red:

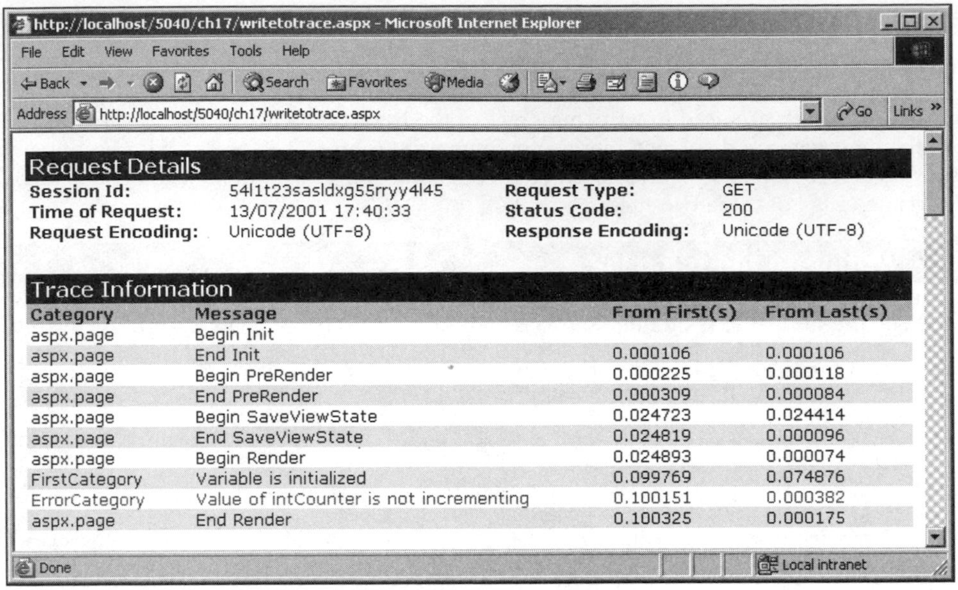
http://localhost/5040/ch17/writetotrace.aspx - Microsoft Internet Explorer
File Edit View Favorites Tools Help
Back Search Favorites Media
Address http://localhost/5040/ch17/writetotrace.aspx
Go Links
Request Details
Session Id: 54l1t23sasldxg55rryy4l45
Time of Request: 13/07/2001 17:40:33
Request Encoding: Unicode (UTF-8)
Request Type: GET
Status Code: 200
Response Encoding: Unicode (UTF-8)
Trace Information
Category Message From First(s) From Last(s)
aspx.page Begin Init
aspx.page End Init 0.000106 0.000106
aspx.page Begin PreRender 0.000225 0.000118
aspx.page End PreRender 0.000309 0.000084
aspx.page Begin SaveViewState 0.024723 0.024414
aspx.page End SaveViewState 0.024819 0.000096
aspx.page Begin Render 0.024893 0.000074
FirstCategory Variable is initialized 0.099769 0.074876
ErrorCategory Value of intCounter is not incrementing 0.100151 0.000382
aspx.page End Render 0.100325 0.000175
Done
Local intranet

How It Works

The first thing we do is to use `Dim` to declare `intCounter` (which we're using as a label), and type it as an integer data type. We then assign a value of `1` to `intCounter`:

```
Dim intCounter as integer
intCounter=1
```

We write a message to the Trace, which says our variable has been initialized:

```
Trace.Write ("FirstCategory", "Variable is initialized")
```

The next three lines of code is a loop, which says that `intCounter` is greater than 10, and that it should have `1` added to it. This function is then looped back to the beginning, so `1` is continually added:

```
do while intCounter > 10
intCounter = intCounter + 1
loop
```

This is obviously going to generate an error, because we have specified that `intCounter=1,` so it cannot be greater than 10. We then introduce our `Trace.Warn` statement, by saying that if `intCounter` is less than `10` (which it is), we should display a warning message:

```
"Value of intCounter is not incrementing"
```

Which is true, because in order for the incrementation loop to work, `intCounter` must be greater than `10`.

```
if intCounter < 10 then
Trace.Warn("ErrorCategory", "Value of intCounter is not incrementing")
```

Note that we're specifying category information in both the `Write` and `Warn` methods.

Application-Level Tracing

As we said earlier, tracing can also be enabled, or disabled, at the application level, in which case the tracing information for all the pages under the application are processed.

The application level tracing setting can be overridden by setting the trace at the page level. For instance, if tracing is enabled at the application level, and a page within this application disables tracing at the page level, then the tracing information will not be displayed for that page.

Application level tracing is set using the `<trace>` section in the configuration file we discussed earlier (web.config). The following is an example of the `<trace>` section:

```
<configuration>
    <system.web>
        <trace enabled="false" requestLimit="10" pageOutput="false"
        traceMode="SortByTime" localOnly="true" />
    </system.web>
</configuration>
```

All of these attributes are discussed in Chapter 20.

Trace.axd

When application level tracing is enabled, the trace information is logged to `Trace.axd`. This file can be accessed using the URL for your application, followed by `trace.axd` – for example:

http://yourwebservername/applicationname/trace.axd

The following figure shows how the `trace.axd` file looks in the browser:

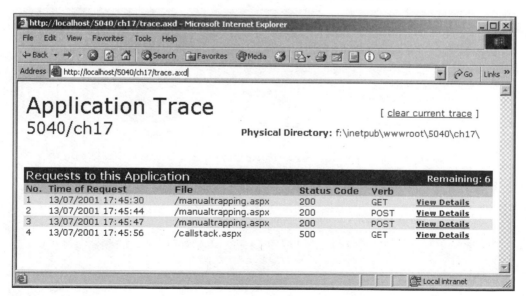

You can see that `trace.axd` provides a summary of each page we requested, and for each page displayed, there is a hyperlink, which will take you to the trace information page for that particular screen.

Handling Errors

So we've looked at what kind of errors can occur, how to avoid them, and how to find them if things do go wrong, but what if the errors just won't go away? Annoyingly, it happens. Don't worry, though, there is a way of dealing with this - we can use an error handling technique to catch them, an even though we can't write a wonder program to fix all bugs on the fly, we can let users know that there is a bug, and not to worry if things don't look right. In this section, we will talk about different error handling techniques that can be used to catch errors, and make our, and the users' life easier.

Unstructured Error Handling

The first technique that we are going to talk about is unstructured error handling. Unstructured error handling uses the On Error statement and the Err object. The On Error statement is used to spot errors when the code is run, and is able to respond to them as you dictate – it handles them. There are two dialects of On Error that you can use, one that allows you to continue execution on the line after the one that has generated the error and the second one directs execution to a custom-made error handler. We'll look at the former first.

Using the On Error Resume Next Statement

A very common error handling approach in previous versions of ASP has been to use the on error resume next statement. When using the on error resume next statement in your page, the page continues its execution from the line following the line in which the error occurred. By just using on error resume next, you could avoid displaying an error message to the users of your application.

The following Try It Out is based on our last example with the loop, and shows an ASP.NET page using the on error resume next statement.

Try It Out – Using on error resume next

1. Open your code editor and type in the following code:

```
<script language="VB" runat="server" >
  Sub UnstructuredError ()
    dim intCounter as integer
    intCounter =1
      for intCounter=1 to 10
      intCounter = intCounter+1
    next
    response.write ("The value of the counter is:" & intCounter & "<br>")
    intCounter = "Storing a string to an integer"
  End Sub

  sub Page_Load()
    on error resume next
    UnstructuredError ()
    response.write ("The Page Execution is completed")
  end sub
</script>
```

2. Save the file as unstructured_error.aspx, and view it using a browser. The following figure shows the result:

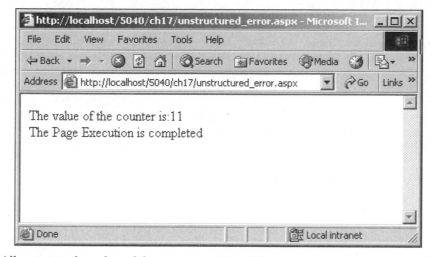

It works. All we see is the value of the counter as 11 and the page execution is completed message.

How It Works

Again, we're creating the integer `intCounter`, and initializing it to a value of 1:

```
Dim intCounter as integer
intCounter =1
```

This time we use a `for loop` construct to increment the value of `intCounter` 10 times:

```
for intCounter=1 to 10
intCounter = intCounter+1
```

The reason we didn't use the `do while` loop from the trace log Try It Out, is because at the end of our loop construct, we want to display the value of `intCounter`. Therefore, we need this value to be at a fixed point – the `do while` loop construct will increment `intCounter` indefinitely, as each time the function is performed, it is looped back and performed again, so `intCounter` would never reach that fixed point. Once we have displayed the value of `intCounter`, we come to the important line. In this line, we are storing a string to a variable of integer data type. Houston, we have a problem:

```
intCounter = "Storing a string to an integer"
```

Then, we call the procedure and return a message that the page execution is completed, to the browser:

```
on error resume next
UnstructuredError ()
response.write ("The Page Execution is completed")
```

> Note that the `on error resume next` statement is placed before the call to the sub. This is because any errors occuring within the sub, will be stacked up to the calling sub. As the first line in the calling procedure is the `on error resume next` statement, the rest of the page (from the `next` keyword) is instructed to execute. So when our error occurs within the `UnstructuredError` subroutine call, everything underneath our `next` marker is still executed.

This may not be prudent in all cases. For instance, consider an online shopping application. Say an online shopping customer is placing an order for 10 items to be delivered next week. During the order processing an error occurs. We have however used the `on error resume next` statement to continue the execution. So the page execution is continued, and the customer is informed that the order is completed. Unfortunately, the items ordered by the customer will never reach them, since the order process did not complete in the first place.

What do we need to do in this case? Instead of displaying an incorrect message that the order is completed, inform the user/customer that there was an error completing the order and provide a toll-free number to call and place the order.

Using the On Error Goto Handler Statement

It is also possible to link the `On Error` statement with the `goto` keyword, and this keyword will indicate either a line number, or a label, which points to a piece of code we want to run when our On Error statement has been triggered by an error. The following code shows an example of using the `On Error goto` statement inside the `Page_Load()` subroutine (although it can be used inside any subroutine):

```
Sub Page_Load()
   On Error Goto OurHandler

  'do something

Exit Sub
OurHandler:

  'Handle the error. Display a message to the user

End Sub
```

The error handler is bolted on to subroutine, after an `Exit Sub` statement. The handler name is followed by a colon and then the code that you wish to run in the event of an error. The name specified in the `OnError Goto` and the name of the handler itself, must both be the same for the code to work as intended.

Let's go back and modify our previous example to catch the error and handle the error ourselves by displaying a message saying that an error as occurred instead of displaying that the page execution is completed.

Try It Out – Using On Error

1. Open up the code you saved as `unstructured_error.aspx`, and modify it in the following way:

```
<script language="VB" runat="server" >
sub UnstructuredError ()
   dim intCounter as integer
   intCounter =1
   for intCounter=1 to 10
       intCounter = intCounter+1
       response.write ("The value of the counter is:" & intCounter & "<br>")
   next
   intCounter = "Storing a string to an integer"
End Sub
```

```
sub Page_Load()
On Error Goto OurHandler
UnstructuredError ()
response.write ("The Page Execution is completed")
exit sub
OurHandler:
    response.write ("An error has occurred while executing this code")
end sub
</script>
```

2. Save the file as `unstructured_error2.aspx`, and run it in your browser. You will see the following (note that we see 2, 4, 6 rather than 1, 2, 3, because every time the value of `intCounter` is incremented by 1 in the for loop, it also has 1 added to it):

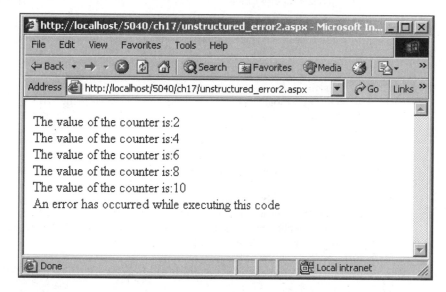

This time, the error in our code triggered our `Handler` message, and did not continue executing the rest of the program.

How It Works

The code has remained almost exactly the same as it was in `Unstructured_Error.aspx`. All we have done is taken out the `on error resume next` statement and replaced it with a simple `On Error` one. Notice that the `On Error` statement is placed at the top of a code block – this tells the program that the `On Error` command applies to the whole page of code. This time, when our error occurs, the `On Error` command is triggered, which points to our `Handler` message. This message is then displayed on the screen, and our imaginary user knows what has happened. You should notice that execution of this subroutine is terminated now, once the error is encountered and that the "page execution is completed" message is never displayed.

There is another way we can inform the user that an error has occurred, but still continue to run the rest of the script, and this is by using the `on error resume next` command in conjunction with the `Err object`.

Using the Err Object

The Err object (which is only available in VB.NET) contains information about runtime errors. Every time an error occurs during page execution, the properties of this object are populated with information pertaining to that error. Note though, that the Err object only contains information about the most recent error; it cannot hold multiple sets of error information at the same time. The following sections summarize the various properties and methods of the Err object:

Member	Description
Err.Number	This property exposes a numeric value representing an error value. It's like an ID field for your error, and associated with it are all the other properties and methods of the Err object. As well as being used to set a numeric value to an error, the Number property can also be used to retrieve one that you set previously.
Err.Description	This property exposes a descriptive message about the error, and can be used to read, or write a description.
Err.Source	This property exposes information about the application that generated the error.
Err.Clear	This method is used to clear any information stored in the different properties of the Err Object. This method can be used to clear the error information after the error has been handled.
Err.Raise	This method is used to generate a runtime error message. When using the raise method, you need to provide the Number you used to identify the error. You also have the option to provide a description, and source information for the error. If you do not provide values for the optional parameters, the values for those parameters are supplied from the existing information in the Err Object, which could be from a previous error. This is a good reason to use the Clear property after each time you use the Err object.

The following example uses the Raise method to generate an error:

```
Err.Raise (vbObjectError + 1000,"Source of the error","Error occurred")
```

Note that we add the error number to the **vbObjectError** constant. A constant is an item that contains a constant value throughout the execution of a program. This also ensures that the error number we raise does not conflict with the numbers of pre-established specific system errors in VB.NET.

With that introduction to the Err object, let's take a look at a worked example. We will modify the previous example, and add the Err object code to handle the error.

Try It Out – Using the Err object

1. Open Unstructured_Error.aspx, and make the following changes to the code:

```
<script language="VB" runat="server" >
  Sub UsingErrObject()
    dim intCounter as integer
    intCounter =1
    for intCounter=1 to 10
      intCounter = intCounter+1
```

```
      next
      response.write ("The value of the counter is : " & intCounter & "<br>")
      intCounter = "Storing a string to an integer"
    End Sub
</script>

<%
on error resume next
UsingErrObject()
if Err.Number <> 0 then
  response.write ("Error occurred : " & "<br>")
  response.write ("Error Description : " & Err.Description & "<br>")
  response.write ("Error Number : " & Err.Number & "<br>")
End if
Err.Clear
response.write ("The Page Execution is completed")
%>
```

2. Save this file as `usingerrobject.aspx`, and view it in your browser. You should see something like the following:

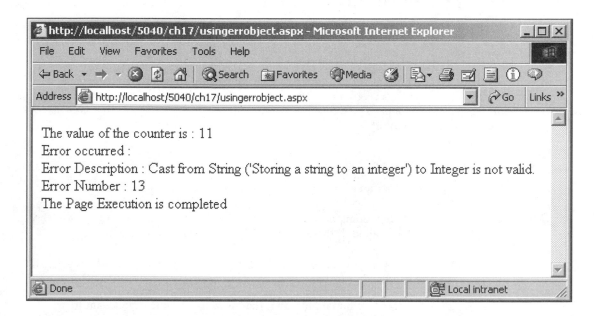

How It Works

The first new line we added creates the new sub, `UsingErrObject`:

```
Sub UsingErrObject()
```

The code itself functions in exactly the same way as `UnstructuredError.aspx`, until we come to call our sub in the HTML block. Here we encounter our `Err` object:

```
if Err.Number <> 0 then
  response.write ("Error occurred : " & "<br>")
  response.write ("Error Description : " & Err.Description & "<br>")
  response.write ("Error Number : " & Err.Number & "<br>")
End if
```

First of all, the number for the error is evaluated. We know an error will occur, because we have entered a string into our integer field, but because we don't know the Number of that particular error, we look for any error that is greater or lesser than zero – in other words is anything but zero.

If this number is found, the following three `response.write` statements will execute. The first one just displays the text **Error Occurred**. The second one requests the error description of the error that occurred, and the third line prints the number of the error.

Finally, we clear our `Err` object:

```
Err.Clear
```

Structured Error Handling

Now we've looked at unstructured error, using `On Error` statement, and the `Err` object, let's now talk about structured error handling. This is a new feature to VB.NET, but is also available in languages such as C++, C# and Java.

So what do we mean by structured error handling? Pretty much just that: handling errors via a particular structure. Lines of code are grouped together, and different handlers are provided to handle different errors within those groups. The following list shows the sequence of events that take place when using structured error handling:

1. Execute one or more lines of code in a group

2. This might execute without an error, or it might generate different kinds of errors.

3. If errors are generated, depending on which error occurs, a corresponding handler, which you will have defined, will be called. If there is no error, no handler will be called.

4. You might have defined a generic handler, which will handle any errors, for which you did not define a specific handler.

From this we can see that there are two important things that need to be done if you want to use structured error handling effectively:

❑   First is to create a group of lines, or block of code

❑   Second, and most important, is to create handlers for the different kinds of errors that could occur when the code block is executed

Before launching into this subject, we need to introduce the concept of exceptions.

Exceptions

An **exception** is any error condition or unexpected behavior that occurs during the execution of a program and consequently disrupts the normal flow of instructions – in fact, the term is just shorthand for "exceptional event". If an error occurs within a method call, the method creates an exception object and hands it off to the runtime system – this object contains information detailing the type of exception that was raised and the state of the program at the time.

> Depending on whether the exception originates from the program itself or from the **CLR, you may or may not be able to recover from the exception. While you can recover from most application exceptions, you can seldom recover from a runtime exception.**

The exception event is **thrown** to the code that calls the event, which can either catch it (resolve the problem), or pass it on up to the code that called that code, and so on up the invocation stack. If it reaches the top of the stack without being caught by a handler along the way, the program will crash. Before talking about how to handle exceptions, we'll breifly introduce you to the exception object, and its properties.

The Exception Object

.NET framework provides a `System.Exception` class, which acts as the base class for all exceptions. The `Exception` class contains properties that inform our understanding of the exception. The following list summarizes the different properties within `Exception` class:

`StackTrace`	This property contains a stack trace (which shows the sequence of nested procedure calls your program has executed). This can be used to determine the location of the error occurrence.
`Message`	This property contains the message about the error.
`InnerException`	This property is used to create and store a series of exceptions during exception handling. For example, imagine if a piece of your code threw an exception. The exception, and its handler, could be stored in the `InnerException property of that handler`. You could then reference the exception, see how it was handled, and, based on that information, perhaps create a more effective handler. This can be very useful when you are reviewing the execution of a piece of troublesome code. `InnerException` can also be used to store an exception that occurred in a previous piece of code.
`Source`	This property contains information about the application that generated the error.
`TargetSite`	This property contains information about the method that throws the exception.
`HelpLink`	This property is used to provide the URL for a file containing help information about the exception that occurred.

The two important exception classes that inherit (derive methods and properties) from `System.Exception` are `ApplicationException` and `SystemException`. The `SystemException` class is thrown by the runtime, and the `ApplicationException` class is thrown by an application.

With this introduction, then, let's look some actual code that makes structured error handling possible.

Using Try/Catch/Finally to catch exceptions

For structured error handling, we will be using the Try...Catch...Finally statement. As explained earlier, our first task in error handling is to group one or more lines of code. This group must be placed within the Try block.

The block of code within the Try is then executed. This may or may not generate an error. If an error does occur during the execution, the Catch block comes into action. The Catch block will contain handlers for the different exceptions that could occur within the code in the Try block. VB.NET executes the exception handler for whatever exception occurs. If a specific handler is not provided, VB.NET will execute a generic handler. If a generic handler is not found, then an error is sent to the client.

The Finally block will be executed either after the error has been handled, or after the code in the Try block has been executed, depending on whether an error occurred or not. The Finally block is typically used to do clean up tasks, such as releasing resources, closing objects and so on.

Note that when using Try block, you should follow it with a Catch block and a Finally block, otherwise the code will result in a syntax error.

The following example shows the structure of the Try...Catch...Finally statement:

```
Try
    'group of one or more lines
    intSum = intNumber1 + intNumber2
Catch
    'handle the error that might occur in the try block
    intSum = 0
Finally
    'clean up code goes here
    intNumber1 = 0
    intNumber2 = 0
End Try
```

Let's get deeper into the details of each block.

Try Block

There is not a lot more to say about the Try block, except that it can contain nested Try...Catch blocks. If an exception occurs within a nested Try block, and the exception is not handled by the nested Catch block, then the exception is tacked up to the outer Try block, where the exception has a chance to be handled by the handler provided in the outer Catch block. So multiple handlers can be established and activated within a nested Try...Catch block.

Catch Block

You can utilize a similar technique to Try...Catch nesting, just within the Catch block. So if you want to handle five different types of exceptions, then you will write five Catch blocks, one to handle each specific exception.

The Catch block is executed in the order it's written, so provide the catch blocks to handle specific exceptions first, and then follow these with your generic exceptions.

The following code block shows an example of handling specific exceptions using the Catch block (e represents an exception):

```
Catch excep as IndexOutOfRangeException
   response.write (e.ToString)
```

In this example, we are handling the IndexOutOfRangeException. This exception occurs when accessing a member of an array that does not exist in that array – in other words, its index is out of the specified range. For instance, say you create an array with 4 elements, but for some reason your code is trying to access the 5th element in the array.

Once we have caught the exception, we use the ToString method of the Exception class to send information about the exception back to the browser. This method provides information such as the error message, the name of the exception, and the stack trace.

Note that the above Catch block will only handle the IndexOutOfRangeException. As we have indicated, it is best to provide exception handlers for all possible exceptions that could occur within the Try block, and also provide a generic handler to handle unexpected exceptions. The following example shows a generic exception handler:

```
Catch excep as exception
   response.write ("Exception Occurred")
```

The Catch block can also be used with a when clause, which handles exceptions when the condition specified in the when clause is true. The following example shows the usage of the when clause:

```
Catch when Err.Number <> 0
   response.write ("Error Occurred: " & "<br>")
   response.write ("Error Number: " & Err.Number & "<br>")
   response.write ("Error Occurred: " & Err.Description & "<br>")
```

In the above example, the when clause checks if the Err object number property is not equal to zero. If the answer to this is true, then a detailed message is sent to the client via the response.write statements.

Finally Block

As we have seen, this block contains cleanup code (such as the closing connection to a database, releasing objects, initializing variables and so on) that should be executed at the end, after the Try or Catch block is executed.

Exit Try

We haven't seen this statement yet, but it's very simple – it's just used to exit out of the Try block, for example:

```
   if intCounter=11 then
   response.write ("Exiting the Try Block" & "<br>")
   exit try
   end if
```

Any errors that occur after this block are effectively ignored, as we have jumped out of the Try block and cannot handle them any more.

Now we've done the theory, let's do the practical.

Try It Out – Using Try...Catch...Finally

1. We're going to modify our `UnstructuredError.aspx` code file again, so open it up and make the following changes:

```vb
<script language="VB" runat="server" >
  Sub StructuredErrorHandling ()
    Try
       dim intCounter as integer
       intCounter =1
       for intCounter=1 to 10
         intCounter = intCounter+1
       next
       response.write ("The value of the counter is:" & intCounter & _
       "<br>")
       intCounter = "Storing a string to an integer"
     'Handler for InvalidCast Exception
     Catch excep as InvalidCastException
       response.write ("Error Occurred"& "<br>" & excep.ToString & "<br>")
     'Catch block using when clause and generic exception handler
     Catch when Err.Number <> 0
       response.write ("Generic Error Occurred" & "<br>")
     Finally
       response.write ("The Page Execution is completed" & "<br>")
     End Try
  End sub
</script>

<%
  StructuredErrorHandling ()
  response.write ("Procedure call completed" & "<br>")
%>
```

2. Save this file as `structurederrorhandling.aspx`, and load it into your browser. The following figure shows the result:

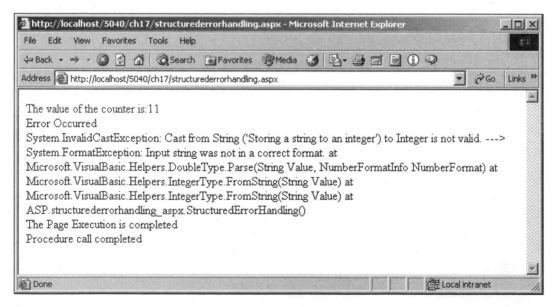

```
The value of the counter is:11
Error Occurred
System.InvalidCastException: Cast from String ('Storing a string to an integer') to Integer is not valid. --->
System.FormatException: Input string was not in a correct format. at
Microsoft.VisualBasic.Helpers.DoubleType.Parse(String Value, NumberFormatInfo NumberFormat) at
Microsoft.VisualBasic.Helpers.IntegerType.FromString(String Value) at
Microsoft.VisualBasic.Helpers.IntegerType.FromString(String Value) at
ASP.structurederrorhandling_aspx.StructuredErrorHandling()
The Page Execution is completed
Procedure call completed
```

How It Works

We began by creating a new sub, and initiating the `Try` block:

```
Sub StructuredErrorHandling ()
  Try
```

We then used the `intCounter` loop as we have done in the past few exercises:

```
dim intCounter as integer
intCounter =1
for intCounter=1 to 10
  intCounter = intCounter+1
next
response.write ("The value of the counter is:" & intCounter & "<br>")
```

We can see that this has happened, because the line was displayed on the screen the code produced. After this, we have our problem line, which generates an error, and this is followed by two `Catch` blocks. The first `Catch` block looks out for incorrect casts in the code, and if one is found, returns a line of text, and the error information to the browser:

```
Catch excep as InvalidCastException
  response.write ("Error Occurred"& "<br>" & exc.ToString & "<br>")
```

Because we cast a string to an integer variable, this error is indeed generated, and our line of text, and error information appears in our browser window. The second `Catch` block is a generic exception handler, which returns the line **Generic Error Occurred**, if any error number is encountered:

```
Catch when Err.Number <> 0
  response.write ("Generic Error Occurred" & "<br>")
```

Because our only error has already been handled, this Catch statement is not triggered. Then comes the `Finally` block, which returns a line to the browser:

```
Finally
  response.write ("The Page Execution is completed" & "<br>")
```

At the end, once the sub has been called, a line is sent to inform the user that the whole procedure is complete:

```
response.write ("Procedure call completed" & "<br>")
```

Again, we see both of these lines in the browser window, which shows that the `Finally` block was executed, despite the error in our code, as was the `response.write` statement within the HTML tags.

Handling Errors Programmatically

We can now handle errors using the `On Error` statement, `Err` object and `Try` statements, but there is still a possibility that some exceptions will sneak through. Amongst other reasons, this might happen because we did not handle all possible exceptions, or we did not provide a generic exception handler. ASP.NET provides us with yet two more methods that can be used to handle any 'unaccounted for' errors, and provide a friendly message to the user, instead the default runtime error screen.

The two methods are:

- ❑ `Page_Error` method
- ❑ `Application_Error` method

Page_Error method

The `Page` class provides this method. Refer to the section called The `Page` Class in Chapter 7 for more information on the `Page` class and its members.

The `Page_Error` method can be used to handle errors at the page level. Every time an unhandled exception occurs, this event gets called. To see how it works, let's take our previous example and modify it to use the `Page_Error` method.

In the above example, we created an error by storing a string to variable of integer datatype, and we used the `Try` statement to handle exceptions. This time, we'll just use the `Page_Error` method to handle the exception:

Try It Out – Using Page_Error

1. Open the code file, `structurederrorhandling.aspx`, and make the following adjustments:

```
<script language="VB" runat="server">
  Sub PageLevelErrorTest()
    dim intCounter as integer
    intCounter =1
    for intCounter=1 to 10
      intCounter = intCounter+1
    next
    response.write ("The value of the counter is:" & intCounter & "<br>")
    intCounter = "Storing a string to an integer"
  End sub

  Sub Page_Error(sender As Object, exc As EventArgs)
    response.write("Error occurred: " & Server.GetLastError().ToString())
    Server.ClearError()
  End Sub

  sub Page_Load()
    PageLevelErrorTest()
  end sub
</script>
```

2. Save the file as `PageLevelError.aspx`, and open it in your browser. You should see something like this:

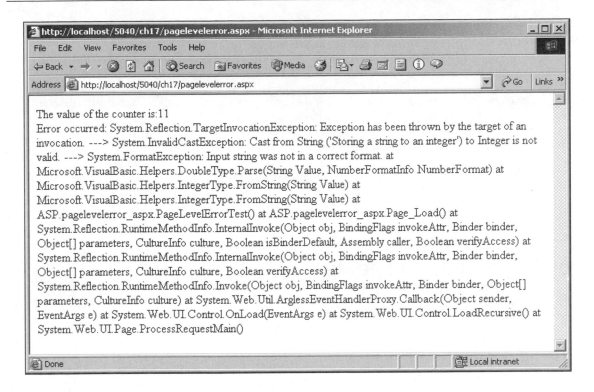

The value of the counter is:11
Error occurred: System.Reflection.TargetInvocationException: Exception has been thrown by the target of an invocation. ---> System.InvalidCastException: Cast from String ('Storing a string to an integer') to Integer is not valid. ---> System.FormatException: Input string was not in a correct format. at Microsoft.VisualBasic.Helpers.DoubleType.Parse(String Value, NumberFormatInfo NumberFormat) at Microsoft.VisualBasic.Helpers.IntegerType.FromString(String Value) at Microsoft.VisualBasic.Helpers.IntegerType.FromString(String Value) at ASP.pagelevelerror_aspx.PageLevelErrorTest() at ASP.pagelevelerror_aspx.Page_Load() at System.Reflection.RuntimeMethodInfo.InternalInvoke(Object obj, BindingFlags invokeAttr, Binder binder, Object[] parameters, CultureInfo culture, Boolean isBinderDefault, Assembly caller, Boolean verifyAccess) at System.Reflection.RuntimeMethodInfo.InternalInvoke(Object obj, BindingFlags invokeAttr, Binder binder, Object[] parameters, CultureInfo culture, Boolean verifyAccess) at System.Reflection.RuntimeMethodInfo.Invoke(Object obj, BindingFlags invokeAttr, Binder binder, Object[] parameters, CultureInfo culture) at System.Web.Util.ArglessEventHandlerProxy.Callback(Object sender, EventArgs e) at System.Web.UI.Control.OnLoad(EventArgs e) at System.Web.UI.Control.LoadRecursive() at System.Web.UI.Page.ProcessRequestMain()

How It Works

We already know about the first half of this code, it's the Page_Error sub that we're interested in. When we create the sub, we specify several things in parentheses:

```
Sub Page_Error(sender As Object, exc As EventArgs)
```

Within the Page_Error method, we are writing a message to the user to say that an error has occurred, and detailed error information is provided using the GetLastError() method of the Server object:

```
response.write("Error occurred: " & Server.GetLastError().ToString())
```

1. *Refer to the ASP.NET Core Objects section in Chapter 10 for more information on the Server object and its members.*

After displaying the message, we free up the server by using the ClearError() method of the Server object.

The Page_Error method is called whenever an unhandled exception is thrown within the page. This method could be used to catch the error, log the error to a log file, notify the administrator of the error using email, or store the error information to a database. We will talk about this in a moment, in the Notification and Logging Section.

Application_Error method

This is the other method that can be used to handle any 'un-accounted for' errors. The `Application_Error` method is similar to the `Page_Error` method, in that, if it is enabled, it is called whenever an unhandled exception is thrown, but from any page under the application. This method is part of the `global.asax` file. Another similarity with the `Page_Error` method, is that `Application_Error` can also be used to log the errors to a log file, notify an administrator using email, or store the error information to a database.

The following example shows the usage of this method:

```
Sub Application_Error(sender As Object, exc As EventArgs)
    'Handle the Error
  'Provide code to log the error or send an email
End Sub
```

Notification and Logging

In this section, we are going to talk about the techniques that are used to log errors to the Windows event log, and notify a site manager or administrator of the occurrence of the error.

Writing To The Event Log

So we now know that any exceptions that are not handled can call the `Application_Error` and `Page_Error` methods. There is another step we can take in handling these unforeseen errors, which involves finding out their occurrence, as this could provide vital clues as to how we handle them in the future.

For instance, say a customer who is ordering a few items from your online shopping center receives an error that the order could not be completed. The site manager should be able to see that an error has occurred, so they can take steps to avoid this error in the future.

To achieve this, errors can be logged in to the Windows event log, which can then be reviewed on a periodic basis. Depending on the nature of the application, the event log could be reviewed every hour, day or week.

System.Diagnostics namespace

The tool that the .NET framework provides for us here is the `System.Diagnostics` namespace, which contains classes that can be used for reading and writing to event logs. Before using the class for accessing event logs, we have to import the `System.Diagnostics` namespace into the program, as shown below:

```
<%@ Import Namespace="System.Diagnostics" %>
```

This line goes at the very top of your code page.

EventLog class

The class that we will use to read and write to the event log is the `EventLog` class. Using this class, we can create a new log, or write entries to an existing log.

First of all, you need to create a log that you can write to, and then you need to specify an event **Source**. A source is a string identifying an individual entry to the log. Creating an event source opens some space in the log for the entry to be recorded. The `CreateEventSource` method can be used to create both a source and a log. In the following example, we create a log called `MyApplicationLog,` and a source called `MyApplicationSource`.

To actually write an entry to the log, we use the `WriteEntry` method, and, as in our last example, provide detailed error information by using the `GetLastError()` method of the `Server` object.

Try It Out – Writing to the Windows error log

1. Type the following code into your code editor:

```
<%@ Import Namespace="System.Diagnostics" %>
<script language="VB" runat="server" >
  Sub EntrytoLog()
    dim intCounter as integer
    intCounter =1
    for intCounter=1 to 10
     intCounter = intCounter+1
    next
    response.write ("The value of the counter is:" & intCounter & "<br>")
    intCounter = "Storing a string to an integer"
      End sub

  Sub Page_Error(sender As Object, exc As EventArgs)
    dim errorMessage as string
    errorMessage = "Error occurred" & Server.GetLastError().ToString()
    Server.ClearError()
    Dim LogName As String = "MyApplicationLog"
    Dim SourceName As String = "MyApplicationSource"
    If (Not EventLog.SourceExists(SourceName))
      EventLog.CreateEventSource(SourceName, LogName)
    End If

    'Insert into Event Log
    Dim MyLog As New EventLog
    MyLog.Source = LogName
    MyLog.WriteEntry(errorMessage, EventLogEntryType.Error)
  End Sub
</script>
<%

  EntrytoLog()
%>
```

2. Save this file as `entrytolog.aspx`, and load it in browser. After the page has loaded, you will see the following:

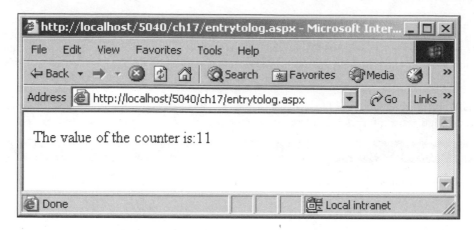

3. However it's not really the display we interested in, but the fact that it has written to a log. To view the contents of the log, open the event viewer. The following figure shows the Event Viewer on my machine:

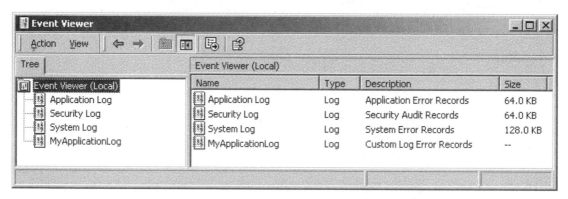

To open event viewer, Click **Start** from the Windows tool bar, then select **Settings**. Click **Control Panel** and the **Control Panel** window appears. Double click on the **Administrative Tools** icon. This will launch the **Administrative Tools** window. Double click on the **Event Viewer** icon to open the **Event Viewer** window

4. In the event viewer, you will see MyApplicationLog listed under the Name column, after System Log. Double click MyApplicationLog to open it, and you will see the Error entry that we made. The figure below shows the entry:

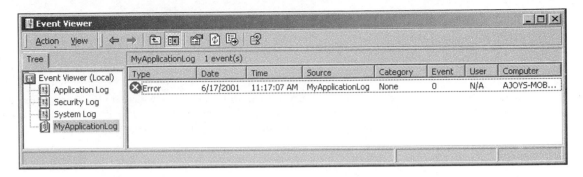

5. Double click on the Error entry to open the Event Properties window, as shown in the figure below. This shows the date and time the entry was made, and the description we provided using the `WriteEntry` method:

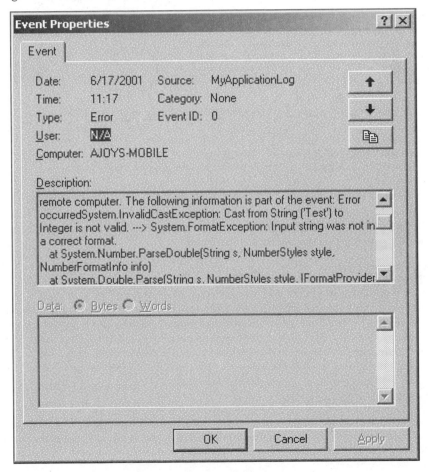

How It Works

The first line to note is the first line itself, as this imports the namespace we will use:

```
<%@ Import Namespace="System.Diagnostics" %>
```

We then establish and loop our familiar `intCounter` variable. After this, we create the `Page_Error` sub, and open it by typing our `errorMessage` variable as a string, and supplying it with a line of text to display, along with error information from the server, before erasing the error from the server:

```
Sub Page_Error(sender As Object, exc As EventArgs)
    dim errorMessage as string
    errorMessage = "Error occurred" & Server.GetLastError().ToString()
    Server.ClearError()
```

Next we define the name of our log, and this particular source, but before creating the two, we check to see if the source already exists:

```
Dim LogName As String = "MyApplicationLog"
Dim SourceName As String = "MyApplicationSource"
If (Not EventLog.SourceExists(SourceName))
  EventLog.CreateEventSource(SourceName, LogName)
```

If the source doesn't already exist, then we proceed to write an entry to the log:

```
Dim MyLog As New EventLog
MyLog.Source = LogName
MyLog.WriteEntry(errorMessage, EventLogEntryType.Error)
```

In the above example, we have used the `EventLog` class to make an entry to the log file under the `Page_Error` method. Alternatively, you could use this class within the `Application_Error` method in the `global.asax` file. Doing this, will create an entry to the log files for any unhandled errors occurring throughout all the pages within the application.

Mailing the site administrator

In our last example, we made an entry to a log file after the occurrence of an error. In the real world this log file could be reviewed at regular intervals, perhaps by a web site manager or administrator. However, this may not be prudent for certain applications. Depending on the nature of the application, the manager or administrator may need to be informed of an error right away. To do this, we could notify the site administrator by sending an email with the details of the error as soon as it happens.

System.Web.Mail namespace

The .NET framework provides a namespace with a set of classes to do this. The `System.Web.Mail` namespace contains three classes that can be used to create and send an email using SMTP:

❑   `MailMessage`

❑   `MailAttachment`

❑   `SmtpMail`.

Before using these classes in our page, we need to import the System.Web.Mail namespace, just as we did with the System.Diagnostics namespace in the last example. Let's look at our three classes in more detail.

MailMessage

The MailMessage class provides properties that are used to create an email. The following table lists the name and purpose of some of the more commonly used members of this class:

\	Use
From	This property is to specify the sender's email address
To	This property is to specify the recipient's email address
Subject	This property is to specify the subject line for the email message
Body	This property is used to set the body of the email message

The syntax when using this class looks like this:

```
mailMessage.From = "senders email address"
    mailMessage.To = "recipients email address"
    mail.Message.Subject = "subject line"
    mailMessage.Body = "body of email message"
```

MailAttachment

This class contains members that are used to create an attachment that is to be sent with the email message.

SmtpMail

This class provides properties that are used to send an email using the SMTP Service. The method we are interested in, at the moment, is the Send method of this class. This method is used to send an email, and the code looks like this:

```
SmtpMail.Send(mailMessage)
```

To show you how a working piece of code, based on the System.Web.Mail namespace, would look, we have modified the previous example to send an email, instead of writing to the log file:

```
<%@ Import Namespace="System.Web.Mail" %>
<script language="VB" runat="server" >
  Sub sendMailTest()
    dim intCounter as integer
    intCounter =1
    for intCounter=1 to 10
    intCounter = intCounter+1
    response.write ("The value of the counter is:" & intCounter & "<br>")
    intCounter = "Storing a string to an integer"
  End sub

  Sub Page_Error(sender As Object, exc As EventArgs)
    dim errorMessage as string
    errorMessage = "Error occurred " & Server.GetLastError().ToString()
    Server.ClearError()
```

```
      'Create an email message
      Dim newMail As New MailMessage
      newMail.From = "fromaddress@yourserver.com"
      newmail.To = "administrator@yourserver.com"
      newMail.Subject = "Error Occurred"
      newMail.Body = errorMessage
      'send the mail to the administrator.
    SmtpMail.Send(newMail)
    End Sub

</script>
<%
 sendMailTest()
%>
```

This code allows email to be sent to the administrator of the server in the event of an error being generated.

Summary

In this chapter, we talked about error handling techniques that can be used when developing ASP.NET applications.

We discussed the different kinds of errors that can occur, techniques for handling errors, including the new tracing feature, handling exceptions using unstructured and structured error handling, and finally, techniques to log the error messages to a log file and notify the site administrator through email.

We saw that adopting good coding practice helps to reduce the number of errors in your code, and that time spent in testing helps us create handlers for recurring errors before the application is moved to the production environment.

Using different error handling techniques helps us to develop applications with fewer bugs, which are, therefore, more successful and competitive.

Web Services

In the days before the Internet started to find its way into every corner of our lives, whenever we wanted to research a subject, the chances are we'd have visited a library to find a book on the topic, possibly visited another library for some more specialized literature, and browsed the relevant periodicals to find the latest articles. While this is still quite possible (if you like that sort of thing), it's usually not necessary. Now that the Internet connects computers containing all sorts of different data sources, it frequently provides us with a one-stop shop for whatever information we might need. In a sense, the Internet has become a "virtual library" for web users.

Web developers face a similar situation. Over the years, we created isolated web applications that were essentially islands unto themselves. Each island became larger and larger, and in its wake, we would often produce large amounts of redundant logic. To overcome this, many developers began using technologies (such as COM and DCOM), that would allow them to build code components once and bundle them up so they could be shared by multiple applications, multiple developers, even between multiple machines.

However, in practice these components were usually very difficult to work with, since they had to be physically distributed and then explicitly registered on each new user's machine. It was possible to share logic around, but it was far from easy.

At the same time, the Web was achieving credibility (not to mention ubiquity) as a useful and reliable medium for the exchange of human-readable information. The logical next step was therefore, to use the same infrastructure to pass around information that was specifically designed for machines to consume – not just GET and POST statements, and simple HTTP headers, but complex data and procedure calls, such as you'd expect to be passed around within an application.

The ASP.NET Web Services model provides us with a simple, straightforward way to do precisely this. Since the Internet has given us a standard method of communication across a global network, web developers can use it to share application logic and therefore reduce the overall amount of code duplication. Not only need we create less logic, but we can also build upon it and extend it. As we'll see, Web Services truly make the Web a "virtual library" of ready-made code for developers.

This chapter will introduce you to ASP.NET Web Services. These are easy to create and use, and possess a programming model that will be very familiar to anyone who has already worked with ASP.NET. It's also a concept that programmers of all levels can learn quickly.

By the end of this chapter, you will have learned:

❑   What a Web Service is and its role in the .NET framework

❑   How to create and use a Web Service

❑   How to describe how a Web Service behaves

❑   How users can discover which Web Services are available

❑   What you need to consider when building a Web Service

Now, lets jump straight in and see the nature of the beast!

What is a Web Service?

Technically speaking, a web service is "a component of programmable application logic that can be accessed using standard web protocols". That is, it's quite similar to the components we considered earlier on, but lets us access all its functionality via the Web. In principle, anyone who can browse the Web can see and use a web service.

Think of a web service as a black box resource that accepts requests from a consumer (some kind of program running on the web client), performs a specific task, and returns the results of that task. In some respects, a search engine such as Google (www.google.com) is a kind of web service – you submit a search expression, and it compiles a list of matching sites, which it sends back to your browser.

Currently the term, web service, is something of a buzzword within the sphere of software development, thanks to a number of new protocols that have opened up the scope of what we can expect web services to do. XML plays a central role in all these technologies, and these **XML Web Services** are something you can expect to hear a great deal about, both now and well into the future.

> **Most of the time, you'll find that when people talk about web services, they're implicitly referring to XML Web Services. This is now so prevalent that many people believe that all web services use XML by definition.**

There's a very important distinction between a web service like Google and the kind of XML Web Service that we're going to be talking about here: on Google, *you* submit the search expression, and *you* read the list of sites that gets sent back. Okay, the browser provides you with a textbox, and parses the response stream so that it looks nice – but it doesn't actually *understand* the information you've submitted, let alone the HTML that Google sends back.

> **Effectively, a conventional search engine acts as an HTML web service.**

If you're using an XML Web Service, you can assume the results will be returned as some kind of XML document, that's explicitly structured and self-describing. It's, therefore, quite straightforward to write a program that interprets these results and perhaps even use the results to formulate a new submission.

As we're going to see, ASP.NET makes it very easy to build XML Web Services, and just as easy to use them – ultimately you only need to reference the Web Service in your code, and you can use it just as if it were a local component. As with normal components, we don't need to know anything about how the service functions, just the tasks it can do, the type of information it needs to do them, and the type of results we're going to get back.

We can use Web Service methods to do just about anything from adding two numbers together, to writing information to a database. The logic they use can be as simple or as complex as we need it to be.

Let's create a simple Web Service to demonstrate just how easy it is.

Try It Out – Creating our first Web Service

In this example, we'll make a Web Service that takes a string input and returns a greeting that includes whatever name we've specified in the input.

1. Create a new file, and enter the following code:

```
<%@ WebService Language="vb" Class="Greetings"%>
Imports System.Web.Services
Public Class Greetings
  <WebMethod()> Public Function Hello(ByVal strName As String) As String
    Return "Hello, " & strName & ". Have a great day!"
  End Function
End Class
```

2. Save this file as `greetings.asmx` in your test directory. Congratulations! You've just created a fully functional Web Service on your local machine!

3. To give it a test run, simply open up your web browser, and request the ASMX file from the appropriate virtual directory – you'll now be presented with a nicely formatted test page, the top of which should look like this:

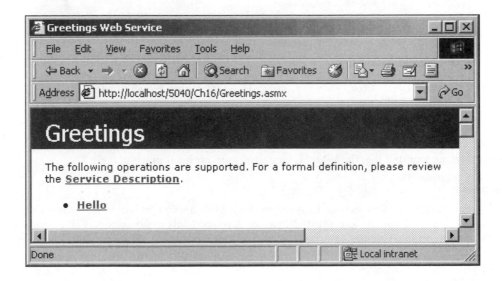

4. Click on the bulleted hyperlink Hello – this is the name of the method we defined in our `Greetings` class above. A new page will be displayed that allows us to enter a name:

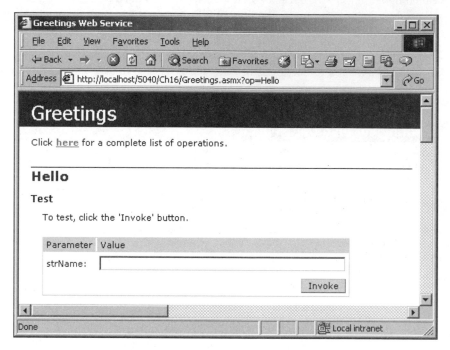

5. Enter your name in the textbox adjacent to the parameter strName, and hit the Invoke button to call our Web Service's `Hello` method. The following result should now appear in a new browser window:

We've now demonstrated that the Web Service works on our local machine.

How It Works

See how easy that was! We used our browser to test a Web Service in both cases. When the test page appeared, we entered a name and pressed Invoke. A request was made to the Web Service to execute the `Hello` method, passing the name we entered as a parameter. Within the method, the Web Service returned a greeting that contained our name. The result was returned inside an XML element called `<string>`.

Let's briefly talk about the code that's in our Web Service. First of all, we can see from the following line that our Web Service is written in VB.NET. We also declare our class name as `Greetings`, which will be important when a consumer wants to use it:

```
<%@ WebService Language="vb" Class="Greetings"%>
```

Our next line gives us access to objects that are needed to build a Web Service:

```
Imports System.Web.Services
```

Finally, we have some logic to actually define the Web Service's functionality:

```
Public Class Greetings
  <WebMethod()> _
  Public Function Hello(strName As String) As String
    Return "Hello, " & strName & ". Have a great day!"
  End Function
End Class
```

Within the `Public Class Greetings` declaration (notice the name here matches the one in the `WebService` declaration above), we define a `Hello` function that simply returns a string based on the parameter `strname`. We prefix this method declaration with a `<WebMethod()>` attribute – this is how we specify that it's to be exposed as a web method, thus making the function visible to the outside world.

With just a few lines of code, we've created a functioning Web Service. We didn't need to specify a format for the result, or write any code to handle any network connections. We didn't even have to register it on the client – all we needed to know was the URL.

Let's take a quick look at how this works in a bit more detail. How are the requests and responses sent to and from a Web Service?

HTTP, XML and Web Services

We've already introduced you (back in Chapter 3) to the basic mechanism by which information is passed back and forth across the Web, so that we can pop a URL in our browser's address bar and request a web page from a remote server. We've also pointed out that ASP.NET Web Services rely on the same mechanism – namely the HTTP request-response system. All the information that we submit to a Web Service is sent as an HTTP Request. Likewise, any information we get back from the Web Service is sent as an HTTP Response:

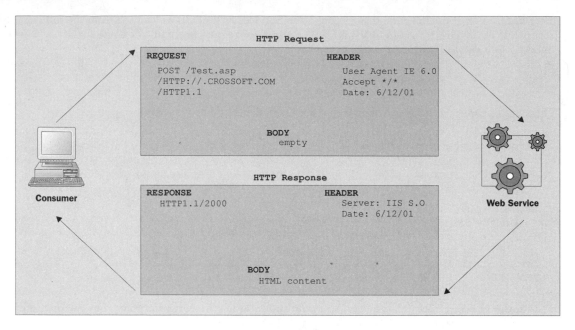

We've already seen that a typical Web Service operates by accepting input from a consumer and using it to produce a result, which is sent back to the consumer as XML. When a consumer makes use of a Web Service's logic, it takes the form of an HTTP request – that's why it's so easy to access from a web browser, which is purpose-built to make such requests.

This request consists of packets of information that are sent to the Web Service (wherever it may reside), and these contain:

❑ Vital information, such as the Web Service's URL and the fact that we're submitting a request (that is, initiating a data exchange that requires a response, rather than simply responding to someone else's request)

❑ Details of the amount of information being sent

❑ The type of document we require back from the Web Service

❑ Information about the consumer, the request date, general configuration statistics, and finally, the data itself.

The Web Service will return an HTTP response with:

❑ A return address for the consumer, and the fact that we're submitting a response and don't expect any further action from the recipient

❑ A success or failure status code, indicating whether or not it received a valid request from the consumer.

❑ Configuration information of its own

❑ Any appropriate data

We can transmit HTTP requests and responses between a Web Service and a consumer as many times as we like, depending on how the interaction between the two has been designed.

So, how exactly does our submitted data get wrapped up in this bundle of HTTP information? As we know from Chapter 3, there are two ways to submit information within an HTTP request, using the GET and POST methods respectively – let's give them each a quick recap.

HTTP GET

This is the simplest way to send data to the client, and probably the most familiar to users of the web. Simple, unstructured information is bundled in with the page as a sequence of **name-value pairs**. These pairings are a simple way to combine all the values in a single string. We can use the `Request.QueryString` collection in our ASP.NET code to access these name-value pairs on the server.

When we tested our `Greetings.Hello` web method just a moment ago, the built-in testing mechanism provided by ASP.NET used HTTP GET to submit the string "Matthew" to the Web Service. Here's the actual GET request that our browser used to access the Web Service when we tested it a moment ago:

```
GET /5040/ch18/greetings.asmx/Hello?strName=Matthew HTTP/1.1
Host: localhost
```

It specifies the GET method, states the page we've requested (including the virtual directory path) along with our query string, and declares that it has structured the request according to version 1.1 of HTTP. It then states the name of the host to which it wants the request submitted, in this case the local machine. The resource requested is:

```
/5040/ch18/greetings.asmx/Hello?strName=Matthew
```

Using this path along with the Host value, we have a full URL:

```
localhost/5040/ch18/greetings.asmx/Hello?strName=Matthew
```

The corresponding response simply specifies the content type we're returning (text/xml) along with the character set and content length. The body of the response then contains the XML we saw earlier:

```
HTTP/1.1 200 OK
Content-Type: text/xml; charset=utf-8
Content-Length: 112


<?xml version="1.0" encoding="utf-8"?>
<string xmlns="http://tempuri.org/">
Hello, Matthew. Have a great day!</string>
```

The response from the server is a 200 message, which is HTTP's success message.

Another common return code is 404, which indicates "File not found." Our HTTP response from the server can also tell us information such as the web server software, the number of bytes to expect, content type, and the type of cookie that will be set.

Note that it's very easy to make a new request on our Web Service by simply editing the query string in the browser's address bar. You might like to try calling up the page again as follows:

http://localhost/5040/ch18/greetings.asmx/Hello?strName=my%20fine%20fellow

HTTP POST

While HTTP GET uses the end of the URL to pass its information from resource to resource, HTTP POST uses the body of the transmission to carry the same name-value pairs. We can retrieve these values using the `Request.Form` collection in ASP.NET. Using POST results in a less-cluttered URL, as well as slightly tighter security, since manipulating the name-value pairs isn't as simple as modifying the URL.

Below is an example of an equivalent POST message being sent to the web server:

```
POST /5040/ch18/greetings.asmx/Hello HTTP/1.1
Host: localhost
Content-Type: application/x-www-form-urlencoded
Content-Length: 15

strName=Matthew
HTTP/1.1 200 OK
```

This time, the request specifies the POST method before stating the page we've requested and the HTTP version. It states the host name and content type (often `application/x-www-form-urlencoded`) and the content length, which now tells the server how many bytes' worth of name-value pairs. This is all followed by the name-value pairs themselves, which are placed on a separate line. The corresponding response from the web server takes exactly the same form as we saw when using the GET method, returning a simple XML document in the response body, with the result of our web method call placed inside a `<string>` element.

That's all well and good so far, but it's still rather limited. Since we ultimately want to use these web methods to replace various local method calls in our applications, we surely need to be able to pass more than strings and integers – what about passing things like data sets and other complex objects?

This is where XML really comes into its own. As we've established, XML plays a vital role in the new model of Web Services. In order to send complex, structured information back and forth between Web Services and consumers, we need to rely on a simple, structured, self-describing data format that they can use to talk to each other. XML provides us with all we need in these respects as well as enormous flexibility.

These powerful new Web Services therefore use XML to describe the data sent from the consumer as well as that being returned. It can also be used to describe the parameters a Web Service expects, and how to find information on Web Services available to consumers on the Internet, and we'll look at these topics shortly. It shields us from having to concern ourselves with which platform the Web Service and consumer reside on, as long as both are on systems that understand XML.

XML is very easy to read and understand, which is handy when we debug our code. However, it can often be verbose since even the simplest of data exchanges can require a significant amount of description. Since we are exchanging all types and structures of data, we must cater for the lowest common denominator. With a common protocol (HTTP/HTTPS) and a common language (XML) that transcend individual machine platforms and operating systems, you should begin to see what a potentially powerful tool Web Services can be.

Simple Object Access Protocol (SOAP)

The **Simple Object Access Protocol** provides a powerful way to call all sorts of remote functions. It wraps up any call-specific information inside an XML element (a **SOAP envelope**) and, therefore, frees us from most of the structural limitations imposed by the HTTP methods we looked at earlier:

```
POST /5040/ch18/greetings.asmx HTTP/1.1
Host: localhost
Content-Type: text/xml; charset=utf-8
Content-Length: length
SOAPAction: "http://tempuri.org/Hello"

<?xml version="1.0" encoding="utf-8"?>
<soap:Envelope
    xmlns:xsi="http://www.w3.org/2001/XMLSchema-instance"
    xmlns:xsd="http://www.w3.org/2001/XMLSchema"
    xmlns:soap="http://schemas.xmlsoap.org/soap/envelope/">
  <soap:Body>
    <Hello xmlns="http://tempuri.org/">
      <strName>Matthew</strName>
    </Hello>
  </soap:Body>
</soap:Envelope>
```

As we can see, the submitted string value "Matthew" is held in a `<strname>` element (identifying the specific parameter being specified in the web method call) and this is nested within a `<Hello>` element (identifying the name of the method we're calling). Sure, it's a little more complex than our previous requests, but that's largely due to the fact that we're only passing a single string value.

Apart from being somewhat more explicit in our request, this approach allows us to submit data in a well-defined structure. Even if we wanted to submit a huge array of complex data objects, the flexibility inherent within this SOAP envelope means that we could. What's more, although the SOAP request is submitted as part of an HTTP POST request, you can see that it's totally separate and self-contained.

> *One consequence of this is that we're not tied to HTTP as a transport protocol – for example, it's quite possible to send this envelope to the web service via SMTP (that is, simply e-mail it to the Web Service). While this is a fascinating and extremely useful option, it's quite a way beyond the scope of this book. If you're interested in finding out more, I suggest you check out* Professional ASP.NET *(Wrox Press, ISBN 1861004558).*

The SOAP response takes a similar form:

```
HTTP/1.1 200 OK
Content-Type: text/xml; charset=utf-8
Content-Length: length

<?xml version="1.0" encoding="utf-8"?>
<soap:Envelope
    xmlns:xsi="http://www.w3.org/2001/XMLSchema-instance"
    xmlns:xsd="http://www.w3.org/2001/XMLSchema"
    xmlns:soap="http://schemas.xmlsoap.org/soap/envelope/">
  <soap:Body>
```

665

```
        <HelloResponse xmlns="http://tempuri.org/">
          <HelloResult>Hello, Matthew. Have a great day!</HelloResult>
        </HelloResponse>
      </soap:Body>
    </soap:Envelope>
```

We can see explicitly that the response string is the result of a call to the Hello method. Again, this result could just as easily take the form of some sort of structured data, and isn't tied into the HTTP response in any way.

When we come to actually *use* Web Services within our ASP.NET logic, it's important to recognize that SOAP is the protocol that they'll use by default. Although at first sight it seems a little more bulky than the other options, it's actually the mechanism that makes it possible to use web methods directly, flexibly, and seamlessly from within our code.

Building an ASP.NET Web Service

We've already defined what a Web Service is and seen an example in action. We've also been introduced to some of the ways in which data can be sent between a Web Service and a consumer using XML and HTTP. Now we'll take a more detailed look at how we put together a Web Service. We'll also start to explore the enormous range of possible uses we can find for Web Services.

As we've seen, we can define a Web Service by simply writing a few lines of code and placing them in an IIS virtual directory, inside a file with an ASMX extension. This extension effectively tells IIS to use aspnet_isapi.dll and lets the ISAPI filter know that we're going to define a Web Service. We can create this just like a standard ASP.NET page, using anything from a text-based editor like Notepad to a full-blown integrated development environment like Visual Studio.NET.

A Web Service definition contains four essential parts:

- ❑ Processing Directive
- ❑ Namespaces
- ❑ Public Class
- ❑ Web-callable methods

Let's take a look at each of these, in turn:

Processing Directive

Within our empty ASMX file, we must let the web server know that we're creating a Web Service. To do this, we enter a directive like the following one at the top of our page:

```
<%@ WebService Language="language" Class="classname"%>
```

As we know, this sort of statement appears at the top of an ASP.NET source file to tell .NET about any settings or constraints that should be applied to whatever object is generated from the file. In this case, the directive tells the compiler the language in which we've written the Web Service, and the name of the class in which it is defined. This might reside in the same file (as it will in this example) or within a separate file (which must be in the \bin directory immediately beneath the Web Application root in which the Web Service lives).

Namespaces

Just as is possible with an ASPX, we can make use of other files' logic within our ASMX page by specifying appropriate namespaces. In this case, we can use the VB.NET command Imports:

```
Imports System.Web.Services
```

Web Services require us to import this namespace as an absolute minimum, as it contains all the necessary classes for Web Services to handle network connection issues and other OS-related tasks.

Public Class

Now we define a Public Class that acts as our container for the methods in our Web Service. Note that the name of this class is effectively the name of the Web Service, and should, therefore, correspond to the Class value we specified in the processing directive:

```
Public Class ClassName
...
End Class
```

Essentially, we're just defining an object class whose methods we're going to expose over the Web. This will ultimately allow us to make remote method calls over the Internet that, to our server, will look like method calls from the same machine.

Web Methods

Methods that we expose for consumption over the Internet are known as web-callable methods or simply **web methods**. By definition a Web Service will expose one or more web methods – of course it can have other methods as well, and these can be protected so that consumers cannot use them directly. The syntax varies slightly depending upon which language is used, but they all tend to follow a similar structure, in VB.NET it is the following:

```
<WebMethod()> Public Function Name(Input As DataType) As DataType
```

We place the WebMethod declaration only before functions we wish to expose to consumers. Those without this declaration cannot be seen.

You may have noticed the set of parentheses following the WebMethod declaration. These are available for providing attributes. This allows us to customize our web-methods in various ways – for example, we can use the CacheDuration attribute to set the number of seconds for which the WebMethod will cache its results. If a consumer requests a result from the Web Service, WebMethod will retrieve the cached copy of these values instead of retrieving them from original sources for the time specified. For example:

```
<WebMethod() CacheDuration=5 >Public Function hello(str as String) As String
```

Creating web methods accounts for the majority of the work when building a Web Service. As we mentioned earlier, it is possible to include more than one web method in an ASMX file, as we'll see in our next example:

Try It Out – Creating a Web Service with Multiple Web Methods

This Web Service contains four web methods that convert inches to centimeters, centimeters to inches, miles to kilometers and kilometers to miles, respectively.

1. Create a new file and enter the following:

```
<%@ WebService Language="VB" Class="MeasurementConversions"%>

Imports System.Web.Services

Public Class MeasurementConversions

  <WebMethod()> _
  Public Function InchesToCentimeters(decInches As Decimal) As Decimal
    Return decInches * 2.54
  End Function

  <WebMethod()> _
  Public Function CentimetersToInches(decCentimeters As Decimal) _
                            As Decimal
    Return decCentimeters / 2.54
  End Function

  <WebMethod()> _
  Public Function MilesToKilometers(decMiles As Decimal) As Decimal
    Return decMiles * 1.61
  End Function

  <WebMethod()> _
  Public Function KilometersToMiles(decKilometers As Decimal) As Decimal
    Return decKilometers / 1.61
  End Function

End Class
```

2. Save the file as MeasurementConversions.asmx in the ch18 directory.

How It Works

In our example, we've created a Web Service that converts between Imperial (English) measurements and Metric measurements.

The first line tells us that the file is a Web Service written in VisualBasic.NET. We have a class name of MeasurementConversions that will be used by consumers to make reference to our Web Service:

```
<%@ WebService Language="VB" Class="MeasurementConversions"%>
```

Next, we import the namespace that allows us to refer to Web Service objects without using fully qualified names:

```
Imports System.Web.Services
```

We then name our class to match the processing directive class name. When we are ready to make remote calls to our Web Service through a consumer, we'll need to know this:

```
Public Class MeasurementConversions
```

Finally, we have the actual `Web methods`. These are separate functions that can be called within a Web Service to return a result. In the first, we pass a value in inches as a `decimal` value and will receive a `decimal` value in centimeters using the standard conversion formula. The second receives a `decimal` in centimeters and converts it to inches:

```
<WebMethod()> _
Public Function InchesToCentimeters(decInches As Decimal) As Decimal
  Return decInches * 2.54
End Function

<WebMethod()> _
Public Function CentimetersToInches(decCentimeters As Decimal) As _
                                    Decimal
  Return decCentimeters / 2.54
End Function
```

The third and fourth Web methods perform similar conversions from miles to kilometers and kilometers to miles, respectively:

```
<WebMethod()> _
Public Function MilesToKilometers(decMiles As Decimal) As Decimal
  Return decMiles * 1.61
End Function

<WebMethod()> _
  Public Function KilometersToMiles(decKilometers As Decimal) As Decimal
    Return decKilometers / 1.61
  End Function
```

We've created a complete Web Service using the **processing directive**, adding **namespaces,** and creating our **Web methods**. Now the big question is "How do we know it works?" It's time to thoroughly try out our Web Service.

Testing your Web Service

As we've seen earlier, the creators of ASP.NET have come up with a great way to test Web Services. All you need is an Internet connection and a browser. In the browser address window, just enter the URL of the Web Service in this way:

http://[path]/[webservice].asmx

The first time our Web Service is accessed, the code will compile on the web server and a new browser window will appear containing some very helpful diagnostic information. This **Web Service Description** page allows us to impersonate a consumer and enter input values to send to the Web Service. As we view the page, we can see information about the Web Service:

- ❑ Names of the Web Service's web-callable functions
- ❑ Request Parameters – the names of all the inputs that the Web Service expects a consumer to supply
- ❑ Response Type – the data types of the result sent by the Web Service to a consumer (for example, `integer`, `string`, `float`, `object`)
- ❑ Fields to enter test values

You'll also see the following message at the top of the test page:

> The following operations are supported. For a formal definition, please review the Service Description.

The Service Description is a comprehensive technical description of all the functionality exposed by the Web Service, and we'll be taking a close look at it later on in the chapter.

Try It Out – Browse to the Conversions test page

So, what happens when we test it our MeasurementConversions web service?

1. Open your browser, and call up the ASMX from the appropriate test directory:

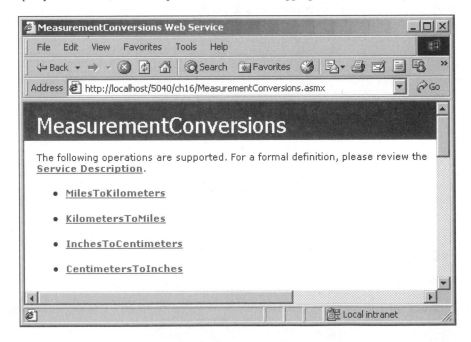

2. Click on the MilesToKilometers method hyperlink:

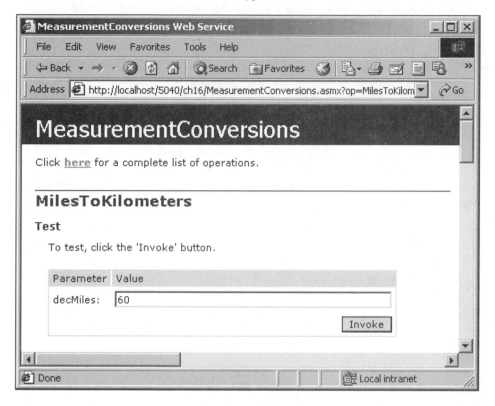

3. Enter a test value in the decMiles value field, of "60"

4. Press Invoke, and a new browser window appears containing our result in kilometers in XML format:

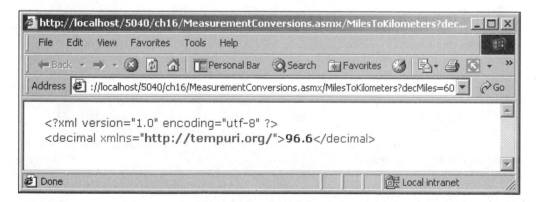

5. Click on the word <u>here</u> in the hyperlink at the top of the test page, and you'll return to the original test screen. You can now repeat this procedure for the other methods shown on the page.

How It Works

When we browse to our test page, we see a screen containing the name of our Web Service and, underneath it, a list of the methods that it exposes. These method names are hyperlinks.

When we click on MilesToKilometers, the Web method test section will appear in the browser window. We are given the name of the parameter, decMiles , and an associated field to enter our test value in. Remember from our example that the data type for MilesToKilometers is a decimal. This is the value that our MeasurementConversions Web Service expects from a consumer. Once the value is entered, we can press the Invoke button to execute the web method. We are impersonating a consuming application when we do this. When we enter the test value 60, it is passed using HTTP as a request to the MilesToKilometers Web method. The value will be multiplied by 1.61 and returned as a decimal. As we've discussed earlier, the result is in XML.

You might say "Sure, our test page tells us what the Web Service's expectations are. But how would a consumer know what they are?"

In the next section, we discuss how to know what a Web Service requires, what it produces and how a consumer can communicate with it.

Using your Web Service

As we've learned, it's essential for consumers to know what parameters to send to a Web Service and what values they should expect it to return. To accomplish this, we use a Web Service Description Language file or **WSDL**. This is an XML file that sets out how interaction between a Web Service and its consumer will occur.

The impact of this WSDL standard is enormous. It is able to define all the interactions of a Web Service, regardless of whether the service is running on Windows, Linux, Unix, or any other platform, and whether it is written in ASP.NET, Java or something else entirely is little short of revolutionary! It means that in future we won't need to concern ourselves with whether our services, or languages, are cross-platform compatible, and instead concentrate on the real issue of writing robust, functional, code – WSDL will take care of declaring the interaction for us.

For instance, if a Web Service expects two specific parameters and returns a single value, the WSDL defines the names, order, and types of each input and output value. Since we know where to find the Web Service using its URL, we don't need to know the physical location, nor the internal logic of the Web Service. With WSDL, we have all the information we need to begin making use of the Web Service functionality within our own applications. It's really that simple!

> **WSDL is the result of several recent improvements to cross-platform standards. At the time of this writing, the WSDL 1.1 specification is currently being reviewed for adoption by the W3C (the World Wide Web Consortium), the Internet technology standards governing body.**

Let's take a quick look at what a WSDL contract looks like using our Measurement Conversion Web Service:

Open up your browser and enter the path:

http://localhost/5040/Ch18/MeasurementConversions.asmx

You'll see the following page:

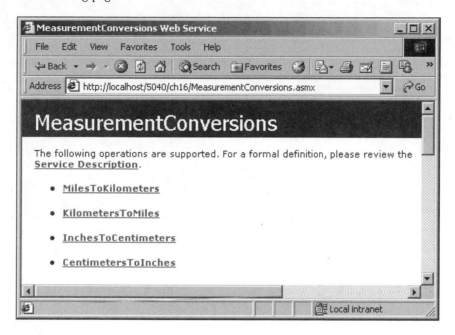

Now, click on the Service Description hyperlink at the top of the page:

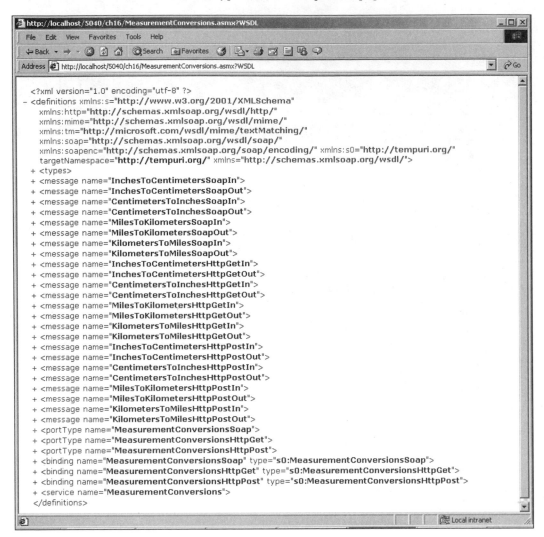

As you can see, there's a lot of information in here (and this is just the collapsed view!). Our web method message names are there and the various HTTP GET, HTTP POST, and SOAP message structures are laid out. These contain the requirements for a consumer to know what parameters are needed to communicate with a Web Service using each message structure.

At the top, the following declaration indicates that the WSDL file is in XML format:

```
<?xml version="1.0" encoding="utf-8" ?>
```

Below that declaration is the `<definitions>` element, which contains various namespaces. Most of these namespaces make reference to SOAP, which we discussed earlier. These must be included in the file in order for SOAP to work correctly:

```
<definitions xmlns:s="http://www.w3.org/2001/XMLSchema"
 xmlns:http="http://schemas.xmlsoap.org/wsdl/http/"
 xmlns:mime="http://schemas.xmlsoap.org/wsdl/mime/"
 xmlns:tm="http://microsoft.com/wsdl/mime/textMatching/"
 xmlns:soap="http://schemas.xmlsoap.org/wsdl/soap/"
 xmlns:soapenc="http://schemas.xmlsoap.org/soap/encoding/"
 xmlns:s0="http://tempuri.org/" targetNamespace="http://tempuri.org/"
 xmlns="http://schemas.xmlsoap.org/wsdl/">
```

The <types> element, that comes next, defines each of the data types that the Web Service expects to receive and return after completion. This is very complex, and almost a science in itself. It is written in XML Schema Definition language, or XSD. You can't see the definitions in our screenshot as its section, like the others, is collapsed.

After this, we have the various one-way transmissions, from a consumer to our Web Service and back again. Our web method message names are in here and the various HTTP GET, HTTP POST, and SOAP message structures are laid out. These contain the requirements for a consumer to know what parameters are required to communicate with a Web Service.

For example, when we expand the message element, we can see the `InchesToCentimeters` web method message structures for SOAP:

```
<message name="InchesToCentimetersSoapIn">
 <part name="parameters" element="s0:InchesToCentimeters" />
</message>
<message name="InchesToCentimetersSoapOut">
 <part name="parameters" element="s0:InchesToCentimetersResponse" />
</message>
```

There are corresponding elements of its HTTP GET and HTTP POST methods. In short, we've got all of the information we need in this file to communicate with our Web Service.

Now that we've discussed the process of building and communicating with web services in detail, let's create something a bit more complex. Our next example will accept a value, and return a result using ADO.NET to retrieve data from an Access database.

Try It Out – ISBN Search Web Service

We'll create a Web Service that returns the title of a book, based on an ISBN that the consumer provides. This will allow our librarian to add a function on his libraries web page to enable his users to search by consuming our Web Service.

This particular service will access a database of books. The database contains information on ISBN and book Titles. Once the details are received from the database, the results will be inserted into a `DataReader` and returned to the consumer in XML.

This example uses the Access database `Library.mdb`, which you can download along with the code samples for this book from www.wrox.com. You should ensure that the file is in the same path as the Web Service that you create:

1. Create a new file in Notepad called `ISBN.asmx`.

2. Add the processing directive and `Imports` statements to the beginning of the file:

```
<%@ WebService Language="vb" Class="ISBN" %>
Imports System.Web.Services
Imports System.Data
Imports System.Data.OleDb
```

3. Web Service-enable this program by adding this code:

```
Public Class ISBN
    Inherits System.Web.Services.WebService

<WebMethod()> _
Public Function BookDetail(ByVal strIsbn As String) As String
  Return GetBookDetails(strIsbn)
End Function
```

4. Enter the following code directly following the `BookDetail` web method. This function performs the database lookup and returns the book title string:

```
Private Function GetBookDetails(ByVal strIsbn As String) As String
 Dim objLibraryDR As OleDbDataReader
 Dim objLibraryConn As OleDbConnection
 Dim objLibraryCmd As OleDbCommand
 Dim strConn As String = "Provider=Microsoft.Jet.OLEDB.4.0;Data Source= _
                " & Server.MapPath("Library.mdb") & ";"
 Dim strSQL As String = "SELECT Title FROM Books WHERE ISBN = '" & _
                         strIsbn & "'"
 Dim strBookTitle As String

 objLibraryConn = New OleDbConnection(strConn)
 objLibraryCmd = New OleDbCommand(strSQL, objLibraryConn)
 objLibraryConn.Open()

 objLibraryDR = _
  objLibraryCmd.ExecuteReader(CommandBehavior.CloseConnection)

 If objLibraryDR.Read() Then
   strBookTitle = objLibraryDR(0)
 Else
   strBookTitle = "Book not found in the database"
 End If
 objLibraryDR.Close()

 Return strBookTitle
End Function

End Class
```

Once we have completed this code entry, we can test our new Web Service. Save this file, then browse to http://localhost/5040/Ch18/isbn.asmx.

Within the `strIsbn` field, enter the ISBN 1861003129. A new browser window will appear containing the following XML:

```
<?xml version="1.0" encoding="utf-8" ?>
<string xmlns="http://tempuri.org/">XSLT Programmers Reference</string>
```

How It Works

Our web service provides what is technically known as a "level of abstraction". This means that the code to do the work of finding our information isn't taken care of by the web-callable method `BookDetails` that we task with finding it. Instead, `BookDetails` calls another, internal, function that we, as consumers, can't see. This function, `GetBookDetails`, does the work of finding the book information and then returns it to `BookDetails`. In turn, `BookDetails` returns it to us:

```
<WebMethod()> _
Public Function BookDetail(ByVal strIsbn As String) As String
  Return GetBookDetails(strIsbn)
End Function

Private Function GetBookDetails(ByVal strIsbn As String) As String
...
End Function
```

We do this because the job of the `GetBookDetails` function remains the same, regardless of which source is making the request. The same function may be called from a non-Web Service source, and we certainly wouldn't want to maintain two separate functions that do the same thing, the difference being only the `<WebMethod>` declaration.

We're using ADO.NET to connect to the `Library.mdb` database, retrieve a book title from its `Books` table based on the ISBN, and store it in a `String` variable.

Keeping the data request simple, we define a connection string (`strConn`), and then open the connection to the database (with `objLibraryConn`):

```
objLibraryConn = New OleDbConnection(strConn)
objLibraryCmd = New OleDbCommand(strSQL, objLibraryConn)
objLibraryConn.Open()
```

Using the `objLibraryCmd` object, we execute the query for a specific ISBN, placing the results in the `objLibraryDR` DataReader:

```
objLibraryDR = objLibraryCmd.ExecuteReader(CommandBehavior.CloseConnection)
```

We then check whether a row was returned, by calling the `Read` method of our DataReader, `objLibraryDR`. If it returns True, we take the first column (column zero, the "Title" column of the database) from the DataReader and place it into `strBookTitle`. Otherwise, if it returns False, we know that the book was not found, and we place a "not found" message in the title value. Then we close our DataReader and return the book title string:

```
If objLibraryDR.Read() Then
  strBookTitle = objLibraryDR(0)
```

```
    Else
      strBookTitle = "Book not found in the database"
    End If

    objLibraryDR.Close()
    Return strBookTitle
```

For more information about ADO.NET, please refer to Chapter 12.

Consuming a Web Service

Now, we've created some Web Services from start to finish using a variety of technologies. The next step is to understand how to include this functionality within a consumer application. To do this, we must first create an interface that will allow the consumer to see all of the web-callable methods and properties exposed by the Web Service. We refer to this interface as a Web Service **proxy**.

How does a proxy work?

A proxy resides on the consumer's machine and acts as a relay between the consumer and the Web Service. When we build a proxy, we use a WSDL file to create a map that tells the consumer what methods are available and how to call them. The consumer then calls the `web method` that is mapped in the proxy, which in turn, makes calls to the actual Web Service over the Internet. The proxy handles all of the network-related work and sending of data, as well as managing the underlying WSDL so the consumer doesn't have to. When we reference the Web Service in the consumer application, it looks as if it's part of the consumer application itself.

Let's take a look at a diagram that illustrates the process:

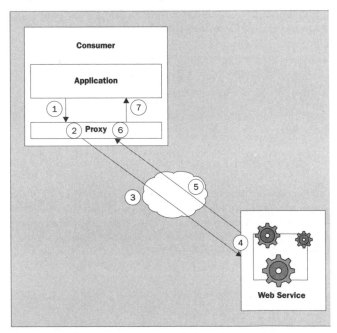

The procedure works as follows:

1. Your application executes a function in the proxy code, passing any appropriate parameters to it, without being concerned that the proxy is going to call a Web Service.

2. The proxy receives this call, and formulates the request that will be sent to the Web Service, using the parameters the consumer has specified.

3. This function call is sent from the proxy to the Web Service. This call can be within the confines of the same machine, across a Local Area Network (LAN), or across the Internet. The method of calling remains the same.

4. The Web Service uses the parameters provided by the proxy to execute its web-callable function and build the result in XML.

5. The resulting data from the Web Service is returned to the proxy at the consumer.

6. The proxy parses the XML returned from the Web Service to retrieve the individual values generated. These values may be as simple as `integers` and strings, or they may define more complex data types.

7. Your application receives the expected values from the proxy function, completely unaware that they resulted from a Web Service call.

In order to make use of a Web Service from an ASP.NET page, our proxy must be created and compiled appropriately. Creating a proxy to a Web Service using the .NET framework tools is very straightforward. These tools make use of WSDL to create a proxy, built in the language of your choice. To demonstrate this, we'll create a new ASP.NET application with which will access our new ISBN Web Service.

Creating a Proxy

Building a proxy is a two-step process:

❑ Generate the proxy source code

❑ Compile the proxy into a run-time library

We'll take a look at how to do this in the following example:

Try It Out – Accessing the ISBN Web Service from a ASP.NET page

In this example, we will build the proxy and a simple page for retrieving book titles from our ISBN Web Service, demonstrating how quickly we can have our Web Service applications up and running.

We'll assume that you've already configured the Windows environment variable PATH, so that it includes a directory path to the executable vbc.exe. If not, you should refer to the section "Configuring your Environment Variables" in Chapter 16, where we looked at how to do this.

You'll now need to follow the same process to add a path to another file called `wsdl.exe`. The exact location of this file will depend on how you've installed ASP.NET, and what version you're using. You should be able to find it by searching under the directory `C:\Program Files`. Add the appropriate path to your PATH environment variables (see Chapter 16) and you're ready to proceed.

1. Navigate to the directory in which your ISBN.asmx file resides, and execute this statement:

```
> wsdl /l:vb /o:ISBNProxy.vb http://localhost/5040/ch18/ISBN.asmx?WSDL
/n:ISBNService
```

You should see these results:

```
Microsoft (R) Web Services Description Language Utility
[Microsoft (R) .NET Framework, Version 1.0.2914.11]
Copyright (C) Microsoft Corp. 1998-2001. All rights reserved.

Writing file 'ISBNProxy.vb'.
```

2. Now let's compile our new proxy code – note that this statement must be entered in full on a single line:

```
> vbc /out:ISBNProxy.dll /t:library
/r:system.web.dll,system.dll,system.xml.dll,system.web.services.dll,system.data.dl
l ISBNProxy.vb
```

You should see these results after executing this:

```
Microsoft (R) Visual Basic.NET Compiler version 7.00.9246
for Microsoft (R) .NET CLR version 1.00.2914.11
Copyright (C) Microsoft Corp 2001. All rights reserved.
```

3. We'll need a binaries directory for our proxy DLL, so unless you have one already, navigate to the directory you're using as the application root (if you're following the steps that we suggested earlier in the book, this will be `C:\BegASPNET`), create a folder in it called `bin`, and copy the newly-created `ISBNProxy.dll` over from the original test directory.

Now that we have a proxy class, and we've moved it to the correct position, we're ready to make use of our ISBN Web Service from within an ASP.NET page. We'll call the page `BookInfo.aspx`, and use it to call the web-callable function `BookDetail` in `ISBN.asmx`. By using a proxy, our reference to the function's namespace will appear as if it were a function within the same page.

4. Create the `BookInfo.aspx` file in your test directory, and enter the following code:

```
<%@ Page Language="vb" Debug="true"%>
<%@ Import namespace="ISBNService" %>

<script language="vb" runat="server">
Private Sub RetrieveBook(ByVal sender As System.Object, ByVal e As _
                         System.EventArgs)
  Dim ws As New ISBNService.ISBN()
```

```
    lblBookTitle.Text = ws.BookDetail(txtISBN.Text)
End Sub
</script>

<html>
  <body>
    <form id="Form1" method="post" runat="server">
      <asp:TextBox id="txtISBN" runat="server"></asp:TextBox>
      <asp:Button id="Button1" runat="server" Text="Submit" _
        OnClick="RetrieveBook"></asp:Button><br />
      <asp:Label id="lblBookTitle" runat="server" Width="152px" _
                    Height="23px"></asp:Label>
    </form>
  </body>
</html>
```

5. Save the file and call it up in your browser. Note that it may take a few seconds for the page to appear, since it is compiled the first time it is accessed. Once this has taken place the ASPX page will execute in the browser:

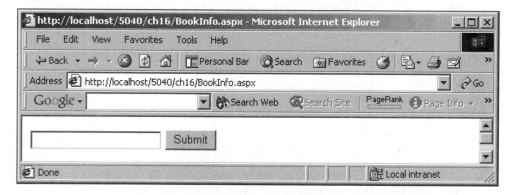

6. Enter an ISBN that we know is in the Books table, such as 1861003129:

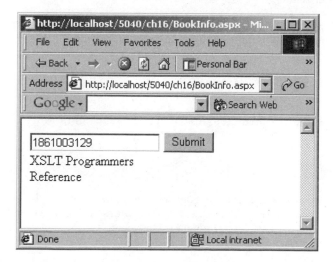

7. Now try an ISBN that you know will not be found, to ensure the proxy is actually working:

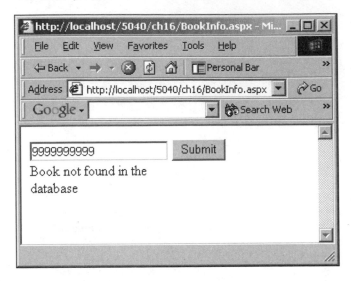

How It Works

When we compiled our proxy to create the `ISBNProxy.dll`, we needed to place it in a `\bin` directory, beneath our application root, as the .NET framework expects to find our DLLs there. We specified this information using the `/out` parameter of the VB compiler, that we ran from the application root:

```
> vbc /out:bin\ISBNProxy.dll /t:library /r:system.web.dll,system.dll,
                         system.xml.dll,system.web.services.dll,
                         system.data.dll ISBNProxy.vb
```

We made use of Web Forms controls on our ASP.NET page. These controls, `<asp:TextBox>`, `<asp:Label>`, and `<asp:Button>`, make up our simple mini-form that makes a very specific call to the `BookDetail` subroutine.

Upon clicking the Submit button, the `RetrieveBook` event fires, as we specified in the OnClick attribute of `<asp:Button>`:

```
<asp:Button id="Button1" runat="server" Text="Submit" _
OnClick="RetrieveBook" /></asp:Button>
```

Within our `RetrieveBook` subroutine, first of all, we create an instance of the proxy that we'll be using:

```
Dim ws As New ISBNService.ISBN()
```

Then it's simply a matter of calling the `BookDetail` function of the `ws` object. With a single line of code, we pass the `String` contents of `txtISBN.text` to the Web Service and receive the book title, placing that `String` into the Label `lblBookTitle.text`:

```
lblBookTitle.Text = ws.BookDetail(txtISBN.Text)
```

Once again, this example proves the simplicity and power of Web Services.

Web Service Discovery

As you begin to build Web Service-integrated applications, it will become increasingly important to locate services that provide the functions you need. Universal Description, Discovery and Integration (UDDI) allows you to do this.

Whenever an industry initiative gains the support of several large industry players, it will likely become mainstream. For this reason, UDDI is positioned to dominate the Web Service discovery field in the future. The UDDI service (http://uddi.microsoft.com) lets businesses register themselves and list their existing Web Services at no charge. Anyone can browse and search the UDDI database for a service that may suit his or her needs. Currently, there are three UDDI implementations, provided by Microsoft, IBM, and Ariba. UDDI provides information, such as contact details (address, phone number, email address, website), business details (DUNS Number and industry sector), and a discovery URL for each service. WSDL is a key component of the UDDI project.

Using http://uddi.microsoft.com/visualstudio/, you can search for businesses that provide Web Services, select the WSDL appropriately, and build your proxies:

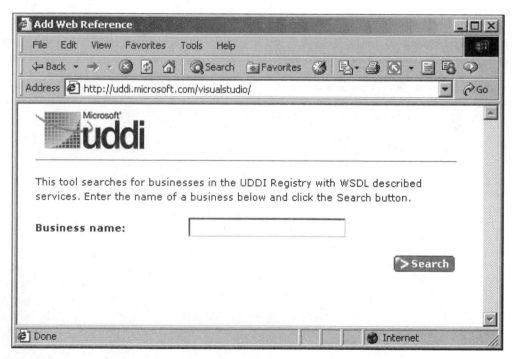

Securing a Web Service

Whether your Web Service is made available on a subscription basis, or is completely free to the public, it is important to consider security. The reasons for securing Web Services can range from simple usage logging to strict access control. If your Web Service provides a very useful feature (of course it will!), it's helpful to keep track of who's using it. While you can log the usage of a Web Service that provides privileged information, more stringent security measures should be taken to make sure that the use of your Web Service is consistent with your purposes.

There are many options for securing web applications and services. Here we'll just discuss some of the most common techniques. These methods are not mutually exclusive, and can be combined to provide a higher level of security.

Username/Password Combination or Registration Keys

By requiring either a username and password pair or a registration key code as an input parameter, you can provide a way to track which consumers are using your Web Service. A simple database table or XML file containing each username/password pair or registration key code is all that's required to provide this kind of security. Considering that no actual authentication of the consumer takes place in this scenario, it is very simple for the client to share the username and password (or registration key) with others. However, when the data provided by the Web Service is not sensitive or proprietary in nature, this security method provides us with a quick and effective option.

Let's examine how we might apply this type of security to our ISBN Web Service.

Try It Out – Securing a Web Service with Username / Password

We will be using the Security database, provided with the code for this book that can be downloaded from www.wrox.com. This contains a very simple Users table consisting of usernames and passwords. Ensure this database is in the same path as the isbn.asmx file we created earlier. All our security will do is attempt to match details from the user with an entry in the Security table.

1. Re-open the ISBN Web Service in Notepad (isbn.asmx), and make the following modifications to the BookDetail web method:

```
<WebMethod ()> _
Public Function BookDetail(ByVal strIsbn As String, _
     ByVal strUsername As String, _
     ByVal strPassword As String) As String
   Dim objSecurityDR As OleDbDataReader
   Dim objSecurityConn As OleDbConnection
   Dim objSecurityCmd As OleDbCommand

   Dim strConn As String = "Provider=Microsoft.Jet.OLEDB.4.0;Data Source="
      strConn += Server.MapPath("Security.mdb") & ";"
   Dim strSQL As String = "select Username from Users where username = '"
      strSQL += strUsername & "' and password = '" & strPassword & "'"

   objSecurityConn = New OleDbConnection(strConn)
   objSecurityCmd = New OleDbCommand(strSQL, objSecurityConn)
   objSecurityConn.Open()
```

```
      objSecurityDR = _
        objSecurityCmd.ExecuteReader(CommandBehavior.CloseConnection)
    If objSecurityDR.Read() Then
        objSecurityDR.Close()
        Return GetBookDetails(strIsbn)
    Else
        objSecurityDR.Close()
        Return "Login to library failed."
    End If
  End Function
  ...
```

2. Save the result as `ISBNSecurity.asmx`.

Notice that we haven't made any changes to `GetBookDetails`. As the core functionality of retrieving the book title from the database hasn't changed. Our goal in this scenario is to provide a gatekeeper that prevents access to the internal logic if the consumer's username and password pair is not found in the database.

Browse to the Web Service to test this newly applied security. The only entry in the security table should have the username librarian and the password secret. This is the only user that is permitted to access our Web Service:

You can add more users by modifying the Security table.

How It Works

We have used nearly the same logic validating the login as we previously used in `GetBookDetails` to look up a book. By adding this logic to the web-callable `BookDetail` function, we completely prevent access to the internal `GetBookDetails` function if the login fails. Upon a failure to login correctly, we return a simple String:

```
    Return "Login to library failed."
```

If the username and password combination is successfully located in the database, the result of the `GetBookDetails` function is returned just as before.

Secure Sockets Layer (SSL)

The most common method of securing information on the Web is the Secure Sockets Layer (SSL). When you make an online purchase, you'll typically see a lock or key icon displayed in the browser's status bar to let you know you're communicating safely. Information passed between the browser and the web site travels in an encrypted form. In the case of Web Services, applying SSL helps ensure that the data traveling between the consumer and endpoint is encrypted, and thus, difficult to intercept.

The beauty of SSL is that it has no affect on the integrity of the data provided by your Web Service. When a value is returned to the consumer it remains the same, regardless of the encryption used in its transportation. The only downside to using SSL is that it does have an effect on the overall performance of your site, as there is more processing required. You can get more information about verifying your identity for use with SSL from a Certificate Authority like Verisign (www.verisign.com).

685

IP Address Restriction

Maintaining an IP address list of all registered users can help us control the use of a Web Service. This approach presents a number of potential issues, the greatest being the never-ending maintenance of IP address ranges for each client. IP address restriction can take place at both hardware and software levels. A hardware application of this security typically involves firewall restrictions to specific IP addresses. Restricting various IP access using software security, often involves keeping a database table of clients and another with associated IP addresses.

Each time a Web Service is accessed, we can get the requestor's IP address and confirm that it exists in the security tables. If a match is located, the Web Service executes normally. Another option for software-based IP-address security is at the web server level. Most web server software permits any number of IP addresses to be restricted or enabled. Within IIS, it's as simple as selecting the properties of a given site and changing the IP restrictions. Since maintaining IP addresses of clients can be terribly cumbersome, as well as overly restrictive (if a consumer's IP address changes frequently), this option is generally not recommended.

Other Considerations

Web Services are bringing about a major paradigm shift, not seen since the early days of the Internet. Because of this, it's very important to recognize that these new conveniences have their own set of advantages and disadvantages. While we won't talk about all the ways to avoid these pitfalls (which would require a book in itself), we will consider some of key issues.

Network Connectivity

A few years ago, the idea of calling a remote function and retrieving a value from it seemed remote. Now that we have Web Services this newfound ability to use, or purchase, a given function from any organization on the Web causes us to think about the issue of Internet connectivity. It's important to realize that not only must your company's Internet connection be reliable, but now we must rely on your Web Service provider's connection to be reliable as well. Furthermore, if a Web Service requires any additional Internet resources, their service vendor's network must also be stable. There are many potential failure points in this arrangement. Often, this can be compounded if a Web Service provider hesitates, or refuses, to disclose who their providers are, since they don't want you going direct to them!

Asynchronous Method Calls

Since SOAP can be transported using SMTP (the email protocol), we can write Web Services that make use of asynchronous method calls. Asynchronous communication is a sort of disconnected, two-way interaction that doesn't require an immediate response. Most programming deals with synchronous communication, where you call a function and wait for it to complete and return a value:

```
Distance_To_Rome = DistanceBetween("Los Angeles", "Rome", "meters")
```

In a situation like this, our application will not continue until the DistanceBetween function completes its logic and returns a value, which is placed in Distance_To_Rome. While this suits our needs most of the time, it is not always appropriate, especially when dealing with web programming. Batch processing, application speed, and anticipated disconnections are three situations where we may wish to consider the possible advantages of asynchronous communication.

The following Visual Basic code snippet illustrates how we might implement asynchronous function calls, using events:

```
...
DistanceBetween("Los Angeles", "Rome", "meters")
...
Private Sub DistanceBetween_CalculationComplete(ByVal Distance as Integer)
  Distance_To_Rome = Distance
End Sub
...
```

If our application contains code such as this, we will issue a request to `DistanceBetween` to calculate the distance between two cites, and then move on with our code. When the `DistanceBetween` object completes its calculation, it fires the `CalculationComplete` event, which allows us to handle the returned value, without making the rest of the application wait.

Because we can call a remote function without the need for immediate response (without breaking an application), our applications can support longer time intervals and handle poorer network conditions, such as dial-up situations. In the case of SMTP, the SOAP request is packaged in an e-mail format and delivered to a mailbox on the server, just as if it was an email composed and addressed to another individual. The specification for SOAP over SMTP defines a process of retrieving this message from the mail server, executing the function required, and mailing the SOAP results again to the consumer, again using SMTP.

Service Hijacking (or Piggybacking)

Once your Web Service is available to the public, you may attract a client who is particularly interested in the service you provide. They're so interested, in fact, that they consider wrapping your powerful Web Service inside of their own and representing it as their own product. Without security safeguards in place (and legal documents as well), a client may repackage your Web Service as if it were their own function, and there's no way for you to detect that this is being done (though you may become suspicious by examining your usage log when your client who occasionally uses your Web Service suddenly shows an enormous increase in activity). Given the level of abstraction that Web Services provide, it would also be nearly impossible for any customers of your unethical client to know who really owns the functionality.

Some organizations use a combination of usage logging or per-use charges. In my opinion, a cleverer way to avoid piggybacking is by using false data tests. We could create an undocumented function within our Web Service that creates a result that only our logic could produce. We would able to determine whether this code is really ours and the client is piggybacking our Web Service or if client is truly using its own logic. An example of implementing a false data test would be a Web Service that provides book information for a given ISBN. As in our ISBN Web Service, we may return some arbitrary details if a certain ISBN is provided and is not associated with a real book. If ISBN "ABCDEFGHI" were entered, special codes or copyright information could be sent as the resulting book title. We could then test this on the piggybacking company we suspect is stealing our web service. Since this hidden functionality would not be published, it would provide a great way to prove that a company was reselling your Web Service's logic without your legal approval.

Provider Solvency

Since the Web Service model is a viable solution, you're probably eager to add their functionality to your core information systems and mission-critical applications. As Web Services become more and more interdependent, it becomes increasingly necessary to research the companies from whom you consume Web Services. You'll want to make sure these providers appear to have what it takes to remain in business. UDDI goes a long way towards helping you with this research by providing company information for each registered Web Service provider (including their DUNS number). In the business world, nothing seems to impact and force sweeping changes more than insolvency, and if you find yourself in the unfortunate circumstance of lost functionality due to a bankrupt Web Service provider, you'll realize how painful the hurried search for a new vendor can be (with little room to bargain with your ex-service's competitors). Although the initial work can be a bit tedious, it is important to know, as far as you can, whether a potential Web Service vendor will still be in business five years from now.

The Interdependency Scenario

The basis for all these and other Web Service considerations is the issue of **interdependency**. The potential exists for you to wake up any given morning, start an application that has worked for years, and find that the Web Service that it relies on is no longer available.

To some extent, thanks to the UDDI search capabilities, you can investigate and assess potential providers, but at the end of the day a degree of faith needs to be put into the services of each provider you choose to consume.

Summary

In this chapter, we've seen that a Web Service exposes its functions as a service that other applications can use. We began by discussing what a Web Service is and how one might be used. We recapped XML and HTTP and their use within the Web Services architecture. Then we delved into the process of building Web Services, and creating and compiling a Web Service proxy. We learned how to use Web Services in an application by incorporating a defined namespace and making use of its methods. Afterwards, we covered how to discover what Web Services we have available to consume. Finally, we considered some of the ways to make a Web Service secure.

As .NET makes programmatic interfaces over the Web more commonplace, we'll gradually be able to see applications sharing and building upon the contributions made by the community of Web Service providers. Web Services will provide a powerful means of seamlessly assembling applications that can span multiple platforms and languages. For the user, a transition is on the horizon from the browser to the more specific applications that make use of Web Services. For the developer, ASP.NET Web Services will make the Internet a programmer's toolbox, with a greater assortment of tools than ever before.

Exercises

1.

    a.   Explain the role of the Simple Object Access Protocol (SOAP) in web services.

    b.   What is the purpose of the WSDL?

    c.   How would you locate a web service that provides the functions you require?

2. Create a Web Service with a class name of `circles` that calculates the area of a circle, the circumference of a circle and the volume of a sphere. (Area = (Pi) r^2; Circumference = 2(Pi)r; Volume of a sphere = 4/3 (Pi)r^3

3. Create a Web Service that connects to the Northwind database and returns Employee's addresses based on their last names.

4. Create an ASP.NET page containing a dropdown listbox in which a user can select names of Northwind employees to return their addresses.

5. Secure the Northwind employee Addresses Web Service so that no unauthorized users have access to it.

Configuration and Optimization

Throughout the course of this book, we've been producing ASP.NET pages that solve a variety of problems. We've looked at basic programming constructs, objects, working with data, and so on. and with each example we've produced, we've examined various ways of producing those results. In this chapter, we'll be looking at how we can improve this process by increasing the performance of our pages through configuration, and through general optimization techniques. We'll also look at other aspects of optimization to improve security, user-friendliness, and to make it easier to debug and manage applications. In particular, we'll look at:

❑ The structure and function of the ASP.NET configuration files, `machine.config` and `web.config`

❑ Customization of areas of those files to increase performance, security, and usability

❑ How to use caching to increase the performance of your server

❑ The use of tracing to debug your code without inserting additional code into it

❑ How to monitor the resources your application is taking up, and gather basic statistics about its operation

This chapter covers some fairly advanced ground, so we'll not be looking at these issues in too much detail, but hopefully we'll set you on the right path to a well-configured and highly-optimized ASP.NET site.

> *If you want to learn more about the advanced topics presented in this chapter, you might want to refer to Professional ASP.NET, Wrox Press ISBN: 1-861004-88-5*

Configuration Overview

ASP.NET has been designed to be easily customizable by adopting XML-based configuration files. These files can be used to configure any component of ASP.NET by editing the file in a text editor. You simply write a piece of code to explain how you'd like ASP.NET to perform a certain operation, and then configure it to run your code instead of its built-in code.

You're not restricted to just defining configuration settings at design- or run-time, either. You can add or change them at any time without any real negative impact on your web server. The new configuration settings you have supplied will simply be activated, with no loss of efficiency for the server.

In this chapter, we're going to be looking at two types of configuration file:

- ❑ The Machine Configuration File – `machine.config` – for machine-wide settings
- ❑ Application Configuration Files – `web.config` – for application specific settings

> *There are a couple more types supported by the .NET framework. These are security configuration files (`enterprisesec.config` and `security.config`). That deal with the tiers of security policy. We won't be covering these here since it's outside the scope of this book.*

Let's take a look at how we can view these configuration files using Internet Explorer.

Browsing .config files

We can easily look at the settings contained in a configuration file using a text editor, because all of the settings are stored as plain text. However, if we open these files in Internet Explorer, you get the ability to expand or collapse nodes on the tree to make a large file more readable. Let's take a look at the `machine.config` file. You can find this at the following location:

```
%SystemRoot%\Microsoft.NET\Framework\v1.0.2914\CONFIG\machine.config
```

If you copy this file and save it as `machine.config.xml` anywhere on your system, then open it up in your browser, you'll see your `machine.config` file displayed in the same way as an XML document.

> **Important note – don't rename the original `machine.config` – ASP.NET relies on this file for its configuration, and it will not run properly without this.**

When your browser loads, you will see small "+" and "-" signs in front of every XML element in the file. These allow you to expand and collapse the hierarchical structure of the XML-based configuration file. This interface makes looking for elements within the file much easier. For example, if you collapse every element in `machine.config` except `<configuration>`, you'll get a graphical display of the basic elements:

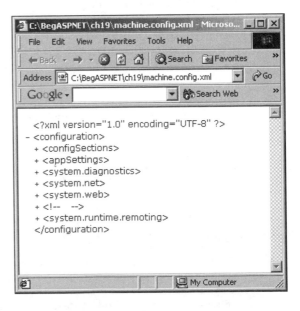

The Configuration Files

We'll be examining two configuration files in this chapter, namely `machine.config` and `web.config`. Your system will probably have one file called `machine.config` on it, and many `web.config` files. `machine.config` contains any machine-specific settings that ASP.NET needs to function, whereas `web.config` contains configuration information for a specific web application, and can override default functionality defined in the base `machine.config` file to provide a customized environment for each application that you produce.

When the page is initialized, the information in `machine.config` is read. Once this has been done, ASP.NET descends to the next level of the hierarchy and reads the individual `web.config` files stored in your web application root directories. These files supply additional configuration information to augment, or override, settings inherited from `machine.config`. Then, ASP.NET will descend to the next level and read `web.config` files stored in your application's child directories below the root. These will be used to augment or override information given either in `machine.config`, or in the root `web.config`. Next, any `web.config` files in child directories below them will be read and acted on in a similar manner. This will continue until all `web.config` files in the tree have been processed. Some of your directories will not have a `web.config` file – in this case, they will inherit their settings from the closest configuration file node in the tree above them.

This can be seen more clearly by looking at the following diagram, of the virtual directories in IIS:

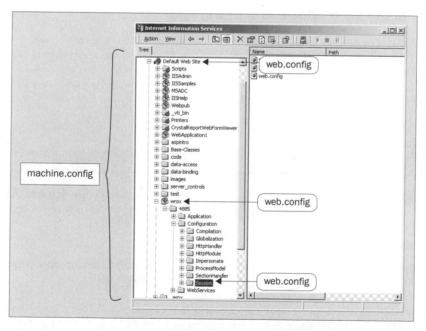

A well-structured setup would store general settings you want taken into account at a machine-wide level in the `machine.config` file, and then override them, when necessary, using `web.config` files specific to the application page or pages that need to do so. This approach is beneficial, as if changes need to be made to the general structure of your application you only need to make alterations to the one `machine.config` file. Likewise, if an individual page needs special settings to function, it can be placed in a child directory with its own `web.config` file, and any changes you make there will affect just that page, and not your whole application or machine.

At runtime, ASP.NET uses the information provided by the configuration files to compute the configuration settings for each application or URL resource. The settings are then cached (see later in the chapter) to allow faster access on subsequent calls. ASP.NET can detect changes made to the configuration files while the web server is running, and will apply the altered version immediately without needing to have the server stopped or rebooted.

ASP.NET protects configuration files from unauthorized snooping by configuring IIS to prevent HTTP access to them. A server error will be returned if any attempt is made to browse these files over HTTP, even if the file does not exist. You can try this for yourself by directing your browser to http://localhost/web.config, where you should get the following message:

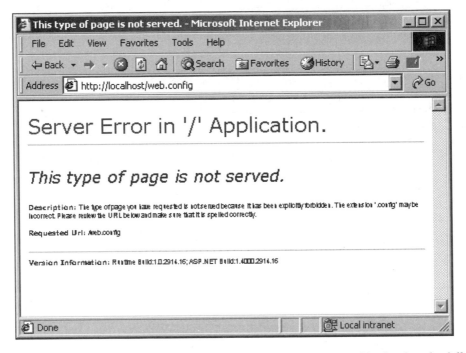

You'll get this same result if you try to browse to global.asax, or any file that has the following extensions: .ascx, .cs, .csproj, .vb, .vbproj, and .webinfo, as they're set up the same way.

Configuration File Rules

We've already mentioned that our configuration files are XML-based files, so now we're going to recap what that means, and how it applies to the well-formedness of these files:

❑ They must have a single unique **root element** that encloses all other elements within it. The root element for both machine.config and web.config is <configuration>.

❑ The elements must be enclosed between corresponding start <start> and end </start> tags. These tags are case-sensitive so <Start> and <start> will be treated differently.

❑ Any attributes, keys or values must be enclosed in double quotes: <add key="data" />.

❑ Elements must be nested and not overlap.

For more information on XML files, see Chapter 7

> **Be very careful when you're editing configuration files, as they affect your server's behavior.**

Configuration File Format

Now that we've refreshed our memory about the basic XML rules that apply to configuration files, we're going to look at the way that these files are structured.

This XML-based structure is most noticeable in `machine.config` where all of the XML elements are declared, and their values set. web.config is usually smaller and only contains a settings section as it is altering elements declared in machine.config, but its XML structure is just as marked.

The configuration files are structurally divided into two main areas. First, there is a **declarations** section, where individual classes are defined to manipulate information. This section is delimited by `<configSections>` tags. Second, there is the **settings** section where values are assigned to the classes declared in the first section. This is delimited by `<sectionSettings>` tags.

It's the `<sectionSettings>` section that we put into `web.config` files to override the values of classes defined in the `machine.config` declarations section. Within these two main groups, there are several subgroups to divide the information up into manageable chunks. The only one that we need to worry about is the `system.web` group, as this is the ASP.NET specific material.

Here's a screenshot of the declarations section, with the `system.web` group expanded:

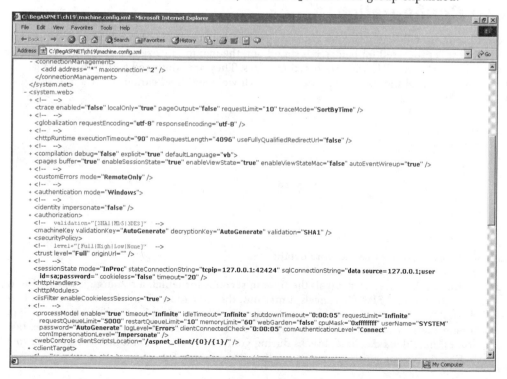

After all the declarations have been made, we move on to the settings section. Here we are establishing the attributes and properties of the declared classes. You don't have to define the settings for elements in the same order that you declared them in the <configSections> tags. You must define settings for every handler you have declared, or an exception will be thrown. You must also take care to ensure that the tags are properly closed and nested, and that any values specified fall into the correct range.

You should note that there is a great deal more structure and detail in these files than we've covered here. Our aim has been to give you a general idea of what these files are and what they look like, so that when we move on to the next section you'll be able to find your way around and tune your system.

The Structure of the Configuration Files

If you look at your machine's machine.config file, you'll see that its declarations and settings are broken up into about 30 blocks of configurations. We're now going to have a quick overview of four of the most useful of these, and point out some of the simple alterations that you might like to make to improve the functioning of your machine.

> **Note all these changes take place in the *settings* section**

General Configuration

This section of our configuration files contains general application configuration settings, such as how long a request is processed for before it is timed out, the maximum size of a request, and whether or not to use a fully qualified URL when re-directing pages. They are contained within the <httpRuntime> tags, and occur within the <system.web> tags, that we mentioned earlier. Here's how you'd set it up in your web.config file:

```
<configuration>
 <system.web>
  <httpRuntime executionTimeout="120"
   maxRequestLength="8192"
   useFullyQualifiedRedirectUrl="false"
  />
 </system.web>
</configuration>
```

Let's look at these settings in a bit more detail:

❑ executionTimeout controls the time in seconds for which a resource is allowed to try to execute before ASP.NET cancels (times out) the execution of the request. 90 seconds is the default value. If you know that a certain process (like a complex database query) will take longer than 90 seconds to execute, increase this value. This is a very useful feature, because if something, like a database, breaks during your code's execution it knows how long to wait before delivering an error message, rather than waiting forever.

❑ `maxRequestLength` specifies the maximum length of a request. 4MB is the default value. If the content requested is larger than 4MB, increase this value. If the content requested never exceeds a lesser value, use that instead. This can be a useful precaution. If your code breaks it will prevent it from dumping great quantities of data to your client, as it will stop when it hits `maxRequestLength`. Also it stops clients trying to request too much information at once and hogging your server's processing time dealing with their requests at the expense of other users.

❑ `useFullyQualifiedRedirectUrl` is not often used. One example of when you need to use this parameter is when you are working with some mobile controls. It indicates whether client-side redirects are fully-qualified, or whether relative redirects are used (which is the default). Certain mobile controls require that you use fully-qualified redirects.

Page Configuration

The page configuration settings give us control over the default behavior of ASP.NET pages. This can include things, such as whether we should buffer output before sending it, and whether or not Session state is enabled for pages within your application. This information is housed within the `<pages>` element in your configuration files. Here's how you'd set it up in your `web.config` file. All values are set to their defaults:

```
<configuration>
  <system.web>
  <pages buffer="true"
  enableSessionState="true"
  enableViewState="true"
  autoEventWireup="true" />
  </system.web>
</configuration>
```

Let's take a closer look at what these settings do:

❑ `buffer` indicates the code execution processing mode. When it is set to `true`, all code is executed before any HTML data in the page is rendered. When it is set to `false`, all code is rendered as it executes. For example, you can turn off buffering if you're running a complex data query that returns results with a slight delay between each record – you could display a table line by line on the page while the page is loading, so that the user is aware of the fact that something is happening.

❑ `EnableSessionState` indicates whether server session variables are available. The default value is `true`, enabling session state. To disable it set the value to `false`. We recommend that you set it to `true`, only if you need to use session variables in your page, as disabling session state improves performance.

❑ `EnableViewState` indicates whether server controls maintain state when the page request ends. When it is set to `true` the Server controls maintain state ("remember" their value); this is the default setting. If it is set to `false`, the server controls don't maintain state (don't "remember" their value). Set it to `true` only if you need controls to maintain state, as again, disabling it improves performance.

❑ `AutoEventWireup` indicates whether ASP.NET fires Page Events, like `Page_Load`, automatically or not. `True` is the default setting for ASP.NET. Changing it to `false` allows custom assemblies to control the firing of Page events.

*False is the default setting for the Visual Studio.NET IDE, since it uses an internal mechanism to control event firing. If you are **not** using VS.NET you must leave it at the default* True.

Application Settings

Application settings allow us to store application configuration details in the configuration files without the need to write our own custom section handlers for them. The key/value pairs declared here are used to populate a table that we can access from within our application. This is a benefit, because configuration files cannot be read over HTTP so it keeps your database connection strings, and so on. away from prying eyes. Here's how you'd set it up in web.config:

```
<configuration>
 <appSettings>
 <add key= "DSN"
  value="server=LSERV; uid=user; pwd=password; database=data" />
 </appSettings>
</configuration>
```

Here a key called "DSN" is being added to the table, and the values in the value section are being associated with it. We will be able to access this information from inside our application. This is done in your ASP.NET script as follows:

```
...
strDataSource = ConfigurationSettings.AppSettings("DSN")
...
```

Custom Errors

While every developer does their best to ensure that pages are thoroughly tested before they are deployed in a full application, errors still happen. When a page has errors that are caught during its compilation by a .NET framework compiler (remember that ASP.NET pages are compiled) ASP.NET generates a syntax error report with information about the error, and sends this information to the browser. On the other hand, if an error occurs while a page is being executed, ASP.NET sends a **Stack Trace** containing information about the error to the browser, which contains information about what it was doing when the error occurred. While this is convenient for us to debug our code, it's not something you want visitors to your site to see, not least because it can reveal detailed information on how our code works, potentially allowing malicious types to find loopholes and exploit them. That aside, we don't want this information to be displayed for our users because this "raw" information is going to disconcert them and bring the quality of our coding into question. Far better for us to make some changes to the way our application handles errors, so the user can be redirected to elsewhere on our site.

You can configure custom error pages for your application using the <customErrors> section of your web.config file, inside the <system.web> tags:

```
<customErrors
  defaultRedirect="url"
  mode="On|Off|RemoteOnly">
  <error statusCode="statuscode" redirect="url"/>
</customErrors>
```

❑ defaultRedirect indicates the default URL to redirect the browser to if an error occurs. This allows your application to recover if a page fails and send your users elsewhere, rather than confront them with a broken page and no links to move on.

❑ mode configures whether custom errors are On, Off, or RemoteOnly. On shows your custom error to everyone when it occurs, regardless of where they are. Off never shows anyone a custom error, and RemoteOnly only shows your custom error to a browser that is not located on your server. You'll need to set this to On in order to test your custom error pages (unless you've access to a browser off the server) after that we recommend you change it to RemoteOnly so your users will see the custom error page and you'll still get the standard error page with all the useful debugging information that it contains.

❑ error subtags can appear as often as required through your custom error element. They are used to define special conditions above and beyond the default re-direct we set up with the defaultRedirect value. They are given an HTTP status code to react to and an URL to redirect to if that status code occurs. This gives you the flexibility to react to different errors differently. For example reacting to 404 Page Not Found, and 403 Access Forbidden errors differently.

The default customErrors configuration option for ASP.NET is RemoteOnly, which means that custom errors are only shown on browsers not located on the server. However no redirect page is specified in the defaults, so the redirection won't work until you set it up in web.config, something like this:

```
<configuration>
<system.web>
  <customerrors
    defaultRedirect = "customerror.aspx"
    mode = "RemoteOnly"
  />
</system.web>
</configuration>
```

Performance Optimization

Some of the options we've just looked at in the previous section are used to improve your system's security (like, for example, using configuration files to house database connection strings), others are for user friendliness (creating customized error pages). But some are simply used to improve the speed at which your ASP.NET applications perform (enabling page buffering, while disabling session state will speed up your pages). Now we're going to look at other ways we can make your application perform faster.

Caching

If you're working on your home PC, and it's connected to the internet via a modem, when you browse a web page for the first time, you may find that the page takes a while to load. Subsequent visits to that page may well be a lot quicker, because the page has been cached on your machine. In a similar way, if one person on a corporate network visits a website, the page may take a while to load. If someone else visits the same page, depending on the settings on the network, they may find that page a lot more quickly, because it has been cached by a network proxy. This method is also used by ASP.NET to cache frequently-used portions of ASP.NET pages on the web server so they don't need to be compiled every time a page is accessed.

However, you probably don't want certain items to be cached indefinitely – for example, if you're running a news site, you want the content on your site to be refreshed at regular intervals to display any new news items. Depending on the nature of your news, you might want it to refresh every half an hour, ten minutes, or even every minute. Any requests that get served during the cached period see the same page, but after the cache duration expires, the old cache is destroyed, and a new page is generated with the updated content. Simply checking for the absence of the item in the cache causes the recreation of the data in the cache. This content is then cached for the required duration and the cycle starts again.

Setting the appropriate time period is of maximum importance. A list of cities and/or zip codes might not need a short expiration period. A list of clients, or a product list, will need regular refreshing over relatively short periods of time. Keep in mind that anything you place in the cache consumes memory, so use the caching feature judiciously.

Output Caching

Output Caching allows caching of any response generated by any request for any application resource. Output caching is very useful when you want to cache the contents of an entire page. On a busy site, caching frequently-accessed pages for even as little as a minute can result in substantial performance gains. While the page lives in the output cache, additional requests for that page are served from the cache without executing and recompiling the code that created the page.

The complete syntax for the Output Cache is this:

```
<%@ OutputCache Duration="#ofseconds" Location="Any | Client |
    Downstream | Server | None" VaryByControl="controlname"
    VaryByCustom="browser | customstring" VaryByHeader="headers"
    VaryByParam="parametername" %>
```

Let's look at some of the most important parameters in more detail:

- ❑ Duration specifies the duration in seconds that the content is allowed to be cached.

- ❑ Location is used to specify which locations are allowed to cache the page. When set to "Server", only the server running the application is allowed to cache the page. A setting of "Downstream" means that any intervening network proxies are allowed to cache a copy of the page. When set to "Client", the browser is allowed to cache the page locally. When set to "Any", any of these caches may be used. Alternatively you could specify a setting of "None", which stops caching from being used.

- ❑ VaryByControl allows controls to be cached on the server, so that they do not have to be rendered every time a page is requested. Using this parameter caches the control specified as it appears on the page. For example, if you have a control that displays a list of news items, these could be cached for ten minutes, simply by caching the control for that long.

- ❑ VaryByCustom allows you to specify whether you want to store different versions of the cache for different browser, or to vary by a specified string. If this parameter is given the value "browser", different caches are created by browser name and major version, which allows you to have different cached versions of a page for different pages. This is particularly useful for when you need to target output differently for different browsers or different devices. It allows you to specify in detail the parts of a page that you want to cache.

❏ `VaryByHeader` enables us to cache pages specified by different HTTP headers, using a semicolon-separated list. When this parameter is set to multiple headers, the output cache will contain a different version of the requested document for each specified header.

❏ `VaryByParam` allows you to vary the caching requirements by specific parameters in the form of a semicolon-separated list of strings. By default, these strings correspond to a query string value, or to a parameter sent with the POST method. When this parameter is set to multiple values, the output cache will contain a different version of the requested document for each specified value. Possible values include "none", "*", and any valid query string or POST parameter name.

This attribute is required when you Output cache ASP.NET pages and/or user controls. A parser error will occur if you don't include it. If you do not want to specify a value to vary cached content by, for example, if you want the complete page cached at all times, set the value to "none". If you want to have a different output cache for all possible parameters, set the value to "*".

Let's have a look at how this works in a quick example.

Try It Out – Output Caching

1. Create an ASPX file containing the following code, and call it `ServerTime.aspx`:

```
<script  runat = "server">
Function ServerTime() As String
  ServerTime = System.DateTime.Now.ToLongTimeString()
End Function
</script>


The time on your web server is : <%=ServerTime %>
```

This code displays the current time on your web server. Call it up in your browser, and verify that the code is working. After a couple of seconds, click your browser's refresh button, and watch the numbers change.

2. Now add the following page directive at the top of your code:

```
<%@ OutputCache Duration="60" VaryByParam="none" %>
<script  runat = "server">
Function ServerTime() As String
  ServerTime = System.DateTime.Now.ToLongTimeString()
End Function
</script>


The time on your web server is : <%=ServerTime %>
```

3. Save your code as `CachedServerTime.aspx`, and call it up in your browser again. To begin with everything looks the same, the code displays the time as before, but when you click the refresh button the time doesn't change, it remains the same. In fact, it will remain the same for 60 seconds. Try it and see!

How It Works

Our `ServerTime.aspx` code example is very simple. It runs a function called `ServerTime()` on your server to get the server's time, and then returns it formatted as a string. This returned information is then displayed to the screen using a line of HTML and some in-line ASP.NET tags;

```
<script runat = "server">
Function ServerTime() As String
   ServerTime = System.DateTime.Now.ToLongTimeString()
End Function
</script>

The time on your web server is : <%=ServerTime %>
```

This code does not specify that it should be cached, so the server processes it anew each time that the page is called. So, when you click the browser's refresh button, it processes the code, and gives you the newly-processed result, so the time changes each time as you press the refresh button.

When the page directive is added this is no longer the case:

```
<%@ OutputCache Duration="60" VaryByParam="none" %>
```

We're instructing the server to cache the output generated by our request for a period of 60 seconds. Any subsequent page requests within that period will be served with the cached version, so the time will remain the same until the cached page expires and it is processed anew. The `VaryByParam` attribute which we saw earlier is set to "none" in this example, meaning that the same page will be delivered from the cache regardless of the parameters delivered with the request (although our example is quite basic, and as a result, it doesn't have any parameters).

Fragment Caching

This allows the caching of portions of a response generated by any request that includes user controls. Sometimes it's not practical to cache an entire page, (for example, if you've got a section for advertisements on a page, or some personalization features that have to be unique to every user). In cases such as these, you may still want portions of the page to be cached, and the remainder to be generated programmatically for each user. If this is the case, it is worthwhile to create user controls frequently for those portions that do not change, so that they can be created once and cached for a defined time period.

For example, to cache all the controls defined in an ASCX (user control) source file, just include this directive in the control itself:

```
<%@ OutputCache Duration="60" VaryByParam="none" %>
```

You don't have to place the `OutputCache` directive in the page in which the controls are called (the ASPX page). All other controls included in the ASCX will automatically be cached for 60 seconds.

If you wanted to cache each of the possible variations of your control's properties, you'd use this directive:

```
<%@ OutputCache Duration="60" VaryByParam="*" %>
```

The asterisk directs the Output Cache to cache a page for every parameter property returned by your control.

Tracing

Tracing is a very useful feature of ASP.NET that lets us follow the execution of our code, and then review it afterwards. This can help us tighten up loose coding and fix bugs. Throughout this book, when we've written code we've traditionally used either `Response.Write` or an ASP.NET `<label>` tag to print information to the screen. They're good as far as they go, but when we use them to debug our code, we're introducing additional code into our program. This is not a good thing to do, as it is often very hard to get this additional code back out again when we want to deploy our application, and it can affect the sequence of operation, meaning you have to adjust your code to accommodate them. Fortunately the `Trace.Write()` object gives us a way of avoid inserting additional code into our applications:

```
Let's explain this with an example.
```

Try It Out – Tracing

1. Here's some code that needs debugging. Call it `TraceCode.aspx`, and save it in your Ch19 directory within your `c:\begaspnet` directory:

```
<script runat = "server">
Public Function Subtract( intFirst As Integer, intSecond As Integer) & _
                                                        As Integer
 return intFirst - intSecond
End Function
</script>

The value of 45 minus 30 is : <%=Subtract(45, 30) %>
```

2. Run this code, to verify it's working, and you'll get this output:

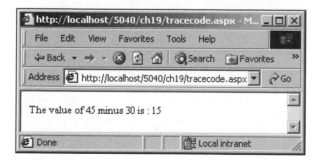

3. Now make the following changes to the code, and save it again:

```
<%@ Page trace= "true" %>
<script runat = "server">
```

```
Public Function Subtract( intFirst As Integer, intSecond As Integer) & _
                                                    As Integer


Trace.Write( " intFirst : ", intFirst)
Trace.Write("intSecond : ", intSecond)
 return intFirst - intSecond
End Function
</script>


The value of 45 minus 30 is : <%=Subtract(45, 30) %>
```

4. When you run it, the output now looks like this:

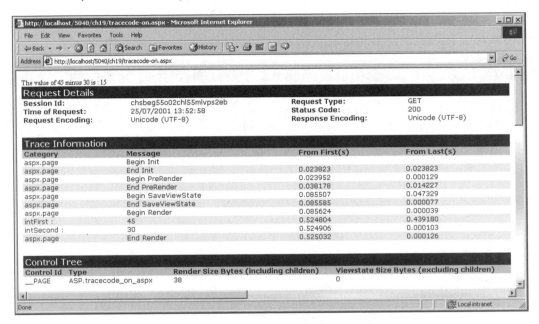

Our page is still at the top, but beneath it a large amount of Trace information is shown, including the values of our variables in the Trace Information section:

How It Works

The code we're using is very simple. We're displaying the returned value of a function that is being fed two values, 45 and 30:

```
<script runat = "server">
Public Function Subtract( intFirst As Integer, intSecond As Integer) & _
                                                    As Integer

 return intFirst - intSecond
End Function
</script>


The value of 45 minus 30 is : <%=Subtract(45, 30) %>
```

To trace the sequence of execution, and the values being used in our code we're adding to Trace.Write statements and a page directive to activate them:

```
<%@ Page trace= "true" %>
<script runat = "server">
Public Function Subtract( intFirst As Integer, intSecond As Integer) & _
                                                    As Integer


Trace.Write( " intFirst : ", intFirst)
Trace.Write("intSecond : ", intSecond)
 return intFirst - intSecond
End Function
</script>


The value of 45 minus 30 is : <%=Subtract(45, 30) %>
```

This provides the following information, as we saw previously:

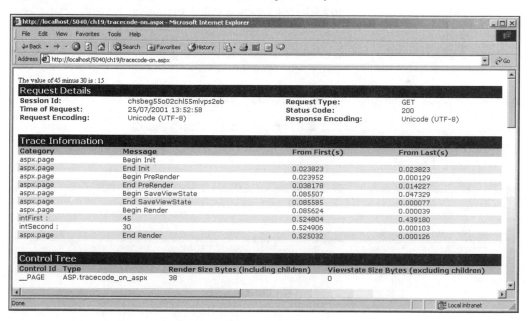

It is the **Trace Information** Section that is of interest to us. It outlines the order in which our page's functionality has been executed. It shows that before getting to our code, and rendering it, a number of other ASP.NET native procedures have been run, including a **PreRender**, and a **SaveViewState** function. We're not using state information in our page, so we might want to think about turning the viewstate function off, as we explained earlier in the chapter to save resources and speed up our code. The trace also confirms, as expected, that our function is using the values we gave it, 45 and 30, for its calculations.

Trace can also be setup in your `web.config` files with code like this:

```
<configuration>
 <system.web>
  <trace
    enabled="true"
    requestLimit = "10"
    pageOutput="false"
    traceMode="SortByTime"
    localOnly = "true"
  />
 </system.web>
</configuration>
```

When we set tracing up in this way (the default value for trace, inherited from machine.config, is false) we can view our trace output using a special tool called trace.axd. This file is a log file that can be used to store the trace results for the last page viewed. This can be called from your browser in the directory for which you have enabled tracing. This method is useful if you don't want to display the actual trace information at the bottom of your page, and want to keep a record of this trace information in a separate file, which is overwritten each time a page is called. Setting the pageOutput directive back to true appends this information back to the bottom of your page.

You can try this out by adding this information to the web.config file in your application root, and then run both your ASPX file and trace.axd from this location.

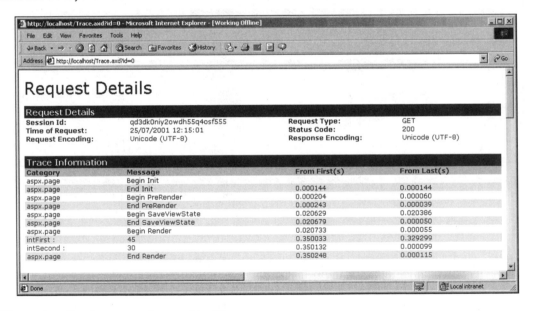

The options for the your web.config file are:

❑ enabled switches tracing on or off at the application level. When it is switched off, you can still set traces for individual pages using the page directive. By default, this is set to False in machine.config.

❑ requestLimit is the total number of trace requests to keep for later viewing with trace.axd. By default, this is set to ten.

❑ `pageOutput` allows you to decide whether you want trace information displaying on every page, as well as being available through `trace.axd`. When it is set to `true`, the tracing information will be added to every page. By default it is set to `false`.

❑ `traceMode` allows you to specify if the trace information is sorted by time or by category. If you sort by category, it will be group information based on the system and `Trace.Write()` settings. By default, this is set to `SortByTime`.

❑ `localOnly` specifies that only requests made through http://localhost/ will be allowed to see the trace information. By default it is set to `true`. This stops your users from viewing your trace information, while letting you view exactly what's going on at the same time.

You can embed `trace.write` statements in your code, while you're debugging your pages to provide useful information when you view a trace on the page. If you turn tracing off on the page, these statements get hidden, and do not need to be removed, because they do not affect the final page output. However, if you find that your application isn't actually performing as it should at a later date, all you need to do is re-enable tracing, and these statements will be used again.

Monitoring the ASP.NET Process

It's always good, especially when you're testing an application, to be able to monitor what the application is doing. Information such as how long the application has been running, how much memory it's using, how many requests it has served, and so on, provide a good insight into how your server is holding up to the demands placed on it by browser requests.

The `ProcessModelInfo` class allows us to monitor part of the ASP.NET process online.

Try-It-Out – Using ProcessModelInfo

1. Save the following code as `ProcessInfo.aspx`, and run it:

```
<html>
<head>
<title>ASP.NET Process Info</title>
</head>
<body>
<script language="VB" runat=server>
Sub Page_Load(sender As Object, e As EventArgs)
Dim history As ProcessInfo() = ProcessModelInfo.GetHistory(10)
Dim i As Integer
 For i = 0 To history.Length -1
   Response.Write ("<table border>")
   Response.Write("<tr><td>ASP.NET Process Start Date and Time<td>" _
   & history(i).StartTime.ToString())
   Response.Write("<tr><td>Process Age ( HH:MM:SS:LongDecimal )<td>" _
   & history(i).Age.ToString())
   Response.Write("<tr><td>Process ID ( The same as in Task Manager )<td>" _
                                     & history(i).ProcessID.ToString())
   Response.Write("<tr><td>Total Request Count (Requests served since" & _
                "the process started)<TD>" _
                & history(i).RequestCount.ToString())
   Response.Write("<tr><td>Peak Memory Used ( KB ) <td>" _
```

```
                        & history(i).PeakMemoryUsed.ToString())
    Response.Write("</table>")
 Next
End Sub
</script>
</body>
</html>
```

2. You should see something like this:

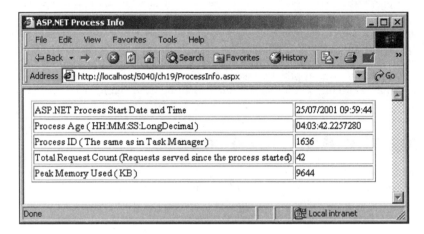

How It Works

The information that we're using here is made available through the GetHistory method of the ProcessModelInfo class. This has several properties, StartTime, Age, ProcessID, RequestCount, and PeakMemoryUsed, which we are displaying in our example. We're placing this information into our history variable here:

```
<html>
<head>
<title>ASP.NET Process Info</title>
</head>
<body>
<script language="VB" runat=server>
Sub Page_Load(sender As Object, e As EventArgs)
Dim history As ProcessInfo() = ProcessModelInfo.GetHistory(10)
Dim i As Integer
```

The number of entries in our table is defined by a For...Next loop that continues for as many items as there are in our history variable. The table itself is constructed using HTML tags:

```
For i = 0 To history.Length -1
  Response.Write ("<table border>")
  Response.Write("<tr><td>ASP.NET Process Start Date and Time<td>" _
  & history(i).StartTime.ToString())
  Response.Write("<tr><td>Process Age ( HH:MM:SS:LongDecimal )<td>" _
```

```
             & history(i).Age.ToString())
      Response.Write("<tr><td>Process ID ( The same as in Task Manager )" & _
                     "<td>" & history(i).ProcessID.ToString())
      Response.Write("<tr><td>Total Request Count (Requests served since" & _
                     "the process started)<TD>" _
                     & history(i).RequestCount.ToString())
      Response.Write("<tr><td>Peak Memory Used ( KB ) <td>" _
                     & history(i).PeakMemoryUsed.ToString())
      Response.Write("</table>")
   Next
   End Sub
   </script>
   </body>
   </html>
```

This can be handy information to have when you are developing your code. The **Peak Memory Used** counter is very useful, to determine whether your test file is consuming too much RAM, and the **Total Request Count** serves as a poor man's page hit counter. Oh, and if the **Process Age** reads 00:0x:xx.x then you know that whatever changes you made to your code have just crashed ASP.NET – oops!

Fear not – the development team at Microsoft did a great job of making process restarts as seamless as possible, so it shouldn't bring your entire machine crashing down, but you'll need to look at the application that caused the fault and fix it, or else your users will be getting errors.

> *I'm indebted to Scott Guthrie, ASP.NET Lead Developer, for pointing the way to this sample. He developed the techniques demonstrated in it, in C#. I merely ported a subset to Visual Basic. Thanks, Scott!*

Tips and Tricks

No configuration guidelines would be complete without offering a list of optimization tips. Here's a brief listing of the tips and examples included in the Microsoft QuickStart samples. If you've not got these installed, they're available from the following sites:

http://www.gotdotnet.com/quickstart/aspplus/
http://docs.aspng.com/quickstart/aspplus/default.aspx
http://aspalliance.com/quickstart/aspplus/
http://www.dotnetjunkies.com/quickstart/default.aspx
http://dev.aspfree.com/quickstart/default.aspx

Don't worry if you don't understand them all! They're being included here so that you can refer back to them throughout your development as a programmer. Think of them as a quick reference guide, that you'll still be able to use as a refresher in the years to come:

❑ **Disable Session State when it is not needed**. Maintaining session state consumes memory and processing time. If you don't need to recall or modify session variables in a page, disable session state for that page.

❏ **Choose your Session State provider carefully**. If you are running just one web server, the fastest and most economical mode of maintaining state is In-Process. Only if you are running a web farm, on more than one machine, should you even consider using SQL Server or the State Server.

❏ **Avoid excessive round trips to the server**. Round-tripping to the server takes time and server resources. You should only round-trip to the server when storing or retrieving data. You can program your controls to generate client-side code, and still use ASP.NET's efficient server controls. Use client-side processing to save server processing time as much as you can.

❏ **Use** `Page.IsPostback` **to avoid extra work on a round trip**. You can use `IsPostback` to determine if a dataset needs to be generated, for example. Generating data is expensive, in terms of processing time. Generating one query on first access and another one on a `POST` can cost you processing time.

❏ **Use server controls sparingly and appropriately**. Even though server controls are very cool, and afford you incredible event-handling capabilities, for simple displays, a simple rendering using `Response.Write` will be far more efficient.

❏ **Avoid excessive server control view state**. The more data you're passing back and forth between the client and the server, the larger the ViewState gets, and the longer it takes for the more resources your consuming. Like Session state, turn this feature off if you don't need to keep state on a page.

❏ **Use** `System.Text.StringBuilder` **for string concatenation**. When you modify a string object using the traditional concatenation methods, you add a new string object for every modification made. That adds up! The new `StringBuilder` object is much more efficient because you use one, and only one, object no matter how many modifications you perform on the string.

❏ **Use early binding in code**. `<%@ Page Language="VB" Strict="true" %>` can be your best friend! This forces early-binding, which in turn forces your code to be more efficient. By having correct typing enforced you prevent costly, inefficient, late-binding. A side benefit is that `Strict` forces you to declare your variables, preventing misplaced values in your code.

❏ **Use SQL stored procedures for data access**. In the .NET Framework, the `SqlConnection` class allows you to have even larger performance gains, since it can actually execute native SQL Server code. Now, not only do you gain the speed of stored procedures but, also, they are executed natively. Performance gains are estimated at 200 to 300% over `OleDb` or `Odbc` connections!

❏ **Use** `SqlDataReader` **for a fast-forward, read-only data cursor**. `SqlDataReader` provides what was known in the ASP world as a "firehose" cursor, which is much faster than other cursors available. In addition, `SqlDataReader` reads data directly from a database connection using Tabular Data Streams (TDS), and allows you to bind server controls directly to data.

❏ **Use Caching features wherever possible**. In high-traffic situations caching data can save you a lot of processing time, since the data will be served from RAM, instead of using precious processing cycles.

❏ **Enable Web gardening for multiprocessor computers**. Why encourage idleness? Enabling the use of all processors available only makes sense, since the more processing power is available to your applications, the more efficient your web server will be.

❏ **Do not forget to disable Debug mode**. Having a compiler watching for errors is the most expensive process that a processor can undertake! *Never* enable debugging on a production box!

Summary

In this chapter, we've covered a lot of ground in the vast topic of configuration and optimization. We looked at `machine.config` and `web.config` and saw how they were structured and their settings hierarchically inherited. Then we looked in more detail at some of the specific settings within those files that you can use to improve the performance, security and user friendliness of your applications.

Next we moved on to look at how we could increase our server's performance through the use of output and fragment caching so that our pages didn't need to be compiled as frequently, before presenting an overview of how we can use the new tracing features to debug our code, while simultaneously avoiding the inclusion of redundant debugging information in our finished production code.

Finally, we briefly looked at the built-in system monitoring information that we can use to assess the performance and suitability of our code, before concluding the chapter with a reference list of recommended performance optimization tips.

The Common System Namespaces

Due to the huge number of classes that make up the .NET class library, we don't have room to list them all, let alone their properties, methods, and events. The SDK provided with the Framework contains a full reference section, which you can access through .NET Framework Reference | .NET Class Library Reference.

To help you find the classes you need, we've provided below a list of the most commonly used namespaces, together with a description of the classes they contain.

Fundamental System Namespaces

System	Fundamental classes and base classes that define commonly-used value and reference data types, events and event handlers, interfaces, attributes, and processing exceptions. Plus services that support data type conversion, method parameter manipulation, mathematics, remote and local program invocation, application environment management, and supervision of managed and unmanaged applications.
System.Collections	Interfaces and classes that define various collections of objects, such as the List, Queue, ArrayList, HashTable, and Dictionary objects.
System.ComponentModel	Classes that are used to implement the run time and design time behavior of components and controls. Includes the base classes and interfaces for implementing attributes, type converters, binding to data sources, and licensing components.
System.Configuration	Classes that are used to configure an assembly and allow custom installers to be created.
System.IO	Classes and types that provide synchronous and asynchronous reading from and writing to data streams and files.
System.Reflection	Classes and interfaces providing a managed view of loaded types, methods, and fields, with the ability to dynamically create and invoke types.
System.Security	Classes that provide the underlying structure for the common language runtime security system, including base classes for permissions.

Table continued on following page

System.Text	Classes representing ASCII, Unicode, UTF-7, and UTF-8 character encodings, abstract base classes for converting blocks of characters to and from blocks of bytes, and a helper class that manipulates and formats String objects without creating intermediate instances.
System.Text.Regular Expressions	Classes that provide access to the .NET Framework regular expression engine.
System.Threading	Classes and interfaces to enable multi-threaded programming, including the `ThreadPool` class, a delegate timer class and the `Mutex` class. Also contains classes for thread scheduling, wait notification, and deadlock resolution.
System.Timers	Contains the programmable `Timer` component, which allows events to be raised at specified intervals.

.NET Languages Namespaces

Microsoft.CSharp	Classes that support compilation and code generation for the C# language.
Microsoft.JScript	Classes that support compilation and code generation for the JScript language.
Microsoft.VisualBasic	Classes that support compilation and code generation for the Visual Basic language.

Data Management Namespaces

System.Data	Classes that constitute the ADO.NET relational data access and management architecture for multiple data sources.
System.Data.OleDb	Classes that support the OLE DB .NET data provider.
System.Data.SqlClient	Classes that support the SQL Server .NET data provider.
System.Data.SqlTypes	Classes for native data types within MS SQL Server.
System.Xml	Classes that provide standards-based support for processing XML.
System.Xml.Schema	Classes that provide standards-based support for processing XML schemas.
System.Xml.XPath	Contains the `XPath` parser and evaluation engine.
System.Xml.Xsl	Classes that provide support for XSL/T transformations.

Debugging and Monitoring Namespaces

System.Diagnostics	Classes for debugging applications and to tracing code execution, starting system processes, reading and writing to event logs, and monitoring system performance using performance counters.
System.Management	Classes for working with Windows Management Instrumentation (WMI).

Application Services Namespaces

System.DirectoryServices	Classes that provide access to Active Directory.
System.EnterpriseServices	Classes that are used to manage component activation and associated activities in an enterprise scenario.
System.Messaging	Classes for working with message queues, sending messages to queues, and receiving or peeking messages from queues. Note, this is not used for SMTP messaging.

Graphics and Printing Namespaces

System.Drawing	Provides access to GDI+ basic graphics functionality.
System.Drawing.Design	Classes that extend design-time user interface logic and drawing.
System.Drawing.Drawing2D	Advanced 2-dimmensional and vector graphics classes.
System.Drawing.Imaging	Advanced GDI+ imaging classes.
System.Drawing.Printing	Classes that allow customized printing.
System.Drawing.Text	Advanced GDI+ typography classes for creating and using fonts.

Fundamental Networking Namespaces

System.Net	Provides simple programming interfaces to many common network protocols. Includes the `WebRequest` and `WebResponse` classes that enable applications to use Internet resources.
System.Net.Sockets	Provides a managed implementation of the Windows Sockets interface in the same way as the Winsock API.

Windows Forms Application Namespaces

System.Windows.Forms	Classes for creating Windows-based executable applications to run under the .NET Framework.
System.Windows.Forms.Design	Classes for extending design-time support for Windows Forms.

Fundamental Web Application Namespaces

System.Web	Classes and interfaces to enable browser/server communication. Includes HTTPRequest and HTTPResponse, and the HTTPServerUtility object that provides access to server-side utilities and processes. Also includes classes for cookie manipulation, file transfer, exception information, and output cache control.
System.Web.Caching	Classes for caching frequently used resources on the server.
System.Web.Configuration	Classes that are used to configure ASP.NET applications.
System.Web.Hosting	Classes for working with application domains, worker requests, and interfacing with IIS.
System.Web.Mail	Classes for creating and managing SMTP email messages and attachments.
System.Web.Security	Classes that implement security in ASP.NET applications.

Web Forms Application Namespaces

System.Web.UI	Classes and interfaces for creating user interface pages and controls in Web applications. Includes the Control base class, the Page class and classes to implement data binding, viewstate management, and control parsing.
System.Web.UI.Design	Classes for extending design-time support for Web Forms.
System.Web.UI.Design. WebControls	Classes for extending design-time support for Web controls.
System.Web.UI.HtmlControls	Classes for creating HTML server controls that map directly to standard HTML elements.
System.Web.UI.WebControls	Classes for creating ASP.NET Web Controls, which provide a consistent and abstract control.

Web Service Application Namespaces

System.Web.Services	Classes for building and using Web Services.
System.Web.Services. Description	Classes for publicly describing Web Services via Service Description Language (SDL).
System.Web.Services. Discovery	Classes for implementing Web Service Discovery.
System.Web.Services. Protocols	Classes that define the data transmission protocols between ASP.NET Web Services and clients.

Language Syntax Comparison in .NET

As well as Visual Basic, the Microsoft .NET Platform current offers built-in support for two other languages, **C#** (pronounced "C Sharp") and **JScript**. The main difference between the three languages is syntactical, but to give you a clearer idea of specific differences, here are the three languages side by side for you to compare. For more information regarding the syntax of the other languages, refer to the complete documentation for the .NET Framework SDK.

	VB	C#	JScript
Variable Declarations	Dim x As Integer Dim s As String Dim s1, s2 As String Dim o 'Implicitly Object Dim obj As New Object() Public name As String	int x; String s; String s1, s2; Object o; Object obj = new Object(); public String name;	var x : int; var s : String; var s1 : String, s2 : String; var o; var obj : Object = new Object(); var name : String;
Statements	Response.Write("foo")	Response.Write("foo");	Response.Write("foo");
Comments	' This is a comment ' This ' is ' a ' multi-line ' comment	// This is a comment /* This is a multi-line comment */	// This is a comment /* This is a multi-line comment */
Accessing Indexed Properties	Dim s, value As String s = Request.QueryString("Name") value = Request.Cookies("Key").Value	String s, value As String; String s = Request.QueryString["Name"]; String value = Request.Cookies["key"];	var s : String = Request.QueryString("Name"); var value : String = Request.Cookies("key");

Declaring Indexed Properties	'Note that default non-indexed properties
	'must be explicitly named in VB
	
	' Default Indexed Property
	Public Default ReadOnly Property
	DefaultProperty(Name As String) As String
	  Get
	    Return CStr(lookuptable(name))
	  End Get
	End Property
		// Default Indexed Property
		public String this[String name] {
		  get {
		    return (String) lookuptable[name];
		  }
		}
			To emulate these properties in JScript it is suggested that function declarations are used instead. Even though the functions can't be accessed using indexed property syntax in CSharp, it'll provide the illusion for VB.
			
			public function Item(name :String) : String {
			  return String(lookuptable(name));
			}

Declaring Simple Properties	JScript does not support the creation of Indexed or Default Indexed properties.
	
	Public Property Name As String
	  Get
	    ...
	    Return ...
	  End Get
	  Set
	    ... = Value
	  End Set
	End Property
		public String name {
		  get {
		    ...
		    return ...;
		  }
		  set {
		    ... = value;
		  }
		}
			function get name() : String {
			  ...
			  return ...;
			}
			function set name(value : String) {
			  ... = value;
			}

	VB	C#	JScript

Declare and Use an Enumeration	`' Declare the Enumeration`
	`Public Enum MessageSize`
	`    Small = 0`
	`    Medium = 1,`
	`    Large = 2`
	`End Enum`
	`' Create a Field or Property`
	`Public MsgSize As MessageSize`
	`' Assign to the property using the Enumeration values`
	`MsgSize = small`
		`// Declare the Enumeration`
		`public enum MessageSize {`
		`    Small = 0,`
		`    Medium = 1,`
		`    Large = 2`
		`}`
		`// Create a Field or Property`
		`public MessageSize msgsize;`
		`// Assign to the property using the Enumeration values`
		`msgsize = Small;`
			`// Declare the Enumeration`
			`public enum MessageSize {`
			`    Small = 0,`
			`    Medium = 1,`
			`    Large = 2`
			`}`
			`// Create a Field or Property`
			`public var msgsize:MessageSize;`
			`// Assign to the property using the Enumeration values`
			`msgsize = Small;`

Enumerating a Collection	`Dim S As String`
	`For Each S In Coll`
	`...`
	`Next`
		`for each ( String s in coll ) {`
		`...`
		`}`
			`var s:String;`
			`for ( s in coll ) {`
			`...`
			`}`

Declare and Use Methods	`' Declare a void return function`
	`Sub Voidfunction()`
	`...`
	`End Sub`
	`' Declare a function that returns a value`
	`Function StringFunction() As String`
	`    ... Return CStr(val)`
	`End Function`
	`' Declare a function that takes and returns values`
	`Function ParmFunction(a As String, b As String) As String`
	`    ... Return CStr(A & B)`
	`End Function`
	`' Use the Functions`
	`VoidFunction()`
	`Dim s1 As String = StringFunction()`
	`Dim s2 As String = ParmFunction("Hello", "World!")`
		`// Declare a void return function`
		`void Voidfunction() {`
		`...`
		`}`
		`// Declare a function that returns a value`
		`String stringfunction() {`
		`    ... return (String) val;`
		`}`
		`// Declare a function that takes and returns values`
		`String parmfunction(String a, String b) {`
		`    ... return (String) (a + b);`
		`}`
		`// Use the Functions`
		`voidfunction();`
		`String s1 = stringfunction();`
		`String s2 = parmfunction("Hello", "World!");`
			`// Declare a void return function`
			`function voidfunction() : void {`
			`...`
			`}`
			`// Declare a function that returns a value`
			`function stringfunction() : String {`
			`    ... return String(val);`
			`}`
			`// Declare a function that takes and returns values`
			`function parmfunction(a:String, b:String) : String {`
			`    ... return String(a + b);`
			`}`
			`// Use the Functions`
			`voidfunction();`
			`var s1:String = stringfunction();`
			`var s2:String = parmfunction("Hello", "World!");`

Custom Attributes	`' Stand-alone attribute`
	`<STAThread>`
	`' Attribute with parameters`
	`<DllImport("ADVAPI32.DLL")>`
	`' Attribute with named parameters`
	`<DllImport("KERNEL32.DLL",`
	`CharSet:=CharSet.Auto)>`
		`// Stand-alone attribute`
		`[STAThread]`
		`// Attribute with parameters`
		`[DllImport("ADVAPI32.DLL")]`
		`// Attribute with named parameters`
		`[DllImport("KERNEL32.DLL",`
		`CharSet=CharSet.Auto]`
			`// Stand-alone attribute`
			`STAThreadAttribute`
			`// Attribute with parameters`
			`DllImportAttribute("ADVAPI32.DLL")`
			`// Attribute with named parameters`
			`DllImportAttribute("KERNEL32.DLL", CharSet=CharSet.Auto)`

Arrays	`Dim a(2) As String`
	`a(0) = "1"`
	`a(1) = "2"`
	`a(2) = "3"`
	
	`Dim a(2,2) As String`
	`a(0,0) = "1"`
	`a(1,0) = "2"`
	`a(2,0) = "3"`
		`String[] a = new String[3];`
		`a[0][0] = "1";`
		`a[1][0] = "2";`
		`a[2][0] = "3";`
		
		`String[][] a = new String[3][3];`
		`a[0][0] = "1";`
		`a[1][0] = "2";`
		`a[2][0] = "3";`
			`var a : String[] = new String[3];`
			`a[0] = "1";`
			`a[1] = "2";`
			`a[2] = "3";`
			
			`var a : String[][] = new String[3][3];`
			`a[0][0] = "1";`
			`a[1][0] = "2";`
			`a[2][0] = "3";`

Table continued on following page

	VB	C#	JScript

Initialization	```Dim s As String = "Hello World"```
	```Dim i As Integer = 1```
	```Dim a() As Double = { 3.00, 4.00, 5.00 }```
		```String s = "Hello World";```
		```int i = 1;```
		```double[] a = { 3.00, 4.00, 5.00 };```
			```var s : String = "Hello World";```
			```var i : int = 1;```
			```var a : double[] = [3.00, 4.00, 5.00];```

If Statements	```If Not (Request.QueryString = Nothing)```
	  ```...```
	```End If```
		```if (Request.QueryString != null) {```
		  ```...```
		```}```
			```if (Request.QueryString != null) {```
			  ```...```
			```}```

Case Statements	```Select Case FirstName```
	  ```Case "John"```
	    ```...```
	  ```Case "Paul"```
	    ```...```
	  ```Case "Ringo"```
	    ```...```
	  ```Case Else```
	    ```...```
	```End Select```
		```switch (FirstName) {```
		  ```case "John" :```
		    ```break;```
		  ```case "Paul" :```
		    ```break;```
		  ```case "Ringo" :```
		    ```break;```
		  ```default:```
		    ```break;```
		```}```
			```switch (FirstName) {```
			  ```case "John" :```
			    ```break;```
			  ```case "Paul" :```
			    ```break;```
			  ```case "Ringo" :```
			    ```break;```
			  ```default:```
			    ```break;```
			```}```

For Loops	```Dim I As Integer```
	```For I = 0 To 2```
	  ```a(I) = "test"```
	```Next```
		```for (int i=0; i<3; i++)```
		  ```a(i) = "test";```
			```for (var i : int = 0; i < 3; i++)```
			  ```a[i] = "test";```

While Loops	```Dim I As Integer```
	```I = 0```
	```Do While I < 3```
	  ```Console.WriteLine(I.ToString())```
	  ```I += 1```
	```Loop```
		```int i = 0;```
		```while (i<3) {```
		  ```Console.WriteLine(i.ToString());```
		  ```i += 1;```
		```}```
			```var i : int = 0;```
			```while (i < 3) {```
			  ```Console.WriteLine(i);```
			  ```i += 1;```
			```}```

Exception Handling	```Try ' Code that throws exceptions```
	```Catch E As OverflowException```
	```Catch a specific exception```
	```Catch E As Exception```
	```' Catch the generic exceptions```
	```Finally Execute some cleanup code```
	```End Try```
		```try { // Code that throws exceptions```
		```} catch(OverflowException e) {```
		  ```Catch a specific exception```
		```} catch(Exception e) {```
		  ```// Catch the generic exceptions```
		```} finally {```
		  ```// Execute some cleanup code```
		```}```
			```try { // Code that throws exceptions```
			```} catch(OverflowException) {```
			  ```Catch a specific exception```
			```} catch(Exception) {```
			  ```// Catch the generic exceptions```
			```} finally {```
			  ```// Execute some cleanup code```
			```}```

	VB	C#	JScript

String Concatenation	' Using Strings
	Dim s1, s2 As String
	s2 &= " world"
	s1 = s2 & " !!!"
	
	' Using StringBuilder class for performance
	Dim s3 As New StringBuilder()
	s3.Append("hello")
	s3.Append(" world")
	s3.Append(" !!!")
		// Using Strings
		String s1;
		String s2 = "hello";
		s2 += " world";
		s1 = s2 + " !!!";
		
		// Using StringBuilder class for performance
		StringBuilder s3 = new StringBuilder();
		s3.Append("hello");
		s3.Append(" world");
		s3.Append(" !!!");
			// Using Strings
			var s1 : String;
			var s2 : String = "hello";
			s2 += " world";
			s1 = s2 + " !!!";
			
			// Using StringBuilder class for performance
			var s3:StringBuilder = new StringBuilder();
			s3.Append("hello");
			s3.Append(" world");
			s3.Append(" !!!");

Event Handlers Delegates	Sub MyButton_Click(Sender As Object, E As EventArgs)
	...
	End Sub
		void MyButton_Click(Object sender, EventArgs E) {
		...
		}
			function MyButton_Click(sender : Object, E : EventArgs) {
			...
			}

Declare Events	' Create a public event
	Public Event MyEvent(Sender as Object, E as EventArgs)
	
	' Create a method for firing the event
	Protected Sub OnMyEvent(E As EventArgs)
	    RaiseEvent MyEvent(Me, E)
	End Sub
		// Create a public event
		public event EventHandler MyEvent;
		
		// Create a method for firing the event
		protected void OnMyEvent(EventArgs e) {
		    MyEvent(this, e);
		}
			JScript does not support the creation of events. JScript may only consume events by declaring Event Handler Delegates and adding those delegates to the Events of another control.

Event Handlers to Events Add/Remove	AddHandler Control.Change, AddressOf Me.ChangeEventHandler RemoveHandler Control.Change, AddressOf Me.ChangeEventHandler	Control.Change += new EventHandler(this.ChangeEventHandler); Control.Change -= new EventHandler(this.ChangeEventHandler);	Control.Change += this.ChangeEventHandler; Control.Change -= this.ChangeEventHandler;
Casting	Dim obj As MyObject Dim iObj As IMyObject obj = Session("Some Value") iObj = CType(obj, IMyObject)	MyObject obj = (MyObject)Session["Some Value"]; IMyObject iObj = obj;	var obj : MyObject = MyObject(Session("Some Value")); var iObj : IMyObject = obj;

Conversion	Dim i As Integer
	Dim s As String
	Dim d As Double
	
	i = 3
	s = i.ToString()
	d = CDbl(s)
	' See also CDbl(...), CStr(...), ...
		int i = 3;
		String s = i.ToString();
		double d = Double.Parse(s);
			var i : int = 3;
			var s : String = i.ToString();
			var d : double = Number(s);

Table continued on following page

	VB	C#	JScript

Class Definition w/ Inheritance	```Imports System```
	```Namespace MySpace```
	``` Public Class Foo :```
	``` Inherits Bar```
	``` Dim x As Integer```
	``` Public Sub New()```
	``` MyBase.New()```
	``` x = 4```
	``` End Sub```
	
	``` Public Sub Add(x As```
	```Integer)```
	``` Me.x = Me.x + x```
	``` End Sub```
	``` Overrides Public```
	```Function GetNum() As```
	```Integer```
	``` Return x```
	``` End Function```
	``` End Class```
	```End Namespace```
	```' vbc /out:libraryvb.dll```
	```/t:library```
	```' library.vb```
		```using System;```
		```namespace MySpace {```
		``` public class Foo : Bar {```
		``` int x;```
		``` public Foo() { x = 4; }```
		``` public void Add(int x) { this.x += x; }```
		``` override public int GetNum() { return```
		```x; }```
		``` }```
		```}```
		```// csc /out:librarycs.dll /t:library```
		```// library.cs```
			```import System;```
			```package MySpace {```
			``` class Foo extends Bar {```
			``` private var x : int;```
			``` function Foo() { x = 4; }```
			``` function Add(x : int) { this.x += x; }```
			``` override function GetNum() : int { return x; }```
			``` }```
			```}```
			```// jsc /out:libraryjs.dll library.js```

Implementing an Interface	```Public Class MyClass :```
	```Implements IEnumerable```
	``` ...```
	``` Function```
	```IEnumerable_GetEnumerator()```
	```As IEnumerator Implements```
	```IEnumerable.GetEnumerator```
	``` ...```
	``` End Function```
	```End Class```
		```public class MyClass : IEnumerable {```
		``` ... IEnumerator IEnumerable.GetEnumerator()```
		``` { ... }```
		```}```
			```public class MyClass implements IEnumerable {```
			``` ... function IEnumerable.GetEnumerator() : IEnumerator {```
			``` ...```
			``` }```
			```}```

Class Definition w/ A Main method	```Imports System```
	```Public Class ConsoleVB```
	``` Public Sub New()```
	``` MyBase.New()```
	``` ...```
	```Console.WriteLine("Object```
	```Created")```
	``` End Sub```
	``` Public Shared Sub Main()```
	``` ...```
	```Console.WriteLine("Hello```
	```World")```
	``` Dim cvb As New```
	```ConsoleVB```
	``` End Sub```
	```End Class```
	```' vbc /out:consolevb.exe```
	```/t:exe console.vb```
		```using System;```
		```public class ConsoleCS {```
		``` public ConsoleCS() {```
		``` Console.WriteLine("Object Created");```
		``` }```
		``` public static void Main (String[] args) {```
		``` Console.WriteLine("Hello World");```
		``` ConsoleCS ccs = new ConsoleCS();```
		``` }```
		```}```
		```// csc /out:consolecs.exe /t:exe console.cs```
			```class ConsoleCS {```
			``` function ConsoleCS() {```
			``` print("Object Created");```
			``` }```
			``` static function Main (args : String[]) {```
			``` print("Hello World");```
			``` var ccs : ConsoleCS = new ConsoleCS();```
			``` }```
			```}```
			```// jsc /out:consolejs.exe /exe console.js```

Standard Module	```Imports System```
	```Public Module ConsoleVB```
	``` Public Sub Main()```
	``` ...```
	```Console.WriteLine("Hello```
	```World")```
	``` End Sub```
	```End Module```
	```' vbc /out:consolevb.exe```
	```/t:exe console.vb```
		```using System;```
		```public class Module {```
		``` public static void Main (String[] args) {```
		``` Console.WriteLine("Hello World");```
		``` }```
		```}```
		```// csc /out:consolecs.exe /t:exe console.cs```
			```print("Hello World");```
			```// jsc /out:consolejs.exe /exe console.js```

A Quick Reference to using the Windows Command Prompt

For many people, DOS is a strange land that ought to be confined to a museum, but if you've never had the joys of playing with DOS prompts for hours on end to tweak the performance of your 286, you might benefit from a quick reference of commonly-used DOS commands. These commands should help you navigate your system from a command-prompt level with more confidence.

We'll start with a tabular listing of common commands, then we'll look at a couple of examples of navigating through your system.

Commands For Controlling the Command Prompt Window

> **If you want to repeat any of the commands you entered previously, press the *up* arrow on your keyboard to scroll through recently used commands**

Command	Usage	Parameters	Description
All commands	`Command /?`	`/?`	This parameter can be included after any DOS command to provide help on the usage and parameters for that command.

CD	`CD directory`
	`CD drive:\directory1\directory2`
	
	`CD ..`
			Changes Directory to the directory specified.

Command	Usage	Parameters	Description
CLS	CLS		Clears the screen
DEL	DEL *file.ext* DEL *.*		Deletes the specified file. The asterisk character (*) can be used as a wild card, hence DEL *.txt will delete all files with a .txt extension in the current directory, whereas, DEL *.* will delete all files in the current directory.
DIR	DIR DIR /W DIR /P DIR /W /P DIR /O:D	/O /P /W	Displays a list of all the files and subdirectories of the directory you are currently working in. The most useful switches for this are /p to page the output (pausing after the screen is full), /w to display in columns across the full width of the page, and /o for ordering the output. You can sort by: ❑ N for name ❑ E for extension ❑ G to group directories first ❑ S for size ❑ D for date and time
FC	FC *sourcefile destinationfile*		Compares the contents of two files and displays the differences between them.
HELP	HELP		Shows the help files.
MOVE	MOVE *drive:\path\sourcefile destination drive\pathpath\file*	/Y /-Y	Moves a file from one location to another. The /Y parameter forces it to supress any warnings about overwriting any existing files, the /-Y parameter makes sure it warns you before replacing files.

.ommand	Usage	Parameters	Description
D	MD *newdirectory*		Creates a new directory as a sub-directory of the directory you are currently working in.
RD	RD *olddirectory*		Deletes a directory from the directory you are currently working in.
REN	REN *source destination*		Renames a file.
TREE	TREE TREE /F	/F	Displays a visual representation of the directory structure of the current active directory. The /F switch displays the files inside each directory.
TYPE	TYPE *file*		Displays the contents of a text file - useful for displaying code from an ASP.NET .aspx, .vb, or .ascx file, because these are stored as text.
XCOPY	XCOPY *source destination*		Copies files and directories from the location specified to a new location (see separate table on XCOPY commands).

Useful Commands for Make Files

Make files are DOS batch files, and are created to simplify working with the command prompt. They're easy to edit (via notepad) so if you make a mistake you don't have to type it all in again – you just run the batch file again:

Command	Usage	Parameters	Description
ECHO	@ECHO OFF ECHO Hello!	ON OFF *message*	The ECHO command is useful for giving the user some feedback if they're running a large batch file. @ECHO OFF will hide all commands being input into the command window, as well as the ECHO command itself. If you omit the @, then the user sees the words ECHO OFF on their screen.

Table continued on following page

Command	Usage	Parameters	Description
FOR	FOR %variable IN (set) DO command		The FOR command is another useful construct for advanced batch file creation. Again, I recommend you study the help files by typing FOR /? for more information.
IF	IF NOT EXIST *filename* XCOPY *source destination*	not errorlevel *number* string1==string2 exist *filename* command	Useful tool for creating conditional statements in a batch file. You could use it to specify various conditions for deploying an application, for example.
REM	REM *This is a comment*		Used for commenting batch file code.
SET	SET *variable=string*	*(too many to list here)*	The SET command is very useful. We can use it to create a variable to hold a string that corresponds to our paths. The SET command is quite versatile, so if you really want to get in to it, type SET /? at the command prompt for a full range of options.
TITLE	TITLE *TitleName*		Used for setting the Title of the current command prompt window.

XCOPY

One of the most useful commands you can use for deploying your ASP.NET applications, is the XCopy command. If you incorporate a number of commands for deploying an application into a batch file, then all your users need to do to deploy the application is simply run a file, and the hard work is done for them. Note that this doesn't set up Virtual Directories – that still needs to be done from the IIS Management Console:

```
XCOPY source destination /option(s)
```

/A	Only copies files with the archive attribute set – to check the status of a file's attributes, use the ATTRIB command (ATTRIB *filename*).
/C	Continues copying even if errors occur.
/D:m-d-y	Copies files changed on or after the specified date. If no date is given, copies only those files whose source time is newer than the destination time.
/E	Copies directories and subdirectories, including empty ones.
/EXCLUDE:*file1 file2 file3*	Copies everything specified, except those files in specific directories that are mentioned here. You can exclude a specific type of file, for example, .txt will exclude all text files. Or you can exclude the contents of a directory. For example, \test\ will exclude copying all files in the test directory.
/F	Displays full source and destination file names while copying.
/H	Copies all hidden or system files in the specified path.
/I	If destination does not exist and copying more than one file, assumes that destination must be a directory.
/K	Preserves any specific file attributes (XCopy normally resets read-only attributes).
/L	Displays all of the files to be copied.
/M	Only copies files with the archive attribute set, then turns off the archive attribute.
/P	Prompts you to confirm whether each destination file should be created before creating it.
/Q	Hides file names while copying.
/R	Overwrites read-only files.
/S	Copies all directories and subdirectories except those which are empty.
/T	Creates a directory structure, but does not copy files. Does not include empty directories or subdirectories. /T /E includes empty directories and subdirectories.
/U	Copies only files that already exist in destination, so useful for updating only those files which have changed. Useful when used with the /Y command to suppress file-overwrite confirmation prompts.
/V	Verifies each new file is created successfully.
/W	Prompts the user to press a key before commencing the copy operation.
/Y	Suppresses prompting to confirm if you want to overwrite an existing destination file.
/-Y	Enables prompting to confirm you want to overwrite an existing destination file.

Examples of using the Command Prompt and Batch Files

Let's have a look at a handful of short examples designed to show how these tools can be used. These aren't designed to be fully-worked examples, so there won't be a lengthy discussion about each one, but they should help to put these concepts into perspective.

Try It Out – Controlling your Environment

1. Create a file in Notepad containing some random text, for example, "The thing I hate most as an author, is constantly having to think of lines of text that don't say Hello World!". Save the file as `test.txt` and place it in the root of your `BegASPNET` directory (if you've followed our convention, this is `C:\BegASPNET`).

2. Open up the command prompt, type the following lines, pressing *Enter* at the end of each line:

```
cd c:\
md test
cd test
dir
xcopy c:\begaspnet\test.txt
dir
type test.txt
```

3. You should see the following on your screen:

How It Works

Let's have a quick look through our code:

```
cd c:\
md test
cd test
dir
```

We changed to the root directory of our C drive. We created a subfolder called test. We changed to the test directory, then we displayed the contents of the directory:

```
xcopy c:\begaspnet\test.txt
dir
type test.txt
```

We then copied the test.txt file we created into this new directory, and re-viewed the contents of the directory to check that the file had copied successfully. Finally, we displayed the contents of our text file on the screen.

Try It out: Working with Batch Files

1. Create a new file in Notepad and add the following text:

```
CLS

REM @echo off

SET source=c:\test\test.txt
SET destination=c:\test\test2.txt

TITLE Trying out a batch file...

IF NOT EXIST %destination% XCOPY %source% %destination% /F

FC %source% %destination%

PAUSE
```

2. Save this as test.bat in your recently-created c:\test directory.

3. Navigate to the c:\test directory using Windows Explorer this time, and double-click on the test.bat file. When prompted, press the F key to indicate that we're using a file, not a directory. You should see the following:

733

```
Trying out a batch file...

C:\test>REM @echo off

C:\test>SET source=c:\test\test.txt

C:\test>SET destination=c:\test\test2.txt

C:\test>TITLE Trying out a batch file...

C:\test>IF NOT EXIST c:\test\test2.txt XCOPY c:\test\test.txt c:\test\test2.txt
/F
Does C:\test\test2.txt specify a file name
or directory name on the target
(F = file, D = directory)? f
C:\test\test.txt -> C:\test\test2.txt
1 File(s) copied

C:\test>FC c:\test\test.txt c:\test\test2.txt
Comparing files C:\TEST\test.txt and C:\TEST\TEST2.TXT
FC: no differences encountered


C:\test>PAUSE
Press any key to continue . . . _
```

4. Now open up your Windows Explorer, and go back to `C:\test`. Delete the newly-created `test2.txt` file, right-click on the `test.bat` file, and select Edit. Change the second line as shown below:

```
CLS

@echo off

SET source=c:\test\test.txt
SET destination=c:\test\test2.txt

TITLE Trying out a batch file...

IF NOT EXIST %destination% XCOPY %source% %destination% /F

FC %source% %destination%

PAUSE
```

5. Double-click on the test.bat file again, responding when prompted and you should see the following:

```
Trying out a batch file...                                    _ □ ✕

Does C:\test\test2.txt specify a file name
or directory name on the target
(F = file, D = directory)? f
C:\test\test.txt -> C:\test\test2.txt
1 File(s) copied
Comparing files C:\TEST\test.txt and C:\TEST\TEST2.TXT
FC: no differences encountered

Press any key to continue . . . _
```

How It Works

Let's run through what our first code did, then look at the differences between this and our second batch:

```
CLS
```

Clear the screen (if you're running the batch file from command prompt, then this is a nice and neat way of starting afresh):

```
REM @echo off
```

Put in a REM statement to comment-out the line we don't want to use just yet (but we'll add it later):

```
SET source=c:\test\test.txt
SET destination=c:\test\test2.txt
```

Set up a couple of variables to save on typing:

```
TITLE Trying out a batch file...
```

Set the title of the active window – you'll notice that the very top of each of the previous screenshots had customized title text in the title bar:

```
IF NOT EXIST %destination% XCOPY %source% %destination% /F

FC %source% %destination%
```

If we've not copied from the original file to create a new file yet, then do the copy, and compare the two files to check that they are identical:

```
PAUSE
```

Finally, provide the user with a prompt to say continue. If you didn't include this and simply double-clicked the icon from Windows Explorer, then when the processing has finished, the window disappears immediately.

When we removed the REM statement, the @echo off declaration hid the input from our batch file, and only displayed the output, which is a useful trick for keeping things a bit more user-friendly.

HTTP 1.1 Error Codes

This appendix lists the client and server error codes with default explanations, provided by Microsoft Internet Information Server; they are included in case you run into errors as you experiment with ASP:

Error Code	Short Text	Explanation
400	Bad Request	Due to malformed syntax, the request could not be understood by the server. The client should not repeat the request without modifications.
401.1	Unauthorized: Logon Failed	This error indicates that the credentials passed to the server do not match the credentials required to log on to the server. Please contact the Web server's administrator to verify that you have permission to access the requested resource.
401.2	Unauthorized: Logon Failed due to server configuration	This error indicates that the credentials passed to the server do not match the credentials required to log on to the server. This is usually caused by not sending the proper WWW-Authenticate header field. Please contact the Web server's administrator to verify that you have permission to access to requested resource.
401.3	Unauthorized: Unauthorized due to ACL on resource	This error indicates that the credentials passed by the client, do not have access to the particular resource on the server. This resource could be either the page or file listed in the address line of the client, or it could be another file on the server that is needed to process the file listed on the address line of the client. Please make a note of the entire address you were trying to access and then contact the Web server's administrator to verify that you have permission to access the requested resource.

Table continued on following page

Error Code	Short Text	Explanation
401.4	Unauthorized: Authorization failed by filter	This error indicates that the Web server has a filter program installed to verify users connecting to the server. The authentication used to connect to the server was denied access by this filter program. Please make a note of the entire address you were trying to access and then contact the Web server's administrator to verify that you have permission to access the requested resource.
401.5	Unauthorized: Authorization failed by ISAPI/CGI app	This error indicates that the address on the Web server you attempted to use has an ISAPI or CGI program installed that verifies user credentials before proceeding. The authentication used to connect to the server was denied access by this program. Please make a note of the entire address you were trying to access and then contact the Web server's administrator to verify that you have permission to access the requested resource.
403.1	Forbidden: Execute Access Forbidden	This error can be caused if you try to execute a CGI, ISAPI, or other executable program from a directory that does not allow programs to be executed. Please contact the Web server's administrator if the problem persists.
403.2	Forbidden: Read Access Forbidden	This error can be caused if there is no default page available and directory browsing has not been enabled for the directory, or if you are trying to display an HTML page that resides in a directory marked for Execute or Script permissions only. Please contact the Web server's administrator if the problem persists.
403.3	Forbidden: Write Access Forbidden	This error can be caused if you attempt to upload to, or modify a file in, a directory that does not allow Write access. Please contact the Web server's administrator if the problem persists.

Error Code	Short Text	Explanation
403.4	Forbidden: SSL required	This error indicates that the page you are trying to access is secured with Secure Sockets Layer (SSL). In order to view it, you need to enable SSL by typing "https://" at the beginning of the address you are attempting to reach. Please contact the Web server's administrator if the problem persists.
403.5	Forbidden: SSL 128 required	This error message indicates that the resource you are trying to access is secured with a 128-bit version of Secure Sockets Layer (SSL). In order to view this resource, you need a browser that supports this level of SSL. Please confirm that your browser supports 128-bit SSL security. If it does, then contact the Web server's administrator and report the problem.
403.6	Forbidden: IP address rejected	This error is caused when the server has a list of IP addresses that are not allowed to access the site, and the IP address you are using is in this list. Please contact the Web server's administrator if the problem persists.
403.7	Forbidden: Client certificate required	This error occurs when the resource you are attempting to access requires your browser to have a client Secure Sockets Layer (SSL) certificate that the server recognizes. This is used for authenticating you as a valid user of the resource. Please contact the Web server's administrator to obtain a valid client certificate.
403.8	Forbidden: Site access denied	This error can be caused if the Web server is not servicing requests, or if you do not have permission to connect to the site. Please contact the Web server's administrator.
403.9	Access Forbidden: Too many users are connected	This error can be caused if the Web server is busy and cannot process your request due to heavy traffic. Please try to connect again later. Please contact the Web server's administrator if the problem persists.

Table continued on following page

Error Code	Short Text	Explanation
403.10	Access Forbidden: Invalid Configuration	There is a configuration problem on the Web server at this time. Please contact the Web server's administrator if the problem persists.
403.11	Access Forbidden: Password Change	This error can be caused if the user has entered the wrong password during authentication. Please refresh the page and try again. Please contact the Web server's administrator if the problem persists.
403.12	Access Forbidden: Mapper Denied Access	Your client certificate map has been denied access to this Web site. Please contact the site administrator to establish client certificate permissions. You can also change your client certificate and retry, if appropriate.
404	Not Found	The Web server cannot find the file or script you asked for. Please check the URL to ensure that the path is correct. Please contact the server's administrator if this problem persists.
405	Method Not Allowed	The method specified in the Request Line is not allowed for the resource identified by the request. Please ensure that you have the proper MIME type set up for the resource you are requesting. Please contact the server's administrator if this problem persists.
406	Not Acceptable	The resource identified by the request can only generate response entities that have content characteristics that are "not acceptable" according to the Accept headers sent in the request. Please contact the server's administrator if this problem persists.
407	Proxy Authentication Required	You must authenticate with a proxy server before this request can be serviced. Please log on to your proxy server, and then try again. Please contact the Web server's administrator if this problem persists.

Error Code	Short Text	Explanation
412	Precondition Failed	The precondition given in one or more of the Request-header fields evaluated to FALSE when it was tested on the server. The client placed preconditions on the current resource meta-information (header field data) to prevent the requested method from being applied to a resource other than the one intended. Please contact the Web server's administrator if the problem persists.
414	Request-URI Too Long	The server is refusing to service the request because the Request-URI is too long. This rare condition is likely to occur only in the following situations:
		A client has improperly converted a POST request to a GET request with long query information.
		A client has encountered a redirection problem (for example, a redirected URL prefix that points to a suffix of itself).
		The server is under attack by a client attempting to exploit security holes present in some servers using fixed-length buffers for reading or manipulating the Request-URI.
		Please contact the Web server's administrator if this problem persists.
500	Internal Server Error	The Web server is incapable of performing the request. Please try your request again later. Please contact the Web server's administrator if this problem persists.
501	Not Implemented	The Web server does not support the functionality required to fulfill the request. Please check your URL for errors, and contact the Web server's administrator if the problem persists.
502	Bad Gateway	The server, while acting as a gateway or proxy, received an invalid response from the upstream server it accessed in attempting to fulfill the request. Please contact the Web server's administrator if the problem persists.

Please note that server error message files are placed in HELP\COMMON folder of Windows.

The ASCII Character Set

The American Standard Code for Information Interchange or ASCII assigns values between 0 and 255 for upper and lower case letters, numeric digits, punctuation marks and other symbols. ASCII characters can be split into the following sections:

- ❑　0 – 31　　　　　Control codes
- ❑　32 – 127　　　　Standard, implementation-independent characters
- ❑　128 – 255　　　 Special symbols, international character sets – generally, non-standard characters.

Control Codes : ASCII Characters 0 - 31

The following table lists and describes the first 32 ASCII characters, often referred to as control codes. The columns show the decimal and hexadecimal ASCII values for each code along with their abbreviated and full names. Descriptions are given to those most in use today.

Decimal	Hexadecimal	Code	Description
000	00	NUL	Null
001	01	SOH	Start Of Heading
002	02	STX	Start of TeXt
003	03	ETX	End of TeXt
004	04	EOT	End Of Transmission
005	05	ENQ	ENQuiry
006	06	ACK	ACKnowledge

Table continued on following page

Decimal	Hexadecimal	Code	Description
007	07	BEL	BELl. Caused teletype machines to ring a bell. Causes a beep in many common terminals and terminal emulation programs.
008	08	BS	BackSpace. Moves the cursor move backwards (left) one space.
009	09	HT	Horizontal Tab. Moves the cursor right to the next tab stop. The spacing of tab stops is dependent on the output device, but is often either 8 or 10 characters wide.
010	0A	LF	Line Feed. Moves the cursor to a new line. On Unix systems, moves to a new line AND all the way to the left.
011	0B	VT	Vertical Tab
012	0C	FF	Form Feed. Advances paper to the top of the next page (if the output device is a printer).
013	0D	CR	Carriage Return. Moves the cursor all the way to the left, but does not advance to the next line.
014	0E	SO	Shift Out
015	0F	SI	Shift In
016	10	DLE	Data Link Escape
017	11	DC1	Device Control 1
018	12	DC2	Device Control 2
019	13	DC3	Device Control 3
020	14	DC4	Device Control 4
021	15	NAK	Negative AcKnowledge
022	16	SYN	SYNchronous idle
023	17	ETB	End of Transmission Block
024	18	CAN	CANcel
025	19	EM	End of Medium
026	1A	SUB	SUBstitute
027	1B	ESC	ESCape
028	1C	FS	File Separator
029	1D	GS	Group Separator
030	1E	RS	Record Separator
031	1F	US	Unit Separator

The Standard ASCII Characters : 32 - 127

ASCII Characters 32 - 127 are the standard, implementation-independent alphanumeric characters we work with every day. The tables below show the characters along with both their decimal and hexadecimal ASCII values.

Characters 32 - 64

The first table, which contains characters 32 - 64, contains the majority of the standard symbolic characters and the numbers from zero to nine.

Decimal	Hexadecimal	Character	Decimal	Hexadecimal	Character
032	20	Space	049	31	1
033	21	!	050	32	2
034	22	"	051	33	3
035	23	#	052	34	4
036	24	$	053	35	5
037	25	%	054	36	6
038	26	&	055	37	7
039	27	'	056	38	8
040	28	(	057	39	9
041	29	)	058	3A	:
042	2A	*	059	3B	;
043	2B	+	060	3C	<
044	2C	,	061	3D	=
045	2D	-	062	3E	>
046	2E	.	063	3F	?
047	2F	/	064	40	@
048	30	0			

Characters 65 - 127

The second table, which contains characters 65 - 127, contains the standard Latin alphabet characters both lower and upper case, separated only by a few characters at 91 - 96 and 123 - 127.

Decimal	Hexadecimal	Character	Decimal	Hexadecimal	Character
065	41	A	097	61	a
066	42	B	098	62	b
067	43	C	099	63	c
068	44	D	100	64	d
069	45	E	101	65	e
070	46	F	102	66	f
071	47	G	103	67	g
072	48	H	104	68	h
073	49	I	105	69	i
074	4A	J	106	6A	j
075	4B	K	107	6B	k
076	4C	L	108	6C	l
077	4D	M	109	6D	m
078	4E	N	110	6E	n
079	4F	O	111	6F	o
080	50	P	112	70	p
081	51	Q	113	71	q
082	52	R	114	72	r
083	53	S	115	73	s
084	54	T	116	74	t
085	55	U	117	75	u
086	56	V	118	76	v
087	57	W	119	77	w
088	58	X	120	78	x
089	59	Y	121	79	y
090	5A	Z	122	7A	z
091	5B	[	123	7B	{

Decimal	Hexadecimal	Character	Decimal	Hexadecimal	Character
092	5C	\	124	7C	|
093	5D	]	125	7D	}
094	5E	^	126	7E	~
095	5F	_	127	7F	delete
096	60	'			

The Non-Standard ASCII Characters : 128 - 255

The second half of the ASCII table holds the non-standard extension set of characters which may vary depending which computer system you may be using. One common – but in no way definitive – example of this extended set is as follows.

Characters 128 - 191

This first table contains characters 128 - 191, abstract symbols that appear in text from time to time.

Decimal	Hexadecimal	Character	Decimal	Hexadecimal	Character
128	80	•	160	A0	non-breaking space
129	81	•	161	A1	¡
130	82	,	162	A2	¢
131	83	f	163	A3	£
132	84	„	164	A4	¤
133	85	…	165	A5	¥
134	86	†	166	A6	¦
135	87	‡	167	A7	§
136	88	ˆ	168	A8	¨
137	89	‰	169	A9	©
138	8A	Š	170	AA	ª
139	8B	‹	171	AB	«
140	8C	Œ	172	AC	¬
141	8D	•	173	AD	-
142	8E	Ž	174	AE	®

Table continued on following page

Decimal	Hexadecimal	Character	Decimal	Hexadecimal	Character
143	8F	•	175	AF	¯
144	90	•	176	B0	°
145	91	'	177	B1	±
146	92	'	178	B2	²
147	93	"	179	B3	³
148	94	•	180	B4	´
149	95	•	181	B5	µ
150	96	–	182	B6	¶
151	97	–	183	B27	·
152	98	~	184	B8	¸
153	99	™	185	B9	¹
154	9A	š	186	BA	º
155	9B	›	187	BB	»
156	9C	œ	188	BC	¼
157	9D	•	189	BD	½
158	9E	Ÿ	190	BE	¾
159	9F	Ÿ	191	BF	¿

Characters 192 - 255

The second table contains characters 192 - 255, variously accented alphabetical characters.

Decimal	Hexadecimal	Character	Decimal	Hexadecimal	Character
192	C0	À	224	E0	à
193	C1	Á	225	E1	á
194	C2	Â	226	E2	â
195	C3	Ã	227	E3	ã
196	C4	Ä	228	E4	ä
197	C5	Å	229	E5	å
198	C6	Æ	230	E6	æ

Decimal	Hexadecimal	Character	Decimal	Hexadecimal	Character
199	C7	Ç	231	E7	ç
200	C8	È	232	E8	è
201	C9	É	233	E9	é
202	CA	Ê	234	EA	ê
203	CB	Ë	235	EB	ë
204	CC	Ì	236	EC	ì
205	CD	Í	237	ED	í
206	CE	Î	238	EE	î
207	CF	Ï	239	EF	ï
208	D0	Ð	240	F0	ð
209	D1	Ñ	241	F1	ñ
210	D2	Ò	242	F2	ò
211	D3	Ó	243	F3	ó
212	D4	Ô	244	F4	ô
213	D5	Õ	245	F5	õ
214	D6	Ö	246	F6	ö
215	D7	×	247	F7	÷
216	D8	Ø	248	F8	ø
217	D9	Ù	249	F9	ù
218	DA	Ú	250	FA	ú
219	DB	Û	251	FB	û
220	DC	Ü	252	FC	ü
221	DD	Ý	253	FD	ý
222	DE	Þ	254	FE	þ
223	DF	ß	255	FF	

References and Further Information

Although .NET is a new product, there are already many Web sites that provide discussion lists, reference information, community support, components, and other useful resources. Some of those that were available when we went to press are listed below.

ASP.NET Web Sites and Discussion Lists

MSDN .Net Start Page	http://msdn.microsoft.com/net/
Visual Studio	http://msdn.microsoft.com/net/
ASP.NET	http://msdn.microsoft.com/net/aspnet/default.asp
Wrox Press ASP discussion list	http://p2p.wrox.com/
Microsoft Framework team Web site	http://www.asp.net/
ASPNG ASP.NET community site	http://www.aspng.com/
A Tale of Two Authors	http://daveandal.com/
.NET Advocacy Discussion Lists	http://discuss.develop.com/dotnet-advocacy.html
.NET101	http://www.dotnet101.com/
.NETWire	http://www.dotnetwire.com/
123aspx.com	http://www.123aspx.com/
411 ASP.NET Directory	http://www.411asp.net/
4GuysFromRolla.com	http://www.4guysfromrolla.com/
ActiveZ.com (in Turkish)	http://activez.cu.edu.tr/
Angry Coder	http://www.angrycoder.com/
ASP Index	http://www.aspin.com/
ASP Wire	http://www.aspwire.com/

ASP101.com	http://www.asp101.com/
aspalliance	http://www.aspalliance.com/
ASPFree.com	http://www.aspfree.com/aspnet/Default.aspx
ASPLists Windows Forms	http://www.asplists.com/asplists/winforms.asp
ASPNextGen.com	http://www.aspnextgen.com/
ASPToday.com	http://www.asptoday.com/
BipinJoshi.com	http://www.bipinjoshi.com/
C# Corner	http://www.c-sharpcorner.com/
C# Corner Discussion Forums	http://www.c-sharpcorner.com/forum/
Code Guru	http://www.codeguru.com/
DevX.com	http://www.devx.com/dotnet/
DOTNET Distribution List	http://discuss.develop.com/dotnet.html
DotNET French .NET news portal	http://www.dotnet-fr.org/
IBuySpy.com	http://www.ibuyspy.com/
KOSOB.com	http://www.kosob.com/
Learn C# The Easy Way	http://learncsharp.cjb.net/
Mailing list DOTNET (in French)	http://www.neoxia.com/fr/mailing-lists.php3
MCPCentral.com	http://www.mcpcentral.com/
St. Louis .NET User Group	http://www.stlnet.org/
The Code Project	http://www.codeproject.com/
ThinkDOTNET	http://www.thinkdotnet.com/
VB-Joker	http://www.vb-joker.com/
VBXML.com	http://www.vbxml.com/
Visual.NET Advisor	http://www.advisor.com/www/VisualNetAdvisor/
VSJ	http://www.net.vsj.co.uk/

Third Party ASP.NET Component Vendors

Software Artisans	http://softwareartisans.com/
Aylo's Charting Engine	http://chart.aylo.com/
Combit	http://www.combit.net/us/default.asp?content=/us/ support/msdotnet.asp

Component Source	http://www.componentsource.com/build/msnet.asp
Dart Communications	http://www.dart.com/dotnet.asp
Dataphor	http://www.dataphor.com/
Desaware Inc.	http://www.desaware.com/net.htm
Developer Express	http://devexpress.com/index.shtm
DevPower Components	http://www.devpower.com/net/
FarPoint Technologies	http://www.fpoint.com/newtech/
Infragistics	http://www.infragistics.com/
LEADTOOLS Imaging Development	http://www.leadtools.com/
Mabry Software	http://www.mabry.com/dotnet.htm
Sax Software Corporation	http://www.saxsoft.net/
Seagate Software	http://www.seagatesoftware.com/ x-jump/scr_net/default.asp
Software FX - Chart FX	http://www.softwarefx.com/
VisualSoft Technologies	http://www.visualmart.com/dotnetreq.asp
WebGecko Software	http://www.webgecko.com/products/dotnet.asp
Xceed Software Inc.	http://www.xceedsoft.com/dotnet/

ASP.NET Hosting

2COOLWEB	http://www.2coolweb.com/
Brinkster.com	http://www.brinkster.com/aspxinfo.asp
Eraserver.net	http://www.eraserver.net/
Extreme Web Works	http://extremewebworks.com/
Franklins.net	http://www.franklins.net/
IIS Host List	http://www.actionjackson.com/hosts/
MaximumASP.com	http://www.maximumasp.com/
ORCSWEB.com	http://www.orcsweb.com/
SecureWebs.com	http://www.securewebs.com/hosting/net.htm

Support, Errata, and p2p.wrox.com

One of the most irritating things about any programming book is when you find that the bit of code that you've just spent an hour typing simply doesn't work. You check it a hundred times to see if you've set it up correctly, and then you notice the spelling mistake in the variable name on the book page. Of course, you can blame the authors for not taking enough care and testing the code, the editors for not doing their job properly, or the proofreaders for not being eagle-eyed enough, but this doesn't get around the fact that mistakes do happen.

We try hard to ensure that no mistakes sneak out into the real world, but we can't promise that this book is 100% error free. What we can do is offer the next best thing by providing you with immediate support and feedback from experts who have worked on the book, and who try to ensure that future editions eliminate these gremlins. We are also committed to supporting you not just while you read the book, but once you start developing applications as well – through our online forums you can put your questions to the authors, reviewers, and fellow industry professionals.

In this appendix we'll look at how to:

- ❑ Enroll in the peer to peer forums at http://p2p.wrox.com
- ❑ Post and check for errata on our main site, http://www.wrox.com
- ❑ E-mail a query, or feedback on our books in general, to our technical support team

Between all three support procedures, you should get an answer to your problem in no time.

The Online Forums at p2p.wrox.com

We provide **programmer to programmer™ support** on mailing lists, forums, and newsgroups, all in addition to our one-to-one e-mail system, which we'll look at in a minute. You can be confident that your query is not just being examined by a support professional, but by the many Wrox authors and other industry experts present on our mailing lists.

How To Enroll For Support

Just follow this four-step system:

1. Go to p2p.wrox.com in your favorite browser:

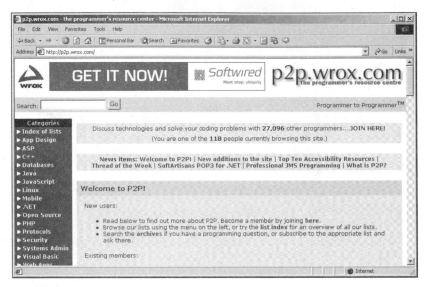

2. Click on the .NET entry in the left hand column. You'll be presented with the lists that are currently available:

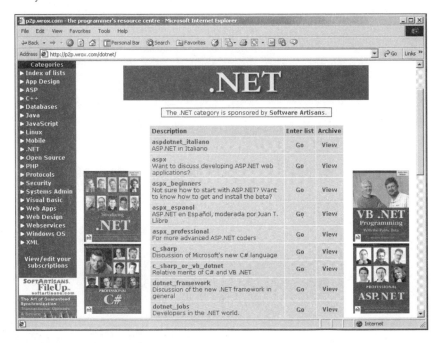

3. Choose to access the list you're interested in by clicking on its entry in the Description column.

4. If you are not a member of the list, you can choose to either view the list without joining it, or create an account in the list, by hitting the respective buttons.

5. If you choose to join, you'll be presented with a form in which you'll need to fill in your e-mail address, name, and a password (of at least 4 digits). Choose how you would like to receive the messages from the list and then hit Subscribe.

6. Congratulations. You're now a member of the mailing list.

Why This System Offers the Best Support

You can choose to join the mailing lists, or you can receive them as a daily digest. If you don't have the time or facility to receive the mailing list, then you can search our online archives.

As these lists are moderated, you can be confident of finding good, accurate information quickly. Mails can be edited or moved by the moderator into the correct place, making this a most efficient resource. Junk and spam mail are deleted, and your own e-mail address is protected by the unique Lyris system from web-bots that can automatically gather up newsgroup mailing list addresses. Any queries about joining or leaving lists, or any query about the list should be sent to listsupport@wrox.com.

Checking the Errata Online at www.wrox.com

The following section will take you step by step through the process of posting errata to our web site to get that help. The sections that follow, therefore, are:

❑ Finding a list of existing errata on the web site

❑ Adding your own errata to the existing list

❑ What happens to your errata once you've posted it (why doesn't it appear immediately)?

There is also a section covering how to e-mail a question for technical support. This comprises:

❑ What your e-mail should include

❑ What happens to your e-mail once we've received it

Finding an Erratum on the Web Site

Before you send in a query, you might be able to save time by finding the answer to your problem on our web site – http://www.wrox.com:

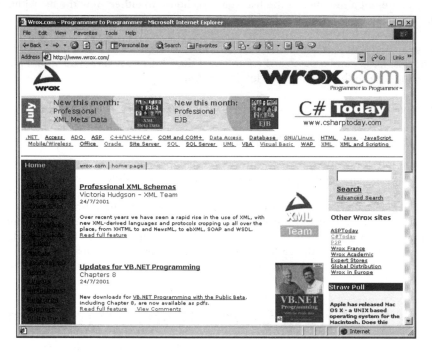

1. Each book we publish has its own page and its own errata sheet. You can get to any book's page by clicking on the subject list below the banner at the top of the page – so for this book click on .NET or ASP.

2. This will list the books available in that subject area. Click on Beginning ASP.NET, and then the Book Errata link.

3. This will take you to the errata page for the book. We update these pages daily to ensure that you have the latest information on bugs and errors. You can get more details on a specific listing by clicking on the link for that error, or you can list all the errata in more detail by clicking on the view all errata link.

Add an Erratum: E-mail Support

If the errata page doesn't solve your problem, then you should contact our customer support team. You can point out an error to put up on the web site, or directly query a problem in the book page with an expert who knows the book in detail. Either click on the submit errata link on the book support page, or send an e-mail to support@wrox.com.

A typical e-mail should include the following things:

- ❏ The **name**, **last four digits of the ISBN**, and **page number** of the problem in the Subject field
- ❏ Your **name**, **contact info** and the **problem** in the body of the message

We won't send you junk mail. We need the details to save your time and ours. When you send an e-mail, it will go through the following chain of support.

Customer Support

Your message is delivered to one of our customer support staff, who are the first people to read it. They have files on most frequently asked questions, and will answer anything general immediately. They answer general questions about the book and the web site.

Editorial

Deeper queries are forwarded to the technical editor responsible for that book. They have experience with the programming language or particular product, and are able to answer detailed technical questions on the subject. Once an issue has been resolved, the editor can post any errata to the web site.

The Authors

Finally, in the unlikely event that the editor can't answer your problem, s/he will forward the request to the author. We try to protect the author from any distractions from writing. However, we are quite happy to forward specific requests to them. Most Wrox authors help with the support on their books. They'll mail the customer and the editor with their response, and again all readers should benefit.

What We Can't Answer

Obviously with an ever-growing range of books and an ever-changing technology base, there is an increasing volume of data requiring support. While we endeavor to answer all questions about the book, we can't answer bugs in your own programs that you've adapted from our code. Do tell us if you're especially pleased with the routine you developed with our help.

How to Tell Us Exactly What You Think

We understand that errors can destroy the enjoyment of a book and can cause many wasted and frustrated hours, so we seek to minimize the distress that they can cause.

You might just wish to tell us how much you liked or loathed the book in question. Or you might have ideas about how this whole process could be improved. In that case you should e-mail feedback@wrox.com. You'll always find a sympathetic ear, no matter what the problem is. Above all you should remember that we do care about what you have to say and we will do our utmost to act upon it.

Index

A Guide to the Index

The index does not cover the Appendices. It is arranged alphabetically, word-by-word, with symbols and numerals preceding the letter A. Angle-bracket tag delimiters and hyphens have been ignored in the alphabetization and acronyms have been preferred to their expansions as main entries, on the grounds that unfamiliar acronyms are easier to construct than to expand.

End Select statement, 197
enterprisesec.config file, 692
entities
database tables, normalization and, 397
XML, 169
entrytolog.aspx file, 649
environment variables
configuration, before compiling components, 563
editing the path statement, 564
HTTP message constituents, 84
PATH, creating a web service proxy, 679
registering, with .NET SDK, 42
equal sign
assignment operator, 142
equality test, 187
Err object, VB.NET
example using, 638
properties and methods of, 638
error categories, 604, 615
Error event, 231
error handling, 634
catching exception events, 641
datatable_errorcheck.aspx page, 426
debugging and, distinguished, 603
identifying error category, 615
oledb_connection.aspx page, 406
programmatic error handling, 645
reading from data sources, 424
specific and generic, 642
sql_connection.aspx page, 409
structured and unstructured techniques, 634
error messages
see also **status codes, HTTP.**
browsers, for badly-formed XML, 171
errors during compilation and during execution, 698
friendly message pages, 619, 645
specifying destination for detailed error information, 619
error prevention
good practice to assist with, 604, 608
identifying vulnerable code sections, 604
<error> subtags
<customErrors> section, 619, 699
ErrorPage property
Page directive, 621
errors
see also **troubleshooting.**
due to trying to work offline, 50
server error caused by code problems, 52
event handlers
ASP.NET button control example, 476
assigned by ASP.NET server controls, 476
browsercheck.aspx page, 334
hashtable1.aspx page, 388
middle stage of page lifecycle, 479
MyCalendar.aspx page, 499, 507
onclick event, 238, 328
onDayRender event, 502
SubmitBtn_Click subroutine, 549
writing subroutines as, 247
event logs
Event Viewer window, 650
mailing the log files for review, 652
event processing
HTML server control feature, 471

Event Properties window
Windows event log, 651
event sources, 649
accessing event logs, 652
Event Viewer window
viewing Windows event logs, 650
event.aspx page, 241
event-driven programming, 230
arithmetical calculation example, 250
ASP.NET and, 229
eventdriven.aspx page, 250
eventhandler.aspx page, 476
EventLog class
CreateEventSource method, 649
WriteEntry method, 649
events
HTML handling of, 236
HTML list of, 237
parameters used by, 243
performed as single discrete action, 233
processed server-side in ASP.NET, 231, 238
processing by browsers and servers, 240
putting code into event subroutines, 234
raised by ASP.NET server controls, 476
real-world examples, 230
server control events, 238, 239
example pages
problems caused by viewing as local file, 46
punctual.aspx, 44
code examined, 45
exception object, 641
exceptions
introduced, 641
execute permissions, 37
execute_reader.aspx page, 415
ExecuteNonQuery method
Command object, 459
ExecuteReader method
Command object, ADO.NET, 410, 411
formating results without using a DataSet, 411
executionTimeout attribute
<httpRuntime> element, 696
Explicit setting
avoiding division by zero errors, 607
Page directive, 609
exponential constant
math.aspx example page, 295
exponential form see **floating-point numbers.**
extending base classes, 555

F

false data tests
detecting web service piggybacking, 687
featuredbook_CB.ascx
used in integrated example for components, 593
featuredbook_CB.vb
used in integrated example for components, 593
featuredbooks.ascx user control file, 542
modifying to use code behind, 549
featuredbooks_CB.ascx file, 551
smaller than featuredbooks.ascx, 554
featuredbooks_CB.vb, 550

X

Effective Data Presentation using ASP.NET Server Control

Introduction

Effective data presentation is not simply a case of presenting the data effectively, but also of efficient retrieval of the data; and to achieve maximum efficiency during paging, we have to take only the data required for display. Here we see two different methods for doing this. While using datagrid's in-built paging functionality, the control displays the navigation buttons (either Next and Previous buttons or numeric page numbers). However every time a user clicks these links, the data source is recreated and re-bound to the DataGrid. The entire data source, not just the page being displayed, is returned. If the table we are paging through has thousands of records in it, all the records are queried, transported to the Web Form, and then a selected few (the current page) are displayed. This results in a serious resource issue on the database.

So by customizing the paging we can control the number of records returned from the database. In this series of two articles I will be demonstrating two methods of implementing a custom paging solution using the ASP.NET and server controls with SQL Server. The page, which we will create, renders ten records per page from the Orders table in the Northwind database. There are two types of page-navigation links:

- ❑ A VCR-style navigation panel, which contains buttons, that allows the user to move to first, last, previous, or next page.

- ❑ Jumps to a specific page type navigation.

Record paging:

Paging through records becomes an essential part of many Web applications, when the application handles large amount of data and all of the data has to be displayed to the user. One of ASP's greatest features is the ease with which an ASP page can access, retrieve, or modify the database information. To achieve this we intermix the HTML and Server-Side Script to present the data effectively. ASP.NET though, the next generation of ASP, offers new means of retrieving data with ADO+ or ADO.Net, along with its full set of complex controls including embedded controls (such as the **Repeater, DataList,** and **DataGrid ASP.NET** controls) with flexible means of binding controls to information in a data store. This approach allows us to bind any control property to information in almost any kind of data store, from the simplest to the most sophisticated, and gives virtually complete control over the data movement, from the data store to the page and back.

DataGrid Web Control:

As the name specifies the DataGrid control presents the data in a tabular manner. The DataGrid ASP.NET server control is a multi-column, data-bound grid, which allows us to define various types of columns, both to layout the contents of the grid and also to add a specific functionality. Such functionality includes selecting, editing or sorting, and can also specify the paging behavior, either by automatically setting the DataGrid paging property to true, or by setting the paging property as desired by customizing the datagrid control programmatically. By manually setting the paging property we can provide our own paging controls, and set the page to display. This option allows us to move to any number of pages at a time, jump to a specific page, and so on. **See Figure 1.**

Why Manual Paging?

The DataGrid server control enables easy paging through data. You can set the DataGrid to use paging, and specify a page size (number of records to display). Each time the page is loaded the Datagrid will recreate the entire data set and automatically move to the appropriate place in the data set. It then displays enough rows to make up one page of the grid.

When we are working with a large dataset, recreating the entire dataset each time is a large waste of resources. In such a case, we should retrieve just the records needed for the page at that time. To allow this, we turn off the automatic paging feature of the grid so that it doesn't assume it is working with the entire data set. We then take responsibility in our own code for retrieving only the data for a single page. So manually setting the paging is effective when large amounts of data have to be displayed.

Customizing the Paging with DataGrid:

The Task of getting the correct ten records lies in a Store Procedure that in turn takes a smart query as its input parameter. The query will be dynamically built each time depending upon the data requested.

Procedure for Paging

```
CREATE PROCEDURE [Sp_Paging]
@ParmQuery Varchar (3000),
@ParmTotalRecs Int output
AS
EXEC(@ParmQuery)
SELECT @ParmTotalRecs = COUNT(*) FROM Orders
```

This stored procedure takes the entire query as an input parameter (@ParmQuery). In addition to this it returns the total number of records from the Orders table as an output parameter (@ParmTotalRecs).

Building Smart Query

```
Select Top 10 OrderId,CustomerId,OrderDate,ShippedDate from Orders where OrderId
in (select top  20 OrderId from Orders Order By OrderId ASC) Order by OrderId Desc
```

The above query is built dynamically, and is passed as an input parameter to the stored procedure Sp_paging. Now lets see the way in which this query works:

Assume that the user needs records between 11 and 20 (the second 10 records), to achieve this a sub-query is used. In the sub-query the top 20 records are selected in ascending order and the bottom 10 records are selected in the main query. Basically the subquery gets the 20 records with the highest quantity, it is then the main query, which selects the TOP 10 records, and reverses the sort order so that it returns the bottom 10 records.

Note: The TOP clause limits the number of rows returned in the result set. This works only with SQL Server. For Oracle database we can use ROWNUM pseudocolumn to get exact records. **See query given below:**

```
SELECT * FROM(SELECT ROWNUM R, A.* FROM(select
OrderId,CustomerId,OrderDate,ShippedDate from Orders) A )WHERE R BETWEEN 11 and 20
```

Designing and Creating Web Forms

```
<%@ Import Namespace="System.Data" %>
<%@ Import Namespace="System.Data.SqlClient" %>
<Html>
<head><Title>Custome Paging</Title>
</head>
<body>
<form runat="server" method="post">
<table border=0 width=742 BgColor=#000000><tr align=center><td align=center>
<table border=0 width=740 BgColor=#ffffff><tr align=center><td align=center>
 <asp:DataGrid runat="server" id="DGpaging"
  Width="740"
  Cellpadding="4"
  Cellspacing="0"
  Gridlines="Horizontal"
  HorizontalAlign="Center"
  HeaderStyle-CssClass="tableHeader"
  ItemStyle-CssClass="tableItem"
  AlternatingItemStyle-BackColor="#00bfff"
  AllowPaging="True"
  AllowCustomPaging="True"
  PageSize="10"
  PagerStyle-Visible="False"
 />
 </td></tr>
 <tr align=center><td align=center>
 <b>Page
     <asp:Label id="CurrentPage" CssClass="pageLinks" runat="server" />
     of
     <asp:Label id="TotalPages" CssClass="pageLinks" runat="server" />
 </td></tr>
<tr align=center><td align=center>
  <asp:LinkButton runat="server" CssClass="pageLinks"
    id="FirstPage" Text="[First Page]"
    OnCommand=" VCRTypeNavigation_OnClick " CommandName="First" />
   <asp:LinkButton runat="server" CssClass="pageLinks"
    id="PreviousPage" Text="[Previous Page]"
    OnCommand=" VCRTypeNavigation_OnClick" CommandName="Prev" />
   <asp:LinkButton runat="server" CssClass="pageLinks"
    id="NextPage" Text="[Next Page]"
```

```
          OnCommand=" VCRTypeNavigation_OnClick" CommandName="Next" />
       <asp:LinkButton runat="server" CssClass="pageLinks"
         id="LastPage" Text="[Last Page]"
          OnCommand=" VCRTypeNavigation_OnClick" CommandName="Last" />
   </td></tr>
   <tr align=center bgcolor="#00008b"><td>
   <asp:label id="PageLabel" runat="server" Font-Name="verdana" Font-Color="#FFFFFF"
   Font-size="10pt" />
   <asp:TextBox id="PageNumber" runat="server" maxlength ="2" Text="1" />
   <asp:button id="gotopage" runat="server"  Text="Go" OnClick = "
   GoTopageNavigation_onClick " />
   </td>
   </tr>
   </table>
   </td></tr></table>
   <Input type="hidden" runat="server" id="TxtReminder">
   <Input type="hidden" runat="server" id="TxtPageNo">
   </form>
   </body>
   </html>
```

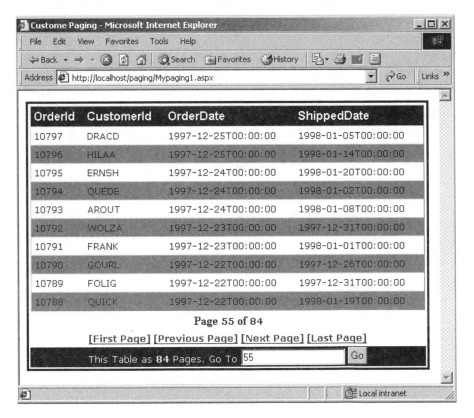

Figure1: The above image shows you the web form design

We place a DataGrid on the web form. Setting the property **allowpaging(default is True)** of the DataGrid to false disables the inbuilt paging property of the DataGrid, but the `PageSize` property is set to the number of pages, here 10, that should be displayed in each page. Since we use our own way of paging through records, we set the `PagerStyle-visible` property to False, which hides the Navigation Links.

Under the DataGrid there are two Label controls. These are used to indicate the current position e.g. page 55 of 84. Below these are the LinkButton controls, which are used to navigate through the data. Each LinkButton specifies an event handled, namely `VCRTypeNavigation_OnClick()`, as its `OnCommand` event handler. The same event handler is used for all the four LinkButtons. Their `CommandName` property is used to determine the navigation through the pages.

Just under the LinkButton are the Label Control, Textbox Control and a Button Control. The button Control specifies an eventhandler namely `GoToPageNavigation_OnClick()` as its `EventArgs`. This helps in Jumping to the page specified in the textbox control. There are two hidden textboxes, which pass the values between pages to build the query dynamically.

Programmatic Part for Paging:

There are three-event handlers and one method. The event handlers are `Page_Load()`, `VCRTypeNavigation_OnClick()`,`GoToPageNavigation_OnClick()` and the method is `BindData()`. The `Page_Load()` event handler is used to set values only during the initial loading of the page. This is as a click on a Button will trigger a `PostBack` event, which is handled by the `VCRTypeNavigation_OnClick()` and `GoToPageNavigation_OnClick()` event handles. The `BindData()` method is the core of the entire code. This is where a call to the stored procedure is made and returns only the data needed.

The page-level variables are `CurrentPageNo`, `StaringPage`, `EndPage` and `Reminder`. These variables either set the values for building a query, or get the values to build a query, and are used in all the events and methods.

BindData() Method

```
Sub BindData()
  Dim myDataSet            As New DataSet()
  Dim myDataSetCommand     As SQLDataSetCommand
  Dim param                As SQLParameter
  Dim ConString            As String
  Dim StrSql               As String
  StrSql="Select top " & StartingPage &" OrderId,CustomerId,OrderDate,ShippedDate
  from orders where orderid in (select top " & Endpage & " orderid from orders order
  by orderid asc) order by orderid desc "

  ConString = "server=localhost;database=Northwind;uid=sa;pwd=;"
  myDataSetCommand = New SQLDataSetCommand("sp_Paging", ConString)
  With myDataSetCommand.SelectCommand
    .CommandType = CommandType.StoredProcedure
    .Parameters.Add(New SQLParameter("@ParmQuery", SqlDBType.VarChar,3000))
    .Parameters.Add(New SQLParameter("@ParmTotalRecs", SqlDBType.Int))
    .Parameters("@ParmTotalRecs").Direction = ParameterDirection.Output
    .Parameters("@ParmQuery").Value =  StrSql
  End With
```

```
        myDataSetCommand.FillSet(myDataSet, "orders")
        DGPaging.DataSource = myDataSet.Tables("orders").DefaultView
        DGPaging.DataBind()
        Reminder= myDataSetCommand.SelectCommand.Parameters("@ParmTotalRecs").Value Mod
        DGPaging.PageSize
        TxtReminder.Value=Reminder
        CurrentPageNumber=TxtPageNo.value.CInt(Expression)
        CurrentPage.Text=TxtPageNo.value
        If Not Page.IsPostBack Then
          TotalPages.Text =
        System.Math.Ceiling(myDataSetCommand.SelectCommand.Parameters("@ParmTotalRecs").Va
        lue/DGPaging.PageSize)
        End If
        PageLabel.Text="<font color=#FFFFFF> This Table as <b> " & TotalPages.Text & "</b>
        Pages.   Go To </font>"
        PageNumber.Text=CurrentPage.Text
        Select Case CurrentPageNumber
          Case 1
            PreviousPage.Enabled = "False"
            NextPage.Enabled="True"
          Case TotalPages.Text.CInt(Expression)
            NextPage.Enabled="False"
            PreviousPage.Enabled="True"
          Case Else
            PreviousPage.Enabled="True"
            NextPage.Enabled="True"
        End Select
        End Sub
```

The `BindData()` method is used to show the `DGPaging` (DataGrid control), which displays the records by calling the Stored Procedure `SP_Paging`. The BindData method uses a `DataSet` and `SQLDataSetCommand` to get the data from the database. A dynamically built query is passed as an input parameter (`@ParmQuery`) to the Procedure. This query is built by setting the `Startingpage` and `Endpage` variables to the pages requested. The hidden fields are used to maintain the state of the page. The `@ParmTotalRecs` parameter is an output parameter, which returns the total number of records in a table, and sets the `Reminder` variable to calculate the total number of page.

Using Select Case evaluator, we either enable or disable the `"Previous Page"` and `"Next Page"` Link Buttons based on the `CurrentPageNumber` value. We certainly do not want a `"Previous Page"` link if the user is looking at the first page. The Enable property of the Link Button determines whether the Text property renders with an `HREF` attribute or not. Either way the text is still displayed.

Page_Load() Event Handler

```
    <Script runat="server" language="vb" >
    Protected CurrentPageNumber As Integer
    Protected StartingPage      As Integer
    Protected Reminder          As Integer
    Protected Endpage           As Integer

    Sub Page_Load(Source As Object, E As EventArgs)
```

```
   If  Not Page.IsPostBack Then
      StartingPage=DGpaging.Pagesize
      EndPage=DGpaging.Pagesize
      TxtPageNo.value=1
      BindData()
   End If
   End Sub
```

A `Page_load()` event is triggered every time a page gets loaded. If the page is not a post back, the `page_load()` event handler calls the method `BindData()` and sets the default values to hidden fields `HiddenStartNo` and `HiddenEndNo` to build the Query. These values are set to show the first ten records in the grid. All other subsequent post backed requests are handled either by `GoTopageNavigation_onClick()` or `VCRTypeNavigation_onClick()` event handlers.

GoTopageNavigation_onClick() Event Handler

```
   Sub GoTopageNavigation_onClick(Source As Object, E As EventArgs)
   Dim PageNo AS Integer
   Reminder=TxtReminder.Value.CInt(Expression)
   TxtPageNo.value=PageNumber.Text.CInt(Expression)
   PageNo=PageNumber.Text.CInt(Expression)
   If PageNo=>TotalPages.Text.CInt(Expression) Then
       If Reminder=0 then
           Startingpage=DGPaging.Pagesize
       Else
           StartingPage=Reminder
     End If
     EndPage=TotalPages.Text.CInt(Expression) * 10
     TxtPageNo.Value=TotalPages.Text.CInt(Expression)
   Else
     Startingpage=DGPaging.Pagesize
     EndPage=PageNo * 10
   End if
   BindData()
   End Sub
```

`GoToPageNavigation_onClick()` event handler is triggered whenever the user clicks on the **Go** submit button, after setting the value in the Textbox `pageNumber`. This event handler checks whether the requested page is the last one, if so it checks for the number of records available in the last page by checking the value in the `TXTReminder` hidden field. If value in `TxtReminder` is greater than zero then that value is set to the `Startingpage` variable. If the requested page is not the last one then the requested page value with the multiple of 10 will be assigned to the `EndPage` variable. The `BindData()` method is called, after setting the values for `StartingPage` and `EndPage`.

VCRTypeNavigation_onClick Event Handler

```
   Sub VCRTypeNavigation_OnClick(Source As Object, E As CommandEventArgs)
    Reminder=TxtReminder.Value.CInt(Expression)
    Select Case e.CommandName
    Case "First"
     StartingPage=DGPaging.Pagesize
```

```
            CurrentPageNumber = 1
            TxtPageNo.value=CurrentPageNumber
            EndPage=CurrentpageNumber * 10
        Case "Last"
          if Reminder=0 then
                Startingpage=DGPaging.Pagesize
          Else
                StartingPage=Reminder
          End If
          CurrentPageNumber = TotalPages.Text.CInt(Expression)
          TxtPageNo.value=CurrentPageNumber
          EndPage=CurrentpageNumber * 10
        Case "Next"
          if CurrentPage.Text.CInt(Expression)+1=TotalPages.Text.CInt(Expression) then
                StartingPage=Reminder
          Else
                StartingPage=DGPaging.Pagesize
          End if
          CurrentPageNumber = CurrentPage.Text.CInt(Expression) +1
          TxtPageNo.value=CurrentPageNumber
          EndPage=CurrentpageNumber * 10
        Case "Prev"
          StartingPage=DGPaging.Pagesize
          CurrentPageNumber = CurrentPage.Text.CInt(Expression) -1
          TxtPageNo.value=CurrentPageNumber
          EndPage=CurrentpageNumber * 10
        End Select
        BindData()
    End Sub
```

`NavigationLink_OnClick()VCRTypeNavigation_OnClick()` event handler is triggered whenever the user clicks on any of the four Link Buttons namely **'First'**, **'Last'**, 'Next' or 'Prev'. Here we simply reset the values for the `CurrentPageNumber`, `StartingPage` and `EndPage` variables depending on the link clicked. In the Last and Next Select Case evaluator we first check whether the requested page is similar to the `GoToPageTypeNagigater_onClick()` Event Handler. The `BindData()` method is called after the values are set.

Summary

In this article we have seen the way of customizing the paging behavior using the ASP.Net's DataGrid, and have also seen two different styles of paging. These paging techniques can also be used in other ASP.Net server controls and also in our classic ASP applications.

In my next article on Effective Data Presentation using ASP.Net Server controls I would like to discuss another paging method. This time using SQL Server 2000's user-defined function, and DataList control, with a simple example of a shopping cart application.

http://msdn.microsoft.com/library/periodic/period00/ASPPlus.htm
http://msdn.microsoft.com/library/periodic/period00/adoplus.htm
http://www.asptoday.com/articles/20000925.htm
http://www.asptoday.com/articles/20000926.htm

p2p.wrox.com
The programmer's resource centre

A unique free service from Wrox Press
with the aim of helping programmers to help each other

Wrox Press aims to provide timely and practical information to today's programmer. P2P is a list server offering a host of targeted mailing lists where you can share knowledge with your fellow programmers and find solutions to your problems. Whatever the level of your programming knowledge, and whatever technology you use, P2P can provide you with the information you need.

ASP
Support for beginners and professionals, including a resource page with hundreds of links, and a popular ASP+ mailing list.

DATABASES
For database programmers, offering support on SQL Server, mySQL, and Oracle.

MOBILE
Software development for the mobile market is growing rapidly. We provide lists for the several current standards, including WAP, WindowsCE, and Symbian.

JAVA
A complete set of Java lists, covering beginners, professionals,and server-side programmers (including JSP, servlets and EJBs)

.NET
Microsoft's new OS platform, covering topics such as ASP+, C#, and general .Net discussion.

VISUAL BASIC
Covers all aspects of VB programming, from programming Office macros to creating components for the .Net platform.

WEB DESIGN
As web page requirements become more complex, programmer sare taking a more important role in creating web sites. For these programmers, we offer lists covering technologies such as Flash, Coldfusion, and JavaScript.

XML
Covering all aspects of XML, including XSLT and schemas.

OPEN SOURCE
Many Open Source topics covered including PHP, Apache, Perl, Linux, Python and more.

FOREIGN LANGUAGE
Several lists dedicated to Spanish and German speaking programmers, categories include .Net, Java, XML, PHP and XML.

How To Subscribe

Simply visit the P2P site, at **http://p2p.wrox.com/**

Select the 'FAQ' option on the side menu bar for more information about the subscription process and our service.

Programmer to Programmer™

wrox

Programmer to Programmer™

Wrox writes books for you. Any suggestions, or ideas about how you want information given in your ideal book will be studied by our team. Your comments are always valued at Wrox.

Free phone in USA 800-USE-WROX
Fax (312) 893 8001

UK Tel.: (0121) 687 4100   Fax: (0121) 687 4101

Beginning ASP .NET – Registration Card

Name _____

Address _____

_____

_____

City _____ State/Region _____

Country _____ Postcode/Zip _____

E-Mail _____

Occupation _____

How did you hear about this book?

☐ Book review (name) _____

☐ Advertisement (name) _____

☐ Recommendation _____

☐ Catalog _____

☐ Other _____

Where did you buy this book?

☐ Bookstore (name) _____ City _____

☐ Computer store (name) _____

☐ Mail order _____

☐ Other _____

What influenced you in the purchase of this book?

☐ Cover Design ☐ Contents ☐ Other (please specify):

How did you rate the overall content of this book?

☐ Excellent ☐ Good ☐ Average ☐ Poor

What did you find most useful about this book? _____

_____

What did you find least useful about this book? _____

_____

Please add any additional comments. _____

_____

What other subjects will you buy a computer book on soon?

_____

What is the best computer book you have used this year?

_____

5040   Check here if you DO NOT want to receive support for this book ■   5040

wrox

Programmer to Programmer™

Note: If you post the bounce back card below in the UK, please send it to:

Wrox Press Limited, Arden House, 1102 Warwick Road,
Acocks Green, Birmingham B27 6HB. UK.

Computer Book Publishers